MW00643636

The Pragmatism Reader

The Pragmatism Reader

FROM PEIRCE THROUGH THE PRESENT

Edited by

Robert B. Talisse and Scott F. Aikin

PRINCETON UNIVERSITY PRESS

PRINCETON AND OXFORD

Copyright © 2011 by Princeton University Press

Published by Princeton University Press,
41 William Street, Princeton, New Jersey 08540

In the United Kingdom: Princeton University Press,
6 Oxford Street, Woodstock, Oxfordshire OX20 1TW

press.princeton.edu

All Rights Reserved

The pragmatism reader : from Peirce through the present / edited by
Robert B. Talisse and Scott F. Aikin.
p. cm.
Includes bibliographical references and index.
ISBN 978-0-691-13705-6 (cloth : alk. paper)—
ISBN 978-0-691-13706-3 (pbk.: alk. paper)
1. Pragmatism. I. Talisse, Robert B. II. Aikin, Scott F.
B832.P768 2011
144'.3—dc22 2010026121

British Library Cataloging-in-Publication Data is available

This book has been composed in Minion Pro

Printed on acid-free paper ∞

Printed in the United States of America

1 3 5 7 9 10 8 6 4 2

CONTENTS

The Pragmatism Reader

Introduction

I

Although the term *pragmatism* is frequently used to characterize some or other highly specific thesis or program, pragmatism is not and never was a school of thought unified around a distinctive doctrine. In fact, the first pragmatists—Charles Peirce, William James, and John Dewey—were divided over what, precisely, pragmatism is. Peirce first proposed the "pragmatic maxim" as a tool for dispensing with metaphysical nonsense; for him, pragmatism was strictly a "method of ascertaining the meanings of hard words and abstract concepts" (CP5.464).[1] The core of this method is the idea that,

> To develop [a thought's] meaning, we have simply to determine what habits it produces, for what a thing means is simply what habits it involves. (CP5.400)

Hence the pragmatic maxim:

> Consider what effects, that might conceivably have practical bearings, we conceive the object of our conception to have. Then our conception of these effects is the whole of our conception of the object. (CP5.402)

For Peirce, pragmatism was a way to clear away philosophical error and start upon the path of properly conducted philosophy. Peirce thought that by analyzing words and statements in terms of "what is tangible and conceivably practical" (CP5.400), one could "dismiss make-believes" (CP5.416) and free philosophy of "senseless jargon" (CP5.401).

Although pragmatism is the beginning of Peirce's philosophy, it is not the whole of Peirce's philosophy. As is well known, Peirce went on to develop original (some might say idiosyncratic) views concerning topics ranging from philosophy of mathematics, logic, and science to phenomenology, semiotics, and aesthetics.

Some twenty years after Peirce introduced the pragmatic maxim, James confessed to being dissatisfied with the narrowness of Peirce's formulation; he proposed a broader application according to which the point of pragmatism is not to detect nonsense, as Peirce had alleged, but rather to settle metaphysical disputes. James proposed that one should include among the "practical effects" of a statement the psychological effects of *believing* it. Thus, whereas Peirce argued that pragmatism renders the doctrine of transubstantiation meaningless, James argued that pragmatism afforded a decisive case in favor of it. James contends that the idea that in the Mass one "feed[s] upon the very substance of divinity" has "tremendous effect" and thus is the "only pragmatic application" of the idea of a substance (WWJ, 392).[2]

Though profoundly influenced by them both, Dewey rejected the views of Peirce and James. According to Dewey, pragmatism was in the business of neither separating out meaningful statements from nonsense nor settling traditional metaphysical disputes. With Peirce, Dewey sought a way of doing philosophy that was unhindered by the traditional puzzles and problematics. But he resisted the Peircean strategy of proposing a test of meaning. Instead, he *socialized* the problems of philosophy, arguing that the traditional philosophical problems naturally arose out of the social and intellectual conditions of a pre-Darwinian age. Dewey contended that, because these conditions no longer obtain, the traditional philosophical problems should be simply abandoned, replaced by new difficulties arising from Darwinian science. He was especially concerned to address the difficulties involved in giving an account of value—moral, aesthetic, epistemic, political—that is consistent with experimental natural science.

In the end, then, Dewey's project owes something to James as well. After all, it was James, not Peirce, who really felt the pinch between the scientific and the normative, between the position of the psychological researcher working in his lab and that of the living human being convinced that the universe was too wild, wondrous, and unruly ever to be brought under the rigid discipline of a scientific theory. However, whereas James endorsed a metaphysical pluralism and an epistemic anti-evidentialism specially designed to leave room for the unruly, the inexplicable, and even the mystical, Dewey, by contrast, proposed a philosophy aimed at fostering equilibrium and continuity in the world. He gave philosophical articulation to the need always to rebuild, reorder, and reconstitute extant materials when they prove disordered, unintelligible, and useless. Dewey saw philosophy as a perpetual effort to *reconstruct* the world according to our current aims and interests. Indeed, he identified *inquiry* or *intelligence* itself with such activity, and he saw philosophy as the systematic attempt to apply intelligence to all varieties of human practice. And, perhaps most importantly, he saw democracy as both the precondition for and the social expression of intelligence.

Dewey's philosophy is thus more systematic and comprehensive than that of either of his pragmatist predecessors. Peirce sought to make our ideas clear and James sought to resolve long-standing metaphysics disputes; Dewey, however, built his pragmatism into a grand philosophical system rooted in Darwinian naturalism. He devised a far-reaching and integrated network of philosophical accounts of experience, logic, existence, language, mind, knowledge, psychology, science, education, value, art, religion, and politics out of his commitment to the Darwinian thought that the fundamental philosophical datum is activity of living creatures interacting with various factors and materials within their environments.

Importantly, this basic Darwinian commitment also drives Dewey's critical stance toward traditional philosophical approaches. According to Dewey, the philosophical lesson of Darwinism is that there are no strict *discontinuities* in nature. He reasons that therefore any philosophy that proceeds from a *dualism* of, say, mind and body, substance and accident, ideal and real, empirical and conceptual, necessary and contingent, fact and value, and experience and reason is not so much in error as simply *obsolete*. In this respect, Dewey breaks with James: his pragmatism is aimed not at reconciling apparently opposed positions but rather at showing that nonpragmatic philosophical programs are nonviable. Again, Dewey shares this much with Peirce. They both saw pragmatism as a critical stance toward the traditional positions, arguments, and categories of philosophy.

Yet we must emphasize that Dewey's attitude toward the philosophical tradition is more extreme than Peirce's. To be sure, Peirce's maxim would have it that many traditional metaphysical statements are nonsense; however, it also leaves a great number of philosophical claims unmolested. For example, Peirce thought that the dispute between nominalism and realism was a *real* philosophical dispute. He proposed his maxim as a way to ensure that legitimate philosophical debates, like the debate between nominalists and realists, could proceed profitably. Dewey, by contrast, aimed his criticisms not at specific statements, but at entire philosophical programs. He dismissed Cartesianism, Kantianism, Humeanism, Platonism, Aristotelianism, and nearly every other philosophical school as instantiations of the common defect of employing some or other dualism. Again, Dewey's charge is that all such approaches are *obsolete*: not meaningless, but useless. Condemning all rival philosophies as hopelessly mired in antiquated categories and thus beyond repair, Dewey proceeded as if they had been decisively vanquished. One need not wait for a rejoinder from a proponent of an obsolete and useless philosophy, much less endeavor to respond to it. Consequently, he declared his own approach "the way, and the only way . . . by which one can freely accept the standpoint and conclusions of modern science" (LW1:4).[3] Whereas Peirce saw pragmatism as a rule for conducting philosophical inquiry, Dewey saw pragmatism as a substantive philosophical program in itself.

These philosophical differences were well recognized by the original pragmatists themselves. The work of James and those he influenced led Peirce in 1905 to officially renounce the term pragmatism; he rebaptized his philosophy *pragmaticism*, a name he hoped was "ugly enough to be safe from kidnappers" (CP5.415). Dewey also distanced himself from James, disapproving of the appeals to his work in James's *Pragmatism: A New Name for Some Old Ways of Thinking* (MW4:107ff.). And in personal correspondence with Dewey, Peirce complained that Dewey's philosophy was "too loose" and employed too many "slipshod arguments" (CP8.180). In any case, Dewey stopped characterizing his view as pragmatism sometime in the early 1920s; in his mature work, he refers to his view as *empirical naturalism* or *instrumentalism* or *experimentalism*.[4]

II

Despite these disputes among the original pragmatists, there is nonetheless a discernible trajectory running from the work of Peirce, James, and Dewey through the middle of the twentieth century to the present. To repeat, there is no distinctive philosophical thesis common to all versions of pragmatism; rather, the pragmatists assembled in this volume share a *common aspiration*. More specifically, the essays collected here represent varied attempts to work out a version of naturalism committed to taking seriously the actual practices of human investigators. That is, the thread tying thinkers otherwise as diverse as Peirce, Nelson Goodman, W.V.O. Quine, Susan Haack, Richard Rorty, Richard Posner, and the others assembled in this volume is the pragmatist aspiration of devising a philosophy that is at once naturalist and humanist, a philosophy that fully respects the modern scientific worldview without thereby losing contact with the world of human practice.[5]

Of course, there is significant dispute among the pragmatists concerning what the world of human practice is like. For some, the most fundamental aspect of human practice is its creative, constructive dimension. We build theories, worldviews, and possibly even worlds themselves. For others, human practice is aimed primarily at communication and coordination with other humans. This inevitably involves *interpretation* and thus *inference*, which in turn might require membership in a community of interpreters or a group of persons disposed to make the same inferences. And for still others, the distinctive element of human life is our cognitive aim of being as right as we can about our world and ourselves. Achieving this end entails not only recognizing the limits of our capacity to know but showing how criteria for correctness need not be exclusively theoretical: the practicability of our theories can be evidence for them, too. As such, the project of inquiry is integrated with our lives not as a special isolated enterprise.

The readings in this volume reflect this (and perhaps an even wider) variety of emphases on the distinctive elements of human experience. To be sure, emphasizing one aspect does not necessarily entail holding the others in contempt or seeing them as derivative. Nelson Goodman is exemplary, as his "Words, Works, Worlds" is an account of creativity and making one's world. Alternately, "The New Riddle of Induction" is a reminder of our cognitive limits and the practical consequences of those limits, namely, that we must "find a way of exercising some control over the hypotheses to be admitted" for confirmation.

This said, Richard Rorty's essays "Solidarity or Objectivity?" and "The Priority of Democracy to Philosophy" are clear cases for the valorization of the aspects of social coordination over the demands for correctness or, as better put, seeing the cognitive aspirations of human practice in the service of social goals. Rorty captures the commitment as follows:

> For pragmatists, the desire for objectivity is not the desire to escape the limitations of one's community, but simply the desire for as much intersubjective agreement as possible, the desire to extend the reference of "us" as far as we can.

The pragmatic enterprise, as Rorty sees it, is conceiving the cognitive demands of knowledge through a social lens. Accordingly, he takes the primary aspects of social life to be that of social coordination.

These three general rubrics of humanism for the pragmatists—clarity, coordination, and correctness—are at issue in each of the selections in this volume. Depending on what aspect of human life the authors take as most significant, their works will follow certain trajectories with the problems they address. And sometimes the authors try to emphasize multiple values. Sidney Hook, Huw Price, and Cheryl Misak see the demands of correctness and those of coordination as mutually informative; consequently, they take politics, conversation, controversy, and inquiry to be continuous. Nelson Goodman and Cornel West articulate the importance of working out philosophical theories that improve our lives, which requires a measure of freedom and spontaneity but also a degree of attentiveness to the needs of one's society. Wilfrid Sellars, W.V.O. Quine, Donald Davidson, and Robert Brandom articulate the ways that our accounts of objectivity and reality arise from the facts of social coordination. Richard Posner, by contrast, takes it that coordination is of singular importance—specifically a coordination that yields the *most efficient* form of social arrangements. C. I. Lewis, Rudolf Carnap, and Susan Haack take it that there are practical criteria for cognitive success but that achieving that success demands often a measure of creativity in coming up with what is proposed and how the evidence is to be assessed. What makes each of these authors *pragmatist* is their emphasis on naturalistic and variously humanistic accounts of philosophical problems and solutions. One of the reasons as to the variety of pragmatisms is the variety of humanisms available to pragmatists.

III

We have said that the essays collected in this volume trace the major developments associated with pragmatism, from its founding to the present. Looking at our table of contents, one notices that we present pragmatism as a highly influential program within mainstream Anglophone philosophy. Moreover, one will notice that we see pragmatism as a *persistent* force throughout the twentieth century and into the present. As it turns out, the conception of pragmatism we have adopted is highly controversial.

According to the dominant narrative regarding pragmatism, the 1940s and 1950s brought an "eclipse" of pragmatism and pragmatist philosophers by more technical forms of philosophizing described variously as "logical positivism," "scientism," or, most generally, "analytic philosophy." The *eclipse narrative*, as we shall call it, is a resurrection story of a familiar stripe: The original pragmatists arrive on the scene around the turn of the twentieth century and attempt to overturn the past by exposing the untenable assumptions underlying traditional philosophy. They offer a radical and new kind of philosophy, one that upsets traditional assumptions and dethrones the status quo. Pragmatism prevails for a brief while, but then the force of tradition reasserts itself, forcing pragmatism underground. Darkness descends. But eventually pragmatism reemerges, due in large measure to the publication of Richard Rorty's groundbreaking 1979 work, *Philosophy and the Mirror of Nature*, which restored the philosophical reputation of John Dewey and opened the field to new work in pragmatism. According to the vast majority of commentators, the past twenty years have seen the "renaissance" of pragmatism.[6]

Like many resurrection stories, the eclipse narrative is also a persecution story. It contends that pragmatism was not refuted but "eclipsed," covered over, put in the background. This element of the story runs as follows. Advances in formal logic associated with Russell and Frege gave rise to faddish intellectual trends that placed the analysis of language at the core of philosophy, thereby making it seem more scientific and rigorous; consequently, the pragmatists, who emphasized experience rather than language, were simply dismissed as confused, imprecise, irrelevant, or worse. The story continues that now we see that the "linguistic turn" characteristic of analytic philosophy was simply an error and that pragmatism has been all along "waiting at the end of the dialectical road" that analytic philosophy had taken fifty years to traverse (Rorty 1982, xviii).

Hence, the renaissance of pragmatism is often seen as a kind of *vindication* of pragmatism, a *victory* over analytic philosophy, a return to sweetness and light. In this way, the eclipse narrative identifies analytic philosophy as a philosophical *villain* and places pragmatism in opposition to it. Even today, it is widely held that the degree to which analytic philosophy represents the mainstream of philosophy in America is the extent to which pragmatism is being marginalized. Consequently, the eclipse narrative tends to foster an attitude of resentment toward professional philosophy that manifests itself in the tendency to demonize analytic philosophy as "narrow," "irrelevant," and "nihilistic," a tendency that Richard Bernstein has rightly criticized as unpragmatic and parochial (1995, 62).[7]

Though it is the dominant understanding of the career of pragmatism, the eclipse narrative is highly dubious. For one thing, those who promote the narrative rarely clarify what they mean by "analytic philosophy," and when a description is offered, it most often rings hollow. Bruce Wilshire, for example, identifies analytic philosophy with "scientism," the view that "only science can know" (2002, 4; cf. McCumber 2001, 49ff.), but it is clear that only the most extreme of the logical positivists, if anyone, ever held such a stark position. More importantly, if we examine the work of the most influential figures in mainstream philosophy from the past sixty years—for example (and excluding those whose work is collected in the present volume), Ludwig Wittgenstein, Bertrand Russell, Karl Popper, John Rawls, John Searle, Daniel Dennett, Charles Taylor, Michael Dummett, and Jürgen Habermas—we find that they either explicitly acknowledge a distinctively pragmatist inheritance or take themselves to be responding critically to identifiably pragmatist arguments. Judged according to the centrality of distinctively pragmatist theses concerning meaning, truth, knowledge, and action to ongoing debates in philosophy, pragmatism is easily among the most successful philosophical trends of the past two centuries. It seems, then, that the eclipse narrative is demonstrably false; pragmatism was alive and well throughout the twentieth century and it continues to be a major force on the philosophical scene.

Against the eclipse narrative, Rorty has claimed that in the years following World War II "all that happened was that the philosophy professors got bored with James and Dewey and latched on to something that looked new and promising" (2004, 284). Although Rorty is correct to reject the eclipse narrative, this rather blasé alternative cannot be the entire story. For one thing, Rorty's account leaves one to wonder why James and Dewey began to look boring and why other options seemed promising. We think Rorty's account should be supplemented along the following lines.

It is worth reminding ourselves of two related facts. First, the alleged eclipse of pragmatism coincides with Dewey's gradual withdrawal from the intellectual scene and eventual death in 1952. Second, the pragmatism that was allegedly eclipsed was primarily Deweyan pragmatism.[8] Accordingly, in order to fill in the story of the career of pragmatism, we need to look again at Dewey's version of pragmatism.

As we mentioned earlier, Dewey explicitly conceived of his pragmatism in revolutionary terms. He thought that the truth of Darwinism required a comprehensive reconstruction of philosophy in which traditional problems of philosophy, and the categories that they presumed, would be discarded; he declared that "we do not solve" the traditional problems of philosophy, we "get over them" (MW4:14). Consequently, Dewey's philosophy begins from a sweeping attack on all of the standard philosophical schools and positions. Perhaps the novelty of Dewey's critique took proponents of these positions by surprise; for Dewey did not simply introduce new considerations into the standing debates, he criticized the presuppositions underlying the debates themselves. Hence, according to Dewey, philosophy's past is composed of a series of mere "puzzles" (LW1:17) to be discarded as "chaff" (LW1:4).

Unlike Rorty, who saw pragmatism as a rejection of philosophy altogether, Dewey's project was not merely critical. Dewey spent his career building a comprehensive philosophical framework based in a distinctively Darwinian brand of pragmatism. By the early 1940s, Dewey had constructed a grand and integrated philosophical system. Indeed, many of Dewey's followers see the systematic nature of Dewey's philosophy as its principal virtue.

What we see in the mid-1900s, however, is a series of new articulations of the old positions that Dewey claimed to have undermined. Frequently, these new articulations were designed to respond to precisely the kind of objections that Dewey had proposed. Consider just a few examples. In the 1950s and 1960s, John Rawls proposed a new methodology for moral theory and a new defense of contractarianism that rejected intuitionism, egoism, utilitarianism, and the metaphysical extravagances of Kantianism. In the late 1950s and following, Roderick Chisholm devised foundationalist epistemology that was also fallibilist. In the 1960s, philosophers of language such as Jerrold Katz and Jerry Fodor drew on Chomsky's work in linguistics to devise a new kind of rationalism and nativism rooted in empirical data. Around the same time, John Searle resuscitated mind-body dualism in a form consistent with naturalism. By the 1970s, powerful new versions of nearly all of the traditional philosophical positions and, importantly, compelling new studies of key historical figures—including Dewey's principal foes, Descartes and Kant—had emerged.

The availability of ostensibly viable new instantiations of traditional positions challenged Dewey's strategy of dismissing entire philosophical schools as premised on a single simple error. New Kantians relied upon the method of reflective equilibrium, not transcendental metaphysics; new foundationalists did not need to embark on a "quest for certainty"; new rationalists could appeal to scientific data in support of their semantics; philosophers of mind could adopt a *property* dualism of mind and body, thereby eschewing the Cartesian metaphysics of dual substances. Whether any of these new positions is philosophically successful is, of course, debatable. Our point is that the development of these views rendered unsustainable Dewey's claim that Darwinism supplied a perspective from which centuries of philosophy could be swept away with a single gesture; it no longer seemed plausible to assert, with Dewey, that his philosophical approach was "the way, and the only way . . . by which one can freely accept the standpoint and conclusions of modern science" (LW1:4). Accordingly, those who favored the kind of pragmatism and naturalism associated with Dewey were driven to abandon Dewey's style of criticism. Pragmatists would have to engage the new developments piecemeal, argument by argument.

This in turn led to a general distrust of the kind of comprehensive philosophical system building in which Dewey engaged. It no longer seemed useful to erect grand systems of philosophy. Most of those active in professional philosophy had come to see that no set of philosophical premises full-bodied enough to support a system was noncontroversial enough to justify the effort of grand system building. The most that pragmatic philosophers could pursue was a defensible account of some more or less specific phenomenon, with the hope that such an account could be shown to hang together with similar accounts of related phenomena. But note that this humbling of philosophical ambition is driven by the utterly *pragmatic* insight that, when no single approach can plausibly claim to be the only responsible way of proceeding, philosophy itself must advance dialectically and in piecemeal fashion, by way of meeting the arguments, challenges, and counterexamples raised by those who do not share one's fundamental philosophical orientation.

Hence, it seems more accurate to say that in the years following World War II, pragmatism was in *crisis*, not eclipse. And the crisis was precipitated by Dewey's own methodology. What was clear at that time was that if pragmatism was to survive, it needed to be reworked, revised in light of new challenges from rival philosophical approaches. Here, the post-Deweyan pragmatist par excellence is Quine. Quine's corpus presents an ongoing development of a few key pragmatist and naturalist insights about science, language, and ontology, and an attempt to fit them together. Importantly, Quine proceeds by way of critical engagement with nonnaturalist critics and interlocutors. It is unsurprising, then, that after Dewey's death Quine quickly rose to become so influential among professional philosophers in America, for he understood that the case for pragmatism was to be made on a case-by-case basis, not by way of a comprehensive philosophical system. For similar reasons, it is no surprise that the Dewey that emerges heroic in Rorty's work is a "therapeutic" Dewey (Rorty 1982, 73), a Dewey shorn of system.

Hence, what is seen by those committed to the eclipse narrative as a turn in professional philosophy toward insularity, irrelevance, and technicality-for-its-own-sake is actually a pragmatically responsible reaction to the sheer plurality of philosophically forceful competitors to pragmatism, a plurality that Dewey had explicitly denied. There was no eclipse or abandonment of pragmatism; rather, the years following Dewey's death corresponded with the period in which pragmatism was forced to confront powerful challenges from opponents who had the opportunity to revise and rework their positions in light of pragmatist criticisms. Once again, we see that, far from being marginalized or excluded, pragmatism remained a highly influential and philosophically powerful force throughout the second half of the twentieth century and through the present. We take it that this assessment is borne out clearly enough in the following pages.

IV

The essays in this volume were selected not only for the influence they have exerted on professional philosophy but also for the directness with which they address familiar philosophical issues. This second selection criterion is crucial. Much of the work on pragmatism has a decidedly metaphilosophical flavor. The pragmatist is often found commenting on the state of professional philosophy, or declaring some traditional area of philosophical inquiry dead, or dismissing long-standing philosophical programs as rooted in some Cartesian or Kantian (and therefore untenable) presupposition. As a kind of naturalism, pragmatism is partly a thesis about the relation of philosophy to the natural sciences; consequently, one should expect pragmatists to engage the questions of the proper aims and methods of philosophy. However, there is a tendency among pragmatists to wax metaphilosophical to the exclusion of all else. This gives the impression that many pragmatists endorse a modified version of the positivist doctrine that all philosophical problems are problems of language: all philosophical problems are problems of metaphilosophy. In its most muscular form, the pragmatist thesis is that, once we understand properly the nature of philosophy, we will discover that there are no philosophical problems anyway.

The tendency to "go meta" obscures the extent to which pragmatists are committed to, and must engage in debates concerning, first-order philosophical claims. Our objective here is to present pragmatism as an engagement with philosophical problems, to show pragmatism at work. When its practitioners "go meta," pragmatism is little more than an appeal to contentious notion of proper philosophical method in order to dismiss a problem. This leaves many (including us) with the suspicion that little or no work as been done. The pragmatist project is viable only on the condition that pragmatist answers to first-order philosophical problems are viable. Only once a philosophical tradition has a successful track record with the problems of philosophy should its practitioners have the right to speak to (or browbeat others regarding) the nature of proper philosophical method. That is, one gets to do metaphilosophy only once one has done well with philosophy. Solving philosophical problems with metaphilosophy, then, gets things entirely backward. As a consequence, excepting the preceding paragraph, there will be little or no metaphilosophical accounts in this volume, but only what we take to be hallmark pragmatist responses to standing philosophical problems.

V

We have assembled this collection both for use in the classroom and as a scholarly resource. Accordingly, all selections are reprinted in full and were originally written as stand-alone pieces rather than as chapters in books developing an extended argument. Before each section, we have added a brief note providing the most general context for the piece. In these, we do not attempt to summarize the content of the article or even state its main thesis; rather, we provide some sense of the role the piece plays in the larger picture of pragmatism that this collection as a whole is trying to call attention to.

In the course of editing this collection we have incurred several debts. We would like to thank Erin Bradfield, Mary Butterfield, Joshua Houston, and Jo Matocha for their editorial assistance. We have also benefited from discussions, comments, and advice from Jody Azzouni, James Bednar, Steve Cahn, Harvey Cormier, Richard Gale, Micah Hester, David Hildebrand, Michael Hodges, Chris King, Cheryl Misak, and Jeffrey Tlumak. Finally, we would like to thank the production staff at Princeton University Press and our editor, Rob Tempio.

Notes

1. We follow the convention in citing Peirce's *Collected Papers*: (volume number.paragraph number).
2. Reference to James's writings are keyed to *The Writings of William James*, edited by John McDermott (1977).
3. References to Dewey's work are keyed the *Collected Works*, which are divided into *Early*, *Middle*, and *Later* works. Citations employ the standard formula: (volume number: page number).
4. For a more complete account of the disagreements between Peirce, James, and Dewey, see Talisse and Aikin 2008, ch. 1.
5. See Aikin 2006 for an account of the details of pragmatist naturalism and humanism.

6. It is nearly impossible to find a current work on pragmatism that does not present some version of this story. See, for example, West 1989, 3; Bernstein 1992; Festenstein 1997, 2; Dickstein 1998, 1; and Westbrook 2005, xii.

7. See Talisse 2007, ch. 7 for further discussion.

8. Peirce was always highly regarded among professional philosophers; however, the full import of his thought could not be estimated, due to the unavailability of a systematic edition of his writings. For this reason, Peirce's pragmatism was never the dominant version. As for James, his pragmatism was never regarded as canonical, and, as we have mentioned, his own articulations of pragmatist themes were largely rejected by subsequent pragmatists, including Dewey.

References

Aikin, Scott. 2006. "Pragmatism, Naturalism, and Phenomenology." *Human Studies* 29: 317–340.

Bernstein, Richard. 1992. "The Resurgence of American Pragmatism." *Social Research* 59: 813–840.

———. 1995. "American Philosophy as a Conflict of Narratives." In Herman Saatkamp, ed., *Rorty and Pragmatism*, 54–67. Nashville: Vanderbilt University Press.

Dewey, John. 1969–1991. *The Collected Works of John Dewey: The Early Works, the Middle Works, the Later Works.* 37 vols. Ed. Jo Ann Boydston. Carbondale: Southern Illinois University Press.

Dickstein, Morris. 1998. "Introduction: Pragmatism Then and Now." In *The Revival of Pragmatism*, ed. Dickstein, 1–18. Durham: Duke University Press.

Festenstein, Matthew. 1997. *Pragmatism and Political Theory.* Chicago: University of Chicago Press.

James, William. 1977. *The Writings of William James.* Ed. John J. McDermott. Chicago: University of Chicago Press.

McCumber, John. 2001. *Time in the Ditch.* Evanston, IL: Northwestern University Press.

Peirce, Charles Sanders. 1931–1958. *The Collected Works of Charles Sanders Peirce.* 8 vols. Ed. Charles Hartshorne, Paul Weiss, and Arthur Burks. Cambridge, MA: Harvard University Press.

Rorty, Richard. 1982. *Consequences of Pragmatism.* Minneapolis: University of Minnesota Press.

———. 2004. Afterword. In *Sidney Hook Reconsidered*, Ed. Matthew Cotter. Amherst: Prometheus Books.

Talisse, Robert B. 2007. *A Pragmatist Philosophy of Democracy.* New York: Routledge.

Talisse, Robert B., and Scott F. Aikin. 2008. *Pragmatism: A Guide for the Perplexed.* London: Continuum.

West, Cornel. 1989. *The American Evasion of Philosophy.* Madison: University of Wisconsin Press.

Westbrook, Robert. 2005. *Democratic Hope.* Ithaca: Cornell University Press.

Wilshire, Bruce. 2002. *Fashionable Nihilism: A Critique of Analytic Philosophy.* Albany: SUNY Press.

This essay was originally published in 1868. Here Peirce launches the kind of attack on Cartesianism that lies at the heart of most subsequent pragmatism.

CHARLES S. PEIRCE

Some Consequences of Four Incapacities

Descartes is the father of modern philosophy, and the spirit of Cartesianism—that which principally distinguishes it from the scholasticism which it displaced—may be compendiously stated as follows:

1. It teaches that philosophy must begin with universal doubt; whereas scholasticism had never questioned fundamentals.
2. It teaches that the ultimate test of certainty is to be found in the individual consciousness; whereas scholasticism had rested on the testimony of sages and of the Catholic Church.
3. The multiform argumentation of the middle ages is replaced by a single thread of inference depending often upon inconspicuous premisses.
4. Scholasticism had its mysteries of faith, but undertook to explain all created things. But there are many facts which Cartesianism not only does not explain but renders absolutely inexplicable, unless to say that "God makes them so" is to be regarded as an explanation.

In some, or all of these respects, most modern philosophers have been, in effect, Cartesians. Now without wishing to return to scholasticism, it seems to me that modern science and modern logic require us to stand upon a very different platform from this.

1. We cannot begin with complete doubt. We must begin with all the prejudices which we actually have when we enter upon the study of philosophy. These prejudices are not to be dispelled by a maxim, for they are things which it does not occur to us *can* be questioned. Hence this initial skepticism will be a mere self-deception, and not real doubt; and no one who follows the Cartesian method will ever be satisfied until he has formally recovered all those beliefs which in form he has given up. It is, therefore, as useless a preliminary as going to the North Pole would be in order to get to Constantinople by coming down regularly upon a meridian. A person may, it is true, in the course of his studies, find reason to doubt what he began by believing; but in that case he doubts because he has a positive reason for it, and not on account of the Cartesian maxim. Let us not pretend to doubt in philosophy what we do not doubt in our hearts.

2. The same formalism appears in the Cartesian criterion, which amounts to this: "Whatever I am clearly convinced of, is true." If I were really convinced, I should have done with reasoning and should require no test of certainty. But thus to make single individuals absolute judges of truth is most pernicious. The result is that metaphysicians will all agree that metaphysics has reached a pitch of certainty far beyond that of the physical sciences;—only they can agree upon nothing else. In sciences in which men come to agreement, when a theory has been broached it is considered to be on probation until this agreement is reached. After it is reached, the question of certainty becomes an idle one, because there is no one left who doubts it. We individually cannot reasonably hope to attain the ultimate philosophy which we pursue; we can only seek it, therefore, for the *community* of philosophers. Hence, if disciplined and candid minds carefully examine a theory and refuse to accept it, this ought to create doubts in the mind of the author of the theory himself.

3. Philosophy ought to imitate the successful sciences in its methods, so far as to proceed only from tangible premisses which can be subjected to careful scrutiny, and to trust rather to the multitude and variety of its arguments than to the conclusiveness of any one. Its reasoning should not form a chain which is no stronger than its weakest link, but a cable whose fibers may be ever so slender, provided they are sufficiently numerous and intimately connected.

4. Every unidealistic philosophy supposes some absolutely inexplicable, unanalyzable ultimate; in short, something resulting from mediation itself not susceptible of mediation. Now that anything is thus inexplicable can only be known by reasoning from signs. But the only justification of an inference from signs is that the conclusion explains the fact. To suppose the fact absolutely inexplicable, is not to explain it, and hence this supposition is never allowable.

In the last number of this journal will be found a piece entitled "Questions concerning certain Faculties claimed for Man," which has been written in this spirit of opposition to Cartesianism. That criticism of certain faculties resulted in four denials, which for convenience may here be repeated:

1. We have no power of Introspection, but all knowledge of the internal world is derived by hypothetical reasoning from our knowledge of external facts.

2. We have no power of Intuition, but every cognition is determined logically by previous cognitions.

3. We have no power of thinking without signs.

4. We have no conception of the absolutely incognizable. These propositions cannot be regarded as certain; and, in order to bring them to a further test, it is now proposed to trace them out to their consequences. We may first consider the first alone; then trace the consequences of the first and second; then see what else will result from assuming the third also; and, finally, add the fourth to our hypothetical premisses.

In accepting the first proposition, we must put aside all prejudices derived from a philosophy which bases our knowledge of the external world on our self-consciousness. We can admit no statement concerning what passes within us except as a hypothesis necessary to explain what takes place in what we commonly call the external world. Moreover when we have upon such grounds assumed one faculty or mode of action of the mind, we cannot, of course, adopt any other hypothesis for the purpose of explaining any fact which can be explained by our first supposition, but must carry the latter as far as it will go. In other words, we must, as far as we can do so without additional hypotheses, reduce all kinds of mental action to one general type.

The class of modifications of consciousness with which we must commence our inquiry must be one whose existence is indubitable, and whose laws are best known, and, therefore (since this knowledge comes from the outside), which most closely follows external facts; that is, it must be some kind of cognition. Here we may hypothetically admit the second proposition of the former paper, according to which there is no absolutely first cognition of any object, but cognition arises by a continuous process. We must begin, then, with a *process* of cognition, and with that process whose laws are best understood and most closely follow external facts. This is no other than the process of valid inference, which proceeds from its premiss, *A*, to its conclusion, *B*, only if, as a matter of fact, such a proposition as *B* is always or usually true when such a proposition as *A* is true. It is a consequence, then, of the first two principles whose results we are to trace out, that we must, as far as we can, without any other supposition than that the mind reasons, reduce all mental action to the formula of valid reasoning.

But does the mind in fact go through the syllogistic process? It is certainly very doubtful whether a conclusion—as something existing in the mind independently, like an image—suddenly displaces two premisses existing in the mind in a similar way. But it is a matter of constant experience, that if a man is made to believe in the premisses, in the sense that he will act from them and will say that they are true, under favorable conditions he will also be ready to act from the conclusion and to say that that is true. Something, therefore, takes place within the organism which is equivalent to the syllogistic process.

A valid inference is either *complete* or *incomplete*. An incomplete inference is one whose validity depends upon some matter of fact not contained in the premisses. This implied fact might have been stated as a premiss, and its relation to the conclusion is the same whether it is explicitly posited or not, since it is at least virtually taken for granted; so that every valid incomplete argument is virtually complete. Complete arguments are divided into *simple* and *complex*. A complex argument is one which from three or more premisses concludes what might have been concluded by successive steps in reasonings each of which is simple. Thus, a complex inference comes to the same thing in the end as a succession of simple inferences.

A complete, simple, and valid argument, or syllogism, is either *apodictic* or *probable*. An apodictic or deductive syllogism is one whose validity depends unconditionally upon the relation of the fact inferred to the facts posited in the premisses. A syllogism whose validity should depend not merely upon its premisses, but upon the existence of some other knowledge, would be impossible; for either this other knowledge would be posited, in which case it would be a part of the premisses, or it would be implicitly assumed, in which case the inference would be incomplete. But a syllogism whose validity depends partly upon the *non-existence* of some other knowledge, is a *probable* syllogism.

A few examples will render this plain. The two following arguments are apodictic or deductive:

1. No series of days of which the first and last are different days of the week exceeds by one a multiple of seven days; now the first and last days of any leap-year are different days of the week, and therefore no leap-year consists of a number of days one greater than a multiple of seven.

2. Among the vowels there are no double letters; but one of the double letters (*w*) is compounded of two vowels: hence, a letter compounded of two vowels is not necessarily itself a vowel.

In both these cases, it is plain that as long as the premisses are true, however other facts may be, the conclusions will be true. On the other hand, suppose that we reason as follows:—"A certain man had the Asiatic cholera. He was in a state of collapse, livid, quite cold, and without perceptible pulse. He was bled copiously. During the process he came out of collapse, and the next morning was well enough to be about. Therefore, bleeding tends to cure the cholera." This is a fair probable inference, provided that the premisses represent our whole knowledge of the matter. But if we knew, for example, that recoveries from cholera were apt to be sudden, and that the physician who had reported this case had known of a hundred other trials of the remedy without communicating the result, then the inference would lose all its validity.

The absence of knowledge which is essential to the validity of any probable argument relates to some question which is determined by the argument itself. This question, like every other, is whether certain objects have certain characters. Hence, the absence of knowledge is either whether besides the objects which, according to the premisses, possess certain characters, any other objects possess them; or, whether besides the characters which, according to the premisses, belong to certain objects, any other characters not necessarily involved in these belong to the same objects. In the former case, the reasoning proceeds as though all the objects which have certain characters were known, and this is *induction*; in the latter case, the inference proceeds as though all the characters requisite to the determination of a certain object or class were known, and this is *hypothesis*. This distinction, also, may be made more plain by examples.

Suppose we count the number of occurrences of the different letters in a certain English book, which we may call *A*. Of course, every new letter which we add to our count will alter the relative number of occurrences of the different letters; but as we proceed with our counting, this change will be less and less. Suppose that we find that as we increase the number of letters counted, the relative number of *e*'s approaches nearly 11 1/4 *per cent* of the whole, that of the *f*s 8 1/2 *per cent*, that of the *a*'s 8 *per cent*, that of the *s*'s 7 1/2 *per cent*, etc. Suppose we repeat the same observations with half a dozen other English writings (which we may designate as *B, C, D, E, F, G*) with the like result. Then we may infer that in every English writing of some length, the different letters occur with nearly those relative frequencies.

Now this argument depends for its validity upon our not knowing the proportion of letters in any English writing besides *A, B, C, D, E, F,* and *G*. For if we know it in respect to *H*, and it is not nearly the same as in the others, our conclusion is destroyed at once; if it is the same, then the legitimate inference is from *A, B, C, D, E, F, G* and *H*, and not from the first seven alone. This, therefore, is an induction.

Suppose, next, that a piece of writing in cipher is presented to us, without the key. Suppose we find that it contains something less than 26 characters, one of which occurs about 11 *per cent* of all the times, another 8 1/2 *per cent*, another 8 *per cent*, and another 7 1/2 *per cent*. Suppose that when we substitute for these *e, t, a* and *s*, respectively, we are able to see how single letters may be substituted for each of the other characters so as to make sense in English, provided, however, that we allow the spelling to be wrong in some cases. If the writing is of any considerable length, we may infer with great probability that this is the meaning of the cipher.

The validity of this argument depends upon there being no other known characters of the writing in cipher which would have any weight in the matter; for if there are—if we know, for example, whether or not there is any other solution of it—this must be allowed its effect in supporting or weakening the conclusion. This, then, is *hypothesis*.

All valid reasoning is either deductive, inductive, or hypothetic; or else it combines two or more of these characters. Deduction is pretty well treated in most logical textbooks; but it will be necessary to say a few words about induction and hypothesis in order to render what follows more intelligible.

Induction may be defined as an argument which proceeds upon the assumption that all the members of a class or aggregate have all the characters which are common to all those members of this class concerning which it is known, whether they have these characters or not; or, in other words, which assumes that that is true of a whole collection which is true of a number of instances taken from it at random. This might be called statistical argument. In the long run, it must generally afford pretty correct conclusions from true premisses. If we have a bag of beans partly black and partly white, by counting the relative proportions of the two colors in several different handfuls, we can approximate more or less to the relative proportions in the whole bag, since a sufficient number of handfuls would constitute all the beans in the bag. The central characteristic and key to induction is, that by taking the conclusion so reached as major premiss of a syllogism, and the proposition stating that such and such objects are taken from the class in question as the minor premiss, the other premiss of the induction will follow from them deductively. Thus, in the above example we concluded that all books in English have about 11 1/4 *per cent* of their letters *e*'s. From that as major premiss, together with the proposition that *A, B, C, D, E, F* and *G* are books in English, it follows deductively that *A, B, C, D, E, F* and *G* have about 11 1/4 *per cent* of their letters *e*'s. Accordingly, induction has been defined by Aristotle as the inference of the major premiss of a syllogism from its minor premiss and conclusion. The function of an induction is to substitute for a series of many subjects, a single one which embraces them and an indefinite number of others. Thus it is a species of "reduction of the manifold to unity."

Hypothesis may be defined as an argument which proceeds upon the assumption that a character which is known necessarily to involve a certain number of others, may be probably predicated of any object which has all the characters which this character is known to involve. Just as induction may be regarded as the inference of the major premiss of a syllogism, so hypothesis may be regarded as the inference of the minor premiss, from the other two propositions. Thus, the example taken above consists of two such inferences of the minor premisses of the following syllogisms:

1. Every English writing of some length in which such and such characters denote *e, t, a,* and *s*, has about 11 1/4 *per cent* of the first sort of marks, 8 1/2 of the second, 8 of the third, and 7 1/2 of the fourth.

This secret writing is an English writing of some length, in which such and such characters denote *e, t, a,* and *s*, respectively:

[Ergo,] This secret writing has about 11 1/4 *per cent* of its characters of the first kind, 8 1/2 of the second, 8 of the third, and 7 1/2 of the fourth.

2. A passage written with such an alphabet makes sense when such and such letters are severally substituted for such and such characters.

This secret writing is written with such an alphabet.

[Ergo,] This secret writing makes sense when such and such substitutions are made.

The function of hypothesis[1] is to substitute for a great series of predicates forming no unity in themselves, a single one (or small number) which involves them all, together (perhaps) with an indefinite number of others. It is, therefore, also a reduction of a manifold to unity. Every deductive syllogism may be put into the form

If *A*, then *B*;
But *A*:
[Ergo,] *B*

And as the minor premiss in this form appears as antecedent or reason of a hypothetical proposition, hypothetic inference may be called reasoning from consequent to antecedent.

The argument from analogy, which a popular writer upon logic calls reasoning from particulars to particulars, derives its validity from its combining the characters of induction and hypothesis, being analyzable either into a deduction or an induction, or a deduction and a hypothesis.

But though inference is thus of three essentially different species, it also belongs to one genus. We have seen that no conclusion can be legitimately derived which could not have been reached by successions of arguments having two premisses each, and implying no fact not asserted.

Either of these premisses is a proposition asserting that certain objects have certain characters. Every term of such a proposition stands either for certain objects or for certain characters. The conclusion may be regarded as a proposition substituted in place of either premiss, the substitution being justified by the fact stated in the other premiss. The conclusion is accordingly derived from either premiss by substituting either a new subject for the subject of the premiss, or a new predicate for the predicate of the premiss, or by both substitutions. Now the substitution of one term for another can be justified only so far as the term substituted represents only what is represented in the term replaced. If, therefore, the conclusion be denoted by the formula,

S is *P;*

and this conclusion be derived, by a change of subject, from a premiss which may on this account be expressed by the formula,

M is *P,*

then the other premiss must assert that whatever thing is represented by S is represented by M, or that

Every *S* is an *M;*

while, if the conclusion, *S* is *P,* is derived from either premiss by a change of predicate, that premiss may be written

S is *M;*

and the other premiss must assert that whatever characters are implied in *P* are implied in *M*, or that

Whatever is *M* is *P*.

In either case, therefore, the syllogism must be capable of expression in the form,

S is *M; M* is *P:*
[Ergo,] *S* is *P*.

Finally, if the conclusion differs from either of its premisses, both in subject and predicate, the form of statement of conclusion and premiss may be so altered that they shall have a common term. This can always be done, for if *P* is the premiss and *C* the conclusion, they may be stated thus:

The state of things represented in *P* is real,
and
The state of things represented in *C* is real.

In this case the other premiss must in some form virtually assert that every state of things such as is represented by *C* is the state of things represented in *P*.

All valid reasoning, therefore, is of one general form; and in seeking to reduce all mental action to the formulæ of valid inference, we seek to reduce it to one single type.

An apparent obstacle to the reduction of all mental action to the type of valid inferences is the existence of fallacious reasoning. Every argument implies the truth of a general principle of inferential procedure (whether involving some matter of fact concerning the subject of argument, or merely a maxim relating to a system of signs), according to which it is a valid argument. If this principle is false, the argument is a fallacy; but neither a valid argument from false premisses, nor an exceedingly weak, but not altogether illegitimate, induction or hypothesis, however its force may be over-estimated, however false its conclusion, is a fallacy.

Now words, taken just as they stand, if in the form of an argument, thereby do imply whatever fact may be necessary to make the argument conclusive; so that to the formal logician, who has to do only with the meaning of the words according to the proper principles of interpretation, and not with the intention of the speaker as guessed at from other indications, the only fallacies should be such as are simply absurd and contradictory, either because their conclusions are absolutely inconsistent with their premisses, or because they connect propositions by a species of illative conjunction, by which they cannot under any circumstances be validly connected.

But to the psychologist an argument is valid only if the premisses from which the mental conclusion is derived would be sufficient, if true, to justify it, either by themselves, or by the aid of other propositions which had previously been held for true. But it is easy to show that all inferences made by man, which are not valid in this sense, belong to four classes, viz,: 1. Those whose premisses are false; 2. Those which have some little force, though only a little; 3. Those which result from confusion of one proposition with another; 4. Those which result from the indistinct apprehension, wrong application, or falsity, of a rule of inference. For, if a man were to commit a fallacy not of either of these classes, he would, from true premisses conceived with perfect distinctness, without being led astray by any prejudice or other judgment serving as a rule of inference, draw a conclusion which had really not the least relevancy. If this could happen, calm consideration and care could be of little use in thinking, for caution only serves to insure our taking all the facts into account, and to make those which we do take account of, distinct; nor can coolness do anything more than to enable us to be cautious, and also to prevent our being affected by a passion in inferring that to be true which we wish were true, or which we fear may be true, or in following some other wrong rule of inference. But experience shows that the calm and careful consideration of the same distinctly conceived premisses (including prejudices) will insure the pronouncement of the same judgment by all men. Now if a fallacy belongs to the first of these four classes and its premisses are false, it is to be presumed that the procedure of the mind from these premisses to the conclusion is either correct, or errs in one of the other three ways; for it cannot be supposed that the mere falsity of the premisses should affect the procedure of reason when that falsity is not known to reason. If the fallacy belongs to the second class and has some force, however little, it is a legitimate probable argument, and belongs to the type of valid inference. If it is of the third class and results from the confusion of one proposition with another, this confusion must be owing to a resemblance between the two propositions; that is to say, the person reasoning, seeing that one proposition has some of the characters which belong to the other, concludes that it has all the essential characters of the other, and is equivalent to it. Now this is a hypothetic inference, which though it may be weak, and though its conclusion happens to be false, belongs to the type of valid inferences; and, therefore, as the *nodus* of the fallacy lies in this confusion, the procedure of the mind in these fallacies of the third class conforms to the formula of valid inference. If the fallacy belongs to the fourth class, it either results from wrongly applying or misapprehending a rule of inference, and so is a fallacy of confusion, or it results from adopting a wrong rule of inference. In this latter case, this rule is in fact taken as a premiss, and therefore the false conclusion is owing merely to the falsity of a premiss. In every fallacy, therefore, possible to the mind of man, the procedure of the mind conforms to the formula of valid inference.

The third principle whose consequences we have to deduce is, that, whenever we think, we have present to the consciousness some feeling, image, conception, or other representation, which serves as a sign. But it follows from our own existence (which is proved by the occurrence of ignorance and error) that everything which is present to us is a phenomenal manifestation of ourselves. This does not prevent its being a phenomenon of something without us, just as a rainbow is at once a manifestation both of the sun and of the rain. When we think, then, we ourselves, as we are at that moment, appear as a sign. Now a sign has, as such, three references: first, it is a sign *to* some thought which interprets it; second, it is a sign *for* some object to which in that thought it is equivalent; third, it is a sign, *in* some respect or quality, which brings it into connection with its object. Let us ask what the three correlates are to which a thought-sign refers.

(1) When we think, to what thought does that thought-sign which is ourself address itself? It may, through the medium of outward expression, which it reaches perhaps only after considerable internal development, come to address itself to thought of another person. But whether this happens or not, it is always interpreted by a subsequent thought of our own. If, after any thought, the current of ideas flows on freely, it follows the law of mental association. In that case, each former thought suggests something to the thought which follows it, i.e., is the sign of something to this latter. Our train of thought may, it is true, be interrupted. But we must remember that, in addition to the principal element of thought at any moment, there are a hundred things in our mind to which but a small fraction of attention or consciousness is conceded. It does not, therefore, follow, because a new constituent of thought gets the uppermost that the train of thought which it displaces is broken off altogether. On the contrary, from our second principle, that there is no intuition or cognition not determined by previous cognitions, it follows that the striking in of a new experience is never an instantaneous affair, but is an *event* occupying time, and coming to pass by a continuous process. Its prominence in consciousness, therefore, must probably be the consummation of a growing process; and if so, there is no sufficient cause for the thought which had been the leading one just before, to cease abruptly and instantaneously.

But if a train of thought ceases by gradually dying out, it freely follows its own law of association as long as it lasts, and there is no moment at which there is a thought belonging to this series, subsequently to which there is not a thought which interprets or repeats it. There is no exception, therefore, to the law that every thought-sign is translated or interpreted in a subsequent one, unless it be that all thought comes to an abrupt and final end in death.

(2) The next question is: For what does the thought-sign stand—what does it name—what is its *suppositum*? The outward thing, undoubtedly, when a real outward thing is thought of. But still, as the thought is determined by a previous thought of the same object, it only refers to the thing through denoting this previous thought. Let us suppose, for example, that Toussaint is thought of, and first thought of as a *Negro*, but not distinctly as a man. If this distinctness is afterwards added, it is through the thought that a *Negro* is a *man*; that is to say, the subsequent thought, *man*, refers to the outward thing by being predicated of that previous thought, *Negro*, which has been had of that thing. If we afterwards think of Toussaint as a general, then we think that this negro, this man, was a general. And so in every case the subsequent thought denotes what was thought in the previous thought.

(3) The thought-sign stands for its object in the respect which is thought; that is to say, this respect is the immediate object of consciousness in the thought, or, in other words, it is the thought itself, or at least what the thought is thought to be in the subsequent thought to which it is a sign.

We must now consider two other properties of signs which are of great importance in the theory of cognition. Since a sign is not identical with the thing signified, but differs from the latter in some respects, it must plainly have some characters which belong to it in itself, and have nothing to do with its representative function. These I call the *material* qualities of the sign. As examples of such qualities, take in the word "man," its consisting of three letters—in a picture, its being flat and without relief. In the second place, a sign must be capable of being connected (not in the reason but really) with another sign of the same object, or with the object itself. Thus, words would be of no value at all unless they could be connected into sentences by means of a real copula which joins signs of the same thing. The usefulness of some signs—as a weathercock, a tally, &c.—consists wholly in their being really connected with the very things they signify. In the case of a picture such a connection is not evident, but it exists in the power of association which connects the picture with the brain-sign which labels it. This real, physical connection of a sign with its object, either immediately or by its connection with another sign, I call the *pure demonstrative application* of the sign. Now the representative function of a sign lies neither in its material quality nor in its pure demonstrative application; because it is something which the sign is, not in itself or in a real relation to its object, but which it is *to a thought*, while both of the characters just defined belong to the sign independently of its addressing any thought. And yet if I take all the things which have certain qualities and physically connect them with another series of things, each to each, they become fit to be signs.

If they are not regarded as such they are not actually signs, but they are so in the same sense, for example, in which an unseen flower can be said to be red, this being also a term relative to a mental affection.

Consider a state of mind which is a conception. It is a conception by virtue of having a *meaning*, a logical comprehension; and if it is applicable to any object, it is because that object has the characters contained in the comprehension of this conception. Now the logical comprehension of a thought is usually said to consist of the thoughts contained in it; but thoughts are events, acts of the mind. Two thoughts are two events separated in time, and one cannot literally be contained in the other. It may be said that all thoughts exactly similar are regarded as one; and that to say that one thought contains another, means that it contains one exactly similar to that other. But how can two thoughts be similar? Two objects can only be *regarded* as similar if they are compared and brought together in the mind. Thoughts have no existence except in the mind; only as they are regarded do they exist. Hence, two thoughts cannot *be* similar unless they are brought together in the mind. But, as to their existence, two thoughts are separated by an interval of time. We are too apt to imagine that we can frame a thought similar to a past thought, by matching it with the latter, as though this past thought were still present to us. But it is plain that the knowledge that one thought is similar to or in any way truly representative of another, cannot be derived from immediate perception, but must be an hypothesis (unquestionably fully justifiable by facts), and that therefore the formation of such a representing thought must be dependent upon a real effective force behind consciousness, and not merely upon a mental comparison. What we must mean, therefore, by saying that one concept is contained in another, is that we normally represent one to be in the other; that is, that we form a particular kind of judgment[2] of which the subject signifies one concept and the predicate the other.

No thought in itself, then, no feeling in itself, contains any others, but is absolutely simple and unanalyzable; and to say that it is composed of other thoughts and feelings, is like saying that a movement upon a straight line is composed of the two movements of which it is the resultant; that is to say, it is a metaphor, or fiction, parallel to the truth. Every thought, however artificial and complex, is, so far as it is immediately present, a mere sensation without parts, and therefore, in itself,[3] without similarity to any other, but incomparable with any other and absolutely *sui generis*. Whatever is wholly incomparable with anything else is wholly inexplicable, because explanation consists in bringing things under general laws or under natural classes. Hence every thought, in so far as it is a feeling of a peculiar sort, is simply an ultimate, inexplicable fact. Yet this does not conflict with my postulate that that fact should be allowed to stand as inexplicable; for, on the one hand, we never can think, "This is present to me," since, before we have time to make the reflection, the sensation is past, and, on the other hand, when once past, we can never bring back the quality of the feeling as it was *in and for itself*, or know what it was like *in itself*, or even discover the existence of this quality except by a corollary from our general theory of ourselves, and then not in its idiosyncrasy, but only as something present. But, as something present, feelings are all alike and require no explanation, since they contain only what is universal. So that nothing which we can truly predicate of feelings is left inexplicable, but only something which we cannot reflectively know. So that we do not fall into the contradiction of making the Mediate immediable. Finally, no present actual thought (which is a mere feeling) has any meaning, any intellectual value; for this lies not in what is actually thought, but in what this thought may be connected with in representation by subsequent thoughts; so that the meaning of a thought is altogether something virtual. It may be objected, that if no thought has any meaning, all thought is without meaning. But this is a fallacy similar to saying, that, if in no one of the successive spaces which a body fills there is room for motion, there is no room for motion throughout the whole. At no one instant in my state of mind is there cognition or representation, but in the relation of my states of mind at different instants there is.[4] In short, the Immediate (and therefore in itself unsusceptible of mediation—the Unanalyzable, the Inexplicable, the Unintellectual) runs in a continuous stream through our lives; it is the sum total of consciousness, whose mediation, which is the continuity of it, is brought about by a real effective force behind consciousness.

Thus, we have in thought three elements: first, the representative function which makes it a *representation;* second, the pure denotative application, or real connection, which brings one thought into *relation* with another; and third, the material quality, or how it feels, which gives thought its *quality.*[5]

That a sensation is not necessarily an intuition, or first impression of sense, is very evident in the case of the sense of beauty; and has been shown, elsewhere, in the case of sound. When the sensation beautiful is determined by previous cognitions, it always arises as a predicate; that is, we think that something is beautiful. Whenever a sensation thus arises in consequence of others, induction shows that those others are more or less complicated. Thus, the sensation of a particular kind of sound arises in consequence of impressions upon the various nerves of the ear being combined in a particular way, and following one another with a certain rapidity. A sensation of color depends upon impressions upon the eye following one another in a regular manner, and with a certain rapidity. The sensation of beauty arises upon a manifold of other impressions. And this will be found to hold good in all cases. Secondly, all these sensations are in themselves simple, or more so than the sensations which give rise to them. Accordingly, a sensation is a simple predicate taken in place of a complex predicate; in other words, it fulfills the function of an hypothesis. But the general principle that every thing to which such and such a sensation belongs, has such and such a complicated series of predicates, is not one determined by reason (as we have seen), but is of an arbitrary nature. Hence, the class of hypothetic inferences which the arising of a sensation resembles, is that of reasoning from definition to definitum, in which the major premiss is of an arbitrary nature. Only in this mode of reasoning, this premiss is determined by the conventions of language, and expresses the occasion upon which a word is to be used; and in the formation of a sensation, it is determined by the constitution of our nature, and expresses the occasions upon which sensation, or a natural mental sign, arises. Thus, the sensation, so far as it represents something, is determined, according to a logical law, by previous cognitions; that is to say, these cognitions determine that there shall be a sensation. But so far as the sensation is a mere feeling of a particular sort, it is determined only by an inexplicable, occult power; and so far, it is not a representation, but only the material quality of a representation. For just as in reasoning from definition to definitum, it is indifferent to the logician how the defined word shall sound, or how many letters it shall contain, so in the case of this constitutional word, it is not determined by an inward law how it shall feel in itself. A feeling, therefore, as a feeling, is merely the *material quality* of a mental sign.

But there is no feeling which is not also a representation, a predicate of something determined logically by the feelings which precede it. For if there are any such feelings not predicates, they are the emotions. Now every emotion has a subject. If a man is angry, he is saying to himself that this or that is vile and outrageous. If he is in joy, he is saying "this is delicious." If he is wondering, he is saying "this is strange." In short, whenever a man feels, he is thinking of *something*. Even those passions which have no definite object—as melancholy—only come to consciousness through tinging *the objects of thought*. That which makes us look upon the emotions more as affections of self than other cognitions, is that we have found them more dependent upon our accidental situation at the moment than other cognitions; but that is only to say that they are cognitions too narrow to be useful. The emotions, as a little observation will show, arise when our attention is strongly drawn to complex and inconceivable circumstances. Fear arises when we cannot predict our fate; joy, in the case of certain indescribable and peculiarly complex sensations. If there are some indications that something greatly for my interest, and which I have anticipated would happen, may not happen; and if, after weighing probabilities, and inventing safeguards, and straining for further information, I find myself unable to come to any fixed conclusion in reference to the future, in the place of that intellectual hypothetic inference which I seek, the feeling of *anxiety* arises. When something happens for which I cannot account, I *wonder*. When I endeavor to realize to myself what I never can do, a pleasure in the future, I *hope*. "I do not understand you," is the phrase of an angry man. The indescribable, the ineffable, the incomprehensible, commonly excite emotion; but nothing is so chilling as a scientific explanation. Thus an emotion is always a simple predicate substituted by an operation of the mind for a highly complicated predicate. Now if we consider that a very complex predicate demands explanation by means of an hypothesis, that that hypothesis must be a simpler predicate substituted for that complex one; and that when we have an emotion, an hypothesis, strictly speaking, is hardly possible—the analogy of the parts played by emotion and hypothesis is very striking. There is, it is true, this difference between an emotion and an intellectual hypothesis, that we have reason to say in the case of the latter, that to whatever the simple hypothetic predicate can be applied, of that the complex predicate is true;

whereas, in the case of an emotion this is a proposition for which no reason can be given, but which is determined merely by our emotional constitution. But this corresponds precisely to the difference between hypothesis and reasoning from definition to definitum, and thus it would appear that emotion is nothing but sensation. There appears to be a difference, however, between emotion and sensation, and I would state it as follows:

There is some reason to think that, corresponding to every feeling within us, some motion takes place in our bodies. This property of the thought-sign, since it has no rational dependence upon the meaning of the sign, may be compared with what I have called the material quality of the sign; but it differs from the latter inasmuch as it is not essentially necessary that it should be felt in order that there should be any thought-sign. In the case of a sensation, the manifold of impressions which precede and determine it are not of a kind, the bodily motion corresponding to which comes from any large ganglion or from the brain, and probably for this reason the sensation produces no great commotion in the bodily organism; and the sensation itself is not a thought which has a very strong influence upon the current of thought except by virtue of the information it may serve to afford. An emotion, on the other hand, comes much later in the development of thought—I mean, further from the first beginning of the cognition of its object—and the thoughts which determine it already have motions corresponding to them in the brain, or the chief ganglion; consequently, it produces large movements in the body, and independently of its representative value, strongly affects the current of thought. The animal motions to which I allude, are, in the first place and obviously, blushing, blenching, staring, smiling, scowling, pouting, laughing, weeping, sobbing, wriggling, flinching, trembling, being petrified, sighing, sniffing, shrugging, groaning, heartsinking, trepidation, swelling of the heart, etc., etc. To these may, perhaps, be added, in the second place, other more complicated actions, which nevertheless spring from a direct impulse and not from deliberation.

That which distinguishes both sensations proper and emotions from the feeling of a thought, is that in the case of the two former the material quality is made prominent, because the thought has no relation of reason to the thoughts which determine it, which exists in the last case and detracts from the attention given to the mere feeling. By there being no relation of reason to the determining thoughts, I mean that there is nothing in the content of the thought which explains why it should arise only on occasion of these determining thoughts. If there is such a relation of reason, if the thought is essentially limited in its application to these objects, then the thought comprehends a thought other than itself; in other words, it is then a complex thought. An incomplex thought can, therefore, be nothing but a sensation or emotion, having no rational character. This is very different from the ordinary doctrine, according to which the very highest and most metaphysical conceptions are absolutely simple. I shall be asked how such a conception of a *being* is to be analyzed, or whether I can ever define *one, two*, and *three*, without a diallelon. Now I shall admit at once that neither of these conceptions can be separated into two others higher than itself; and in that sense, therefore, I fully admit that certain very metaphysical and eminently intellectual notions are absolutely simple. But though these concepts cannot be defined by genus and difference, there is another way in which they can be defined. All determination is by negation; we can first recognize any character only by putting an object which possesses it into comparison with an object which possesses it not. A conception, therefore, which was quite universal in every respect would be unrecognizable and impossible. We do not obtain the conception of Being, in the sense implied in the copula, by observing that all the things which we can think of have something in common, for there is no such thing to be observed. We get it by reflecting upon signs—words or thoughts; we observe that different predicates may be attached to the same subject, and that each makes some conception applicable to the subject; then we imagine that a subject has something true of it merely because a predicate (no matter what) is attached to it—and that we call Being. The conception of being is, therefore, a conception about a sign—a thought, or word; and since it is not applicable to every sign, it is not primarily universal, although it is so in its mediate application to things. Being, therefore, may be defined; it may be defined, for example, as that which is common to the objects included in any class, and to the objects not included in the same class. But it is nothing new to say that metaphysical conceptions are primarily and at bottom thoughts about words, or thoughts about thoughts; it is the doctrine both of Aristotle (whose categories are parts of speech) and of Kant (whose categories are the characters of different kinds of propositions).

Sensation and the power of abstraction or attention may be regarded as, in one sense, the sole constituents of all thought. Having considered the former, let us now attempt some analysis of the latter. By the force of attention, an emphasis is put upon one of the objective elements of consciousness. This emphasis is, therefore, not itself an object of immediate consciousness; and in this respect it differs entirely from a feeling. Therefore, since the emphasis, nevertheless, consists in some effect upon consciousness, and so can exist only so far as it affects our knowledge; and since an act cannot be supposed to determine that which precedes it in time, this act can consist only in the capacity which the cognition emphasized has for producing an effect upon memory, or otherwise influencing subsequent thought. This is confirmed by the fact that attention is a matter of continuous quantity; for continuous quantity, so far as we know it, reduces itself in the last analysis to time. Accordingly, we find that attention does, in fact, produce a very great effect upon subsequent thought. In the first place, it strongly affects memory, a thought being remembered for a longer time the greater the attention originally paid to it. In the second place, the greater the attention, the closer the connection and the more accurate the logical sequence of thought. In the third place, by attention a thought may be recovered which has been forgotten. From these facts, we gather that attention is the power by which thought at one time is connected with and made to relate to thought at another time; or, to apply the conception of thought as a sign, that it is the *pure demonstrative application* of a thought-sign.

Attention is roused when the same phenomenon presents itself repeatedly on different occasions, or the same predicate in different subjects. We see that *A* has a certain character, that *B* has the same, *C* has the same; and this excites our attention, so that we say, "*These* have this character." Thus attention is an act of induction; but it is an induction which does not increase our knowledge, because our "these" covers nothing but the instances experienced. It is, in short, an argument from enumeration.

Attention produces effects upon the nervous system. These effects are habits, or nervous associations. A habit arises, when, having had the sensation of performing a certain act, *m*, on several occasions *a, b, c*, we come to do it upon every occurrence of the general event, *l*, of which *a, b* and *c* are special cases. That is to say, by the cognition that

Every case of *a, b*, or *c*, is a case of *m*,

is determined the cognition that

Every case of *l* is a case of *m*.

Thus the formation of a habit is an induction, and is therefore necessarily connected with attention or abstraction. Voluntary actions result from the sensations produced by habits, as instinctive actions result from our original nature.

We have thus seen that every sort of modification of consciousness—Attention, Sensation, and Understanding—is an inference. But the objection may be made that inference deals only with general terms, and that an image, or absolutely singular representation, cannot therefore be inferred.

"Singular" and "individual" are equivocal terms. A singular may mean that which can be but in one place at one time. In this sense it is not opposed to general. *The sun* is a singular in this sense, but, as is explained in every good treatise on logic, it is a general term. I may have a very general conception of Hermolaus Barbarus, but still I conceive him only as able to be in one place at one time. When an image is said to be singular, it is meant that it is absolutely determinate in all respects. Every possible character, or the negative thereof, must be true of such an image. In the words of the most eminent expounder of the doctrine, the image of a man "must be either of a white, or a black, or a tawny; a straight or a crooked; a tall, or a low, or a middle-sized man." It must be of a man with his mouth open or his mouth shut, whose hair is precisely of such and such a shade, and whose figure has precisely such and such proportions. No statement of Locke has been so scouted by all friends of images as his denial that the "idea" of a triangle must be either of an obtuse-angled, right-angled, or acute-angled triangle. In fact, the image of a triangle must be of one, each of whose angles is of a certain number of degrees, minutes, and seconds.

This being so, it is apparent that no man has a *true* image of the road to his office, or of any other real thing. Indeed he has no image of it at all unless he can not only recognize it, but imagines it (truly or falsely) in all its infinite details. This being the case, it becomes very doubtful whether we ever have any such thing as an image in our imagination. Please, reader, to look at a bright red book, or other brightly colored object, and then to shut your eyes and say whether you see that color, whether brightly or faintly—whether, indeed, there is anything like sight there. Hume and the other followers of Berkeley maintain that there is no difference between the sight and the memory of the red book except in "their different degrees of force and vivacity." "The colors which the memory employs," says Hume, "are faint and dull compared with those in which our original perceptions are clothed." If this were a correct statement of the difference, we should remember the book as being less red than it is; whereas, in fact, we remember the color with very great precision for a few moments (please to test this point, reader), although we do not see anything like it. We carry away absolutely nothing of the color except the *consciousness that we could recognize it*. As a further proof of this, I will request the reader to try a little experiment. Let him call up, if he can, the image of a horse—not of one which he has ever seen, but of an imaginary one—and before reading further let him by contemplation fix the image in his memory. . . . Has the reader done as requested?[6] for I protest that it is not fair play to read further without doing so.—Now, the reader can say in general of what color that horse was, whether grey, bay, or black. But he probably cannot say *precisely* of what shade it was. He cannot state this as exactly as he could just after having *seen* such a horse. But why, if he had an image in his mind which no more had the general color than it had the particular shade, has the latter vanished so instantaneously from his memory while the former still remains? It may be replied, that we always forget the details before we do the more general characters; but that this answer is insufficient is, I think, shown by the extreme disproportion between the length of time that the exact shade of something looked at is remembered as compared with that instantaneous oblivion to the exact shade of the thing imagined, and the but slightly superior vividness of the memory of the thing seen as compared with the memory of the thing imagined.

The nominalists, I suspect, confound together thinking a triangle without thinking that it is either equilateral, isosceles, or scalene, and thinking a triangle without thinking whether it is equilateral, isosceles, or scalene.

It is important to remember that we have no intuitive power of distinguishing between one subjective mode of cognition and another; and hence often think that something is presented to us as a picture, while it is really constructed from slight data by the understanding. This is the case with dreams, as is shown by the frequent impossibility of giving an intelligible account of one without adding something which we feel was not in the dream itself. Many dreams, of which the waking memory makes elaborate and consistent stories, must probably have been in fact mere jumbles of these feelings of the ability to recognize this and that which I have just alluded to.

I will now go so far as to say that we have no images even in actual perception. It will be sufficient to prove this in the case of vision; for if no picture is seen when we look at an object, it will not be claimed that hearing, touch, and the other senses, are superior to sight in this respect. That the picture is not painted on the nerves of the retina is absolutely certain, if, as physiologists inform us, these nerves are needle-points pointing to the light and at distances considerably greater than the *minimum visible*. The same thing is shown by our not being able to perceive that there is a large blind spot near the middle of the retina. If, then, we have a picture before us when we see, it is one constructed by the mind at the suggestion of previous sensations. Supposing these sensations to be signs, the understanding by reasoning from them could attain all the knowledge of outward things which we derive from sight, while the sensations are quite inadequate to forming an image or representation absolutely determinate. If we have such an image or picture, we must have in our minds a representation of a surface which is only a part of every surface we see, and we must see that each part, however small, has such and such a color. If we look from some distance at a speckled surface, it seems as if we did not see whether it were speckled or not; but if we have an image before us, it must appear to us either as speckled, or as not speckled. Again, the eye by education comes to distinguish minute differences of color; but if we see only absolutely determinate images, we must, no less before our eyes are trained than afterwards, see each color as particularly such and such a shade. Thus to suppose that we have an image before us when we see, is not only a hypothesis which explains nothing whatever, but is one which actually creates difficulties which require new hypotheses in order to explain them away.

One of these difficulties arises from the fact that the details are less easily distinguished than, and forgotten before, the general circumstances. Upon this theory, the general features exist in the details: the details are, in fact, the whole picture. It seems, then, very strange that that which exists only secondarily in the picture should make more impression than the picture itself. It is true that in an old painting the details are not easily made out; but this is because we know that the blackness is the result of time, and is no part of the picture itself. There is no difficulty in making out the details of the picture as it looks at present; the only difficulty is in guessing what it used to be. But if we have a picture on the retina, the minutest details are there as much as, nay, more than, the general outline and significancy of it. Yet that which must actually be seen, it is extremely difficult to recognize; while that which is only abstracted from what is seen is very obvious.

But the conclusive argument against our having any images, or absolutely determinate representations in perception, is that in that case we have the materials in each such representation for an infinite amount of conscious cognition, which we yet never become aware of. Now there is no meaning in saying that we have something in our minds which never has the least effect on what we are conscious of knowing. The most that can be said is, that when we see we are put in a condition in which we are able to get a very large and perhaps indefinitely great amount of knowledge of the visible qualities of objects.

Moreover, that perceptions are not absolutely determinate and singular is obvious from the fact that each sense is an abstracting mechanism. Sight by itself informs us only of colors and forms. No one can pretend that the images of sight are determinate in reference to taste. They are, therefore, so far general that they are neither sweet nor non-sweet, bitter nor non-bitter, having savor nor insipid.

The next question is whether we have any general conceptions except in judgments. In perception, where we know a thing as existing, it is plain that there is a judgment that the thing exists, since a mere general concept of a thing is in no case a cognition of it as existing. It has usually been said, however, that we can call up any concept without making any judgment; but it seems that in this case we only arbitrarily suppose ourselves to have an experience. In order to conceive the number 7, I suppose, that is, I arbitrarily make the hypothesis or judgment, that there are certain points before my eyes, and I judge that these are seven. This seems to be the most simple and rational view of the matter, and I may add that it is the one which has been adopted by the best logicians. If this be the case, what goes by the name of the association of images is in reality an association of judgments. The association of ideas is said to proceed according to three principles—those of resemblance, of contiguity, and of causality.

But it would be equally true to say that signs denote what they do on the three principles of resemblance, contiguity, and causality. There can be no question that anything is a sign of whatever is associated with it by resemblance, by contiguity, or by causality: nor can there be any doubt that any sign recalls the thing signified. So, then, the association of ideas consists in this, that a judgment occasions another judgment, of which it is the sign. Now this is nothing less nor more than inference.

Everything in which we take the least interest creates in us its own particular emotion, however slight this may be. This emotion is a sign and a predicate of the thing. Now, when a thing resembling this thing is presented to us, a similar emotion arises; hence, we immediately infer that the latter is like the former. A formal logician of the old school may say, that in logic no term can enter into the conclusion which had not been contained in the premisses, and that therefore the suggestion of something new must be essentially different from inference. But I reply that that rule of logic applies only to those arguments which are technically called completed. We can and do reason—

Elias was a man;
[Ergo,] He was mortal.

And this argument is just as valid as the full syllogism, although it is so only because the major premiss of the latter happens to be true. If to pass from the judgment "Elias was a man" to the judgment "Elias was mortal," without actually saying to one's self that "All men are mortal," is not inference, then the term "inference" is used in so restricted a sense that inferences hardly occur outside of a logic-book.

What is here said of association by resemblance is true of all association. All association is by signs. Everything has its subjective or emotional qualities, which are attributed either absolutely or relatively, or by conventional imputation to anything which is a sign of it. And so we reason,

The sign is such and such;
[Ergo,] The sign is that thing.

This conclusion receiving, however, a modification, owing to other considerations, so as to become—

The sign is almost (is representative of) that thing.

We come now to the consideration of the last of the four principles whose consequences we were to trace; namely, that the absolutely incognizable is absolutely inconceivable. That upon Cartesian principles the very realities of things can never be known in the least, most competent persons must long ago have been convinced. Hence the breaking forth of idealism, which is essentially anti-Cartesian, in every direction, whether among empiricists (Berkeley, Hume), or among noologists (Hegel, Fichte). The principle now brought under discussion is directly idealistic; for, since the meaning of a word is the conception it conveys, the absolutely incognizable has no meaning because no conception attaches to it. It is, therefore, a meaningless word; and, consequently, whatever is meant by any term as "the real" is cognizable in some degree, and so is of the nature of a cognition, in the objective sense of that term.

At any moment we are in possession of certain information, that is, of cognitions which have been logically derived by induction and hypothesis from previous cognitions which are less general, less distinct, and of which we have a less lively consciousness. These in their turn have been derived from others still less general, less distinct, and less vivid; and so on back to the ideal first,[7] which is quite singular, and quite out of consciousness. This ideal first is the particular thing-in-itself. It does not exist *as such*. That is, there is no thing which is in-itself in the sense of not being relative to the mind, though things which are relative to the mind doubtless are, apart from that relation. The cognitions which thus reach us by this infinite series of inductions and hypotheses (which though infinite *a parte ante logice*, is yet as one continuous process not without a beginning *in time*) are of two kinds, the true and the untrue, or cognitions whose objects are *real* and those whose objects are *unreal*. And what do we mean by the real? It is a conception which we must first have had when we discovered that there was an unreal, an illusion; that is, when we first corrected ourselves. Now the distinction for which alone this fact logically called, was between an *ens* relative to private inward determinations, to the negations belonging to idiosyncrasy, and an *ens* such as would stand in the long run. The real, then, is that which, sooner or later, information and reasoning would finally result in, and which is therefore independent of the vagaries of me and you. Thus, the very origin of the conception of reality shows that this conception essentially involves the notion of a COMMUNITY, without definite limits, and capable of a definite increase of knowledge. And so those two series of cognition—the real and the unreal—consist of those which, at a time sufficiently future, the community will always continue to re-affirm; and of those which, under the same conditions, will ever after be denied. Now, a proposition whose falsity can never be discovered, and the error of which therefore is absolutely incognizable, contains, upon our principle, absolutely no error. Consequently, that which is thought in these cognitions is the real, as it really is. There is nothing, then, to prevent our knowing outward things as they really are, and it is most likely that we do thus know them in numberless cases, although we can never be absolutely certain of doing so in any special case.

But it follows that since no cognition of ours is absolutely determinate, generals must have a real existence. Now this scholastic realism is usually set down as a belief in metaphysical fictions. But, in fact, a realist is simply one who knows no more recondite reality than that which is represented in a true representation. Since, therefore, the word "man" is true of something, that which "man" means is real. The nominalist must admit that man is truly applicable to something; but he believes that there is beneath this a thing in itself, an incognizable reality. His is the metaphysical figment. Modern nominalists are mostly superficial men, who do not know, as the more thorough Roscellinus and Occam did, that a reality which has no representation is one which has no relation and no quality. The great argument for nominalism is that there is no man unless there is some particular man. That, however, does not affect the realism of Scotus; for although there is no man of whom all further determination can be denied, yet there is a man, abstraction being made of all further determination. There is a real difference between man irrespective of what the other determinations may be, and man with this or that particular series of determinations, although undoubtedly this difference is only relative to the mind and not *in re*. Such is the position of Scotus.[8] Occam's great objection is, there can be no real distinction which is not *in re*, in the thing-in-itself; but this begs the question for it is itself based only on the notion that reality is something independent of representative relation.[9]

Such being the nature of reality in general, in what does the reality of the mind consist? We have seen that the content of consciousness, the entire phenomenal manifestation of mind, is a sign resulting from inference. Upon our principle, therefore, that the absolutely incognizable does not exist, so that the phenomenal manifestation of a substance is the substance, we must conclude that the mind is a sign developing according to the laws of inference. What distinguishes a man from a word? There is a distinction doubtless. The material qualities, the forces which constitute the pure denotative application, and the meaning of the human sign, are all exceedingly complicated in comparison with those of the word. But these differences are only relative. What other is there? It may be said that man is conscious, while a word is not. But consciousness is a very vague term. It may mean that emotion which accompanies the reflection that we have animal life. This is a consciousness which is dimmed when animal life is at its ebb in old age, or sleep, but which is not dimmed when the spiritual life is at its ebb; which is the more lively the better *animal* a man is, but which is not so, the better *man* he is. We do not attribute this sensation to words, because we have reason to believe that it is dependent upon the possession of an animal body. But this consciousness, being a mere sensation, is only a part of the *material quality* of the man-sign. Again, consciousness is sometimes used to signify the *I think*, or unity in thought; but the unity is nothing but consistency, or the recognition of it. Consistency belongs to every sign, so far as it is a sign; and therefore every sign, since it signifies primarily that it is a sign, signifies its own consistency. The man-sign acquires information, and comes to mean more than he did before. But so do words. Does not electricity mean more now than it did in the days of Franklin? Man makes the word, and the word means nothing which the man has not made it mean, and that only to some man. But since man can think only by means of words or other external symbols, these might turn round and say: "You mean nothing which we have not taught you, and then only so far as you address some word as the interpretant of your thought." In fact, therefore, men and words reciprocally educate each other; each increase of a man's information involves and is involved by, a corresponding increase of a word's information.

Without fatiguing the reader by stretching this parallelism too far, it is sufficient to say that there is no element whatever of man's consciousness which has not something corresponding to it in the word; and the reason is obvious. It is that the word or sign which man uses is the man himself. For, as the fact that every thought is a sign, taken in conjunction with the fact that life is a train of thought, proves that man is a sign; so, that every thought is an *external* sign, proves that man is an external sign. That is to say, the man and the external sign are identical, in the same sense in which the words *homo* and *man* are identical. Thus my language is the sum total of myself; for the man is the thought.

It is hard for man to understand this, because he persists in identifying himself with his will, his power over the animal organism, with brute force. Now the organism is only an instrument of thought. But the identity of a man consists in the consistency of what he does and thinks, and *consistency* is the intellectual character of a thing; that is, is its expressing something.

Finally, as what anything really is, is what it may finally come to be known to be in the ideal state of complete information, so that reality depends on the ultimate decision of the community; so thought is what it is, only by virtue of its addressing a future thought which is in its value as thought identical with it, though more developed. In this way, the existence of thought now depends on what is to be hereafter; so that it has only a potential existence, dependent on the future thought of the community.

The individual man, since his separate existence is manifested only by ignorance and error, so far as he is anything apart from his fellows, and from what he and they are to be, is only a negation. This is man,

> . . . proud man,
> Most ignorant of what he's most assured,
> His glassy essence.

Notes

1. Several persons versed in logic have objected that I have here quite misapplied the term *hypothesis*, and that what I so designate is an argument from *analogy*. It is a sufficient reply to say that the example of the cipher has been given as an apt illustration of hypothesis by Descartes (Rule 10, *Oeuvres choisies*: Paris, 1865, page 334), by Leibniz (*Nouveaux Essais*, lib. 4, ch. 12, §13, Ed. Erdmann, p. 383 *b*), and (as I learn from D. Stewart; *Works*, vol. 3, pp. 305 et seqq.) by Gravesande, Boscovich, Hartley, and G. L. Le Sage. The term *Hypothesis* has been used in the following senses: 1. For the theme or proposition forming the subject of discourse. 2. For an assumption. Aristotle divides *theses* or propositions adopted without any reason into definitions and hypotheses. The latter are propositions stating the existence of something. Thus the geometer says, "Let there be a triangle." 3. For a condition in a general sense. We are said to seek other things than happiness *ex hypotheseos*, conditionally. The best republic is the ideally perfect, the second the best on earth, the third the best *ex hypotheseos*, under the circumstances. Freedom is the *hypothesis* or condition of democracy. 4. For the antecedent of a hypothetical proposition. 5. For an oratorical question which assumes facts. 6. In the *Synopsis* of Psellus, for the reference of a subject to the things it denotes. 7. Most commonly in modern times, for the conclusion of an argument from consequence and consequent to antecedent. This is my use of the term. 8. For such a conclusion when too weak to be a theory accepted into the body of a science.

I give a few authorities to support the seventh use:

Chauvin.—Lexicon Rationale, 1st Ed.—"Hypothesis est propositio, quæ assumitur ad probandum aliam veritatem incognitam. Requirunt multi, ut hæc hypothesis vera esse cognoscatur, etiam antequam appareat, an alia ex ea deduci possint. Verum aiunt alii, hoc unum desiderari, ut hypothesis pro vera admittatur, quod nempe ex hac talia deducitur, quæ respondent phænomenis, et satisfaciunt omnibus difficultatibus, quæ hac parte in re, et in iis quæ de ea apparent, occurrebant."

Newton.—"Hactenus phænomena coelorum et maris nostri per vim gravitatis exposui, sed causam gravitatis nondum assignavi. . . . Rationem vero harum gravitatis proprietatum ex phænomenis nondum potui deducere, et hypotheses non fingo. Quicquid enim ex phænomenis non deducitur, *hypothesis* vocanda est. . . . In hac Philosophiâ Propositiones deducuntur ex phænomenis, et redduntur generates per inductionem." *Principia. Ad fin.*

Sir Wm. Hamilton.—"Hypotheses, that is, propositions which are assumed with probability, in order to explain or prove something else which cannot otherwise be explained or proved."—*Lectures on Logic* (Am. Ed.), p. 188.

"The name of *hypothesis* is more emphatically given to provisory suppositions, which serve to explain the phenomena in so far as observed, but which are only asserted to be true, if ultimately confirmed by a complete induction." —Ibid., p. 364.

"When a phenomenon is presented which can be explained by no principle afforded through experience, we feel discontented and uneasy; and there arises an effort to discover some cause which may, at least provisionally, account for the outstanding phenomenon; and this cause is finally recognized as valid and true, if, through it, the given phenomenon is found to obtain a full and perfect explanation. The judgment in which a phenomenon is referred to such a problematic cause, is called a *Hypothesis*."—Ibid., pp. 449, 450. See also *Lectures on Metaphysics*, p. 117.

J. S. Mill.—"An hypothesis is any supposition which we make (either without actual evidence, or on evidence avowedly insufficient), in order to endeavor to deduce from it conclusions in accordance with facts which are known to be real; under the idea that if the conclusions to which the hypothesis leads are known truths, the hypothesis itself either must be, or at least is likely to be true."—*Logic* (6th Ed.), vol. 2, p. 8.

Kant.—"*If all the consequents of a cognition are true, the cognition itself is true.* . . . It is allowable, therefore, to conclude from consequent to a reason, but without being able to determine this reason. From the complexus of all consequents alone can we conclude the truth of a determinate reason. . . . The difficulty with this *positive* and *direct* mode of inference (*modus ponens*) is that the totality of the consequents cannot be apodeictically recognized, and that we are therefore led by this mode of inference only to a probable and *hypothetically* true cognition (*Hypotheses*)."—*Logik* by Jäsche; *Werke*, Ed. Rosenk. and Sch., vol. 3, p. 221.

"A hypothesis is the judgment of the truth of a reason on account of the sufficiency of the consequents." —Ibid., p. 262.

Herbart.—"We can make hypotheses, thence deduce consequents, and afterwards see whether the latter accord with experience. Such suppositions are termed hypotheses."—*Einleitung; Werke*, vol. 1, p. 53.

Beneke.—"Affirmative inferences from consequent to antecedent, or hypotheses."—*System der Logik*, vol. 2, p. 103.

There would be no difficulty in greatly multiplying these citations.

2. A judgment concerning a minimum of information, for the theory of which see my paper on Comprehension and Extension, in the *Proceedings of the American Academy of Arts and Sciences*, vol. 7, p. 426.

3. Observe that I say *in itself.* I am not so wild as to deny that my sensation of red today is like my sensation of red yesterday. I only say that the similarity can *consist* only in the physiological force behind consciousness—which leads me to say, I recognize this feeling the same as the former one, and so does not consist in a community of sensation.

4. Accordingly, just as we say that a body is in motion, and not that motion is in a body we ought to say that we are in thought and not that thoughts are in us.

5. On quality, relation, and representation, see *Proceedings of the American Academy of Arts and Sciences*, vol. 7, p. 293.

6. No person whose native tongue is English will need to be informed that contemplation is essentially (1) protracted, (2) voluntary, and (3) an action, and that it is never used for that which is set forth to the mind in this act. A foreigner can convince himself of this by the proper study of English writers. Thus, Locke (*Essay concerning Human Understanding*, Book II, chap. 19, § 1) says, "If it [an idea] be held there [in view] long under attentive consideration, 'tis *Contemplation*"; and again (*Ibid.*, Book II, chap. 10, § 1) "keeping the *Idea* which is brought into it [the mind] for some time actually in view, which is called *Contemplation*." This term is therefore unfitted to translate *Anschauung*; for this latter does not imply an act which is necessarily protracted or voluntary, and denotes most usually a mental presentation, sometimes a faculty, less often the reception of an impression in the mind, and seldom, if ever, an action. To the translation of *Anschauung* by intuition, there is, at least, no such insufferable objection. Etymologically, the two words precisely correspond. The original philosophical meaning of

intuition was a cognition of the present manifold in that character; and it is now commonly used, as a modern writer says, "to include all the products of the perceptive (external or internal) and imaginative faculties; every act of consciousness, in short, of which the immediate object is an *individual*, thing, act, or state of mind, presented under the condition of distinct existence in space and time." Finally, we have the authority of Kant's own example for translating his *Anschauung* by *Intuitus*; and indeed this is the common usage of Germans writing Latin. Moreover, *intuitiv* frequently replaces *anschauend* or *anschaulich*. If this constitutes a misunderstanding of Kant, it is one which is shared by himself and nearly all his countrymen.

7. By an ideal, I mean the limit which the possible cannot attain.

8. "Eadem natura est, quæ in existentia per gradum singularitatis est determinata, et in intellectu, hoc est ut habet relationem ad intellectum ut cognitum ad cognoscens, est indeterminata."—*Quaestiones Subtillissimae*, lib. 7, qu. 18.

9. See his argument *Summa logices*, part. 1, cap. 16.

In this 1877 paper from Popular Science Monthly, *Peirce sets out the doubt-belief model of inquiry and defends the method of science.*

CHARLES S. PEIRCE

The Fixation of Belief

I

Few persons care to study logic, because everybody conceives himself to be proficient enough in the art of reasoning already. But I observe that this satisfaction is limited to one's own ratiocination, and does not extend to that of other men.

We come to the full possession of our power of drawing inferences, the last of all our faculties; for it is not so much a natural gift as a long and difficult art. The history of its practice would make a grand subject for a book. The medieval schoolman, following the Romans, made logic the earliest of a boy's studies after grammar, as being very easy. So it was as they understood it. Its fundamental principle, according to them, was, that all knowledge rests either on authority or reason; but that whatever is deduced by reason depends ultimately on a premiss derived from authority. Accordingly, as soon as a boy was perfect in the syllogistic procedure, his intellectual kit of tools was held to be complete.

To Roger Bacon, that remarkable mind who in the middle of the thirteenth century was almost a scientific man, the schoolmen's conception of reasoning appeared only an obstacle to truth. He saw that experience alone teaches anything—a proposition which to us seems easy to understand, because a distinct conception of experience has been handed down to us from former generations; which to him likewise seemed perfectly clear, because its difficulties had not yet unfolded themselves. Of all kinds of experience, the best, he thought, was interior illumination, which teaches many things about Nature which the external senses could never discover, such as the transubstantiation of bread.

Four centuries later, the more celebrated Bacon, in the first book of his *Novum Organum*, gave his clear account of experience as something which must be open to verification and reexamination. But, superior as Lord Bacon's conception is to earlier notions, a modern reader who is not in awe of his grandiloquence is chiefly struck by the inadequacy of his view of scientific procedure. That we have only to make some crude experiments, to draw up briefs of the results in certain blank forms, to go through these by rule, checking off everything disproved and setting down the alternatives, and that thus in a few years physical science would be finished up—what an idea! "He wrote on science like a Lord Chancellor," indeed, as Harvey, a genuine man of science said.

The early scientists, Copernicus, Tycho Brahe, Kepler, Galileo, Harvey, and Gilbert, had methods more like those of their modern brethren. Kepler undertook to draw a curve through the places of Mars;[1] and to state the times occupied by the planet in describing the different parts of that curve; but perhaps his greatest service to science was in impressing on men's minds that this was the thing to be done if they wished to improve astronomy; that they were not to content themselves with inquiring whether one system of epicycles was better than another but that they were to sit down to the figures and find out what the curve, in truth, was. He accomplished this by his incomparable energy and courage, blundering along in the most inconceivable way (to us), from one irrational hypothesis to another, until, after trying twenty-two of these, he fell, by the mere exhaustion of his invention, upon the orbit which a mind well furnished with the weapons of modern logic would have tried almost at the outset.

In the same way, every work of science great enough to be well remembered for a few generations affords some exemplification of the defective state of the art of reasoning of the time when it was written; and each chief step in science has been a lesson in logic. It was so when Lavoisier and his contemporaries took up the study of Chemistry. The old chemist's maxim had been, "*Lege, lege, lege, labora, ora, et relege.*" Lavoisier's method was not to read and pray, but to dream that some long and complicated chemical process would have a certain effect, to put it into practice with dull patience, after its inevitable failure, to dream that with some modification it would have another result, and to end by publishing the last dream as a fact: his way was to carry his mind into his laboratory, and literally to make of his alembics and cucurbits instruments of thought, giving a new conception of reasoning as something which was to be done with one's eyes open, in manipulating real things instead of words and fancies.

The Darwinian controversy is, in large part, a question of logic. Mr. Darwin proposed to apply the statistical method to biology. The same thing has been done in a widely different branch of science, the theory of gases. Though unable to say what the movements of any particular molecule of gas would be on a certain hypothesis regarding the constitution of this class of bodies, Clausius and Maxwell were yet able, eight years before the publication of Darwin's immortal work, by the application of the doctrine of probabilities, to predict that in the long run such and such a proportion of the molecules would, under given circumstances, acquire such and such velocities; that there would take place, every second, such and such a relative number of collisions, etc.; and from these propositions were able to deduce certain properties of gases, especially in regard to their heat-relations. In like manner, Darwin, while unable to say what the operation of variation and natural selection in any individual case will be, demonstrates that in the long run they will, or would, adapt animals to their circumstances. Whether or not existing animal forms are due to such action, or what position the theory ought to take, forms the subject of a discussion in which questions of fact and questions of logic are curiously interlaced.

II

The object of reasoning is to find out, from the consideration of what we already know, something else which we do not know. Consequently, reasoning is good if it be such as to give a true conclusion from true premisses, and not otherwise. Thus, the question of validity is purely one of fact and not of thinking. A being the facts stated in the premisses and B being that concluded, the question is, whether these facts are really so related that if A were B would generally be. If so, the inference is valid; if not, not. It is not in the least the question whether, when the premisses are accepted by the mind, we feel an impulse to accept the conclusion also. It is true that we do generally reason correctly by nature. But that is an accident; the true conclusion would remain true if we had no impulse to accept it; and the false one would remain false, though we could not resist the tendency to believe in it.

We are, doubtless, in the main logical animals, but we are not perfectly so. Most of us, for example, are naturally more sanguine and hopeful than logic would justify. We seem to be so constituted that in the absence of any facts to go upon we are happy and self-satisfied; so that the effect of experience is continually to contract our hopes and aspirations. Yet a lifetime of the application of this corrective does not usually eradicate our sanguine disposition. Where hope is unchecked by any experience, it is likely that our optimism is extravagant. Logicality in regard to practical matters (if this be understood, not in the old sense, but as consisting in a wise union of security with fruitfulness of reasoning) is the most useful quality an animal can possess, and might, therefore, result from the action of natural selection; but outside of these it is probably of more advantage to the animal to have his mind filled with pleasing and encouraging visions, independently of their truth; and thus, upon unpractical subjects, natural selection might occasion a fallacious tendency of thought.

That which determines us, from given premisses, to draw one inference rather than another, is some habit of mind, whether it be constitutional or acquired, The habit is good or otherwise, according as it produces true conclusions from true premisses or not; and an inference is regarded as valid or not, without reference to the truth or falsity of its conclusion specially, but according as the habit which determines it is such as to produce true conclusions in general or not. The particular habit of mind which governs this or that inference may be formulated in a proposition whose truth depends on the validity of the inferences which the habit determines; and such a formula is called a *guiding principle* of inference. Suppose, for example, that we observe that a rotating disk of copper quickly comes to rest when placed between the poles of a magnet, and we infer that this will happen with every disk of copper. The guiding principle is, that what is true of one piece of copper is true of another. Such a guiding principle with regard to copper would be much safer than with regard to many other substances—brass, for example.

A book might be written to signalize all the most important of these guiding principles of reasoning. It would probably be, we must confess, of no service to a person whose thought is directed wholly to practical subjects, and whose activity moves along thoroughly-beaten paths. The problems that present themselves to such a mind are matters of routine which he has learned once for all to handle in learning his business. But let a man venture into an unfamiliar field, or where his results are not continually checked by experience, and all history shows that the most masculine intellect will ofttimes lose his orientation and waste his efforts in directions which bring him no nearer to his goal, or even carry him entirely astray. He is like a ship in the open sea, with no one on board who understands the rules of navigation. And in such a case some general study of the guiding principles of reasoning would be sure to be found useful.

The subject could hardly be treated, however, without being first limited; since almost any fact may serve as a guiding principle. But it so happens that there exists a division among facts, such that in one class are all those which are absolutely essential as guiding principles, while in the others are all which have any other interest as objects of research. This division is between those which are necessarily taken for granted in asking why a certain conclusion is thought to follow from certain premisses, and those which are not implied in such a question. A moment's thought will show that a variety of facts are already assumed when the logical question is first asked. It is implied, for instance, that there are such states of mind as doubt and belief—that a passage from one to the other is possible, the object of thought remaining the same, and that this transition is subject to some rules by which all minds are alike bound. As these are facts which we must already know before we can have any clear conception of reasoning at all, it cannot be supposed to be any longer of much interest to inquire into their truth or falsity. On the other hand, it is easy to believe that those rules of reasoning which are deduced from the very idea of the process are the ones which are the most essential; and, indeed, that so long as it conforms to these it will, at least, not lead to false conclusions from true premisses. In point of fact, the importance of what may be deduced from the assumptions involved in the logical question turns out to be greater than might be supposed, and this for reasons which it is difficult to exhibit at the outset. The only one which I shall here mention is, that conceptions which are really products of logical reflection, without being readily seen to be so, mingle with our ordinary thoughts, and are frequently the causes of great confusion. This is the case, for example, with the conception of quality. A quality as such is never an object of observation. We can see that a thing is blue or green, but the quality of being blue and the quality of being green are not things which we see; they are products of logical reflections. The truth is, that common-sense, or thought as it first emerges above the level of the narrowly practical, is deeply imbued with that bad logical quality to which the epithet *metaphysical* is commonly applied; and nothing can clear it up but a severe course of logic.

III

We generally know when we wish to ask a question and when we wish to pronounce a judgment, for there is a dissimilarity between the sensation of doubting and that of believing.

But this is not all which distinguishes doubt from belief. There is a practical difference. Our beliefs guide our desires and shape our actions. The Assassins, or followers of the Old Man of the Mountain, used to rush into death at his least command, because they believed that obedience to him would insure everlasting felicity. Had they doubted this, they would not have acted as they did. So it is with every belief, according to its degree. The feeling of believing is a more or less sure indication of there being established in our nature some habit which will determine our actions. Doubt never has such an effect.

Nor must we overlook a third point of difference. Doubt is an uneasy and dissatisfied state from which we struggle to free ourselves and pass into the state of belief; while the latter is a calm and satisfactory state which we do not wish to avoid, or to change to a belief in anything else.[2] On the contrary, we cling tenaciously, not merely to believing, but to believing just what we do believe.

Thus, both doubt and belief have positive effects upon us, though very different ones. Belief does not make us act at once, but puts us into such a condition that we shall behave in some certain way, when the occasion arises. Doubt has not the least such active effect, but stimulates us to inquiry until it is destroyed. This reminds us of the irritation of a nerve and the reflex action produced thereby; while for the analogue of belief, in the nervous system, we must look to what are called nervous associations—for example, to that habit of the nerves in consequence of which the smell of a peach will make the mouth water.

IV

The irritation of doubt causes a struggle to attain a state of belief. I shall term this struggle *inquiry*, though it must be admitted that this is sometimes not a very apt designation.

The irritation of doubt is the only immediate motive for the struggle to attain belief. It is certainly best for us that our beliefs should be such as may truly guide our actions so as to satisfy our desires; and this reflection will make us reject every belief which does not seem to have been so formed as to insure this result. But it will only do so by creating a doubt in the place of that belief. With the doubt, therefore, the struggle begins, and with the cessation of doubt it ends. Hence, the sole object of inquiry is the settlement of opinion. We may fancy that this is not enough for us, and that we seek, not merely an opinion, but a true opinion. But put this fancy to the test, and it proves groundless; for as soon as a firm belief is reached we are entirely satisfied, whether the belief be true or false. And it is clear that nothing out of the sphere of our knowledge can be our object, for nothing which does not affect the mind can be the motive for mental effort. The most that can be maintained is, that we seek for a belief that we shall *think* to be true. But we think each one of our beliefs to be true, and, indeed, it is mere tautology to say so.

That the settlement of opinion is the sole end of inquiry is a very important proposition. It sweeps away, at once, various vague and erroneous conceptions of proof. A few of these may be noticed here.

1. Some philosophers have imagined that to start an inquiry it was only necessary to utter a question whether orally or by setting it down upon paper, and have even recommended us to begin our studies with questioning everything! But the mere putting of a proposition into the interrogative form does not stimulate the mind to any struggle after belief. There must be a real and living doubt, and without this all discussion is idle.
2. It is a very common idea that a demonstration must rest on some ultimate and absolutely indubitable propositions. These, according to one school, are first principles of a general nature; according to another, are first sensations. But, in point of fact, an inquiry, to have that completely satisfactory result called demonstration, has only to start with propositions perfectly free from all actual doubt. If the premisses are not in fact doubted at all, they cannot be more satisfactory than they are.
3. Some people seem to love to argue a point after all the world is fully convinced of it. But no further advance can be made. When doubt ceases, mental action on the subject comes to an end; and, if it did go on, it would be without a purpose.

V

If the settlement of opinion is the sole object of inquiry, and if belief is of the nature of a habit, why should we not attain the desired end, by taking as answer to a question any we may fancy, and constantly reiterating it to ourselves, dwelling on all which may conduce to that belief, and learning to turn with contempt and hatred from anything that might disturb it? This simple and direct method is really pursued by many men. I remember once being entreated not to read a certain newspaper lest it might change my opinion upon free-trade. "Lest I might be entrapped by its fallacies and misstatements," was the form of expression. "You are not," my friend said, "a special student of political economy. You might, therefore, easily be deceived by fallacious arguments upon the subject. You might, then, if you read this paper, be led to believe in protection. But you admit that free-trade is the true doctrine; and you do not wish to believe what is not true." I have often known this system to be deliberately adopted. Still oftener, the instinctive dislike of an undecided state of mind, exaggerated into a vague dread of doubt, makes men cling spasmodically to the views they already take. The man feels that, if he only holds to his belief without wavering, it will be entirely satisfactory. Nor can it be denied that a steady and immovable faith yields great peace of mind. It may, indeed, give rise to inconveniences, as if a man should resolutely continue to believe that fire would not burn him, or that he would be eternally damned if he received his *ingesta* otherwise than through a stomach-pump. But then the man who adopts this method will not allow that its inconveniences are greater than its advantages. He will say, "I hold steadfastly to the truth, and the truth is always wholesome." And in many cases it may very well be that the pleasure he derives from his calm faith overbalances any inconveniences resulting from its deceptive character. Thus, if it be true that death is annihilation, then the man who believes that he will certainly go straight to heaven when he dies, provided he have fulfilled certain simple observances in this life, has a cheap pleasure which will not be followed by the least disappointment. A similar consideration seems to have weight with many persons in religious topics, for we frequently hear it said, "Oh, I could not believe so-and-so, because I should be wretched if I did." When an ostrich buries its head in the sand as danger approaches, it very likely takes the happiest course. It hides the danger, and then calmly says there is no danger; and, if it feels perfectly sure there is none, why should it raise its head to see? A man may go through life, systematically keeping out of view all that might cause a change in his opinions, and if he only succeeds—basing his method, as he does, on two fundamental psychological laws—I do not see what can be said against his doing so. It would be an egotistical impertinence to object that his procedure is irrational, for that only amounts to saying that his method of settling belief is not ours. He does not propose to himself to be rational, and, indeed, will often talk with scorn of man's weak and illusive reason. So let him think as he pleases.

But this method of fixing belief, which may be called the method of tenacity, will be unable to hold its ground in practice. The social impulse is against it. The man who adopts it will find that other men think differently from him, and it will be apt to occur to him, in some saner moment, that their opinions are quite as good as his own, and this will shake his confidence in his belief This conception, that another man's thought or sentiment may be equivalent to one's own, is a distinctly new step, and a highly important one. It arises from an impulse too strong in man to be suppressed, without danger of destroying the human species. Unless we make ourselves hermits, we shall necessarily influence each other's opinions; so that the problem becomes how to fix belief, not in the individual merely, but in the community.

Let the will of the state act, then, instead of that of the individual. Let an institution be created which shall have for its object to keep correct doctrines before the attention of the people, to reiterate them perpetually, and to teach them to the young;

having at the same time power to prevent contrary doctrines from being taught, advocated, or expressed. Let all possible causes of a change of mind be removed from men's apprehensions. Let them be kept ignorant, lest they should learn of some reason to think otherwise than they do. Let their passions be enlisted, so that they may regard private and unusual opinions with hatred and horror. Then, let all men who reject the established belief be terrified into silence. Let the people turn out and tar-and-feather such men, or let inquisitions be made into the manner of thinking of suspected persons, and when they are found guilty of forbidden beliefs, let them be subjected to some signal punishment. When complete agreement could not otherwise be reached, a general massacre of all who have not thought in a certain way has proved a very effective means of settling opinion in a country. If the power to do this be wanting, let a list of opinions be drawn up, to which no man of the least independence of thought can assent, and let the faithful be required to accept all these propositions, in order to segregate them as radically as possible from the influence of the rest of the world.

This method has, from the earliest times, been one of the chief means of upholding correct theological and political doctrines, and of preserving their universal or catholic character. In Rome, especially, it has been practised from the days of Numa Pompilius to those of Pius Nonus. This is the most perfect example in history; but wherever there is a priesthood—and no religion has been without one—this method has been more or less made use of. Wherever there is an aristocracy, or a guild, or any association of a class of men whose interests depend, or are supposed to depend, on certain propositions, there will be inevitably found some traces of this natural product of social feeling. Cruelties always accompany this system; and when it is consistently carried out, they become atrocities of the most horrible kind in the eyes of any rational man. Nor should this occasion surprise, for the officer of a society does not feel justified in surrendering the interests of that society for the sake of mercy, as he might his own private interests. It is natural, therefore, that sympathy and fellowship should thus produce a most ruthless power.

In judging this method of fixing belief, which may be called the method of authority, we must, in the first place, allow its immeasurable mental and moral superiority to the method of tenacity. Its success is proportionately greater; and, in fact, it has over and over again worked the most majestic results. The mere structures of stone which it has caused to be put together—in Siam, for example, in Egypt, and in Europe—have many of them a sublimity hardly more than rivaled by the greatest works of Nature. And, except the geological epochs, there are no periods of time so vast as those which are measured by some of these organized faiths. If we scrutinize the matter closely, we shall find that there has not been one of their creeds which has remained always the same; yet the change is so slow as to be imperceptible during one person's life, so that individual belief remains sensibly fixed. For the mass of mankind, then, there is perhaps no better method than this. If it is their highest impulse to be intellectual slaves, then slaves they ought to remain.

But no institution can undertake to regulate opinions upon every subject. Only the most important ones can be attended to, and on the rest men's minds must be left to the action of natural causes. This imperfection will be no source of weakness so long as men are in such a state of culture that one opinion does not influence another—that is, so long as they cannot put two and two together. But in the most priest-ridden states some individuals will be found who are raised above that condition. These men possess a wider sort of social feeling; they see that men in other countries and in other ages have held to very different doctrines from those which they themselves have been brought up to believe; and they cannot help seeing that it is the mere accident of their having been taught as they have, and of their having been surrounded with the manners and associations they have, that has caused them to believe as they do and not far differently. Nor can their candour resist the reflection that there is no reason to rate their own views at a higher value than those of other nations and other centuries; thus giving rise to doubts in their minds.

They will further perceive that such doubts as these must exist in their minds with reference to every belief which seems to be determined by the caprice either of themselves or of those who originated the popular opinions. The willful adherence to a belief, and the arbitrary forcing of it upon others, must, therefore, both be given up. A different new method of settling opinions must be adopted, that shall not only produce an impulse to believe, but shall also decide what proposition it is which is to be believed. Let the action of natural preferences be unimpeded, then, and under their influence let men, conversing together and regarding matters in different lights, gradually develop beliefs in harmony with natural causes. This method resembles that by which conceptions of art have been brought to maturity. The most perfect example of it is to be found in the history of metaphysical philosophy. Systems of this sort have not usually rested upon any observed facts, at least not in any great degree. They have been chiefly adopted because their fundamental propositions seemed "agreeable to reason." This is an apt expression; it does not mean that which agrees with experience, but that which we find ourselves inclined to believe. Plato, for example, finds it agreeable to reason that the distances of the celestial spheres from one another should be proportional to the different lengths of strings which produce harmonious chords. Many philosophers have been led to their main conclusions by considerations like this; but this is the lowest and least developed form which the method takes, for it is clear that another man might find Kepler's theory, that the celestial spheres are proportional to the inscribed and circumscribed spheres of the different regular solids, more agreeable to *his* reason. But the shock of opinions will soon lead men to rest on preferences of a far more universal nature. Take, for example, the doctrine that man only acts selfishly—that is, from the consideration that acting in one way will afford him more pleasure than acting in another. This rests on no fact in the world, but it has had a wide acceptance as being the only reasonable theory.

This method is far more intellectual and respectable from the point of view of reason than either of the others which we have noticed. But its failure has been the most manifest. It makes of inquiry something similar to the development of taste; but taste, unfortunately, is always more or less a matter of fashion, and accordingly metaphysicians have never come to any fixed agreement, but the pendulum has swung backward and forward between a more material and a more spiritual philosophy, from the earliest times to the latest. And so from this, which has been called the *a priori* method, we are driven, in Lord Bacon's phrase, to a true induction. We have examined into this *a priori* method as something which promised to deliver our opinions from their accidental and capricious element. But development, while it is a process which eliminates the effect of some casual circumstances, only magnifies that of others. This method, therefore, does not differ in a very essential way from that of authority. The government may not have lifted its finger to influence my convictions; I may have been left outwardly quite free to choose, we will say, between monogamy and polygamy, and, appealing to my conscience only, I may have concluded that the latter practice is in itself licentious. But when I come to see that the chief obstacle to the spread of Christianity among a people of as high culture as the Hindoos has been a conviction of the immorality of our way of treating women, I cannot help seeing that, though governments do not interfere, sentiments in their development will be very greatly determined by accidental causes. Now, there are some people, among whom I must suppose that my reader is to be found, who, when they see that any belief of theirs is determined by any circumstance extraneous to the facts, will from that moment not merely admit in words that that belief is doubtful, but will experience a real doubt of it, so that it ceases to be a belief.

To satisfy our doubts, therefore, it is necessary that a method should be found by which our beliefs may be determined by nothing human, but by some external permanency—by something upon which our thinking has no effect. Some mystics imagine that they have such a method in a private inspiration from on high. But that is only a form of the method of tenacity, in which the conception of truth as something public is not yet developed. Our external permanency would not be external, in our sense, if it was restricted in its influence to one individual. It must be something which affects, or might affect, every man. And, though these affections are necessarily as various as are individual conditions, yet the method must be such that the ultimate conclusion of every man shall be the same. Such is the method of science. Its fundamental hypothesis, restated in more familiar language, is this: There are Real things, whose characters are entirely independent of our opinions about them; those Reals affect our senses according to regular laws, and, though our sensations are as different as are our relations to the objects, yet, by taking advantage of the laws of perception, we can ascertain by reasoning how things really and truly are; and any man, if he have sufficient experience and he reason enough about it, will be led to the one True conclusion. The new conception here involved is that of Reality. It may be asked how I know that there are any Reals. If this hypothesis is the sole support of my method of inquiry, my method of inquiry must not be used to support my hypothesis. The reply is this: 1. If investigation cannot be regarded as proving that there are

Real things, it at least does not lead to a contrary conclusion; but the method and the conception on which it is based remain ever in harmony. No doubts of the method, therefore, necessarily arise from its practice, as is the case with all the others. 2. The feeling which gives rise to any method of fixing belief is a dissatisfaction at two repugnant propositions. But here already is a vague concession that there is some *one* thing which a proposition should represent. Nobody, therefore, can really doubt that there are Reals, for, if he did, doubt would not be a source of dissatisfaction. The hypothesis, therefore, is one which every mind admits. So that the social impulse does not cause men to doubt it. 3. Everybody uses the scientific method about a great many things, and only ceases to use it when he does not know how to apply it. 4. Experience of the method has not led us to doubt it, but, on the contrary, scientific investigation has had the most wonderful triumphs in the way of settling opinion. These afford the explanation of my not doubting the method or the hypothesis which it supposes; and not having any doubt, nor believing that anybody else whom I could influence has, it would be the merest babble for me to say more about it. If there be anybody with a living doubt upon the subject, let him consider it.

To describe the method of scientific investigation is the object of this series of papers. At present I have only room to notice some points of contrast between it and other methods of fixing belief.

This is the only one of the four methods which presents any distinction of a right and a wrong way. If I adopt the method of tenacity, and shut myself out from all influences, whatever I think necessary to doing this, is necessary according to that method. So with the method of authority: the state may try to put down heresy by means which, from a scientific point of view, seem very ill-calculated to accomplish its purposes; but the only test *on that method* is what the state thinks; so that it cannot pursue the method wrongly. So with the *a priori* method. The very essence of it is to think as one is inclined to think. All metaphysicians will be sure to do that, however they may be inclined to judge each other to be perversely wrong. The Hegelian system recognizes every natural tendency of thought as logical, although it be certain to be abolished by counter-tendencies. Hegel thinks there is a regular system in the succession of these tendencies, in consequence of which, after drifting one way and the other for a long time, opinion will at last go right. And it is true that metaphysicians do get the right ideas at last; Hegel's system of Nature represents tolerably the science of his day; and one may be sure that whatever scientific investigation shall have put out of doubt will presently receive *a priori* demonstration on the part of the metaphysicians. But with the scientific method the case is different. I may start with known and observed facts to proceed to the unknown; and yet the rules which I follow in doing so may not be such as investigation would approve. The test of whether I am truly following the method is not an immediate appeal to my feelings and purposes, but, on the contrary, itself involves the application of the method. Hence it is that bad reasoning as well as good reasoning is possible; and this fact is the foundation of the practical side of logic.

It is not to be supposed that the first three methods of settling opinion present no advantage whatever over the scientific method. On the contrary, each has some peculiar convenience of its own. The *a priori* method is distinguished for its comfortable conclusions. It is the nature of the process to adopt whatever belief we are inclined to, and there are certain flatteries to the vanity of man which we all believe by nature, until we are awakened from our pleasing dream by rough facts. The method of authority will always govern the mass of mankind; and those who wield the various forms of organized force in the state will never be convinced that dangerous reasoning ought not to be suppressed in some way. If liberty of speech is to be untrammeled from the grosser forms of constraint, then uniformity of opinion will be secured by a moral terrorism to which the respectability of society will give its thorough approval. Following the method of authority is the path of peace. Certain non-conformities are permitted; certain others (considered unsafe) are forbidden. These are different in different countries and in different ages; but, wherever you are, let it be known that you seriously hold a tabooed belief, and you may be perfectly sure of being treated with a cruelty less brutal but more refined than hunting you like a wolf. Thus, the greatest intellectual benefactors of mankind have never dared, and dare not now, to utter the whole of their thought; and thus a shade of *prima facie* doubt is cast upon every proposition which is considered essential to the security of society. Singularly enough, the persecution does not all come from without; but a man torments himself and is oftentimes most distressed at finding himself believing propositions which he has been brought up to regard with aversion. The peaceful and sympathetic man will, therefore, find it hard to resist the temptation to submit his opinions to authority. But most of all I admire the method of tenacity for its strength, simplicity, and directness. Men who pursue it are distinguished for their decision of character, which becomes very easy with such a mental rule. They do not waste time in trying to make up their minds what they want, but, fastening like lightning upon whatever alternative comes first, they hold to it to the end, whatever happens, without an instant's irresolution. This is one of the splendid qualities which generally accompany brilliant, unlasting success. It is impossible not to envy the man who can dismiss reason, although we know how it must turn out at last.

Such are the advantages which the other methods of settling opinion have over scientific investigation. A man should consider well of them; and then he should consider that, after all, he wishes his opinions to coincide with the fact, and that there is no reason why the results of those three first methods should do so. To bring about this effect is the prerogative of the method of science. Upon such considerations he has to make his choice—a choice which is far more than the adoption of any intellectual opinion, which is one of the ruling decisions of his life, to which, when once made, he is bound to adhere. The force of habit will sometimes cause a man to hold on to old beliefs, after he is in a condition to see that they have no sound basis. But reflection upon the state of the case will overcome these habits, and he ought to allow reflection its full weight. People sometimes shrink from doing this, having an idea that beliefs are wholesome which they cannot help feeling rest on nothing. But let such persons suppose an analogous though different case from their own. Let them ask themselves what they would say to a reformed Mussulman who should hesitate to give up his old notions in regard to the relations of the sexes; or to a reformed Catholic who should still shrink from reading the Bible. Would they not say that these persons ought to consider the matter fully, and clearly understand the new doctrine, and then ought to embrace it, in its entirety? But, above all, let it be considered that what is more wholesome than any particular belief is integrity of belief, and that to avoid looking into the support of any belief from a fear that it may turn out rotten is quite as immoral as it is disadvantageous. The person who confesses that there is such a thing as truth, which is distinguished from falsehood simply by this, that if acted on it should, on full consideration, carry us to the point we aim at and not astray, and then, though convinced of this, dares not know the truth and seeks to avoid it, is in a sorry state of mind indeed.

Notes

1. Not quite so, but as nearly so as can be told in a few words.
2. I am not speaking of secondary effects occasionally produced by the interference of other impulses.

In this 1878 paper from Popular Science Monthly, *Peirce proposes the pragmatic maxim and articulates his "end of inquiry" conception of truth.*

CHARLES S. PEIRCE

How to Make Our Ideas Clear

I

Whoever has looked into a modern treatise on logic of the common sort, will doubtless remember the two distinctions between *clear* and *obscure* conceptions, and between *distinct* and *confused* conceptions. They have lain in the books now for nigh two centuries, unimproved and unmodified, and are generally reckoned by logicians as among the gems of their doctrine.

A clear idea is defined as one which is so apprehended that it will be recognized wherever it is met with, and so that no other will be mistaken for it. If it fails of this clearness, it is said to be obscure.

This is rather a neat bit of philosophical terminology; yet, since it is clearness that they were defining, I wish the logicians had made their definition a little more plain. Never to fail to recognize an idea, and under no circumstances to mistake another for it, let it come in how recondite a form it may, would indeed imply such prodigious force and clearness of intellect as is seldom met with in this world. On the other hand, merely to have such an acquaintance with the idea as to have become familiar with it, and to have lost all hesitancy in recognizing it in ordinary cases, hardly seems to deserve the name of clearness of apprehension, since after all it only amounts to a subjective feeling of mastery which may be entirely mistaken. I take it, however, that when the logicians speak of "clearness," they mean nothing more than such a familiarity with an idea, since they regard the quality as but a small merit, which needs to be supplemented by another, which they call *distinctness*.

A distinct idea is defined as one which contains nothing which is not clear. This is technical language; by the *contents* of an idea logicians understand whatever is contained in its definition. So that an idea is *distinctly* apprehended, according to them, when we can give a precise definition of it, in abstract terms. Here the professional logicians leave the subject; and I would not have troubled the reader with what they have to say, if it were not such a striking example of how they have been slumbering through ages of intellectual activity, listlessly disregarding the enginery of modern thought, and never dreaming of applying its lessons to the improvement of logic. It is easy to show that the doctrine that familiar use and abstract distinctness make the perfection of apprehension has its only true place in philosophies which have long been extinct; and it is now time to formulate the method of attaining to a more perfect clearness of thought, such as we see and admire in the thinkers of our own time.

When Descartes set about the reconstruction of philosophy, his first step was to (theoretically) permit scepticism and to discard the practice of the schoolmen of looking to authority as the ultimate source of truth. That done, he sought a more natural fountain of true principles, and thought he found it in the human mind; thus passing, in the directest way, from the method of authority to that of apriority, as described in my first paper ["The Fixation of Belief"]. Self-consciousness was to furnish us with our fundamental truths, and to decide what was agreeable to reason. But since, evidently, not all ideas are true, he was led to note, as the first condition of infallibility, that they must be clear. The distinction between an idea *seeming* clear and really being so, never occurred to him. Trusting to introspection, as he did, even for a knowledge of external things, why should he question its testimony in respect to the contents of our own minds? But then, I suppose, seeing men, who seemed to be quite clear and positive, holding opposite opinions upon fundamental principles, he was further led to say that clearness of ideas is not sufficient, but that they need also to be distinct, i.e., to have nothing unclear about them. What he probably meant by this (for he did not explain himself with precision) was, that they must sustain the test of dialectical examination; that they must not only seem clear at the outset, but that discussion must never be able to bring to light points of obscurity connected with them.

Such was the distinction of Descartes, and one sees that it was precisely on the level of his philosophy. It was somewhat developed by Leibnitz. This great and singular genius was as remarkable for what he failed to see as for what he saw. That a piece of mechanism could not do work perpetually without being fed with power in some form, was a thing perfectly apparent to him; yet he did not understand that the machinery of the mind can only transform knowledge, but never originate it, unless it be fed with facts of observation. He thus missed the most essential point of the Cartesian philosophy, which is, that to accept propositions which seem perfectly evident to us is a thing which, whether it be logical or illogical, we cannot help doing. Instead of regarding the matter in this way, he sought to reduce the first principles of science to two classes, those which cannot be denied without self-contradiction, and those which result from the principle of sufficient reason (of which more anon), and was apparently unaware of the great difference between his position and that of Descartes. So he reverted to the old trivialities of logic; and, above all, abstract definitions played a great part in his philosophy. It was quite natural, therefore, that on observing that the method of Descartes labored under the difficulty that we may seem to ourselves to have clear apprehensions of ideas which in truth are very hazy, no better remedy occurred to him than to require an abstract definition of every important term. Accordingly, in adopting the distinction of *clear* and *distinct* notions, he described the latter quality as the clear apprehension of everything contained in the definition; and the books have ever since copied his words. There is no danger that his chimerical scheme will ever again be over-valued. Nothing new can ever be learned by analyzing definitions. Nevertheless, our existing beliefs can be set in order by this process, and order is an essential element of intellectual economy, as of every other. It may be acknowledged, therefore, that the books are right in making familiarity with a notion the first step toward clearness of apprehension, and the defining of it the second. But in omitting all mention of any higher perspicuity of thought, they simply mirror a philosophy which was exploded a hundred years ago. That much-admired "ornament of logic"—the doctrine of clearness and distinctness—may be pretty enough, but it is high time to relegate to our cabinet of curiosities the antique *bijou*, and to wear about us something better adapted to modern uses.

The very first lesson that we have a right to demand that logic shall teach us is, how to make our ideas clear; and a most important one it is, depreciated only by minds who stand in need of it. To know what we think, to be masters of our own meaning, will make a solid foundation for great and weighty thought. It is most easily learned by those whose ideas are meagre and restricted; and far happier they than such as wallow helplessly in a rich mud of conceptions. A nation, it is true, may, in the course of generations, overcome the disadvantage of an excessive wealth of language and its natural concomitant, a vast, unfathomable deep of ideas. We may see it in history, slowly perfecting its literary forms, sloughing at length its metaphysics, and, by virtue of the untirable patience which is often a compensation, attaining great excellence in every branch of mental acquirement. The page of history is not yet unrolled that is to tell us whether such a people will or will not in the long run prevail over one whose ideas (like the words of their language) are few, but which possesses a wonderful mastery over those which it has. For an individual, however, there can be no question that a few clear ideas are worth more than many confused ones. A young man would hardly be persuaded to sacrifice the greater part of his thoughts to save the rest; and the muddled head is the least apt to see the necessity of such a sacrifice. Him we can usually only commiserate, as a person with a congenital defect. Time will help him, but intellectual maturity with regard to clearness is apt to come rather late. This seems an unfortunate arrangement of Nature, inasmuch as clearness is of less use to a man settled in life, whose errors have in great measure had their effect, than it would be to one whose path lay before him. It is terrible to see how a single unclear idea, a single formula without meaning, lurking in a young man's head, will sometimes act like an obstruction of inert matter in an artery, hindering the nutrition of the brain, and condemning its victim to pine away in the fullness of his intellectual vigor and in the midst of intellectual plenty. Many a man has cherished for years as his hobby some vague shadow of an idea, too meaningless to be positively false; he has, nevertheless, passionately loved it, has made it his companion by day and by night, and has given to it his strength and his life, leaving all other occupations for its sake, and in short has lived with it and for it, until it has become, as it were, flesh of his flesh and bone of his bone; and then he has waked up some bright morning to find it gone, clean vanished away like the beautiful Melusina of the fable, and the essence of his life gone with it. I have myself known such a man; and who can tell how many histories of circle-squarers, metaphysicians, astrologers, and what not, may not be told in the old German story?

II

The principles set forth in the first part of this essay lead, at once, to a method of reaching a clearness of thought of higher grade than the "distinctness" of the logicians. It was there noticed that the action of thought is excited by the irritation of doubt, and ceases when belief is attained; so that the production of belief is the sole function of thought. All these words, however, are too strong for my purpose. It is as if I had described the phenomena as they appear under a mental microscope. Doubt and Belief, as the words are commonly employed, relate to religious or other grave discussions. But here I use them to designate the starting of any question, no matter how small or how great, and the resolution of it. If, for instance, in a horse-car, I pull out my purse and find a five-cent nickel and five coppers, I decide, while my hand is going to the purse, in which way I will pay my fare. To call such a question Doubt, and my decision Belief, is certainly to use words very disproportionate to the occasion. To speak of such a doubt as causing an irritation which needs to be appeased, suggests a temper which is uncomfortable to the verge of insanity. Yet, looking at the matter minutely, it must be admitted that, if there is the least hesitation as to whether I shall pay the five coppers or the nickel (as there will be sure to be, unless I act from some previously contracted habit in the matter), though irritation is too strong a word, yet I am excited to such small mental activity as may be necessary to deciding how I shall act. Most frequently doubts arise from some indecision, however momentary, in our action. Sometimes it is not so. I have, for example, to wait in a railway-station, and to pass the time I read the advertisements on the walls. I compare the advantages of different trains and different routes which I never expect to take, merely fancying myself to be in a state of hesitancy, because I am bored with having nothing to trouble me. Feigned hesitancy, whether feigned for mere amusement or with a lofty purpose, plays a great part in the production of scientific inquiry. However the doubt may originate, it stimulates the mind to an activity which may be slight or energetic, calm or turbulent. Images pass rapidly through consciousness, one incessantly melting into another, until at last, when all is over—it may be in a fraction of a second, in an hour, or after long years—we find ourselves decided as to how we should act under such circumstances as those which occasioned our hesitation. In other words, we have attained belief.

In this process we observe two sorts of elements of consciousness, the distinction between which may best be made clear by means of an illustration. In a piece of music there are the separate notes, and there is the air. A single tone may be prolonged for an hour or a day, and it exists as perfectly in each second of that time as in the whole taken together; so that, as long as it is sounding, it might be present to a sense from which everything in the past was as completely absent as the future itself. But it is different with the air, the performance of which occupies a certain time, during the portions of which only portions of it are played. It consists in an orderliness in the succession of sounds which strike the ear at different times; and to perceive it there must be some continuity of consciousness which makes the events of a lapse of time present to us. We certainly only perceive the air by hearing the separate notes; yet we cannot be said to directly hear it, for we hear only what is present at the instant, and an orderliness of succession cannot exist in an instant. These two sorts of objects, what we are *immediately* conscious of and what we are *mediately* conscious of, are found in all consciousness. Some elements (the sensations) are completely present at every instant so long as they last, while others (like thought) are actions having beginning, middle, and end, and consist in a congruence in the succession of sensations which flow through the mind. They cannot be immediately present to us, but must cover some portion of the past or future. Thought is a thread of melody running through the succession of our sensations.

We may add that just as a piece of music may be written in parts, each part having its own air, so various systems of relationship of succession subsist together between the same sensations. These different systems are distinguished by having different motives, ideas, or functions. Thought is only one such system, for its sole motive, idea, and function is to produce belief, and whatever does not concern that purpose belongs to some other system of relations. The action of thinking may incidentally have other results; it may serve to amuse us, for example, and among *dilettanti* it is not rare to find those who have so perverted thought to the purposes of pleasure that it seems to vex them to think that the questions upon which they delight to exercise it may ever get finally settled; and a positive discovery which takes a favorite subject out of the arena of literary debate is met with ill-concealed dislike. This disposition is the very debauchery of thought. But the soul and meaning of thought, abstracted from the other elements which accompany it, though it may be voluntarily thwarted, can never be made to direct itself toward anything but the production of belief. Thought in action has for its only possible motive the attainment of thought at rest; and whatever does not refer to belief is no part of the thought itself.

And what, then, is belief? It is the demi-cadence which closes a musical phrase in the symphony of our intellectual life. We have seen that it has just three properties: First, it is something that we are aware of; second, it appeases the irritation of doubt; and, third, it involves the establishment in our nature of a rule of action, or, say for short, a *habit*. As it appeases the irritation of doubt, which is the motive for thinking, thought relaxes, and comes to rest for a moment when belief is reached. But, since belief is a rule for action, the application of which involves further doubt and further thought, at the same time that it is a stopping-place, it is also a new starting-place for thought. That is why I have permitted myself to call it thought at rest, although thought is essentially an action. The *final* upshot of thinking is the

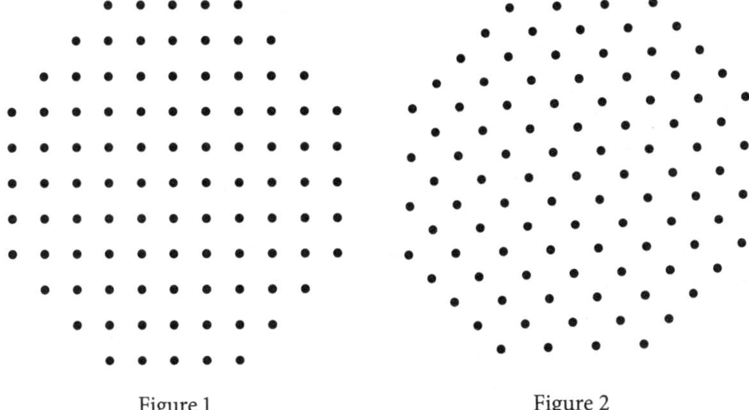

Figure 1 Figure 2

exercise of volition, and of this thought no longer forms a part: but belief is only a stadium of mental action, an effect upon our nature due to thought, which will influence future thinking.

The essence of belief is the establishment of a habit; and different beliefs are distinguished by the different modes of action to which they give rise. If beliefs do not differ in this respect, if they appease the same doubt by producing the same rule of action, then no mere differences in the manner of consciousness of them can make them different beliefs, any more than playing a tune in different keys is playing different tunes. Imaginary distinctions are often drawn between beliefs which differ only in their mode of expression;—the wrangling which ensues is real enough, however. To believe that any objects are arranged among themselves as in Fig. 1, and to believe that they are arranged in Fig. 2, are one and the same belief; yet it is conceivable that a man should assert one proposition and deny the other. Such false distinctions do as much harm as the confusion of beliefs really different, and are among the pitfalls of which we ought constantly to beware, especially when we are upon metaphysical ground. One singular deception of this sort, which often occurs, is to mistake the sensation produced by our own unclearness of thought for a character of the object we are thinking. Instead of perceiving that the obscurity is purely subjective, we fancy that we contemplate a quality of the object which is essentially mysterious; and if our conception be afterward presented to us in a clear form we do not recognize it as the same, owing to the absence of the feeling of unintelligibility. So long as this deception lasts, it obviously puts an impassable barrier in the way of perspicuous thinking; so that it equally interests the opponents of rational thought to perpetuate it, and its adherents to guard against it.

Another such deception is to mistake a mere difference in the grammatical construction of two words for a distinction between the ideas they express. In this pedantic age, when the general mob of writers attend so much more to words than to things, this error is common enough. When I just said that thought is an *action*, and that it consists in a *relation*, although a person performs an action but not a relation, which can only be the result of an action, yet there was no inconsistency in what I said, but only a grammatical vagueness.

From all these sophisms we shall be perfectly safe so long as we reflect that the whole function of thought is to produce habits of action; and that whatever there is connected with a thought, but irrelevant to its purpose, is an accretion to it, but no part of it. If there be a unity among our sensations which has no reference to how we shall act on a given occasion, as when we listen to a piece of music, why we do not call that thinking. To develop its meaning, we have, therefore, simply to determine what habits it produces, for what a thing means is simply what habits it involves. Now, the identity of a habit depends on how it might lead us to act, not merely under such circumstances as are likely to arise, but under such as might possibly occur, no matter how improbable they may be. What the habit is depends on *when* and *how* it causes us to act. As for the *when*, every stimulus to action is derived from perception; as for the *how*, every purpose of action is to produce some sensible result. Thus, we come down to what is tangible and conceivably practical, as the root of every real distinction of thought, no matter how subtile it may be; and there is no distinction of meaning so fine as to consist in anything but a possible difference of practice.

To see what this principle leads to, consider in the light of it such a doctrine as that of transubstantiation. The Protestant churches generally hold that the elements of the sacrament are flesh and blood only in a tropical sense; they nourish our souls as meat and the juice of it would our bodies.

But the Catholics maintain that they are literally just meat and blood; although they possess all the sensible qualities of wafercakes and diluted wine. But we can have no conception of wine except what may enter into a belief, either—

1. That this, that, or the other, is wine; or,
2. That wine possesses certain properties.

Such beliefs are nothing but self-notifications that we should, upon occasion, act in regard to such things as we believe to be wine according to the qualities which we believe wine to possess. The occasion of such action would be some sensible perception, the motive of it to produce some sensible result. Thus our action has exclusive reference to what affects the senses, our habit has the same bearing as our action, our belief the same as our habit, our conception the same as our belief; and we can consequently mean nothing by wine but what has certain effects, direct or indirect, upon our senses; and to talk of something as having all the sensible characters of wine, yet being in reality blood, is senseless jargon. Now, it is not my object to pursue the theological question; and having used it as a logical example I drop it, without caring to anticipate the theologian's reply. I only desire to point out how impossible it is that we should have an idea in our minds which relates to anything but conceived sensible effects of things. Our idea of anything *is* our idea of its sensible effects; and if we fancy that we have any other we deceive ourselves, and mistake a mere sensation accompanying the thought for a part of the thought itself. It is absurd to say that thought has any meaning unrelated to its only function. It is foolish for Catholics and Protestants to fancy themselves in disagreement about the elements of the sacrament, if they agree in regard to all their sensible effects, here and hereafter.

It appears, then, that the rule for attaining the third grade of clearness of apprehension is as follows: Consider what effects, that might conceivably have practical bearings, we conceive the object of our conception to have. Then, our conception of these effects is the whole of our conception of the object.

III

Let us illustrate this rule by some examples; and, to begin with the simplest one possible, let us ask what we mean by calling a thing *hard.* Evidently that it will not be scratched by many other substances. The whole conception of this quality, as of every other, lies in its conceived effects. There is absolutely no difference between a hard thing and a soft thing so long as they are not brought to the test. Suppose, then, that a diamond could be crystallized in the midst of a cushion of soft cotton, and should remain there until it was finally burned up. Would it be false to say that that diamond was soft? This seems a foolish question, and would be so, in fact, except in the realm of logic. There such questions are often of the greatest utility as serving to bring logical principles into sharper relief than real discussions ever could. In studying logic we must not put them aside with hasty answers, but must consider them with attentive care, in order to make out the principles involved. We may, in the present case, modify our question, and ask what prevents us from saying that all hard bodies remain perfectly soft until they are touched, when their hardness increases with the pressure until they are scratched. Reflection will show that the reply is this: there would be no *falsity* in such modes of speech. They would involve a modification of our present usage of speech with regard to the words hard and soft, but not of their meanings. For they represent no fact to be different from what it is; only they involve arrangements of facts which would be exceedingly maladroit. This leads us to remark that the question of what would occur under circumstances which do not actually arise is not a question of fact, but only of the most perspicuous arrangement of them. For example, the question of free-will and fate in its simplest form, stripped of verbiage, is something like this: I have done something of which I am ashamed; could I, by an effort of the will, have resisted the temptation, and done otherwise? The philosophical reply is, that this is not a question of fact, but only of the arrangement of facts. Arranging them so as to exhibit what is particularly pertinent to my question—namely, that I ought to blame myself for having done wrong—it is perfectly true to say that, if I had willed to do otherwise than I did, I should have done otherwise. On the other hand, arranging the facts so as to exhibit another important consideration, it is equally true that, when a temptation has once been allowed to work, it will, if it has a certain force, produce its effect, let me struggle how I may. There is no objection to a contradiction in what would result from a false supposition. The *reductio ad absurdum* consists in showing that contradictory results would follow from a hypothesis which is consequently judged to be false. Many questions are involved in the free-will discussion, and I am far from desiring to say that both sides are equally right. On the contrary, I am of opinion that one side denies important facts, and that the other does not. But what I do say is, that the above single question was the origin of the whole doubt; that, had it not been for this question, the controversy would never have arisen; and that this question is perfectly solved in the manner which I have indicated.

Let us next seek a clear idea of Weight. This is another very easy case. To say that a body is heavy means simply that, in the absence of opposing force, it will fall. This (neglecting certain specifications of how it will fall, etc., which exist in the mind of the physicist who uses the word) is evidently the whole conception of weight. It is a fair question whether some particular facts may not *account* for gravity; but what we mean by the force itself is completely involved in its effects.

This leads us to undertake an account of the idea of Force in general. This is the great conception which, developed in the early part of the seventeenth century from the rude idea of a cause, and constantly improved upon since, has shown us how to explain all the changes of motion which bodies experience, and how to think about all physical phenomena; which has given birth to modern science, and changed the face of the globe; and which, aside from its more special uses, has played a principal part in directing the course of modern thought, and in furthering modern social development. It is, therefore, worth some pains to comprehend it. According to our rule, we must begin by asking what is the immediate use of thinking about force; and the answer is, that we thus account for changes of motion. If bodies were left to themselves, without the intervention of forces, every motion would continue unchanged both in velocity and in direction. Furthermore, change of motion never takes place abruptly; if its direction is changed, it is always through a curve without angles; if its velocity alters, it is by degrees. The gradual changes which are constantly taking place are conceived by geometers to be compounded together according to the rules of the parallelogram of forces. If the reader does not already know what this is, he will find it, I hope, to his advantage to endeavor to follow the following explanation; but if mathematics are insupportable to him, pray let him skip three paragraphs rather than that we should part company here.

A *path* is a line whose beginning and end are distinguished. Two paths are considered to be equivalent, which, beginning at the same point, lead to the same point. Thus *the two paths*, *A B C D E* and *A F G H E*, are equivalent. Paths which do not begin at the same point are considered to be equivalent provided that, on moving either of them without turning it, but keeping it always parallel to its original position, when its beginning coincides with that of the other path, the ends also coincide. Paths are considered as geometrically added together, when one begins where the other ends; thus the path *A E* is conceived to be a sum of *A B*, *B C*, *C D*, and *D E*. In

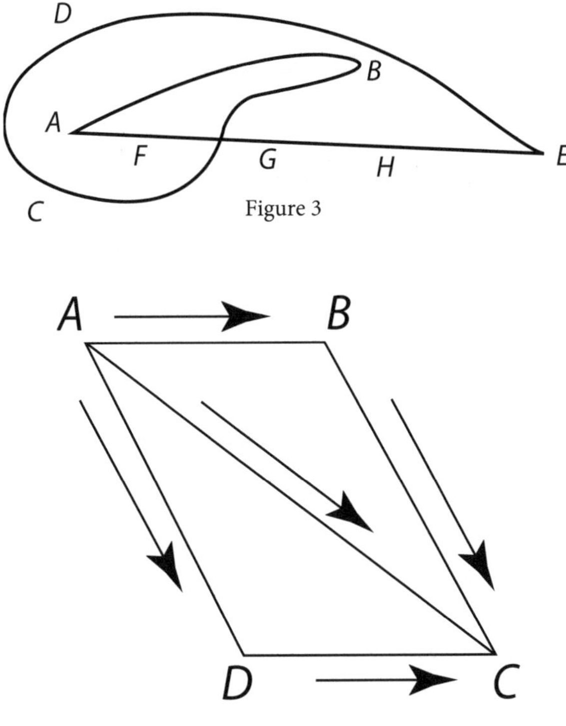

Figure 3

Figure 4

the parallelogram of Fig. 4 the diagonal *A C* is the sum of *A B* and *B C*; or, since *A D* is geometrically equivalent to *B C*, *A C* is the geometrical sum of *A B* and *A D*.

All this is purely conventional. It simply amounts to this: that we choose to call paths having the relations I have described equal or added. But, though it is a convention, it is a convention with a good reason. The rule for geometrical addition may be applied not only to paths, but to any other things which can be represented by paths. Now, as a path is determined by the varying direction and distance of the point which moves over it from the starting-point, it follows that anything which from its beginning to its end is determined by a varying direction and a varying magnitude is capable of being represented by a line. Accordingly, *velocities* may be represented by lines, for they have only directions and rates. The same thing is true of *accelerations*, or changes of velocities. This is evident enough in the case of velocities; and it becomes evident for accelerations if we consider that precisely what velocities are to positions—namely, states of change of them—that accelerations are to velocities.

The so-called "parallelogram of forces" is simply a rule for compounding accelerations. The rule is, to represent the accelerations by paths, and then to geometrically

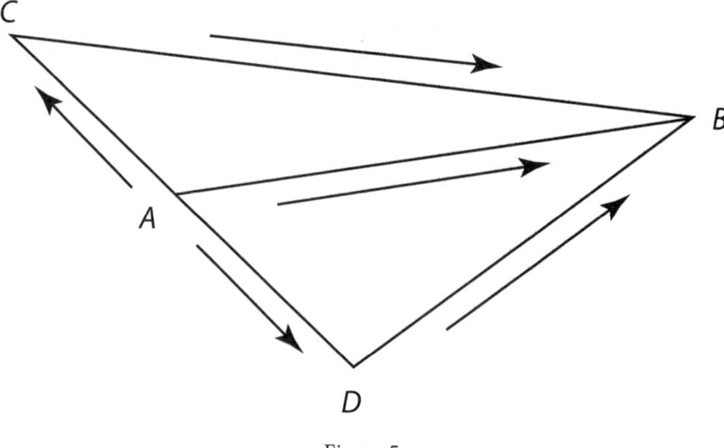

Figure 5

add the paths. The geometers, however, not only use the "parallelogram of forces" to compound different accelerations, but also to resolve one acceleration into a sum of several. Let *A B* (Fig. 5) be the path which represents a certain acceleration—say, such a change in the motion of a body that at the end of one second the body will, under the influence of that change, be in a position different from what it would have had if its motion had continued unchanged such that a path equivalent to *A B* would lead from the latter position to the former. This acceleration may be considered as the sum of the accelerations represented by *A C* and *C B*. It may also be considered as the sum of the very different accelerations represented by *A D* and *D B*, where *A D* is almost the opposite of *A C*. And it is clear that there is an immense variety of ways in which *A B* might be resolved into the sum of two accelerations.

After this tedious explanation, which I hope, in view of the extraordinary interest of the conception of force, may not have exhausted the reader's patience, we are prepared at last to state the grand fact which this conception embodies. This fact is that if the actual changes of motion which the different particles of bodies experience are each resolved in its appropriate way, each component acceleration is precisely such as is prescribed by a certain law of Nature, according to which bodies, in the relative positions which the bodies in question actually have at the moment,[1] always receive certain accelerations, which, being compounded by geometrical addition, give the acceleration which the body actually experiences.

This is the only fact which the idea of force represents, and whoever will take the trouble clearly to apprehend what this fact is, perfectly comprehends what force is. Whether we ought to say that a force *is* an acceleration, or that it *causes* an acceleration, is a mere question of propriety of language, which has no more to do with our real meaning than the difference between the French idiom "*Il fait froid*" and its English equivalent "*It is cold*" Yet it is surprising to see how this simple affair has muddled men's minds. In how many profound treatises is not force spoken of as a "mysterious entity," which seems to be only a way of confessing that the author despairs of ever getting a clear notion of what the word means! In a recent admired work on Analytic Mechanics it is stated that we understand precisely the effect of force, but what force itself is we do not understand! This is simply a self-contradiction. The idea which the word force excites in our minds has no other function than to affect our actions, and these actions can have no reference to force otherwise than through its effects. Consequently, if we know what the effects of force are, we are acquainted with every fact which is implied in saying that a force exists, and there is nothing more to know. The truth is, there is some vague notion afloat that a question may mean something which the mind cannot conceive; and when some hair-splitting philosophers have been confronted with the absurdity of such a view, they have invented an empty distinction between positive and negative conceptions, in the attempt to give their non-idea a form not obviously nonsensical. The nullity of it is sufficiently plain from the considerations given a few pages back; and, apart from those considerations, the quibbling character of the distinction must have struck every mind accustomed to real thinking.

IV

Let us now approach the subject of logic, and consider a conception which particularly concerns it, that of *reality*. Taking clearness in the sense of familiarity, no idea could be clearer than this. Every child uses it with perfect confidence, never dreaming that he does not understand it. As for clearness in its second grade, however, it would probably puzzle most men, even among those of a reflective turn of mind, to give an abstract definition of the real. Yet such a definition may perhaps be reached by considering the points of difference between reality and its opposite, fiction. A figment is a product of somebody's imagination; it has such characters as his thought impresses upon it. That those characters are independent of how you or I think is an external reality. There are, however, phenomena within our own minds, dependent upon our thought, which are at the same time real in the sense that we really think them. But though their characters depend on how we think, they do not depend on what we think those characters to be. Thus, a dream has a real existence as a mental phenomenon, if somebody has really dreamt it; that he dreamt so and so, does not depend on what anybody thinks was dreamt, but is completely independent of all opinion on the subject. On the other hand, considering, not the fact of dreaming, but the thing dreamt, it retains its peculiarities by virtue of no other fact than that it was dreamt to possess them. Thus we may define the real as that whose characters are independent of what anybody may think them to be.

But, however satisfactory such a definition may be found, it would be a great mistake to suppose that it makes the idea of reality perfectly clear. Here, then, let us apply our rules. According to them, reality, like every other quality, consists in the peculiar sensible effects which things partaking of it produce. The only effect which real things have is to cause belief, for all the sensations which they excite emerge into consciousness in the form of beliefs. The question therefore is, how is true belief (or belief in the real) distinguished from false belief (or belief in fiction). Now, as we have seen in the former paper ["The Fixation of Belief"], the ideas of truth and falsehood, in their full development, appertain exclusively to the experiential method of settling opinion. A person who arbitrarily chooses the propositions which he will adopt can use the word truth only to emphasize the expression of his determination to hold on to his choice. Of course, the method of tenacity never prevailed exclusively; reason is too natural to men for that. But in the literature of the dark ages we find some fine examples of it. When Scotus Erigena is commenting upon a poetical passage in which hellebore is spoken of as having caused the death of Socrates, he does not hesitate to inform the inquiring reader that Helleborus and Socrates were two eminent Greek philosophers, and that the latter, having been overcome in argument by the former, took the matter to heart and died of it! What sort of an idea of truth could a man have who could adopt and teach, without the qualification of a perhaps, an opinion taken so entirely at random? The real spirit of Socrates, who I hope would have been delighted to have been "overcome in argument," because he would have learned something by it, is in curious contrast with the naive idea of the glossist, for whom (as for "the born missionary" of today) discussion would seem to have been simply a struggle. When philosophy began to awake from its long slumber, and before theology completely dominated it, the practice seems to have been for each professor to seize upon any philosophical position he found unoccupied and which seemed a strong one, to intrench himself in it, and to sally forth from time to time to give battle to the others. Thus, even the scanty records we possess of those disputes enable us to make out a dozen or more opinions held by different teachers at one time concerning the question of nominalism and realism. Read the opening part of the Historia Calamitatum of Abelard, who was certainly as philosophical as any of his contemporaries, and see the spirit of combat which it breathes. For him, the truth is simply his particular stronghold. When the method of authority prevailed, the truth meant little more than the Catholic faith. All the efforts of the scholastic doctors are directed toward harmonizing their faith in Aristotle and their faith in the Church, and one may search their ponderous folios through without finding an argument which goes any further. It is noticeable that where different faiths flourish side by side, renegades are looked upon with contempt even by the party whose belief they adopt; so completely has the idea of loyalty replaced that of truth-seeking. Since the time of Descartes, the defect in the conception of truth has been less apparent. Still, it will sometimes strike a scientific man that the philosophers have been less intent on finding out what the facts are, than on inquiring what belief is most in harmony with their system. It is hard to convince a follower of the *a priori* method by adducing facts; but show him that an opinion he is defending is inconsistent with what he has laid down elsewhere, and he will be very apt to retract it. These minds do not seem to believe that disputation is ever to cease; they seem to think that the opinion which is natural for one man is not so for another, and that belief will, consequently, never be settled. In contenting themselves with fixing their own opinions by a method which would lead another man to a different result, they betray their feeble hold of the conception of what truth is.

On the other hand, all the followers of science are animated by a cheerful hope that the processes of investigation, if only pushed far enough, will give one certain solution to each question to which they apply it. One man may investigate the velocity of light by studying the transits of Venus and the aberration of the stars; another by the oppositions of Mars and the eclipses of Jupiter's satellites; a third by the method of Fizeau; a fourth by that of Foucault; a fifth by the motions of the curves of Lissajoux; a sixth, a seventh, an eighth, and a ninth, may follow the different methods of comparing the measures of statical and dynamical electricity. They may at first obtain different results, but, as each perfects his method and his processes, the results are found to move steadily together toward a destined centre. So with all scientific research. Different minds may set out with the most antagonistic views, but the progress of investigation carries them by a force outside of themselves to one and the same conclusion. This activity of thought by which we are carried, not where we wish, but to a fore-ordained goal, is like the operation of destiny. No modification of the point of view taken, no selection of other facts for study, no natural bent of mind even, can enable a man to escape the predestinate opinion. This great hope is embodied in the conception of truth and reality. The opinion which is fated[2] to be ultimately agreed to by all who investigate, is what we mean by the truth, and the object represented in this opinion is the real. That is the way I would explain reality.

But it may be said that this view is directly opposed to the abstract definition which we have given of reality, inasmuch as it makes the characters of the real depend on what is ultimately thought about them. But the answer to this is that, on the one hand, reality is independent, not necessarily of thought in general, but only of what you or I or any finite number of men may think about it; and that, on the other hand, though the object of the final opinion depends on what that opinion is, yet what that opinion is does not depend on what you or I or any man thinks. Our perversity and that of others may indefinitely postpone the settlement of opinion; it might even conceivably cause an arbitrary proposition to be universally accepted as long as the human race should last. Yet even that would not change the nature of the belief, which alone could be the result of investigation carried sufficiently far; and if, after the extinction of our race, another should arise with faculties and disposition for investigation, that true opinion must be the one which they would ultimately come to. "Truth crushed to earth shall rise again," and the opinion which would finally result from investigation does not depend on how anybody may actually think. But the reality of that which is real does depend on the real fact that investigation is destined to lead, at last, if continued long enough, to a belief in it.

But I may be asked what I have to say to all the minute facts of history, forgotten never to be recovered, to the lost books of the ancients, to the buried secrets.

> Full many a gem of purest ray serene
> The dark, unfathomed caves of ocean bear;
> Full many a flower is born to blush unseen,
> And waste its sweetness on the desert air.

Do these things not really exist because they are hopelessly beyond the reach of our knowledge? And then, after the universe is dead (according to the prediction of some scientists), and all life has ceased forever, will not the shock of atoms continue though there will be no mind to know it? To this I reply that, though in no possible state of knowledge can any number be great enough to express the relation between the amount of what rests unknown to the amount of the known, yet it is unphilosophical to suppose that, with regard to any given question (which has any clear meaning), investigation would not bring forth a solution of it, if it were carried far enough. Who would have said, a few years ago, that we could ever know of what substances stars are made whose light may have been longer in reaching us than the human race has existed? Who can he sure of what we shall not know in a few hundred years? Who can guess what would be the result of continuing the pursuit of science for ten thousand years, with the activity of the last hundred? And if it were to go on for a million, or a billion, or any number of years you please, how is it possible to say that there is any question which might not ultimately be solved?

But it may be objected, "Why make so much of these remote considerations, especially when it is your principle that only practical distinctions have a meaning?" Well, I must confess that it makes very little difference whether we say that a stone on the bottom of the ocean, in complete darkness, is brilliant or not—that is to say, that it *probably* makes no difference, remembering always that that stone *may* be fished up tomorrow. But that there are gems at the bottom of the sea, flowers in the untraveled desert, etc., are propositions which, like that about a diamond being hard when it is not pressed, concern much more the arrangement of our language than they do the meaning of our ideas.

It seems to me, however, that we have, by the application of our rule, reached so clear an apprehension of what we mean by reality, and of the fact which the idea rests on, that we should not, perhaps, be making a pretension so presumptuous as it would be singular, if we were to offer a metaphysical theory of existence for universal acceptance among those who employ the scientific method of fixing belief. However, as metaphysics is a subject much more curious than useful, the knowledge of which, like that of a sunken reef, serves chiefly to enable us to keep clear of it, I will not trouble the reader with any more Ontology at this moment. I have already been led much farther into that path than I should have desired; and I have given the reader such a dose of mathematics, psychology, and all that is most abstruse, that I fear he may already have left me, and that what I am now writing is for the compositor and proof-reader exclusively. I trusted to the importance of the subject. There is no royal road to logic, and really valuable ideas can only be had at the price of close attention. But I know that in the matter of ideas the public prefer the cheap and nasty; and in my next paper ["The Doctrine of Chances"] I am going to return to the easily intelligible, and not wander from it again. The reader who has been at the pains of wading through this paper, shall be rewarded in the next one by seeing how beautifully what has been developed in this tedious way can be applied to the ascertainment of the rules of scientific reasoning.

We have, hitherto, not crossed the threshold of scientific logic. It is certainly important to know how to make our ideas clear, but they may be ever so clear without being true. How to make them so, we have next to study. How to give birth to those vital and procreative ideas which multiply into a thousand forms and diffuse themselves everywhere, advancing civilization and making the dignity of man, is an art not yet reduced to rules, but of the secret of which the history of science affords some hints.

Notes

1. Possibly the velocities also have to be taken into account.
2. Fate means merely that which is sure to come true, and can nohow be avoided. It is a superstition to suppose that a certain sort of events are ever fated, and it is another to suppose that the word fate can never be freed from its superstitious taint. We are all fated to die.

This paper was delivered to the University of California (Berkeley) Philosophical Union in 1898. Here James refers to Peirce as pragmatism's founder and offers a broader interpretation of the pragmatic maxim.

WILLIAM JAMES

Philosophical Conceptions and Practical Results

I will seek to define with you merely what seems to be the most likely direction in which to start upon the trail of truth. Years ago this direction was given to me by an American philosopher whose home is in the East, and whose published works, few as they are and scattered in periodicals, are no fit expression of his powers. I refer to Mr. Charles S. Peirce, with whose very existence as a philosopher I dare say many of you are unacquainted. He is one of the most original of contemporary thinkers; and the principle of practicalism—or pragmatism, as he called it, when I first heard him enunciate it at Cambridge in the early '70's—is the clue or compass by following which I find myself more and more confirmed in believing we may keep our feet upon the proper trail.

Peirce's principle, as we may call it, may be expressed in a variety of ways, all of them very simple. In the *Popular Science Monthly* for January, 1878, he introduces it as follows: The soul and meaning of thought, he says, can never be made to direct itself towards anything but the production of belief, belief being the demicadence which closes a musical phrase in the symphony of our intellectual life. Thought in movement has thus for its only possible motive the attainment of thought at rest. But when our thought about an object has found its rest in belief, then our action on the subject can firmly and safely begin. Beliefs, in short, are really rules for action; and the whole function of thinking is but: one step in the production of habits of action. If there were any part of a thought that made no difference in the thought's practical consequences, then that part would be no proper element of the thought's significance. Thus the same thought may be clad in different words; but if the different words suggest no different conduct, they are mere outer accretions, and have no part in the thought's meaning. If, however, they determine conduct differently, they are essential elements of the significance. "Please open the door," and, "*Veuillez ouvrir la porte*" in French, mean just the same thing; but "D—n you, open the door," although in English, *means* something very different. Thus to develop a thought's meaning we need only determine what conduct it is fitted to produce; that conduct is for us its sole significance. And the tangible fact at the root of all our thought-distinctions, however subtle, is that there is no one of them so fine as to consist in anything but a possible difference of practice. To attain perfect clearness in our thoughts of an object, then, we need only consider what effects of a conceivably practical kind the object may involve—what sensations we are to expect from it, and what reactions we must prepare. Our conception of these effects, then, is for us the whole of our conception of the object, so far as that conception has positive significance at all.

This is the principle of Peirce, the principle of pragmatism. I think myself that it should be expressed more broadly than Mr. Peirce expresses it. The ultimate test for us of what a truth means is indeed the conduct it dictates or inspires. But it inspires that conduct because it first foretells some particular turn to our experience which shall call for just that conduct from us. And I should prefer for our purposes this evening to express Peirce's principle by saying that the effective meaning of any philosophic proposition can always be brought down to some particular consequence, in our future practical experience, whether active or passive; the point lying rather in the fact that the experience must be particular, than in the fact that it must be active.

To take in the importance of this principle, one must get accustomed to applying it to concrete cases. Such use as I am able to make of it convinces me that to be mindful of it in philosophical disputations tends wonderfully to smooth out misunderstandings and to bring in peace. If it did nothing else, then, it would yield a sovereignly valuable rule of method for discussion. So I shall devote the rest of this precious hour with you to its elucidation, because I sincerely think that if you once grasp it, it will shut your steps out from many an old false opening, and head you in the true direction for the trail.

One of its first consequences is this. Suppose there are two different philosophical definitions, or propositions, or maxims, or what not, which seem to contradict each other, and about which men dispute. If, by supposing the truth of the one, you can foresee no conceivable practical consequence to anybody at any time or place, which is different from what you would foresee if you supposed the truth of the other, why then the difference between the two propositions is no difference,—it is only a specious and verbal difference, unworthy of further contention. Both formulas mean radically the same thing, although they may say it in such different words. It is astonishing to see how many philosophical disputes collapse into insignificance the moment you subject them to this simple test. There can be no difference which doesn't make a difference—no difference in abstract truth which does not express itself in a difference of concrete fact, and of conduct consequent upon the fact, imposed on somebody, somehow, somewhere, and somewhen. It is true that a certain shrinkage of values often seems to occur in our general formulas when we measure their meaning in this prosaic and practical way. They diminish. But the vastness that is merely vagueness is a false appearance of importance, and not a vastness worth retaining. The *x*'s, *y*'s, and *z*'s always do shrivel, as I have heard a learned friend say, whenever at the end of your algebraic computation they change into so many plain *a*'s, *b*'s, and *c*'s; but the whole function of algebra is, after all, to get them into that more definite shape; and the whole function of philosophy ought to be to find out what definite difference it will make to you and me, at definite instants of our life, if this world-formula or that world-formula be the one which is true.

If we start off with an impossible case, we shall perhaps all the more clearly see the use and scope of our principle. Let us, therefore, put ourselves, in imagination, in a position from which no forecasts of consequence, no dictates of conduct, can possibly be made, so that the principle of pragmatism finds no field of application. Let us, I mean, assume that the present moment is the absolutely last moment of the world, with bare nonentity beyond it, and no hereafter for either experience or conduct.

Now I say that in that case there would be no sense whatever in some of our most urgent and envenomed philosophical and religious debates. The question is, "Is matter the producer of all things, or is a God there too?" would, for example, offer a perfectly idle and insignificant alternative if the world were finished and no more of it to come. Many of us, most of us, I think, now feel as if a terrible coldness and deadness would come over the world were we forced to believe that no informing spirit or purpose had to do with it, but it merely accidentally had come. The actually experienced details of fact might be the same on either hypothesis, some sad, some joyous; some rational, some odd and grotesque; but without a God behind them, we think they would have something ghastly, they would tell no genuine story, there would be no speculation in those eyes that they do glare with. With the God, on the other hand, they would grow solid, warm, and altogether full of real significance. But I say that such an alternation of feelings, reasonable enough in a consciousness that is prospective, as ours now is, and whose world is partly yet to come, would be absolutely senseless and irrational in a purely retrospective consciousness summing up a world already past. For such a consciousness, no emotional interest could attach to the alternative. The problem would be purely intellectual; and if unaided matter could, with any scientific plausibility, be shown to cipher out the actual facts, then not the faintest shadow ought to cloud the mind, of regret for the God that by the same ciphering would prove needless and disappear from our belief.

For just consider the case sincerely, and say what would be the *worth* of such a God if he *were* there, with his work accomplished and his world run down. He would be worth no more than just that world was worth. To that amount of result, with its mixed merits and defects, his creative power could attain, but go no farther. And since there is to be no future; since the whole value and meaning of the world has been already paid in and actualized in the feelings that went with it in the passing, and now go with it in the ending; since it draws no supplemental significance (such as our real world draws) from its function of preparing something yet to come; why then, by it we take God's measure, as it were. He is the Being who could once for all do *that*; and for that much we are thankful to him, but for nothing more. But now, on the contrary hypothesis, namely, that the bits of matter following their "laws" could make that world and do no less, should we not be just as thankful to them? Wherein should we suffer loss, then, if we dropped God as an hypothesis and made the matter alone responsible? Where would the special deadness, "crassness," and ghastliness come in?

And how, experience being what it is once for all, would God's presence in it make it any more "living," any richer in our sight?

Candidly, it is impossible to give any answer to this question. The actually experienced world is supposed to be the same in its details on either hypothesis, "the same, for our praise or blame," as Browning says. It stands there indefeasibly; a gift which can't be taken back. Calling matter the cause of it retracts no single one of the items that have made it up, nor does calling God the cause augment them. They are the God or the atoms, respectively, of just that and no other world. The God, if there, has been doing just what atoms could do—appearing in the character of atoms, so to speak—and earning such gratitude as is due to atoms, and no more. If his presence lends no different turn or issue to the performance, it surely can lend it no increase of dignity. Nor would indignity come to it were he absent, and did the atoms remain the only actors on the stage. When a play is once over, and the curtain down, you really make it no better by claiming an illustrious genius for its author, just as you make it no worse by calling him a common hack.

Thus if no future detail of experience or conduct is to be deduced from our hypothesis, the debate between materialism and theism becomes quite idle and insignificant. Matter and God in that event mean exactly the same thing—the power, namely, neither more nor less, that can make just this mixed, imperfect, yet completed world—and the wise man is he who in such a case would turn his back on such a supererogatory discussion. Accordingly most men instinctively—and a large class of men, the so-called positivists or scientists, deliberately—do turn their backs on philosophical disputes from which nothing in the line of definite future consequences can be seen to follow. The verbal and empty character of our studies is surely a reproach with which you of the Philosophical Union are but too sadly familiar. An escaped Berkeley student said to me at Harvard the other day,—he had never been in the philosophical department here,—"Words, words, words, are all that you philosophers care for." We philosophers think it all unjust; and yet, if the principle of pragmatism be true, it is a perfectly sound reproach unless the metaphysical alternatives under investigation can be shown to have alternative practical outcomes, however delicate and distant these may be. The common man and the scientist can discover no such outcomes. And if the metaphysician can discern none either, the common man and scientist certainly are in the right of it, as against him. His science is then but pompous trifling; and the endowment of a professorship for such a being would be something really absurd.

Accordingly, in every genuine metaphysical debate some practical issue, however remote, is really involved. To realize this, revert with me to the question of materialism or theism; and place yourselves this time in the real world we live in, the world that has a future, that is yet uncompleted whilst we speak. In this unfinished world the alternative of "materialism or theism?" is intensely practical; and it is worth while for us to spend some minutes of our hour in seeing how truly this is the case.

How, indeed, does the programme differ for us, according as we consider that the facts of experience up to date are purposeless configurations of atoms moving according to eternal elementary laws, or that on the other hand they are due to the providence of God? As far as the past facts go, indeed there is no difference. These facts are in, are bagged, are captured; and the good that's in them is gained, be the atoms or be the God their cause. There are accordingly many materialists about us to-day who, ignoring altogether the future and practical aspects of the question, seek to eliminate the odium attaching to the word materialism, and even to eliminate the word itself, by showing that, if matter could give birth to all these gains, why then matter, functionally considered, is just as divine an entity as God, in fact coalesces with God, is what you mean by God. Cease, these persons advise us, to use either of these terms, with their outgrown opposition. Use terms free of the clerical connotations on the one hand; of the suggestion of grossness, coarseness, ignobility, on the other. Talk of the primal mystery, of the unknowable energy, of the one and only power, instead of saying either God or matter. This is the course to which Mr. Spencer urges us at the end of the first volume of his *Psychology*. In some well-written pages he there shows us that a "matter" so infinitely subtile, and performing motions as inconceivably quick and fine as modern science postulates in her explanations, has no trace of grossness left. He shows that the conception of spirit, as we mortals hitherto have framed it, is itself too gross to cover the exquisite complexity of Nature's facts. Both terms, he says are but symbols, pointing to that one unknowable reality in which their oppositions cease.

Throughout these remarks of Mr. Spencer, eloquent, and even noble in a certain sense, as they are, he seems to think that the dislike of ordinary man to materialism comes from a purely æsthetic disdain of matter, as something gross in itself, and vile and despicable. Undoubtedly such an æsthetic disdain of matter has played a part in philosophic history. But it forms no part whatever of an intelligent modern man's dislikes. Give him a matter bound forever by its laws to lead our world nearer and nearer to perfection, and any rational man will worship that matter as readily as Mr. Spencer worships his own so-called unknowable power. It not only has made for righteousness up to date, but it will make for righteousness forever; and that is all we need. Doing practically all that a God can do, it is equivalent to God, its function is a God's function, and in a world in which a God would be superfluous; from such a world a God could never lawfully be missed.

But *is* the matter by which Mr. Spencer's process of cosmic evolution is carried on any such principle of never-ending perfection as this? Indeed it is not, for the future end of every cosmically evolved thing or system of things is tragedy; and Mr. Spencer, in confining himself to the æsthetic and ignoring the practical side of the controversy, has really contributed nothing serious to its relief. But apply now our principle of practical results, and see what a vital significance the question of materialism or theism immediately acquires.

Theism and materialism, so indifferent when taken retrospectively, point when we take them prospectively to wholly different practical consequences, to opposite outlooks of experience. For, according to the theory of mechanical evolution, the laws of redistribution of matter and motion, though they are certainly to thank for all the good hours which our organisms have ever yielded us and for all the ideals which our minds now frame, are yet fatally certain to undo their work again, and to redissolve everything that they have once evolved. You all know the picture of the last foreseeable state of the dead universe, as evolutionary science gives it forth. I cannot state it better than in Mr. Balfour's words: "The energies of our system will decay, the glory of the sun, will be dimmed, and the earth, tideless and inert, will no longer tolerate the race which has for a moment disturbed its solitude. Man will go down into the pit, and all his thoughts will perish. The uneasy consciousness which in this obscure corner has for a brief space broken the contented silence of the universe, will be at rest. Matter will know itself no longer. 'Imperishable monuments' and 'immortal deeds,' death itself, and love stronger than death, will be as if they had not been. Nor will anything that is, be better or worse for all that the labor, genius, devotion, and suffering of man have striven through countless ages to effect."[1]

That is the sting of it, that in the vast driftings of the cosmic weather, though many a jewelled shore appears, and many an enchanted cloud-bank floats away, long lingering ere it be dissolved—even as our world now lingers, for our joy—yet when these transient products are gone, nothing, absolutely *nothing* remains, to represent those particular qualities, those elements of preciousness which they may have enshrined. Dead and gone are they, gone utterly from the very sphere and room of being. Without an echo; without a memory; without an influence on aught that may come after, to make it care for similar ideals. This utter final wreck and tragedy is of the essence of scientific materialism as at present understood. The lower and not the higher forces are the eternal forces, or the last surviving forces within the only cycle of evolution which we can definitely see. Mr. Spencer believes this as much as any one; so why should he argue with us as if we were making silly æsthetic objections to the "grossness" of "matter and motion,"—the principles of his philosophy,—when what really dismays us in it is the disconsolateness of its ulterior practical results?

No, the true objection to materialism is not positive but negative. It would be farcical at this day to make complaint of it for what it *is*, for "grossness." Grossness is what grossness *does*—we now know *that*. We make complaint of it, on the contrary, for what it is *not*—not a permanent warrant for our more ideal interests, not a fulfiller of our remotest hopes.

The notion of God, on the other hand, however inferior it may be in clearness to those mathematical notions so current in mechanical philosophy, has at least this practical superiority over them, that it guarantees an ideal order that shall be permanently preserved. A world with a God in it to say the last word, may indeed burn up or freeze, but we then think of Him as still mindful of the old ideals and sure to bring them elsewhere to fruition; so that, where He is, tragedy is only provisional and partial, and shipwreck and dissolution not the absolutely final things. This need of an eternal moral order is one of the deepest needs of our breast. And those poets, like Dante and Wordsworth, who live on the conviction of such an order, owe to that fact the extraordinary tonic and consoling power of their verse. Here then, in these different emotional and practical appeals, in these adjustments of our concrete attitudes of hope and expectation, and all the delicate consequences which their differences entail, lie the real meanings of materialism and theism—not in hairsplitting abstractions about matter's inner essence, or about the metaphysical attributes of God. Materialism means simply the denial that the moral order is eternal, and the cutting off of ultimate hopes; theism means the affirmation of an eternal moral order and the letting loose of hope. Surely here is an issue genuine enough, for any one who feels it; and, as long as men are men, it will yield matter for serious philosophic debate. Concerning this question, at any rate, the positivists and pooh-pooh-ers of metaphysics are in the wrong.

But possibly some of you may still rally to their defence. Even whilst admitting that theism and materialism make different prophecies of the world's future, you may yourselves pooh-pooh the difference as something so infinitely remote as to mean nothing for a sane mind. The essence of a sane mind, you may say, is to take shorter views, and to feel no concern about such chimæras as the latter end of the world. Well, I can only say that if you say this, you do injustice to human nature. Religious melancholy is not disposed of by a simple flourish of the word "insanity." The absolute things, the last things, the overlapping things, are the truly philosophic concern; all superior minds feel seriously about them, and the mind with the shortest views is simply the mind of the more shallow man.

However, I am willing to pass over these very distant outlooks on the ultimate, if any of you so insist. The theistic controversy can still serve to illustrate the principle of pragmatism for us well enough, without driving us so far afield. If there be a God, it is not likely that he is confined solely to making differences in the world's latter end; he probably makes differences all along its course. Now the principle of practicalism says that the very meaning of the conception of God lies in those differences which must be made in our experience if the conception be true. God's famous inventory of perfections, as elaborated by dogmatic theology, either means nothing, says our principle, or it implies certain definite things that we can feel and do at particular moments of our lives, things which we could not feel and should not do were no God present and were the business of the universe carried on by material atoms instead. So far as our conceptions of the Deity involve no such experiences, so far they are meaningless and verbal,—scholastic entities and abstractions, as the positivists say, and fit objects for their scorn. But so far as they do involve such definite experiences, God means something for us, and may be real.

Now if we look at the definitions of God made by dogmatic theology, we see immediately that some stand and some fall when treated by this test. God, for example, as any orthodox text-book will tell us, is a being existing not only *per se*, or by himself, as created beings exist, but *a se*, or from himself; and out of this "aseity" flow most of his perfections. He is for example, necessary; absolute; infinite in all respects; and single. He is simple, not compounded of essence and existence, substance and accident, actuality and potentiality, or subject and attributes, as are other things. He belongs to no genus; he is inwardly and outwardly unalterable; he knows and wills all things, and first of all his own infinite self, in one indivisible eternal act. And he is absolutely self-sufficing, and infinitely happy. Now in which one of us practical Americans here assembled does this conglomeration of attributes awaken any sense of reality? And if in no one, then why not? Surely because such attributes awaken no responsive active feelings and call for no particular conduct of our own. How does God's "aseity" come home to *you?* What specific thing can I do to adapt myself to his "simplicity"? Or how determine our behavior henceforward if his "felicity" is anyhow absolutely complete? In the '50's and '60's Captain Mayne Reid was the great writer of boys' books of out-of-door adventure. He was forever ex-tolling the hunters and field-observers of living animals' habits, and keeping up a fire of invective against the "closet-naturalists," as he called them, the collectors and classifiers, and handlers of skeletons and skins. When I was a boy I used to think that a closet-naturalist must be the vilest type of wretch under the sun. But surely the systematic theologians are the closet-naturalists of the Deity, even in Captain Mayne Reid's sense. Their orthodox deduction of God's attributes is nothing but a shuffling and matching of pedantic dictionary-adjectives, aloof from morals, aloof from human needs, something that might be worked out from the mere word "God" by a logical machine of wood and brass as well as by a man of flesh and blood. The attributes which I have quoted have absolutely nothing to do with religion, for religion is a living practical affair. Other parts, indeed, of God's traditional description do have practical connection with life, and have owed all their historic importance to that fact. His omniscience, for example, and his justice. With the one he sees us in the dark, with the other he rewards and punishes what he sees. So do his ubiquity and eternity and unalterability appeal to our confidence, and his goodness banish our fears. Even attributes of less meaning to this present audience have in past times so appealed. One of the chief attributes of God, according to the orthodox theology, is his infinite love of himself, proved by asking the question, "By what but an infinite object can an infinite affection be appeased?" An immediate consequence of this primary self-love of God is the orthodox dogma that the manifestation of his own glory is God's primal purpose in creation; and that dogma has certainly made very efficient practical connection with life. It is true that we ourselves are tending to outgrow this old monarchical conception of a Deity with his "court" and pomp—"his state is kingly, thousands to his bidding speed," etc.—but there is no denying the enormous influence it has had over ecclesiastical history, nor, by repercussion, over the history of European states. And yet even these more real and significant attributes have the trail of the serpent over them as the books on theology have actually worked them out. One feels that, in the theologians' hands, they are only a set of dictionary-adjectives, mechanically deduced; logic has stepped into the place of vision, professionalism into that of life. Instead of bread we get a stone; instead of a fish, a serpent. Did such a conglomeration of abstract general terms give really the gist of our knowledge of the Deity, divinity-schools might indeed continue to flourish, but religion, vital religion, would have taken its flight from this world. What keeps religion going is something else than abstract definitions and systems of logically concatenated adjectives, and something different from faculties of theology and their professors. All these things are after-effects, secondary accretions upon a mass of concrete religious experiences, connecting themselves with feeling and conduct that renew themselves in *saecula saeculorum* in the lives of humble private men. If you ask what these experiences are, they are conversations with the unseen, voices and visions, responses to prayer, changes of heart, deliverances from fear, inflowings of help, assurances of support, whenever certain persons set their own internal attitude in certain appropriate ways. The power comes and goes and is lost, and can be found only in a certain definite direction, just as if it were a concrete material thing. These direct experiences of a wider spiritual life with which our superficial consciousness is continuous, and with which it keeps up an intense commerce, form the primary mass of direct religious experience on which all hearsay religion rests, and which furnishes that notion of an ever-present God, out of which systematic theology thereupon proceeds to make capital in its own unreal pedantic way. What the word "God" means is just those passive and active experiences of your life. Now, my friends, it is quite immaterial to my purpose whether you yourselves enjoy and venerate these experiences, or whether you stand aloof, and, viewing them in others, suspect them of being illusory and vain. Like all other human experiences, they too certainly share in the general liability to illusion and mistake. They need not be infallible. But they are certainly the originals of the God-idea, and theology is the translation; and you remember that I am now using the God-idea merely as an example, not to discuss as to its truth or error, but only to show how well the principle of pragmatism works. That the God of systematic theology should exist or not exist is a matter of small practical moment. At most it means that you may continue uttering certain abstract words and that you must stop using others. But if the God of these particular experiences be false, it is an awful thing for you, if you are one of those whose lives are stayed on such experiences. The theistic controversy, trivial enough if we take it merely academically and theologically, is of tremendous significance if we test it by its results for actual life.

I can best continue to recommend the principle of practicalism to you by keeping in the neighborhood of this theological idea. I reminded you a few minutes ago that the old monarchical notion of the Deity as a sort of Louis the Fourteenth of the Heavens is losing nowadays much of its ancient prestige. Religious philosophy, like all philosophy, is growing more and more idealistic. And in the philosophy of the Absolute, so called, that post-Kantian form of idealism which is carrying so many of our higher minds before it, we have the triumph of what in old times was summarily disposed of as the pantheistic heresy,—I mean the conception of God, not as the extraneous creator, but as the indwelling spirit and substance of the world. I know not where one can find a more candid, more clear, or, on the whole, more persuasive statement of this theology of Absolute Idealism than in the addresses made before this very Union three years ago by your own great Californian philosopher (whose colleague at Harvard I am proud to be), Josiah Royce. His contributions to the resulting volume, *The Conception of God*, form a very masterpiece of popularization. Now you will remember, many of you, that in the discussion that followed Professor Royce's first address, the debate turned largely on the ideas of unity and plurality, and on the question whether, if God be One in All and All in All, "One with the unity of a single instant," as Royce calls it, "forming in His wholeness one luminously transparent moment," any room is left for real morality or freedom. Professor Howison, in particular, was earnest in urging that morality and freedom are relations between a manifold of selves, and that under the régime of Royce's monistic Absolute Thought "no true manifold of selves is or can be provided for." I will not go into any of the details of that particular discussion, but just ask you to consider for a moment whether, in general, any discussion about monism or pluralism, any argument over the unity of the universe, would not necessarily be brought into a shape where it tends to straighten itself out, by bringing our principle of practical results to bear.

The question whether the world is at bottom One or Many is a typical metaphysical question. Long has it raged! In its crudest form it is an exquisite example of the *loggerheads* of metaphysics. "I say it is one great fact," Parmenides and Spinoza exclaim. "I say it is many little facts," reply the atomists and associationists. "I say it is both one and many, many in one," say the Hegelians; and in the ordinary popular discussions we rarely get beyond this barren reiteration by the disputants of their pet adjectives of number. But is it not first of all clear that when we take such an adjective as "One" absolutely and abstractly, its meaning is so vague and empty that it makes no difference whether we affirm or deny it? Certainly this universe is not the mere number One; and yet you can number it "one," if you like, in talking about it as contrasted with other possible worlds numbered "two" and "three" for the occasion. What exact thing do you *practically* mean by "One," when you call the universe One, is the first question you must ask. In what ways does the oneness come home to your own personal life? By what difference does it express itself in your experience? How can you act differently towards a universe which is one? Inquired into in this way, the unity might grow clear and be affirmed in some ways and denied in others, and so cleared up, even though a certain vague and worshipful portentousness might disappear from the notion of it in the process.

For instance, one practical result that follows when we have one thing to handle, is that we can pass from one part of it to another without letting go of the thing. In this sense oneness must be partly denied and partly affirmed of our universe. Physically we can pass continuously in various manners from one part of it to another part. But logically and psychically the passage seems less easy, for there is no obvious transition from one mind to another, or from minds to physical things. You have to step off and get on again; so that in these ways the world is not one, as measured by that practical test.

Another practical meaning of oneness is susceptibility of collection. A collection is one, though the things that compose it be many. Now, can we practically "collect" the universe? Physically, of course we cannot. And mentally we cannot, if we take it concretely in its details. But if we take it summarily and abstractly, then we collect it mentally whenever we refer to it, even as I do now when I fling the term "universe" at it, and so seem to leave a mental ring around it. It is plain however, that such abstract noetic unity (as one might call it) is practically an extremely insignificant thing.

Again, oneness may mean generic sameness, so that you can treat all parts of the collection by one rule and get the same results. It is evident that in this sense the oneness of our world is incomplete, for in spite of much generic sameness in its elements and items, they still remain of many irreducible kinds. You can't pass by mere logic all over the field of it.

Its elements have, however, an affinity or commensurability with each other, are not wholly irrelevant, but can be compared, and fit together after certain fashions. This again might practically mean that they were one *in origin*, and that, tracing them backwards, we should find them arising in a single primal causal fact. Such unity of origin would have definite practical consequences, would have them for our scientific life at least.

I can give only these hasty superficial indications of what I mean when I say that it tends to clear up the quarrel between monism and pluralism to subject the notion of unity to such practical tests. On the other hand, it does but perpetuate strife and misunderstanding to continue talking of it in an absolute and mystical way. I have little doubt myself that this old quarrel might be completely smoothed out to the satisfaction of all claimants, if only the maxim of Peirce were methodically followed here. The current monism on the whole still keeps talking in too abstract a way. It says the world must be either pure disconnectedness, no universe at all, or absolute unity. It insists that there is no stopping-place half way. Any connection whatever, says this monism, is only possible if there be still more connection, until at last we are driven to admit the absolutely total connection required. But this absolutely total connection either means nothing, is the mere word "one" spelt long; or else it means the sum of all the partial connections that can possibly be conceived. I believe that when we thus attack the question, and set ourselves to search for these possible connections, and conceive each in a definite practical way, the dispute is already in a fair way to be settled beyond the chance of misunderstanding, by a compromise in which the Many and the One both get their lawful rights.

But I am in danger of becoming technical; so I must stop right here, and let you go.

I am happy to say that it is the English-speaking philosophers who first introduced the custom of interpreting the meaning of conceptions by asking what difference they make for life. Mr. Peirce has only expressed in the form of an explicit maxim what their sense for reality led them all instinctively to do. The great English way of investigating a conception is to ask yourself right off, "What is it *known as?* In what facts does it result? What is its *cash-value*, in terms of particular experience? and what special difference would come into the world according as it were true or false?" Thus does Locke treat the conception of personal identity. What you mean by it is just your chain of memories, says he. That is the only concretely verifiable part of its significance. All further ideas about it, such as the oneness or manyness of the spiritual substance on which it is based, are therefore void of intelligible meaning; and propositions touching such ideas may be indifferently affirmed or denied. So Berkeley with his "matter." The cash-value of matter is our physical sensations. That is what it is known as, all that we concretely verify of its conception. That therefore is the whole meaning of the word "matter"—any other pretended meaning is mere wind of words. Hume does the same thing with causation. It is known as habitual antecedence, and tendency on our part to look for something definite to come. Apart from this practical meaning it has no significance whatever, and books about it may be committed to the flames, says Hume. Stewart and Brown, James Mill, John Mill, and Bain, have followed more or less consistently the same method; and Shadworth Hodgson has used it almost as explicitly as Mr. Peirce. These writers have many of them no doubt been too sweeping in their negations; Hume, in particular, and James Mill, and Bain. But when all is said and done, it was they, not Kant, who introduced "the critical method" into philosophy, the one method fitted to make philosophy a study worthy of serious men. For what seriousness can possibly remain in debating philosophic propositions that will never make an appreciable difference to us in action? And what matters it, when all propositions are practically meaningless, which of them be called true or false?

The shortcomings and the negations and baldnesses of the English philosophers in question come, not from their eye to merely practical results, but solely from their failure to track the practical results completely enough to see how far they extend. Hume can be corrected and built out, and his beliefs enriched, by using Humian principles exclusively, and without making any use of the circuitous and ponderous artificialities of Kant. It is indeed a somewhat pathetic matter, as it seems to me, that this is not the course which the actual history of philosophy has followed. Hume had no English successors of adequate ability to complete him and correct his negations; so it happened, as a matter of fact, that building out of critical philosophy has mainly been left to thinkers who were under the influence of Kant. Even in England and this country it is with Kantian catch-words and categories that the fuller view of life is pursued, and in our universities it is the courses in transcendentalism that kindle the enthusiasm of the more ardent students, whilst the courses in English philosophy are committed to a secondary place. I cannot think that this is exactly as it should be. And I say this not out of national jingoism, for jingoism has no place in philosophy; or out of excitement over the great Anglo-American alliance against the world, of which we nowadays hear so much—though heaven knows that to that alliance I wish a Godspeed. I say it because I sincerely believe that the English spirit in philosophy is intellectually, as well as practically and morally, on the saner, sounder, and truer path. Kant's mind is the rarest and most intricate of all possible antique bric-a-brac museums, and connoisseurs and dilettanti will always wish to visit it and see the wondrous and racy contents. The temper of the dear old man about his work is perfectly delectable. And yet he is really—although I shrink with some terror from saying such a thing before some of you here present—at bottom a mere curio, a "specimen." I mean by this a perfectly definite thing: I believe that Kant bequeaths to us not one single conception which is both indispensable to philosophy and which philosophy either did not possess before him, or was not destined inevitably to acquire after him through the growth of men's reflection upon the hypotheses by which science interprets nature. The true line of philosophic progress lies, in short, it seems to me, not so much *through* Kant as *round* him to the point where now we stand. Philosophy can perfectly well outflank him, and build herself up into adequate fulness by prolonging more directly the older English lines.

Notes

Address before the Philosophical Union of the University of California, August 26, 1898. We here follow its first printing in *The University Chronicle* I (1898) 289–309 (omitting the first four and the last paragraphs). Reprinted in *Collected Essays and Review* 406–37.

1. *The Foundations of Belief*, p. 30.

The sixth lecture from the series that would be published in 1907 as Pragmatism: A New Name for Some Old Ways of Thinking. *In it, James defends the idea that truth is what "works."*

WILLIAM JAMES

Pragmatism's Conception of Truth

When Clerk-Maxwell was a child it is written that he had a mania for having everything explained to him, and that when people put him off with vague verbal accounts of any phenomenon he would interrupt them impatiently by saying, "Yes; but I want you to tell me the *particular go* of it!" Had his question been about truth, only a pragmatist could have told him the particular go of it. I believe that our contemporary pragmatists, especially Messrs. Schiller and Dewey, have given the only tenable account of this subject. It is a very ticklish subject, sending subtle rootlets into all kinds of crannies, and hard to treat in the sketchy way that alone befits a public lecture. But the Schiller-Dewey view of truth has been so ferociously attacked by rationalistic philosophers, and so abominably misunderstood, that here, if anywhere, is the point where a clear and simple statement should be made.

I fully expect to see the pragmatist view of truth run through the classic stages of a theory's career. First, you know, a new theory is attacked as absurd; then it is admitted to be true, but obvious and insignificant; finally it is seen to be so important that its adversaries claim that they themselves discovered it. Our doctrine of truth is at present in the first of these three stages, with symptoms of the second stage having begun in certain quarters. I wish that this lecture might help it beyond the first stage in the eyes of many of you.

Truth, as any dictionary will tell you, is a property of certain of our ideas. It means their 'agreement' as falsity means their disagreement, with 'reality.' Pragmatists and intellectualists both accept this definition as a matter of course. They begin to quarrel only after the question is raised as to what may precisely be meant by the term 'agreement' and what by the term 'reality' when reality is taken as something for our ideas to agree with.

In answering these questions the pragmatists are more analytic and painstaking, the intellectualists more offhand and irreflective. The popular notion is that a true idea must copy its reality. Like other popular views, this one follows the analogy of the most usual experience. Our true ideas of sensible things do indeed copy them. Shut your eyes and think of yonder clock on the wall, and you get just such a true picture or copy of its dial. But your idea of its 'works' (unless you are a clock-maker) is much less of a copy, yet it passes muster, for it in no way clashes with the reality. Even though it should shrink to the mere word 'works' that word still serves you truly; and when you speak of the 'time-keeping function' of the clock, or of its spring's 'elasticity,' it is hard to see exactly what your ideas can copy.

You perceive that there is a problem here. Where our ideas can not copy definitely their object, what does agreement with that object mean? A Berkeleian idealist might say that they are true whenever they are what God means that we ought to think about that object. But transcendental idealism holds the copy-view all through. Its doctrine is that our ideas possess truth just in proportion as they approach to being copies of the absolute's eternal way of thinking.

These views, you see, invite pragmatistic discussion. But the great assumption of the intellectualists is that truth means essentially an inert static relation. When you've got your true idea of anything, there's an end of the matter. You're in possession; you *know;* you've fulfilled your thinking destiny. You are where you ought to be mentally; you have obeyed your categorical imperative; and nothing more need follow on that climax of your rational destiny. Epistemologically you are in equilibrium.

Pragmatism, on the other hand, asks its usual question. "Grant an idea or belief to be true," it says, "what concrete difference will its being true make in any one's actual life? How will the truth be realized? What experiences will be different from those which would obtain if the belief were false? What, in short, is the truth's cash value in experiential terms?"

The moment pragmatism asks this question, it sees the answer: *True ideas are those that we can validate, corroborate and verify. False ideas are those that we can not.* That is the practical difference it makes to us to have true ideas; that, therefore, is the meaning of truth, for it is all that truth is known as.

This thesis is what I have to defend. The truth of an idea is not a stagnant property inherent in it. Truth *happens* to an idea. It *becomes* true, is *made* true by events. Its verity *is* in fact an event, a process, the process, namely, of its verifying itself, its veri-*fication.* Its validity is the process of its valid-*ation.*

This trivial-sounding thesis has results which it will take the rest of my hour to explain.

Let me begin by reminding you of the fact that the possession of true thoughts means everywhere the possession of invaluable instruments of action; and that our duty to gain truth, so far from being a blank command from out of the blue, or a 'stunt' self-imposed by our intellect, can account for itself by excellent practical reasons.

The importance to human life of having true beliefs about matters of fact is a thing too notorious. We live in a world of realities that can be infinitely useful or infinitely harmful. Ideas that tell us which of them to expect count as the true ideas in all this primary sphere of verification, and the pursuit of such ideas is a primary human duty. The possession of truth, so far from being here an end in itself, is only a preliminary means towards other vital satisfactions. If I am lost in the woods and starved, and find what looks like a cow-path, it is of the utmost importance that I should think of a human habitation at the end of it, for if I do so and follow it, I save myself. The true thought is useful here because the house which is its object is useful. The practical value of true ideas is thus primarily derived from the practical importance of their objects to us. Their objects are, indeed, not important at all times. I may on another occasion have no use for the house; and then my idea of it, however verifiable, will be practically irrelevant, and had better remain latent. Yet since almost any object may some day become temporarily important, the advantage of having a general stock of *extra* truths, of ideas that shall be true of merely possible situations, is obvious. We store such extra truths away in our memories, and with the overflow we fill our books of reference. Whenever such an extra truth becomes practically relevant to one of our emergencies, it passes from cold-storage to do work in the world, and our belief in it grows active. You can say of it then either that 'it is useful because it is true' or that 'it is true because it is useful.' Both these phrases mean exactly the same thing, namely, that here is an idea that gets fulfilled and can be verified. Truth is the name for what starts the verification-process, use is the name for what completes it. True ideas would never have been singled out as such, would never have acquired a class-name, least of all a name suggesting value, unless they had been useful from the outset.

From this simple cue pragmatism gets her general notion of truth as something essentially bound up with the way in which one moment in our experience may lead us towards other moments which it will be worth while to have been led to. Primarily, and on the common-sense level, the truth of a state of mind means this function of *a leading that is worth while*. When a moment in our experience of any kind whatever inspires us with a thought that is true, that means that sooner or later we dip by that thought's guidance into the particulars of experience again and make advantageous connection with them. This is a vague enough statement, but I beg you to retain it, for it is essential.

Our experience meanwhile is all shot through with regularities. One bit of it can warn us to get ready for another bit, can 'intend' or be 'significant of' that remoter object. The object's advent is the significance's verification. Truth, in these cases, meaning nothing but eventual verification, is manifestly incompatible with waywardness on our part. Woe to him whose beliefs play fast and loose with the order which realities follow in his experience: They will lead him nowhere or else make false connections.

By 'realities' or 'objects' here, we mean either 'things' of common sense, sensibly present, or else common-sense relations, such as dates, places, distances, kinds, activities. Following our mental image of a house along the cow-path, we actually come to see the house; we get the image's full verification. Such simply verified leadings are certainly the originals and prototypes of the truth-process. Experience offers indeed other forms of truth-process, but they are all conceivable as primary verifications arrested, multiplied or substituted one for another.

Take, for instance, yonder object on the wall. You and I consider it to be a 'clock,' although no one of us has seen the hidden works that make it one. We let our notion pass for true without attempting to verify. If truth mean verification-process essentially, ought we then to call such unverified truths as this abortive? No, for they form the overwhelmingly large number of the truths we live by. Indirect as well as direct verifications pass muster. Where circumstantial evidence is sufficient, we can go without eye-witnessing. Just as we here assume Japan to exist without ever having been there, because it *works* to do so, everything we know conspiring with the belief, and nothing interfering, so we assume that thing to be a clock. We *use* it as a clock, regulating the length of our lecture by it. The verification of the assumption here means its leading to no frustration or contradiction. Verifi*ability* of wheels and weights and pendulum is as good as verification. For one truth-process completed there are a million in our lives that function in this state of nascency. They turn us *towards* direct verification; lead us into the surroundings of the objects they envisage; and then, if everything runs on harmoniously, we are so sure that verification is possible that we omit it, and are usually justified by all that happens.

Truth lives, in fact, for the most part on a credit system. Our thoughts and beliefs 'pass' so long as nothing challenges them, just as bank notes pass so long as nobody refuses them. But this all points to direct face-to-face verifications somewhere, without which the fabric of truth collapses like a financial system with no cash basis whatever. You accept my verification of one thing, I yours of another. We trade on each other's truth. Beliefs verified concretely by *somebody* are the posts of the whole superstructure.

Another great reason for waiving complete verification in the usual business of life is that all things exist in kinds and not singly. Our world is found once for all to have that peculiarity. So that when we have once directly verified our ideas about one specimen of a kind, we consider ourselves free to apply them to other specimens without verification. A mind that habitually discerns the kind of thing before it, and acts by the law of the kind immediately, without pausing to verify, will be a 'true' mind in ninety-nine out of a hundred emergencies, proved so by its conduct fitting everything it meets, and getting no refutation.

Indirectly or only potentially verifying processes may thus be true as well as full verification-processes. They work as true processes would work, give us the same advantages, and claim our recognition for the same reasons. All this on the commonsense level of matters of fact, which we are alone considering.

But matters of fact are not our only stock in trade. *Relations among ideas* form another sphere where true and false beliefs obtain, and here the beliefs are absolute, or unconditional. When they are true they bear the name either of definitions or of principles. It is either a principle or a definition that 1 and 1 make 2, that 2 and 1 make 3, and so on; that white differs less from gray than it does from black; that when the cause begins to act the effect also commences. Such propositions hold of all possible 'ones' of all conceivable 'whites' and 'grays' and 'causes.' The objects here are mental objects. Their relations are obvious at a glance, and no sense-verification is necessary. Moreover, once true, always true, of those same mental objects. Truth here has an 'eternal' character. If you can find a concrete thing anywhere that is 'one' or 'white' or 'gray,' or an 'effect,' then your principles will everlastingly apply to it. The only risk is in the finding. It is but one more case of ascertaining the kind, and applying the law of its kind to the particular object. You are sure to get truth if you can but name the kind rightly, for your principles hold good of everything of that kind without exception. If they failed to obtain concretely, you would say that you had classed your objects wrongly.

In this realm of mental relations, truth again is an affair of leading. We pass from one abstract idea to another, framing in the end great systems of logical and mathematical truth, under the respective terms of which the sensible facts of experience eventually arrange themselves, so that our eternal truths hold good of realities also. This marriage of fact and theory is endlessly useful. What we say is here already true in advance of special verification, if we have subsumed our objects rightly. Our ready-made ideal framework for all sorts of possible objects follows from the very structure of our thinking. We can no more play fast and loose with these abstract relations than we can do so with our sense-experiences. They coerce us; we must treat them consistently, whether or not we like the results. The rules of addition apply to our debts as rigorously as to our assets. The hundredth decimal of π is predetermined ideally now, though no one may have computed it. If we should ever need the figure in our dealings with an actual circle we should need to have it given rightly, calculated by the usual rules; for it is the same kind of truth that those rules elsewhere calculate.

Between the coercions of the sensible order and those of the ideal order, our mind is thus wedged tightly. Our ideas must agree with realities, be such realities concrete or abstract, be they facts or be they principles, under penalty of endless inconsistency and frustration.

So far, intellectualists can raise no protest. They can only say that we have barely touched the skin of the matter.

Realities mean, then, either concrete facts, or abstract kinds of things, and relations perceived intuitively between them. But what now does 'agreement' with such realities mean?—to quote again the definition of truth that is current.

Here it is that pragmatism and intellectualism begin to part company. Primarily, no doubt, to agree means to copy, but we saw that the mere word 'clock' would do instead of a mental picture of its works, and that of many realities our ideas can only be symbols and not copies. 'Past time,' 'power,' 'spontaneity,'—how can our mind copy such realities?

To 'agree' in the widest sense with a reality, *can only mean to be guided either straight up to it or into its surroundings, or to be put into such working touch with it as to handle either it or something connected with it better than if we disagreed.* Better either intellectually or practically! And often agreement will only mean the negative fact that nothing contradictory from the quarter of that reality comes to interfere with the way in which our ideas guide us elsewhere. To copy a reality is, indeed, one way of agreeing with it, but it is far from being essential. The essential thing is the process of being guided. Any idea that helps us to deal with either the reality or its belongings, that doesn't entangle our progress in frustrations, that *fits*, in fact, and adapts our life to the reality's whole setting, will agree sufficiently to meet the requirement. It will hold true of that reality.

Thus, *names* are just as 'true' or 'false' as definite mental pictures are. They set up similar verification-processes, and lead to fully equivalent practical results.

All human thinking gets discursified; we exchange ideas; we lend and borrow verifications, get them from one another by means of social intercourse. All truth thus gets verbally built out, stored up, and made available for every one. Hence, we must *talk* consistently just as we must *think* consistently; for both in talk and thought we deal with kinds. Names are arbitrary, but once understood, they must be kept to. We mustn't now call Abel 'Cain' or Cain 'Abel.' If we do, we ungear ourselves from the book of Genesis, and from all its connections with the universe of speech and fact down to the present time. We throw ourselves out of whatever truth that whole system may embody.

The overwhelming majority of our true ideas admit of no direct or face-to-face verification—those of past history, for example, as of Cain and Abel. The stream of time can be remounted only verbally, or verified indirectly by the present prolongations or effects of what the past harbored. Yet if they agree with these verbalities and effects, we can know that our ideas of the past are true. *As true as past time itself was,* so true was Julius Caesar, so true were antediluvian monsters, all in their proper dates and settings. That past time itself was, is guaranteed by its coherence with everything that's present. True as the present *is*, the past *was* also.

Agreement thus turns out to be essentially an affair of leading—leading that is useful because it is into quarters that contain objects that are important. True ideas lead us into useful verbal and conceptual quarters as well as directly up to useful sensible termini. They lead to consistency, stability and flowing human intercourse. They lead away from eccentricity and isolation, from foiled and barren thinking. The untrammeled flowing of the leading-process, its general freedom from clash and contradiction, passes for its indirect verification: but all roads lead to Rome, and in the end, and eventually, all true processes must lead to the face of directly verifying sensible experiences *somewhere.*

Such is the large loose way in which the pragmatist interprets the word agreement. He treats it altogether practically. He lets it cover any process of conduction from a present idea to a future terminus, provided only it run prosperously. It is only thus that 'scientific' ideas, flying as they do beyond common sense, can be said to agree with their realities. It is as *if* reality were made of ether, atoms or electrons, but we mustn't think so literally. The term 'energy' doesn't even pretend to stand for anything 'objective.' It is only a way of measuring the surface of phenomena so as to *string* their changes on a simple formula.

Yet in the choice of these man-made formulas we can not be capricious any more than we can be capricious on the common-sense practical level. We must find a theory that will *work*; and that means something extremely difficult; for our theory must mediate between all previous truths and certain new experiences. It must derange common sense and previous belief as little as possible, and it must lead to some sensible terminus or other that can be verified exactly. To 'work' means both these things; and the squeeze is so tight that there is little loose play for any theory. They are wedged and controlled as nothing else is. Yet sometimes alternative theoretic formulas are equally compatible with all the truths we know, and then we choose between them for subjective reasons. We choose the kind of theory to which we are already partial; we follow 'elegance' or 'economy.' Clerk-Maxwell somewhere says it would be 'poor scientific taste' to choose the more complex of two equally well-evidenced conceptions; and you will all agree with him. Truth here is what gives us the maximum possible sum of satisfactions, taste included, but consistency both with previous truth and with novel fact is always the most imperious claimant.

I have led you through a very sandy desert. But now, if I may be allowed so vulgar an expression, we begin to taste the milk in the cocoanut. Our rationalist critics here discharge their batteries upon us, and to reply to them will take us out from all this dryness into full sight of a momentous philosophical alternative.

Our account of truth is an account of truths in the plural, of processes of leading, realized *in rebus*, and having only this quality in common, that they *pay*. They pay by guiding us into or towards some part of a system that dips at numerous points into sense-percepts, which we may copy mentally or not, but with which at any rate we are now in the kind of commerce vaguely designated as verification. Truth for us is simply a collective name for verification-processes, just as health, wealth, strength, etc., are names for other processes connected with life, and also pursued because it pays to pursue them. Truth is *made*, just as health, wealth and strength are made, in the course of experience.

Here rationalism is instantaneously up in arms against us. I can imagine a rationalist to talk as follows:

"Truth is not made," he will say; "it absolutely obtains, being a unique relation that does not wait upon any process, but shoots straight over the head of experience, and hits its reality every time. Our belief that yon thing on the wall is a clock is true already, although no one in the whole history of the world should verify it. The abstract quality of standing in that transcendent relation is what makes any thought true that possesses it, whether or not there be verification. You pragmatists put the cart before the horse in making truth's being reside in verification-processes. These are merely signs of its being, merely our lame ways of ascertaining, after the fact, which of our ideas already has possessed the wondrous quality. The quality itself is timeless, like all essences and natures. Thoughts partake of it directly, as they partake of falsity or of irrelevancy. It can't be analyzed away into pragmatic consequences."

The whole plausibility of this rationalist tirade is due to the fact to which we have already paid so much attention. In our world, namely, abounding as it does in things of similar kinds and similarly associated, one verification serves for others of its kind, and one great use of knowing things is to be led not so much to them as to their associates, especially to human talk about them. The quality of truth, obtaining *ante rem*, pragmatically means, then, the fact that in such a world innumerable ideas work better by their indirect or possible than by their direct and actual verification. Truth *ante rem* means only verifiability, then; or else it is a case of the stock rationalist delusion of treating the *name* of a concrete phenomenal reality as an independent metaphysical entity, and placing it behind the reality as its explanation. Professor Mach quotes somewhere an epigram of Lessing's:

> Sagt Hänschen Schlau zu Vetter Fritz,
> "Wie kommt es, Vetter Fritzen,
> Dass grad' die reichsten in der Welt,
> Das meiste Geld besitzem?"

Hänschen Schlau here treats the principle 'wealth' as something distinct from the facts denoted by the man's being rich. It antedates them; the facts become only a sort of secondary coincidence with the rich man's essential nature.

In the case of 'wealth' we all see the fallacy. We know that wealth is but a name for concrete processes that certain men's lives play a part in, and not a natural excellence found in Messrs. Rockefeller and Carnegie, but not in the rest of us.

Like wealth, health also lives *in rebus*. It is a name for processes, as digestion, circulation, sleep, etc., that go on happily, though in this instance we are more inclined to think of it as a principle and say the man digests and sleeps so well because he is so healthy.

With 'strength' we are, I think, more rationalistic still, decidedly inclined to treat it as an excellence preexisting in the man and explanatory of the herculean performances of his muscles.

With 'truth' most people go over the border entirely, and treat the rationalistic account as self-evident. But really all these words in *th* are exactly similar. Truth exists *ante rem* just as much and as little as the other things do.

The scholastics made much of the distinction between habit and act. Health *in actu* means, among other things, good sleeping and digesting. But a healthy man need not always be sleeping, or always digesting, any more than a wealthy man need be always handling money, or a strong man always lifting weights. All such qualities sink to the status of 'habits' between their times of exercise; and similarly truth becomes a habit of certain of our ideas and beliefs in their intervals of rest from verifying activity. But that activity is the root of the whole matter, and the condition of there being any habit to exist in the intervals.

'The true,' to put it very briefly, is only the expedient in the way of our thinking, just as 'the right' is only the expedient in the way of our behaving. Expedient in almost any fashion; and expedient in the long run and on the whole, of course; for what meets expediently all the experience in sight won't necessarily meet all farther experiences equally satisfactorily. Experience, as we know, has ways of *boiling over*, and making us correct our present formulas.

The 'absolutely' true, meaning what no further experience will ever alter, is that ideal vanishing-point towards which we imagine that all our temporary truths will some day converge. It runs on all fours with the perfectly wise man, and with the absolutely complete experience; and, like these other ideals, it may never fully eventuate or materialize. We have to live to-day by what truth we can get to-day, and be ready to-morrow to call it falsehood. Ptolemaic astronomy, Euclidean space, Aristotelian logic, scholastic metaphysics, were expedient for centuries, but human experience has boiled over those limits, and we now call these things only relatively true, or true within those borders of experience. 'Absolutely' they are false; for we know that those limits were casual, and might have been transcended by past theorists just as they are by present thinkers.

When new experiences lead to retrospective judgments, using the past tense, what these judgments utter *was* true, even though no past thinker had been led there. We live forwards, a Danish thinker has said, but we understand backwards. The present sheds a backward light on the world's previous processes. They may have been truth-processes for the actors in them. They are not so for one who knows the later revelations of the story.

This regulative notion of a potential better truth to be established later, possibly to be established some day absolutely, and having powers of retroactive legislation, turns its face, like all pragmatist notions, towards concreteness of fact and towards the future. Like the half-truths, the absolute truth will have to be *made*, made as a relation incidental to the growth of a mass of verification-experience, to which the half-true ideas are all along contributing their quota.

I have already insisted on the fact that truth is made largely out of previous truths. Men's beliefs at any time are so much experience *funded*. But they are themselves parts of the sum total of the world's experience, and become matter, therefore, for the next day's funding operations. So far as reality means experienceable reality, both it and the truths men gain about it are everlastingly in process of mutation—mutation towards a definite goal, it may be—but still mutation.

Mathematicians can solve problems with two variables. On the Newtonian theory, for instance, acceleration varies with distance, but distance also varies with acceleration. In the realm of truth-processes facts come independently and determine our beliefs provisionally. But these beliefs make us act, and as fast as they do so, they bring new facts into sight which redetermine the beliefs accordingly. So the whole coil and ball of truth, as it rolls up, is the product of a double influence. Truths emerge from facts; but they dip forward into facts again and add to them; which facts again create or reveal new truth (the word is indifferent) and so on *ad infinitum*. The facts themselves meanwhile are not true. They simply *are*. Truth is the function of beliefs that start and terminate among them.

The case is like a snowball's growth, due, as it is, to the distribution of the snow on the one hand, and to the direction of the boy's successive pushes on the other, with these factors codetermining each other incessantly.

The most fateful point of difference between being a rationalist and being a pragmatist is now fully in sight. Experience is in mutation, and our psychological ascertainments of truth are in mutation—so much rationalism will allow; but never that either reality itself or truth itself is mutable. Reality stands complete and ready-made from all eternity, rationalism insists, and the agreement of our ideas with it is that unique and timeless virtue in them of which she has already told us. As that intrinsic excellence, their truth has nothing to do with our experiences. It adds nothing to the content of experience. It makes no difference to reality itself; it is supervenient, inert, static, a reflection merely. It doesn't *exist*, it *holds* or *obtains*; it belongs to another dimension from that of facts and fact-relations, belongs, in short, to the epistemological dimension—and with that big word rationalism closes the discussion.

Thus, just as pragmatism faces forward to the future, so does rationalism here again face backward to a past eternity. True to her inveterate habit, rationalism reverts to 'principles' and thinks that when an abstraction once is named, we own a solution.

The tremendous pregnancy in the way of consequences for life of this radical difference of outlook will only become apparent in my later lectures. I wish meanwhile to close this lecture by showing that rationalism's sublimity does not save it from inanity.

When, namely, you ask rationalists, instead of accusing pragmatism of desecrating the notion of truth, to define it themselves by saying exactly what *they* understand by it, the only positive attempts I can think of are these two:

1. "Truth is the system of propositions which have an unconditional claim to be recognized as valid."[1]

2. Truth is a name for all those judgments which we find ourselves under obligation to make by a kind of imperative duty.[2]

The first thing that strikes one in such definitions is their unutterable triviality. They are absolutely true, of course, but absolutely insignificant until you handle them pragmatically. What do you mean by 'claim' here, and what do you mean by 'duty'? As summary names for the concrete reasons why thinking in true ways is overwhelmingly expedient and good for mortal men, it is all right to talk of claims on reality's part to be agreed with, and of obligations on our part to agree. We feel both the claims and the obligations, and we feel them for just those reasons.

But the rationalists who talk of claim and obligation expressly say that they have nothing to do with our practical interests or personal reasons. Our reasons for agreeing are psychological facts, they say, relative to each thinker, and to the accidents of his life. They are his evidence merely, they are no part of the life of truth itself. That life transacts itself in a purely logical or epistemological, as distinguished from a psychological, dimension, and its claims antedate and exceed all personal motivations whatsoever. Though neither man nor God should ever *ascertain* truth, the word would still have to be defined as that which *ought* to be ascertained and recognized.

There never was a more exquisite example of an idea abstracted from the concretes of experience and then used to oppose and negate what it was abstracted from.

Philosophy and common life abound in similar instances. The 'sentimentalist fallacy' is to shed tears over abstract justice and generosity, beauty, etc., and never to know these qualities when you meet them in the street, because the circumstances make them vulgar. Thus I read in the privately printed biography of an eminently rationalistic mind: "It was strange that with such admiration for beauty in the abstract, my brother had no enthusiasm for fine architecture, for beautiful painting, or for flowers." And in almost the last philosophic work I have read, I find such passages as the following: "Justice is ideal, solely ideal. Reason conceives that it ought to exist, but experience shows that it can not. . . . Truth, which ought to be, can not be. . . . Reason is deformed by experience. As soon as reason enters experience, it becomes contrary to reason."

The rationalist's fallacy here is exactly like the sentimentalist's. Both extract a quality from the muddy particulars of experience, and find it so pure when extracted that they contrast it with each and all its muddy instances as an opposite and higher nature. All the while it is *their* nature. It is the nature of truths to be validated, verified. It pays for our ideas to be validated. Our obligation to seek truth is part of our general obligation to do what pays. The payments true ideas bring are the sole *why* of our duty to follow them. Identical whys exist in the case of wealth and health.

Truth makes no other kind of claim and imposes no other kind of ought than health and wealth do. All these claims are conditional; the concrete benefits we gain are what we mean by calling the pursuit a duty. In the case of truth, untrue beliefs work as perniciously in the long run as true beliefs work beneficially. Talking abstractly, the quality 'true' may thus be said to grow absolutely precious, and the quality 'untrue' absolutely damnable. The one may be called good, the other bad, unconditionally. We ought to think the true, we ought to shun the false, imperatively.

But if we treat all this abstraction literally and oppose it to its mother soil in experience, see what a preposterous position we work ourselves into.

We can not then take a step forward in our actual thinking. When shall I acknowledge this truth and when that? Shall the acknowledgment be loud?—or silent? If sometimes loud, sometimes silent, which *now?* When may a truth go into cold-storage in the encyclopedia? and when shall it come out for battle? Must I constantly be repeating the truth 'twice two are four' because of its eternal claim on recognition? or is it sometimes irrelevant? Must my thoughts dwell night and day on my personal sins and blemishes, because I truly have them?—or may I sink and ignore them in order to be a decent social unit, and not a mass of morbid melancholy and apology?

It is quite evident that our obligation to acknowledge truth, so far from being unconditional, is tremendously conditioned. Truth, with a big T, and in the singular, claims abstractly to be recognized, of course; but concrete truths in the plural need be recognized only when their recognition is expedient. A truth must always be preferred to a falsehood when both relate to the situation; but when neither does, truth is as little of a duty as falsehood. If you ask me what o'clock it is and I tell you that I live at 95 Irving Street, my answer may indeed be true, but you don't see why it is my duty to give it. A false address would be as much to the purpose.

With this admission that there are conditions that limit the application of the abstract imperative, the pragmatistic treatment of truth sweeps back upon us in its fullness. Our duty to agree with reality is seen to be grounded in a perfect jungle of concrete expediencies.

When Berkeley had explained what people meant by matter, people thought that he denied matter's existence. When Messrs. Schiller and Dewey now explain what people mean by truth, they are accused of denying *its* existence. These pragmatists destroy all objective standards, critics say, and put foolishness and wisdom on one level. A favorite formula for describing Mr. Schiller's doctrines and mine is that we are persons who think that by saying whatever you find it pleasant to say and calling it truth you fulfill every pragmatistic requirement.

I leave it to you to judge whether this be not an impudent slander. Pent in, as the pragmatist, more than any one else, sees himself to be, between the whole body of funded truths squeezed from the past, and the coercions of the world of sense about him, who so well as he feels the immense pressure of objective control under which our minds perform their operations? We have heard much of late of the uses of the imagination in science. It is high time to urge the use of a little imagination in philosophy. The unwillingness of some of our critics to read any but the silliest and stupidest of possible meanings into our statements is as discreditable to their imaginations as anything I know in recent philosophic history. Schiller says the true is that which 'works.' Thereupon he is treated as one who limits verification to the lowest material utilities. Dewey says truth is what gives 'satisfaction.' He is treated as one who believes in calling everything true which, if it were true, would be pleasant.

Our critics certainly need more imagination of realities. I have honestly tried to stretch my own imagination and to read the best possible meaning into the rationalist conception, but I have to confess that it still completely baffles me. The notion of a reality calling on us to 'agree' with it, and that for no reasons, but simply because its claim is 'unconditional' or 'transcendent' is one that I can make neither head nor tail of. I try to imagine myself as the sole reality in the world, and then to imagine what more I would 'claim' if I were allowed to. When you suggest the possibility of my claiming that a mind should come into being from out of the void inane and stand and copy me, I can indeed imagine what the copying might mean, but I can conjure up no motive. What good it would do me to be copied, or what good it would do that mind to copy me, if practical consequences are expressly and in principle ruled out as motives for the claim (as they are by our rationalist authorities) I can not fathom. And when we get beyond copying, and fall back on unnamed forms of agreeing that are expressly denied to be either copyings or leadings or fittings, or any other processes pragmatically definable, the *what* of the 'agreement' claimed becomes as unintelligible as the why of it. Neither content nor motive can be imagined for it. It is an absolutely meaningless abstraction.[3]

Surely in this field of truth it is the pragmatists and not the rationalists who are the more genuine defenders of the universe's rationality.

Notes

The sixth of a course of eight lectures on 'Pragmatism' delivered at the Lowell Institute, Boston, November–December, 1906.

1. A. E. Taylor, *Philosophical Review*, Vol. XIV, p. 288.
2. H. Rickert, 'Der Gegenstand der Erkenntniss,' chapter on 'Die Urtheilsnothwendigkeit.'
3. I am not forgetting that Professor Rickert long ago gave up the notion of truth being founded on agreement with reality. Reality, according to him, is whatever agrees with truth, and truth is founded solely on our primal duty. This fantastic flight, together with Mr. Joachim's candid confession of failure in his book 'The Nature of Truth,' seem to me to mark the bankruptcy of rationalism when dealing with this subject. Naturally I could not, in a popular lecture, pursue my subject into such intricacies.

This paper was delivered to students at Yale and Brown, and published in 1896; here James argues against evidentialism and in favor of the claim that under certain conditions one's "passional nature" may determine one's belief even in the absence of evidence.

WILLIAM JAMES

The Will to Believe

In the recently published Life by Leslie Stephen of his brother, Fitz-James, there is an account of a school to which the latter went when he was a boy. The teacher, a certain Mr. Guest, used to converse with his pupils in this wise: "Gurney, what is the difference between justification and sanctification?—Stephen, prove the omnipotence of God " etc. In the midst of our Harvard freethinking and indifference we are prone to imagine that here at your good old orthodox College conversation continues to be somewhat upon this order; and to show you that we at Harvard have not lost all interest in these vital subjects, I have brought with me tonight something like a sermon on justification by faith to read to you,—I mean an essay in justification *of* faith, a defence of our right to adopt a believing attitude in religious matters, in spite of the fact that our merely logical intellect may not have been coerced. 'The Will to Believe,' accordingly, is the title of my paper.

I have long defended to my own students the lawfulness of voluntarily adopted faith; but as soon as they have got well imbued with the logical spirit, they have as a rule refused to admit my contention to be lawful philosophically, even though in point of fact they were personally all the time chock-full of some faith or other themselves. I am all the while, however, so profoundly convinced that my own position is correct, that your invitation has seemed to me a good occasion to make my statements more clear. Perhaps your minds will be more open than those with which I have hitherto had to deal. I will be as little technical as I can, though I must begin by setting up some technical distinctions that will help us in the end.

I

Let us give the name of *hypothesis* to anything that may be proposed to our belief; and just as the electricians speak of live and dead wires, let us speak of any hypothesis as either *live* or *dead*. A live hypothesis is one which appeals as a real possibility to him to whom it is proposed. If I ask you to believe in the Mahdi, the notion makes no electric connection with your nature,—it refuses to scintillate with any credibility at all. As an hypothesis it is completely dead. To an Arab, however (even if he be not one of the Madhi's followers), the hypothesis is among the mind's possibilities: it is alive. This shows that deadness and liveness in an hypothesis are not intrinsic properties, but relations to the individual thinker. They are measured by his willingness to act. The maximum of liveness in hypothesis means willingness to act irrevocably. Practically, that means belief; but there is some believing tendency wherever there is willingness to act at all.

Next, let us call the decision between two hypotheses an *option*. Options may be of several kinds. They may be—1, *living* or *dead*; 2, *forced* or *avoidable*; 3, *momentous* or *trivial*; and for our purpose we may call an option a *genuine* option when it is the forced, living, and momentous kind.

1. A living option is one in which both hypotheses are live ones. If I say to you: "Be a theosophist or be a Mohammedan," it is probably a dead option, because for you neither hypothesis is likely to be alive. But if I say: "Be an agnostic or be Christian," it is otherwise: trained as you are, each hypothesis makes some appeal, however small, to your belief.

2. Next, if I say to you: "Choose between going out with your umbrella or without it," I do not offer you a genuine option, for it is not forced. You can easily avoid it by not going out at all. Similarly, if I say, "Either love me or hate me," "Either call my theory true or call it false," your option is avoidable. You may remain indifferent to me, neither loving nor hating, and you may decline to offer any judgment as to my theory. But if I say, "Either accept this truth or go without it," I put on you a forced option, for there is no standing place outside of the alternative. Every dilemma based on a complete logical disjunction, with no possibility of not choosing, is an option of this forced kind.

3. Finally, if I were Dr. Nansen and proposed to you to join my North Pole expedition, your option would be momentous; for this would probably be your only similar opportunity, and your choice now would either exclude you from the North Pole sort of immortality altogether or put at least the chance of it into your hands. He who refuses to embrace a unique opportunity loses the prize as surely as if he tried and failed. *Per contra*, the option is trivial when the opportunity is not unique, when the stake is insignificant, or when the decision is reversible if it later prove unwise. Such trivial options abound in the scientific life. A chemist finds an hypothesis live enough to spend a year in its verification: he believes in it to that extent. But if his experiments prove inconclusive either way, he is quit for his loss of time, no vital harm being done.

It will facilitate our discussion if we keep all these distinctions well in mind.

II

The next matter to consider is the actual psychology of human opinion. When we look at certain facts, it seems as if our passional and volitional nature lay at the root of all our convictions. When we look at others, it seems as if they could do nothing when the intellect had once said its say. Let us take the latter facts up first.

Does it not seem preposterous on the very face of it to talk of our opinions being modifiable at will? Can our will either help or hinder our intellect in its perceptions of truth? Can we, by just willing it, believe that Abraham Lincoln's existence is a myth, and that the portraits of him in McClure's Magazine are all of some one else? Can we, by any effort of our will, or by any strength of wish that it were true, believe ourselves well and about when we are roaring with rheumatism in bed, or feel certain that the sum of the two one-dollar bills in our pocket must be a hundred dollars? We can *say* any of these things, but we are absolutely impotent to believe them; and of just such things is the whole fabric of the truths that we do believe in made up,—matters of fact, immediate or remote, as Hume said, and relations between ideas, which are either there or not there for us if we see them so, and which if not there cannot be put there by any action of our own.

In Pascal's Thoughts there is a celebrated passage known in literature as Pascal's wager. In it he tries to force us into Christianity by reasoning as if our concern with truth resembled our concern with the stakes in a game of chance. Translated freely his words are these: You must either believe or not believe that God is—which will you do? Your human reason cannot say. A game is going on between you and the nature of things which at the day of judgment will bring out either heads or tails. Weigh what your gains and your losses would be if you should stake all you have on heads, or God's existence: if you win in such case, you gain eternal beatitude; if you lose, you lose nothing at all. If there were an infinity of chances, and only one for God in this wager, still you ought to stake your all on God; for though you surely risk a finite loss by this procedure, any finite loss is reasonable, even a certain one is reasonable, if there is but the possibility of infinite gain. Go, then, and take holy water, and have masses said; belief will come and stupefy your scruples,—*Cela vous fera croire et vous abêtira*. Why should you not? At bottom, what have you to lose?

You probably feel that when religious faith expresses itself thus, in the language of the gaming-table, it is put to its last tramps. Surely Pascal's own personal belief in masses and holy water had far other springs; and this celebrated page of his is but an argument for others, a last desperate snatch at a weapon against the hardness of the unbelieving heart. We feel that a faith in masses and holy water adopted wilfully after such a mechanical calculation would lack the inner soul of faith's reality; and if we were of the Deity, we should probably take pleasure in cutting off believers from their infinite reward. It is evident that unless there be some pre-existing tendency to believe in masses and holy water, the option offered to the will by Pascal is not a living option. Certainly no Turk ever took to masses and holy water on its account; and even to us Protestants these seem such foregone impossibilities that Pascal's logic, invoked for them specifically, leaves us unmoved. As well might the Mahdi write to us, saying, "I am the Expected One whom God has created in his effulgence. You shall be infinitely happy if you confess me; otherwise you shall be cut off from the light of the sun. Weigh, then, your infinite gain if I am genuine against your finite sacrifice if I am not!" His logic would be that of Pascal; but he would vainly use it on us, for the hypothesis he offers us is dead. No tendency to act on it exists in us to any degree.

The talk of believing by our volition seems, then, from one point of view, simply silly. From another point of view it is worse than silly, it is vile. When one turns to the magnificent edifice of the physical sciences, and sees how it was reared; what thousands of disinterested moral lives of men lie buried in its mere foundations; what patience and postponement, what choking down of preference, what submission to the icy laws of outer fact are wrought into its very stones and mortar; how absolutely impersonal it stands in its vast augustness,—then how besotted and contemptible seems every little sentimentalist who comes blowing his voluntary smoke-wreaths, and pretending to decide things from out of his private dream! Can we wonder if those bred in the rugged and manly school of science should feel like spewing such subjectivism out of their mouths? The whole system of loyalties which grow up in the schools of science go dead against its toleration; so that it is only natural that those who have caught the scientific fever should pass over to the opposite extreme, and write sometimes as if the incorruptibly truthful intellect ought positively to prefer bitterness and unacceptableness to the heart in its cup.

It fortifies my soul to know
That, thou I perish, Truth is so—

sings Clough, while Huxley exclaims: "My only consolation lies in the reflection that, however bad our posterity may become, so far as they hold the plain rule of not pretending to believe what they have no reason to believe, because it may be to their advantage so to pretend [the word 'pretend' is surely here redundant], they will not have reached the lowest depth of immorality." And that delicious *enfant terrible* Clifford writes: "Belief is desecrated when given to unproved and unquestioned statements for the solace and private pleasure of the believer. . . . Whoso would deserve well of his fellows in this matter will guard the purity of his belief with a very fanaticism of jealous care, lest at any time it should rest on an unworthy object, and catch a stain which can never be wiped away. . . . If [a] belief has been accepted on insufficient evidence [even though the belief be true, as Clifford on the same page explains] the pleasure is a stolen one. . . . It is sinful because it is stolen in defiance of our duty to mankind. That duty is to guard ourselves from such beliefs as from a pestilence which may shortly master our own body and then spread to the rest of the town. . . . It is wrong always, everywhere, and for every one, to believe anything upon insufficient evidence."

III

All this strikes one as healthy, even when expressed, as by Clifford, with somewhat too much of robustious pathos in the voice. Free-will and simple wishing do seem, in the matter of our credences, to be only fifth wheels to the coach. Yet if any one should thereupon assume that intellectual insight is what remains after wish and will and sentimental preference have taken wing, or that pure reason is what then settles our opinions, he would fly quite as directly in the teeth of the facts.

It is only our already dead hypotheses that our willing nature is unable to bring to life again. But what has made them dead for us is for the most part a previous action of our willing nature of an antagonistic kind. When I say 'willing nature,' I do not mean only such deliberate volitions as may have set up habits of belief that we cannot now escape from,—I mean all such factors of belief as fear and hope, prejudice and passion, imitation and partisanship, the circumpressure of our caste and set. As a matter of fact we find ourselves believing, we hardly know how or why. Mr. Balfour gives the name of 'authority' to all those influences, born of the intellectual climate, that make hypotheses possible or impossible for us, alive or dead. Here in this room, we all of us believe in molecules and the conservation of energy, in democracy and necessary progress, in Protestant Christianity and the duty of fighting for 'the doctrine of the immortal Monroe,' all for no reasons worthy of the name. We see into these matters with no more inner clearness, and probably with much less, than any disbeliever in them might possess. His unconventionality would probably have some grounds to show for its conclusions; but for us, not insight, but the *prestige* of the opinions, is what makes the spark shoot from them and light up our sleeping magazines of faith. Our reason is quite satisfied, in nine hundred and ninety-nine cases out of every thousand of us, if it can find a few arguments that will do to recite in case our credulity is criticised by some one else. Our faith is faith in some one else's faith, and in the greatest matters this is most the case. Our belief in truth itself for instance, that there is a truth, and that our minds and it are made for each other,—what is it but a passionate affirmation of desire, in which our social system backs us up? We want to have a truth; we want to believe that our experiments and studies and discussions must put us in a continually better and better position towards it; and on this line we agree to fight out our thinking lives. But if a pyrrhonistic sceptic asks us *how we know* all this, can our logic find a reply? No! certainly it cannot. It is just one volition against another,—we willing to go in for life upon a trust or assumption which he, for his part, does not care to make.

As a rule we disbelieve all facts and theories for which we have no use. Clifford's cosmic emotions find no use for Christian feelings. Huxley belabors the bishops because there is no use for sacerdotalism in his scheme of life. Newman, on the contrary, goes over to Romanism, and finds all sorts of reasons good for staying there, because a priestly system is for him an organic need and delight. Why do so few 'scientists' even look at the evidence for telepathy, so called? Because they think, as a leading biologist, now dead, once said to me, that even if such a thing were true, scientists ought to band together to keep it suppressed and concealed. It would undo the uniformity of Nature and all sorts of other things without which scientists cannot carry on their pursuits. But if this very man had been shown something which as a scientist he might *do* with telepathy, he might not only have examined the evidence, but even have found it good enough. This very law which the logicians would impose upon us—if I may give the name of logicians to those who would rule out our willing nature here—is based on nothing but their own natural wish to exclude all elements for which they, in their professional quality of logicians, can find no use.

Evidently, then, our non-intellectual nature does influence our convictions. There are passional tendencies and volitions which run before and others which come after belief, and it is only the latter that are too late for the fair; and they are not too late when the previous passional work has been already in their own direction. Pascal's argument, instead of being powerless, then seems a regular clincher, and is the last stroke needed to make our faith in masses and holy water complete. The state of things is evidently far from simple; and pure insight and logic, whatever they might do ideally, are not the only things that really do produce our creeds.

IV

Our next duty, having recognized this mixed-up state of affairs, is to ask whether it be simply reprehensible and pathological, or whether, on the contrary, we must treat it as a normal element in making up our minds. The thesis I defend is, briefly stated, this: *Our passional nature not only lawfully may, but must, decide an option between propositions, whenever it is a genuine option that cannot by its nature be decided on intellectual grounds; for to say, under such circumstances, "Do not decide, but leave the question open," is itself a passional decision,—just like deciding yes or no,—and is attended with the same risk of losing the truth.* The thesis thus abstractly expressed will, I trust, soon become quite clear. But I must first indulge in a bit more of preliminary work.

V

It will be observed that for the purposes of this discussion we are on 'dogmatic' ground,—ground, I mean, which leaves systematic philosophical scepticism altogether out of account. The postulate that there is truth, and that it is the destiny of our minds to attain it, we are deliberately resolving to make, though the sceptic will not make it. We part company with him, therefore, absolutely, at this point. But the faith that truth exists, and that our minds can find it may be held in two ways. We may talk of the *empiricist* way and of the *absolutist* way of believing in truth. The absolutists in this matter say that we not only can attain to knowing truth, but we can *know when* we have attained to knowing it; while the empiricists think that although we may attain it, we cannot infallibly know when. To *know* is one thing, and to know for certain *that* we know is another. One may hold to the first being possible without the second;

hence the empiricists and the absolutists, although neither of them is a sceptic in the usual philosophic sense of the term, show very different degrees of dogmatism in their lives.

If we look at the history of opinions, we see that the empiricist tendency has largely prevailed in science, while in philosophy the absolutist tendency has had everything its own way. The characteristic sort of happiness, indeed, which philosophies yield has mainly consisted in the conviction felt by each successive school or system that by it bottom-certitude had been attained. "Other philosophies are collections of opinions, mostly false; *my* philosophy gives standing-ground forever,"—who does not recognize in this the key-note of every system worthy of the name? A system, to be a system at all, must come as a closed system, reversible in this or that detail, perchance, but in its essential features never!

Scholastic orthodoxy, to which one must always go when one wishes to find perfectly clear statement, has beautifully elaborated this absolutist conviction in a doctrine which it calls that of 'objective evidence.' If, for example, I am unable to doubt that I now exist before you, that two is less than three, or that if all men are mortal then I am mortal too, it is because these things illumine my intellect irresistibly. The final ground of this objective evidence possessed by certain propositions is the *adequatio intellectus nostri cum re* [the agreement of our intellect with the thing known]. The certitude it brings involves an *aptitudinem ad extorquendam certum assensum* [an aptitude for extorting a certain assent from our intellect] on the part of the truth envisaged, and on the side of the subject a *quietem in cognitione* [a quiet rest in knowledge], when once the object is mentally received, that leaves no possibility of doubt behind; and in the whole transaction nothing operates but the *entitas ipsa* [entity itself] of the object and the *entitas ipsa* of the mind. We slouchy modern thinkers dislike to talk in Latin,—indeed, we dislike to talk in set terms at all; but at bottom our own state of mind is very much like this whenever we uncritically abandon ourselves: You believe in objective evidence, and I do. Of some things we feel that we are certain: we know, and we know that we do know. There is something that gives a click inside of us, a bell that strikes twelve, when the hands of our mental clock have swept the dial and meet over the meridian hour. The greatest empiricists among us are only empiricists on reflection: when left to their instincts, they dogmatize like infallible popes. When the Cliffords tell us how sinful it is to be Christians on such 'insufficient evidence,' insufficiency is really the last thing they have in mind. For them the evidence is absolutely sufficient, only it makes the other way. They believe so completely in an anti-christian order of the universe that there is no living option: Christianity is a dead hypothesis from the start.

VI

But now, since we are all such absolutists by instinct, what in our quality of students of philosophy ought we to do about the fact? Shall we espouse and indorse it? Or shall we treat it as a weakness of our nature from which we must free ourselves, if we can?

I sincerely believe that the latter course is the only one we can follow as reflective men. Objective evidence and certitude are doubtless very fine ideals to play with, but where on this moonlit and dream-visited planet are they found? I am, therefore, myself a complete empiricist so far as my theory of human knowledge goes. I live, to be sure, by the practical faith that we must go on experiencing and thinking over our experience, for only thus can our opinions grow more true; but to hold any one of them—I absolutely do not care which—as if it never could be reinterpretable or corrigible, I believe to be a tremendously mistaken attitude, and I think that the whole history of philosophy will bear me out. There is but one indefectibly certain truth, and that is the truth that pyrrhonistic scepticism itself leaves standing,—the truth that the present phenomenon of consciousness exists. That, however, is the bare starting-point of knowledge, the mere admission of a stuff to be philosophized about. The various philosophies are but so many attempts at expressing what this stuff really is. And if we repair to our libraries what disagreement do we discover! Where is a certainly true answer found? Apart from abstract propositions of comparison (such as two and two are the same as four), propositions which tell us nothing by themselves about concrete reality, we find no proposition ever regarded by any one as evidently certain that has not either been called a falsehood, or at least had its truth sincerely questioned by some one else. The transcending of the axioms of geometry, not in play but earnest, by certain of our contemporaries (as Zöllner and Charles H. Hinton), and the rejection of the whole Aristotelian logic by the Hegelians, are striking instances in point.

No concrete test of what is really true has ever been agreed upon. Some make the criterion external to the moment of perception, putting it either in revelation, the *consensus gentium* [the agreement of all nations], the instincts of the heart, or the systematized experience of the race. Others make the perceptive moment its own test,—Descartes, for instance, with his clear and distinct ideas guaranteed by the veracity of God; Reid with his 'common-sense;' and Kant with his forms of synthetic judgment *a priori*. The inconceivability of the opposite; the capacity to be verified by sense; the possession of complete organic unity or self-relation, realized when a thing is its own other,—are standards which, in turn, have been used. The much lauded objective evidence is never triumphantly there; it is a mere aspiration or *Grenzbegriff* [limit or ideal notion] marking the infinitely remote ideal of our thinking life. To claim that certain truths now possess it, is simply to say that when you think them true and they are true, then their evidence is objective, otherwise it is not. But practically one's conviction that the evidence one goes by is of the real objective brand, is only one more subjective opinion added to the lot. For what a contradictory array of opinions have objective evidence and absolute certitude been claimed! The world is rational through and through,—its existence is an ultimate brute fact; there is a personal God,—a personal God is inconceivable; there is an extra-mental physical world immediately known,—the mind can only know its own ideas; a moral imperative exists,—obligation is only the resultant of desires; a permanent spiritual principle is in every one,—there are only shifting states of mind;—there is an endless chain of causes,—there is an absolute first cause; —an eternal necessity,—a freedom; —a purpose,—no purpose;—a primal One,—a primal Many; a universal continuity, —an essential discontinuity in things, an infinity,—no infinity. There is this,—there is that; there is indeed nothing which some one has not thought absolutely true, while his neighbor deemed it absolutely false; and not an absolutist among them seems ever to have considered that the trouble may all the time be essential, and that the intellect, even with truth directly in its grasp, may have no infallible signal for knowing whether it be truth or no. When, indeed, one remembers that the most striking practical application to life of the doctrine of objective certitude has been the conscientious labors of the Holy Office of the Inquisition, one feels less tempted than ever to lend the doctrine a respectful ear.

But please observe, now, that when as empiricists we give up the doctrine of objective certitude, we do not thereby give up the quest or hope of truth itself. We still pin our faith on its existence, and still believe that we gain an ever better position towards it by systematically continuing to roll up experiences and think. Our great difference from the scholastic lies in the way we face. The strength of his system lies in the principles, the origin, the *terminus a quo* [the beginning point] of his thought; for us the strength is in the outcome, the upshot, the *terminus ad quem* [the end result]. Not where it comes from but what it leads to is to decide. It matters not to an empiricist from what quarter an hypothesis may come to him: he may have acquired it by fair means or by foul; passion may have whispered or accident suggested it; but if the total drift of thinking continues to confirm it, that is what he means by its being true.

VII

One more point, small but important, and our preliminaries are done. There are two ways of looking at our duty in the matter of opinion,—ways entirely different, and yet ways about whose difference the theory of knowledge seems hitherto to have shown very little concern. *We must know the truth; and we must avoid error*,—these are our first and great commandments as would-be knowers; but they are not two ways of stating an identical commandment, they are two separable laws. Although it may indeed happen that when we believe the truth *A*, we escape as an incidental consequence from believing the falsehood *B*, it hardly ever happens that by merely disbelieving *B* we necessarily believe *A*. We may in escaping *B* fall into believing other falsehoods, *C* or *D*, just as bad as *B*; or we may escape *B* by not believing anything at all, not even *A*.

Believe truth! Shun error!—these, we see, are two materially different laws; and by choosing between them we may end by coloring differently our whole intellectual life. We may regard the chase for truth as paramount, and the avoidance of error as secondary; or we may, on the other hand, treat the avoidance of error as more imperative, and let truth take its chance. Clifford, in the instructive passage which I have quoted, exhorts us to the latter course. Believe nothing, he tells us, keep your mind in suspense forever, rather than by closing it on insufficient evidence incur the awful risk of believing lies. You, on the other hand, may think that the risk of being in error is a very small matter when compared with the blessings of real knowledge, and be ready to be duped many times in your investigation rather than postpone indefinitely the chance of guessing true. I myself find it impossible to go with Clifford. We must remember that these feelings of our duty about either truth or error are in any case only expressions of our passional life. Biologically considered, our minds are as ready to grind out falsehood as veracity, and he who says, "Better go without belief forever than believe a lie!" merely shows his own preponderant private horror of becoming a dupe. He may be critical of many of his desires and fears, but this fear he slavishly obeys. He cannot imagine any one questioning its binding force. For my own part, I have also a horror of being duped; but I can believe that worse things than being duped may happen to a man in this world: so Clifford's exhortation has to my ears a thoroughly fantastic sound. It is like a general informing his soldiers that it is better to keep out of battle forever than to risk a single wound. Not so are victories either over enemies or over nature gained. Our errors are surely not such awfully solemn things. In a world where we are so certain to incur them in spite of all our caution, a certain lightness of heart seems healthier than this excessive nervousness on their behalf. At any rate, it seems the fittest thing for the empiricist philosopher.

VIII

And now, after all this introduction, let us go straight at our question. I have said, and now repeat it, that not only as a matter of fact do we find our passional nature influencing us in our opinions, but that there are some options between opinions in which this influence must be regarded both as an inevitable and as a lawful determinant of our choice.

I fear here that some of you my hearers will begin to scent danger, and lend an inhospitable ear. Two first steps of passion you have indeed had to admit as necessary,—we must think so as to avoid dupery, and we must think so as to gain truth; but the surest path to those ideal consummations, you will probably consider, is from now onwards to take no further passional step.

Well, of course, I agree as far as the facts will allow. Wherever the option between losing truth and gaining it is not momentous, we can throw the chance of *gaining truth* away, and at any rate save ourselves from any chance of *believing falsehood*, by not making up our minds at all till objective evidence has come. In scientific questions, this is almost always the case; and even in human affairs in general, the need of acting is seldom so urgent that a false belief to act on is better than no belief at all.

Law courts, indeed, have to decide on the best evidence attainable for the moment, because a judge's duty is to make law as well as to ascertain it, and (as a learned judge once said to me) few cases are worth spending much time over: the great thing is to have them decided on *any* acceptable principle, and got out of the way. But in our dealings with objective nature we obviously are recorders, not makers, of the truth; and decisions for the mere sake of deciding promptly and getting on to the next business would be wholly out of place. Throughout the breadth of physical nature facts are what they are quite independently of us, and seldom is there any such hurry about them that the risks of being duped by believing a premature theory need be faced. The questions here are always trivial options, the hypotheses are hardly living (at any rate not living for us spectators), the choice between believing truth or falsehood is seldom forced. The attitude of sceptical balance is therefore the absolutely wise one if we would escape mistakes. What difference, indeed, does it make to most of us whether we have or have not a theory of the Röntgen rays [x-rays], whether we believe or not in mind-stuff, or have a conviction about the causality of conscious states? It makes no difference. Such options are not forced on us. On every account it is better not to make them, but still keep weighing reasons *pro et contra* with an indifferent hand.

I speak, of course, here of the purely judging mind. For purposes of discovery such indifference is to be less highly recommended, and science would be far less advanced than she is if the passionate desires of individuals to get their own faiths confirmed had been kept out of the game. See for example the sagacity which Spencer and Weismann now display. On the other hand, if you want an absolute duffer in an investigation, you must, after all, take the man who has no interest whatever in its results: he is the warranted incapable, the positive fool. The most useful investigator, because the most sensitive observer, is always he whose eager interest in one side of the question is balanced by an equally keen nervousness lest he become deceived.[1] Science has organized this nervousness into a regular *technique*, her so-called method of verification; and she has fallen so deeply in love with the method that one may even say she has ceased to care for truth by itself at all. It is only truth as technically verified that interests her. The truth of truths might come in merely affirmative form, and she would decline to touch it. Such truth as that, she might repeat with Clifford, would be stolen in defiance of her duty to mankind. Human passions, however, are stronger than technical rules. "*Le coeur a ses raisons*" as Pascal says, "*que la raison ne connait pas*" [The heart has its reasons which the mind does not understand]; and however indifferent to all but the bare rules of the game the umpire, the abstract intellect, may be, the concrete players who furnish him the materials to judge of are usually, each one of them, in love with some pet 'live hypothesis' of his own. Let us agree, however, that wherever there is no forced option, the dispassionately judicial intellect with no pet hypothesis, saving us, as it does, from dupery at any rate, ought to be our ideal.

The question next arises: Are there not somewhere forced options in our speculative questions, and can we (as men who may be interested at least as much in positively gaining truth as in merely escaping dupery) always wait with impunity till the coercive evidence shall have arrived? It seems *a priori* improbable that the truth should be so nicely adjusted to our needs and powers as that. In the great boarding-house of nature, the cakes and the butter and the syrup seldom come out so even and leave the plates so clean. Indeed, we should view them with scientific suspicion if they did.

IX

Moral questions immediately present themselves as questions whose solution cannot wait for sensible proof. A moral question is a question not of what sensibly exists, but of what is good, or would be good if it did exist. Science can tell us what exists; but to compare the *worths*, both of what exists and of what does not exist, we must consult not science, but what Pascal calls our heart. Science herself consults her heart when she lays it down that the infinite ascertainment of fact and correction of false belief are the supreme goods for man. Challenge the statement, and science can only repeat it oracularly, or else prove it by showing that such ascertainment and correction bring man all sorts of other goods which man's heart in torn decides. The question of having moral beliefs at all or not having them is decided by our will. Are our moral preferences true or false, or are they only odd biological phenomena, making things good or bad for *us*, but in themselves indifferent? How can your pure intellect decide? If your heart does not want a world of moral reality, your head will assuredly never make you believe in one. Mephistophelian scepticism, indeed, will satisfy the head's play-instincts much better than any rigorous idealism can. Some men (even at the student age) are so naturally cool-hearted that the moralistic hypothesis never has for them any pungent life, and in their supercilious presence the hot young moralist always feels strangely ill at ease. The appearance of knowingness is on their side, of *naiveté* and gullibility on his. Yet, in the inarticulate heart of him, he clings to it that he is not a dupe, and that there is a realm in which (as Emerson says) all their wit and intellectual superiority is no better than the cunning of a fox. Moral scepticism can no more be refuted or proved by logic than intellectual scepticism can. When we stick to it that there is truth (be it of either kind), we do so with our whole nature, and resolve to stand or fall by the results. The sceptic with his whole nature adopts the doubting attitude; but which of us is the wiser, Omniscience only knows.

Turn now from these wide questions of good to a certain class of questions of fact, questions concerning personal relations, states of mind between one man and another. *Do you like me or not?*—for example. Whether you do or not depends, in countless instances, on whether I meet you half-way, am willing to assume that you must like me, and show you trust and expectation. The previous faith on my part in your liking's existence is in such cases what makes your liking come. But if I stand aloof, and refuse to budge an inch until I have objective evidence, until you shall have done something apt, as the absolutists say, *ad extorquendum assensum meum*, ten to one your liking never comes. How many women's hearts are vanquished by the mere sanguine insistence of some man that they must love him! He will not consent to the hypothesis that they cannot. The desire for a certain kind of truth here brings about that special truth's existence; and so it is in innumerable cases of other sorts. Who gains promotions, boons, appointments, but the man in whose life they are seen to play the part of live hypotheses, who discounts them, sacrifices other things for their sake before they have come, and takes risks for them in advance? His faith acts on the powers above him as a claim, and creates its own verification.

A social organism of any sort whatever, large or small, is what it is because each member proceeds to his own duty with a trust that the other members will simultaneously do theirs. Wherever a desired result is achieved by the co-operation of many independent persons, its existence as a fact is a pure consequence of the precursive faith in one another of those immediately concerned. A government, an army, a commercial system, a ship, a college, an athletic team, all exist on this condition, without which not only is nothing achieved, but nothing is even attempted. A whole train of passengers (individually brave enough) will be looted by a few highwaymen, simply because the latter can count on one another, while each passenger fears that if he makes a movement of resistance, he will be shot before any one else backs him up. If we believed that the whole car-full would rise at once with us, we should each severally rise, and train-robbing would never even be attempted. There are, then, cases where a fact cannot come at all unless a preliminary faith exists in its coming. *And where faith in a fact can help create the fact*, that would be an insane logic which should say that faith running ahead of scientific evidence is the 'lowest kind of immorality' into which a thinking being can fall. Yet such is the logic by which our scientific absolutists pretend to regulate our lives!

X

In truths dependent on our personal action, then, faith based on desire is certainly a lawful and possibly an indispensable thing.

But now, it will be said, these are all childish human cases, and have nothing to do with great cosmic matters, like the question of religious faith. Let us then pass on to that. Religions differ so much in their accidents that in discussing the religious question we must make it very generic and broad. What then do we now mean by the religious hypothesis? Science says things are; morality says some things are better than other things; and religion says essentially two things.

First, she says that the best things are the more eternal things, the overlapping things, the things in the universe that throw the last stone, so to speak, and say the final word. "Perfection is eternal,"—this phrase of Charles Secrétan seems a good way of putting this first affirmation of religion, an affirmation which obviously cannot yet be verified scientifically at all.

The second affirmation of religion is that we are better off even now if we believe her first affirmation to be true.

Now, let us consider what the logical elements of this situation are *in case the religious hypothesis in both its branches be really true.* (Of course, we must admit that possibility at the outset. If we are to discuss the question at all, it must involve a living option. If for any of you religion be a hypothesis that cannot, by any living possibility be true, then you need go no farther. I speak to the 'saving remnant' alone.) So proceeding, we see, first, that religion offers itself as a *momentous* option. We are supposed to gain, even now, by our belief, and to lose by our nonbelief, a certain vital good. Secondly, religion is a *forced* option, so far as that good goes. We cannot escape the issue by remaining sceptical and waiting for more light, because, although we do avoid error in that way *if religion be untrue*, we lose the good, *if it be true*, just as certainly as if we positively chose to disbelieve. It is as if a man should hesitate indefinitely to ask a certain woman to marry him because he was not perfectly sure that she would prove an angel after he brought her home. Would he not cut himself off from that particular angel-possibility as decisively as if he went and married some one else? Scepticism, then, is not avoidance of option; it is option of a certain particular kind of risk. *Better risk loss of truth than chance of error,*—that is your faith-vetoer's exact position. He is actively playing his stake as much as the believer is; he is backing the field against the religious hypothesis, just as the believer is backing the religious hypothesis against the field. To preach scepticism to us as a duty until 'sufficient evidence' for religion be found, is tantamount therefore to telling us, when in presence of the religious hypothesis, that to yield to our fear of its being error is wiser and better than to yield to our hope that it may be true. It is not intellect against all passions, then; it is only intellect with one passion laying down its law. And by what, forsooth, is the supreme wisdom of this passion warranted? Dupery for dupery, what proof is there that dupery through hope is so much worse than dupery through fear? I, for one, can see no proof; and I simply refuse obedience to the scientist's command to imitate his kind of option, in a case where my own stake is important enough to give me the right to choose my own form of risk. If religion be true and the evidence for it be still insufficient, I do not wish, by putting your extinguisher upon my nature (which feels to me as if it had after all some business in this matter), to forfeit my sole chance in life of getting upon the winning side,—that chance depending, of course, on my willingness to run the risk of acting as if my passional need of taking the world religiously might be prophetic and right.

All this is on the supposition that it really may be prophetic and right, and that, even to us who are discussing the matter, religion is a live hypothesis which may be true. Now, to most of us religion comes in a still further way that makes a veto on our active faith even more illogical. The more perfect and more eternal aspect of the universe is represented in our religions as having personal form. The universe is no longer a mere *It* to us, but a *Thou,* if we are religious; and any relation that may be possible from person to person might be possible here. For instance, although in one sense we are passive portions of the universe, in another we show a curious autonomy, as if we were small active centres on our own account. We feel, too, as if the appeal of religion to us were made to our own active good-will, as if evidence might be forever withheld from us unless we met the hypothesis half-way. To take a trivial illustration: just as a man who in a company of gentlemen made no advances, asked a warrant for every concession, and believed no one's word without proof, would cut himself off by such churlishness from all the social rewards that a more trusting spirit would earn,—so here, one who should shut himself up in snarling logicality and try to make the gods extort his recognition willy-nilly, or not get it at all, might cut himself off forever from his only opportunity of making the gods' acquaintance. This feeling, forced on us we know not whence, that by obstinately believing that there are gods (although not to do so would be so easy both for our logic and our life) we are doing the universe the deepest service we can, seems part of the living essence of the religious hypothesis. If the hypothesis were true in all its parts, including this one, then pure intellectualism, with its veto on our making willing advances, would be an absurdity; and some participation of our sympathetic nature would be logically required. I, therefore, for one, cannot see my way to accepting the agnostic rules for truth-seeking, or wilfully agree to keep my willing nature out of the game. I cannot do so for this plain reason, that *a rule of thinking which would absolutely prevent me from acknowledging certain kinds of truth if those kinds of truth were really there, would be an irrational rule.* That for me is the long and short of the formal logic of the situation, no matter what the kinds of truth might materially be.

I confess I do not see how this logic can be escaped. But sad experience makes me fear that some of you may still shrink from radically saying with me, *in abstracto*, that we have the right to believe at our own risk any hypothesis that is live enough to tempt our will. I suspect, however, that if this is so, it is because you have got away from the abstract logical point of view altogether, and are thinking (perhaps without realizing it) of some particular religious hypothesis which for you is dead. The freedom to 'believe what we will' you apply to the case of some patent superstition; and the faith you think of is the faith defined by the schoolboy when he said, "Faith is when you believe something that you know ain't true." I can only repeat that this is misapprehension. *In concreto*, the freedom to believe can only cover living options which the intellect of the individual cannot by itself resolve; and living options never seem absurdities to him who has them to consider. When I look at the religious question as it really puts itself to concrete men, and when I think of all the possibilities which both practically and theoretically it involves, then this command that we shall put a stopper on our heart, instincts, and courage, and *wait*—acting of course meanwhile more or less as if religion were *not* true[2]—till doomsday, or till such time as our intellect and senses working together may have raked in evidence enough,—this command, I say, seems to me the queerest idol ever manufactured in the philosophic cave. Were we scholastic absolutists, there might be more excuse. If we had an infallible intellect with its objective certitudes, we might feel ourselves disloyal to such a perfect organ of knowledge in not trusting to it exclusively, in not waiting for its releasing word. But if we are empiricists, if we believe that no bell in us tolls to let us know for certain when truth is in our grasp, then it seems a piece of idle fantasticality to preach so solemnly our duty of waiting for the bell. Indeed we *may* wait if we will,—I hope you do not think that I am denying that,—but if we do so, we do so at our peril as much as if we believed. In either case we *act*, taking our life in our hands. No one of us ought to issue vetoes to the other, nor should we bandy words of abuse. We ought, on the contrary, delicately and profoundly to respect one another's mental freedom: then only shall we bring about the intellectual republic; then only shall we have that spirit of inner tolerance without which all our outer tolerance is soulless, and which is empiricism's glory; then only shall we live and let live, in speculative as well as in practical things.

I began by a reference to Fitz James Stephen: let me end by a quotation from him, "What do you think of yourself? What do you think of the world? . . . These are questions with which all must deal as it seems good to them. They are riddles of the Sphinx, and in some way or other we must deal with them. . . . In all important transactions of life we have to take a leap in the dark. . . . If we decide to leave the riddles unanswered, that is a choice; if we waver in our answer, that, too, is a choice: but whatever choice we make, we make it at our peril. If a man chooses to turn his back altogether on God and the future, no one can prevent him; no one can show beyond reasonable doubt that *he* is mistaken. If a man thinks otherwise and acts as he thinks, I do not see that any one can prove that he is mistaken. Each must act as he thinks best; and if he is wrong, so much the worse for him. We stand on a mountain pass in the midst of whirling snow and blinding mist through which we get glimpses now and then of paths which may be deceptive. If we stand still we shall be frozen to death. If we take the wrong road we shall be dashed to pieces. We do not certainly know whether there is any right one. What must we do? 'Be strong and of a good courage.' Act for the best, hope for the best, and take what comes. . . . If death ends all, we cannot meet death better."[3]

Notes

An Address to the Philosophical Clubs of Yale and Brown Universities. Published in the New World, June, 1896.

1. Compare Wilfrid Ward's Essay, "The Wish to Believe," in his *Witnesses to the Unseen*, Macmillan & Co., 1893.

2. Since belief is measured by action, he who forbids us to believe religion to be true, necessarily also forbids us to act as we should if we did believe it to be true. The whole defence of

religious faith hinges upon action. If the action required or inspired by the religious hypothesis is in no way different from that dictated by the naturalistic hypothesis, then religious faith is a pure superfluity, better pruned away, and controversy about its legitimacy is a piece of idle trifling, unworthy of serious minds. I myself believe, of course, that the religious hypothesis gives to the world an expression which specifically determines our reactions, and makes them in a large part unlike what they might be on a purely naturalistic scheme of belief.

3. *Liberty, Equality, Fraternity*, p. 353, second edition. London, 1874.

Originally published in 1917, this paper criticizes traditional empiricism's conception of experience and lays the groundwork for Dewey's pragmatic naturalism.

JOHN DEWEY

The Need for a Recovery of Philosophy

Intellectual advance occurs in two ways. At times increase of knowledge is organized about old conceptions, while these are expanded, elaborated and refined, but not seriously revised, much less abandoned. At other times, the increase of knowledge demands qualitative rather than quantitative change; alteration, not addition. Men's minds grow cold to their former intellectual concerns; ideas that were burning fade; interests that were urgent seem remote. Men face in another direction; their older perplexities are unreal; considerations passed over as negligible loom up. Former problems may not have been solved, but they no longer press for solution.

Philosophy is no exception to the rule. But it is unusually conservative—not, necessarily, in proffering solutions, but in clinging to problems. It has been so allied with theology and theological morals as representatives of men's chief interests, that radical alteration has been shocking. Men's activities took a decidedly new turn, for example, in the seventeenth century, and it seemed as if philosophy, under the lead of thinkers like Bacon and Descartes, was to execute an about-face. But, in spite of the ferment, it turned out that many of the older problems were but translated from Latin into the vernacular or into the new terminology furnished by science.

The association of philosophy with academic teaching has reinforced this intrinsic conservatism. Scholastic philosophy persisted in universities after men's thoughts outside of the walls of colleges had moved in other directions. In the last hundred years intellectual advances of science and politics have in like fashion been crystallized into material of instruction and now resist further change. I would not say that the spirit of teaching is hostile to that of liberal inquiry, but a philosophy which exists largely as something to be taught rather than wholly as something to be reflected upon is conducive to discussion of views held by others rather than to immediate response. Philosophy when taught inevitably magnifies the history of past thought, and leads professional philosophers to approach their subject-matter through its formulation in received systems. It tends, also, to emphasize points upon which men have divided into schools, for these lend themselves to retrospective definition and elaboration. Consequently, philosophical discussion is likely to be a dressing out of antithetical traditions, where criticism of one view is thought to afford proof of the truth of its opposite (as if formulation of views guaranteed logical exclusives). Direct preoccupation with contemporary difficulties is left to literature and politics.

If changing conduct and expanding knowledge ever required a willingness to surrender not merely old solutions but old problems it is now. I do not mean that we can turn abruptly away from all traditional issues. This is impossible; it would be the undoing of the one who attempted it. Irrespective of the professionalizing of philosophy, the ideas philosophers discuss are still those in which Western civilization has been bred. They are in the backs of the heads of educated people. But what serious-minded men not engaged in the professional business of philosophy most want to know is what modifications and abandonments of intellectual inheritance are required by the newer industrial, political, and scientific movements. They want to know what these newer movements mean when translated into general ideas. Unless professional philosophy can mobilize itself sufficiently to assist in this clarification and redirection of men's thoughts, it is likely to get more and more sidetracked from the main currents of contemporary life.

This essay may, then, be looked upon as an attempt to forward the emancipation of philosophy from too intimate and exclusive attachment to traditional problems. It is not in intent a criticism of various solutions that have been offered, but raises a question *as to the genuineness, under the present conditions of science and social life, of the problems.*

The limited object of my discussion will, doubtless, give an exaggerated impression of my conviction as to the artificiality of much recent philosophizing. Not that I have wilfully exaggerated in what I have said, but that the limitations of my purpose have led me not to say many things pertinent to a broader purpose. A discussion less restricted would strive to enforce the genuineness, in their own context, of questions now discussed mainly because they have been discussed rather than because contemporary conditions of life suggest them. It would also be a grateful task to dwell upon the precious contributions made by philosophic systems which as a whole are impossible. In the course of the development of unreal premises and the discussion of artificial problems, points of view have emerged which are indispensable possessions of culture. The horizon has been widened; ideas of great fecundity struck out; imagination quickened; a sense of the meaning of things created. It may even be asked whether these accompaniments of classic systems have not often been treated as a kind of guarantee of the systems themselves. But while it is a sign of an illiberal mind to throw away the fertile and ample ideas of a Spinoza, a Kant, or a Hegel, because their setting is not logically adequate, it is surely a sign of an undisciplined one to treat their contributions to culture as confirmations of premises with which they have no necessary connection.

I

A criticism of current philosophizing from the standpoint of the traditional quality of its problems must begin somewhere, and the choice of a beginning is arbitrary.

It has appeared to me that the notion of experience implied in the questions most actively discussed gives a natural point of departure. For, if I mistake not, it is just the inherited view of experience common to the empirical school and its opponents which keeps alive many discussions even of matters that on their face are quite remote from it, while it is also this view which is most untenable in the light of existing science and social practice. Accordingly I set out with a brief statement of some of the chief contrasts between the orthodox description of experience and that congenial to present conditions.

(i) In the orthodox view, experience is regarded primarily as a knowledge-affair. But to eyes not looking through ancient spectacles, it assuredly appears as an affair of the intercourse of a living being with its physical and social environment. (ii) According to tradition experience is (at least primarily) a psychical thing, infected throughout by "subjectivity." What experience suggests about itself is a genuinely objective world which enters into the actions and sufferings of men and undergoes modifications through their responses. (iii) So far as anything beyond a bare present is recognized by the established doctrine, the past exclusively counts. Registration of what has taken place, reference to precedent, is believed to be the essence of experience. Empiricism is conceived of as tied up to what has been, or is, "given." But experience in its vital form is experimental, an effort to change the given; it is characterized by projection, by reaching forward into the unknown; connexion with a future is its salient trait. (iv) The empirical tradition is committed to particularism. Connexions and continuities are supposed to be foreign to experience, to be by-products of dubious validity. An experience that is an undergoing of an environment and a striving for its control in new directions is pregnant with connexions. (v) In the traditional notion experience and thought are antithetical terms. Inference, so far as it is other than a revival of what has been given in the past, goes beyond experience; hence it is either invalid, or else a measure of desperation by which, using experience as a springboard, we jump out to a world of stable things and other selves. But experience, taken free of the restrictions imposed by the older concept, is full of inference. There is, apparently, no conscious experience without inference; reflection is native and constant.

These contrasts, with a consideration of the effect of substituting the account of experience relevant to modern life for the inherited account, afford the subject-matter of the following discussion.

Suppose we take seriously the contribution made to our idea of experience by biology,—not that recent biological science discovered the facts, but that it has so emphasized them that there is no longer an excuse for ignoring them or treating them as negligible. Any account of experience must now fit into the consideration that experiencing means living; and that living goes on in and because of an environing medium, not in a vacuum. Where there is experience, there is a living being. Where there is life, there is a double connexion maintained with the environment. In part, environmental energies constitute organic functions; they enter into them. Life is not possible without such direct support by the environment. But while all organic changes depend upon the natural energies of the environment for their origination and occurrence, the natural energies sometimes carry the organic functions prosperously forward, and sometimes act counter to their continuance. Growth and decay, health and disease, are alike continuous with activities of the natural surroundings. The difference lies in the bearing of what happens upon future life-activity. From the standpoint of this future reference environmental incidents fall into groups: those favorable to life-activities, and those hostile.

The successful activities of the organism, those within which environmental assistance is incorporated, react upon the environment to bring about modifications favorable to their own future. The human being has upon his hands the problem of responding to what is going on around him so that these changes will take one turn rather than another, namely, that required by its own further functioning. While backed in part by the environment, its life is anything but a peaceful exhalation of environment. It is obliged to struggle—that is to say, to employ the direct support given by the environment in order indirectly to effect changes that would not otherwise occur. In this sense, life goes on by means of controlling the environment. Its activities must change the changes going on around it; they must neutralize hostile occurrences; they must transform neutral events into cooperative factors or into an efflorescence of new features.

Dialectic developments of the notion of self-preservation, of the *conatus essendi*, often ignore all the important facts of the actual process. They argue as if self-control, self-development, went on directly as a sort of unrolling push from within. But life endures only in virtue of the support of the environment. And since the environment is only incompletely enlisted in our behalf, self-preservation—or self-realization or whatever—is always indirect—always an affair of the way in which our present activities affect the direction taken by independent changes in the surroundings. Hindrances must be turned into means.

We are also given to playing loose with the conception of adjustment, as if that meant something fixed—a kind of accommodation once for all (ideally at least) of the organism *to* an environment. But as life requires the fitness of the environment to the organic functions, adjustment to the environment means not passive acceptance of the latter, but acting so that the environing changes take a certain turn. The "higher" the type of life, the more adjustment takes the form of an adjusting of the factors of the environment to one another in the interest of life; the less the significance of living, the more it becomes an adjustment to a given environment till at the lower end of the scale the differences between living and the nonliving disappear.

These statements are of an external kind. They are about the conditions of experience, rather than about experiencing itself. But assuredly experience as it concretely takes place bears out the statements. Experience is primarily a process of undergoing: a process of standing something; of suffering and passion, of affection, in the literal sense of these words. The organism has to endure, to undergo, the consequences of its own actions. Experience is no slipping along in a path fixed by inner consciousness.

Private consciousness is an incidental outcome of experience of a vital objective sort; it is not its source. Undergoing, however, is never mere passivity. The most patient patient is more than a receptor. He is also an agent—a reactor, one trying experiments, one concerned with undergoing in a way which may influence what is still to happen. Sheer endurance, side-stepping evasions, are, after all, ways of treating the environment with a view to what such treatment will accomplish. Even if we shut ourselves up in the most clam-like fashion, we are doing something; our passivity is an active attitude, not an extinction of response. Just as there is no assertive action, no aggressive attack upon things as they are, which is all action, so there is no undergoing which is not on our part also a going on and a going through.

Experience, in other words, is a matter of *simultaneous* doings and sufferings. Our undergoings are experiments in varying the course of events; our active tryings are trials and tests of ourselves. This duplicity of experience shows itself in our happiness and misery, our successes and failures. Triumphs are dangerous when dwelt upon or lived off from; successes use themselves up. Any achieved equilibrium of adjustment with the environment is precarious because we cannot evenly keep pace with changes in the environment. These are so opposed in direction that we must choose. We must take the risk of casting in our lot with one movement or the other. Nothing can eliminate all risk, all adventure; the one thing doomed to failure is to try to keep even with the whole environment at once—that is to say, to maintain the happy moment when all things go our way.

The obstacles which confront us are stimuli to variation, to novel response, and hence are occasions of progress. If a favor done us by the environment conceals a threat, so its disfavor is a potential means of hitherto unexperienced modes of success. To treat misery as anything but misery, as for example a blessing in disguise or a necessary factor in good, is disingenuous apologetics. But to say that the progress of the race has been stimulated by ills undergone, and that men have been moved by what they suffer to search out new and better courses of action is to speak veraciously.

The preoccupation of experience with things which are coming (are now coming, not just to come) is obvious to any one whose interest in experience is empirical. Since we live forward; since we live in a world where changes are going on whose issue means our weal or woe; since every act of ours modifies these changes and hence is fraught with promise, or charged with hostile energies—what should experience be but a future implicated in a present! Adjustment is no timeless state; it is a continuing process. To say that a change takes time may be to say something about the event which is external and uninstructive. But adjustment of organism to environment takes time in the pregnant sense; every step in the process is conditioned by reference to further changes which it effects. What is going on in the environment is the concern of the organism; not what is already "there" in accomplished and finished form. In so far as the issue of what is going on may be affected by intervention of the organism, the moving event is a challenge which stretches the agent-patient to meet what is coming. Experiencing exhibits things in their unterminated aspect moving toward determinate conclusions. The finished and done with is of import as affecting the future, not on its own account: in short, because it is not, really, done with.

Anticipation is therefore more primary than recollection; projection than summoning of the past; the prospective than the retrospective. Given a world like that in which we live, a world in which environing changes are partly favorable and partly callously indifferent, and experience is bound to be prospective in import; for any control attainable by the living creature depends upon what is done to alter the state of things. Success and failure are the primary "categories" of life; achieving of good and averting of ill are its supreme interests; hope and anxiety (which are not self-enclosed states of feeling, but active attitudes of welcome and wariness) are dominant qualities of experience. Imaginative forecast of the future is this forerunning quality of behavior rendered available for guidance in the present. Day-dreaming and castle-building and esthetic realization of what is not practically achieved are offshoots of this practical trait, or else practical intelligence is a chastened fantasy. It makes little difference. Imaginative recovery of the bygone is indispensable to successful invasion of the future, but its status is that of an instrument. To ignore its import is the sign of an undisciplined agent; but to isolate the past, dwelling upon it for its own sake and giving it the eulogistic name of knowledge, is to substitute the reminiscence of old-age for effective intelligence. The movement of the agent-patient to meet the future is partial and passionate; yet detached and impartial study of the past is the only alternative to luck in assuring success to passion.

II

This description of experience would be but a rhapsodic celebration of the commonplace were it not in marked contrast to orthodox philosophical accounts. The contrast indicates that traditional accounts have not been empirical, but have been deductions, from unnamed premises, of what experience *must* be. Historic empiricism has been empirical in a technical and controversial sense. It has said, Lord, Lord, Experience, Experience; but in practice it has served ideas *forced into* experience, not *gathered from* it.

The confusion and artificiality thereby introduced into philosophical thought is nowhere more evident than in the empirical treatment of relations or dynamic continuities. The experience of a living being struggling to hold its own and make its way in an environment, physical and social, partly facilitating and partly obstructing its actions, is of necessity a matter of ties and connexions, of bearings and uses. The very point of experience, so to say, is that it doesn't occur in a vacuum; its agent-patient instead of being insulated and disconnected is bound up with the movement of things by most intimate and pervasive bonds. Only because the organism is in and of the world, and its activities correlated with those of other things in multiple ways, is it susceptible to undergoing things and capable of trying to reduce objects to means of securing its good fortune. That these connexions are of diverse kinds is irresistibly proved by the fluctuations which occur in its career. Help and hindrance, stimulation and inhibition, success and failure mean specifically different modes of correlation. Although the actions of things in the world are taking place in one continuous stretch of existence, there are all kinds of specific affinities, repulsions, and relative indifferences.

Dynamic connexions are qualitatively diverse, just as are the centers of action. *In this sense*, pluralism, not monism, is an established empirical fact. The attempt to establish monism from consideration of the very nature of a relation is a mere piece of dialectics. Equally dialectical is the effort to establish by a consideration of the nature of relations an ontological Pluralism of Ultimates: *simple and independent beings*. To attempt to get results from a consideration of the "external" nature of relations is of a piece with the attempt to deduce results from their "internal" character. Some things are relatively insulated from the influence of other things; some things are easily invaded by others; some things are fiercely attracted to conjoin their activities with those of others. Experience exhibits every kind of connexion[1] from the most intimate to mere external juxtaposition.

Empirically, then, active bonds or continuities of all kinds, together with static discontinuities, characterize existence. To deny this qualitative heterogeneity is to reduce the struggles and difficulties of life, its comedies and tragedies to illusion: to the non-being of the Greeks or to its modern counterpart, the "subjective." Experience is an affair of facilitations and checks, of being sustained and disrupted, being let alone, being helped and troubled, of good fortune and defeat in all the countless qualitative modes which these words pallidly suggest. The existence of genuine connexions of all manner of heterogeneity cannot be doubted. Such words as conjoining, disjoining, resisting, modifying, saltatory, and ambulatory (to use James' picturesque term) only hint at their actual heterogeneity.

Among the revisions and surrenders of historic problems demanded by this feature of empirical situations, those centering in the rationalistic-empirical controversy may be selected for attention. The implications of this controversy are twofold: First, that connexions are as homogeneous in fact as in name; and, secondly, if genuine, are all due to thought, or, if empirical, are arbitrary by-products of past particulars. The stubborn particularism of orthodox empiricism is its outstanding trait; consequently the opposed rationalism found no justification of bearings, continuities, and ties save to refer them in gross to the work of a hyper-empirical Reason.

Of course, not all empiricism prior to Hume and Kant was sensationalistic, pulverizing "experience" into isolated sensory qualities or simple ideas. It did not all follow Locke's lead in regarding the entire content of generalization as the "workmanship of the understanding." On the Continent, prior to Kant, philosophers were content to draw a line between empirical generalizations regarding matters of fact and necessary universals applying to truths of reason. But logical atomism was implicit even in this theory. Statements referring to empirical fact were mere quantitative summaries of particular instances. In the sensationalism which sprang from Hume (and which was left unquestioned by Kant as far as any strictly empirical element was concerned) the implicit particularism was made explicit. But the doctrine that sensations and ideas are so many separate existences was not derived from observation nor from experiment. It was a logical deduction from a prior unexamined concept of the nature of experience. From the same concept it followed that the appearance of stable objects and of general principles of connexion was but an appearance.[2]

Kantianism, then, naturally invoked universal bonds to restore objectivity. But, in so doing, it accepted the particularism of experience and proceeded to supplement it from non-empirical sources. A sensory manifold being all which is really empirical in experience, a reason which transcends experience must provide synthesis. The net outcome might have suggested a correct account of experience. For we have only to forget the apparatus by which the net outcome is arrived at, to have before us the experience of the plain man—a diversity of ceaseless changes connected in all kinds of ways, static and dynamic. This conclusion would deal a deathblow to both empiricism and rationalism. For, making clear the non-empirical character of the alleged manifold of unconnected particulars, it would render unnecessary the appeal to functions of the understanding in order to connect them. With the downfall of the traditional notion of experience, the appeal to reason to supplement its defects becomes superfluous.

The tradition was, however, too strongly entrenched; especially as it furnished the subject-matter of an alleged science of states of mind which were directly known in their very presence. The historic outcome was a new crop of artificial puzzles about relations; it fastened upon philosophy for a long time the quarrel about the *a priori* and the *a posteriori* as its chief issue. The controversy is to-day quiescent. Yet it is not at all uncommon to find thinkers modern in tone and intent who regard any philosophy of experience as necessarily committed to denial of the existence of genuinely general propositions, and who take empiricism to be inherently averse to the recognition of the importance of an organizing and constructive intelligence.

The quiescence alluded to is in part due, I think, to sheer weariness. But it is also due to a change of standpoint introduced by biological conceptions; and particularly the discovery of biological continuity from the lower organisms to man. For a short period, Spencerians might connect the doctrine of evolution with the old problem, and use the long temporal accumulation of "experiences" to generate something which, for human experience, is *a priori*. But the tendency of the biological way of thinking is neither to confirm or negate the Spencerian doctrine, but to shift the issue. In the orthodox position *a posteriori* and *a priori* were affairs of knowledge. But it soon becomes obvious that while there is assuredly something *a priori*—that is to say, native, unlearned, original—in human experience, that something is *not* knowledge, but is activities made possible by means of established connexions of neurones. This empirical fact does not solve the orthodox problem; it dissolves it. It shows that the problem was misconceived, and solution sought by both parties in the wrong direction.

Organic instincts and organic retention, or habit-forming, are undeniable factors in actual experience. They are factors which effect organization and secure continuity. They are among the specific facts which a description of experience cognizant of the correlation of organic action with the action of other natural objects will include. But while fortunately the contribution of biological science to a truly empirical description of experiencing has outlawed the discussion of the *a priori* and *a posteriori*, the transforming effect of the same contributions upon other issues has gone unnoticed, save as pragmatism has made an effort to bring them to recognition.

III

The point seriously at issue in the notion of experience common to both sides in the older controversy thus turns out to be the place of thought or intelligence in experience. Does reason have a distinctive office? Is there a characteristic order of relations contributed by it?

Experience, to return to our positive conception, is primarily what is undergone in connexion with activities whose import lies in their objective consequences—their bearing upon future experiences. Organic functions deal with things as things in course, in operation, in a state of affairs not yet given or completed. What is done with, what is just "there," is of concern only in the potentialities which it may indicate. As ended, as wholly given, it is of no account. But as a sign of what may come, it becomes an indispensable factor in behavior dealing with changes, the outcome of which is not yet determined.

The only power the organism possesses to control its own future depends upon the way its present responses modify changes which are taking place in its medium. A living being may be comparatively impotent, or comparatively free. It is all a matter of the way in which its present reactions to things influence the future reactions of things upon it. Without regard to its wish or intent every act it performs makes some difference in the environment. The change may be trivial as respects its own career and fortune. But it may also be of incalculable importance; it may import harm, destruction, or it may procure well-being.

Is it possible for a living being to increase its control of welfare and success? Can it manage, in any degree, to assure its future? Or does the amount of security depend wholly upon the accidents of the situation? Can it learn? Can it gain ability to assure its future in the present? These questions center attention upon the significance of reflective intelligence in the process of experience. The extent of an agent's capacity for inference, its power to use a given fact as a sign of something not yet given, measures the extent of its ability systematically to enlarge its control of the future.

A being which can use given and finished facts as signs of things to come; which can take given things as evidences of absent things, can, in that degree, forecast the future; it can form reasonable expectations. It is capable of achieving ideas; it is possessed of intelligence. For use of the given or finished to anticipate the consequence of processes going on is precisely what is meant by "ideas," by "intelligence."

As we have already noted, the environment is rarely all of a kind in its bearing upon organic welfare; its most whole-hearted support of life-activities is precarious and temporary. Some environmental changes are auspicious; others are menacing. The secret of success—that is, of the greatest attainable success—is for the organic response to cast in its lot with present auspicious changes to strengthen them and thus to avert the consequences flowing from occurrences of ill-omen. Any reaction is a venture; it involves risk. We always build better or worse than we can foretell. But the organism's fateful intervention in the course of events is blind, its choice is random, except as it can employ what happens to it as a basis of inferring what is likely to happen later. In the degree in which it can read future results in present on-goings, its responsive choice, its partiality to this condition or that, become intelligent. Its bias grows reasonable. It can deliberately, intentionally, participate in the direction of the course of affairs. Its foresight of different futures which result according as this or that present factor predominates in the shaping of affairs permits it to partake intelligently instead of blindly and fatally in the consequences its reactions give rise to. Participate it must, and to its own weal or woe. Inference, the use of what happens, to anticipate what will—or at least may—happen, makes the difference between directed and undirected participation. And this capacity for inferring is precisely the same as that use of natural occurrences for the discovery and determination of consequences—the formation of new dynamic connexions—which constitutes knowledge.

The fact that thought is an intrinsic feature of experience is fatal to the traditional empiricism which makes it an artificial by-product. But for that same reason it is fatal to the historic rationalisms whose justification was the secondary and retrospective position assigned to thought by empirical philosophy. According to the particularism of the latter, thought was inevitably only a bunching together of hard-and-fast separate items; thinking was but the gathering together and tying of items already completely given, or else an equally artificial untying—a mechanical adding and subtracting of the given. It was but a cumulative registration, a consolidated merger; generality was a matter of bulk, not of quality. Thinking was therefore treated as lacking constructive power; even its organizing capacity was but simulated, being in truth but arbitrary pigeonholing. Genuine projection of the novel, deliberate variation and invention, are idle fictions in such a version of experience. If there ever was creation, it all took place at a remote period. Since then the world has only recited lessons.

The value of inventive construction is too precious to be disposed of in this cavalier way. Its unceremonious denial afforded an opportunity to assert that in addition to experience the subject has a ready-made faculty of thought or reason which transcends experience. Rationalism thus accepted the account of experience given by traditional empiricism, and introduced reason as extra-empirical. There are still thinkers who regard any empiricism as necessarily committed to a belief in a cut-and-dried reliance upon disconnected precedents, and who hold that all systematic organization of past experiences for new and constructive purposes is alien to strict empiricism.

Rationalism never explained, however, how a reason extraneous to experience could enter into helpful relation with concrete experiences. By definition, reason and experience were antithetical, so that the concern of reason was not the fruitful expansion and guidance of the course of experience, but a realm of considerations too sublime to touch, or be touched by, experience. Discreet rationalists confined themselves to theology and allied branches of abstruse science, and to mathematics. Rationalism would have been a doctrine reserved for academic specialists and abstract formalists had it not assumed the task of providing an apologetics for traditional morals and theology, thereby getting into touch with actual human beliefs and concerns. It is notorious that historic empiricism was strong in criticism and in demolition of outworn beliefs, but weak for purposes of constructive social direction. But we frequently overlook the fact that whenever rationalism cut free from conservative apologetics, it was also simply an instrumentality for pointing out inconsistencies and absurdities in existing beliefs—a sphere in which it was immensely useful, as the Enlightenment shows. Leibniz and Voltaire were contemporary rationalists in more senses than one.[3]

The recognition that reflection is a genuine factor within experience and an indispensable factor in that control of the world which secures a prosperous and significant expansion of experience undermines historic rationalism as assuredly as it abolishes the foundations of historic empiricism. The bearing of a correct idea of the place and office of reflection upon modern idealisms is less obvious, but no less certain.

One of the curiosities of orthodox empiricism is that its outstanding speculative problem is the existence of an "external world." For in accordance with the notion that experience is attached to a private subject as its exclusive possession, a world like the one in which we appear to live must be "external" to experience instead of being its subject-matter. I call it a curiosity, for if anything seems adequately grounded empirically it is the existence of a world which resists the characteristic functions of the subject of experience; which goes its way, in some respects, independently of these functions, and which frustrates our hopes and intentions. Ignorance which is fatal; disappointment; the need of adjusting means and ends to the course of nature, would seem to be facts sufficiently characterizing empirical situations as to render the existence of an external world indubitable.

That the description of experience was arrived at by forcing actual empirical facts into conformity with dialectic developments from a concept of a knower outside of the real world of nature is testified to by the historic alliance of empiricism and idealism.[4] According to the most logically consistent editions of orthodox empiricism, all that can be experienced is the fleeting, the momentary, mental state. That alone is absolutely and indubitably present; therefore, it alone is cognitively certain. It alone is *knowledge*. The existence of the past (and of the future), of a decently stable world and of other selves—indeed, of one's own self—falls outside this datum of experience. These can be arrived at only by inference which is "ejective"—a name given to an alleged type of inference that jumps from experience, as from a springboard, to something beyond experience.

I should not anticipate difficulty in showing that this doctrine is, dialectically, a mass of inconsistencies. Avowedly it is a doctrine of desperation, and as such it is cited here to show the desperate straits to which ignoring empirical facts has reduced a doctrine of experience. More positively instructive are the objective idealisms which have been the offspring of the marriage between the "reason" of historic rationalism and the alleged immediate psychical stuff of historic empiricism. These idealisms have recognized the genuineness of connexions and the impotency of "feeling." They have then identified connexions with logical or rational connexions, and thus treated "the real World" as a synthesis of sentient consciousness by means of a rational self-consciousness introducing objectivity: stability and universality of reference.

Here again, for present purposes, criticism is unnecessary. It suffices to point out that the value of this theory is bound up with the genuineness of the problem of which it purports to be a solution. If the basic concept is a fiction, there is no call for the solution. The more important point is to perceive how far the "thought" which figures in objective idealism comes from meeting the empirical demands made upon actual thought. Idealism is much less formal than historic rationalism. It treats thought, or reason, as constitutive of experience by means of uniting and constructive functions, not as just concerned with a realm of eternal truths apart from experience. On such a view thought certainly loses its abstractness and remoteness. But, unfortunately, in thus gaining the whole world it loses its own self. A world already, in its intrinsic structure, dominated by thought is not a world in which, save by contradiction of premises, thinking has anything to do.

That the doctrine logically results in making change unreal and error unaccountable are consequences of importance in the technique of professional philosophy; in the denial of empirical fact which they imply they seem to many a *reductio ad absurdum* of the premises from which they proceed. But, after all, such consequences are of only professional import. What is serious, even sinister, is the implied sophistication regarding the place and office of reflection in the scheme of things. A doctrine which exalts thought in name while ignoring its efficacy in fact (that is, its use in bettering life) is a doctrine which cannot be entertained and taught without serious peril. Those who are not concerned with professional philosophy but who are solicitous for intelligence as a factor in the amelioration of actual conditions can but look askance at any doctrine which holds that the entire scheme of things is already, if we but acquire the knack of looking at it aright, fixedly and completely rational. It is a striking manifestation of the extent in which philosophies have been compensatory in quality.[5] But the matter cannot be passed over as if it were simply a question of not grudging a certain amount of consolation to one amid the irretrievable evils of life. For as to these evils no one knows how many are retrievable; and a philosophy which proclaims the ability of a dialectic theory of knowledge to reveal the world as already and eternally a self-luminous rational whole, contaminates the scope and use of thought at its very spring. To substitute the otiose insight gained by manipulation of a formula for the slow coöperative work of a humanity guided by reflective intelligence is more than a technical blunder of speculative philosophers.

A practical crisis may throw the relationship of ideas to life into an exaggerated Brocken-like spectral relief, where exaggeration renders perceptible features not ordinarily noted. The use of force to secure narrow because exclusive aims is no novelty in human affairs. The deploying of all the intelligence at command in order to increase the effectiveness of the force used is not so common, yet presents nothing intrinsically remarkable. The identification of force—military, economic, and administrative—with moral necessity and moral culture is, however, a phenomenon not likely to exhibit itself on a wide scale except where intelligence has already been suborned by an idealism which identifies "the actual with the rational," and thus finds the measure of reason in the brute event determined by superior force. If we are to have a philosophy which will intervene between attachment to rule of thumb muddling and devotion to a systematized subordination of intelligence to preëxistent ends, it can be found only in a philosophy which finds the ultimate measure of intelligence in consideration of a desirable future and in search for the means of bringing it progressively into existence. When professed idealism turns out to be a narrow pragmatism—narrow because taking for granted the finality of ends determined by historic conditions—the time has arrived for a pragmatism which shall be empirically idealistic, proclaiming the essential connexion of intelligence with the unachieved future—with possibilities involving a transfiguration.

IV

Why has the description of experience been so remote from the facts of empirical situations? To answer this question throws light upon the submergence of recent philosophizing in epistemology—that is, in discussions of the nature, possibility, and limits of knowledge in general, and in the attempt to reach conclusions regarding the ultimate nature of reality from the answers given to such questions.

The reply to the query regarding the currency of a non-empirical doctrine of experience (even among professed empiricists) is that the traditional account is derived from a conception once universally entertained regarding the subject or bearer or center of experience. The description of experience has been forced into conformity with this prior conception; it has been primarily a deduction from it, actual empirical facts being poured into the moulds of the deductions. The characteristic feature of this prior notion is the assumption that experience centers in, or gathers about, or proceeds from a center or subject which is outside the course of natural existence, and set over against it:—it being of no importance, for present purposes, whether this antithetical subject is termed soul, or spirit, or mind, or ego, or consciousness, or just knower or knowing subject.

There are plausible grounds for thinking that the currency of the idea in question lies in the form which men's religious preoccupations took for many centuries. These were deliberately and systematically otherworldly. They centered about a Fall which was not an event in nature, but an aboriginal catastrophe that corrupted Nature; about a redemption made possible by supernatural means; about a life in another world—essentially, not merely spatially, Other. The supreme drama of destiny took place in a soul or spirit which, under the circumstances, could not be conceived other than as non-natural—extra-natural, if not, strictly speaking, supernatural. When Descartes and others broke away from medieval interests, they retained as commonplaces its intellectual apparatus: Such as, knowledge is exercised by a power that is extra-natural and set over against the world to be known. Even if they had wished to make a complete break, they had nothing to put as knower in the place of the soul. It may be doubted whether there was any available empirical substitute until science worked out the fact that physical changes are functional correlations of energies, and that man is continuous with other forms of life, and until social life had developed an intellectually free and responsible individual as its agent.

But my main point is not dependent upon any particular theory as to the historic origin of the notion about the bearer of experience. The point is there on its own account. The essential thing is that the bearer was conceived as outside of the world; so that experience consisted in the bearer's being affected through a type of operations not found anywhere in the world, while knowledge consists in surveying the world, looking at it, getting the view of a spectator.

The theological problem of attaining knowledge of God as ultimate reality was transformed in effect into the philosophical problem of the possibility of attaining knowledge of reality. For how is one to get beyond the limits of the subject and subjective occurrences? Familiarity breeds credulity oftener than contempt. How can a problem be artificial when men have been busy discussing it almost for three hundred years? But if the assumption that experience is something set over against the world is contrary to fact, then the problem of how self or mind or subjective experience or consciousness can reach knowledge of an external world is assuredly a meaningless problem. Whatever questions there may be about knowledge, they will not be the kind of problems which have formed epistemology.

The problem of knowledge as conceived in the industry of epistemology is the problem of knowledge *in general*—of the possibility, extent, and validity of knowledge in general. What does this "in general" mean? In ordinary life there are problems a-plenty of knowledge in particular; every conclusion we try to reach, theoretical or practical, affords such a problem. But there is no problem of knowledge in general. I do not mean, of course, that general statements cannot be made about knowledge, or that the problem of attaining these general statements is not a genuine one. On the contrary, specific instances of success and failure in inquiry exist, and are of such a character that one can discover the conditions conducing to success and failure. Statement of these conditions constitutes logic, and is capable of being an important aid in proper guidance of further attempts at knowing. But this logical problem of knowledge is at the opposite pole from the epistemological. Specific problems are about right conclusions to be reached—which means, in effect, right ways of going about the business of inquiry. They imply a difference between knowledge and error consequent upon right and wrong methods of inquiry and testing; not a difference between experience and the world. The problem of knowledge *überhaupt* exists because it is assumed that there is a knower in general, who is outside of the world to be known, and who is defined in terms antithetical to the traits of the world. With analogous assumptions, we could invent and discuss a problem of digestion in general. All that would be required would be to conceive the stomach and food-material as inhabiting different worlds. Such an assumption would leave on our hands the question of the possibility, extent, nature, and genuineness of any transaction between stomach and food.

But because the stomach and food inhabit a continuous stretch of existence, because digestion is but a correlation of diverse activities in one world, the problems of digestion are specific and plural: What are the particular correlations which constitute it? How does it proceed in different situations? What is favorable and what unfavorable to its best performance?—and so on. Can one deny that if we were to take our clue from the present empirical situation, including the scientific notion of evolution (biological continuity) and the existing arts of control of nature, subject and object would be treated as occupying the same natural world as unhesitatingly as we assume the natural conjunction of an animal and its food? Would it not follow that knowledge is one way in which natural energies coöperate? Would there be airy problem save discovery of the peculiar structure of this coöperation, the conditions under which it occurs to best effect, and the consequences which issue from its occurrence?

It is a commonplace that the chief divisions of modern philosophy, idealism in its different kinds, realisms of various brands, so-called common-sense dualism, agnosticism, relativism, phenomenalism, have grown up around the epistemological problem of the general relation of subject and object. Problems not openly epistemological, such as whether the relation of changes in consciousness to physical changes is one of interaction, parallelism, or automatism have the same origin. What becomes of philosophy, consisting largely as it does of different answers to these questions, in case the assumptions which generate the questions have no empirical standing? Is it not time that philosophers turned from the attempt to determine the comparative merits of various replies to the questions to a consideration of the claims of the questions?

When dominating religious ideas were built up about the idea that the self is a stranger and pilgrim in this world; when morals, falling in line, found true good only in inner states of a self inaccessible to anything but its own private introspection; when political theory assumed the finality of disconnected and mutually exclusive personalities, the notion that the bearer of experience is antithetical to the world instead of being in and of it was congenial. It at least had the warrant of other beliefs and aspirations. But the doctrine of biological continuity or organic evolution has destroyed the scientific basis of the conception. Morally, men are now concerned with the amelioration of the conditions of the common lot in this world. Social sciences recognize that associated life is not a matter of physical juxtaposition, but of genuine intercourse—of community of experience in a non-metaphorical sense of community. Why should we longer try to patch up and refine and stretch the old solutions till they seem to cover the change of thought and practice? Why not recognize that the trouble is with the problem?

A belief in organic evolution which does not extend unreservedly to the way in which the subject of experience is thought of, and which does not strive to bring the entire theory of experience and knowing into line with biological and social facts, is hardly more than Pickwickian. There are many, for example, who hold that dreams, hallucinations, and errors cannot be accounted for at all except on the theory that a self (or "consciousness") exercises a modifying influence upon the "real object." The logical assumption is that consciousness is outside of the real object; that it is something different in kind, and therefore has the power of changing "reality" into appearance, of introducing "relativities" into things as they are in themselves—in short, of infecting real things with subjectivity. Such writers seem unaware of the fact that this assumption makes consciousness supernatural in the literal sense of the word; and that, to say the least, the conception can be accepted by one who accepts the doctrine of biological continuity only after every other way of dealing with the facts has been exhausted.

Realists, of course (at least some of the Neo-realists), deny any such miraculous intervention of consciousness. But they[6] admit the reality of the problem; denying only this particular solution, they try to find some other way out, which will still preserve intact the notion of knowledge as a relationship of a general sort between subject and object.

Now dreams and hallucinations, errors, pleasures, and pains, possibly "secondary" qualities, do not occur save where there are organic centers of experience. They cluster about a subject. But to treat them as things which inhere exclusively in the subject; or as posing the problem of a distortion of *the* real object by a knower set over against the world, or as presenting facts to be explained primarily as cases of contemplative knowledge, is to testify that one has still to learn the lesson of evolution in its application to the affairs in hand.

If biological development be accepted, the subject of experience is at least an animal, continuous with other organic forms in a process of more complex organization. An animal in turn is at least continuous with chemico-physical processes which, in living things, are so organized as really to constitute the activities of life with all their defining traits. And experience is not identical with brain action; it is the entire organic agent-patient in all its interaction with the environment, natural and social. The brain is primarily an organ of a certain kind of behavior, not of knowing the world. And to repeat what has already been said, experiencing *is* just certain modes of interaction, of correlation, of natural objects among which the organism happens, so to say, to be one. It follows with equal force that experience means primarily not knowledge, but ways of doing and suffering. Knowing must be described by discovering what particular mode—qualitatively unique—of doing and suffering it is. As it is, we find experience assimilated to a non-empirical concept of knowledge, derived from an antecedent notion of a spectator outside of the world.[7]

In short, the epistemological fashion of conceiving dreams, errors, "relativities," etc., depends upon the isolation of mind from intimate participation with other changes in the same continuous nexus. Thus it is like contending that when a bottle bursts, the bottle is, in some self-contained miraculous way, exclusively responsible. Since it is the nature of a bottle to be whole so as to retain fluids, bursting is an abnormal event—comparable to an hallucination. Hence it cannot belong to the "real" bottle; the "subjectivity" of glass is the cause. It is obvious that since the breaking of glass is a case of specific correlation of natural energies, its accidental and abnormal character has to do with *consequences*, not with causation. Accident is interference with the consequences for which the bottle is intended. The bursting considered apart from its bearing on these consequences is on a plane with any other occurrence in the wide world. But from the standpoint of a desired future, bursting is an anomaly, an interruption of the course of events.

The analogy with the occurrence of dreams, hallucinations, etc., seems to me exact. Dreams are not something outside of the regular course of events; they are in and of it. They are not cognitive distortions of real things; they are *more* real things. There is nothing abnormal in their existence, any more than there is in the bursting of a bottle.[8] But they may be abnormal, from the standpoint of their influence, of their operation as stimuli in calling out responses to modify the future. Dreams have often been taken as prognostics of what is to happen; they have modified conduct. A hallucination may lead a man to consult a doctor; such a consequence is right and proper. But the consultation indicates that the subject regarded it as an indication of consequences which he feared: as a symptom of a disturbed life. Or the hallucination may lead him to anticipate consequences which in fact flow only from the possession of great wealth. Then the hallucination is a disturbance of the normal course of events; the occurrence is wrongly *used* with reference to eventualities.

To regard reference to use and to desired and intended consequences as involving a "subjective" factor is to miss the point, for this has regard to the future. The uses to which a bottle are put are not mental; they do not consist of physical states; they are further correlations of natural existences. Consequences in use are genuine natural events; but they do not occur without the intervention of behavior involving anticipation of a future. The case is not otherwise with an hallucination. The differences it makes are in any case differences in the course of the one continuous world. The important point is whether they are good or bad differences. To use the hallucination as a sign of organic lesions that menace health means the beneficial result of seeing a physician; to respond to it as a sign of consequences such as actually follow only from being persecuted is to fall into error—to be abnormal. The persecutors are "unreal"; that is, there are no things which act as persecutors act; but the hallucination exists. Given its conditions it is as natural as any other event, and poses only the same kind of problem as is put by the occurrence of, say, a thunderstorm. The "unreality" of persecution is not, however, a subjective matter; it means that conditions do not exist for producing the *future* consequences which are now anticipated and reacted to. Ability to anticipate future consequences and to respond to them as stimuli to present behavior may well *define* what is meant by a mind or by "consciousness."[9] But this is only a way of saying just what kind of a real or natural existence the subject is; it is not to fall back on a preconception about an unnatural subject in order to characterize the occurrence of error.

Although the discussion may be already labored, let us take another example—the occurrence of disease. By definition it is pathological, abnormal. At one time in human history this abnormality was taken to be something dwelling in the intrinsic nature of the event—in its existence irrespective of future consequences. Disease was literally extra-natural and to be referred to demons or to magic. No one to-day questions its naturalness—its place in the order of natural events. Yet it is abnormal—for it operates to effect results different from those which follow from health. The difference is a genuine empirical difference, not a mere mental distinction. From the standpoint of bearing on a subsequent course of events disease is unnatural, in spite of the naturalness of its occurrence and origin.

The habit of ignoring reference to the future is responsible for the assumption that to admit human participation in any form is to admit the "subjective" in a sense which alters the objective into the phenomenal. There have been those who, like Spinoza, regarded health and disease, good and ill, as equally real and equally unreal. However, only a few consistent materialists have included truth along with error as merely phenomenal and subjective. But if one does not regard movement toward possible consequences as genuine, wholesale denial of existential validity to all these distinctions is the only logical course. To select truth as objective and error as "subjective" is, on this basis, an, unjustifiably partial procedure. Take everything as fixedly given, and both truth and error are arbitrary insertions into fact. Admit the genuineness of changes going on, and capacity for its direction through organic action based on foresight, and both truth and falsity are alike existential. It is human to regard the course of events which is in line with our own efforts as the *regular* course of events, and interruptions as abnormal, but this partiality of human desire is itself a part of what actually takes place.

It is now proposed to take a particular case of the alleged epistemological predicament for discussion, since the entire ground cannot be covered. I think, however, the instance chosen is typical, so that the conclusion reached may be generalized.

The instance is that of so-called relativity in perception. There are almost endless instances; the stick bent in water; the whistle changing pitch with change of distance from the ear; objects doubled when the eye is pushed; the destroyed star still visible, etc., etc. For our consideration we may take the case of a spherical object that presents itself to one observer as a flat circle, to another as a somewhat distorted elliptical surface. This situation gives empirical proof, so it is argued, of the difference between a real object and mere appearance. Since there is but one object, the existence of two *subjects* is the sole differentiating factor. Hence the two appearances of the one real object is proof of the intervening distorting action of the subject. And many of the Neo-realists who deny the difference in question, admit the case to be one of knowledge and accordingly to constitute an epistemological problem. They have in consequence developed wonderfully elaborate schemes of sundry kinds to maintain "epistemological monism" intact.

Let us try to keep close to empirical facts. In the first place the two unlike appearances of the one sphere are physically necessary because of the laws of reaction of light. If the one sphere did *not* assume these two appearances under given conditions, we should be confronted with a hopelessly irreconcilable discrepancy in the behavior of natural energy. That the result is natural is evidenced by the fact that two cameras—or other arrangements of apparatus for reflecting light—yield precisely the same results. Photographs are as genuinely physical existences as the original sphere; and they exhibit the two geometrical forms.

The statement of these facts makes no impression upon the confirmed epistemologist; he merely retorts that as long as it is admitted that the organism is the cause of a sphere being seen, from different points, as a circular and as an elliptical surface, the essence of his contention—the modification of the real object by the subject—is admitted. To the question why the same logic does not apply to photographic records he makes, as far as I know, no reply at all.

The source of the difficulty is not hard to see. The objection assumes that the alleged modifications of *the* real object are cases of *knowing* and hence attributable to the influence of a *knower*. Statements which set forth the doctrine will always be found to refer to the organic factor, to the eye, as an observer or a percipient. Even when reference is made to a lens or a mirror, language is sometimes used which suggests that the writer's naïveté is sufficiently gross to treat these physical factors as if they were engaged in perceiving the sphere. But as it is evident that the lens operates as a physical factor in correlation with other physical factors—notably light—so it ought to be evident that the intervention of the optical apparatus of the eye is a purely non-cognitive matter. The relation in question is not one between a sphere and a would-be knower of it, unfortunately condemned by the nature of the knowing apparatus to alter the thing he would know; it is an affair of the dynamic interaction of two physical agents in producing a third thing, an effect;—an affair of precisely the same kind as in any physical conjoint action, say the operation of hydrogen and oxygen in producing water. To regard the eye as primarily a knower, an observer, of things, is as crass as to assign that function to a camera. But unless the eye (or optical apparatus, or brain, or organism) be so regarded, there is absolutely no problem of observation or of knowledge in the case of the occurrence of elliptical and circular surfaces. Knowledge does not enter into the affair at all till *after* these forms of refracted light have been produced. About them there is nothing unreal. Light is really, physically, existentially, refracted into these forms. If the same spherical form upon refracting light to physical objects in two quite different positions produced the same geometric forms, there would, indeed, be something to marvel at—as there would be if wax produced the same results in contact simultaneously with a cold body and with a warm one. Why talk about *the real* object in relation to a *knower* when what is given is one real thing in dynamic connection with another real thing?

The way of dealing with the case will probably meet with a retort; at least, it has done so before. It has been said that the account given above and the account of traditional subjectivism differ only verbally. The essential thing in both, so it is said, is the admission that an activity of a self or subject or organism makes a difference in the real object. Whether the subject makes this difference in the very process of knowing or makes it prior to the act of knowing is a minor matter; what is important is that the known thing has, by the time it is known, been "subjectified."

The objection gives a convenient occasion for summarizing the main points of the argument. On the one hand, the retort of the objector depends upon talking about *the* real object. Employ the term "*a* real object," and the change produced by the activity characteristic of the optical apparatus is of just the same kind as that of the camera lens or that of any other physical agency. Every event in the world marks a difference made to one existence in active conjunction with some other existence. And, as for the alleged subjectivity, if subjective is used merely as an adjective to designate the specific activity of a particular existence, comparable, say, to the term feral, applied to tiger, or metallic, applied to iron, then of course reference to subjective is legitimate. But it is also tautological. It is like saying that flesh eaters are carnivorous. But the term "subjective" is so consecrated to other uses, usually implying invidious contrast with objectivity (while subjective in the sense just suggested means specific mode *of* objectivity), that it is difficult to maintain this innocent sense. Its use in any disparaging way in the situation before us—any sense implicating contrast with a real object—assumes that the organism *ought* not to make any difference when it operates in conjunction with other things. Thus we run to earth that assumption that the subject is heterogeneous from every other natural existence; it is to be the one otiose, inoperative thing in a moving world—our old assumption of the self as outside of things.[10]

What and where is knowledge in the case we have been considering? Not, as we have already seen, in the production of forms of light having a circular and elliptical surface. These forms are natural happenings. They may enter into knowledge or they may not, according to circumstances. Countless such refractive changes take place without being noted.[11] When they become subject-matter for knowledge, the inquiry they set on foot may take on an indefinite variety of forms. One may be interested in ascertaining more about the structural peculiarities of the forms themselves; one may be interested in the mechanism of their production; one may find problems in projective geometry, or in drawing and painting—all depending upon the specific matter-of-fact context. The forms may be *objectives* of knowledge—of reflective examination—or they may be means of knowing something else. It may happen—under some circumstances it does happen—that the objective of inquiry is the nature of the geometric form which, when refracting light, gives rise to these other forms. In this case the sphere is the thing known, and in this case, the forms of light are signs or evidence of the conclusion to be drawn. There is no more reason for supposing that they *are* (mis) knowledges of the sphere—that the sphere is necessarily and from the start what one is trying to know—than for supposing that the position of the mercury in the thermometer tube is a cognitive distortion of atmospheric pressure. In each case (that of the mercury and that of, say, a circular surface) the primary datum is a physical happening. In each case it may be used, upon occasion, as a sign or evidence of the nature of the causes which brought it about. Given the position in question, the circular form would be an intrinsically *unreliable* evidence of the nature and position of the spherical body only in case it, as the direct datum of perception, were *not* what it is—a circular form.

I confess that all this seems so obvious that the reader is entitled to inquire into the motive for reciting such plain facts. Were it not for the persistence of the epistemological problem it would be an affront to the reader's intelligence to dwell upon them. But as long as such facts as we have been discussing furnish the subject-matter with which philosophizing is peculiarly concerned, these commonplaces must be urged and reiterated. They bear out two contentions which are important at the juncture, although they will lose special significance as soon as these are habitually recognized: Negatively, a prior and non-empirical notion of the self is the source of the prevailing belief that experience as such is primarily cognitional—a knowledge affair; positively, *knowledge is always a matter of the use that is made of experienced natural events*, a use in which given things are treated as indications of what will be experienced under different conditions.

Let us make one effort more to clear up these points. Suppose it is a question of knowledge of water. The thing to be known does not present itself primarily as a matter of knowledge-and-ignorance at all. It occurs as a stimulus to action and as the source of certain undergoings. It is something to react to:—to drink, to wash with, to put out fire with, and also something that reacts unexpectedly to our reactions, that makes us undergo disease, suffocation, drowning. In this twofold way, water or anything else enters into experience. Such presence in experience has of itself nothing to do with knowledge or consciousness; nothing that is in the sense of depending upon them, though it has everything to do with knowledge and consciousness in the sense that the latter depends upon prior experience of this non-cognitive sort. Man's experience is what it is because his response to things (even successful response) and the reactions of things to his life, are so radically different from knowledge. The difficulties and tragedies of life, the stimuli to acquiring knowledge, lie in the radical disparity of presence-in-experience and presence-in-knowing. Yet the immense importance of knowledge experience, the fact that turning presence-in-experience over into presence-in-a-knowledge-experience is the sole mode of control of nature, has systematically hypnotized European philosophy since the time of Socrates into thinking that all experiencing is a mode of knowing, if not good knowledge, then a low-grade or confused or implicit knowledge.

When water is an adequate stimulus to action or when its reactions oppress and overwhelm us, it remains outside the scope of knowledge. When, however, the bare presence of the thing (say, as optical stimulus) ceases to operate directly as stimulus to response and begins to operate in connection with a forecast of the consequences it will effect when responded to, it begins to acquire meaning—to be known, to be an object. It is noted as something which is wet, fluid, satisfies thirst, allays uneasiness, etc. The conception that we begin with a known visual quality which is thereafter enlarged by adding on qualities apprehended by the other senses does not rest upon experience; it rests upon making experience conform to the notion that every experience *must* be a cognitive noting. As long as the visual stimulus operates as a stimulus on its own account, there is no apprehension, no noting, of color or light at all. To much the greater portion of sensory stimuli we react in precisely this wholly non-cognitive way. In the attitude of suspended response in which consequences are anticipated, the direct stimulus becomes a sign or index of something else—and thus matter of noting or apprehension or acquaintance, or whatever term may be employed. This difference (together, of course, with the consequences which go with it) is the difference which the natural event of knowing makes to the natural event of direct organic stimulation. It is no change of a reality into an unreality, of an object into something subjective; it is no secret, illicit, or epistemological transformation; it is a genuine acquisition of new and distinctive features through entering into relations with things with which it was not formerly connected—namely, possible and future things.

But, replies some one so obsessed with the epistemological point of view that he assumes that the prior account is a rival epistemology in disguise, all this involves no change in Reality, no difference made to Reality. Water was all the time all the things it is ever found out to be. Its real nature has not been altered by knowing it; any such alteration means a misknowing.

In reply let it be said,—once more and finally,—there is no assertion or implication about *the* real object, or *the* real world or *the* reality. Such an assumption goes with that epistemological universe of discourse which has to be abandoned in an empirical universe of discourse. The change is of *a* real object. An incident of the world operating as a physiologically direct stimulus is assuredly a reality. Responded to, it produces specific consequences in virtue of the response. Water is not drunk unless somebody drinks it; it does not quench thirst unless a thirsty person drinks it—and so on. Consequences occur whether one is aware of them or not; they are integral facts in experience. But let one of these consequences be anticipated and let it, as anticipated, become an indispensable element in the stimulus, and then there is a known object. It is not that knowing *produces* a change, but that it *is* a change of the specific kind described. A serial process, the successive portions of which are as such incapable of simultaneous occurrence, is telescoped and condensed into an object, a unified inter-reference of contemporaneous properties, most of which express potentialities rather than completed data.

Because of this change, an *object* possesses truth or error (which the physical occurrence as such never has); it is classifiable as fact or fantasy; it is of a sort or kind, expresses an essence or nature, possesses implications, etc., etc. That is to say, it is marked by specifiable *logical* traits not found in physical occurrences as such. Because objective idealisms have seized upon these traits as constituting the very essence of Reality is no reason for proclaiming that they are ready-made features of physical happenings, and hence for maintaining that knowing is nothing but an appearance of things on a stage for which "consciousness" supplies the footlights. For only the epistemological predicament leads to "presentations" being regarded as cognitions of things which were previously unpresented. In any empirical situation of everyday life or of science, knowledge signifies something stated or inferred of another thing. Visible water is not a more or less erroneous presentation of H_2O, but H_2O is a knowledge about the thing we see, drink, wash with, sail on, and use for power.

A further point and the present phase of discussion terminates. Treating knowledge as a presentative relation between the knower and object makes it necessary to regard the mechanism of *presentation* as constituting the act of knowing. Since things may be presented in sense-perception, in recollection, in imagination and in conception, and since the mechanism in every one of these four styles of presentation is sensory-cerebral the problem of knowing becomes a mind-body problem.[12] The psychological, or physiological, mechanism of presentation involved in seeing a chair, remembering what I ate yesterday for luncheon, imagining the moon the size of a cart wheel, conceiving a mathematical continuum is identified with the operation of knowing. The evil consequences are twofold. The problem of the relation of mind and body has become a part of the problem of the possibility of knowledge in general, to the further complication of a matter already hopelessly constrained. Meantime the actual process of knowing, namely, operations of controlled observation, inference, reasoning, and testing, the only process with *intellectual* import, is dismissed as irrelevant to the theory of knowing. The methods of knowing practised in daily life and science are excluded from consideration in the philosophical theory of knowing. Hence the constructions of the latter become more and more elaborately artificial because there is no definite check upon them. It would be easy to quote from epistemological writers statements to the effect that these processes (which supply the only empirically verifiable facts of knowing) are *merely* inductive in character, or even that they are of purely psychological significance. It would be difficult to find a more complete inversion of the facts than in the latter statement, since presentation constitutes in fact the psychological affair. A confusion of logic with physiological physiology has bred hybrid epistemology, with the amazing result that the technique of effective inquiry is rendered irrelevant to the theory of knowing, and those physical events involved in the occurrence of data for knowing are treated as if they constituted the act of knowing.

V

What are the bearings of our discussion upon the conception of the present scope and office of philosophy? What do our conclusions indicate and demand with reference to philosophy itself? For the philosophy which reaches such conclusions regarding knowledge and mind must apply them, sincerely and whole-heartedly, to its idea of its own nature. For philosophy claims to be one form or mode of knowing. If, then, the conclusion is reached that knowing is a way of employing empirical occurrences with respect to increasing power to direct the consequences which flow from things, the application of the conclusion must be made to philosophy itself. It, too, becomes not a contemplative survey of existence nor an analysis of what is past and done with, but an outlook upon future possibilities with reference to attaining the better and averting the worse. Philosophy must take, with good grace, its own medicine.

It is easier to state the negative results of the changed idea of philosophy than the positive ones. The point that occurs to mind most readily is that philosophy will have to surrender all pretension to be peculiarly concerned with ultimate reality, or with reality as a complete (i.e., completed) whole: with *the* real object. The surrender is not easy of achievement. The philosophic tradition that comes to us from classic Greek thought and that was reinforced by Christian philosophy in the Middle Ages discriminates philosophical knowing from other modes of knowing by means of an alleged peculiarly intimate concern with supreme, ultimate, true reality. To deny this trait to philosophy seems to many to be the suicide of philosophy; to be a systematic adoption of skepticism or agnostic positivism.

The pervasiveness of the tradition is shown in the fact that so vitally a contemporary thinker as Bergson, who finds a philosophic revolution involved in abandonment of the traditional identification of the truly real with the fixed (an identification inherited from Greek thought), does not find it in his heart to abandon the counterpart identification of philosophy with search for the truly Real; and hence finds it necessary to substitute an ultimate and absolute flux for an ultimate and absolute permanence. Thus his great empirical services in calling attention to the fundamental importance of considerations of time for problems of life and mind get compromised with a mystic, non-empirical "Intuition"; and we find him preoccupied with solving, by means of his new idea of ultimate reality, the traditional problems of realities-in-themselves and phenomena, matter and mind, free-will and determinism, God and the world. Is not that another evidence of the influence of the classic idea about philosophy?

Even the new realists are not content to take their realism as a plea for approaching subject-matter directly instead of through the intervention of epistemological apparatus; they find it necessary first to determine the status of *the* real object. Thus they too become entangled in the problem of the possibility of error, dreams, hallucinations, etc., in short, the problem of evil. For I take it that an uncorrupted realism would accept such things as real events, and find in them no other problems than those attending the consideration of any real occurrence—namely, problems of structure, origin, and operation.

It is often said that pragmatism, unless it is content to be a contribution to mere methodology, must develop a theory of Reality. But the chief characteristic trait of the pragmatic notion of reality is precisely that no theory of Reality in general, *überhaupt*, is possible or needed. It occupies the position of an emancipated empiricism or a thoroughgoing naïve realism. It finds that "reality" is a *denotative* term, a word used to designate indifferently everything that happens. Lies, dreams, insanities, deceptions, myths, theories are all of them just the events which they specifically are. Pragmatism is content to take its stand with science; for science finds all such events to be subject-matter of description and inquiry—just like stars and fossils, mosquitoes and malaria, circulation and vision. It also takes its stand with daily life, which finds that such things really have to be reckoned with as they occur interwoven in the texture of events.

The only way in which the term reality can ever become more than a blanket denotative term is through recourse to specific events in all their diversity and thatness. Speaking summarily, I find that the retention by philosophy of the notion of a Reality feudally superior to the events of everyday occurrence is the chief source of the increasing isolation of philosophy from common sense and science. For the latter do not operate in any such region. As with them of old, philosophy in dealing with real difficulties finds itself still hampered by reference to realities more real, more ultimate, than those which directly happen.

I have said that identifying the cause of philosophy with the notion of superior reality is the cause of an *increasing* isolation from science and practical life. The phrase reminds us that there was a time when the enterprise of science and the moral interests of men both moved in a universe invidiously distinguished from that of ordinary occurrence. While all that happens is equally real—since it really happens—happenings are not of equal worth. Their respective consequences, their import, varies tremendously. Counterfeit money, although real (or rather *because* real), is really different from valid circulatory medium, just as disease is really different from health; different in specific structure and so different in consequences. In occidental thought, the Greeks were the first to draw the distinction between the genuine and the spurious in a generalized fashion and to formulate and enforce its tremendous significance for the conduct of life. But since they had at command no technique of experimental analysis and no adequate technique of mathematical analysis, they were compelled to treat the difference of the true and the false, the dependable and the deceptive, as signifying two kinds of existence, the truly real and the apparently real.

Two points can hardly be asserted with too much emphasis. The Greeks were wholly right in the feeling that questions of good and ill, as far as they fall within human control, are bound up with discrimination of the genuine from the spurious, of "being" from what only pretends to be. But because they lacked adequate instrumentalities for coping with this difference in specific situations, they were forced to treat the difference as a wholesale and rigid one. Science was concerned with vision of ultimate and true reality; opinion was concerned with getting along with apparent realities. Each had its appropriate region permanently marked off. Matters of opinion could never become matters of science; their intrinsic nature forbade. When the practice of science went on under such conditions, science and philosophy were one and the same thing. Both had to do with ultimate reality in its rigid and insuperable difference from ordinary occurrences.

We have only to refer to the way in which medieval life wrought the philosophy of an ultimate and supreme reality into the context of practical life to realize that for centuries political and moral interests were bound up with the distinction between the absolutely real and the relatively real. The difference was no matter of a remote technical philosophy, but one which controlled life from the cradle to the grave, from the grave to the endless life after death. By means of a vast institution, which in effect was state as well as church, the claims of ultimate reality were enforced; means of access to it were provided. Acknowledgment of The Reality brought security in this world and salvation in the next. It is not necessary to report the story of the change which has since taken place. It is enough for our purposes to note that none of the modern philosophies of a superior reality, or *the* real object, idealistic or realistic, holds that its insight makes a difference like that between sin and holiness, eternal condemnation and eternal bliss. While in its own context the philosophy of ultimate reality entered into the vital concerns of men, it now tends to be an ingenious dialectic exercised in professorial corners by a few who have retained ancient premises while rejecting their application to the conduct of life.

The increased isolation from science of any philosophy identified with the problem of *the* real is equally marked. For the growth of science has consisted precisely in the invention of an equipment, a technique of appliances and procedures, which, accepting all occurrences as homogeneously real, proceeds to distinguish the authenticated from the spurious, the true from the false, by specific modes of treatment in specific situations. The procedures of the trained engineer, of the competent physician, of the laboratory expert, have turned out to be the only ways of discriminating the counterfeit from the valid. And they have revealed that the difference is not one of antecedent fixity of existence, but one of mode of treatment and of the consequences thereon attendant. After mankind has learned to put its trust in specific procedures in order to make its discriminations between the false and the true, philosophy arrogates to itself the enforcement of the distinction at its own cost.

More than once, this essay has intimated that the counterpart of the idea of invidiously real reality is the spectator notion of knowledge. If the knower, however defined, is set over against the world to be known, knowing consists in possessing a transcript, more or less accurate but otiose, of real things. Whether this transcript is preservative in character (as realists say) or whether it is by means of states of consciousness which represent things (as subjectivists say), is a matter of great importance in its own context. But, in another regard, this difference is negligible in comparison with the point in which both agree. Knowing is viewing from outside. But if it be true that the self or subject of experience is part and parcel of the course of events, it follows that the self *becomes* a knower. It becomes a mind in virtue of a distinctive way of partaking in the course of events. The significant distinction is no longer between the knower *and* the world; it is between different ways of being in and of the movement of things; between a brute physical way and a purposive, intelligent way.

There is no call to repeat in detail the statements which have been advanced. Their net purport is that the directive presence of future possibilities in dealing with existent conditions is what is meant by knowing; that the self becomes a knower or mind when anticipation of future consequences operates as its stimulus. What we are now concerned with is the effect of this conception upon the nature of philosophic knowing.

As far as I can judge, popular response to pragmatic philosophy was moved by two quite different considerations. By some it was thought to provide a new species of sanctions, a new mode of apologetics, for certain religious ideas whose standing had been threatened. By others, it was welcomed because it was taken as a sign that philosophy was about to surrender its otiose and speculative remoteness; that philosophers were beginning to recognize that philosophy is of account only if, like everyday knowing and like science, it affords guidance to action and thereby makes a difference in the event. It was welcomed as a sign that philosophers were willing to have the worth of their philosophizing measured by responsible tests.

I have not seen this point of view emphasized, or hardly recognized, by professional critics. The difference of attitude can probably be easily explained. The epistemological universe of discourse is so highly technical that only those who have been trained in the history of thought think in terms of it. It did not occur, accordingly, to nontechnical readers to interpret the doctrine that the meaning and validity of thought are fixed by differences made in consequences and in satisfactoriness, to mean consequences in personal feelings. Those who were professionally trained, however, took the statement to mean that consciousness or mind in the mere act of looking at things modifies them. It understood the doctrine of test of validity by consequences to mean that apprehensions and conceptions are true if the modifications affected by them were of an emotionally desirable tone.

Prior discussion should have made it reasonably clear that the source of this misunderstanding lies in the neglect of temporal considerations. The change made in things by the self in knowing is not immediate and, so to say, cross-sectional. It is longitudinal—in the redirection given to changes already going on. Its analogue is found in the changes which take place in the development of, say, iron ore into a watch-spring, not in those of the miracle of transubstantiation. For the static, cross-sectional, non-temporal relation of subject and object, the pragmatic hypothesis substitutes apprehension of a thing in terms of the results in other things which it is tending to effect. For the unique epistemological relation, it substitutes a practical relation of a familiar type:—responsive behavior which changes in time the subject-matter to which it applies. The unique thing about the responsive behavior which constitutes knowing is the specific difference which marks it off from other modes of response, namely, the part played in it by anticipation and prediction. Knowing is the act, stimulated by this foresight, of securing and averting consequences. The success of the achievement measures the standing of the foresight by which response is directed. The popular impression that pragmatic philosophy means that philosophy shall develop ideas relevant to the actual crises of life, ideas influential in dealing with them and tested by the assistance they afford, is correct.

Reference to practical response suggests, however, another misapprehension. Many critics have jumped at the obvious association of the word pragmatic with practical. They have assumed that the intent is to limit all knowledge, philosophic included, to promoting "action," understanding by action, either just any bodily movement, or those bodily movements which conduce to the preservation and grosser well-being of the body. James' statement that general conceptions must "cash in" has been taken (especially by European critics) to mean that the end and measure of intelligence lies in the narrow and coarse utilities which it produces. Even an acute American thinker, after first criticizing pragmatism as a kind of idealistic epistemology, goes on to treat it as a doctrine which regards intelligence as a lubricating oil facilitating the workings of the body.

One source of the misunderstanding is suggested by the fact that "cashing in" to James meant that a general idea must always be capable of verification in specific existential cases. The notion of "cashing in" says nothing about the breadth or depth of the specific consequences. As an empirical doctrine, it could not say anything about them in general; the specific cases must speak for themselves. If one conception is verified in terms of eating beefsteak, and another in terms of a favorable credit balance in the bank, that is not because of anything in the theory, but because of the specific nature of the conceptions in question, and because there exist particular events like hunger and trade. If there are also existences in which the most liberal esthetic ideas and the most generous moral conceptions can be verified by specific embodiment, assuredly so much the better. The fact that a strictly empirical philosophy was taken by so many critics to imply an *a priori* dogma about the kind of consequences capable of existence is evidence, I think, of the inability of many philosophers to think in concretely empirical terms. Since the critics were themselves accustomed to get results by manipulating the concepts of "consequences" and of "practice," they assumed that even a would-be empiricist must be doing the same sort of thing. It will, I suppose, remain for a long time incredible to some that a philosopher should really intend to go to specific experiences to determine of what scope and depth practice admits, and what sort of consequences the world permits to come into being. Concepts are so clear; it takes so little time to develop their implications; experiences are so confused, and it requires so much time and energy to lay hold of them. And yet these same critics charge pragmatism with adopting subjective and emotional standards!

As a matter of fact, the pragmatic theory of intelligence means that the function of mind is to project new and more complex ends—to free experience from routine and from caprice. Not the use of thought to accomplish purposes already given either in the mechanism of the body or in that of the existent state of society, but the use of intelligence to liberate and liberalize action, is the pragmatic lesson. Action restricted to given and fixed ends may attain great technical efficiency; but efficiency is the only quality to which it can lay claim. Such action is mechanical (or becomes so), no matter what the scope of the preformed end, be it the Will of God or *Kultur*. But the doctrine that intelligence develops within the sphere of action for the sake of possibilities not yet given is the opposite of a doctrine of mechanical efficiency. Intelligence *as* intelligence is inherently forward-looking; only by ignoring its primary function does it become a mere means for an end already given. The latter is servile, even when the end is labeled moral, religious, or esthetic. But action directed to ends to which the agent has not previously been attached inevitably carries with it a quickened and enlarged spirit. A pragmatic intelligence is a creative intelligence, not a routine mechanic.

All this may read like a defense of pragmatism by one concerned to make out for it the best case possible. Such is not, however, the intention. The purpose is to indicate the extent to which intelligence frees action from a mechanically instrumental character. Intelligence is, indeed, instrumental *through* action to the determination of the qualities of future experience. But the very fact that the concern of intelligence is with the future, with the as-yet-unrealized (and with the given and the established only as conditions of the realization of possibilities), makes the action in which it takes effect generous and liberal; free of spirit. Just that action which extends and approves intelligence has an intrinsic value of its own in being instrumental:—the intrinsic value of being informed with intelligence in behalf of the enrichment of life. By the same stroke, intelligence becomes truly liberal: knowing is a human undertaking, not an esthetic appreciation carried on by a refined class or a capitalistic possession of a few learned specialists, whether men of science or of philosophy.

More emphasis has been put upon what philosophy is not than upon what it may become. But it is not necessary, it is not even desirable, to set forth philosophy as a scheduled program. There are human difficulties of an urgent, deep-seated kind which may be clarified by trained reflection, and whose solution may be forwarded by the careful development of hypotheses. When it is understood that philosophic thinking is caught up in the actual course of events, having the office of guiding them towards a prosperous issue, problems will abundantly present themselves. Philosophy will not solve these problems; philosophy is vision, imagination, reflection—and these functions, apart from action, modify nothing and hence resolve nothing. But in a complicated and perverse world, action which is not informed with vision, imagination, and reflection, is more likely to increase confusion and conflict than to straighten things out. It is not easy for generous and sustained reflection to become a guiding and illuminating method in action. Until it frees itself from identification with problems which are supposed to depend upon Reality as such, or its distinction from a world of Appearance, or its relation to a Knower as such, the hands of philosophy are tied. Having no chance to link its fortunes with a responsible career by suggesting things to be tried, it cannot identify itself with questions which actually arise in the vicissitudes of life. Philosophy recovers itself when it ceases to be a device for dealing with the problems of philosophers and becomes a method, cultivated by philosophers, for dealing with the problems of men.

Emphasis must vary with the stress and special impact of the troubles which perplex men. Each age knows its own ills, and seeks its own remedies. One does not have to forecast a particular program to note that the central need of any program at the present day is an adequate conception of the nature of intelligence and its place in action. Philosophy cannot disavow responsibility for many misconceptions of the nature of intelligence which now hamper its efficacious operation. It has at least a negative task imposed upon it. It must take away the burdens which it has laid upon the intelligence of the common man in struggling with his difficulties. It must deny and eject that intelligence which is naught but a distant eye, registering in a remote and alien medium the spectacle of nature and life. To enforce the fact that the emergence of imagination and thought is relative to the connexion of the sufferings of men with their doings is of itself to illuminate those sufferings and to instruct those doings. To catch mind in its connexion with the entrance of the novel into the course of the world is to be on the road to see that intelligence is itself the most promising of all novelties, the revelation of the meaning of that transformation of past into future which is the reality of every present. To reveal intelligence as the organ for the guidance of this transformation, the sole director of its quality, is to make a declaration of present untold significance for action. To elaborate these convictions of the connexion of intelligence with what men undergo because of their doings and with the emergence and direction of the creative, the novel, in the world is of itself a program which will keep philosophers busy until something more worth while is forced upon them. For the elaboration has to be made through application to all the disciplines which have an intimate connexion with human conduct:—to logic, ethics, esthetics, economics, and the procedure of the sciences formal and natural.

I also believe that there is a genuine sense in which the enforcement of the pivotal position of intelligence in the world and thereby in control of human fortunes (so far as they are manageable) is the peculiar problem in the problems of life which come home most closely to ourselves—to ourselves living not merely in the early twentieth century but in the United States. It is easy to be foolish about the connexion of thought with national life. But I do not see how any one can question the distinctively national color of English, or French, or German philosophies. And if of late the history of thought has come under the domination of the German dogma of an inner evolution of ideas, it requires but a little inquiry to convince oneself that that dogma itself testifies to a particularly nationalistic need and origin. I believe that philosophy in America will be lost between chewing a historic cud long since reduced to woody fiber, or an apologetics for lost causes (lost to natural science), or a scholastic, schematic formalism, unless it can somehow bring to consciousness America's own needs and its own implicit principle of successful action.

This need and principle, I am convinced, is the necessity of a deliberate control of policies by the methods, of intelligence, an intelligence which is not the faculty of intellect, honored in text-books and neglected elsewhere, but which is the sum-total of impulses, habits, emotions, records, and discoveries which forecast what is desirable and undesirable in future possibilities, and which contrive ingeniously in behalf of imagined good. Our life has no background of sanctified categories upon which we may fall back; we rely upon precedent as authority only to our own undoing—for with us there is such a continuously novel situation that final reliance upon precedent entails some class interest guiding us by the nose whither it will. British empiricism, with its appeal to what has been in the past, is, after all, only a kind of *a priorism*. For it lays down a fixed rule for future intelligence to follow; and only the immersion of philosophy in technical learning prevents our seeing that this is the essence of *a priorism*.

We pride ourselves upon being realistic, desiring a hardheaded cognizance of facts, and devoted to mastering the means of life. We pride ourselves upon a practical idealism, a lively and easily moved faith in possibilities as yet unrealized, in willingness to make sacrifice for their realization. Idealism easily becomes a sanction of waste and carefulness, and realism a sanction of legal formalism in behalf of things as they are—the rights of the possessor. We thus tend to combine a loose and ineffective optimism with assent to the doctrine of take who take can: a deification of power. All peoples at all times have been narrowly realistic in practice and have then employed idealization to cover up in sentiment and theory their brutalities. But never, perhaps, has the tendency been so dangerous and so tempting as with ourselves. Faith in the power of intelligence to imagine a future which is the projection of the desirable in the present, and to invent the instrumentalities of its realization, is our salvation. And it is a faith which must be nurtured and made articulate: surely a sufficiently large task for our philosophy.

Notes

1. The word relation suffers from ambiguity. I am speaking here of connexion, dynamic and functional interaction. "Relation" is a term used also to express logical reference. I suspect that much of the controversy about internal and external relations is due to this ambiguity. One passes at will from existential connexions of things to logical relationship of terms.

Such an identification of existences with terms is congenial to idealism, but is paradoxical in a professed realism.

2. There is some gain in substituting a doctrine of flux and interpenetration of psychical states, à la Bergson, for that of rigid discontinuity. But the substitution leaves untouched the fundamental misstatement of experience, the conception of experience as directly and primarily "inner" and psychical.

3. Mathematical science in its formal aspects, or as a branch of formal logic, has been the empirical stronghold of rationalism. But an empirical empiricism, in contrast with orthodox deductive empiricism, has no difficulty in establishing its jurisdiction as to deductive functions.

4. It is a shame to devote the word idealism, with its latent moral, practical connotations, to a doctrine whose tenets are the denial of the existence of a physical world, and the psychical character of all objects—at least as far as they are knowable. But I am following usage, not attempting to make it.

5. See Dr. Kallen's essay, below. [Kallen, "Value and Existence in Philosophy, Art, and Religion," in *Creative Intelligence*, by Dewey et al., New York : Henry Holt Company, 1917, pp. 409–467.]

6. The "they" means the "some" of the prior sentence—those whose realism is epistemological, instead of being a plea for taking the facts of experience as we find them without refraction through epistemological apparatus.

7. It is interesting to note that some of the realists who have assimilated the cognitive relation to other existential relations in the world (instead of treating it as an unique or epistemological relation) have been forced in support of their conception of knowledge as a "preservative" or spectatorial affair to extend the defining features of the latter to all relations among things, and hence to make all the "real" things in the world pure "simples, " wholly independent of one another. So conceived the doctrine of external relations appears to be rather the doctrine of complete externality of *things*. Aside from this point, the doctrine is interesting for its dialectical ingenuity and for the elegant development of assumed premises, rather than convincing on account of empirical evidence supporting it.

8. In other words, there is a general "problem of error" only because there is a general problem of evil, concerning which see Dr. Kallen's essay, below. [Kallen, "Value and Existence in Philosophy, Art, and Religion."]

9. Compare the paper by Professor Bode. [Bode, "Consciousness and Psychology," in *Creative Intelligence*, by Dewey, pp. 228–281.]

10. As the attempt to retain the epistemological problem and yet to reject idealistic and relativistic solutions has forced some Neo-realists into the doctrine of isolated and independent simples, so it has also led to a doctrine of Eleatic pluralism. In order to maintain the doctrine the subject makes no difference to anything else, it is held that no ultimate real makes any difference to anything else—all this rather than surrender once for all the genuineness of the problem and to follow the lead of empirical subject-matter.

11. There is almost no end to the various dialectic developments of the epistemological situation. When it is held that all the relations of the type in question are cognitive, and yet it is recognized (as it must be) that many such "transformations" go unremarked, the theory is supplemented by introducing "unconscious" psychical modifications.

12. Conception-presentation has, of course, been made by many in the history of speculation an exception to this statement; "pure" memory is also made an exception by Bergson. To take cognizance of this matter would, of course, accentuate, not relieve, the difficulty remarked upon in the text.

In this 1910 essay, Dewey argues that Darwinism renders many of the traditional categories and problems of philosophy obsolete. We "do not solve" the traditional philosophical problems, we "get over them."

JOHN DEWEY

The Influence of Darwinism on Philosophy

I

That the publication of the "Origin of Species" marked an epoch in the development of the natural sciences is well known to the layman. That the combination of the very words origin and species embodied an intellectual revolt and introduced a new intellectual temper is easily overlooked by the expert. The conceptions that had reigned in the philosophy of nature and knowledge for two thousand years, the conceptions that had become the familiar furniture of the mind, rested on the assumption of the superiority of the fixed and final; they rested upon treating change and origin as signs of defect and unreality. In laying hands upon the sacred ark of absolute permanency, in treating the forms that had been regarded as types of fixity and perfection as originating and passing away, the "Origin of Species" introduced a mode of thinking that in the end was bound to transform the logic of knowledge, and hence the treatment of morals, politics, and religion.

No wonder, then, that the publication of Darwin's book, a half century ago, precipitated a crisis. The true nature of the controversy is easily concealed from us, however, by the theological clamor that attended it. The vivid and popular features of the anti-Darwinian row tended to leave the impression that the issue was between science on one side and theology on the other. Such was not the case—the issue lay primarily within science itself, as Darwin himself early recognized. The theological outcry he discounted from the start, hardly noticing it save as it bore upon the "feelings of his female relatives." But for two decades before final publication he contemplated the possibility of being put down by his scientific peers as a fool or as crazy; and he set, as the measure of his success, the degree in which he should affect three men of science: Lyell in geology, Hooker in botany, and Huxley in zoology.

Religious considerations lent fervor to the controversy, but they did not provoke it. Intellectually, religious emotions are not creative but conservative. They attach themselves readily to the current view of the world and consecrate it. They steep and dye intellectual fabrics in the seething vat of emotions; they do not form their warp and woof. There is not, I think, an instance of any large idea about the world being independently generated by religion. Although the ideas that rose up like armed men against Darwinism owed their intensity to religious associations, their origin and meaning are to be sought in science and philosophy, not in religion.

II

Few words in our language foreshorten intellectual history as much as does the word species. The Greeks, in initiating the intellectual life of Europe, were impressed by characteristic traits of the life of plants and animals; so impressed indeed that they made these traits the key to defining nature and to explaining mind and society. And truly, life is so wonderful that a seemingly successful reading of its mystery might well lead men to believe that the key to the secrets of heaven and earth was in their hands. The Greek rendering of this mystery, the Greek formulation of the aim and standard of knowledge, was in the course of time embodied in the word species, and it controlled philosophy for two thousand years. To understand the intellectual face-about expressed in the phrase "Origin of Species," we must, then, understand the long dominant idea against which it is a protest.

Consider how men were impressed by the facts of life. Their eyes fell upon certain things slight in bulk, and frail in structure. To every appearance, these perceived things were inert and passive. Suddenly, under certain circumstances, these things—henceforth known as seeds or eggs or germs—begin to change, to change rapidly in size, form, and qualities. Rapid and extensive changes occur, however, in many things—as when wood is touched by fire. But the changes in the living thing are orderly; they are cumulative; they tend constantly in one direction; they do not, like other changes, destroy or consume, or pass fruitless into wandering flux; they realize and fulfil. Each successive stage, no matter how unlike its predecessor, preserves its net effect and also prepares the way for a fuller activity on the part of its successor. In living beings, changes do not happen as they seem to happen elsewhere, any which way; the earlier changes are regulated in view of later results. This progressive organization does not cease till there is achieved a true final term, a τελὸς, a completed, perfected end. This final form exercises in turn a plenitude of functions, not the least noteworthy of which is production of germs like those from which it took its own origin, germs capable of the same cycle of self-fulfilling activity.

But the whole miraculous tale is not yet told. The same drama is enacted to the same destiny in countless myriads of individuals so sundered in time, so severed in space, that they have no opportunity for mutual consultation and no means of interaction. As an old writer quaintly said, "things of the same kind go through the same formalities"—celebrate, as it were, the same ceremonial rites.

This formal activity which operates throughout a series of changes and holds them to a single course; which subordinates their aimless flux to its own perfect manifestation; which, leaping the boundaries of space and time, keeps individuals distant in space and remote in time to a uniform type of structure and function: this principle seemed to give insight into the very nature of reality itself. To it Aristotle gave the name, εἶδος. This term the scholastics translated as *species*.

The force of this term was deepened by its application to everything in the universe that observes order in flux and manifests constancy through change. From the casual drift of daily weather, through the uneven recurrence of seasons and unequal return of seed time and harvest, up to the majestic sweep of the heavens—the image of eternity in time—and from this to the unchanging pure and contemplative intelligence beyond nature lies one unbroken fulfilment of ends. Nature as a whole is a progressive realization of purpose strictly comparable to the realization of purpose in any single plant or animal.

The conception of εἶδος, species, a fixed form and final cause, was the central principle of knowledge as well as of nature. Upon it rested the logic of science. Change as change is mere flux and lapse; it insults intelligence. Genuinely to know is to grasp a permanent end that realizes itself through changes, holding them thereby within the metes and bounds of fixed truth. Completely to know is to relate all special forms to their one single end and good: pure contemplative intelligence. Since, however, the scene of nature which directly confronts us is in change, nature as directly and practically experienced does not satisfy the conditions of knowledge. Human experience is in flux, and hence the instrumentalities of sense-perception and of inference based upon observation are condemned in advance. Science is compelled to aim at realities lying behind and beyond the processes of nature, and to carry on its search for these realities by means of rational forms transcending ordinary modes of perception and inference.

There are, indeed, but two alternative courses. We must either find the appropriate objects and organs of knowledge in the mutual interactions of changing things; or else, to escape the infection of change, *we must* seek them in some transcendent and supernal region. The human mind, deliberately as it were, exhausted the logic of the changeless, the final, and the transcendent, before it essayed adventure on the pathless wastes of generation and transformation. We dispose all too easily of the efforts of the schoolmen to interpret nature and mind in terms of real essences, hidden forms, and occult faculties, forgetful of the seriousness and dignity of the ideas that lay behind. We dispose of them by laughing at the famous gentleman who accounted for the fact that opium put people to sleep on the ground it had a dormitive faculty. But the doctrine, held in our own day, that knowledge of the plant that yields the poppy consists in referring the peculiarities of an individual to a type, to a universal form, a doctrine so firmly established that any other method of knowing was conceived to be unphilosophical and unscientific, is a survival of precisely the same logic. This identity of conception in the scholastic and anti-Darwinian theory may well suggest greater sympathy for what has become unfamiliar as well as greater humility regarding the further unfamiliarities that history has in store.

Darwin was not, of course, the first to question the classic philosophy of nature and of knowledge. The beginnings of the revolution are in the physical science of the sixteenth and seventeenth centuries. When Galileo said: "It is my opinion that the earth is very noble and admirable by reason of so many and so different alterations and generations which are incessantly made therein," he expressed the changed temper that was coming over the world; the transfer of interest from the permanent to the changing. When Descartes said: "The nature of physical things is much more easily conceived when they are beheld coming gradually into existence, than when they are only considered as produced at once in a finished and perfect state," the modern world became self-conscious of the logic that was henceforth to control it, the logic of which Darwin's "Origin of Species" is the latest scientific achievement. Without the methods of Copernicus, Kepler, Galileo, and their successors in astronomy, physics, and chemistry, Darwin would have been helpless in the organic sciences. But prior to Darwin the impact of the new scientific method upon life, mind, and politics, had been arrested, because between these ideal or moral interests and the inorganic world intervened the kingdom of plants and animals. The gates of the garden of life were barred to the new ideas; and only through this garden was there access to mind and politics. The influence of Darwin upon philosophy resides in his having conquered the phenomena of life for the principle of transition, and thereby freed the new logic for application to mind and morals and life. When he said of species what Galileo had said of the earth, *e pur se muove*, he emancipated, once for all, genetic and experimental ideas as an organon of asking questions and looking for explanations.

III

The exact bearings upon philosophy of the new logical outlook are, of course, as yet, uncertain and inchoate. We live in the twilight of intellectual transition. One must add the rashness of the prophet to the stubbornness of the partizan to venture a systematic exposition of the influence upon philosophy of the Darwinian method. At best, we can but inquire as to its general bearing—the effect upon mental temper and complexion, upon that body of half-conscious, half-instinctive intellectual aversions and preferences which determine, after all, our more deliberate intellectual enterprises. In this vague inquiry there happens to exist as a kind of touchstone a problem of long historic currency that has also been much discussed in Darwinian literature. I refer to the old problem of design *versus* chance, mind *versus* matter, as the causal explanation, first or final, of things.

As we have already seen, the classic notion of species carried with it the idea of purpose. In all living forms, a specific type is present directing the earlier stages of growth to the realization of its own perfection. Since this purposive regulative principle is not visible to the senses, it follows that it must be an ideal or rational force. Since, however, the perfect form is gradually approximated through the sensible changes, it also follows that in and through a sensible realm a rational ideal force is working out its own ultimate manifestation. These inferences were extended to nature: (*a*) She does nothing in vain; but all for an ulterior purpose, (*b*) Within natural sensible events there is therefore contained a spiritual causal force, which as spiritual escapes perception, but is apprehended by an enlightened reason, (*c*) The manifestation of this principle brings about a subordination of matter and sense to its own realization, and this ultimate fulfilment is the goal of nature and of man. The design argument thus operated in two directions. Purposefulness accounted for the intelligibility of nature and the possibility of science, while the absolute or cosmic character of this purposefulness gave sanction and worth to the moral and religious endeavors of man. Science was underpinned and morals authorized by one and the same principle, and their mutual agreement was eternally guaranteed.

This philosophy remained, in spite of sceptical and polemic outbursts, the official and the regnant philosophy of Europe for over two thousand years. The expulsion of fixed first and final causes from astronomy, physics, and chemistry had indeed given the doctrine something of a shock. But, on the other hand, increased acquaintance with the details of plant and animal life operated as a counterbalance and perhaps even strengthened the argument from design. The marvelous adaptations of organisms to their environment, of organs to the organism, of unlike parts of a complex organ—like the eye—to the organ itself; the foreshadowing by lower forms of the higher; the preparation in earlier stages of growth for organs that only later had their functioning—these things were increasingly recognized with the progress of botany, zoology, paleontology, and embryology. Together, they added such prestige to the design argument that by the late eighteenth century it was, as approved by the sciences of organic life, the central point of theistic and idealistic philosophy.

The Darwinian principle of natural selection cut straight under this philosophy. If all organic adaptations are due simply to constant variation and the elimination of those variations which are harmful in the struggle for existence that is brought about by excessive reproduction, there is no call for a prior intelligent causal force to plan and preordain them. Hostile critics charged Darwin with materialism and with making chance the cause of the universe.

Some naturalists, like Asa Gray, favored the Darwinian principle and attempted to reconcile it with design. Gray held to what may be called design on the installment plan. If we conceive the "stream of variations" to be itself intended, we may suppose that each successive variation was designed from the first to be selected. In that case, variation, struggle, and selection simply define the mechanism of "secondary causes" through which the "first cause" acts; and the doctrine of design is none the worse off because we know more of its *modus operandi*.

Darwin could not accept this mediating proposal. He admits or rather he asserts that it is "impossible to conceive this immense and wonderful universe including man with his capacity of looking far backwards and far into futurity as the result of blind chance or necessity."[1] But nevertheless he holds that since variations are in useless as well as useful directions, and since the latter are sifted out simply by the stress of the conditions of struggle for existence, the design argument as applied to living beings is unjustifiable; and its lack of support there deprives it of scientific value as applied to nature in general. If the variations of the pigeon, which under artificial selection give the pouter pigeon, are not preordained for the sake of the breeder, by what logic do we argue that variations resulting in natural species are pre-designed?[2]

IV

So much for some of the more obvious facts of the discussion of design *versus* chance, as causal principles of nature and of life as a whole. We brought up this discussion, you recall, as a crucial instance. What does our touchstone indicate as to the bearing of Darwinian ideas upon philosophy? In the first place, the new logic outlaws, flanks, dismisses—what you will—one type of problems and substitutes for it another type. Philosophy forswears inquiry after absolute origins and absolute finalities in order to explore specific values and the specific conditions that generate them.

Darwin concluded that the impossibility of assigning the world to chance as a whole and to design in its parts indicated the insolubility of the question. Two radically different reasons, however, may be given as to why a problem is insoluble. One reason is that the problem is too high for intelligence; the other is that the question in its very asking makes assumptions that render the question meaningless. The latter alternative is unerringly pointed to in the celebrated case of design *versus* chance. Once admit that the sole verifiable or fruitful object of knowledge is the particular set of changes that generate the object of study together with the consequences that then flow from it, and no intelligible question can be asked about what, by assumption, lies outside. To assert—as is often asserted—that specific values of particular truth, social bonds and forms of beauty, if they can be shown to be generated by concretely knowable conditions, are meaningless and in vain; to assert that they are justified only when they and their particular causes and effects have all at once been gathered up into some inclusive first cause and some exhaustive final goal, is intellectual atavism. Such argumentation is reversion to the logic that explained the extinction of fire by water through the formal essence of aqueousness and the quenching of thirst by water through the final cause of aqueousness. Whether used in the case of the special event or that of life as a whole, such logic only abstracts some aspect of the existing course of events in order to reduplicate it as a petrified eternal principle by which to explain the very changes of which it is the formalization.

When Henry Sidgwick casually remarked in a letter that as he grew older his interest in what or who made the world was altered into interest in what kind of a world it is anyway, his voicing of a common experience of our own day illustrates also the nature of that intellectual transformation effected by the Darwinian logic. Interest shifts from the wholesale essence back of special changes to the question of how special changes serve and defeat concrete purposes; shifts from an intelligence that shaped things once for all to the particular intelligences which things are even now shaping; shifts from an ultimate goal of good to the direct increments of justice and happiness that intelligent administration of existent conditions may beget and that present carelessness or stupidity will destroy or forego.

In the second place, the classic type of logic inevitably set philosophy upon proving that life *must* have certain qualities and values—no matter how experience presents the matter—because of some remote cause and eventual goal. The duty of wholesale justification inevitably accompanies all thinking that makes the meaning of special occurrences depend upon something that once and for all lies behind them. The habit of derogating from present meanings and uses prevents our looking the facts of experience in the face; it prevents serious acknowledgment of the evils they present and serious concern with the goods they promise but do not as yet fulfil. It turns thought to the business of finding a wholesale transcendent remedy for the one and guarantee for the other. One is reminded of the way many moralists and theologians greeted Herbert Spencer's recognition of an unknowable energy from which welled up the phenomenal physical processes without and the conscious operations within. Merely because Spencer labeled his unknowable energy "God," this faded piece of metaphysical goods was greeted as an important and grateful concession to the reality of the spiritual realm. Were it not for the deep hold of the habit of seeking justification for ideal values in the remote and transcendent, surely this reference of them to an unknowable absolute would be despised in comparison with the demonstrations of experience that knowable energies are daily generating about us precious values.

The displacing of this wholesale type of philosophy will doubtless not arrive by sheer logical disproof, but rather by growing recognition of its futility. Were it a thousand times true that opium produces sleep because of its dormitive energy, yet the inducing of sleep in the tired, and the recovery to waking life of the poisoned, would not be thereby one least step forwarded. And were it a thousand times dialectically demonstrated that life as a whole is regulated by a transcendent principle to a final inclusive goal, none the less truth and error, health and disease, good and evil, hope and fear in the concrete, would remain just what and where they now are. To improve our education, to ameliorate our manners, to advance our politics, we must have recourse to specific conditions of generation.

Finally, the new logic introduces responsibility into the intellectual life. To idealize and rationalize the universe at large is after all a confession of inability to master the courses of things that specifically concern us. As long as mankind suffered from this impotency, it naturally shifted a burden of responsibility that it could not carry over to the more competent shoulders of the transcendent cause. But if insight into specific conditions of value and into specific consequences of ideas is possible, philosophy must in time become a method of locating and interpreting the more serious of the conflicts that occur in life, and a method of projecting ways for dealing with them: a method of moral and political diagnosis and prognosis.

The claim to formulate *a priori* the legislative constitution of the universe is by its nature a claim that may lead to elaborate dialectic developments. But it is also one that removes these very conclusions from subjection to experimental test, for, by definition, these results make no differences in the detailed course of events. But a philosophy that humbles its pretensions to the work of projecting hypotheses for the education and conduct of mind, individual and social, is thereby subjected to test by the way in which the ideas it propounds work out in practice. In having modesty forced upon it, philosophy also acquires responsibility.

Doubtless I seem to have violated the implied promise of my earlier remarks and to have turned both prophet and partizan. But in anticipating the direction of the transformations in philosophy to be wrought by the Darwinian genetic and experimental logic, I do not profess to speak for any save those who yield themselves consciously or unconsciously to this logic. No one can fairly deny that at present there are two Effects of the Darwinian mode of thinking. On the one hand, there are making many sincere and vital efforts to revise our traditional philosophic conceptions in accordance with its demands. On the other hand, there is as definitely a recrudescence of absolutistic philosophies; an assertion of a type of philosophic knowing distinct from that of the sciences, one which opens to us another kind of reality from that to which the sciences give access; an appeal through experience to something that essentially goes beyond experience. This reaction affects popular creeds and religious movements as well as technical philosophies. The very conquest of the biological sciences by the new ideas has led many to proclaim an explicit and rigid separation of philosophy from science.

Old ideas give way slowly; for they are more than abstract logical forms and categories. They are habits, predispositions, deeply engrained attitudes of aversion and preference. Moreover, the conviction persists—though history shows it to be a hallucination—that all the questions that the human mind has asked are questions that can be answered in terms of the alternatives that the questions themselves present. But in fact intellectual progress usually occurs through sheer abandonment of questions together with both of the alternatives they assume—an abandonment that results from their decreasing vitality and a change of urgent interest. We do not solve them: we get over them. Old questions are solved by disappearing, evaporating, while new questions corresponding to the changed attitude of endeavor and preference take their place. Doubtless the greatest dissolvent in contemporary thought, of old questions, the greatest precipitant of new methods, new intentions, new problems, is the one effected by the scientific revolution that found its climax in the "Origin of Species."

Notes

A lecture in a course of public lectures on "Charles Darwin and His Influence on Science," given at Columbia University in the winter and spring of 1909. Reprinted from the *Popular Science Monthly* for July, 1909.

1. "Life and Letters," Vol. I., p. 282; cf. 285.

2. "Life and Letters," Vol. II., pp. 146, 170, 245; Vol. I., pp. 283–84. See also the closing portion of his "Variations of Animals and Plants under Domestication."

This 1939 address encapsulates Dewey's conception of participatory and progressive democracy.

JOHN DEWEY

Creative Democracy—The Task before Us

Under present circumstances I cannot hope to conceal the fact that I have managed to exist eighty years. Mention of the fact may suggest to you a more important fact—namely, that events of the utmost significance for the destiny of this country have taken place during the past four-fifths of a century, a period that covers more than half of its national life in its present form. For obvious reasons I shall not attempt a summary of even the more important of these events. I refer here to them because of their bearing upon the issue to which this country committed itself when the nation took shape—the creation of democracy, an issue which is now as urgent as it was a hundred and fifty years ago when the most experienced and wisest men of the country gathered to take stock of conditions and to create the political structure of a self-governing society.

For the net import of the changes that have taken place in these later years is that ways of life and institutions which were once the natural, almost the inevitable, product of fortunate conditions have now to be won by conscious and resolute effort. Not all the country was in a pioneer state eighty years ago. But it was still, save perhaps in a few large cities, so close to the pioneer stage of American life that the traditions of the pioneer, indeed of the frontier, were active agencies in forming the thoughts and shaping the beliefs of those who were born into its life. In imagination at least the country was still having an open frontier, one of unused and unappropriated resources. It was a country of physical opportunity and invitation. Even so, there was more than a marvelous conjunction of physical circumstances involved in bringing to birth this new nation. There was in existence a group of men who were capable of readapting older institutions and ideas to meet the situations provided by new physical conditions—a group of men extraordinarily gifted in political inventiveness.

At the present time, the frontier is moral, not physical. The period of free lands that seemed boundless in extent has vanished. Unused resources are now human rather than material. They are found in the waste of grown men and women who are without the chance to work, and in the young men and young women who find doors closed where there was once opportunity. The crisis that one hundred and fifty years ago called out social and political inventiveness is with us in a form which puts a heavier demand on human creativeness.

At all events this is what I mean when I say that we now have to re-create by deliberate and determined endeavor the kind of democracy which in its origin one hundred and fifty years ago was largely the product of a fortunate combination of men and circumstances. We have lived for a long time upon the heritage that came to us from the happy conjunction of men and events in an earlier day. The present state of the world is more than a reminder that we have now to put forth every energy of our own to prove worthy of our heritage. It is a challenge to do for the critical and complex conditions of today what the men of an earlier day did for simpler conditions.

If I emphasize that the task can be accomplished only by inventive effort and creative activity, it is in part because the depth of the present crisis is due in considerable part to the fact that for a long period we acted as if our democracy were something that perpetuated itself automatically; as if our ancestors had succeeded in setting up a machine that solved the problem of perpetual motion in politics. We acted as if democracy were something that took place mainly at Washington and Albany—or some other state capital—under the impetus of what happened when men and women went to the polls once a year or so—which is a somewhat extreme way of saying that we have had the habit of thinking of democracy as a kind of political mechanism that will work as long as citizens were reasonably faithful in performing political duties.

Of late years we have heard more and more frequently that this is not enough; that democracy is a way of life. This saying gets down to hard pan. But I am not sure that something of the externality of the old idea does not cling to the new and better statement. In any case we can escape from this external way of thinking only as we realize in thought and act that democracy is a *personal* way of individual life; that it signifies the possession and continual use of certain attitudes, forming personal character and determining desire and purpose in all the relations of life. Instead of thinking of our own dispositions and habits as accommodated to certain institutions we have to learn to think of the latter as expressions, projections and extensions of habitually dominant personal attitudes.

Democracy as a personal, an individual, way of life involves nothing fundamentally new. But when applied it puts a new practical meaning in old ideas. Put into effect it signifies that powerful present enemies of democracy can be successfully met only by the creation of personal attitudes in individual human beings; that we must get over our tendency to think that its defense can be found in any external means whatever, whether military or civil, if they are separated from individual attitudes so deep-seated as to constitute personal character.

Democracy is a way of life controlled by a working faith in the possibilities of human nature. Belief in the Common Man is a familiar article in the democratic creed. That belief is without basis and significance save as it means faith in the potentialities of human nature as that nature is exhibited in every human being irrespective of race, color, sex, birth and family, of material or cultural wealth. This faith may be enacted in statutes, but it is only on paper unless it is put in force in the attitudes which human beings display to one another in all the incidents and relations of daily life. To denounce Naziism for intolerance, cruelty and stimulation of hatred amounts to fostering insincerity if, in our personal relations to other persons, if, in our daily walk and conversation, we are moved by racial, color or other class prejudice; indeed, by anything save a generous belief in their possibilities as human beings, a belief which brings with it the need for providing conditions which will enable these capacities to reach fulfillment. The democratic faith in human equality is belief that every human being, independent of the quantity or range of his personal endowment, has the right to equal opportunity with every other person for development of whatever gifts he has. The democratic belief in the principle of leadership is a generous one. It is universal. It is belief in the capacity of every person to lead his own life free from coercion and imposition by others provided right conditions are supplied.

Democracy is a way of personal life controlled not merely by faith in human nature in general but by faith in the capacity of human beings for intelligent judgment and action if proper conditions are furnished. I have been accused more than once and from opposed quarters of an undue, a Utopian, faith in the possibilities of intelligence and in education as a correlate of intelligence. At all events, I did not invent this faith. I acquired it from my surroundings as far as those surroundings were animated by the democratic spirit. For what is the faith of democracy in the role of consultation, of conference, of persuasion, of discussion, in formation of public opinion, which in the long run is self-corrective, except faith in the capacity of the intelligence of the common man to respond with commonsense to the free play of facts and ideas which are secured by effective guarantees of free inquiry, free assembly and free communication? I am willing to leave to upholders of totalitarian states of the right and the left the view that faith in the capacities of intelligence is Utopia. For the faith is so deeply embedded in the methods which are intrinsic to democracy that when a professed democrat denies the faith he convicts himself of treachery to his profession.

When I think of the conditions under which men and women are living in many foreign countries today, fear of espionage, with danger hanging over the meeting of friends for friendly conversation in private gatherings, I am inclined to believe that the heart and final guarantee of democracy is in free gatherings of neighbors on the street corner to discuss back and forth what is read in uncensored news of the day, and in gatherings of friends in the living rooms of houses and apartments to converse freely with one another. Intolerance, abuse, calling of names because of differences of opinion about religion or politics or business, as well as because of differences of race, color, wealth or degree of culture are treason to the democratic way of life. For everything which bars freedom and fullness of communication sets up barriers that divide human beings into sets and cliques, into antagonistic sects and factions, and thereby undermines the democratic way of life. Merely legal guarantees of the civil liberties of free belief, free expression, free assembly are of little avail if in daily life freedom of communication, the give and take of ideas, facts, experiences, is choked by mutual suspicion, by abuse, by fear and hatred. These things destroy the essential condition of the democratic way of living even more effectually than open coercion which—as the example of totalitarian states proves—is effective only when it succeeds in breeding hate, suspicion, intolerance in the minds of individual human beings.

Finally, given the two conditions just mentioned, democracy as a way of life is controlled by personal faith in personal day-by-day working together with others. Democracy is the belief that even when needs and ends or consequences are different for each individual, the habit of amicable cooperation—which may include, as in sport, rivalry and competition—is itself a priceless addition to life. To take as far as possible every conflict which arises—and they are bound to arise—out of the atmosphere and medium of force, of violence as a means of settlement into that of discussion and of intelligence is to treat those who disagree—even profoundly—with us as those from whom we may learn, and in so far, as friends. A genuinely democratic faith in peace is faith in the possibility of conducting disputes, controversies and conflicts as cooperative undertakings in which both parties learn by giving the other a chance to express itself, instead of having one party conquer by forceful suppression of the other—a suppression which is none the less one of violence when it takes place by psychological means of ridicule, abuse, intimidation, instead of by overt imprisonment or in concentration camps. To cooperate by giving differences a chance to show themselves because of the belief that the expression of difference is not only a right of the other persons but is a means of enriching one's own life-experience, is inherent in the democratic personal way of life.

If what has been said is charged with being a set of moral commonplaces, my only reply is that that is just the point in saying them. For to get rid of the habit of thinking of democracy as something institutional and external and to acquire the habit of treating it as a way of personal life is to realize that democracy is a moral ideal and so far as it becomes a fact is a moral fact. It is to realize that democracy is a reality only as it is indeed a commonplace of living.

Since my adult years have been given to the pursuit of philosophy, I shall ask your indulgence if in concluding I state briefly the democratic faith in the formal terms of a philosophic position. So stated, democracy is belief in the ability of human experience to generate the aims and methods by which further experience will grow in ordered richness. Every other form of moral and social faith rests upon the idea that experience must be subjected at some point or other to some form of external control; to some "authority" alleged to exist outside the processes of experience. Democracy is the faith that the process of experience is more important than any special result attained, so that special results achieved are of ultimate value only as they are used to enrich and order the ongoing process. Since the process of experience is capable of being educative, faith in democracy is all one with faith in experience and education. All ends and values that are cut off from the ongoing process become arrests, fixations. They strive to fixate what has been gained instead of using it to open the road and point the way to new and better experiences.

If one asks what is meant by experience in this connection my reply is that it is that free interaction of individual human beings with surrounding conditions, especially the human surroundings, which develops and satisfies need and desire by increasing knowledge of things as they are. Knowledge of conditions as they are is the only solid ground for communication and sharing; all other communication means the subjection of some persons to the personal opinion of other persons. Need and desire—out of which grow purpose and direction of energy—go beyond what exists, and hence beyond knowledge, beyond science. They continually open the way into the unexplored and unattained future.

Democracy as compared with other ways of life is the sole way of living which believes wholeheartedly in the process of experience as end and as means; as that which is capable of generating the science which is the sole dependable authority for the direction of further experience and which releases emotions, needs and desires so as to call into being the things that have not existed in the past. For every way of life that fails in its democracy limits the contacts, the exchanges, the communications, the interactions by which experience is steadied while it is also enlarged and enriched. The task of this release and enrichment is one that has to be carried on day by day. Since it is one that can have no end till experience itself comes to an end, the task of democracy is forever that of creation of a freer and more humane experience in which all share and to which all contribute.

In this essay from 1938, Hook lays out an argument for participatory democracy based in a pragmatist epistemology.

SIDNEY HOOK

The Democratic Way of Life

The greatest tribute to democracy as an ideal of social life is unwittingly paid to it in the *apologias* of the dictators of the modern world—Hitler, Stalin, and Mussolini. For all of them insist in the shrillest tones that the regimes they control are actually, despite appearances, democracies "in a higher sense." For example, Mussolini in a public address delivered at Berlin in September 1937, proclaimed that "the greatest and soundest democracies which exist in the world today are Italy and Germany"; while Stalin, after the worst blood purge in history, praises the constitution that bears his name—a constitution that openly provides (in Section 126) for the control of all socio-political institutions by the minority Communist Party—as the most democratic in all history. And here in America, due to the needs of the foreign policy of the various dictatorships, their partisans now wrap up their program of blood and steel in the American flag and make a great verbal play about being defenders of American democracy. Thus, in a letter to the *New York Times* (July 20, 1938) Mr. Fritz Kuhn speaks of Americans who have become members of his German *Bund* (Nazis) "because of their faith in its devotion to the institutions of the United States." With even greater fanfare the American Communist Party has proclaimed its love of democracy to the death on the assumption that Americans neither read nor have memories. Both pronouncements merely reflect the necessities of foreign policy of Germany and Russia respectively.

That the greatest enemies of democracy should feel compelled to render demagogic lip-allegiance to it is an eloquent sign of the inherent plausibility of democratic ideals to the modern mind, and of their universal appeal. But that its enemies, apparently with some success, should have the audacity to flaunt the principles they have so outrageously betrayed in practice, is just as eloquent a sign that these principles are ambiguous. Agreement where there is no clarity merely cloaks differences; it does not settle them. Sooner or later it breeds confusion and confusion breeds distrust. In the end there grows up a venomous rancor which is so intent upon destroying the enemy that it is blind to what the real differences are.

The analysis of the concept of democracy is not merely, then, a theoretical problem for the academician. The ordinary man who says he believes in democracy must clearly understand what he means by it. Otherwise the genuine issues that divide men will be lost in the welter of emotive words which demagogues skillfully evoke to conceal their true intentions. There is such a thing as the ethics of words. And of all the words in our political vocabulary none is in greater need of precise analysis and scrupulous use than "democracy."

Anyone can use a word as a sign for any idea provided he makes adequately clear what he means by it. For example, if a man says, "By democracy I mean a government in which the name of the ruler begins with a D," we can smile at his peculiar definition and pass on. We need not dispute his usage if he always accompanies it with a parenthetical explanation of what he understands by the term. However, if he introduces the term into a political discussion without stating explicitly the special meaning it has for him, we have every scientific and moral right to object. For where words of a certain kind are already in use, to employ them as signs of new meanings without posting, so to speak, a clear public notice, is to be guilty of a form of counterfeit. New verbal signs can always be found for new meanings.

Democracy is a term which has customarily been associated with certain *historical* practices and with certain writings in the history of culture. Instead of beginning with arbitrary nominal definitions, it would be preferable to describe and critically evaluate the growth of democracy in Western Europe from its origins in the Greek city (slave) states to the present. But this could only be essayed in a systematic treatise.

The third alternative—one which we shall here follow—is to begin with a definition which formally is acceptable to most people who distinguish democracy from other forms of political organization, and which is in consonance with at least traditional American usage. We shall then indicate what it implies as far as the structure of other present-day social institutions is concerned, what techniques of settling differences it commits us to, and what fundamental ethical values are presupposed. In this way we shall combine the advantages of an analytical and "contemporary-historical" treatment.

1. The Definition Explored

A democratic society is one where the government rests upon the freely given consent of the governed. Some ambiguity attaches to every term in this preliminary definition. The least ambiguous is the term "governed." By "the governed" is meant those adult participating members of the community, with their dependents, whose way of life is affected by what the government does or leaves undone. By "the government" is primarily intended the law-and-policy-making agencies, legislative, executive, and judicial, whose activities control the life of the community. In the first instance, then, government is a political concept; but in certain circumstances it may refer to social and economic organizations whose policies affect the lives of a large number of individuals. In saying that the government rests upon the "consent" of the governed, it is meant that at certain fixed periods its policies are submitted to the governed for approval or disapproval. By "freely given" consent of the governed is meant that no coercion, direct or indirect, is brought to bear upon the governed to elicit their approval or disapproval. A government that "rests upon" the freely given consent of the governed is one which *in fact* abides by the expression of this approval or disapproval.

A direct consequence of this definition may be that there is no complete democracy anywhere in the world. This no more prevents our employing the term intelligently and making comparative evaluation than the fact that no one is "perfectly healthy" prevents us from making the concept "health" basic to medical theory and practice. There is no absolutely fat man, but we can easily tell whether one man is fatter than another. So long as our definition enables us to order existing communities in a series of greater or less democracy, our definition is adequate.

If a democratic government rests upon the freely given consent of the governed, then it cannot be present where institutional arrangements—whether political or nonpolitical—obviously obstruct the registering or the implementing of the common consent. We do not have to settle any metaphysical questions about the nature of freedom in order to be able to tell when consent is not free. A plebiscite or election which is held at the point of a bayonet, or in which one can only vote "Yes," or in which no opposition candidates are permitted, obviously does not express freely given consent. These are only the crudest violations of the democratic ideal, but they are sufficient to make the pretense that the present-day regimes in Italy, Russia, and Germany are democratic sound almost obscene.

There are less obvious but no less effective ways of coercively influencing the expression of consent. A threat, for example, to deprive the governed of their jobs or means of livelihood, by a group which has the power to do so, would undermine a democracy even if its name were retained. In fact, every overt form of economic pressure, since it is experienced directly by the individual and since so many other phases of his life are dependent upon economic security, is an overt challenge to democracy. Where the political forms of democracy function within a society in which economic controls are not subject to political control, there is always a standing threat to democracy. For in such a society the possibility exists that economic pressure may strongly influence the expression of consent. Where it cannot influence the expression of consent, it may subvert or prevent its execution. This is particularly true in modern societies in which social instruments of production, necessary for the livelihood of many, are privately owned by the few. A political democracy cannot function properly where differences in economic power are so great that one group can determine the weal or woe of another by nonpolitical means. Genuine political democracy, therefore, entails the right of the governed, through their representatives, to control economic policy. In this sense, it might be said that where there is no economic democracy—a phrase which will be explained later—there can be no genuine and widespread political democracy. The exact degree of economic control necessary to political democracy will vary with changing conditions. It is clear that today modern economic organization plays such a dominant role in social life that political democracy cannot be implemented if it is unable to control economic policy.

A further consequence of "freely given consent" is the absence of a monopoly of education where education includes all agencies of cultural transmission, especially the press. Important as is the majority principle for a democracy, the expression of consent by the majority is not free if it is deprived of access to sources of information, if it can read *only* the official interpretation, if it can hear *only* one voice in classroom, pulpit, and radio—if, in short, all critical opposition is branded as treason to be extirpated by heresy trials, by re-education in concentration camps, and by execution squads. The individual has no more freedom of action when his mind is deliberately tied by ignorance than when his hands are tied with rope. The very dependence of modern man upon the printed word, greater than ever before in history, makes the public right to critical dissent all the more necessary if common consent is to be free. Not many years ago this would have been a commonplace. Today apologists have so muddied the waters of truth that its reaffirmation must be stressed.

2. Positive Conditions for Democracy

So far we have been considering conditions in the absence of which democracy cannot exist. But the effective working of a democracy demands the presence of a number of other conditions. Among these, the active participation of the governed in the processes of government is primary.

By active participation is meant not the attempt to do the specific work of officials but free discussion and consultation on public policies, and voluntary co-operation in the execution of mandates reached through the democratic process. Where the governed feel that they have no stake in the government, indifference results. And political indifference may be called the dry-rot of democracy. "The food of feeling," as Mill well says, "is action. . . . Let a person have nothing to do for his country, and he will not care for it."

The country or community, however, is never a homogeneous whole. There may be common interests, but the conceptions of the common interest are never common. Nor in this world can all interests ever in fact be common. If they were, government would be a mere administrative detail. The variety of interests that is always to be found makes necessary that no interest be excluded from voicing its demands, even though these demands may, in the process of democratic deliberation, be compromised or rejected. The only historical alternative to the participation of the masses in the processes of government is the ancient, artful, and uncertain technique of "bread and circuses." That the modern bread is smeared with oleomargarine and the modern circuses are cinematic makes no essential difference. Such a technique conceals differences and trouble centers; whereas the methods of participation and consultation uncover them, articulate new social needs, and suggest instrumentalities for handling them. The wisest policy cannot succeed in face of popular indifference or hostility. Even those who believe that the professionally wise men or experts must do the governing exclude at their own peril those whom they would govern from their counsels.

Another requirement for the effective working of democracy is the presence of mechanisms which permit prompt action, through delegated authority, in crucial situations. What constitutes a crucial situation and what specific administrative mechanisms are best adapted to meet it cannot be settled in advance. But it is clear that there is nothing incompatible with democracy in freely delegating specific functions to authority provided that at a certain fixed time an accounting is made to the governed who alone have the prerogative of renewing or abrogating the grant of authority.

Today the very existence of democracy depends upon its ability to act decisively in its own defense. Effective defense against a foreign totalitarian enemy may require extraordinary and exceptional measures of coordination and control. Some fear that this is the road to totalitarianism. It *may* be. But the alternative is *certain* totalitarianism. So long as democratic communities are threatened by totalitarian states, they must make provision, openly and after discussion, for delegation of authority to responsible individuals to undertake technical defense in a crisis.

That such grants of authority may be abused goes without saying. It may even be acknowledged that there is no absolute guarantee against the risks of usurpation. But unless these risks are sometimes taken, democratic government may be destroyed by evils whose urgency will not wait until the close of prolonged debate. Common sense recognizes this in case of flood and plague. Flood and plague have their social analogues. *But whatever the crisis may be, the recognition that it is a crisis must come from the governed or their delegated representatives; grants of power must be renewed democratically; and the governed cannot, without destroying their democracy, proclaim that the crisis is permanent.*

The fact that the preservation of democracy sometimes demands the delegation of far-reaching authority, and the fact that the possession of such authority may corrupt those who wield it, reinforces another positive requirement of democracy. To understand this requirement we must take note of the psychological effects of holding power, and the historical evidence which indicates that many democratic organizations, sooner or later, become instruments of a minority group which, identifying its own special interests with the interests of the organization as a whole, keeps power by fraud, myth, and force. Taken literally, Lord Acton's maxim, "Power always corrupts and absolute power corrupts absolutely," is an exaggeration. But there is sufficient truth in it to give us pause when we are about to invest individuals or groups with great power, even temporarily. Similarly, Robert Michels's "iron law of oligarchy," according to which democrats may be victorious but democracy never, goes beyond the data he has assembled. But no one can read his powerful case studies and the data presented by other writers like Pareto, Machajaski, and Nomad without realizing how plausible Michels's induction is. And when we add to this the degeneration, under our very eyes, of the Russian Revolution—a revolution which began avowedly as a workers' democracy, developed into the dictatorship of the Communist Party *over* the proletariat, and finally took form as the bloody rule of a camarilla that has piled up more corpses in a few years than did the Roman emperors in as many centuries of Christian persecution—the lesson is driven home with sickening force.

This lesson is that a positive requirement of a working democracy is an intelligent distrust of its leadership, a skepticism, stubborn but not blind, of all demands for the enlargement of power, and an emphasis upon critical method in every phase of education and social life. This skepticism, like other forms of vigilance, may often seem irritating to leaders who are convinced of their good intentions. The skepticism, however, is not of their intentions but of the objective consequences of their power. Where skepticism is replaced by uncritical enthusiasm and the many-faceted deifications which our complex society makes possible, a fertile emotional soil for dictatorship has been prepared. The most convincing aspect of Plato's analysis of the cycle of political decay in the eighth book of his *Republic* is the transition from a hero-worshiping democracy to an absolute tyranny.

Another positive requirement of democracy we have already referred to as economic democracy. By economic democracy is meant the power of the community, organized as producers and consumers, to determine the basic question of the objectives of economic development. Such economic democracy presupposes some form of social ownership and planning; but whether the economy is to be organized in a single unit or several, whether it is to be highly centralized or not, are experimental questions. There are two criteria to decide such questions. One is the extent to which a specific form of economic organization or ownership makes possible an abundance of goods and services for the greatest number, without which formal political democracy is necessarily limited in its functions, if not actually endangered. The other is the extent to which a specific form of economic organization preserves and strengthens the conditions of the democratic process already described.

Certain kinds of economic planning may give the security of a jail—in which, in exchange for freedom, the inmates are given food, clothing, and shelter of sorts. But any type of planned society which does not provide for the freest criticism, for diversity, for creative individuality, for catholicity of taste, cannot ever guarantee real security. In such a society the "security" is conditional upon accepting arbitrary bureaucratic decree as the law of life. This is conspicuously true wherever the instruments of promotion are socialized by a nondemocratic state. When Stalin tells us that "the dictatorship of the proletariat is *substantially* the dictatorship of the [Communist] Party," he is telling us that the Russian worker can purchase a problematic security only insofar as he accepts this Party dictatorship.[1]

The upshot, then, of our analysis is that just as political democracy is incomplete without some form of economic democracy, so there can be no genuine economic democracy without political democracy. Some may call this socialism. But it is certainly not the "socialism" of either Hitler or Stalin. Nor, despite the fears of frightened tories, of Roosevelt,

3. The Argument against Democracy

Our discussion would be incomplete if we did not consider the chief objections which have been urged against democracy by some of the outstanding thinkers of the past and present. Most of these objections are variants of two fundamental arguments—practical and theoretical.

The practical argument, from the time of Plato down, stresses the imperfections in the actual working of democracy. It draws up a detailed indictment of the blundering inefficiencies of democracies, the influence of demagogy and prejudice in the formulation of their policies, and the operation of certain political mechanisms which place the power of selection of the rulers of the community, actually, in the hands of a minority. And from this largely accurate description of the way in which democracies do in fact work, it is concluded that democracy must be scrapped for another alternative.

The description may be granted without justifying the conclusion. For unless we know the precise nature of the alternative and how *it* works out in practice, we may legitimately reply that the cure for the evils of democracy is better democracy. This is not a catch phrase. For by better democracy is meant the realization of the conditions and requirements already outlined—or, at the very least, the struggle for them.

And what are the alternatives to democracy with its imperfections? All alternatives turn out upon analysis to involve some form of benevolent despotism—whether a personal or a class or a party despotism. Now the fatal objection to a benevolent despotism of any sort—aside from the fact that people with different interests have different ideas of what constitutes benevolence—is that no one knows how long the despotism will remain benevolent, not even the despot himself. We may appeal from Philip drunk to Philip sober, but who is to keep Philip sober?

Not a single benevolent act of a despot recorded in history but can be matched with scores of malevolent acts. For every guilty man a dictator spares there are thousands of innocent men he dooms. The *ideal* benevolent despotism is a mere figment of the imagination; and even as an ideal, it is no more promising than *ideal* democracy. Moreover, it is wrong to compare the ideal form of benevolent despotism with the actual practice of democracy. If we intelligently compare the practices of both, whether in antiquity or in the modern world, the lovers of democracy need not fear the outcome.

The second type of argument against democracy, the theoretical, is really presupposed by the first. It holds that, the ultimate end of government being human welfare, only those having the best knowledge and highest intelligence are qualified for the difficult pursuit of discovering the nature of human welfare. Since the problems of government are largely administrative, demanding knowledge and intelligence, and since an effective democracy presupposes the possession of both knowledge and intelligence by the majority of the population, which even the lover of democracy must admit is rarely the case, democracy must be rejected. Plato put the nub of the argument in a metaphor: Who would propose that, setting out on a perilous journey, we should *elect* the pilot of the ship? And yet the pilot of the ship of state has a task infinitely more difficult, and the course of the vessel is beset by many more perils. What rhyme or reason exists, therefore, for electing him? Or as Santayana, a direct lineal descendant of Plato in political philosophy, put it, "It is knowledge and knowledge only that may rule by divine right."

Space permits only a brief indication of the Achilles-heel of this argument. While there may be experts in knowledge of fact, there are no experts in wisdom of policy. Ultimate welfare presupposes that there is an "ultimate good." But a conclave of philosophers gathered together to determine the nature of the ultimate good would resemble nothing so much as the Tower of Babel. Wisdom of policy depends upon knowledge of one's interests. It is true that some men are not clear as to what their own interests are. But it is arrant presumption for other men to pretend to them that they know what their interests "really" are, or what they should be. A parent dealing with children may sometimes be justified in asserting that he knows better than they what their real interests are; but any ruler who justifies his abrogation of democratic control by proclaiming that he knows what the real interests of the governed are better than they do themselves is therewith telling them that they are no more responsible than children. Besides oppressing them, he is insulting them, for he envisages their childhood as perpetual. It is not accidental that we call dictatorial government paternal. In paternal government, however, there is more authority than affection. The paternal ruler often takes his political children for guinea pigs upon whom he can try peculiar experiments. Their peculiarity lies in the fact that, whatever their outcome, the present generation of guinea pigs never recovers.

True, there may be no wisdom in electing a pilot or a cobbler. But in the last analysis, as even Plato was compelled to recognize, it is the user and not the maker who is the best judge of work done. Who wears the shoe knows best where it pinches. On this homely truth every theoretical attack on democracy founders.

4. The Values and Method of Democracy

And democracy is more than a pattern of institutional behavior. Democracy is an affirmation of certain attitudes and values which are more important than any particular set of institutions, because those attitudes and values must serve as the sensitive directing controls of institutional change.

Every mechanism of democratic government has a critical point at which it may run wild. It may be formally perfect but actually murderous. For example, the principle of majority rule is a necessary condition of a working democracy. But a majority can oppress a minority. Numbers, even less than knowledge, give divine right, or immunity from folly. A government resting upon the consent of the majority may not therewith be good government—as the tragic history of the oppression of minorities testifies. To the lessons of that history no one can be indifferent; for every member of the community is part of a minority at some point or on some issue. The persecution of the Jews during the last two thousand years is sufficient evidence that political forms by themselves are no safeguards for a minority—even when it is innocent, unarmed, and culturally creative.

It is helpful but hardly sufficient to insist that democratic communities must provide for self-government by voluntary organized minorities on all questions which concern the minority rather than the community at large. It is not sufficient because minorities are often in opposition on communal issues, and the very willingness to extend autonomy on "local" issues is contingent upon acceptance of the values of democracy as a way of life.

Now there are three related values which are central to democracy as a way of life.

The first is found in many variant formulations, but common to them all is the belief that every individual should be regarded as possessing intrinsic worth or dignity. The social corollary of this recognition is that equal opportunities of development should be provided for the realization of individual talents and capacities. To believe in the equality of opportunities does not mean to believe in the equality of talents. But it does carry with it a recognition that, under conditions of modern technology, marked inequalities in the distribution of wealth or in standards of living are prejudicial to equal opportunities of development. If it is absurd to ask that identical technical opportunities be accorded the artist and the engineer, the machinist and the administrator, it is not absurd to expect that their living conditions be approximately the same. The ideal of equality is not something to be mechanically applied. But it must function as a regulative principle of distribution. Otherwise endemic conflicts, latent in all human associations, take such acute forms that they imperil the very existence of democracy.

The belief in the equal right of all members of the community to develop their personalities must be complemented by a belief in the value of difference, variety, uniqueness. In a democracy differences of interest and achievements must not be merely suffered, they must be encouraged. The healthy zest arising from the conflict and interchange of ideas and personal tastes in a free society is a much more fruitful source of new and significant experiences than the peace of dull, dead uniformity. Of course there are limits to difference as there are to specialization. For however different people are, they live in a common world, they must communicate in a common language, and accept the common constraints which safeguard the species from extinction. In nondemocratic societies this fact that men are always bound in some way by the necessities of living together is used as a premise for constructing vast techniques of repression to choke off differences in almost every way. In democratic societies, however, the same prime fact must serve rather as a condition for enlarging the scope of variation, free play, growth, and experiment.

No matter what the values are to which a democracy is committed, situations will arise in which these values conflict or are challenged by still other values. A decision made in one situation does not necessarily stand for all other situations. The ultimate commitment of a democracy, then, must be a faith in some method by which these conflicts are resolved. Since the method must be the test of all values, it would not be inaccurate to call it the basic value in the democratic way of life. This method is the method of intelligence, of critical scientific inquiry. In a democracy it must be directed to all issues, to all conflicts, if democracy is not to succumb to the dangers which threaten it from both within and without. It is not mere chance that the greatest philosopher of experimental empiricism—John Dewey—is also the greatest philosopher of democracy.

To say that the method of intelligence is essential to the democratic process seems like worrying a commonplace. But not when it is realized how revolutionary the impact would be of giving the method of intelligence institutional force in education, economics, law, and politics. Policies would be treated as hypotheses, not as dogmas; customary practices as generalizations, not as God-given truths. A generation trained in schools where emphasis was placed upon method, method, and still more method, could hardly be swayed by current high-pressured propaganda. The very liberties granted by free institutions in a democracy provide opportunities for special interests to forge powerful instruments to undermine it. The most insidious of all devices for overthrowing democratic institutions is to acquire protective coloration by hypocritical espousal of democracy, to occupy strategic posts, and to open the gates after the Trojan horse is safely within the city. There is no protection against this save the critically armed mind which is immune to rhetoric and parades, and which does *not* give the fanatic a tolerant kind of credit for being sincere in his belief that the end justifies any means.

Those who believe in democracy must distinguish intelligently and act resolutely. First of all, they must distinguish between honest opposition *within* the framework of the democratic process and the opposition, subsidized and controlled by the totalitarian enemies of democracy, which is a form of treason to everything democrats hold dear. Opposition of the first kind, no matter how mistaken, must be tolerated, if for no other reason than that we cannot be sure that it is not we who are mistaken. Opposition of the second kind, no matter what protective coloration it wears—and it will usually be found wrapped up in counterfeit symbols of patriotism or in recently acquired vestments of the Bill of Rights—must be swiftly dealt with if democracy is to survive.

Minorities know that the majority may be tyrannical. The tyranny of the mass flows from its insensitiveness to the consequences of means and methods, not only for the minority but for itself. An insistence upon evidence, relevance, and deliberation is not incompatible with action; it is incompatible only with blind action. The method of intelligence cuts under the fanaticisms which make a fetish of ends, by stressing the conditions and consequences of their use. It both uncovers and enforces responsibilities in social life. It, and it alone, can distinguish between social conflicts which are negotiable and those which are irreconcilable, and the degree of each. Where conflicts are negotiable, it approaches social problems as difficulties to be solved by experiment and analysis, not as battles to be fought out in the heat of blood lust.

What alternative method can be embraced by a society which permits and encourages plural values and plural associations? The more intelligence is liberated in a democratic community, the greater its control of nature and the sources of wealth; the greater its control of nature, the greater possibility of diversifying interests, values, and associations; the greater diversification, the more necessary the function of intelligence to mediate, integrate, and harmonize.

Notes

Originally published as "Democracy as a Way of Life," *Southern Review* 4 (Summer 1938): 46–57. Reprinted by permission of the Estate of Sidney Hook.

1. The quotation is from a speech of Stalin. Compare his *Leninism* (New York: International Publishers, 1928), page 33. That the dictatorship of the Party is not a specifically Russian doctrine but an integral part of the Leninist (not Marxist) theory is clear from the "Theses and Resolutions" of the Communist International. Compare also, for the American variant, the following passage from William Z. Foster's *Towards Soviet America* (New York: Coward-McCann, 1932): "Under the [proletarian] dictatorship, all the capitalistic parties—Republican, Democratic, Progressive, Socialist [*sic*]—will be liquidated, and the Communist Party functioning alone as the Party of the toiling masses" (page 275). And yet the Communist Party has such a profound contempt for the Intelligence of the American public, and of its own members, that it publicly proclaims itself as the heir of the traditions of Jefferson!

Originally published in 1923, this paper contains the core of Lewis's synthesis of Kant and pragmatism.

C. I. LEWIS

A Pragmatic Conception of the *A Priori*

The conception of the *a priori* points two problems which are perennial in philosophy: the part played in knowledge by the mind itself, and the possibility of "necessary truth" or of knowledge "independent of experience." But traditional conceptions of the *a priori* have proved untenable. That the mind approaches the flux of immediacy with some godlike foreknowledge of principles which are legislative for experience, that there is any natural light or any innate ideas, it is no longer possible to believe.

Nor shall we find the clue to the *a priori* in any compulsion of the mind to incontrovertible truth or any peculiar kind of demonstration which establishes first principles. All truth lays upon the rational mind the same compulsion to belief; as Mr. Bosanquet has pointed out, this character belongs to all propositions or judgments once their truth is established.

The difficulties of the conception are due, I believe, to two mistakes: whatever is *a priori* is necessary, but we have misconstrued the relation of necessary truth to mind. And the *a priori* is independent of experience, but in so taking it, we have misunderstood its relation to empirical fact. What is *a priori* is necessary truth not because it compels the mind's acceptance, but precisely because it does not. It is given experience, brute fact, the *a posteriori* element in knowledge which the mind must accept willy-nilly. The *a priori* represents an attitude in some sense freely taken, a stipulation of the mind itself, and a stipulation which might be made in some other way if it suited our bent or need. Such truth is necessary as opposed to contingent, not as opposed to voluntary. And the *a priori* is independent of experience not because it prescribes a form which the data of sense must fit, or anticipates some preëstablished harmony of experience with the mind, but precisely because it prescribes nothing to experience. That is *a priori* which is true, *no matter what.* What it anticipates is not the given, but our attitude toward it: it concerns the uncompelled initiative of mind or, as Josiah Royce would say, our categorical ways of acting.

The traditional example of the *a priori par excellence* is the laws of logic. These can not be derived from experience since they must first be taken for granted in order to prove them. They make explicit our general modes of classification. And they impose upon experience no real limitation. Sometimes we are asked to tremble before the spectre of the "alogical," in order that we may thereafter rejoice that we are saved from this by the dependence of reality upon mind. But the "alogical" is pure bogey, a word without a meaning. What kind of experience could defy the principle that everything must either be or not be, that nothing can both be and not be, or that if *x* is *y* and *y* is *z*, then *x* is *z*? If anything imaginable or unimaginable could violate such laws, then the ever-present fact of change would do it every day. The laws of logic are purely formal; they forbid nothing but what concerns the use of terms and the corresponding modes of classification and analysis. The law of contradiction tells us that nothing can be both white and not-white, but it does not and can not tell us whether black is not-white, or soft or square is not-white. To discover *what contradicts what* we must always consult the character of experience. Similarly the law of the excluded middle formulates our decision that whatever is not designated by a certain term shall be designated by its negative. It declares our purpose to make, for every term, a complete dichotomy of experience, instead—as we might choose—of classifying on the basis of a tripartite division into opposites (as black and white) and the middle ground between the two. Our rejection of such tripartite division represents only our penchant for simplicity.

Further laws of logic are of similar significance. They are principles of procedure, the parliamentary rules of intelligent thought and speech. Such laws are independent of experience because they impose no limitations whatever upon it. They are legislative because they are addressed to ourselves—because definition, classification, and inference represent no operations of the objective world, but only our own categorical attitudes of mind.

And further, the ultimate criteria of the laws of logic are pragmatic. Those who suppose that there is, for example, *a* logic which everyone would agree to if he understood it and understood himself, are more optimistic than those versed in the history of logical discussion have a right to be. The fact is that there are several logics, markedly different, each self-consistent in its own terms and such that whoever, using it, avoids false premises, will never reach a false conclusion. Mr. Russell, for example, bases *his* logic on an implication relation such that if twenty sentences be cut from a newspaper and put in a hat, and then two of these be drawn at random, one of them will certainly imply the other, and it is an even bet that the implication will be mutual. Yet upon a foundation so remote from ordinary modes of inference the whole structure of *Principia Mathematica* is built. This logic—and there are others even more strange—is utterly consistent and the results of it entirely valid. Over and above all questions of consistency, there are issues of logic which can not be determined—nay, can not even be argued—except on pragmatic grounds of conformity to human bent and intellectual convenience. That we have been blind to this fact, itself reflects traditional errors in the conception of the *a priori*.

We may note in passing one less important illustration of the *a priori*—the proposition "true by definition." Definitions and their immediate consequences, analytic propositions generally, are necessarily true, true under all possible circumstances. Definition is legislative because it is in some sense arbitrary. Not only is the meaning assigned to words more or less a matter of choice—that consideration is relatively trivial—but the manner in which the precise classifications which definition embodies shall be effected is something not dictated by experience. If experience were other than it is, the definition and its corresponding classification might be inconvenient, fantastic, or useless, but it could not be false. Mind makes classifications and determines meanings; in so doing it creates the *a priori* truth of analytic judgments. But that the manner of this creation responds to pragmatic considerations is so obvious that it hardly needs pointing out.

If the illustrations so far given seem trivial or verbal, that impression may be corrected by turning to the place which the *a priori* has in mathematics and in natural science. Arithmetic, for example, depends *en toto* upon the operation of counting or correlating, a procedure which can be carried out at will in any world containing identifiable things—even identifiable ideas—regardless of the further characters of experience. Mill challenged this *a priori* character of arithmetic. He asked us to suppose a demon sufficiently powerful and maleficent so that every time two things were brought together with two other things, this demon should always introduce a fifth. The implication which he supposed to follow is that under such circumstances 2 + 2 = 5 would be a universal law of arithmetic. But Mill was quite mistaken. In such a world we should be obliged to become a little clearer than is usual about the distinction between arithmetic and physics, that is all. If two black marbles were put in the same urn with two white ones, the demon could take his choice of colors, but it would be evident that there were more black marbles or more white ones than were put in. The same would be true of all objects in any wise identifiable. We should simply find ourselves in the presence of an extraordinary physical law, which we should recognize as universal in our world, that whenever two things were brought into proximity with two others, an additional and similar thing was always created by the process. Mill's world would be physically most extraordinary. The world's work would be enormously facilitated if hats or locomotives or tons of coal could be thus multiplied by anyone possessed originally of two pairs. But the laws of mathematics would remain unaltered. It is because this is true that arithmetic is *a priori*. Its laws prevent *nothing*; they are compatible with anything which happens or could conceivably happen in nature. They would be true in any possible world. Mathematical addition is not a physical transformation. Physical changes which result in an increase or decrease of the countable things involved are matters of everyday occurrence. Such physical processes present us with phenomena in which the purely mathematical has to be separated out by abstraction. Those laws and those laws only have necessary truth which we are prepared to maintain, no matter what. It is because we shall always separate out that part of the phenomenon not in conformity with arithmetic and designate it by some other category—physical change, chemical reaction, optical illusion—that arithmetic is *a priori*.

The *a priori* element in science and in natural law is greater than might be supposed. In the first place, all science is based upon definitive concepts. The formulation of these concepts is, indeed, a matter determined by the commerce between our intellectual or our pragmatic interests and the nature of experience. Definition is classification. The scientific search is for such classification as will make it possible to correlate appearance and behavior, to discover law, to penetrate to the "essential nature" of things in order that behavior may become predictable. In other words, if definition is unsuccessful, as early scientific definitions mostly have been, it is because the classification thus set up corresponds with no natural cleavage and does not correlate with any important uniformity of behavior. A name itself must represent *some* uniformity in experience or it names nothing. What does not repeat itself or recur in intelligible fashion is not a thing. Where the definitive uniformity is a clue to other uniformities, we have successful scientific definition. Other definitions can not be said to be false; they are merely useless. In scientific classification the search is, thus, for *things worth naming*. But the naming, classifying, defining activity is essentially prior to investigation. We can not interrogate experience in general. Until our meaning is definite and our classification correspondingly exact, experience can not conceivably answer our questions.

In the second place, the fundamental laws of any science—or those treated as fundamental—are *a priori* because they formulate just such definitive concepts or categorical tests by which alone investigation becomes possible. If the lightning strikes the railroad track at two places, A and B, how shall we tell whether these events are simultaneous? "We . . . require a definition of simultaneity such that this definition supplies us with the method by means of which . . . we can decide whether or not both the lightning strokes occurred simultaneously. As long as this requirement is not satisfied, I allow myself to be deceived as a physicist (and of course the same applies if I am not a physicist), when I imagine that I am able to attach a meaning to the statement of simultaneity. . . .

"After thinking the matter over for some time you then offer the following suggestion with which to test simultaneity. By measuring along the rails, the connecting line *AB* should be measured up and an observer placed at the mid-point *M* of the distance *AB*. This observer should be supplied with an arrangement (*e.g.*, two mirrors inclined at 90°) which allows him visually to observe both places *A* and *B* at the same time. If the observer perceives the two flashes at the same time, then they are simultaneous.

"I am very pleased with this suggestion, but for all that I can not regard the matter as quite settled, because I feel constrained to raise the following objection: 'Your definition would certainly be right, if I only knew that the light by means of which the observer at *M* perceives the lightning flashes travels along the length *A–M* with the same velocity as along the length *B–M*. But an examination of this supposition would only be possible if we already had at our disposal the means of measuring time. It would thus appear as though we were moving here in a logical circle.'

"After further consideration you cast a somewhat disdainful glance at me—and rightly so—and you declare: 'I maintain my previous definition nevertheless, because in reality it assumes absolutely nothing about light. There is only *one* demand to be made of the definition of simultaneity, namely, that in every real case it must supply us with an empirical decision as to whether or not the conception which has to be defined is fulfilled. That light requires the same time to traverse the path *A–M* as for the path *B–M* is in reality *neither a supposition nor a hypothesis* about the physical nature of light, but a *stipulation* which I can make of my own freewill in order to arrive at a definition of simultaneity' . . . We are thus led also to a definition of 'time' in physics."[1]

As this example from the theory of relativity well illustrates, we can not even ask the questions which discovered law would answer until we have first by *a priori* stipulation formulated definitive criteria. Such concepts are not verbal definitions, nor classifications merely; they are themselves laws which prescribe a certain uniformity of behavior to whatever is thus named. Such definitive laws are *a priori;* only so can we enter upon the investigation by which further laws are sought. Yet it should also be pointed out that such *a priori* laws are subject to abandonment if the structure which is built upon them does not succeed in simplifying our interpretation of phenomena. If, in the illustration given, the relation "simultaneous with," as defined, should not prove transitive—if event *A* should prove simultaneous with *B*, and *B* with *C*, but not *A* with *G*—this definition would certainly be rejected.

And thirdly, there is that *a priori* element in science—as in other human affairs—which constitutes the criteria of the real as opposed to the unreal in experience. An object itself is a uniformity. Failure to behave in certain categorical ways marks it as unreal. Uniformities of the type called "natural law" are the clues to reality and unreality. A mouse which disappears where no hole is, is no real mouse; a landscape which recedes as we approach is but illusion. As the queen remarked in the episode of the wishing-carpet: "If this were real, then it would be a miracle. But miracles do not happen. Therefore I shall wake presently." That the uniformities of natural law are the only reliable criteria of the real, is inescapable. But such a criterion is *ipso facto a priori.* No conceivable experience could dictate the alteration of a law so long as failure to obey that law marked the content of experience as unreal.

This is one of the puzzles of empiricism. We deal with experience: what any reality may be which underlies experience, we have to learn. What we desire to discover is natural law, the formulation of those uniformities which obtain amongst the real. But experience as it comes to us contains not only the real but all the content of illusion, dream, hallucination, and mistake. The *given* contains both real and unreal, confusingly intermingled. If we ask for uniformities of this unsorted experience, we shall not find them. Laws which characterize all experience, of real and unreal both, are non-existent and would in any case be worthless. What we seek are the uniformities of the *real;* but *until we have such laws, we can not sift experience and segregate the real.*

The obvious solution is that the enrichment of experience, the separation of the real from the illusory or meaningless, and the formulation of natural law, all grow up together. If the criteria of the real are *a priori*, that is not to say that no conceivable character of experience would lead to alteration of them. For example, spirits can not be photographed. But if photographs of spiritistic phenomena, taken under properly guarded conditions, should become sufficiently frequent, this *a priori* dictum would be called in question. What we should do would be to redefine our terms. Whether "spook" was spirit or matter, whether the definition of "spirit" or of "matter" should be changed; all this would constitute one interrelated problem. We should reopen together the question of definition or classification, of criteria for this sort of real, and of natural law. And the solution of one of these would mean the solution of all. Nothing could *force* a redefinition of spirit or of matter. A sufficiently fundamental relation to human bent, to human interests, would guarantee continuance unaltered even in the face of unintelligible and baffling experiences. In such problems, the mind finds itself uncompelled save by its own purposes and needs. I *may* categorize experience as I will; but *what* categorical distinctions will best serve my interests and objectify my own intelligence? What the mixed and troubled experience shall be—that is beyond me. But what I shall do with it—that is my own question, when the character of experience is sufficiently before me. I am coerced only by my own need to understand.

It would indeed be inappropriate to characterize as *a priori* a law which we are wholly prepared to alter in the light of further experience, even though in an isolated case we should discard as illusory any experience which failed to conform. But the crux of the situation lies in this; beyond such principles as those of logic, which we seem fully prepared to maintain no matter what, there must be further and more particular criteria of the real prior to any investigation of nature whatever. We can not even interrogate experience without a network of categories and definitive concepts. And we must further be prepared to say what experimental findings will answer what questions, and how. Without tests which represent anterior principle, there is no question which experience could answer at all. Thus the most fundamental laws in any category—or those which we regard as most fundamental—are *a priori,* even though continued failure to render experience intelligible in such terms might result eventually in the abandonment of that category altogether. Matters so comparatively small as the behavior of Mercury and of starlight passing the sun's limb may, if there be persistent failure to bring them within the field of previously accepted modes of explanation, result in the abandonment of the independent categories of space and time. But without the definitions, fundamental principles, and tests, of the type which constitute such categories, no experience whatever could prove or disprove anything. And to that mind which should find independent space and time absolutely necessary conceptions, no possible experiment could prove the principles of relativity. "There must be some error in the experimental findings, or some law not yet discovered," represents an attitude which can never be rendered impossible. And the only sense in which it could be proved unreasonable would be the pragmatic one of comparison with another method of categorical analysis which more successfully reduced all such experience to order and law.

At the bottom of all science and all knowledge are categories and definitive concepts which represent fundamental habits of thought and deep-lying attitudes which the human mind has taken in the light of its total experience. But a new and wider experience may bring about some alteration of these attitudes, even though by themselves they dictate nothing as to the content of experience, and no experience can conceivably prove them invalid.

Perhaps some will object to this conception on the ground that only such principles should be designated *a priori* as the human mind *must* maintain, no matter what; that if, for example, it is shown possible to arrive at a consistent doctrine of physics in terms of relativity, even by the most arduous reconstruction of our fundamental notions, then the present conceptions are by that fact shown not to be *a priori*. Such objection is especially likely from those who would conceive the *a priori* in terms of an absolute mind or an absolutely universal human nature. We should readily agree that a decision by popular approval or a congress of scientists or anything short of such a test as would bring to bear the full weight of human capacity and interest, would be ill-considered as having to do with the *a priori*. But we wish to emphasize two facts: first, that in the field of those conceptions and principles which have altered in human history, there are those which could neither be proved nor disproved by any experience, but represent the uncompelled initiative of human thought—that without this uncompelled initiative no growth of science, nor any science at all, would be conceivable. And second, that the difference between such conceptions as are, for example, concerned in the decision of relativity versus absolute space and time, and those more permanent attitudes such as are vested in the laws of logic, there is only a difference of degree. The dividing line between the *a priori* and the *a posteriori* is that between principles and definitive concepts which *can* be maintained in the face of all experience and those genuinely empirical generalizations which *might* be proven flatly false. The thought which both rationalism and empiricism have missed is that there are principles, representing the initiative of mind, which, impose upon experience no limitations whatever, but that such conceptions are still subject to alteration on pragmatic grounds when the expanding boundaries of experience reveal their infelicity as intellectual instruments.

Neither human experience nor the human mind has a character which is universal, fixed, and absolute. "The human mind" does not exist at all save in the sense that all humans are very much alike in fundamental respects, and that the language habit and the enormously important exchange of ideas has greatly increased our likeness in those respects which are here in question. Our categories and definitions are peculiarly social products, reached in the light of experiences which have much in common, and beaten out, like other pathways, by the coincidence of human purposes and the exigencies of human coöperation. Concerning the *a priori* there need be neither universal agreement nor complete historical continuity. Conceptions, such as those of logic, which are least likely to be affected by the opening of new ranges of experience, represent the most stable of our categories; but none of them is beyond the possibility of alteration.

Mind contributes to experience the element of order, of classification, categories, and definition. Without such, experience would be unintelligible. Our knowledge of the validity of these is simply consciousness of our own fundamental ways of acting and our own intellectual intent. Without this element, knowledge is impossible, and it is here that whatever truths are necessary and independent of experience must be found. But the commerce between our categorical ways of acting, our pragmatic interests, and the particular character of experience, is closer than we have realized. No explanation of any one of these can be complete without consideration of the other two.

Pragmatism has sometimes been charged with oscillating between two contrary notions; the one, that experience is "through and through malleable to our purpose" the other, that facts are "hard" and uncreated by the mind. We here offer a mediating conception: through all our knowledge runs the element of the *a priori*, which is indeed malleable to our purpose and responsive to our need. But throughout, there is also that other element of experience which is "hard," "independent," and unalterable to our will.

Notes

Read at the meeting of the American Philosophical Association, Dec. 27, 1922.

1. Einstein, *Relativity*, pp. 26–28: italics are the author's.

This essay was first published in Erkenntnis in 1968 and later served as the first chapter of Ways of Worldmaking. *In it, Goodman argues that the development of symbolic systems is the crucial element of cognitive life.*

NELSON GOODMAN

Words, Works, Worlds

1. Questions

Countless worlds made from nothing by use of symbols—so might a satirist summarize some of Cassirer's major themes. These themes—the multiplicity of worlds, the speciousness of 'the given', the creative power of the understanding, the variety and formative function of symbols—are also integral to my own thinking. Sometimes, though, I forget that they have been so eloquently set forth by Cassirer,[1] partly perhaps because his emphasis on myth, his concern with the comparative study of cultures, and his talk of the human spirit have been mistakenly associated with current trends toward mystical obscurantism, anti-intellectual intuitionism, or anti-scientific humanism. Actually these attitudes are as alien to Cassirer as to my own skeptical, analytic, constructionalist orientation.

My aim in what follows is less to defend certain theses that Cassirer and I share than to take a hard look at some crucial questions they raise. In just what sense are there many worlds? What distinguishes genuine from spurious worlds? What are worlds made of? How are they made, and what role do symbols play in the making? And how is worldmaking related to knowing? These questions must be faced even if full and final answers are far off.

2. Versions and Visions

As intimated by William James's equivocal title *A Pluralistic Universe*, the issue between monism and pluralism tends to evaporate under analysis. If there is but one world, it embraces a multiplicity of contrasting aspects; if there are many worlds, the collection of them all is one. The one world may be taken as many, or the many worlds taken as one; whether one or many depends on the way of taking.

Why, then, does Cassirer stress the multiplicity of worlds? In what important and often neglected sense are there many worlds? Let it be clear that the question here is not of the possible worlds that many of my contemporaries, especially those near Disneyland, are busy making and manipulating. We are not speaking in terms of multiple possible alternatives to a single actual world but of multiple actual worlds. How to interpret such terms as "real", "unreal", "fictive", and "possible" is a subsequent question.

Consider, to begin with, the fact that the statements "the sun always moves" and "the sun never moves", though equally true, are at odds with each other. Shall we say, then, that they describe different worlds, and indeed that there are as many different worlds as there are such mutually exclusive truths? Rather, we are inclined to regard the two strings of words not as complete statements with truth-values of their own but as elliptical for some such statements as "Under frame of reference *A*, the sun always moves" and "Under frame of reference *B*, the sun never moves"—statements that may both be true of the same world.

Frames of reference, though, belong less to what is described than to systems of description; and each of the two statements relates what is described to such a system. If I ask about the world, you can offer to tell me how it is under one or more frames of reference; but if I insist that you tell me how it is apart from all frames, what can you say? We are confined to ways of describing whatever is described. Our universe, so to speak, consists of these ways rather than of a world or of worlds.

The alternative descriptions of motion, all of them in much the same terms and routinely transformable into one another, provide only a minor and rather pallid example of diversity in accounts of the world. Much more striking is the vast variety of versions and visions in the several sciences, in the works of different painters and writers, and in our perceptions as informed by these, by circumstances, and by our own insights, interests, and past experiences. Even with all illusory or wrong or dubious versions dropped, the rest exhibit new dimensions of disparity. Here we have no neat set of frames of reference, no ready rules for transforming physics, biology, and psychology into one another, and no way at all of transforming any of these into Van Gogh's vision, or Van Gogh's into Canaletto's. Such of these versions as are depictions rather than descriptions have no truth-value in the literal sense, and cannot be combined by conjunction. The difference between juxtaposing and conjoining two statements has no evident analogue for two pictures or for a picture and a statement. The dramatically contrasting versions of the world can of course be accommodated by relativization: each is right under a given system—for a given science, a given artist, or a given perceiver and situation. Here again we turn from describing or depicting 'the world' to talking of descriptions and depictions, but now without even the consolation of intertranslatability among or any evident organization of the several systems in question.

Yet doesn't a right version differ from a wrong one just in applying to the world, so that rightness itself depends upon and implies a world? On the contrary, 'the world' depends upon rightness. We cannot test a version by comparing it with a world undescribed, undepicted, unperceived, but only by other means that I shall discuss later. While we may speak of determining what versions are right as 'learning about the world', 'the world' supposedly being that which all right versions describe, all we learn about the world is contained in right versions of it; and while the underlying world, bereft of these, need not be denied to those who love it, it is perhaps on the whole a world well lost. For some purposes, we may want to define a relation that will so sort versions into clusters that each cluster constitutes a world and the members of the cluster are versions of that world; but for many purposes, right world-descriptions and world-depictions and world-perceptions, the ways-the-world-is, or just versions can be treated as our worlds.[2]

Since the fact that there are many different world-versions is hardly debatable, and the question how many if any worlds-in-themselves there are is virtually empty, in what nontrivial sense are there, as Cassirer and like-minded pluralists insist, many worlds? Just this, I think that many different world-versions are of independent interest and importance, without any requirement or presumption of reducibility to a single base. The pluralist, far from being anti-scientific, accepts the sciences at full value. His typical adversary is the monopolistic materialist or physicalist who maintains that one system, physics, is preeminent and all-inclusive, such that every other version must eventually be reduced to it or rejected as false or meaningless. If all right versions could somehow be reduced to one and only one, that one might with some semblance of plausibility[3] be regarded as the only truth about the only world. But the evidence for such reducibility is negligible, and even the claim is nebulous since physics itself is fragmentary and unstable and the kind and consequences of reduction envisaged are vague. (How do you go about reducing Constable's or James Joyce's world-view to physics?) I am the last person likely to underrate construction and reduction.[4] A reduction from one system to another can make a genuine contribution to understanding the interrelationships among world-versions; but reduction in any reasonably strict sense is rare, almost always partial, and seldom if ever unique. To demand full and sole reducibility to physics or any other one version is to forego nearly all other versions. The pluralists' acceptance of versions other than physics implies no relaxation of rigor but a recognition that standards different from yet no less exacting than those applied in science are appropriate for appraising what is conveyed in perceptual or pictorial or literary versions.

So long as contrasting right versions not all reducible to one are countenanced, unity is to be sought not in an ambivalent or neutral something beneath these versions but in an overall organization embracing them. Cassirer undertakes the search through a cross-cultural study of the development of myth, religion, language, art, and science. My approach is rather through an analytic study of types and functions of symbols and symbol systems. In neither case should a unique result be anticipated; universes of worlds as well as worlds themselves may be built in many ways.

3. How Firm a Foundation?

The non-Kantian theme of multiplicity of worlds is closely akin to the Kantian theme of the vacuity of the notion of pure content. The one denies us a unique world, the other the common stuff of which worlds are made. Together these theses defy our intuitive demand for something stolid underneath, and threaten to leave us uncontrolled, spinning out our own inconsequent fantasies.

The overwhelming case against perception without conception, the pure given, absolute immediacy, the innocent eye, substance as substratum, has been so fully and frequently set forth—by Berkeley, Kant, Cassirer, Gombrich,[5] Bruner,[6] and many others—as to need no restatement here. Talk of unstructured content or an unconceptualized given or a substratum without properties is self-defeating; for the talk imposes structure, conceptualizes, ascribes properties. Although conception without perception is merely *empty*, perception without conception is *blind* (totally inoperative). Predicates, pictures, other labels, schemata, survive want of application, but content vanishes without form. We can have words without a world but no world without words or other symbols.

The many stuffs—matter, energy, waves, phenomena—that worlds are made of are made along with the worlds. But made from what? Not from nothing, after all, but *from other worlds*. Worldmaking as we know it always starts from worlds already on hand; the making is a remaking. Anthropology and developmental psychology may study social and individual histories of such world-building, but the search for a universal or necessary beginning is best left to theology.[7] My interest here is rather with the processes involved in building a world out of others.

With false hope of a firm foundation gone, with the world displaced by worlds that are but versions, with substance dissolved into function, and with the given acknowledged as taken, we face the questions how worlds are made, tested, and known.

4. Ways of Worldmaking

Without presuming to instruct the gods or other worldmakers, or attempting any comprehensive or systematic survey, I want to illustrate and comment on some of the processes that go into worldmaking. Actually, I am concerned more with certain relationships among worlds than with how or whether particular worlds are made from others.

(a) Composition and Decomposition

Much but by no means all worldmaking consists of taking apart and putting together, often conjointly: on the one hand, of dividing wholes into parts and partitioning kinds into subspecies, analyzing complexes into component features, drawing distinctions; on the other hand, of composing wholes and kinds out of parts and members and subclasses, combining features into complexes, and making connections. Such composition and decomposition is normally effected or assisted or consolidated by the application of labels: names, predicates, gestures, pictures, etc. Thus, for example, temporally diverse events are brought together under a proper name or identified, as making up 'an object' or 'a person'; or snow is sundered into several materials under terms of the Eskimo vocabulary. Metaphorical transfer—for example, where taste predicates are applied to sounds—may effect a double reorganization, both re-sorting the new realm of application and relating it to the old one.

Identification rests upon organization into entities and kinds. The response to the question "same or not the same?" must always be "same what?"[8] Different so-and-sos may be the same such-and-such: what we point to or indicate, verbally or otherwise, may be different events but the same object, different towns but the same state, different members but the same club or different clubs but the same members, different innings but the same ball game. 'The ball-in-play' of a single game may be comprised of temporal segments of a dozen or more baseballs. The psychologist asking the child to judge constancy when one vessel is emptied into another must be careful to specify *what* constancy is in question—constancy of volume or depth or shape or kind of material, etc.[9] Identity or constancy in a world is identity with respect to what is within that world as organized.

Motley entities cutting across each other in complicated patterns may belong to the same world. We do not make a new world every time we take things apart or put them together in another way; but worlds may differ in that not everything belonging to one belongs to the other. The world of the Eskimo who has not grasped the comprehensive concept of snow differs not only from the world of the Samoan but also from the world of the New Englander who has not grasped the Eskimo's distinctions. In other cases, worlds differ in response to theoretical rather than practical needs. A world with points as elements cannot be the Whiteheadian world having points as certain classes of nesting volumes, or having points as certain pairs of interesting lines or as certain triples of intersecting planes. That the points of our everyday world can be equally well defined in any of these ways does not mean that a point can be identified in any one world with a nest of volumes and a pair of lines and a triple of planes; for all these are different from each other. Again the world of a system taking minimal concrete phenomena as atomic cannot admit qualities as atomic parts of these concreta.[10]

Repetition as well as identification is relative to organization. A world may be unmanageably heterogeneous or unbearably monotonous according to how events are sorted into kinds. Whether or not today's experiment repeats yesterday's, however much the two events may differ, depends upon whether they test a common hypothesis; as Sir George Thomson puts it:

> There will always be something different. . . . What it comes to when you say you repeat an experiment is that you repeat all the features of an experiment which a theory determines are relevant. In other words you repeat the experiment: as an example of the theory.[11]

Likewise, two musical performances that differ drastically are nevertheless performances of the same work if they conform to the same score. The notational system distinguishes constitutive from contingent features, thus picking out the performance-kinds that count as works.[12] And things 'go on in the same way' or not according to what is regarded as the same way; 'now I can go on',[13] in Wittgenstein's sense, when I have found a familiar pattern, or a tolerable variation of one, that fits and goes beyond the cases given. Induction requires taking some classes to the exclusion of others as relevant kinds. Only so e.g., do our observations of emeralds exhibit any regularity and confirm that all emeralds are green rather than that all are grue (i.e. examined before a given date and green, or not so examined and blue).[14] The uniformity of nature we marvel at or the unreliability we protest belongs to a world of our own making.

In these latter cases, worlds differ in the relevant kinds comprised in them. I say "relevant" rather than "natural" for two reasons: first, "natural" is an inapt term to cover not only biological species but such artificial kinds as musical works, psychological experiments, and types of machinery; and second, "natural" suggests some absolute categorical or psychological priority while the kinds in question are rather habitual or traditional or devised for a new purpose.

(b) Weighting

While we may say that in the cases discussed some relevant kinds of one world are missing from another, we might perhaps better say that the two worlds contain just the same classes sorted differently into relevant and irrelevant kinds. Some relevant kinds of the one world, rather than being absent from the other, are present as irrelevant kinds; some differences among worlds are not so much in entities comprised as in emphasis or accent, and these differences are no less consequential. Just as to stress all syllables is to stress none, so to take all classes as relevant kinds is to take none as such. In one world there may be many kinds serving different purposes; but conflicting purposes may make for irreconcilable accents and contrasting worlds, as may conflicting conceptions of what kinds serve a given purpose. Grue cannot be a relevant kind for induction in the same world as green; for that would preclude some of the decisions, right or wrong, that constitute inductive inference.

Some of the most striking contrasts of emphasis appear in the arts. Many of the differences among portrayals by Daumier, Ingres, Michelangelo, and Rouault are differences in aspects accentuated. What counts as emphasis, of course, is departure from the relative prominence accorded the several features in the current world of our everyday seeing. With changing interests and new insights, the visual weighting of features of bulk or line or stance or light alters, and yesterday's level world seems strangely perverted—yesterday's realistic calendar landscape becomes a repulsive caricature.

These differences in emphasis, too, amount to a difference in relevant kinds recognized. Several portrayals of the same subject may thus place it according to different categorical schemata. Like a green emerald and a grue one, even if the same emerald, a Piero della Francesca *Christ* and a Rembrandt one belong to worlds organized into different kinds.

Works of art, though, characteristically illustrate rather than name or describe relevant kinds. Even where the ranges of application—the things described or depicted—coincide, the features or kinds exemplified or expressed may be very different. A line drawing of softly draped cloth may exemplify rhythmic linear patterns; and a poem with no words for sadness and no mention of a sad person may in the quality of its language be sad, and poignantly express sadness. The distinction between saying or representing on the one hand and showing or exemplifying on the other becomes even more evident in the case of abstract painting and music and dance that have no subject-matter but nevertheless manifest—exemplify or express—forms and feelings. Exemplification and expression, though running in the opposite direction from denotation—that is, from the symbol to a literal or metaphorical feature of it instead of to something the symbol applies to—are no less symbolic referential functions and instruments of worldmaking.[15]

Emphasis or weighting is not always binary as is a sorting into relevant and irrelevant kinds or into important and unimportant features. Ratings of relevance, importance, utility, value often yield hierarchies rather than dichotomies. Such weightings are also instances of a particular type of ordering.

(c) Ordering

Worlds not differing in entities or emphasis may differ in ordering; for example, the worlds of different constructional systems differ in order of derivation. As nothing is at rest or is in motion apart from a frame of reference so nothing is primitive or is derivationally prior to anything apart from a constructional system. However, derivation unlike motion is of little immediate practical interest; and thus in our everyday world, although we almost always adopt a frame of reference at least temporarily, we seldom adopt a derivational basis. Earlier I said that the difference between a world having points as pairs of lines and a world having lines as composed of points is that the latter but not the former admits as entities nonlinear elements comprised within lines. But alternatively we may say that these worlds differ in their derivational ordering of lines and points of the not-derivationally-ordered world of daily discourse.

Orderings of a different sort pervade perception and practical cognition. The standard ordering of brightness in color follows the linear increase in physical intensity of light; but the standard ordering of hues curls the straight line of increasing wavelength into a circle. Order includes periodicity as well as proximity; and the standard ordering of tones is by pitch and octave. Orderings alter with circumstances and objectives. Much as the nature of shapes changes under different geometries, so do perceived patterns change under different orderings; the patterns perceived under a twelve-tone scale are quite different from those perceived under the traditional eight-tone scale, and rhythms depend upon the marking off into measures.

Radical reordering of another sort occurs in constructing a static image from the input from scanning a picture, or of a unified and comprehensive image of an object or a city from temporally and spatially and qualitatively heterogeneous observations and other items of information.[16] Some very fast readers recreate normal word-ordering from a series of fixations that proceed down the left-hand page and then up the right-hand page of a book.[17] And spatial order in a map or a score is translated into the temporal sequence of a trip or a performance.

All measurement, furthermore, is based upon order. Indeed, only through suitable arrangements and groupings can we handle vast quantities of material perceptually or cognitively. Gombrich discusses the decimal periodization of historical time into decades, centuries, and millennia.[18] Daily time is marked off into twenty-four hours, and each of these into sixty minutes of sixty seconds each. Whatever else may be said of these modes of organization, they are not 'found in the world' but *built into a world*. Ordering, as well as composition and decomposition and weighting of wholes and kinds, participates in worldmaking.

(d) Deletion and Supplementation

Also, the making of one world out of another usually involves some extensive weeding out and filling in—actual excision of some old and supply of some new material. Our capacity for overlooking is virtually unlimited, and what we do take in usually consists of significant fragments and clues that need massive supplementation. Artists often make skilfull use of this; a lithograph by Giacometti fully presents a walking man by sketches of the head, hands, and feet only in just the right postures and positions against an expanse of blank paper, and a drawing by Katharine Sturgis conveys a hockey player in action by a single charged line.

That we find what we are prepared to find, what we look for or what forcefully affronts our expectations, that we are blind to what neither serves nor counters our interests, is a commonplace of everyday life and is amply attested by psychological experiments.[19] In the painful experience of proofreading and the more pleasurable one of watching a skilled magician, we incurably miss something that is there and see something that is not there. Memory edits more ruthlessly; a person with equal command of two languages may remember a learned list of items while forgetting in which language they were listed.[20] And even within what we do perceive and remember, we dismiss as illusory or negligible what cannot be fitted into the architecture of the world we are building.

The scientist is no less drastic, rejecting or purifying most of the entities and events of the world of ordinary things while generating quantities of filling for curves suggested by sparse data, and erecting elaborate structures on the basis of meagre observations. Thus does he build a world conforming to his chosen concepts and obeying his universal laws.

Replacement of a so-called analog by a so-called digital system involves deletion in the articulation of separate steps; for example, to use a digital thermometer with readings in tenths of a degree is to recognize no temperature as lying between 90 and 90.1 degrees. Similar deletion occurs under standard musical notation, which recognizes no pitch between *c* and *c#* and no duration between a sixty-fourth and a one-hundred-and-twenty-eighth note. On the other hand, supplementation occurs when, say, an analog replaces a digital instrument for measuring mileage, or when a violinist performs from a score.

Perhaps the most spectacular cases of supplementation, though, are found in the perception of motion. Sometimes motion in the perceptual world results from intricate and abundant fleshing out of the physical stimuli. Psychologists have long known of what is called the 'phi phenomenon': under carefully controlled conditions, if two spots of light are flashed a short distance apart and in quick succession, the viewer normally sees a spot of light moving continuously along a path from the first position to the second. That is remarkable enough in itself since of course the direction of motion cannot have been determined prior to the second flash; but perception has even greater creative power. Paul Kolers has recently shown[21] that if the first stimulus spot is circular and the second square, the seen moving spot transforms smoothly from circle to square; and transformations between two-dimensional and three-dimensional shapes are often effected without trouble. Moreover, if a barrier of light is interposed between the two stimulus spots, the moving spot detours around the barrier. But what happens if the first flash is, say, red and the second pink (or blue)? Kolers and von Grünau[22] have found that, almost incredibly, while the seen spot moves and transforms its shape smoothly as before, it stays red to about the middle of the path and then abruptly changes to pink (or blue)! Just why these supplementations occur as they do is a fascinating subject for speculation.[23]

(e) Deformation

Finally, some changes are reshapings or deformations that may according to point of view be considered either corrections or distortions. The physicist smooths out the simplest rough curve that fits all his data. Vision stretches a line, ending with arrowheads pointing *in* while shrinking a physically equal line ending with arrowheads pointing *out*, and tends to expand the size of a smaller more valuable coin in relation to that of a larger less valuable one.[24] Caricaturists often go beyond overemphasis to actual distortion. Picasso starting from Velasquez's *Las Meninas*, and Brahms starting from a theme of Haydn's, work magical variations that amount to revelations.

These then are ways that worlds are made. I do not say *the* ways. My classification is not offered as comprehensive or clearcut or mandatory. Not only do the processes illustrated often occur in combination but the examples chosen sometimes fit equally well under more than one heading; for example, some changes may be considered alternatively as reweightings or reorderings or reshapings or as all of these, and some deletions are also matters of differences in composition. All I have tried to do is to suggest something of the variety of processes in constant use. While a tighter systematization could surely be developed, none can be ultimate; for as remarked earlier, there is no more a unique world of worlds than there is a unique world.

5. Trouble with Truth

With all this freedom to divide and combine, emphasize, order, delete, fill in and fill out, and even distort, what are the objectives and the constraints? What are the criteria for success in making a world?

Insofar as a version is verbal and consists of statements, truth may be relevant. But truth cannot be defined or tested by agreement with 'the world'; for not only do truths differ for different worlds but the nature of agreement between a version and a world apart from it is notoriously nebulous. Rather—speaking loosely and without trying to answer either Pilate's question or Tarski's—a version is true when it offends no unyielding beliefs and none of its own precepts. Among beliefs unyielding at a given time may be long-lived reflections of laws of logic, short-lived reflections of recent observations, and other convictions and prejudices ingrained with varying degrees of firmness. Among precepts, for example, may be choices among alternative frames of reference, weightings, and derivational bases. But the line between beliefs and precepts is neither sharp nor stable. Beliefs are framed in concepts informed by precepts; and if a Boyle ditches his data for a smooth curve just missing them all, we may say either that observational volume and pressure are different properties from theoretical volume and pressure or that the truths about volume and pressure differ in the two worlds of observation and theory. And the staunchest belief tends in time to admit alternatives; "the earth is at rest" passed from dogma to dependence upon precept.

Truth, far from being a solemn and severe master, is a docile and obedient servant. The scientist who supposes that he is single-mindedly dedicated to the search for truth deceives himself. He is unconcerned with the trivial truths he could grind out endlessly; and he looks to the multifaceted and irregular results of observations for little more than suggestions of overall structures and significant generalizations. He seeks system, simplicity, scope; and when satisfied on these scores he tailors truth to fit.[25] He as much decrees as discovers the laws he sets forth, as much designs as discerns the patterns he delineates.

Truth, moreover, pertains solely to what is said, and literal truth solely to what is said literally. We have seen, though, that worlds are made not only by what is said literally but also by what is said metaphorically, and not only by what is said either literally or metaphorically but also by what is exemplified and expressed—by what is shown as well as what is said. In a scientific treatise, only literal truth may count;

but in a poem or novel, metaphorical or allegorical truth may matter more, for even a literally false statement may be metaphorically true[26] and may mark or make new associations and discriminations, change emphases, effect exclusions and additions. And statements whether literally or metaphorically true or false may show what they do not say, may work as trenchant literal or metaphorical examples of unmentioned features and feelings. In Vachel Lindsay's *The Congo*, for example, the pulsating pattern of drumbeats is insistently exhibited rather than described.

Finally, for nonverbal versions and even for verbal versions without statements, truth is irrelevant. We risk confusion when we speak of pictures or predicates as "true of" what they depict or apply to; they have no truth-value, and may represent or denote some things and not others, while a statement does have truth-value and is true of everything if of anything.[27] And a nonrepresentational picture such as a Mondrian says nothing, denotes nothing, pictures nothing, and is neither true nor false, but shows much. Nevertheless, showing or exemplifying, like denoting, is a referential function; and much the same considerations count for pictures as for the concepts or predicates of a theory: their relevance and their revelations, their force and their fit—in sum their *rightness*. Rather than speaking of pictures as true or false we might better speak of theories as right or wrong; for the truth of the laws of a theory is but one special feature and is often, as we have seen, overridden in importance by the cogency and compactness and comprehensiveness, the informativeness and organizing power of the whole system.

"The truth, the whole truth, and nothing but the truth" would thus be a perverse and paralyzing policy for any worldmaker. The whole truth would be too much; it is too vast, variable, and clogged with trivia. The truth alone would be too little, for some right versions are not true—being either false or neither true nor false—and even for true versions rightness may matter more.

6. Relative Reality

Shouldn't we now return to sanity from all this mad proliferation of worlds? Shouldn't we stop speaking of right versions as if each were, or had, its own world, and recognize all as versions of one and the same neutral and underlying world? The world thus regained, as remarked earlier, is a world without kinds or order or motion or rest or pattern—a world not worth fighting for or against.

We might, though, take the real world to be that of some one of the alternative right versions (or groups of them bound together by some principle of reducibility or translatability) and regard all others as versions of that same world differing from the standard version in accountable ways. The physicist takes his world as the real one, attributing the deletions, additions, irregularities, emphases, of other versions to the imperfections of perception, the urgencies of practice, or poetic license. The phenomenalist regards the perceptual world as fundamental, and the excisions, abstractions, simplifications and distortions of other versions as resulting from scientific or practical or artistic concerns. For the man-in-the-street, most versions from science, art, and perception depart in some ways from the familiar serviceable world he has jerry-built from fragments of scientific and artistic tradition and from his own struggle for survival. This world, indeed, is the one most often taken as real; for reality in a world, like realism in a picture, is largely a matter of habit.

Ironically, then, our passion for *one* world is satisfied, at different times and for different purposes, in *many* different ways. Not only motion, derivation, weighting, order, but even reality is relative. And so also, of course, is fiction; for so long as one world is designated as real, one version or integrated group of versions as the standard of reality, differing versions are considered to be at least in part either false or figurative, and ontological disparities to be the result of omitting real or adding fictive entities. Incidentally, with one world designated as real, merely-possible worlds might naturally be identified with divergent true or right versions; but for some contemporary philosophers, merely-possible worlds seem rather to be identified with false versions or 'state-descriptions' constructed from the same vocabulary as the only true one.

That reality is relative, worlds and right versions many, does not imply that all alternatives are equally good for every or indeed for any purpose, or that every alternative is much good for some purpose or other, and by no means precludes preference among versions. Not even a fly is likely to take one of his wing-tips as a fixed point; we do not welcome molecules or concreta as elements of our everyday world, or combine tomatoes and triangles and typewriters and tyrants and tornadoes into a single kind; the physicist will count none of these among his fundamental particles; the painter who sees like the man-in-the-street will have more popular than artistic success. And the same philosopher who here meta-philosophically contemplates a vast variety of worlds finds that only versions meeting the demands of a dogged and deflationary nominalism suit his purposes in constructing philosophical systems.

Moreover, while readiness to recognize alternative worlds may be liberating, and suggestive of new avenues of exploration, a willingness to welcome all worlds builds none. Mere acknowledgement of the many available frames of reference provides us with no map of the motions of heavenly bodies; acceptance of the eligibility of alternative bases produces no scientific theory or philosophical system; awareness of varied ways of seeing paints no pictures. A broad mind is no substitute for hard work.

7. Notes on Knowing

What I have been saying bears on the nature of knowledge. On these terms, knowing cannot be exclusively or even primarily a matter of determining what is true. Discovery often amounts, as when I place a piece in a jigsaw puzzle, not to arrival at a proposition for declaration or defense, but to finding a fit. Much of knowing aims at something other than true, or any, belief. An increase in acuity of insight or in range of comprehension, rather than a change in belief, occurs when we find in a pictured forest a face we already knew was there, or learn to distinguish stylistic differences among works already classified by artist or composer or writer, or study a picture or a concerto or a treatise until we see or hear or grasp features and structures we could not discern before. Such growth in knowledge is not by formation or fixation of belief[28] but by the advancement of understanding.[29]

Furthermore, if worlds are as much made as found, so also knowing is as much remaking as reporting. All the processes of worldmaking I have discussed enter into knowing. Perceiving motion, we have seen, often consists in producing it. Discovering laws involves drafting them. Recognizing patterns is very much a matter of inventing and imposing them. Comprehension and creation go on together.

I may not have given adequate answers to the questions I raised at the start; and you may feel that I have used far too freely all the processes I have described, from decomposition through deletion to distortion. But even if you feel that what I have said is not true, I hope you may find some of it right.

Notes

Written for delivery at the meeting in honor of the 100th anniversary of the birth of Ernst Cassirer, held at the University of Hamburg on October 21, 1974.

1. E.g. in *Language and Myth*, translated by Suzanne Langer (Harper, 1946).
2. Cf. 'The Way the World Is' (1960), in my *Problem and Projects* [hereinafter *PP*] (Bobbs-Merrill, 1972), pp. 24–32.
3. But not much; for no one type of reducibility serves all purposes.
4. Cf. 'The Revision of Philosophy' (1956), in *PP*, pp. 5–23; and also my *The Structure of Appearance* [hereinafter *SA*] (Bobbs-Merrill, second ed., 1966).
5. In *Art and Illusion* (Pantheon Books, 1960), E. H. Gombrich argues in many passages against the notion of 'the innocent eye'.
6. See the essays in Jerome S. Bruner's *Beyond the Information Given* [hereinafter *BI*] ed. by Jeremy M. Anglin (W. W. Norton, 1973), Chapter I.
7. Cf. *SA*, pp. 127–145; and 'Sense and Certainty' (1952) and The Epistemological Argument' (1967), in *PP*, pp. 6–75. We might take construction of a history of successive development of worlds to involve application of something like a Kantian regulative principle, and the search for a first world thus to be as misguided as the search for a first moment of time.
8. This does not, as sometimes is supposed, require any modification of the Leibniz formula for identity, but merely reminds us that the answer to a question "Is this the same as that?" may depend upon whether the "this" and the "that" in the question refer to thing or event or color or species, etc.
9. See *BI*, pp. 331–340.
10. See further *SA*, pp. 3–22, 132–135, 142–145.
11. In 'Some Thoughts on Scientific Method' (1963), in *Boston Studies in the Philosophy of Science*, Vol. II (Humanities Press, 1965), p. 85.

12. See my *Languages of Art* [hereinafter *LA*] (Bobbs-Merrill, 1968), pp. 115–130.

13. Discussion of what this means occupies many sections, from about Section 142 on, of Ludwig Wittgenstein's *Philosophical Investigations*, translated by G.E.M. Anscombe (Blackwell, 1953). I am not suggesting that the answer I give here is Wittgenstein's.

14. See my *Fact, Fiction, and Forecast* (Bobbs-Merrill, third ed., 1973), pp. 72–80.

15. On exemplification and expression as referential relations see *LA*, pp. 50–57, 87–95.

16. See *The Image of the City* by Kevin Lynch (Cambridge, Technology Press, 1960).

17. See E. Llewellyn Thomas, 'Eye Movements in Speed Reading', in *Speed Reading: Practices and Procedures* (University of Delaware Press,1962), pp. 104–114.

18. In *Zeit, Zahl, und Zeichen*, written for delivery at the meeting mentioned in the unnumbered note above.

19. See 'On Perceptual Readiness' (1957), in *BI*, pp. 7–42.

20. See Paul Kolers, 'Bilinguals and Information Processing', *Scientific American* 218 (1968), 78–86.

21. *Aspects of Motion Perception* (Pergamon Press, 1972), pp. 47ff.

22. This result is reported in 'Visual Construction of Color is Digital', forthcoming in *Science*. I am grateful to the authors, in the Department of Psychology at the University of Toronto, for permission to cite this paper prior to its publication.

23. I plan to write a paper 'Essay on a New Fact of Vision', on this matter.

24. See 'Value and Need as Organizing Factors in Perception' (1947), in *BI*, pp. 43–56.

25. See 'Science and Simplicity' (1963), in *PP*, pp. 337–346.

26. See *LA*, pp. 51,68–70.

27. E.g. "2 + 2 = 4" is true of everything in that for every *x*, *x* is such that 2 + 2 = 4. A statement *S* will normally not be *true about x* unless *S* is about *x* in one of the senses of "about" defined in 'About' (*PP*, pp. 246–272); but definition of "about" depends essentially on features of statements that have no reasonable analogues for pictures.

28. I allude here to Charles S. Peirce's paper 'The Fixation of Belief' (1877), in *Collected Papers of Charles Sanders Peirce*, Harvard University Press, Vol. 5 (1934), pp. 223–247.

29. On the nature and importance of understanding in the broader sense, see M. Polanyi, *Personal Knowledge* (University of Chicago Press, 1960).

After proposing an analysis of the "old" riddle of induction posed by Hume, Goodman raises, and then tries to answer, a "new" riddle of induction, which centers on the question of why certain kinds of predicates function in inductive inference and others do not.

NELSON GOODMAN

The New Riddle of Induction

1. The Old Problem of Induction

At the close of the preceding lecture, I said that today I should examine how matters stand with respect to the problem of induction. In a word, I think they stand ill. But the real difficulties that confront us today are not the traditional ones. What is commonly thought of as the Problem of Induction has been solved, or dissolved; and we face new problems that are not as yet very widely understood. To approach them, I shall have to run as quickly as possible over some very familiar ground.

The problem of the validity of judgments about future or unknown cases arises, as Hume pointed out, because such judgments are neither reports of experience nor logical consequences of it. Predictions, of course, pertain to what has not yet been observed. And they cannot be logically inferred from what has been observed; for what *has* happened imposes no logical restrictions on what *will* happen. Although Hume's dictum that there are no necessary connections of matters of fact has been challenged at times, it has withstood all attacks. Indeed, I should be inclined not merely to agree that there are no necessary connections of matters of fact, but to ask whether there are any necessary connections at all[1]—but that is another story.

Hume's answer to the question how predictions are related to past experience is refreshingly non-cosmic. When an event of one kind frequently follows upon an event of another kind in experience, a habit is formed that leads the mind, when confronted with a new event of the first kind, to pass to the idea of an event of the second kind. The idea of necessary connection arises from the felt impulse of the mind in making this transition.

Now if we strip this account of all extraneous features, the central point is that to the question "Why one prediction rather than another?", Hume answers that the elect prediction is one that accords with a past regularity, because this regularity has established a habit. Thus among alternative statements about a future moment, one statement is distinguished by its consonance with habit and thus with regularities observed in the past. Prediction according to any other alternative is errant.

How satisfactory is this answer? The heaviest criticism has taken the righteous position that Hume's account at best pertains only to the source of predictions, not their legitimacy; that he sets forth the circumstances under which we make given predictions—and in this sense explains why we make them—but leaves untouched the question of our license for making them. To trace origins, runs the old complaint, is not to establish validity: the real question is not why a prediction is in fact made but how it can be justified. Since this seems to point to the awkward conclusion that the greatest of modern philosophers completely missed the point of his own problem, the idea has developed that he did not really take his solution very seriously, but regarded the main problem as unsolved and perhaps as insoluble. Thus we come to speak of 'Hume's problem' as though he propounded it as a question without answer.

All this seems to me quite wrong. I think Hume grasped the central question and considered his answer to be passably effective. And I think his answer is reasonable and relevant, even if it is not entirely satisfactory. I shall explain presently. At the moment, I merely want to record a protest against the prevalent notion that the problem of justifying induction, when it is so sharply dissociated from the problem of describing how induction takes place, can fairly be called Hume's problem.

I suppose that the problem of justifying induction has called forth as much fruitless discussion as has any halfway respectable problem of modern philosophy. The typical writer begins by insisting that some way of justifying predictions must be found, proceeds to argue that for this purpose we need some resounding universal law of the Uniformity of Nature, and then inquires how this universal principle itself can be justified. At this point, if he is tired, he concludes that the principle must be accepted as an indispensable assumption; or if he is energetic and ingenious, he goes on to devise some subtle justification for it. Such an invention, however, seldom satisfies anyone else; and the easier course of accepting an unsubstantiated and even dubious assumption much more sweeping than any actual predictions we make seems an odd and expensive way of justifying them.

2. Dissolution of the Old Problem

Understandably, then, more critical thinkers have suspected that there might be something awry with the problem we are trying to solve. Come to think of it, what precisely would constitute the justification we seek? If the problem is to explain how we know that certain predictions will turn out to be correct, the sufficient answer is that we don't know any such thing. If the problem is to *find* some way of distinguishing antecedently between true and false predictions, we are asking for prevision rather than for philosophical explanation. Nor does it help matters much to say that we are merely trying to show that or why certain predictions are *probable*. Often it is said that while we cannot tell in advance whether a prediction concerning a given throw of a die is true, we can decide whether the prediction is a probable one. But if this means determining how the prediction is related to actual frequency distributions of future throws of the die, surely there is no way of knowing or proving this in advance. On the other hand, if the judgment that the prediction is probable has nothing to do with subsequent occurrences, then the question remains in what sense a probable prediction is any better justified than an improbable one.

Now obviously the genuine problem cannot be one of attaining unattainable knowledge or of accounting for knowledge that we do not in fact have. A better understanding of our problem can be gained by looking for a moment at what is involved in justifying non-inductive inferences. How do we justify a *de*duction? Plainly, by showing that it conforms to the general rules of deductive inference. An argument that so conforms is justified or valid, even if its conclusion happens to be false. An argument that violates a rule is fallacious even if its conclusion happens to be true. To justify a deductive conclusion therefore requires no knowledge of the facts it pertains to. Moreover, when a deductive argument has been shown to conform to the rules of logical inference, we usually consider it justified without going on to ask what justifies the rules. Analogously, the basic task in justifying an inductive inference is to show that it conforms to the general rules of *in*duction. Once we have recognized this, we have gone a long way towards clarifying our problem.

Yet, of course, the rules themselves must eventually be justified. The validity of a deduction depends not upon conformity to any purely arbitrary rules we may contrive, but upon conformity to valid rules. When we speak of *the* rules of inference we mean the valid rules—or better, *some* valid rules, since there may be alternative sets of equally valid rules. But how is the validity of rules to be determined? Here again we encounter philosophers who insist that these rules follow from some self-evident axiom, and others who try to show that the rules are grounded in the very nature of the human mind. I think the answer lies much nearer the surface. Principles of deductive inference are justified by their conformity with accepted deductive practice. Their validity depends upon accordance with the particular deductive inferences we actually make and sanction. If a rule yields inacceptable inferences, we drop it as invalid. Justification of general rules thus derives from judgments rejecting or accepting particular deductive inferences.

This looks flagrantly circular. I have said that deductive inferences are justified by their conformity to valid general rules, and that general rules are justified by their conformity to valid inferences. But this circle is a virtuous one. The point is that rules and particular inferences alike are justified by being brought into agreement with each other. *A rule is amended if it yields an inference we are unwilling to accept; an inference is rejected if it violates a rule we are unwilling to amend.* The process of justification is the delicate one of making mutual adjustments between rules and accepted inferences; and in the agreement achieved lies the only justification needed for either.

All this applies equally well to induction. An inductive inference, too, is justified by conformity to general rules, and a general rule by conformity to accepted inductive inferences. Predictions are justified if they conform to valid canons of induction; and the canons are valid if they accurately codify accepted inductive practice.

A result of such analysis is that we can stop plaguing ourselves with certain spurious questions about induction. We no longer demand an explanation for guarantees that we do not have, or seek keys to knowledge that we cannot obtain. It dawns upon us that the traditional smug insistence upon a hard-and-fast line between justifying induction and describing ordinary inductive practice distorts the problem. And we owe belated apologies to Hume. For in dealing with the question how normally accepted inductive judgments are made, he was in fact dealing with the question of inductive validity.[2] The validity of a prediction consisted for him in its arising from habit, and thus in its exemplifying some past regularity. His answer was incomplete and perhaps not entirely correct; but it was not beside the point. The problem of induction is not a problem of demonstration but a problem of defining the difference between valid and invalid predictions.

This clears the air but leaves a lot to be done. As principles of *de*ductive inference, we have the familiar and highly developed laws of logic; but there are available no such precisely stated and well-recognized principles of inductive inference. Mill's canons hardly rank with Aristotle's rules of the syllogism, let alone with *Principia Mathematica*. Elaborate and valuable treatises on probability usually leave certain fundamental questions untouched. Only in very recent years has there been any explicit and systematic work upon what I call the constructive task of confirmation theory.

3. The Constructive Task of Confirmation Theory

The task of formulating rules that define the difference between valid and invalid inductive inferences is much like the task of defining any term with an established usage. If we set out to define the term "tree", we try to compose out of already understood words an expression that will apply to the familiar objects that standard usage calls trees, and that will not apply to objects that standard usage refuses to call trees. A proposal that plainly violates either condition is rejected; while a definition that meets these tests may be adopted and used to decide cases that are not already settled by actual usage. Thus the interplay we observed between rules of induction and particular inductive inferences is simply an instance of this characteristic dual adjustment between definition and usage, whereby the usage informs the definition, which in turn guides extension of the usage.

Of course this adjustment is a more complex matter than I have indicated. Sometimes, in the interest of convenience or theoretical utility, we deliberately permit a definition to run counter to clear mandates of common usage. We accept a definition of "fish" that excludes whales. Similarly we may decide to deny the term "valid induction" to some inductive inferences that are commonly considered valid, or apply the term to others not usually so considered. A definition may modify as well as extend ordinary usage.[3]

Some pioneer work on the problem of defining confirmation or valid induction has been done by Professor Hempel.[4] Let me remind you briefly of a few of his results. Just as deductive logic is concerned primarily with a relation between statements—namely the consequence relation—that is independent of their truth or falsity, so inductive logic as Hempel conceives it is concerned primarily with a comparable relation of confirmation between statements. Thus the problem is to define the relation that obtains between any statement S_1 and another S_2 if and only if S_1 may properly be said to confirm S_2 in any degree.

With the question so stated, the first step seems obvious. Does not induction proceed in just the opposite direction from deduction? Surely some of the evidence statements that inductively support a general hypothesis are consequences of it. Since the consequence relation is already well defined by deductive logic, will we not be on firm ground in saying that confirmation embraces the converse relation? The laws of deduction in reverse will then be among the laws of induction.

Let's see where this leads us. We naturally assume further that whatever confirms a given statement confirms also whatever follows from that statement.[5] But if we combine this assumption with our proposed principle, we get the embarrassing result that every statement confirms every other. Surprising as it may be that such innocent beginnings lead to such an intolerable conclusion, the proof is very easy. Start with any statement S_1. It is a consequence of, and so by our present criterion confirms, the conjunction of S_1 and any statement whatsoever—call it S_2. But the confirmed conjunction, S_1S_2, of course has S_2 as a consequence. Thus every statement confirms all statements.

The fault lies in careless formulation of our first proposal. While some statements that confirm a general hypothesis are consequences of it, not all its consequences confirm it. This may not be immediately evident; for indeed we do in some sense furnish support for a statement when we establish one of its consequences. We settle one of the questions about it. Consider the heterogeneous conjunction:

> 8497 is a prime number and the other side of the moon is flat and Elizabeth the First was crowned on a Tuesday.

To show that any one of the three component statements is true is to support the conjunction by reducing the net undetermined claim. But support[6] of this kind is not confirmation; for establishment of one component endows the whole statement with no credibility that is transmitted to other component statements. Confirmation of a hypothesis occurs only when an instance imparts to the hypothesis some credibility that is conveyed to other instances. Appraisal of hypotheses, indeed, is incidental to prediction, to the judgment of new cases on the basis of old ones.

Our formula thus needs tightening. This is readily accomplished, as Hempel points out, if we observe that a hypothesis is genuinely confirmed only by a statement that is an instance of it in the special sense of entailing not the hypothesis itself but its relativization or restriction to the class of entities mentioned by that statement. The relativization of a general hypothesis to a class results from restricting the range of its universal and existential quantifiers to the members of that class. Less technically, what the hypothesis says of all things the evidence statement says of one thing (or of one pair or other *n*-ad of things). This obviously covers the confirmation of the conductivity of all copper by the conductivity of a given piece; and it excludes confirmation of our heterogeneous conjunction by any of its components. And, when taken together with the principle that what confirms a statement confirms all its consequences, this criterion does not yield the untoward conclusion that every statement confirms every other.

New difficulties promptly appear from other directions, however. One is the infamous paradox of the ravens. The statement that a given object, say this piece of paper, is neither black nor a raven confirms the hypothesis that all non-black things are non-ravens. But this hypothesis is logically equivalent to the hypothesis that all ravens are black. Hence we arrive at the unexpected conclusion that the statement that a given object is neither black nor a raven confirms the hypothesis that all ravens are black. The prospect of being able to investigate ornithological theories without going out in the rain is so attractive that we know there must be a catch in it. The trouble this time, however, lies not in faulty definition, but in tacit and illicit reference to evidence not stated in our example. Taken by itself, the statement that the given object is neither black nor a raven confirms the hypothesis that everything that is not a raven is not black as well as the hypothesis that everything that is not black is not a raven. We tend to ignore the former hypothesis because we know it to be false from abundant other evidence—from all the familiar things that are not ravens but are black. But we are required to assume that no such evidence is available. Under this circumstance, even a much stronger hypothesis is also obviously confirmed: that nothing is either black or a raven. In the light of this confirmation of the hypothesis that there are no ravens, it is no longer surprising that under the artificial restrictions of the example, the hypothesis that all ravens are black is also confirmed. And the prospects for indoor ornithology vanish when we notice that under these same conditions, the contrary hypothesis that no ravens are black is equally well confirmed.[7]

On the other hand, our definition does err in not forcing us to take into account all the *stated* evidence. The unhappy results are readily illustrated. If two compatible evidence statements confirm two hypotheses, then naturally the conjunction of the evidence statements should confirm the conjunction of the hypotheses.[8] Suppose our evidence consists of the statements E_1 saying that a given thing *b* is black, and E_2 saying that a second thing *c* is not black. By our present definition, E_1 confirms the hypothesis that everything is black, and E_2 the hypothesis that everything is non-black. The conjunction of these perfectly compatible evidence statements will then confirm the self-contradictory hypothesis that everything is both black and non-black. Simple as this anomaly is, it requires drastic modification of our definition. What given evidence confirms is not what we arrive at by generalizing from separate items of it, but—roughly speaking—what we arrive at by generalizing from the total stated evidence. The central idea for an improved definition is that, within certain limitations, what is asserted to be true for the narrow universe of the evidence statements is confirmed for the whole universe of discourse. Thus if our evidence is E_1 and E_2, neither the hypothesis that all things are black nor the hypothesis that all things are non-black is confirmed; for neither is true for the evidence-universe consisting of *b* and *c*. Of course, much more careful formulation is needed, since some statements that are true of the evidence-universe—such as that there is only one black thing—are obviously not confirmed for the whole universe. These matters are taken care of by the studied formal definition that Hempel develops on this basis; but we cannot and need not go into further detail here.

No one supposes that the task of confirmation-theory has been completed. But the few steps I have reviewed—chosen partly for their bearing on what is to follow—show how things move along once the problem of definition displaces the problem of justification. Important and long-unnoticed questions are brought to light and answered; and we are encouraged to expect that the many remaining questions will in time yield to similar treatment.

But our satisfaction is shortlived. New and serious trouble begins to appear.

4. The New Riddle of Induction

Confirmation of a hypothesis by an instance depends rather heavily upon features of the hypothesis other than its syntactical form. That a given piece of copper conducts electricity increases the credibility of statements asserting that other pieces of copper conduct electricity, and thus confirms the hypothesis that all copper conducts electricity. But the fact that a given man now in this room is a third son does not increase the credibility of statements asserting that other men now in this room are third sons, and so does not confirm the hypothesis that all men now in this room are third sons. Yet in both cases our hypothesis is a generalization of the evidence statement. The difference is that in the former case the hypothesis is a *lawlike* statement; while in the latter case, the hypothesis is a merely contingent or accidental generality. Only a statement that is *lawlike*—regardless of its truth or falsity or its scientific importance—is capable of receiving confirmation from an instance of it; accidental statements are not. Plainly, then, we must look for a way of distinguishing lawlike from accidental statements.

So long as what seems to be needed is merely a way of excluding a few odd and unwanted cases that are inadvertently admitted by our definition of confirmation, the problem may not seem very hard or very pressing. We fully expect that minor defects, will be found in our definition and that the necessary refinements will have to be worked out patiently one after another. But some further examples will show that our present difficulty is of a much graver kind.

Suppose that all emeralds examined before a certain time *t* are green.[9] At time *t* then, our observations support the hypothesis that all emeralds are green; and this is in accord with our definition of confirmation. Our evidence statements assert that emerald *a* is green, that emerald *b* is green, and so on; and each confirms the general hypothesis that all emeralds are green. So far, so good.

Now let me introduce another predicate less familiar than "green". It is the predicate "grue" and it applies to all things examined before *t* just in case they are green but to other things just in case they are blue. Then at time *t* we have, for each evidence statement asserting that a given emerald is green, a parallel evidence statement asserting that that emerald is grue. And the statements that emerald *a* is grue, that emerald *b* is grue, and so on, will each confirm the general hypothesis that all emeralds are grue. Thus according to our definition, the prediction that all emeralds subsequently examined will be green and the prediction that all will be grue are alike confirmed by evidence statements describing the same observations. But if an emerald subsequently examined is grue, it is blue and hence not green. Thus although we are well aware which of the two incompatible predictions is genuinely confirmed, they are equally well confirmed according to our present definition. Moreover, it is clear that if we simply choose an appropriate predicate, then on the basis of these same observations we shall have equal confirmation, by our definition, for any prediction whatever about other emeralds—or indeed about anything else.[10] As in our earlier example, only the predictions subsumed under lawlike hypotheses are genuinely confirmed; but we have no criterion as yet for determining lawlikeness. And now we see that without some such criterion, our definition not merely includes a few unwanted cases, but is so completely ineffectual that it virtually excludes nothing. We are left once again with the intolerable result that anything confirms anything. This difficulty cannot be set aside as an annoying detail to be taken care of in due course. It has to be met before our definition will work at all.

Nevertheless, the difficulty is often slighted because on the surface there seem to be easy ways of dealing with it. Sometimes, for example, the problem is thought to be much like the paradox of the ravens. We are here again, it is pointed out, making tacit and illegitimate use of information outside the stated evidence: the information, for example, that different samples of one material are usually alike in conductivity, and the information that different men in a lecture audience are usually not alike in the number of their older brothers. But while it is true that such information is being smuggled in, this does not by itself settle the matter as it settles the matter of the ravens. There the point was that when the smuggled information is forthrightly declared, its effect upon the confirmation of the hypothesis in question is immediately and properly registered by the definition we are using. On the other hand, if to our initial evidence we add statements concerning the conductivity of pieces of other materials or concerning the number of older brothers of members of other lecture audiences, this will not in the least affect the confirmation, according to our definition, of the hypothesis concerning copper or of that concerning this lecture audience. Since our definition is insensitive to the bearing upon hypotheses of evidence so related to them, even when the evidence is fully declared, the difficulty about accidental hypotheses cannot be explained away on the ground that such evidence is being surreptitiously taken into account.

A more promising suggestion is to explain the matter in terms of the effect of this other evidence not directly upon the hypothesis in question but *in*directly through other hypotheses that *are* confirmed, according to our definition, by such evidence. Our information about other materials does by our definition confirm such hypotheses as that all pieces of iron conduct electricity, that no pieces of rubber do, and so on; and these hypotheses, the explanation runs, impart to the hypothesis that all pieces of copper conduct electricity (and also to the hypothesis that none do) the character of lawlikeness—that is, amenability to confirmation by direct positive instances when found. On the other hand, our information about other lecture audiences *dis*confirms many hypotheses to the effect that all the men in one audience are third sons, or that none are; and this strips any character of lawlikeness from the hypothesis that all (or the hypothesis that none) of the men in *this* audience are third sons. But clearly if this course is to be followed, the circumstances under which hypotheses are thus related to one another will have to be precisely articulated.

The problem, then, is to define the relevant way in which such hypotheses must be alike. Evidence for the hypothesis that all iron conducts electricity enhances the lawlikeness of the hypothesis that all zirconium conducts electricity, but does not similarly affect the hypothesis that all the objects on my desk conduct electricity. Wherein lies the difference? The first two hypotheses fall under the broader hypothesis—call it "*H*"—that every class of things of the same material is uniform in conductivity; the first and third fall only under some such hypothesis as—call it "*K*"—that every class of things that are either all of the same material or all on a desk is uniform in conductivity. Clearly the important difference here is that evidence for a statement affirming that one of the classes covered by *H* has the property in question increases the credibility of any statement affirming that another such class has this property; while nothing of the sort holds true with respect to *K*. But this is only to say that *H* is lawlike and *K* is not. We are faced anew with the very problem we are trying to solve: the problem of distinguishing between lawlike and accidental hypotheses.

The most popular way of attacking the problem takes its cue from the fact that accidental hypotheses seem typically to involve some spatial or temporal restriction, or reference to some particular individual. They seem to concern the people in some particular room, or the objects on some particular person's desk; while lawlike hypotheses characteristically concern all ravens or all pieces of copper whatsoever. Complete generality is thus very often supposed to be a sufficient condition of lawlikeness; but to define this complete generality is by no means easy. Merely to require that the hypothesis contain no term naming, describing, or indicating a particular thing or location will obviously not be enough. The troublesome hypothesis that all emeralds are grue contains no such term; and where such a term does occur, as in hypotheses about men in *this room*, it can be suppressed in favor of some predicate (short or long, new or old) that contains no such term but applies only to exactly the same things. One might think, then, of excluding not only hypotheses that actually contain terms for specific individuals but also all hypotheses that are equivalent to others that do contain such terms. But, as we have just seen, to exclude only hypotheses of which *all* equivalents contain such terms is to exclude nothing. On the other hand, to exclude all hypotheses that have *some* equivalent containing such a term is to exclude everything; for even the hypothesis

All grass is green

has as an equivalent

All grass in London or elsewhere is green.

The next step, therefore, has been to consider ruling out predicates of certain kinds. A syntactically universal hypothesis is lawlike, the proposal runs, if its predicates are 'purely qualitative' or 'non-positional'.[11] This will obviously accomplish nothing if a purely qualitative predicate is then conceived either as one that is equivalent to some expression free of terms for specific individuals, or as one that is equivalent to no expression that contains such a term; for this only raises again the difficulties just pointed out. The claim appears to be rather that at least in the case of a simple enough predicate we can readily determine by direct inspection of its meaning whether or not it is purely qualitative. But even aside from obscurities in the notion of 'the meaning' of a predicate, this claim seems to me wrong. I simply do not know how to tell whether a predicate is qualitative or positional, except perhaps by completely begging the question at issue and asking whether the predicate is 'well-behaved'—that is, whether simple syntactically universal hypotheses applying it are lawlike.

This statement will not go unprotected. "Consider", it will be argued, "the predicates 'blue' and 'green' and the predicate 'grue' introduced earlier, and also the predicate 'bleen' that applies to emeralds examined before time *t* just in case they are blue and to other emeralds just in case they are green. Surely it is clear", the argument runs, "that the first two are purely qualitative and the second two are not; for the meaning of each of the latter two plainly involves reference to a specific temporal position." To this I reply that indeed I do recognize the first two as well-behaved predicates admissible in lawlike hypotheses, and the second two as ill-behaved predicates. But the argument that the former but not the latter are purely qualitative seems to me quite unsound. True enough, if we start with "blue" and "green", then "grue" and "bleen" will be explained in terms of "blue" and "green" and a temporal term. But equally truly, if we start with "grue" and "bleen", then "blue" and "green" will be explained in terms of "grue" and "bleen" and a temporal term; "green", for example, applies to emeralds examined before time *t* just in case they are grue, and to other emeralds just in case they are bleen. Thus qualitativeness is an entirely relative matter and does not by itself establish any dichotomy of predicates. This relativity seems to be completely overlooked by those who contend that the qualitative character of a predicate is a criterion for its good behavior.

Of course, one may ask why we need worry about such unfamiliar predicates as "grue" or about accidental hypotheses in general, since we are unlikely to use them in making predictions. If our definition works for such hypotheses as are normally employed, isn't that all we need? In a sense, yes; but only in the sense that we need no definition, no theory of induction, and no philosophy of knowledge at all. We get along well enough without them in daily life and in scientific research. But if we seek a theory at all, we cannot excuse gross anomalies resulting from a proposed theory by pleading that we can avoid them in practice. The odd cases we have been considering are clinically pure cases that, though seldom encountered in practice, nevertheless display to best advantage the symptoms of a widespread and destructive malady.

We have so far neither any answer nor any promising clue to an answer to the question what distinguishes lawlike or confirmable hypotheses from accidental or non-confirmable ones; and what may at first have seemed a minor technical difficulty has taken on the stature of a major obstacle to the development of a satisfactory theory of confirmation. It is this problem that I call the new riddle of induction.

5. The Pervasive Problem of Projection

At the beginning of this lecture, I expressed the opinion that the problem of induction is still unsolved, but that the difficulties that face us today are not the old ones; and I have tried to outline the changes that have taken place. The problem of justifying induction has been displaced by the problem of defining confirmation, and our work upon this has left us with the residual problem of distinguishing between confirmable and non-confirmable hypotheses. One might say roughly that the first question was "Why does a positive instance of a hypothesis give any grounds for predicting further instances?"; that the newer question was "What is a positive instance of a hypothesis?"; and that the crucial remaining question is "What hypotheses are confirmed by their positive instances?"

The vast amount of effort expended on the problem of induction in modern times has thus altered our afflictions but hardly relieved them. The original difficulty about induction arose from the recognition that anything may follow upon anything. Then, in attempting to define confirmation in terms of the converse of the consequence relation, we found ourselves with the distressingly similar difficulty that our definition would make any statement confirm any other. And now, after modifying our definition drastically, we still get the old devastating result that any statement will confirm any statement. Until we find a way of exercising some control over the hypotheses to be admitted, our definition makes no distinction whatsoever between valid and invalid inductive inferences.

The real inadequacy of Hume's account lay not in his descriptive approach but in the imprecision of his description. Regularities in experience, according to him, give rise to habits of expectation; and thus it is predictions conforming to past regularities that are normal or valid. But Hume overlooks the fact that some regularities do and some do not establish such habits; that predictions based on some regularities are valid while predictions based on other regularities are not. Every word you have heard me say has occurred prior to the final sentence of this lecture; but that does not, I hope, create any expectation that every word you will hear me say will be prior to that sentence. Again, consider our case of emeralds. All those examined before time *t* are green; and this leads us to expect, and confirms the prediction, that the next one will be green. But also, all those examined are grue; and this does not lead us to expect, and does not confirm the prediction, that the next one will be grue. Regularity in greenness confirms the prediction of further cases; regularity in grueness does not. To say that valid predictions are those based on past regularities, without being able to say *which* regularities, is thus quite pointless. Regularities are where you find them, and you can find them anywhere. As we have seen, Hume's failure to recognize and deal with this problem has been shared even by his most recent successors.

As a result, what we have in current confirmation theory is a definition that is adequate for certain cases that so far can be described only as those for which it is adequate. The theory works where it works. A hypothesis is confirmed by statements related to it in the prescribed way provided it is so confirmed. This is a good deal like having a theory that tells us that the area of a plane figure is one-half the base times the altitude, without telling us for what figures this holds. We must somehow find a way of distinguishing lawlike hypotheses, to which our definition of confirmation applies, from accidental hypotheses, to which it does not.

Today I have been speaking solely of the problem of induction, but what has been said applies equally to the more general problem of projection. As pointed out earlier, the problem of prediction from past to future cases is but a narrower version of the problem of projecting from any set of cases to others. We saw that a whole cluster of troublesome problems concerning dispositions and possibility can be reduced to this problem of projection. That is why the new riddle of induction, which is more broadly the problem of distinguishing between projectible and non-projectible hypotheses, is as important as it is exasperating.

Our failures teach us, I think, that lawlike or projectible hypotheses cannot be distinguished on any merely syntactical grounds or even on the ground that these hypotheses are somehow purely general in meaning. Our only hope lies in re-examining the problem once more and looking for some new approach. This will be my course in the final lecture.

Notes

"The New Riddle of Induction" reprinted by permission of the publisher from *Fact, Fiction, and Forecast* by Nelson Goodman, pp. 59–83, Cambridge, Mass.: Harvard University Press, Copyright © 1979, 1983 by Nelson Goodman.

1. Although this remark is merely an aside, perhaps I should explain for the sake of some unusually sheltered reader that the notion of a necessary connection of ideas, or of an absolutely analytic statement, is no longer sacrosanct. Some, like Quine and White, have forthrightly attacked the notion; others, like myself, have simply discarded it; and still others have begun to feel acutely uncomfortable about it.

2. A hasty reader might suppose that my insistence here upon identifying the problem of justification with a problem of description is out of keeping with my parenthetical insistence in the preceding lecture that the goal of philosophy is something quite different from the mere description of ordinary or scientific procedure. Let me repeat that the point urged there was that the organization of the explanatory account need not reflect the manner or order in which predicates are adopted in practice. It surely must describe practice, however, in the sense that the extensions of predicates as explicated must conform in certain ways to the extensions of the same predicates as applied in practice. Hume's account is a description in just this sense. For it is an attempt to set forth the circumstances under which those inductive judgments are made that are normally accepted as valid; and to do that is to state necessary and sufficient conditions for, and thus to define, valid induction. What I am maintaining above is that the problem of justifying induction is not something over and above the problem of describing or defining valid induction.

3. For a fuller discussion of definition in general see Chapter I of *The Structure of Appearance*.

4. The basic article is 'A Purely Syntactical Definition of Confirmation' cited in Note $I._{10}$. A much less technical account is given in 'Studies in the Logic of Confirmation', *Mind*, n.s., vol. 54 (1945), pp. 1–26 and 97–121. Later work by Hempel and others on defining *degree* of confirmation does not concern us here.

5. I am not here asserting that this is an indispensable requirement upon a definition of confirmation. Since our commonsense assumptions taken in combination quickly lead us to absurd conclusions, some of these assumptions have to be dropped; and different theorists may make different decisions about which to drop and which to preserve. Hempel gives up the converse consequence condition, while Carnap (*Logical Foundations of Probability*, Chicago and London, 1950, pp. 474–6) drops both the consequence condition and the converse consequence condition. Such differences of detail between different treatments of confirmation do not affect the central points I am making in this lecture.

6. Any hypothesis is 'supported' by its own positive instances; but support—or better, direct factual support—is only one factor in confirmation. This factor has been separately studied by John G. Kemeny and Paul Oppenheim in 'Degree of Factual Support', *Philosophy of Science*, vol. 19 (1952), pp. 307–24. As will appear presently, my concern in these lectures is primarily with certain other important factors in confirmation, some of them quite generally neglected.

7. An able and thorough exposition of this paragraph is given by Israel Scheffler in his *Anatomy of Inquiry*, New York, 1963, pp. 286–91.

8. The status of the conjunction condition is much like that of the consequence condition—see note 5. Although Carnap drops the conjunction condition also (p. 394), he adopts for different reasons the requirement we find needed above: that the total available evidence must always be taken into account (pp. 211–13).

9. Although the example used is different, the argument to follow is substantially the same as that set forth in my note 'A Query on Confirmation'. [*Journal of Philosophy*, vol. XLIII (1946), pp. 383–385.]

10. For instance, we shall have equal confirmation, by our present definition, for the prediction that roses subsequently examined will be blue. Let "emerose" apply just to emeralds examined before time *t* and to roses examined later. Then all emeroses so far examined are grue, and this confirms the hypothesis that all emeroses are grue and hence the prediction that roses subsequently examined will be blue. The problem raised by such antecedents has been little noticed, but is no easier to meet than that raised by similarly perverse consequents.

11. Carnap took this course in his paper 'On the Application of Inductive Logic', *Philosophy and Phenomenological Research*, vol. 8 (1947), pp. 133–47, which is in part a reply to my 'A Query on Confirmation'. The discussion was continued in my note 'On Infirmities of Confirmation Theory', *Philosophy and Phenomenological Research*, vol. 8 (1947), pp. 149–51; and in Carnap's 'Reply to Nelson Goodman', same journal, same volume, pp. 461–2.

In this seminal paper, Quine attacks two doctrines at the heart of traditional empiricism: the analytic-synthetic distinction and verificationism.

W.V.O. QUINE

Two Dogmas of Empiricism

Modern empiricism has been conditioned in large part by two dogmas. One is a belief in some fundamental cleavage between truths which are *analytic*, or grounded in meanings independently of matters of fact, and truths which are *synthetic*, or grounded in fact. The other dogma is *reductionism*: the belief that each meaningful statement is equivalent to some logical construct upon terms which refer to immediate experience. Both dogmas, I shall argue, are ill founded. One effect of abandoning them is, as we shall see, a blurring of the supposed boundary between speculative metaphysics and natural science. Another effect is a shift toward pragmatism.

I. Background for Analyticity

Kant's cleavage between analytic and synthetic truths was foreshadowed in Hume's distinction between relations of ideas and matters of fact, and in Leibniz's distinction between truths of reason and truths of fact. Leibniz spoke of the truths of reason as true in all possible worlds. Picturesqueness aside, this is to say that the truths of reason are those which could not possibly be false. In the same vein we hear analytic statements defined as statements whose denials are self-contradictory. But this definition has small explanatory value; for the notion of self-contradictoriness, in the quite broad sense needed for this definition of analyticity, stands in exactly the same need of clarification as does the notion of analyticity itself.[1] The two notions are the two sides of a single dubious coin.

Kant conceived of an analytic statement as one that attributes to its subject no more than is already conceptually contained in the subject. This formulation has two shortcomings: it limits itself to statements of subject-predicate form, and it appeals to a notion of containment which is left at a metaphorical level. But Kant's intent, evident more from the use he makes of the notion of analyticity than from his definition of it, can be restated thus: a statement is analytic when it is true by virtue of meanings and independently of fact. Pursuing this line, let us examine the concept of *meaning* which is presupposed.

We must observe to begin with that meaning is not to be identified with naming, or reference. Consider Frege's example of 'Evening Star' and 'Morning Star'. Understood not merely as a recurrent evening apparition but as a body, the Evening Star is the planet Venus, and the Morning Star is the same. The two singular terms *name* the same thing. But the meanings must be treated as distinct, since the identity 'Evening Star = Morning Star' is a statement of fact established by astronomical observation. If 'Evening Star' and 'Morning Star' were alike in meaning, the identity 'Evening Star = Morning Star' would be analytic.

Again there is Russell's example of 'Scott' and 'the author of *Waverley*'. Analysis of the meanings of words was by no means sufficient to reveal to George IV that the person named by these two singular terms was one and the same.

The distinction between meaning and naming is no less important at the level of abstract terms. The terms '9' and 'the number of planets' name one and the same abstract entity but presumably must be regarded as unlike in meaning; for astronomical observation was needed, and not mere reflection on meanings, to determine the sameness of the entity in question.

Thus far we have been considering singular terms. With general terms, or predicates, the situation is somewhat different but parallel. Whereas a singular term purports to name an entity, abstract or concrete, a general term does not; but a general term is *true of* an entity, or of each of many, or of none. The class of all entities of which a general term is true is called the *extension* of the term. Now paralleling the contrast between the meaning of a singular term and the entity named, we must distinguish equally between the meaning of a general term and its extension. The general terms 'creature with a heart' and 'creature with a kidney', e.g., are perhaps alike in extension but unlike in meaning.

Confusion of meaning with extension, in the case of general terms, is less common than confusion of meaning with naming in the case of singular terms. It is indeed a commonplace in philosophy to oppose intension (or meaning) to extension, or, in a variant vocabulary, connotation to denotation.

The Aristotelian notion of essence was the forerunner, no doubt, of the modern notion of intension or meaning. For Aristotle it was essential in men to be rational, accidental to be two-legged. But there is an important difference between this attitude and the doctrine of meaning. From the latter point of view it may indeed be conceded (if only for the sake of argument) that rationality is involved in the meaning of the word 'man' while two-leggedness is not; but two-leggedness may at the same time be viewed as involved in the meaning of 'biped' while rationality is not. Thus from the point of view of the doctrine of meaning it makes no sense to say of the actual individual, who is at once a man and a biped, that his rationality is essential and his two-leggedness accidental or vice versa. Things had essences, for Aristotle, but only linguistic forms have meanings. Meaning is what essence becomes when it is divorced from the object of reference and wedded to the word.

For the theory of meaning the most conspicuous question is as to the nature of its objects: what sort of things are meanings? They are evidently intended to be ideas, somehow—mental ideas for some semanticists, Platonic ideas for others. Objects of either sort are so elusive, not to say debatable, that there seems little hope of erecting a fruitful science about them. It is not even clear, granted meanings, when we have two and when we have one; it is not clear when linguistic forms should be regarded as *synonymous*, or alike in meaning, and when they should not. If a standard of synonymy should be arrived at, we may reasonably expect that the appeal to meanings as entities will not have played a very useful part in the enterprise.

A felt need for meant entities may derive from an earlier failure to appreciate that meaning and reference are distinct. Once the theory of meaning is sharply separated from the theory of reference, it is a short step to recognizing as the business of the theory of meaning simply the synonymy of linguistic forms and the analyticity of statements; meanings themselves, as obscure intermediary entities, may well be abandoned.

The description of analyticity as truth by virtue of meanings started us off in pursuit of a concept of meaning. But now we have abandoned the thought of any special realm of entities called meanings. So the problem of analyticity confronts us anew.

Statements which are analytic by general philosophical acclaim are not, indeed, far to seek. They fall into two classes. Those of the first class, which may be called *logically true*, are typified by:

(1) No unmarried man is married.

The relevant feature of this example is that it is not merely true as it stands, but remains true under any and all reinterpretations of 'man' and 'married'. If we suppose a prior inventory of *logical* particles, comprising 'no', 'un-', 'not', 'if', 'then', 'and', etc., then in general a logical truth is a statement which is true and remains true under all reinterpretations of its components other than the logical particles.

But there is also a second class of analytic statements, typified by:

(2) No bachelor is married.

The characteristic of such a statement is that it can be turned into a logical truth by putting synonyms for synonyms; thus (2) can be turned into (1) by putting 'unmarried man' for its synonym 'bachelor'. We still lack a proper characterization of this second class of analytic statements, and therewith of analyticity generally, inasmuch as we have had in the above description to lean on a notion of "synonymy" which is no less in need of clarification than analyticity itself.

In recent years Carnap has tended to explain analyticity by appeal to what he calls state-descriptions.[2] A state-description is any exhaustive assignment of truth values to the atomic, or noncompound, statements of the language. All other statements of the language are, Carnap assumes, built up of their component clauses by means of the familiar logical devices, in such a way that the truth value of any complex statement is fixed for each state-description by specifiable logical laws. A statement is then explained as analytic when it comes out true under every state-description. This account is an adaptation of Leibniz's "true in all possible worlds." But note that this version of analyticity serves its purpose only if the atomic statements of the language are, unlike 'John is a bachelor' and 'John is married', mutually independent. Otherwise there would be a state-description which assigned truth to 'John is a bachelor' and falsity to 'John is married', and consequently 'All bachelors are married' would turn out synthetic rather than analytic under the proposed criterion. Thus the criterion of analyticity in terms of state-descriptions serves only for languages devoid of extralogical synonym-pairs, such as 'bachelor' and 'unmarried man': synonym-pairs of the type which give rise to the "second class" of analytic statements. The criterion in terms of state-descriptions is a reconstruction at best of logical truth.

I do not mean to suggest that Carnap is under any illusions on this point. His simplified model language with its state-descriptions is aimed primarily not at the general problem of analyticity but at another purpose, the clarification of probability and induction. Our problem, however, is analyticity; and here the major difficulty lies not in the first class of analytic statements, the logical truths, but rather in the second class, which depends on the notion of synonymy.

II. Definition

There are those who find it soothing to say that the analytic statements of the second class reduce to those of the first class, the logical truths, by *definition*; 'bachelor', e.g., is *defined* as 'unmarried man'. But how do we find that 'bachelor' is defined as 'unmarried man'? Who defined it thus, and when? Are we to appeal to the nearest dictionary, and accept the lexicographer's formulation as law? Clearly this would be to put the cart before the horse. The lexicographer is an empirical scientist, whose business is the recording of antecedent facts; and if he glosses 'bachelor' as 'unmarried man' it is because of his belief that there is a relation of synonymy between these forms, implicit in general or preferred usage prior to his own work. The notion of synonymy presupposed here has still to be clarified, presumably in terms relating to linguistic behavior. Certainly the "definition" which is the lexicographer's report of an observed synonymy cannot be taken as the ground of the synonymy.

Definition is not, indeed, an activity exclusively of philologists. Philosophers and scientists frequently have occasion to "define" a recondite term by paraphrasing it into terms of a more familiar vocabulary. But ordinarily such a definition, like the philologist's, is pure lexicography, affirming a relationship of synonymy antecedent to the exposition in hand.

Just what it means to affirm synonymy, just what the interconnections may be which are necessary and sufficient in order that two linguistic forms be properly describable as synonymous, is far from clear; but, whatever these interconnections may be, ordinarily they are grounded in usage. Definitions reporting selected instances of synonymy come then as reports upon usage.

There is also, however, a variant type of definitional activity which does not limit itself to the reporting of pre-existing synonymies. I have in mind what Carnap calls *explication*—an activity to which philosophers are given, and scientists also in their more philosophical moments. In explication the purpose is not merely to paraphrase the definiendum into an outright synonym, but actually to improve upon the definiendum by refining or supplementing its meaning. But even explication, though not merely reporting a pre-existing synonymy between definiendum and definiens, does rest nevertheless on *other* pre-existing synonymies. The matter may be viewed as follows. Any word worth explicating has some contexts which, as wholes, are clear and precise enough to be useful; and the purpose of explication is to preserve the usage of these favored contexts while sharpening the usage of other contexts. In order that a given definition be suitable for purposes of explication, therefore, what is required is not that the definiendum in its antecedent usage be synonymous with the definiens, but just that each of these favored contexts of the definiendum, taken as a whole in its antecedent usage, be synonymous with the corresponding context of the definiens.

Two alternative definientia may be equally appropriate for the purposes of a given task of explication and yet not be synonymous with each other; for they may serve interchangeably within the favored contexts but diverge elsewhere. By cleaving to one of these definientia rather than the other, a definition of explicative kind generates, by fiat, a relationship of synonymy between definiendum and definiens which did not hold before. But such a definition still owes its explicative function, as seen, to pre-existing synonymies.

There does, however, remain still an extreme sort of definition which does not hark back to prior synonymies at all; viz., the explicitly conventional introduction of novel notations for purposes of sheer abbreviation. Here the definiendum becomes synonymous with the definiens simply because it has been created expressly for the purpose of being synonymous with the definiens. Here we have a really transparent case of synonymy created by definition; would that all species of synonymy were as intelligible. For the rest, definition rests on synonymy rather than explaining it.

The word 'definition' has come to have a dangerously reassuring sound, due no doubt to its frequent occurrence in logical and mathematical writings. We shall do well to digress now into a brief appraisal of the role of definition in formal work.

In logical and mathematical systems either of two mutually antagonistic types of economy may be striven for, and each has its peculiar practical utility. On the one hand we may seek economy of practical expression: ease and brevity in the statement of multifarious relationships. This sort of economy calls usually for distinctive concise notations for a wealth of concepts. Second, however, and oppositely, we may seek economy in grammar and vocabulary; we may try to find a minimum of basic concepts such that, once a distinctive notation has been appropriated to each of them, it becomes possible to express any desired further concept by mere combination and iteration of our basic notations. This second sort of economy is impractical in one way, since a poverty in basic idioms tends to a necessary lengthening of discourse. But it is practical in another way: it greatly simplifies theoretical discourse *about* the language, through minimizing the terms and the forms of construction wherein the language consists.

Both sorts of economy, though prima facie incompatible, are valuable in their separate ways. The custom has consequently arisen of combining both sorts of economy by forging in effect two languages, the one a part of the other. The inclusive language, though redundant in grammar and vocabulary, is economical in message lengths, while the part, called *primitive notation*, is economical in grammar and vocabulary. Whole and part are correlated by rules of translation whereby each idiom not in primitive notation is equated to some complex built up of primitive notation. These rules of translation are the so-called *definitions* which appear in formalized systems. They are best viewed not as adjuncts to one language but as correlations between two languages, the one a part of the other.

But these correlations are not arbitrary. They are supposed to show how the primitive notations can accomplish all purposes, save brevity and convenience, of the redundant language. Hence the definiendum and its definiens may be expected, in each case, to be related in one or another of the three ways lately noted. The definiens may be a faithful paraphrase of the definiendum into the narrower notation, preserving a direct synonymy as of antecedent usage; or the definiens may, in the spirit of explication, improve upon the antecedent usage of the definiendum; or finally, the definiendum may be a newly created notation, newly endowed with meaning here and now.

In formal and informal work alike, thus, we find that definition—except in the extreme case of the explicitly conventional introduction of new notations—hinges on prior relationships of synonymy. Recognizing then that the notion of definition does not hold the key to synonymy and analyticity, let us look further into synonymy and say no more of definition.

III. Interchangeability

A natural suggestion, deserving close examination, is that the synonymy of two linguistic forms consists simply in their interchangeability in all contexts without change of truth value; interchangeability, in Leibniz's phrase, *salva veritate*. Note that synonyms so conceived need not even be free from vagueness, as long as the vaguenesses match.

But it is not quite true that the synonyms 'bachelor' and 'unmarried man' are everywhere interchangeable *salva veritate*. Truths which become false under substitution of 'unmarried man' for 'bachelor' are easily constructed with help of 'bachelor of arts' or 'bachelor's buttons'. Also with help of quotation, thus:

'Bachelor' has less than ten letters.

Such counterinstances can, however, perhaps be set aside by treating the phrases 'bachelor of arts' and 'bachelor's buttons' and the quotation "bachelor" each as a single indivisible word and then stipulating that the interchangeability *salva veritate* which is to be the touchstone of synonymy is not supposed to apply to fragmentary occurrences inside of a word. This account of synonymy, supposing it acceptable on other counts, has indeed the drawback of appealing to a prior conception of "word" which can be counted on to present difficulties of formulation in its turn. Nevertheless some progress might be claimed in having reduced the problem of synonymy to a problem of wordhood. Let us pursue this line a bit, taking "word" for granted.

The question remains whether interchangeability *salva veritate* (apart from occurrences within words) is a strong enough condition for synonymy, or whether, on the contrary, some nonsynonymous expressions might be thus interchangeable. Now let us be clear that we are not concerned here with synonymy in the sense of complete identity in psychological associations or poetic quality; indeed no two expressions are synonymous in such a sense. We are concerned only with what may be called *cognitive synonymy*. Just what this is cannot be said without successfully finishing the present study; but we know something about it from the need which arose for it in connection with analyticity in Section I. The sort of synonymy needed there was merely such that any analytic statement could be turned into a logical truth by putting synonyms for synonyms. Turning the tables and assuming analyticity, indeed, we could explain cognitive synonymy of terms as follows (keeping to the familiar example): to say that 'bachelor' and 'unmarried man' are cognitively synonymous is to say no more nor less than that the statement:

(3) All and only bachelors are unmarried men

is analytic.[3]

What we need is an account of cognitive synonymy not presupposing analyticity—if we are to explain analyticity conversely with help of cognitive synonymy as undertaken in Section I. And indeed such an independent account of cognitive synonymy is at present up for consideration, viz., interchangeability *salva veritate* everywhere except within words. The question before us, to resume the thread at last, is whether such interchangeability is a sufficient condition for cognitive synonymy. We can quickly assure ourselves that it is, by examples of the following sort. The statement:

(4) Necessarily all and only bachelors are bachelors

is evidently true, even supposing 'necessarily' so narrowly construed as to be truly applicable only to analytic statements. Then, if 'bachelor' and 'unmarried man' are interchangeable *salva veritate*, the result

(5) Necessarily, all and only bachelors are unmarried men

of putting 'unmarried man' for an occurrence of 'bachelor' in (4) must, like (4), be true. But to say that (5) is true is to say that (3) is analytic, and hence that 'bachelor' and 'unmarried men' are cognitively synonymous.

Let us see what there is about the above argument that gives it its air of hocus-pocus. The condition of interchangeability *salva veritate* varies in its force with variations in the richness of the language at hand. The above argument supposes we are working with a language rich enough to contain the adverb 'necessarily', this adverb being so construed as to yield truth when and only when applied to an analytic statement. But can we condone a language which contains such an adverb? Does the adverb really make sense? To suppose that it does is to suppose that we have already made satisfactory sense of 'analytic'. Then what are we so hard at work on right now?

Our argument is not flatly circular, but something like it. It has the form, figuratively speaking, of a closed curve in space.

Interchangeability *salva veritate* is meaningless until relativized to a language whose extent is specified in relevant respects. Suppose now we consider a language containing just the following materials. There is an indefinitely large stock of one- and many-place predicates, mostly having to do with extralogical subject matter. The rest of the language is logical. The atomic sentences consist each of a predicate followed by one or more variables; and the complex sentences are built up of atomic ones by truth functions and quantification. In effect such a language enjoys the benefits also of descriptions and class names and indeed singular terms generally, these being contextually definable in known ways.[4] Such a language can be adequate to classical mathematics and indeed to scientific discourse generally, except in so far as the latter involves debatable devices such as modal adverbs and contrary-to-fact conditionals. Now a language of this type is *extensional*, in this sense: any two predicates which *agree extensionally* (i.e., are true of the same objects) are interchangeable *salva veritate*.

In an extensional language, therefore, interchangeability *salva veritate* is no assurance of cognitive synonymy of the desired type. That 'bachelor' and 'unmarried man' are interchangeable *salva veritate* in an extensional language assures us of no more than that (3) is true. There is no assurance here that the extensional agreement of 'bachelor' and 'unmarried man' rests on meaning rather than merely on accidental matters of fact, as does extensional agreement of 'creature with a heart' and 'creature with a kidney'.

For most purposes extensional agreement is the nearest approximation to synonymy we need care about. But the fact remains that extensional agreement falls far short of cognitive synonymy of the type required for explaining analyticity in the manner of Section I. The type of cognitive synonymy required there is such as to equate the synonymy of 'bachelor' and 'unmarried man' with the analyticity of (3), not merely with the truth of (3).

So we must recognize that interchangeability *salva veritate*, if construed in relation to an extensional language, is not a sufficient condition of cognitive synonymy in the sense needed for deriving analyticity in the manner of Section I. If a language contains an intensional adverb 'necessarily' in the sense lately noted, or other particles to the same effect, then interchangeability *salva veritate* in such a language does afford a sufficient condition of cognitive synonymy; but such a language is intelligible only if the notion of analyticity is already clearly understood in advance.

The effort to explain cognitive synonymy first, for the sake of deriving analyticity from it afterward as in Section I, is perhaps the wrong approach. Instead we might try explaining analyticity somehow without appeal to cognitive synonymy. Afterward we could doubtless derive cognitive synonymy from analyticity satisfactorily enough if desired. We have seen that cognitive synonymy of 'bachelor' and 'unmarried man' can be explained as analyticity of (3). The same explanation works for any pair of one-place predicates, of course, and it can be extended in obvious fashion to many-place predicates. Other syntactical categories can also be accommodated in fairly parallel fashion. Singular terms may be said to be cognitively synonymous when the statement of identity formed by putting '=' between them is analytic. Statements may be said simply to be cognitively synonymous when their biconditional (the result of joining them by 'if and only if') is analytic.[5] If we care to lump all categories into a single formulation, at the expense of assuming again the notion of "word" which was appealed to early in this section, we can describe any two linguistic forms as cognitively synonymous when the two forms are interchangeable (apart from occurrences within "words") *salva* (no longer *veritate* but) *analyticitate*. Certain technical questions arise, indeed, over cases of ambiguity or homonymy; let us not pause for them, however, for we are already digressing. Let us rather turn our backs on the problem of synonymy and address ourselves anew to that of analyticity.

IV. Semantical Rules

Analyticity at first seemed most naturally definable by appeal to a realm of meanings. On refinement, the appeal to meanings gave way to an appeal to synonymy or definition. But definition turned out to be a will-o'-the-wisp, and synonymy turned out to be best understood only by dint of a prior appeal to analyticity itself. So we are back at the problem of analyticity.

I do not know whether the statement 'Everything green is extended' is analytic. Now does my indecision over this example really betray an incomplete understanding, an incomplete grasp of the "meanings", of 'green' and 'extended'? I think not. The trouble is not with 'green' or 'extended' but with 'analytic'.

It is often hinted that the difficulty in separating analytic statements from synthetic ones in ordinary language is due to the vagueness of ordinary language and that the distinction is clear when we have a precise artificial language with explicit "semantical rules." This, however, as I shall now attempt to show, is a confusion.

The notion of analyticity about which we are worrying is a purported relation between statements and languages: a statement S is said to be *analytic for* a language L, and the problem is to make sense of this relation generally, i.e., for variable 'S' and 'L'. The point that I want to make is that the gravity of this problem is not perceptibly less for artificial languages than for natural ones. The problem of making sense of the idiom '*S* is analytic for *L*', with variable '*S*' and '*L*', retains its stubbornness even if we limit the range of the variable '*L*' to artificial languages. Let me now try to make this point evident.

For artificial languages and semantical rules we look naturally to the writings of Carnap. His semantical rules take various forms, and to make my point I shall have to distinguish certain of the forms. Let us suppose, to begin with, an artificial language L_0 whose semantical rules have the form explicitly of a specification, by recursion or otherwise, of all the analytic statements of L_0. The rules tell us that such and such statements, and only those, are the analytic statements of L_0. Now here the difficulty is simply that the rules contain the word 'analytic', which we do not understand! We understand what expressions the rules attribute analyticity to, but we do not understand what the rules attribute to those expressions. In short, before we can understand a rule which begins "A statement *S* is analytic for language L_0 if and only if . . .," we must understand the general relative term 'analytic for'; we must understand '*S* is analytic for *L*' where '*S*' and '*L*' are variables.

Alternatively we may, indeed, view the so-called rule as a conventional definition of a new simple symbol 'analytic-for-L_0', which might better be written untendentiously as '*K*' so as not to seem to throw light on the interesting word 'analytic'. Obviously any number of classes *K*, *M*, *N*, etc. of statements of L_0 can be specified for various purposes or for no purpose; what does it mean to say that *K*, as against *M*, *N*, etc., is the class of the "analytic" statements of L_0?

By saying what statements are analytic for L_0 we explain 'analytic-for-L_0' but not 'analytic', not 'analytic for'. We do not begin to explain the idiom '*S* is analytic for *L*' with variable '*S*' and '*L*', even though we be content to limit the range of '*L*' to the realm of artificial languages.

Actually we do know enough about the intended significance of 'analytic' to know that analytic statements are supposed to be true. Let us then turn to a second form of semantical rule, which says not that such and such statements are analytic but simply that such and such statements are included among the truths. Such a rule is not subject to the criticism of containing the un-understood word 'analytic'; and we may grant for the sake of argument that there is no difficulty over the broader term 'true'. A semantical rule of this second type, a rule of truth, is not supposed to specify all the truths of the language; it merely stipulates, recursively or otherwise, a certain multitude of statements which, along with others unspecified, are to count as true. Such a rule may be conceded to be quite clear. Derivatively, afterward, analyticity can be demarcated thus: a statement is analytic if it is (not merely true but) true according to the semantical rule.

Still there is really no progress. Instead of appealing to an unexplained word 'analytic', we are now appealing to an unexplained phrase 'semantical rule'. Not every true statement which says that the statements of some class are true can count as a semantical rule—otherwise *all* truths would be "analytic" in the sense of being true according to semantical rules. Semantical rules are distinguishable, apparently, only by the fact of appearing on a page under the heading 'Semantical Rules'; and this heading is itself then meaningless.

We can say indeed that a statement is *analytic-for-*L_0 if and only if it is true according to such and such specifically appended "semantical rules," but then we find ourselves back at essentially the same case which was originally discussed: "*S* is analytic-for-L_0 if and only if. . . ." Once we seek to explain '*S* is analytic for *L*' generally for variable '*L*' (even allowing limitation of '*L*' to artificial languages), the explanation 'true according to the semantical rules of *L*' is unavailing; for the relative term 'semantical rule of' is as much in need of clarification, at least, as 'analytic for'.

It might conceivably be protested that an artificial language *L* (unlike a natural one) is a language in the ordinary sense *plus* a set of explicit semantical rules—the whole constituting, let us say, an ordered pair; and that the semantical rules of *L* then are specifiable simply as the second component of the pair *L*. But, by the same token and more simply, we might construe an artificial language *L* outright as an ordered pair whose second component is the class of its analytic statements; and then the analytic statements of *L* become specifiable simply as the statements in the second component of *L*. Or better still, we might just stop tugging at our bootstraps altogether.

Not all the explanations of analyticity known to Carnap and his readers have been covered explicitly in the above considerations, but the extension to other forms is not hard to see. Just one additional factor should be mentioned which sometimes enters: sometimes the semantical rules are in effect rules of translation into ordinary language, in which case the analytic statements of the artificial language are in effect recognized as such from the analyticity of their specified translations in ordinary language. Here certainly there can be no thought of an illumination of the problem of analyticity from the side of the artificial language.

From the point of view of the problem of analyticity the notion of an artificial language with semantical rules is a *feu follet par excellence*. Semantical rules determining the analytic statements of an artificial language are of interest only in so far as we already understand the notion of analyticity; they are of no help in gaining this understanding.

Appeal to hypothetical languages of an artificially simple kind could conceivably be useful in clarifying analyticity, if the mental or behavioral or cultural factors relevant to analyticity—whatever they may be—were somehow sketched into the simplified model. But a model which takes analyticity merely as in irreducible character is unlikely to throw light on the problem of explicating analyticity.

It is obvious that truth in general depends on both language and extralinguistic fact. The statement 'Brutus killed Caesar' would be false if the world had been different in certain ways, but it would also be false if the word 'killed' happened rather to have the sense of 'begat'. Hence the temptation to suppose in general that the truth of a statement is somehow analyzable into a linguistic component and a factual component. Given this supposition, it next seems reasonable that in some statements the factual component should be null; and these are the analytic statements. But, for all its *a priori* reasonableness, a boundary between analytic and synthetic statements simply has not been drawn. That there is such a distinction to be drawn at all is an unempirical dogma of empiricists, a metaphysical article of faith.

V. The Verification Theory and Reductionism

In the course of these somber reflections we have taken a dim view first of the notion of meaning, then of the notion of cognitive synonymy, and finally of the notion of analyticity. But what, it may be asked, of the verification theory of meaning? This phrase has established itself so firmly as a catchword of empiricism that we should be very unscientific indeed not to look beneath it for a possible key to the problem of meaning and the associated problems.

The verification theory of meaning, which has been conspicuous in the literature from Peirce onward, is that the meaning of a statement is the method of empirically confirming or infirming it. An analytic statement is that limiting case which is confirmed no matter what.

As urged in Section I, we can as well pass over the question of meanings as entities and move straight to sameness of meaning, or synonymy. Then what the verification theory says is that statements are synonymous if and only if they are alike in point of method of empirical confirmation or infirmation.

This is an account of cognitive synonymy not of linguistic forms generally, but of statements.[6] However, from the concept of synonymy of statements we could derive the concept of synonymy for other linguistic forms, by considerations somewhat similar to those at the end of Section III. Assuming the notion of "word," indeed, we could explain any two forms as synonymous when the putting of the one form for an occurrence of the other in any statement (apart from occurrences within "words") yields a synonymous statement. Finally, given the concept of synonymy thus for linguistic forms generally, we could define analyticity in terms of synonymy and logical truth as in Section I. For that matter, we could define analyticity more simply in terms of just synonymy of statements together with logical truth; it is not necessary to appeal to synonymy of linguistic forms other than statements. For a statement may be described as analytic simply when it is synonymous with a logically true statement.

So, if the verification theory can be accepted as an adequate account of statement synonymy, the notion of analyticity is saved after all. However, let us reflect. Statement synonymy is said to be likeness of method of empirical confirmation or infirmation. Just what are these methods which are to be compared for likeness? What, in other words, is the nature of the relationship between a statement and the experiences which contribute to or detract from its confirmation?

The most naive view of the relationship is that it is one of direct report. This is *radical reductionism*. Every meaningful statement is held to be translatable into a statement (true or false) about immediate experience. Radical reductionism, in one form or another, well antedates the verification theory of meaning explicitly so-called. Thus Locke and Hume held that every idea must either originate directly in sense experience or else be compounded of ideas thus originating; and taking a hint from Tooke[7] we might rephrase this doctrine in semantical jargon by saying that a term, to be significant at all, must be either a name of a sense datum or a compound of such names or an abbreviation of such a compound. So stated, the doctrine remains ambiguous as between sense data as sensory events and sense data as sensory qualities; and it remains vague as to the admissible ways of compounding. Moreover, the doctrine is unnecessarily and intolerably restrictive in the term-by-term critique which it imposes. More reasonably, and without yet exceeding the limits of what I have called radical reductionism, we may take full statements as our significant units—thus demanding that our statements as wholes be translatable into sense-datum language, but not that they be translatable term by term.

This emendation would unquestionably have been welcome to Locke and Hume and Tooke, but historically it had to await two intermediate developments. One of these developments was the increasing emphasis on verification or confirmation, which came with the explicitly so-called verification theory of meaning. The objects of verification or confirmation being statements, this emphasis gave the statement an ascendency over the word or term as unit of significant discourse. The other development, consequent upon the first, was Russell's discovery of the concept of incomplete symbols defined in use.

Radical reductionism, conceived now with statements as units, sets itself the task of specifying a sense-datum language and showing how to translate the rest of significant discourse, statement by statement, into it. Carnap embarked on this project in the *Aufbau*.[8]

The language which Carnap adopted as his starting point was not a sense-datum language in the narrowest conceivable sense, for it included also the notations of logic, up through higher set theory. In effect it included the whole language of pure mathematics. The ontology implicit in it (i.e., the range of values of its variables) embraced not only sensory events but classes, classes of classes, and so on. Empiricists there are who would boggle at such prodigality. Carnap's starting point is very parsimonious, however, in its extralogical or sensory part. In a series of constructions in which he exploits the resources of modern logic with much ingenuity, he succeeds in defining a wide array of important additional sensory concepts which, but for his constructions, one would not have dreamed were definable on so slender a basis. Carnap was the first empiricist who, not content with asserting the reducibility of science to terms of immediate experience, took serious steps toward carrying out the reduction.

Even supposing Carnap's starting point satisfactory, his constructions were, as he himself stressed, only a fragment of the full program. The construction of even the simplest statements about the physical world was left in a sketchy state. Carnap's suggestions on this subject were, despite their sketchiness, very suggestive. He explained spatio-temporal point-instants as quadruples of real numbers and envisaged assignment of sense qualities to point-instants according to certain canons. Roughly summarized, the plan was that qualities should be assigned to point-instants in such a way as to achieve the laziest world compatible with our experience. The principle of least action was to be our guide in constructing a world from experience.

Carnap did not seem to recognize, however, that his treatment of physical objects fell short of reduction not merely through sketchiness, but in principle. Statements of the form 'Quality *q* is at point-instant *x; y; z; t*' were, according to his canons, to be apportioned truth values in such a way as to maximize and minimize certain overall features, and with growth of experience the truth values were to be progressively revised in the same spirit. I think this is a good schematization (deliberately oversimplified, to be sure) of what science really does; but it provides no indication, not even the sketchiest, of how a statement of the form 'Quality *q* is at *x; y; z; t*' could ever be translated into Carnap's initial language of sense data and logic. The connective 'is at' remains an added undefined connective; the canons counsel us in its use but not in its elimination.

Carnap seems to have appreciated this point afterward; for in his later writings he abandoned all notion of the translatability of statements about the physical world into statements about immediate experience. Reductionism in its radical form has long since ceased to figure in Carnap's philosophy.

But the dogma of reductionism has, in a subtler and more tenuous form, continued to influence the thought of empiricists. The notion lingers that to each statement, or each synthetic statement, there is associated a unique range of possible sensory events such that the occurrence of any of them would add to the likelihood of truth of the statement, and that there is associated also another unique range of possible sensory events whose occurrence would detract from that likelihood. This notion is of course implicit in the verification theory of meaning.

The dogma of reductionism survives in the supposition that each statement, taken in isolation from its fellows, can admit of confirmation or infirmation at all. My countersuggestion, issuing essentially from Carnap's doctrine of the physical world in the *Aufbau*, is that our statements about the external world face the tribunal of sense experience not individually but only as a corporate body.

The dogma of reductionism, even in its attenuated form, is intimately connected with the other dogma: that there is a cleavage between the analytic and the synthetic. We have found ourselves led, indeed, from the latter problem to the former through the verification theory of meaning. More directly, the one dogma clearly supports the other in this way: as long as it is taken to be significant in general to speak of the confirmation and infirmation of a statement, it seems significant to speak also of a limiting kind of statement which is vacuously confirmed, *ipso facto*, come what may; and such a statement is analytic.

The two dogmas are, indeed, at root identical. We lately reflected that in general the truth of statements does obviously depend both upon language and upon extralinguistic fact; and we noted that this obvious circumstance carries in its train, not logically but all too naturally, a feeling that the truth of a statement is somehow analyzable into a linguistic component and a factual component. The factual component must, if we are empiricists, boil down to a range of confirmatory experiences. In the extreme case where the linguistic component is all that matters, a true statement is analytic. But I hope we are now impressed with how stubbornly the distinction between analytic and synthetic has resisted any straightforward drawing. I am impressed also, apart from prefabricated examples of black and white balls in an urn, with how baffling the problem has always been of arriving at any explicit theory of the empirical confirmation of a synthetic statement. My present suggestion is that it is nonsense, and the root of much nonsense, to speak of a linguistic component and a factual component in the truth of any individual statement. Taken collectively, science has its double dependence upon language and experience; but this duality is not significantly traceable into the statements of science taken one by one.

Russell's concept of definition in use was, as remarked, an advance over the impossible term-by-term empiricism of Locke and Hume. The statement, rather than the term, came with Russell to be recognized as the unit accountable to an empiricist critique. But what I am now urging is that even in taking the statement as unit we have drawn our grid too finely. The unit of empirical significance is the whole of science.

VI. Empiricism without the Dogmas

The totality of our so-called knowledge or beliefs, from the most casual matters of geography and history to the profoundest laws of atomic physics or even of pure mathematics and logic, is a man-made fabric which impinges on experience only along the edges. Or, to change the figure, total science is like a field of force whose boundary conditions are experience. A conflict with experience at the periphery occasions readjustments in the interior of the field. Truth values have to be redistributed over some of our statements. Re-evaluation of some statements entails re-evaluation of others, because of their logical interconnections—the logical laws being in turn simply certain further statements of the system, certain further elements of the field. Having re-evaluated one statement we must re-evaluate some others, whether they be statements logically connected with the first or whether they be the statements of logical connections themselves. But the total field is so undetermined by its boundary conditions, experience, that there is much latitude of choice as to what statements to re-evaluate in the light of any single contrary experience. No particular experiences are linked with any particular statements in the interior of the field, except indirectly through considerations of equilibrium affecting the field as a whole.

If this view is right, it is misleading to speak of the empirical content of an individual statement—especially if it be a statement at all remote from the experiential periphery of the field. Furthermore it becomes folly to seek a boundary between synthetic statements, which hold contingently on experience, and analytic statements which hold come what may. Any statement can be held true come what may, if we make drastic enough adjustments elsewhere in the system. Even a statement very close to the periphery can be held true in the face of recalcitrant experience by pleading hallucination or by amending certain statements of the kind called logical laws. Conversely, by the same token, no statement is immune to revision. Revision even of the logical law of the excluded middle has been proposed as a means of simplifying quantum mechanics; and what difference is there in principle between such a shift and the shift whereby Kepler superseded Ptolemy, or Einstein Newton, or Darwin Aristotle?

For vividness I have been speaking in terms of varying distances from a sensory periphery. Let me try now to clarify this notion without metaphor. Certain statements, though *about* physical objects and not sense experience, seem peculiarly germane to sense experience—and in a selective way: some statements to some experiences, others to others. Such statements, especially germane to particular experiences, I picture as near the periphery. But in this relation of "germaneness" I envisage nothing more than a loose association reflecting the relative likelihood, in practice, of our choosing one statement rather than another for revision in the event of recalcitrant experience. For example, we can imagine recalcitrant experiences to which we would surely be inclined to accommodate our system by re-evaluating just the statement that there are brick houses on Elm Street, together with related statements on the same topic. We can imagine other recalcitrant experiences to which we would be inclined to accommodate our system by re-evaluating just the statement that there are no centaurs, along with kindred statements. A recalcitrant experience can, I have already urged, be accommodated by any of various alternative re-evaluations in various alternative quarters of the total system; but, in the cases which we are now imagining, our natural tendency to disturb the total system as little as possible would lead us to focus our revisions upon these specific statements concerning brick houses or centaurs. These statements are felt, therefore, to have a sharper empirical reference than highly theoretical statements of physics or logic or ontology. The latter statements may be thought of as relatively centrally located within the total network, meaning merely that little preferential connection with any particular sense data obtrudes itself.

As an empiricist I continue to think of the conceptual scheme of science as a tool, ultimately, for predicting future experience in the light of past experience. Physical objects are conceptually imported into the situation as convenient intermediaries—not by definition in terms of experience, but simply as irreducible posits comparable, epistemologically, to the gods of Homer. Let me interject that for my part I do, qua lay physicist, believe in physical objects and not in Homer's gods; and I consider it a scientific error to believe otherwise. But in point of epistemological footing the physical objects and the gods differ only in degree and not in kind. Both sorts of entities enter our conception only as cultural posits. The myth of physical objects is epistemologically superior to most in that it has proved more efficacious than other myths as a device for working a manageable structure into the flux of experience.

Imagine, for the sake of analogy, that we are given the rational numbers. We develop an algebraic theory for reasoning about them, but we find it inconveniently complex, because certain functions such as square root lack values for some arguments. Then it is discovered that the rules of our algebra can be much simplified by conceptually augmenting our ontology with some mythical entities, to be called irrational numbers. All we continue to be really interested in, first and last, are rational numbers; but we find that we can commonly get from one law about rational numbers to another much more quickly and simply by pretending that the irrational numbers are there too.

I think this a fair account of the introduction of irrational numbers and other extensions of the number system. The fact that the mythical status of irrational numbers eventually gave way to the Dedekind-Russell version of them as certain infinite classes of ratios is irrelevant to my analogy. That version is impossible anyway as long as reality is limited to the rational numbers and not extended to classes of them.

Now I suggest that experience is analogous to the rational numbers and that the physical objects, in analogy to the irrational numbers, are posits which serve merely to simplify our treatment of experience. The physical objects are no more reducible to experience than the irrational numbers to rational numbers, but their incorporation into the theory enables us to get more easily from one statement about experience to another.

The salient differences between the positing of physical objects and the positing of irrational numbers are, I think, just two. First, the factor of simplification is more overwhelming in the case of physical objects than in the numerical case. Second, the positing of physical objects is far more archaic, being indeed coeval, I expect, with language itself. For language is social and so depends for its development upon intersubjective reference.

Positing does not stop with macroscopic physical objects. Objects at the atomic level and beyond are posited to make the laws of macroscopic objects, and ultimately the laws of experience, simpler and more manageable; and we need not expect or demand full definition of atomic and subatomic entities in terms of macroscopic ones, any more than definition of macroscopic things in terms of sense data. Science is a continuation of common sense, and it continues the common-sense expedient of swelling ontology to simplify theory.

Physical objects, small and large, are not the only posits. Forces are another example; and indeed we are told nowadays that the boundary between energy and matter is obsolete. Moreover, the abstract entities which are the substance of mathematics—ultimately classes and classes of classes and so on up—are another posit in the same spirit. Epistemologically these are myths on the same footing with physical objects and gods, neither better nor worse except for differences in the degree to which they expedite our dealings with sense experiences.

The over-all algebra of rational and irrational numbers is under-determined by the algebra of rational numbers, but is smoother and more convenient; and it includes the algebra of rational numbers as a jagged or gerrymandered part. Total science, mathematical and natural and human, is similarly but more extremely underdetermined by experience. The edge of the system must be kept squared with experience; the rest, with all its elaborate myths or fictions, has as its objective the simplicity of laws.

Ontological questions, under this view, are on a par with questions of natural science. Consider the question whether to countenance classes as entities. This, as I have argued elsewhere,[9] is the question whether to quantify with respect to variables which take classes as values. Now Carnap has maintained[10] that this is a question not of matters of fact but of choosing a convenient language form, a convenient conceptual scheme or framework for science. With this I agree, but only on the proviso that the same be conceded regarding scientific hypotheses generally. Carnap has recognized[11] that he is able to preserve a double standard for ontological questions and scientific hypotheses only by assuming an absolute distinction between the analytic and the synthetic; and I need not say again that this is a distinction which I reject.

Some issues do, I grant, seem more a question of convenient conceptual scheme and others more a question of brute fact. The issue over there being classes seems more a question of convenient conceptual scheme; the issue over there being centaurs, or brick houses on Elm Street, seems more a question of fact. But I have been urging that this difference is only one of degree, and that it turns upon our vaguely pragmatic inclination to adjust one strand of the fabric of science rather than another in accommodating some particular recalcitrant experience. Conservatism figures in such choices, and so does the quest for simplicity.

Carnap, Lewis, and others take a pragmatic stand on the question of choosing between language forms, scientific frameworks; but their pragmatism leaves off at the imagined boundary between the analytic and the synthetic. In repudiating such a boundary I espouse a more thorough pragmatism. Each man is given a scientific heritage plus a continuing barrage of sensory stimulation; and the considerations which guide him in warping his scientific heritage to fit his continuing sensory promptings are, where rational, pragmatic.

Notes

Much of this paper is devoted to a critique of analyticity which I have been urging orally and in correspondence for years past. My debt to the other participants in those discussions, notably Carnap, Church, Goodman, Tarski, and White, is large and indeterminate. White's excellent essay "The Analytic and the Synthetic: An Untenable Dualism," in *John Dewey: Philosopher of Science and Freedom* (New York, 1950), says much of what needed to be said on the topic; but in the present paper I touch on some further aspects of the problem. I am grateful to Dr. Donald L. Davidson for valuable criticism of the first draft.

1. See White, op. cit., p, 324.

2. R. Carnap, *Meaning and Necessity* (Chicago, 1947), pp. 9ff.; *Logical Foundations of Probability* (Chicago, 1950), pp. 70ff.

3. This is cognitive synonymy in a primary, broad sense. Carnap (*Meaning and Necessity*, pp. 56ff.) and Lewis (*Analysis of Knowledge and Valuation* [La Salle, Ill., 1946], pp. 83ff.) have suggested how, once this notion is at hand, a narrower sense of cognitive synonymy which is preferable for some purposes can in turn be derived. But this special ramification of concept-building lies aside from the present purposes and must not be confused with the broad sort of cognitive synonymy here concerned.

4. See, e.g., my *Mathematical Logic* (New York, 1940; Cambridge, Mass., 1947), sec. 24, 26, 27; or *Methods of Logic* (New York, 1950), sec. 37 ff.

5. The 'if and only if' itself is intended in the truth functional sense. See Carnap, *Meaning and Necessity*, p, 14.

6. The doctrine can indeed be formulated with terms rather than statements as the units. Thus C. I. Lewis describes the meaning of a term as "*a criterion in mind*, by reference to which one is able to apply or refuse to apply the expression in question in the case of presented, or imagined, things or situations" (*op. cit.*, p. 133).

7. John Horne Tooke, *The Diversions of Purley* (London, 1776; Boston, 1806), I, ch. ii.

8. R. Carnap, *Der logische Aufbau der Welt* (Berlin, 1928).

9. E.g., in "Notes on Existence and Necessity," *Journal of Philosophy*, XL (1943), 113–127.

10. Carnap, "Empiricism, Semantics, and Ontology," *Revue internationale de philosophie*, IV (1950), 20–40.

11. *Op. cit.*, p. 32, footnote.

In this paper Quine offers a solution to the paradox of non-being by way of an extension of Russell's theory of definite descriptions and the concept of "ontological commitment."

W.V.O. QUINE

On What There Is

A curious thing about the ontological problem is its simplicity. It can be put in three Anglo-Saxon monosyllables: "What is there?" It can be answered, moreover, in a word—"Everything"—and everyone will accept this answer as true. However, this is merely to say that there is what there is. There remains room for disagreement over cases; and so the issue has stayed alive down the centuries.

Suppose now that two philosophers, McX and I, differ over ontology. Suppose McX maintains there is something which I maintain there is not. McX can, quite consistently with his own point of view, describe our difference of opinion by saying that I refuse to recognize certain entities. I should protest of course that he is wrong in his formulation of our disagreement, for I maintain that there are no entities, of the kind which he alleges, *for* me to recognize; but my finding him wrong in his formulation of our disagreement is unimportant, for I am committed to considering him wrong in his ontology anyway.

When *I* try to formulate our difference of opinion, on the other hand, I seem to be in a predicament. I cannot admit that there are some things which McX countenances and I do not, for in admitting that there are such things I should be contradicting my own rejection of them.

It would appear, if this reasoning were sound, that in any ontological dispute the proponent of the negative side suffers the disadvantage of not being able to admit that his opponent disagrees with him.

This is the old Platonic riddle of non-being. Non-being must in some sense be, otherwise what is it that there is not? This tangled doctrine might be nicknamed *Plato's beard;* historically it has proved tough, frequently dulling the edge of Occam's razor.

It is some such line of thought that leads philosophers like McX to impute being where they might otherwise be quite content to recognize that there is nothing. Thus, take Pegasus. If Pegasus *were* not, McX argues, we should not be talking about anything when we use the word; therefore it would be nonsense to say even that Pegasus is not. Thinking to show thus that the denial of Pegasus cannot be coherently maintained, he concludes that Pegasus is.

McX cannot, indeed, quite persuade himself that any region of space-time, near or remote, contains a flying horse of flesh and blood. Pressed for further details on Pegasus, then, he says that Pegasus is an idea in men's minds. Here, however, a confusion begins to be apparent. We may for the sake of argument concede that there is an entity, and even a unique entity (though this is rather implausible), which is the mental Pegasus-idea; but this mental entity is not what people are talking about when they deny Pegasus.

McX never confuses the Parthenon with the Parthenon-idea. The Parthenon is physical; the Parthenon-idea is mental (according any way to McX's version of ideas, and I have no better to offer). The Parthenon is visible; the Parthenon-idea is invisible. We cannot easily imagine two things more unlike, and less liable to confusion, than the Parthenon and the Parthenon-idea. But when we shift from the Parthenon to Pegasus, the confusion sets in—for no other reason than that McX would sooner be deceived by the crudest and most flagrant counterfeit than grant the non-being of Pegasus.

The notion that Pegasus must be, because it would otherwise be nonsense to say even that Pegasus is not, has been seen to lead McX into an elementary confusion. Subtler minds, taking the same precept as their starting point, come out with theories of Pegasus which are less patently misguided than McX's, and correspondingly more difficult to eradicate. One of these subtler minds is named, let us say, Wyman. Pegasus, Wyman maintains, has his being as an unactualized possible. When we say of Pegasus that there is no such thing, we are saying, more precisely, that Pegasus does not have the special attribute of actuality. Saying that Pegasus is not actual is on a par, logically, with saying that the Parthenon is not red; in either case we are saying something about an entity whose being is unquestioned.

Wyman, by the way, is one of those philosophers who have united in ruining the good old word 'exist'. Despite his espousal of unactualized possibles, he limits the word 'existence' to actuality—thus preserving an illusion of ontological agreement between himself and us who repudiate the rest of his bloated universe. We have all been prone to say, in our common-sense usage of 'exist', that Pegasus does not exist, meaning simply that there is no such entity at all. If Pegasus existed he would indeed be in space and time, but only because the word 'Pegasus' has spatio-temporal connotations, and not because 'exists' has spatio-temporal connotations. If spatio-temporal reference is lacking when we affirm the existence of the cube root of 27, this is simply because a cube root is not a spatio-temporal kind of thing, and not because we are being ambiguous in our use of 'exist'. However, Wyman, in an ill-conceived effort to appear agreeable, genially grants us the non-existence of Pegasus and then, contrary to what *we* meant by non-existence of Pegasus, insists that Pegasus *is*. Existence is one thing, he says, and subsistence is another. The only way I know of coping with this obfuscation of issues is to *give* Wyman the word 'exist'. I'll try not to use it again; I still have 'is'. So much for lexicography; let's get back to Wyman's ontology.

Wyman's overpopulated universe is in many ways unlovely. It offends the aesthetic sense of us who have a taste for desert landscapes, but this is not the worst of it. Wyman's slum of possibles is a breeding ground for disorderly elements. Take, for instance, the possible fat man in that doorway; and, again, the possible bald man in that doorway. Are they the same possible man, or two possible men? How do we decide? How many possible men are there in that doorway? Are there more possible thin ones than fat ones? How many of them are alike? Or would their being alike make them one? Are no *two* possible things alike? Is this the same as saying that it is impossible for two things to be alike? Or, finally, is the concept of identity simply inapplicable to unactualized possibles? But what sense can be found in talking of entities which cannot meaningfully be said to be identical with themselves and distinct from one another? These elements are well nigh incorrigible. By a Fregean therapy of individual concepts, some effort might be made at rehabilitation; but I feel we'd do better simply to clear Wyman's slum and be done with it.

Possibility, along with the other modalities of necessity and impossibility and contingency, raises problems upon which I do not mean to imply that we should turn our backs. But we can at least limit modalities to whole statements. We may impose the adverb 'possibly' upon a statement as a whole, and we may well worry about the semantical analysis of such usage; but little real advance in such analysis is to be hoped for in expanding our universe to include so-called *possible entities*. I suspect that the main motive for this expansion is simply the old notion that Pegasus, e.g., must be because it would otherwise be nonsense to say even that he is not.

Still, all the rank luxuriance of Wyman's universe of possibles would seem to come to naught when we make a slight change in the example and speak not of Pegasus but of the round square cupola on Berkeley College. If, unless Pegasus were, it would be nonsense to say that he is not, then by the same token, unless the round square cupola on Berkeley College were, it would be nonsense to say that it is not. But, unlike Pegasus, the round square cupola on Berkeley College cannot be admitted even as an unactualized *possible*. Can we drive Wyman now to admitting also a realm of unactualizable impossibles? If so, a good many embarrassing questions could be asked about them. We might hope even to trap Wyman in contradictions, by getting him to admit that certain of these entities are at once round and square. But the wily Wyman chooses the other horn of the dilemma and concedes that it is nonsense to say that the round square cupola on Berkeley College is not. He says that the phrase 'round square cupola' is meaningless.

Wyman was not the first to embrace this alternative. The doctrine of the meaninglessness of contradictions runs away back. The tradition survives, moreover, in writers such as Wittgenstein who seem to share none of Wyman's motivations. Still I wonder whether the first temptation to such a doctrine may not have been substantially the motivation which we have observed in Wyman. Certainly the doctrine has no intrinsic appeal; and it has led its devotees to such quixotic extremes as that of challenging the method of proof by *reductio ad absurdum*—a challenge in which I seem to detect a quite striking *reductio ad absurdum eius ipsius*.

Moreover, the doctrine of meaninglessness of contradictions has the severe methodological drawback that it makes it impossible, in principle, ever to devise an effective test of what is meaningful and what is not. It would be forever impossible for us to devise systematic ways of deciding whether a string of signs made sense—even to us individually, let alone other people—or not. For, it follows from a discovery in mathematical logic, due to Church, that there can be no generally applicable test of contradictoriness.

I have spoken disparagingly of Plato's beard, and hinted that it is tangled. I have dwelt at length on the inconveniences of putting up with it. It is time to think about taking steps.

Russell, in his theory of so-called singular descriptions, showed clearly how we might meaningfully use seeming names without supposing that the entities allegedly named be. The names to which Russell's theory directly applies are complex descriptive names such as 'the author of *Waverly*', 'the present King of France', 'the round square cupola on Berkeley College'. Russell analyzes such phrases systematically as fragments of the whole sentences in which they occur. The sentence 'The author of *Waverly* was a poet', e.g., is explained as a whole as meaning 'Someone (better: something) wrote *Waverly* and was a poet, and nothing else wrote Waverly'. (The point of this added clause is to affirm the uniqueness which is implicit in the word 'the', in 'the author of *Waverly*'.) The sentence 'The round square cupola on Berkeley College is pink' is explained as 'Something is round and square and is a cupola on Berkeley College and is pink, and nothing else is round and square and a cupola on Berkeley College'.

The virtue of this analysis is that the seeming name, a descriptive phrase, is paraphrased *in context* as a so-called incomplete symbol. No unified expression is offered as an analysis of the descriptive phrase, but the statement as a whole which was the context of that phrase still gets its full quota of meaning—whether true or false.

The unanalyzed statement 'The author of *Waverly* was a poet' contains a part, 'the author of *Waverly*', which is wrongly supposed by McX and Wyman to demand objective reference in order to be meaningful at all. But in Russell's translation, 'Something wrote Waverly and was a poet and nothing else wrote Waverly', the burden of objective reference which had been put upon the descriptive phrase is now taken over by words of the kind that logicians call bound variables, variables of quantification: namely, words like 'something', 'nothing', 'everything'. These words, far from purporting to be names specifically of the author of *Waverly*, do not purport to be names at all; they refer to entities generally, with a kind of studied ambiguity peculiar to themselves. These quantificational words or bound variables are of course a basic part of language, and their meaningfulness, at least in context, is not to be challenged. But their meaningfulness in no way presupposes there being either the author of *Waverly* or the round square cupola on Berkeley College or any other specifically preassigned objects.

Where descriptions are concerned, there is no longer any difficulty in affirming or denying being. 'There is the author of *Waverly*' is explained by Russell as meaning 'Someone (or, more strictly, something) wrote *Waverly* and nothing else wrote *Waverly*'. 'The author of *Waverly* is not' is explained, correspondingly, as the alternation 'Either each thing failed to write *Waverly* or two or more things wrote *Waverly*'. This alternation is false, but meaningful; and it contains no expression purporting to designate the author of *Waverly*. The statement 'The round square cupola on Berkeley College is not' is analyzed in similar fashion. So the old notion that statements of nonbeing defeat themselves goes by the board. When a statement of being or non-being is analyzed by Russell's theory of descriptions, it ceases to contain any expression which even purports to name the alleged entity whose being is in question, so that the meaningfulness of the statement no longer can be thought to presuppose that there be such an entity.

Now what of 'Pegasus'? This being a word rather than a descriptive phrase, Russell's argument does not immediately apply to it. However, it can easily be made to apply. We have only to rephrase 'Pegasus' as a description, in any way that seems adequately to single out our idea: say 'the winged horse that was captured by Bellerophon'. Substituting such a phrase for 'Pegasus', we can then proceed to analyze the statement 'Pegasus is', or 'Pegasus is not', precisely on the analogy of Russell's analysis of 'The author of *Waverly* is' and 'The author of *Waverly* is not'.

In order thus to subsume a one-word name or alleged name such as 'Pegasus' under Russell's theory of description, we must of course be able first to translate the word into a description. But this is no real restriction. If the notion of Pegasus had been so obscure or so basic a one that no pat translation into a descriptive phrase had offered itself along familiar lines, we could still have availed ourselves of the following artificial and trivial-seeming device: we could have appealed to the *ex hypothesi* unanalyzable, irreducible attribute of *being Pegasus*, adopting, for its expression, the verb 'is-Pegasus', or 'pegasizes'. The noun 'Pegasus' itself could then be treated as derivative, and identified after all with a description: 'the thing that is-Pegasus', 'the thing that pegasizes'.

If the importing of such a predicate as 'pegasizes' seems to commit us to recognizing that there is a corresponding attribute, pegasizing, in Plato's heaven or in the mind of men, well and good. Neither we nor Wyman nor McX have been contending, thus far, about the being or non-being of universals, but rather about that of Pegasus. If in terms of pegasizing we can interpret the noun 'Pegasus' as a description subject to Russell's theory of descriptions, then we have disposed of the old notion that Pegasus cannot be said not to be without presupposing that in some sense Pegasus is.

Our argument is now quite general. McX and Wyman supposed that we could not meaningfully affirm a statement of the form 'So-and-so is not', with a simple or descriptive singular noun in place of 'so-and-so', unless so-and-so be. This supposition is now seen to be quite generally groundless, since the singular noun in question can always be expanded into a singular description, trivially or otherwise, and then analyzed out a la Russell.

We cannot conclude, however, that man is henceforth free of all ontological commitments. We commit ourselves outright to an ontology containing numbers when we say there are prime numbers between 1000 and 1010; we commit ourselves to an ontology containing centaurs when we say there are centaurs; and we commit ourselves to an ontology containing Pegasus when we say Pegasus is. But we do not commit ourselves to an ontology containing Pegasus or the author of *Waverly* or the round square cupola on Berkeley College when we say that Pegasus or the author of *Waverly* or the cupola in question is not. We need no longer labor under the delusion that the meaningfulness of a statement containing a singular term presupposes an entity named by the term. A singular term need not name to be significant.

An inkling of this might have dawned on Wyman and McX even without benefit of Russell if they had only noticed—as so few of us do—that there is a gulf between *meaning* and *naming* even in the case of a singular term which is genuinely a name of an object. Frege's example will serve: the phrase 'Evening Star' names a certain large physical object of spherical form, which is hurtling through space some scores of millions of miles from here. The phrase 'Morning Star' names the same thing, as was probably first established by some observant Babylonian. But the two phrases cannot be regarded as having the same meaning; otherwise that Babylonian could have dispensed with his observations and contented himself with reflecting on the meanings of his words. The meanings, then, being different from one another, must be other than the named object, which is one and the same in both cases.

Confusion of meaning with naming not only made McX think he could not meaningfully repudiate Pegasus; a continuing confusion of meaning with naming no doubt helped engender his absurd notion that Pegasus is an idea, a mental entity. The structure of his confusion is as follows. He confused the alleged *named object* Pegasus with the *meaning* of the word 'Pegasus', therefore concluding that Pegasus must be in order that the word have meaning. But what sorts of things are meanings? This is a moot point; however, one might quite plausibly explain meanings as ideas in the mind, supposing we can make clear sense in turn of the idea of ideas in the mind. Therefore Pegasus, initially confused with a meaning, ends up as an idea in the mind. It is the more remarkable that Wyman, subject to the same initial motivation as McX, should have avoided this particular blunder and wound up with unactualized possibles instead.

Now let us turn to the ontological problem of universals: the question whether there are such entities as attributes, relations, classes, numbers, functions. McX, characteristically enough, thinks there are. Speaking of attributes, he says: "There are red houses, red roses, red sunsets; this much is pre-philosophical common-sense in which we must all agree. These houses, roses, and sunsets, then, have something in common; and this which they have in common is all I mean by the attribute of redness." For McX, thus, there being attributes is even more obvious and trivial than the obvious and trivial fact of there being red houses, roses, and sunsets. This, I think, is characteristic of metaphysics, or at least of that part of metaphysics called ontology: one who regards a statement on this subject as true at all must regard it as trivially true. One's ontology is basic to the conceptual scheme by which he interprets all experiences, even the most commonplace ones. Judged within some particular conceptual scheme—and how else is judgment possible?—an ontological statement goes without saying, standing in need of no separate justification at all. Ontological statements follow immediately from all manner of casual statements of commonplace fact, just as—from the point of view, anyway, of McX's conceptual scheme—'There is an attribute' follows from 'There are red houses, red roses, red sunsets.'

Judged in another conceptual scheme, an ontological statement which is axiomatic to McX's mind may, with equal immediacy and triviality, be adjudged false. One may admit that there are red houses, roses, and sunsets, but deny, except as a popular and misleading manner of speaking, that they have anything in common. The words 'houses', 'roses', and 'sunsets' denote each of sundry individual entities which are houses and roses and sunsets, and the word 'red' or 'red object' denotes each of sundry individual entities which are red houses, red roses, red sunsets; but there is not, in addition, any entity whatever, individual or otherwise, which is named by the word 'redness', nor, for that matter, by the word 'househood', 'rose-hood', 'sunsethood'. That the houses and roses and sunsets are all of them red may be taken as ultimate and irreducible, and it may be held that McX is no better off, in point of real explanatory power, for all the occult entities which he posits under such names as 'redness'.

One means by which McX might naturally have tried to impose his ontology of universals on us was already removed before we turned to the problem of universals. McX cannot argue that predicates such as 'red' or 'is-red', which we all concur in using, must be regarded as names each of a single universal entity in order that they be meaningful at all. For, we have seen that being a name of something is a much more special feature than being meaningful. He cannot even charge us—at least not by *that* argument—with having posited an attribute of pegasizing by our adoption of the predicate 'pegasizes'.

However, McX hits upon a different stratagem. "Let us grant," he says, "this distinction between meaning and naming of which you make so much. Let us even grant that 'is red', 'pegasizes', etc., are not names of attributes. Still, you admit they have meanings. But these *meanings*, whether they are *named* or not, are still universals, and I venture to say that some of them might even be the very things that I call attributes, or something to much the same purpose in the end."

For McX, this is an unusually penetrating speech; and the only way I know to counter it is by refusing to admit meanings. However, I feel no reluctance toward refusing to admit meanings, for I do not thereby deny that words and statements are meaningful. McX and I may agree to the letter in our classification of linguistic forms into the meaningful and the meaningless, even though McX construes meaningfulness as the *having* (in some sense of 'having') of some abstract entity which he calls a meaning, whereas I do not. I remain free to maintain that the fact that a given linguistic utterance is meaningful (or *significant*, as I prefer to say so as not to invite hypostasis of meanings as entities) is an ultimate and irreducible matter of fact; or, I may undertake to analyze it in terms directly of what people do in the presence of the linguistic utterance in question and other utterances similar to it.

The useful ways in which people ordinarily talk or seem to talk about meanings boil down to two: the *having* of meanings, which is significance, and *sameness* of meaning, or synonymy. What is called *giving* the meaning of an utterance is simply the uttering of a synonym, couched, ordinarily, in clearer language than the original. If we are allergic to meanings as such, we can speak directly of utterances as significant or insignificant, and as synonymous or heteronymous one with another. The problem of explaining these adjectives 'significant' and 'synonymous' with some degree of clarity and rigor—preferably, as I see it, in terms of behavior—is as difficult as it is important. But the explanatory value of special and irreducible intermediary entities called meanings is surely illusory.

Up to now I have argued that we can use singular terms significantly in sentences without presupposing that there be the entities which those terms purport to name. I have argued further that we can use general terms, e.g., predicates, without conceding them to be names of abstract entities. I have argued further that we can view utterances as significant, and as synonymous or heteronymous with one another, without countenancing a realm of entities called meanings. At this point McX begins to wonder whether there is any limit at all to our ontological immunity. Does *nothing* we may say commit us to the assumption of universals or other entities which we may find unwelcome?

I have already suggested a negative answer to this question, in speaking of bound variables, or variables of quantification, in connection with Russell's theory of descriptions. We can very easily involve ourselves in ontological commitments, by saying, e.g., that *there is something* (bound variable) which red houses and sunsets have in common; or that *there is something* which is a prime number between 1000 and 1010. But this is, essentially, the only way we can involve ourselves in ontological commitments: by our use of bound variables. The use of alleged names is no criterion, for we can repudiate their namehood at the drop of a hat unless the assumption of a corresponding entity can be spotted in the things we affirm in terms of bound variables. Names are in fact altogether immaterial to the ontological issue, for I have shown, in connection with 'Pegasus' and 'pegasize', that names can be converted to descriptions, and Russell has shown that descriptions can be eliminated. Whatever we say with help of names can be said in a language which shuns names altogether. To be is, purely and simply, to be the value of a variable. In terms, of the categories of traditional grammar, this amounts roughly to saying that to be is to be in the range of reference of a pronoun. Pronouns are the basic media of reference; nouns might better have been named pro-pronouns. The variables of quantification, 'something', 'nothing', 'everything', range over our whole ontology, whatever it may be; and we are convicted of a particular ontological presupposition if, and only if, the alleged presupposition has to be reckoned among the entities over which our variables range in order to render one of our affirmations true.

We may say, e.g., that some dogs are white, and not thereby commit ourselves to recognizing either doghood or whiteness as entities. 'Some dogs are white' says that some things that are dogs are white; and, in order that this statement be true, the things over which the bound variable 'something' ranges must include some white dogs, but need not include doghood or whiteness. On the other hand, when we say that some zoological species are cross-fertile, we are committing ourselves to recognizing as entities the several species themselves, abstract though they be. We remain so committed at least until we devise some way of so paraphrasing the statement as to show that the seeming reference to species on the part of our bound variable was an avoidable manner of speaking.

If I have been seeming to minimize the degree to which in our philosophical and unphilosophical discourse we involve ourselves in ontological commitments, let me then emphasize that classical mathematics, as the example of primes between 1000 and 1010 clearly illustrates, is up to its neck in commitments to an ontology of abstract entities. Thus it is that the great mediaeval controversy over universals has flared up anew in the modern philosophy of mathematics. The issue is clearer now than of old, because we now have a more explicit standard whereby to decide what ontology a given theory or form of discourse is committed to: a theory is committed to those and only those entities to which the bound variables of the theory must be capable of referring in order that the affirmations made in the theory be true.

Because this standard of ontological presupposition did not emerge clearly in the philosophical tradition, the modern philosophical mathematicians have not on the whole recognized that they were debating the same old problem of universals in a newly clarified form. But the fundamental cleavages among modern points of view on foundations of mathematics do come down pretty explicitly to disagreements as to the range of entities to which the bound variables should be permitted to refer.

The three main mediaeval points of view regarding universals are designated by historians as *realism, conceptualism*, and *nominalism*. Essentially these same three doctrines reappear in twentieth-century surveys of the philosophy of mathematics under the new names *logicism*, *intuitionism*, and *formalism*.

Realism, as the word is used in connection with the mediaeval controversy over universals, is the Platonic doctrine that universals or abstract entities have being independently of the mind; the mind may discover them but cannot create them. *Logicism*, represented by such latter-day Platonists as Frege, Russell, Whitehead, Church, and Carnap, condones the use of bound variables to refer to abstract entities known and unknown, specifiable and unspecifiable, indiscriminately.

Conceptualism holds that there are universals but they are mind-made. *Intuitionism*, espoused in modern times in one form or another by Poincaré, Brouwer, Weyl, and others, countenances the use of bound variables to refer to abstract entities only when those entities are capable of being cooked up individually from ingredients specified in advance. As Fraenkel has put it, logicism holds that classes are discovered while intuitionism holds that they are invented—a fair statement indeed of the old opposition between realism and conceptualism. This opposition is no mere quibble; it makes an essential difference in the amount of classical mathematics to which one is willing to subscribe. Logicists, or realists, are able on their assumptions to get Cantor's ascending orders of infinity; intuitionists are compelled to stop with the lowest order of infinity, and, as an indirect consequence, to abandon even some of the classical laws of real numbers. The modern controversy between logicism and intuitionism arose, in fact, from disagreements over infinity.

Formalism, associated with the name of Hilbert, echoes intuitionism in deploring the logicist's unbridled recourse to universals. But formalism also finds intuitionism unsatisfactory. This could happen for either of two opposite reasons. The formalist might, like the logicist, object to the crippling of classical mathematics; or he might, like the *nominalists* of old, object to admitting abstract entities at all, even in the restrained sense of mind-made entities. The upshot is the same: the formalist keeps classical mathematics as a play of insignificant notations. This play of notations can still be of utility—whatever utility it has already shown itself to have as a crutch for physicists and technologists. But utility need not imply significance, in any literal linguistic sense. Nor need the marked success of mathematicians in spinning out theorems, and in finding objective bases for agreement with one another's results, imply significance. For, an adequate basis for agreement among mathematicians can be found simply in the rules which govern the manipulation of the notations—these syntactical rules being, unlike the notations themselves, quite significant and intelligible.[1]

I have argued that the sort of ontology we adopt can be consequential—notably in connection with mathematics, although this is only an example. Now how are we to adjudicate among rival ontologies? Certainly the answer is not provided by the semantical formula "To be is to be the value of a variable"; this formula serves rather, conversely, in testing the conformity of a given remark or doctrine to a prior ontological standard. We look to bound variables in connection with ontology not in order to know what there is, but in order to know what a given remark or doctrine, ours or someone else's, *says* there is; and this much is quite properly a problem involving language. But what there is another question.

In debating over what there is, there are still reasons for operating on a semantical plane. One reason is to escape from the predicament noted at the beginning of the paper: the predicament of my not being able to admit that there are things which McX countenances and I do not. So long as I adhere to my ontology, as opposed to McX's, I cannot allow my bound variables to refer to entities which belong to McX's ontology and not to mine. I can, however, consistently describe our disagreement by characterizing the statements which McX affirms. Provided merely that my ontology countenances linguistic forms, or at least concrete inscriptions and utterances, I can talk about McX's sentences.

Another reason for withdrawing to a semantical plane is to find common ground on which to argue. Disagreement in ontology involves basic disagreement in conceptual schemes; yet McX and I, despite these basic disagreements, find that our conceptual schemes converge sufficiently in their intermediate and upper ramifications to enable us to communicate successfully on such topics as politics, weather, and, in particular, language. In so far as our basic controversy over ontology can be translated upward into a semantical controversy about words and what to do with them, the collapse of the controversy into question-begging may be delayed.

It is no wonder, then, that ontological controversy should tend into controversy over language. But we must not jump to the conclusion that what there is depends on words. Translatability of a question into semantical terms is no indication that the question is linguistic. To see Naples is to bear a name which, when prefixed to the words 'sees Naples', yields a true sentence; still there is nothing linguistic about seeing Naples.

Our acceptance of an ontology is, I think, similar in principle to our acceptance of a scientific theory, say a system of physics: we adopt, at least insofar as we are reasonable, the simplest conceptual scheme into which the disordered fragments of raw experience can be fitted and arranged. Our ontology is determined once we have fixed upon the over-all conceptual scheme which is to accommodate science in the broadest sense; and the considerations which determine a reasonable construction of any part of that conceptual scheme, e.g. the biological or the physical part, are not different in kind from the considerations which determine a reasonable construction of the whole. To whatever extent the adoption of any system of scientific theory may be said to be a matter of language, the same—but no more—may be said of the adoption of an ontology.

But simplicity, as a guiding principle in constructing conceptual schemes, is not a clear and unambiguous idea; and it is quite capable of presenting a double or multiple standard. Imagine, e.g., that we have devised the most economical set of concepts adequate to the play-by-play reporting of immediate experience. The entities under this scheme—the values of bound variables—are, let us suppose, individual subjective events of sensation or reflection. We should still find, no doubt, that a physicalistic conceptual scheme, purporting to talk about external objects, offers great advantages in simplifying our over-all reports. By bringing together scattered sense events and treating them as perceptions of one object, we reduce the complexity of our stream of experience to a manageable conceptual simplicity. The rule of simplicity is indeed our guiding maxim in assigning sense data to objects: we associate an earlier and a later round sensum with the same so-called penny, or with two different so-called pennies, in obedience to the demands of maximum simplicity in our total world-picture.

Here we have two competing conceptual schemes, a phenomenalistic one and a physicalistic one. Which should prevail? Each has its advantages; each has its special simplicity in its own way. Each, I suggest, deserves to be developed. Each may be said, indeed, to be the more fundamental, though in different senses: the one is epistemologically, the other physically, fundamental.

The physical conceptual scheme simplifies our account of experience because of the way myriad scattered sense events come to be associated with single so-called objects; still there is no likelihood that each sentence about physical objects can actually be translated, however deviously and complexly, into the phenomenalistic language. Physical objects are postulated entities which round out and simplify our account of the flux of experience, just as the introduction of irrational numbers simplifies laws of arithmetic. From the point of view of the conceptual scheme of the elementary arithmetic of rational numbers alone, the broader arithmetic of rational and irrational numbers would have the status of a convenient myth, simpler than the literal truth (namely the arithmetic of rationals) and yet containing that literal truth as a scattered part. Similarly, from a phenomenalistic point of view, the conceptual scheme of physical objects is a convenient myth, simpler than the literal truth and yet containing that literal truth as a scattered part.

Now what of classes or attributes of physical objects, in turn? A platonistic ontology of this sort is, from the point of view of a strictly physicalistic conceptual scheme, as much of a myth as that physicalistic conceptual scheme itself was for phenomenalism. This higher myth is a good and useful one, in turn, in so far as it simplifies our account of physics. Since mathematics is an integral part of this higher myth, the utility of this myth for physical science is evident enough. In speaking of it nevertheless as a myth, I echo that philosophy of mathematics to which I alluded earlier under the name of formalism. But my present suggestion is that an attitude of formalism may with equal justice be adopted toward the physical conceptual scheme, in turn, by the pure aesthete or phenomenalist.

The analogy between the myth of mathematics and the myth of physics is, in some additional and perhaps fortuitous ways, strikingly close. Consider, for example, the crisis which was precipitated in the foundations of mathematics, at the turn of the century, by the discovery of Russell's paradox and other antinomies of set theory. These contradictions had to be obviated by unintuitive, *ad hoc* devices; our mathematical myth-making became deliberate and evident to all. But what of physics? An antinomy arose between the undular and the corpuscular accounts of light; and if this was not as out-and-out a contradiction as Russell's paradox, I suspect that the reason is merely that physics is not as out-and-out as mathematics. Again, the second great modern crisis in the foundations of mathematics—precipitated in 1931 by Gödel's proof that there are bound to be undecidable statements in arithmetic—has its companion-piece in physics in Heisenberg's indeterminacy principle.

In earlier pages I undertook to show that some common arguments in favor of certain ontologies are fallacious. Further, I advanced an explicit standard whereby to decide what the ontological commitments of a theory are. But the question what ontology actually to adopt still stands open, and the obvious counsel is tolerance and an experimental spirit. Let us by all means see how much of the physicalistic conceptual scheme can be reduced to a phenomenalistic one; still physics also naturally demands pursuing, irreducible *in toto* though it be. Let us see how, or to what degree, natural science may be rendered independent of platonistic mathematics; but let us also pursue mathematics and delve into its platonistic foundations.

From among the various conceptual schemes best suited to these various pursuits, one—the phenomenalistic—claims epistemological priority. Viewed from within the phenomenalistic conceptual scheme, the ontologies of physical objects and mathematical objects are myths. The quality of myth, however, is relative; relative, in this case, to the epistemological point of view. This point of view is one among various, corresponding to one among our various interests and purposes.

Notes

This is a revised version of a paper which was presented before the Graduate Philosophy Club of Yale University on May 7, 1948. The latter paper, in turn, was a revised version of one which was presented before the Graduate Philosophical Seminary of Princeton University on March 15.

1. See Goodman and Quine, "Steps toward a constructive nominalism," *Journal of Symbolic Logic*, vol. 12 (1947), pp. 97–122.

In this paper Quine proposes a solution to Goodman's "new riddle of induction" based in Darwinian considerations.

W.V.O. QUINE

Natural Kinds

What tends to confirm an induction? This question has been aggravated on the one hand by Hempel's puzzle of the non-black non-ravens,[1] and exacerbated on the other by Goodman's puzzle of the grue emeralds.[2] I shall begin my remarks by relating the one puzzle to the other, and the other to an innate flair that we have for natural kinds. Then I shall devote the rest of the paper to reflections on the nature of this notion of natural kinds and its relation to science.

Hempel's puzzle is that just as each black raven tends to confirm the law that all ravens are black, so each green leaf, being a non-black non-raven, should tend to confirm the law that all non-black things are non-ravens, that is, again, that all ravens are black. What is paradoxical is that a green leaf should count toward the law that all ravens are black.

Goodman propounds his puzzle by requiring us to imagine that emeralds, having been identified by some criterion other than color, are now being examined one after another and all up to now are found to be green. Then he proposes to call anything *grue* that is examined today or earlier and found to be green or is not examined before tomorrow and is blue. Should we expect the first one examined tomorrow to be green, because all examined up to now were green? But all examined up to now were also grue; so why not expect the first one tomorrow to be grue, and therefore blue?

The predicate "green," Goodman says,[3] is *projectible*; "grue" is not. He says this by way of putting a name to the problem. His step toward solution is his doctrine of what he calls entrenchment,[4] which I shall touch on later. Meanwhile the terminological point is simply that projectible predicates are predicates ζ and η whose shared instances all do count, for whatever reason, toward confirmation of $\ulcorner$All ζ are $\eta\urcorner$.

Now I propose assimilating Hempel's puzzle to Goodman's by inferring from Hempel's that the complement of a projectible predicate need not be projectible. "Raven" and "black" are projectible; a black raven does count toward "All ravens are black." Hence a black raven counts also, indirectly, toward "All non-black things are non-ravens," since this says the same thing. But a green leaf does not count toward "All non-black things are non-ravens," nor, therefore, toward "All ravens are black"; "non-black" and "non-raven" are not projectible. "Green" and "leaf" are projectible, and the green leaf counts toward "All leaves are green" and "All green things are leaves";

but only a black raven can confirm "All ravens are black," the complements not being projectible.

If we see the matter in this way, we must guard against saying that a statement ⌜All ζ are η⌝ is lawlike only if ζ and η are projectible. "All non-black things are non-ravens" is a law despite its non-projectible terms, since it is equivalent to "All ravens are black." Any statement is lawlike that is logically *equivalent* to ⌜All ζ are η⌝ for some projectible ζ and η.[5]

Having concluded that the complement of a projectible predicate need not be projectible, we may ask further whether there is *any* projectible predicate whose complement is projectible. I can conceive that there is not, when complements are taken strictly. We must not be misled by limited or relative complementation; "male human" and "non-male human" are indeed both projectible.

To get back now to the emeralds, why do we expect the next one to be green rather than grue? The intuitive answer lies in similarity, however subjective. Two green emeralds are more similar than two grue ones would be if only one of the grue ones were green. Green things, or at least green emeralds, are a kind.[6] A projectible predicate is one that is true of all and only the things of a kind. What makes Goodman's example a puzzle, however, is the dubious scientific standing of a general notion of similarity, or of kind.

The dubiousness of this notion is itself a remarkable fact. For surely there is nothing more basic to thought and language than our sense of similarity; our sorting of things into kinds. The usual general term, whether a common noun or a verb or an adjective, owes its generality to some resemblance among the things referred to. Indeed, learning to use a word depends on a double resemblance: first, a resemblance between the present circumstances and past circumstances in which the word was used, and second, a phonetic resemblance between the present utterance of the word and past utterances of it. And every reasonable expectation depends on resemblance of circumstances, together with our tendency to expect similar causes to have similar effects.

The notion of a kind and the notion of similarity or resemblance seem to be variants or adaptations of a single notion. Similarity is immediately definable in terms of kind; for, things are similar when they are two of a kind. The very words for "kind" and "similar" tend to run in etymologically cognate pairs. Cognate with "kind" we have "akin" and "kindred." Cognate with "like" we have "ilk." Cognate with "similar" and "same" and "resemble" there are "*sammeln*" and "assemble," suggesting a gathering into kinds.

We cannot easily imagine a more familiar or fundamental notion than this, or a notion more ubiquitous in its applications. On this score it is like the notions of logic: like identity, negation, alternation, and the rest. And yet, strangely, there is something logically repugnant about it. For we are baffled when we try to relate the general notion of similarity significantly to logical terms. One's first hasty suggestion might be to say that things are similar when they have all or most or many properties in common. Or, trying to be less vague, one might try defining comparative similarity—"*a* is more similar to *b* than to *c*"—as meaning that *a* shares more properties with *b* than with *c*. But any such course only reduces our problem to the unpromising task of settling what to count as a property.

The nature of the problem of what to count as a property can be seen by turning for a moment to set theory. Things are viewed as going together into sets in any and every combination describable and indescribable. Any two things are joint members of any number of sets. Certainly then we cannot define "*a* is more similar to *b* than to *c*" to mean that *a* and *b* belong jointly to more sets than *a* and *c* do. If properties are to support this line of definition where sets do not, it must be because properties do not, like sets, take things in every random combination. It must be that properties are shared only by things that are significantly similar. But properties in such a sense are no clearer than kinds. To start with such a notion of property, and define similarity on that basis, is no better than accepting similarity as undefined.

The contrast between properties and sets which I suggested just now must not be confused with the more basic and familiar contrast between properties, as intensional, and sets as extensional. Properties are intensional in that they may be counted as distinct properties even though wholly coinciding in respect of the things that have them. There is no call to reckon kinds as intensional. Kinds can be seen as sets, determined by their members. It is just that not all sets are kinds.

If similarity is taken simple-mindedly as a yes-or-no affair, with no degrees, then there is no containing of kinds within broader kinds. For, as remarked, similarity now simply means belonging to some one same kind. If all colored things comprise a kind, then all colored things count as similar, and the set of all red things is too narrow to count as a kind. If on the other hand the set of all red things counts as a kind, then colored things do not all count as similar, and the set of all colored things is too broad to count as a kind. We cannot have it both ways. Kinds can, however, overlap; the red things can comprise one kind, the round another.

When we move up from the simple dyadic relation of similarity to the more serious and useful triadic relation of comparative similarity, a correlative change takes place in the notion of kind. Kinds come to admit now not only of overlapping but also of containment one in another. The set of all red things and the set of all colored things can now both count as kinds; for all colored things can now be counted as resembling one another more than some things do, even though less, on the whole, than red ones do.

At this point, of course, our trivial definition of similarity as sameness of kind breaks down; for almost any two things could count now as common members of some broad kind or other, and anyway we now want to define comparative or triadic similarity. A definition that suggests itself is this: *a* is more similar to *b* than to *c* when *a* and *b* belong jointly to more kinds than *a* and *c* do. But even this works only for finite systems of kinds.

The notion of kind and the notion of similarity seemed to be substantially one notion. We observed further that they resist reduction to less dubious notions, as of logic or set theory. That they at any rate be definable each in terms of the other seems little enough to ask. We just saw a somewhat limping definition of comparative similarity in terms of kinds. What now of the converse project, definition of kind in terms of similarity?

One may be tempted to picture a kind, suitable to a comparative similarity relation, as any set which is "qualitatively spherical" in this sense: it takes in exactly the things that differ less than so-and-so much from some central norm. If without serious loss of accuracy we can assume that there are one or more actual things (*paradigm cases*) that nicely exemplify the desired norm, and one or more actual things (*foils*) that deviate just barely too much to be counted into the desired kind at all, then our definition is easy: *the kind with paradigm a and foil b* is the set of all the things to which *a* is more similar than *a* is to *b*. More generally, then, a set may be said to be a kind if and only if there are *a* and *b*, known or unknown, such that the set is the kind with paradigm *a* and foil *b*.

If we consider examples, however, we see that this definition does not give us what we want as kinds. Thus take red. Let us grant that a central shade of red can be picked as norm. The trouble is that the paradigm cases, objects in just that shade of red, can come in all sorts of shapes, weights, sizes, and smells. Mere degree of overall similarity to any one such paradigm case will afford little evidence of degree of redness, since it will depend also on shape, weight, and the rest. If our assumed relation of comparative similarity were just comparative chromatic similarity, then our paradigm-and-foil definition of kind would indeed accommodate redkind. What the definition will not do is distill purely chromatic kinds from mixed similarity.

A different attempt, adapted from Carnap, is this: a set is a kind if all its members are more similar to one another than they all are to any one thing outside the set. In other words, each non-member differs more from some member than that member differs from any member. However, as Goodman showed in a criticism of Carnap,[7] this construction succumbs to what Goodman calls the difficulty of imperfect community. Thus consider the set of all red round things, red wooden things, and round wooden things. Each member of this set resembles each other member somehow: at least in being red, or in being round, or in being wooden, and perhaps in two or all three of these respects or others. Conceivably, moreover, there is no one thing outside the set that resembles every member of the set to even the least of these degrees. The set then meets the proposed definition of kind. Yet surely it is not what anyone means by a kind. It admits yellow croquet balls and red rubber balls while excluding yellow rubber balls.

The relation between similarity and kind, then, is less clear and neat than could be wished. Definition of similarity in terms of kind is halting, and definition of kind in terms of similarity is unknown. Still the two notions are in an important sense correlative. They vary together. If we reassess something *a* as less similar to *b* than to *c*, where it had counted as more similar to *b* than to *c*, surely we will correspondingly permute *a*, *b*, and *c* in respect of their assignment to kinds; and conversely.

I have stressed how fundamental the notion of similarity or of kind is to our thinking, and how alien to logic and set theory. I want to go on now to say more about how fundamental these notions are to our thinking, and something also about their nonlogical roots. Afterward I want to bring out how the notion of similarity or of kind changes as science progresses. I shall suggest that it is a mark of maturity of a branch of science that the notion of similarity or kind finally dissolves, so far as it is relevant to that branch of science. That is, it ultimately submits to analysis in the special terms of that branch of science and logic.

For deeper appreciation of how fundamental similarity is, let us observe more closely how it figures in the learning of language. One learns by *ostension* what presentations to call yellow; that is, one learns by hearing the word applied to samples. All he has to go on, of course, is the similarity of further cases to the samples. Similarity being a matter of degree, one has to learn by trial and error how reddish or brownish or greenish a thing can be and still be counted yellow. When he finds he has applied the word too far out, he can use the false cases as samples to the contrary; and then he can proceed to guess whether further cases are yellow or not by considering whether they are more similar to the in-group or the out-group. What one thus uses, even at this primitive stage of learning, is a fully functioning sense of similarity, and relative similarity at that: *a* is more similar to *b* than to *c*.

All these delicate comparisons and shrewd inferences about what to call yellow are, in Sherlock Holmes's terminology, elementary. Mostly the process is unconscious. It is the same process by which an animal learns to respond in distinctive ways to his master's commands or other discriminated stimulations.

The primitive sense of similarity that underlies such learning has, we saw, a certain complexity of structure: *a* is more similar to *b* than to *c*. Some people have thought that it has to be much more complex still: that it depends irreducibly on *respects*, thus similarity in color, similarity in shape, and so on. According to this view, our learning of yellow by ostension would have depended on our first having been told or somehow apprised that it was going to be a question of color. Now hints of this kind are a great help, and in our learning we often do depend on them. Still one would like to be able to show that a single general standard of similarity, but of course comparative similarity, is all we need, and that respects can be abstracted afterward. For instance, suppose the child has learned of a yellow ball and block that they count as yellow, and of a red ball and block that they do not, and now he has to decide about a yellow cloth. Presumably he will find the cloth more similar to the yellow ball and to the yellow block than to the red ball or red block; and he will not have needed any prior schooling in colors and respects. Carnap undertook to show long ago how some respects, such as color, could by an ingenious construction be derived from a general similarity notion;[8] however, this development is challenged, again, by Goodman's difficulty of imperfect community.

A standard of similarity is in some sense innate. This point is not against empiricism; it is a commonplace of behavioral psychology. A response to a red circle, if it is rewarded, will be elicited again by a pink ellipse more readily than by a blue triangle; the red circle resembles the pink ellipse more than the blue triangle. Without some such prior spacing of qualities, we could never acquire a habit; all stimuli would be equally alike and equally different. These spacings of qualities, on the part of men and other animals, can be explored and mapped in the laboratory by experiments in conditioning and extinction.[9] Needed as they are for all learning, these distinctive spacings cannot themselves all be learned; some must be innate.

If then I say that there is an innate standard of similarity, I am making a condensed statement that can be interpreted, and truly interpreted, in behavioral terms. Moreover, in this behavioral sense it can be said equally of other animals that they have an innate standard of similarity too. It is part of our animal birthright. And, interestingly enough, it is characteristically animal in its lack of intellectual status. At any rate we noticed earlier how alien the notion is to mathematics and logic.

This innate qualitative spacing of stimulations was seen to have one of its human uses in the ostensive learning of words like "yellow." I should add as a cautionary remark that this is not the only way of learning words, nor the commonest; it is merely the most rudimentary way. It works when the question of the reference of a word is a simple question of spread: how much of our surroundings counts as yellow, how much counts as water, and so on. Learning a word like "apple" or "square" is more complicated, because here we have to learn also where to say that one apple or square leaves off and another begins. The complication is that apples do not add up to an apple, nor squares, generally, to a square. "Yellow" and "water" are mass terms, concerned only with spread; "apple" and "square" are terms of divided reference, concerned with both spread and individuation. Ostension figures in the learning of terms of this latter kind too, but the process is more complex.[10] And then there are all the other sorts of words, all those abstract and neutral connectives and adverbs and all the recondite terms of scientific theory; and there are also the grammatical constructions themselves to be mastered. The learning of these things is less direct and more complex still. There are deep problems in this domain, but they lie aside from the present topic.

Our way of learning "yellow," then, gives less than a full picture of how we learn language. Yet more emphatically, it gives less than a full picture of the human use of an innate standard of similarity, or innate spacing of qualities. For, as remarked, every reasonable expectation depends on similarity. Again on this score, other animals are like man. Their expectations, if we choose so to conceptualize their avoidance movements and salivation and pressing of levers and the like, are clearly dependent on their appreciation of similarity. Or, to put matters in their methodological order, these avoidance movements and salivation and pressing of levers and the like are typical of what we have to go on in mapping the animals' appreciation of similarity, their spacing of qualities.

Induction itself is essentially only more of the same: animal expectation or habit formation. And the ostensive learning of words is an implicit case of induction. Implicitly the learner of "yellow" is working inductively toward a general law of English verbal behavior, though a law that he will never try to state; he is working up to where he can in general judge when an English speaker would assent to "yellow" and when not.

Not only is ostensive learning a case of induction; it is a curiously comfortable case of induction, a game of chance with loaded dice. At any rate this is so if, as seems plausible, each man's spacing of qualities is enough like his neighbor's. For the learner is generalizing on his yellow samples by similarity considerations, and his neighbors have themselves acquired the use of the word "yellow", in their day, by the same similarity considerations. The learner of "yellow" is thus making his induction in a friendly world. Always, induction expresses our hope that similar causes will have similar effects; but when the induction is the ostensive learning of a word, that pious hope blossoms into a foregone conclusion. The uniformity of people's quality spaces virtually assures that similar presentations will elicit similar verdicts.

It makes one wonder the more about other inductions, where what is sought is a generalization not about our neighbor's verbal behavior but about the harsh impersonal world. It is reasonable that our quality space should match our neighbor's, we being birds of a feather; and so the general trustworthiness of induction in the ostensive learning of words was a put-up job. To trust induction as a way of access to the truths of nature, on the other hand, is to suppose, more nearly, that our quality space matches that of the cosmos. The brute irrationality of our sense of similarity, its irrelevance to anything in logic and mathematics, offers little reason to expect that this sense is somehow in tune with the world—a world which, unlike language, we never made. Why induction should be trusted, apart from special cases such as the ostensive learning of words, is the perennial philosophical problem of induction.

One part of the problem of induction, the part that asks why there should be regularities in nature at all, can, I think, be dismissed. *That* there are or have been regularities, for whatever reason, is an established fact of science; and we cannot ask better than that. *Why* there have been regularities is an obscure question, for it is hard to see what would count as an answer. What does make clear sense is this other part of the problem of induction: why does our innate subjective spacing of qualities accord so well with the functionally relevant groupings in nature as to make our inductions tend to come out right? Why should our subjective spacing of qualities have a special purchase on nature and a lien on the future?

There is some encouragement in Darwin. If people's innate spacing of qualities is a gene-linked trait, then the spacing that has made for the most successful inductions will have tended to predominate through natural selection.[11] Creatures inveterately wrong in their inductions have a pathetic but praiseworthy tendency to die before reproducing their kind.

At this point let me say that I shall not be impressed by protests that I am using inductive generalizations, Darwin's and others, to justify induction, and thus reasoning in a circle. The reason I shall not be impressed by this is that my position is a naturalistic one; I see philosophy not as an *a priori* propaedeutic or groundwork for science, but as continuous with science. I see philosophy and science as in the same boat—a boat which, to revert to Neurath's figure as I so often do, we can rebuild only at sea while staying afloat in it. There is no external vantage point, no first philosophy. All scientific findings, all scientific conjectures that are at present plausible, are therefore in my view as welcome for use in philosophy as elsewhere. For me then the problem of induction is a problem about the world: a problem of how we, as we now are (by our present scientific lights), in a world we never made, should stand better than random or coin-tossing chances of coming out right when we predict by inductions which are based on our innate, scientifically unjustified similarity standard. Darwin's natural selection is a plausible partial explanation.

It may, in view of a consideration to which I next turn, be almost explanation enough. This consideration is that induction, after all, has its conspicuous failures. Thus take color. Nothing in experience, surely, is more vivid and conspicuous than color and its contrasts. And the remarkable fact, which has impressed scientists and philosophers as far back at least as Galileo and Descartes, is that the distinctions that matter for basic physical theory are mostly independent of color contrasts. Color impresses man; raven black impresses Hempel; emerald green impresses Goodman. But color is cosmically secondary. Even slight differences in sensory mechanisms from species to species, Smart remarks,[12] can make overwhelming differences in the grouping of things by color. Color is king in our innate quality space, but undistinguished in cosmic circles. Cosmically, colors would not qualify as kinds.

Color is helpful at the food-gathering level. Here it behaves well under induction, and here, no doubt, has been the survival value of our color-slanted quality space. It is just that contrasts that are crucial for such activities can be insignificant for broader and more theoretical science. If man were to live by basic science alone, natural selection would shift its support to the color-blind mutation.

Living as he does by bread and basic science both, man is torn. Things about his innate similarity sense that are helpful in the one sphere can be a hindrance in the other. Credit is due man's inveterate ingenuity, or human sapience, for having worked around the blinding dazzle of color vision and found the more significant regularities elsewhere. Evidently natural selection has dealt with the conflict by endowing man doubly: with both a color-slanted quality space and the ingenuity to rise above it.

He has risen above it by developing modified systems of kinds, hence modified similarity standards for scientific purposes. By the trial-and-error process of theorizing he has re-grouped things into new kinds which prove to lend themselves to many inductions better than the old.

A crude example is the modification of the notion of fish by excluding whales and porpoises. Another taxonomic example is the grouping of kangaroos, opossums, and marsupial mice in a single kind, marsupials, while excluding ordinary mice. By primitive standards the marsupial mouse is more similar to the ordinary mouse than to the kangaroo; by theoretical standards the reverse is true.

A theoretical kind need not be a modification of an intuitive one. It may issue from theory full-blown, without antecedents; for instance the kind which comprises positively charged particles.

We revise our standards of similarity or of natural kinds on the strength, as Goodman remarks,[13] of second-order inductions. New groupings, hypothetically adopted at the suggestion of a growing theory, prove favorable to inductions and so become "entrenched." We newly establish the projectibility of some predicate, to our satisfaction, by successfully trying to project it. In induction nothing succeeds like success.

Between an innate similarity notion or spacing of qualities and a scientifically sophisticated one, there are all gradations. Sciences, after all, differs from common sense only in degree of methodological sophistication. Our experiences from earliest infancy are bound to have overlaid our innate spacing of qualities by modifying and supplementing our grouping habits little by little, inclining us more and more to an appreciation of theoretical kinds and similarities, long before we reach the point of studying science systematically as such. Moreover, the later phases do not wholly supersede the earlier; we retain different similarity standards, different systems of kinds, for use in different contexts. We all still say that a marsupial mouse is more like an ordinary mouse than a kangaroo, except when we are concerned with genetic matters. Something like our innate quality space continues to function alongside the more sophisticated regroupings that have been found by scientific experience to facilitate induction.

We have seen that a sense of similarity or of kinds is fundamental to learning in the widest sense—to language learning, to induction, to expectation. Toward a further appreciation of how utterly this notion permeates our thought, I want now to point out a number of other very familiar and central notions which seem to depend squarely on this one. They are notions that are definable in terms of similarity, or kinds, and further irreducible.

A notable domain of examples is the domain of dispositions, such as Carnap's example of solubility in water. To say of some individual object that it is soluble in water is not to say merely that it always dissolves when in water, because this would be true by default of any object, however insoluble, if it merely happened to be destined never to get into water. It is to say rather that it *would* dissolve if it were in water; but this account brings small comfort, since the device of a subjunctive conditional involves all the perplexities of disposition terms and more. Thus far I simply repeat Carnap.[14] But now I want to point out what could be done in this connection with the notion of kind. Intuitively, what qualifies a thing as soluble though it never gets into water is that it is of the same kind as the things that actually did or will dissolve; it is similar to them. Strictly we can't simply say "*the* same kind," nor simply "similar," when we have wider and narrower kinds, less and more similarity. Let us then mend our definition by saying that the soluble things are the common members of *all* such kinds. A thing is soluble if *each* kind that is broad enough to embrace all actual victims of solution embraces it too.

Graphically the idea is this: we make a set of all the sometime victims, all the things that actually did or will dissolve in water, and then we add just enough other things to round the set out into a kind. This is the water-soluble kind.

If this definition covers just the desired things, the things that are really soluble in water, it owes its success to a circumstance that could be otherwise. The needed circumstance is that a sufficient variety of things actually get dissolved in water to assure their not all falling under any one kind narrower than the desired water-soluble kind itself. But it is a plausible circumstance, and I am not sure that its accidental character is a drawback. If the trend of events had been otherwise, perhaps the solubility concept would not have been wanted.

However, if I seem to be defending this definition, I must now hasten to add that of course it has much the same fault as the definition which used the subjunctive conditional. This definition uses the unreduced notion of kind, which is certainly not a notion we want to rest with either; neither theoretical kind nor intuitive kind. My purpose in giving the definition is only to show the link between the problem of dispositions and the problem of kinds.

As between theoretical and intuitive kinds, certainly the theoretical ones are the ones wanted for purposes of defining solubility and other dispositions of scientific concern. Perhaps "amiable" and "reprehensible" are disposition terms whose definitions should draw rather on intuitive kinds.

In considering the disposition of solubility we observed a link first with the subjunctive conditional and then with the notion of kind. This suggests comparing also the two end terms, so as to see the connection between the subjunctive conditional and the notion of kind. We had then, on the one side, the subjunctive conditional "If *x* were in water it would dissolve"; and on the other side, in terms of kinds, we had "Each kind that embraces all things that ever get into water and dissolve, embraces *x*." Here we have equated a sample subjunctive conditional to a sentence about kinds. We can easily enough generalize the equivalence to cover a significant class of subjunctive conditionals: the form "If *x* were an *F* then *x* would be a *G*" gets equated to "Each kind that embraces all *Fs* that are *Gs* embraces *x*." Notice that the *Fs* themselves, here, would not be expected to constitute a kind; nor the *Gs*; nor the *Fs* which are *Gs*. But you take the fewest things you can which, added to the *Fs* which are *Gs*, suffice to round the set out to a kind. Then *x* is one of these few additional things; this is the interpretation we get of the subjunctive conditional "If *x* were an *F* then *x* would be a *G*."

One might try this formula out on other examples, and study it for possible light on subjunctive conditionals more generally. Some further insight into this queer idiom might thus be gained. But let us remember that we are still making uncritical use of the unreduced notion of kind. My purpose, again, is only to show the link between these matters.

Another dim notion, which has intimate connections with dispositions and subjunctive conditionals, is the notion of cause; and we shall see that it too turns on the notion of kinds. Hume explained cause as invariable succession, and this makes sense as long as the cause and effect are referred to by general terms. We can say that fire causes heat, and we can mean thereby, as Hume would have it, that each event classifiable under the head of fire is followed by an event classifiable under the head of heat, or heating up. But this account, whatever its virtues for these general causal statements, leaves singular causal statements unexplained.

What does it mean to say that the kicking over of a lamp in Mrs. Leary's barn caused the Chicago fire? It cannot mean merely that the event at Mrs. Leary's belongs to a set, and the Chicago fire belongs to a set, such that there is invariable succession between the two sets: every member of the one set is followed by a member of the other. This paraphrase is trivially true and too weak. Always, if one event happens to be followed by another, the two belong to *certain* sets between which there is invariable succession. We can rig the sets arbitrarily. Just put any arbitrary events in the first set, including the first of the two events we are interested in; and then in the other set put the second of those two events, together with other events that happen to have occurred just after the other members of the first set.

Because of this way of trivialization, a singular causal statement says no more than that the one event was followed by the other. That is, it says no more if we use the definition just now contemplated; which, therefore, we must not. The trouble with that definition is clear enough: it is the familiar old trouble of the promiscuity of sets. Here, as usual, kinds, being more discriminate, enable us to draw distinctions where sets do not. To say that one event caused another is to say that the two events are of *kinds* between which there is invariable succession. If this correction does not yet take care of Mrs. Leary's cow, the fault is only with invariable succession itself, as affording too simple a definition of general causal statements; we need to hedge it around with provisions for partial or contributing causes and a good deal else. That aspect of the causality problem is not my concern. What I wanted to bring out is just the relevance of the notion of kinds, as the needed link between singular and general causal statements.

We have noticed that the notion of kind, or similarity, is crucially relevant to the notion of disposition, to the subjunctive conditional, and to singular causal statements. From a scientific point of view these are a pretty disreputable lot. The notion of kind, or similarity, is equally disreputable. Yet some such notion, some similarity sense, was seen to be crucial to all learning, and central in particular to the processes of inductive generalization and prediction which are the very life of science. It appears that science is rotten to the core.

Yet there may be claimed for this rot a certain undeniable fecundity. Science reveals hidden mysteries, predicts successfully, and works technological wonders. If this is the way of rot, then rot is rather to be prized and praised than patronized.

Rot, actually, is not the best model here. A better model is human progress. A sense of comparative similarity, I remarked earlier, is one of man's animal endowments.

Insofar as it fits in with regularities of nature, so as to afford us reasonable success in our primitive inductions and expectations, it is presumably an evolutionary product of natural selection. Secondly, as remarked, one's sense of similarity or one's system of kinds develops and changes and even turns multiple as one matures, making perhaps for increasingly dependable prediction. And at length standards of similarity set in which are geared to theoretical science. This development is a development away from the immediate, subjective, animal sense of similarity to the remoter objectivity of a similarity determined by scientific hypotheses and posits and constructs. Things are similar in the later or theoretical sense to the degree that they are interchangeable parts of the cosmic machine revealed by science.

This progress of similarity standards, in the course of each individual's maturing years, is a sort of recapitulation in the individual of the race's progress from muddy savagery. But the similarity notion even in its theoretical phase is itself a muddy notion still. We have offered no definition of it in satisfactory scientific terms. We of course have a behavioral definition of what counts, for a given individual, as similar to what, or as more similar to what than to what; we have this for similarity old and new, human and animal. But it is no definition of what it means really for *a* to be more similar to *b* than to *c*; really, and quite apart from this or that psychological subject.

Did I already suggest a definition to this purpose, metaphorically, when I said that things are similar to the extent that they are interchangeable parts of the cosmic machine? More literally, could things be said to be similar in proportion to how much of scientific theory would remain true on interchanging those things as objects of reference in the theory? This only hints a direction; consider for instance the dimness of "how much theory." Anyway the direction itself is not a good one; for it would make similarity depend in the wrong way on theory. A man's judgments of similarity do and should depend on his theory, on his beliefs; but similarity itself, what the man's judgments purport to be judgments of, purports to be an objective relation in the world. It belongs in the subject matter not of our theory of theorizing about the world, but of our theory of the world itself. Such would be the acceptable and reputable sort of similarity concept, if it could be defined.

It does get defined in bits: bits suited to special branches of science. In this way, on many limited fronts, man continues his rise from savagery, sloughing off the muddy old notion of kind or similarity piecemeal, a vestige here and a vestige there. Chemistry, the home science of water-solubility itself, is one branch that has reached this stage. Comparative similarity of the sort that matters for chemistry can be stated outright in chemical terms, that is, in terms of chemical composition. Molecules will be said to *match* if they contain atoms of the same elements in the same topological combinations. Then, in principle, we might get at the comparative similarity of objects *a* and *b* by considering how many pairs of matching molecules there are, one molecule from *a* and one from *b* each time, and how many unmatching pairs. The ratio gives even a theoretical measure of relative similarity, and thus abundantly explains what it is for *a* to be more similar to *b* than to *c*. Or we might prefer to complicate our definition by allowing also for degrees in the matching of molecules; molecules having almost equally many atoms, or having atoms whose atomic numbers or atomic weights are almost equal, could be reckoned as matching better than others. At any rate a lusty chemical similarity concept is assured.

From it, moreover, an equally acceptable concept of kinds is derivable, by the paradigm-and-foil definition noted early in this paper. For it is a question now only of distilling purely chemical kinds from purely chemical similarity; no admixture of other respects of similarity interferes. We thus exonerate water-solubility, which, the last time around, we had reduced no further than to an unexplained notion of kind. Therewith also the associated subjunctive conditional, "If this were in water it would dissolve," gets its bill of health.

The same scientific advances that have thus provided a solid underpinning for the definition of solubility in terms of kinds, have also, ironically enough, made that line of definition pointless by providing a full understanding of the mechanism of solution. One can redefine water-solubility by simply describing the structural conditions of that mechanism. This embarrassment of riches is, I suspect, a characteristic outcome. That is, once we can legitimize a disposition term by defining the relevant similarity standard, we are apt to know the mechanism of the disposition, and so bypass the similarity. Not but that the similarity standard is worth clarifying too, for its own sake or for other purposes.

Philosophical or broadly scientific motives can impel us to seek still a basic and absolute concept of similarity, along with such fragmentary similarity concepts as suit special branches of science. This drive for a cosmic similarity concept is perhaps identifiable with the age-old drive to reduce things to their elements. It epitomizes the scientific spirit, though dating back to the pre-Socratics: to Empedocles with his theory of four elements, and above all to Democritus with his atoms. The modern physics of elementary particles, or of hills in space-time, is a more notable effort in this direction.

This idea of rationalizing a single notion of relative similarity, throughout its cosmic sweep, has its metaphysical attractions. But there would remain still need also to rationalize the similarity notion more locally and superficially, so as to capture only such similarity as is relevant to some special science. Our chemistry example is already a case of this, since it stops short of full analysis into neutrons, electrons, and the other elementary particles.

A more striking example of superficiality, in this good sense, is afforded by taxonomy, say in zoology. Since learning about the evolution of species, we are in a position to define comparative similarity suitably for this science by consideration of family trees. For a theoretical measure of the degree of similarity of two individual animals we can devise some suitable function that depends on proximity and frequency of their common ancestors. Or a more significant concept of degree of similarity might be devised in terms of genes. When kind is construed in terms of any such similarity concept, fishes in the corrected, whale-free sense of the word qualify as a kind while fishes in the more inclusive sense do not.

Different similarity measures, or relative similarity notions, best suit different branches of science; for there are wasteful complications in providing for finer gradations of relative similarity than matter for the phenomena with which the particular science is concerned. Perhaps the branches of science could be revealingly classified by looking to the relative similarity notion that is appropriate to each. Such a plan is reminiscent of Felix Klein's so-called *Erlangerprogramm* in geometry, which involved characterizing the various branches of geometry by what transformations were irrelevant to each. But a branch of science would only qualify for recognition and classification under such a plan when it had matured to the point of clearing up its similarity notion. Such branches of science would qualify further as unified, or integrated into our inclusive systematization of nature, only insofar as their several similarity concepts were *compatible*; capable of meshing, that is, and differing only in the fineness of their discriminations.

Disposition terms and subjunctive conditionals in these areas, where suitable senses of similarity and kind are forthcoming, suddenly turn respectable; respectable and, in principle, superfluous. In other domains they remain disreputable and practically indispensable. They may be seen perhaps as unredeemed notes; the theory that would clear up the unanalyzed underlying similarity notion in such cases is still to come. An example is the disposition called intelligence—the ability, vaguely speaking, to learn quickly and to solve problems. Sometime, whether in terms of proteins or colloids or nerve nets or overt behavior, the relevant branch of science may reach the stage where a similarity notion can be constructed capable of making even the notion of intelligence respectable. And superfluous.

In general we can take it as a very special mark of the maturity of a branch of science that it no longer needs an irreducible notion of similarity and kind. It is that final stage where the animal vestige is wholly absorbed into the theory. In this career of the similarity notion, starting in its innate phase, developing over the years in the light of accumulated experience, passing then from the intuitive phase into theoretical similarity, and finally disappearing altogether, we have a paradigm of the evolution of unreason into science.

Notes

1. C. G. Hempel, *Aspects of Scientific Explanation and Other Essays* (New York: Free Press, 1965), p. 15.

2. Nelson Goodman, *Fact, Fiction, and Forecast* (Cambridge, Mass., 1955, or New York: Bobbs-Merrill, 1965), p. 74. I am indebted to Goodman and to Burton Dreben for helpful criticisms of earlier drafts of the present paper.

3. Goodman, *Fact*, pp. 82 f.

4. *Ibid.*, pp. 95 ff.

5. I mean this only as a sufficient condition of lawlikeness. See Donald Davidson, "Emeroses by other names," *Journal of Philosophy* 63 (1966), 778–780.

6. This relevance of kind is noted by Goodman, *Fact*, first edition, pp. 119 f.; second edition, pp. 121 f.

7. Nelson Goodman, *The Structure of Appearance*, 2d ed. (New York: Bobbs-Merrill, 1966), pp. 163 f.

8. Rudolf Carnap, *The Logical Structure of the World* (California, 1967), pp. 141–147. (German edition 1928).

9. See my *Word and Object*, pp. 83 f., for further discussion and references.

10. See *Word and Object*, pp. 90–95.

11. This was noted by S. Watanabe on the second page of his paper "Une explication mathématique du classement d'objets," in S. Dockx and P. Bernays, eds., *Information and Prediction in Science* (New York: Academy Press, 1965).

12. J. J. C. Smart, *Philosophy and Scientific Realism* (New York: Humanities, 1963), pp. 68–72.

13. Goodman, *Fact*, pp. 95 ff.

14. Carnap, "Testability and meaning," *Philosophy of Science* 3 (1936), 419–471; 4 (1937), 1–40.

This piece is addressed to many of the same questions Quine addresses in "On What There Is." Carnap promotes a distinction between "internal" and "external" interpretations of questions of the form "Do x's exist?"

RUDOLF CARNAP

Empiricism, Semantics, and Ontology

1. The Problem of Abstract Entities

Empiricists are in general rather suspicious with respect to any kind of abstract entities like properties, classes, relations, numbers, propositions, etc. They usually feel much more in sympathy with nominalists than with realists (in the medieval sense). As far as possible they try to avoid any reference to abstract entities and to restrict themselves to what is sometimes called a nominalistic language, i.e., one not containing such references. However, within certain scientific contexts it seems hardly possible to avoid them. In the case of mathematics, some empiricists try to find a way out by treating the whole of mathematics as a mere calculus, a formal system for which no interpretation is given or can be given. Accordingly, the mathematician is said to speak not about numbers, functions, and infinite classes, but merely about meaningless symbols and formulas manipulated according to given formal rules. In physics it is more difficult to shun the suspected entities, because the language of physics serves for the communication of reports and predictions and hence cannot be taken as a mere calculus. A physicist who is suspicious of abstract entities may perhaps try to declare a certain part of the language of physics as uninterpreted and uninterpretable, that part which refers to real numbers as space-time coordinates or as values of physical magnitudes, to functions, limits, etc. More probably he will just speak about all these things like anybody else but with an uneasy conscience, like a man who in his everyday life does with qualms many things which are not in accord with the high moral principles he professes on Sundays. Recently the problem of abstract entities has arisen again in connection with semantics, the theory of meaning and truth. Some semanticists say that certain expressions designate certain entities, and among these designated entities they include not only concrete material things but also abstract entities, e.g., properties as designated by predicates and propositions as designated by sentences.[1] Others object strongly to this procedure as violating the basic principles of empiricism and leading back to a metaphysical ontology of the Platonic kind.

It is the purpose of this article to clarify this controversial issue. The nature and implications of the acceptance of a language referring to abstract entities will first be discussed in general; it will be shown that using such a language does not imply embracing a Platonic ontology but is perfectly compatible with empiricism and strictly scientific thinking. Then the special question of the role of abstract entities in semantics will be discussed. It is hoped that the clarification of the issue will be useful to those who would like to accept abstract entities in their work in mathematics, physics, semantics, or any other field; it may help them to overcome nominalistic scruples.

2. Frameworks of Entities

Are there properties, classes, numbers, propositions? In order to understand more clearly the nature of these and related problems, it is above all necessary to recognize a fundamental distinction between two kinds of questions concerning the existence or reality of entities. If someone wishes to speak in his language about a new kind of entities, he has to introduce a system, of new ways of speaking, subject to new rules; we shall call this procedure the construction of a *framework* for the new entities in question. And now we must distinguish two kinds of questions of existence: first, questions of the existence of certain entities of the new kind *within the framework*; we call them *internal questions*; and second, questions concerning the existence or reality of *the framework itself*, called *external questions*. Internal questions and possible answers to them are formulated with the help of the new forms of expressions. The answers may be found either by purely logical methods or by empirical methods, depending upon whether the framework is a logical or a factual one. An external question is of a problematic character which is in need of closer examination.

The World of Things

Let us consider as an example the simplest framework dealt with in the everyday language: the spatio-temporally ordered system of observable things and events. Once we have accepted this thing-language and thereby the framework of things, we can raise and answer internal questions, e.g., "Is there a white piece of paper on my desk?", "Did King Arthur actually live?", "Are unicorns and centaurs real or merely imaginary?", and the like. These questions are to be answered by empirical investigations. Results of observations are evaluated according to certain rules as confirming or disconfirming evidence for possible answers. (This evaluation is usually carried out, of course, as a matter of habit rather than a deliberate, rational procedure. But it is possible, in a rational reconstruction, to lay down explicit rules for the evaluation. This is one of the main tasks of a pure, as distinguished from a psychological epistemology.) The concept of reality occurring in these internal questions is an empirical, scientific, non-metaphysical concept. To recognize something as a real thing or event means to succeed in incorporating it into the framework of things at a particular space-time position so that it fits, together with the other things recognized as real, according to the rules of the framework.

From these questions we must distinguish the external question of the reality of the thing world itself. In contrast to the former questions, this question is raised neither by the man in the street nor by scientists, but only by philosophers. Realists give an affirmative answer, subjective idealists a negative one, and the controversy goes on for centuries without ever being solved. And it cannot be solved because it is framed in a wrong way. To be real in the scientific sense means to be an element of the framework; hence this concept cannot be meaningfully applied to the framework itself. Those who raise the question of the reality of the thing world itself have perhaps in mind not a theoretical question as their formulation seems to suggest, but rather a practical question, a matter of a practical decision concerning the structure of our language. We have to make the choice whether or not to accept and use the forms of expression for the framework in question.

In the case of this particular example, there is usually no deliberate choice because we all have accepted the thing-language early in our lives as a matter of course. Nevertheless, we may regard it as a matter of decision in this sense: we are free to choose to continue using the thing language or not; in the latter case we could restrict ourselves to a language of sense-data and other "phenomenal" entities, or construct an alternative to the customary thing language with another structure, or, finally, we could refrain from speaking. If someone decides to accept the thing language, there is no objection against saying that he has accepted the world of things. But this must not be interpreted as if it meant his acceptance of a *belief* in the reality of the thing world; there is no such belief or assertion or assumption, because it is not a theoretical question. To accept the thing world means nothing more than to accept a certain form of language, in other words, to accept rules for forming statements and for testing, accepting, or rejecting them. Thus the acceptance of the thing language leads, on the basis of observations made, also to the acceptance, belief, and assertion of certain statements. But the thesis of the reality of the thing world cannot be among these statements, because it cannot be formulated in the thing language or, it seems, in any other theoretical language.

The decision of accepting the thing language, although itself not of a cognitive nature, will nevertheless usually be influenced by theoretical knowledge, just like any other deliberate decision concerning the acceptance of linguistic or other rules. The purposes for which the language is intended to be used, for instance, the purpose of communicating factual knowledge, will determine which factors are relevant for the decision. The efficiency, fruitfulness, and simplicity of the use of the thing language may be among the decisive factors. And the questions concerning these qualities are indeed of a theoretical nature. But these questions cannot be identified with the question of realism. They are not yes-no questions but questions of degree. The thing language in the customary form works indeed with a high degree of efficiency for most purposes of everyday life. This is a matter of fact, based upon the content of our experiences. However, it would be wrong to describe this situation by saying: "The fact of the efficiency of the thing language is confirming evidence for the reality of the thing world"; we should rather say instead: "This fact makes it advisable to accept the thing language".

The System of Numbers

As an example of a framework which is of a logical rather than a factual nature let us take the system of natural numbers. This system is established by introducing into the language new expressions with suitable rules: (1) numerals like "five" and sentence forms like "there are five books on the table"; (2) The general term "number" for the new entities, and sentence forms like "five is a number"; (3) expressions for properties of numbers (e.g., "odd", "prime"), relations (e.g., "greater than"), and functions (e.g., "plus"), and sentence forms like "two plus three is five"; (4) numerical variables ("*m*", "n", etc.) and quantifiers for universal sentences ("for every *n*, . . .") and existential sentences ("there is an n such that . . .") with the customary deductive rules.

Here again there are internal questions, e.g., "Is there a prime number greater than hundred?" Here, however, the answers are found, not by empirical investigation based on observations, but by logical analysis based on the rules for the new expressions. Therefore the answers are here analytic, i.e., logically true.

What is now the nature of the philosophical question concerning the existence or reality of numbers? To begin with, there is the internal question which, together with the affirmative answer, can be formulated in the new terms, say, by "There are numbers" or, more explicitly, "There is an *n* such that *n* is a number". This statement follows from the analytic statement "five is a number" and is therefore itself analytic. Moreover, it is rather trivial (in contradistinction to a statement like "There is a prime number greater than a million", which is likewise analytic but far from trivial), because, it does not say more than that the new system is not empty; but this is immediately seen from the rule which states that words like "five" are substitutable for the new variables. Therefore nobody who meant the question "Are there numbers?" in the internal sense would either assert or even seriously consider a negative answer. This makes it plausible to assume that those philosophers who treat the question of the existence of numbers as a serious philosophical problem and offer lengthy arguments on either side, do not have in mind the internal question. And, indeed, if we were to ask them: "Do you mean the question as to whether the system of numbers, if we were to accept it, would be found to be empty or not?", they would probably reply: "Not at all; we mean a question prior to the acceptance of the new framework". They might try to explain what they mean by saying that it is a question of the ontological status of numbers; the question whether or not numbers have a certain metaphysical characteristic called reality (but a kind of ideal reality, different from the material reality of the thing world) or subsistence or status of "independent entities". Unfortunately, these philosophers have so far not given a formulation of their question in terms of the common scientific language. Therefore our judgement must be that they have not succeeded in giving to the external question and to the possible answers any cognitive content. Unless and until they supply a clear cognitive interpretation, we are justified in our suspicion that their question is a pseudo-question, that is, one disguised in the form of a theoretical question while in fact it is non-theoretical; in the present case it is the practical problem whether or not to incorporate into the language the new linguistic forms which represent the framework of numbers.

The Framework of Propositions

New variables, "*p*", "*q*", etc., are introduced with a rule to the effect that any (declarative) sentence may be substituted for a variable of this kind; this includes, in addition to the sentences of the original thing language, also all general sentences with variables of any kind which may have been introduced into the language. Further, the general term "proposition" is introduced, "*p* is a proposition" may be defined by "*p* or not *p*" (or by any other sentence form yielding only analytic sentences). Therefore, every sentence of the form ". . . is a proposition" (where any sentence may stand in the place of the dots) is analytic. This holds, for example, for the sentence:

(*a*) "Chicago is large is a proposition".

(We disregard here the fact that the rules of English grammar require not a sentence but a that-clause as the subject of another sentence; accordingly, instead of (a) we should have to say "That Chicago is large is a proposition".) Predicates may be admitted whose argument expressions are sentences; these predicates may be either extensional (e.g., the customary truth-functional connectives) or not (e.g., modal predicates like "possible", "necessary", etc.). With the help of the new variables, general sentences may be formed, e.g.,

(*b*) "For every *p*, either *p* or not-*p*".

(*c*) "There is a *p* such that *p* is not necessary and not-*p* is not necessary".

(*d*) "There is a *p* such that *p* is a proposition".

(*c*) and (*d*) assert internal existence. The statement "There are propositions" may be meant in the sense of (*d*); in this case it is analytic (since it follows from (*a*)) and even trivial. If, however, the statement is meant in an external sense, then it is non-cognitive.

It is important to notice that the system of rules for the linguistic expressions of the propositional framework (of which only a few rules have here been briefly indicated) is sufficient for the introduction of the framework. Any further explanations as to the nature of the propositions (i.e., the elements of the framework indicated, the values of the variables "*p*", "*q*", etc.) are theoretically unnecessary because, if correct, they follow from the rules. For example, are propositions mental events (as in Russell's theory)? A look at the rules shows us that they are not, because otherwise existential statements would be of the form: "If the mental state of the person in question fulfills such and such conditions, then there is a *p* such that . . .". The fact that no references to mental conditions occur in existential statements (like (*c*), (*d*), etc.) shows that propositions are not mental entities. Further, a statement of the existence of linguistic entities (e.g., expressions, classes of expressions, etc.) must contain a reference to a language. The fact that no such reference occurs in the existential statements here, shows that propositions are not linguistic entities. The fact that in these statements no reference to a subject (an observer or knower) occurs (nothing like: "There is a *p* which is necessary for Mr. *X* "), shows that the propositions (and their properties, like necessity, etc.) are not subjective. Although characterizations of these or similar kinds are, strictly speaking, unnecessary, they may nevertheless be practically useful. If they are given, they should be understood, not as ingredient parts of the system, but merely as marginal notes with the purpose of supplying to the reader helpful hints or convenient pictorial associations which may make his learning of the use of the expressions easier than the bare system of the rules would do. Such a characterization is analogous to an extra-systematic explanation which a physicist sometimes gives to the beginner. He might, for example, tell him to imagine the atoms of a gas as small balls rushing around with great speed, or the electromagnetic field and its oscillations as quasi-elastic tensions and vibrations in an ether. In fact, however, all that can accurately be said about atoms or the field is implicitly contained in the physical laws of the theories in question.[2]

The Framework of Thing Properties

The thing language contains words like "red", "hard", "stone", "house", etc., which are used for describing what things are like. Now we may introduce new variables, say "*f*", "*g*", etc., for which those words are substitutable and furthermore the general term "property". New rules are laid down which admit sentences like "Red is a property", "Red is a color", "These two pieces of paper have at least one color in common" (i.e., "There is an *f* such that *f* is a color, and . . ."). The last sentence is an internal assertion. It is of an empirical, factual nature. However, the external statement, the philosophical statement of the reality of properties—a special case of the thesis of the reality of universals—is devoid of cognitive content.

The Frameworks of Integers and Rational Numbers

Into a language containing the framework of natural numbers we may introduce first the (positive and negative) integers as relations among natural numbers and then the rational numbers as relations among integers. This involves introducing new types of variables, expressions substitutable for them and the general terms "integer" and "rational number".

The Framework of Real Numbers

On the basis of the rational numbers, the real numbers may be introduced as classes of a special kind (segments) of rational numbers (according to the method developed by Dedekind and Frege). Here again a new type of variables is introduced, expressions substitutable for them (e.g., "√2"), and the general term "real number".

The Framework of a Spatio-Temporal Coordinate System for Physics

The new entities are the space-time points. Each is an ordered quadruple of four real numbers, called its coordinates, consisting of three spatial and one temporal coordinates. The physical state of a spatio-temporal point or region is described either with the help of qualitative predicates (e.g., "hot") or by ascribing numbers as values of a physical magnitude (e.g., mass, temperature, and the like). The step from the framework of things (which does not contain space-time points but only extended objects with spatial and temporal relations between them) to the physical coordinate system is again a matter of decision. Our choice of certain features, although itself not theoretical, is suggested by theoretical knowledge, either logical or factual. For example, the choice of real numbers rather than rational numbers or integers as coordinates is not much influenced by the facts of experience but mainly due to considerations of mathematical simplicity. The restriction to rational coordinates would not be in conflict with any experimental knowledge we have, because the result of any measurement is a rational number. However, it would prevent the use of ordinary geometry (which says, e.g., that the diagonal of a square with the side 1 has the irrational value √2) and thus lead to great complications. On the other hand, the decision to use three rather than two or four spatial coordinates is strongly suggested, but still not forced upon us, by the result of common observations. If certain events allegedly observed in spiritualistic séances, e.g., a ball moving out of a sealed box, were confirmed beyond any reasonable doubt, it might seem advisable to use four spatial coordinates. Internal questions are here, in general, empirical questions to be answered by empirical investigations. On the other hand, the external questions of the reality of physical space and physical time are pseudo-questions. A question like "Are there (really) space-time points?" is ambiguous. It may be meant as an internal question; then the affirmative answer is, of course, analytic and trivial. Or it may be meant in the external sense; "Shall we introduce such and such forms into our language?"; in this case it is not a theoretical but a practical question, a matter of decision rather than assertion, and hence the proposed formulation would be misleading. Or finally, it may be meant in the following sense: "Are our experiences such that the use of the linguistic forms in question will be expedient and fruitful?" This is a theoretical question of a factual, empirical nature. But it concerns a matter of degree; therefore a formulation in the form "real or not?" would be inadequate.

3. What Does Acceptance of a Framework Mean?

Let us now summarize the essential characteristics of situations involving the introduction of a new framework of entities, characteristics which are common to the various examples outlined above.

The acceptance of a framework of new entities is represented in the language by introduction of new forms of expressions to be used according to a new set of rules. There may be new names for particular entities of the kind in question; but some such names may already occur in the language before the introduction of the new framework. (Thus, for example, the thing language contains certainly words of the type of "blue" and "house" before the framework of properties is introduced; and it may contain words like "ten" in sentences of the form "I have ten fingers" before the framework of numbers is introduced.) The latter fact shows that the occurrence of constants of the type in question—regarded as names of entities of the new kind after the new framework is introduced—is not a sure sign of the acceptance of the framework. Therefore the introduction of such constants is not to be regarded as an essential step in the introduction of the framework. The two essential steps are rather the following. First, the introduction of a general term, a predicate of higher level, for the new kind of entities, permitting us to say of any particular entity that it belongs to this kind (e.g., "Red is a *property*", "Five is a *number*"). Second, the introduction of variables of the new type. The new entities are values of these variables; the constants (and the closed compound expressions, if any) are substitutable for the variables.[3] With the help of the variables, general sentences concerning the new entities can be formulated.

After the new forms are introduced into the language, it is possible to formulate with their help internal questions and possible answers to them. A question of this kind may be either empirical or logical; accordingly a true answer is either factually true or analytic.

From the internal questions we must clearly distinguish external questions, i.e., philosophical questions concerning the existence or reality of the framework itself. Many philosophers regard a question of this kind as an ontological question which must be raised and answered *before* the introduction of the new language forms. The latter introduction, they believe, is legitimate only if it can be justified by an ontological insight supplying an affirmative answer to the question of reality. In contrast to this view, we take the position that the introduction of the new ways of speaking does not need any theoretical justification because it does not imply any assertion of reality. We may still speak (and have done so) of "the acceptance of the framework" or "the acceptance of the new entities" since this form of speech is customary; but one must keep in mind that these phrases do not mean for us anything more than acceptance of the new linguistic forms. Above all, they must not be interpreted as referring to an assumption, belief, or assertion of "the reality of the entities." There is no such assertion. An alleged statement of the reality of the framework of entities is a pseudo-statement without cognitive content. To be sure, we have to face at this point an important question; but it is a practical, not a theoretical question; it is the question of whether or not to accept the new linguistic forms. The acceptance cannot be judged as being either true or false because it is not an assertion. It can only be judged as being more or less expedient, fruitful, conducive to the aim for which the language is intended. Judgments of this kind supply the motivation for the decision of accepting or rejecting the framework.[4]

Thus it is clear that the acceptance of a framework must not be regarded as implying a metaphysical doctrine concerning the reality of the entities in question. It seems to me due to a neglect of this important distinction that some contemporary nominalists label the admission of variables of abstract types as "platonism".[5] This is, to say the least, an extremely misleading terminology. It leads to the absurd consequence, that the position of everybody who accepts the language of physics with its real number variables (as a language of communication, not merely as a calculus) would be called platonistic, even if he is a strict empiricist who rejects platonic metaphysics.

A brief historical remark may here be inserted. The non-cognitive character of the questions which we have called here external questions was recognized and emphasized already by the Vienna Circle under the leadership of Moritz Schlick, the group from which the movement of logical empiricism originated. Influenced by ideas of Ludwig Wittgenstein, the Circle rejected both the thesis of the reality of the external world and the thesis of its irreality as pseudo-statements;[6] the same was the case for both the thesis of the reality of universals (abstract entities, in our present terminology) and the nominalistic thesis that they are not real and that their alleged names are not names of anything but merely *flatus vocis*. (It is obvious that the apparent negation of a pseudo-statement must also be a pseudo-statement.) It is therefore not correct to classify the members of the Vienna Circle as nominalists, as is sometimes done. However, if we look at the basic anti-metaphysical and pro-scientific attitude of most nominalists (and the same holds for many materialists and realists in the modern sense), disregarding their occasional pseudo-theoretical formulations, then it is, of course, true to say that the Vienna Circle was much closer to those philosophers than to their opponents.

4. Abstract Entities in Semantics

The problem of the legitimacy and the status of abstract entities has recently again led to controversial discussions in connection with semantics. In a semantical meaning analysis certain expressions in a language are often said to designate (or name or denote or signify or refer to) certain extra-linguistic entities.[7] As long as physical things or events (e.g., Chicago or Caesar's death) are taken as designata (entities designated), no serious doubts arise. But strong objections have been raised, especially by some empiricists, against abstract entities as designata, e.g., against semantical statements of the following kind:

(1) "The word 'red' designates a property of things";
(2) "The word 'color' designates a property of properties of things";
(3) "The word 'five' designates a number";
(4) "The word 'odd' designates a property of numbers";
(5) "The sentence 'Chicago is large' designates a proposition."

Those who criticize these statements do not, of course, reject the use of the expressions in question, like "red" or "five"; nor would they deny that these expressions are meaningful. But to be meaningful, they would say, is not the same as having a meaning in the sense of an entity designated. They reject the belief, which they regard as implicitly presupposed by those semantical statements, that to each expression of the types in question (adjectives like "red", numerals like "five", etc.) there is a particular real entity to which the expression stands in the relation of designation. This belief is rejected as incompatible with the basic principles of empiricism or of scientific thinking. Derogatory labels like "Platonic realism", "hypostatization", or "'Fido'-Fido principle" are attached to it. The latter is the name given by Gilbert Ryle[8] to the criticized belief, which, in his view, arises by a naive inference of analogy: just as there is an entity well known to me, viz. my dog Fido, which is designated by the name "Fido", thus there must be for every meaningful expression a particular entity to which it stands in the relation of designation or naming, i.e., the relation exemplified by "Fido"-Fido. The belief criticized is thus a case of hypostatization, i.e., of treating as names expressions which are not names. While "Fido" is a name, expressions like "red", "five", etc. are said not to be names, not to designate anything.

Our previous discussions concerning the acceptance of frameworks enables us now to clarify the situation with respect to abstract entities as designata. Let us take as an example the statement:

(*a*) "'Five' designates a number."

The formulation of this statement presupposes that our language L contains the forms of expressions corresponding to what we have called the framework of numbers, in particular, numerical variables and the general term "number". If L contains these forms, the following is an analytic statement in L:

(*b*) "Five is a number."

Further, to make the statement (*a*) possible, L must contain an expression like "designates" or "is a name of" for the semantical relation of designation. If suitable rules for this term are laid down, the following is likewise analytic:

(*c*) "'Five' designates five."

(Generally speaking, any expression of the form "'. . .' designates . . ." is an analytic statement provided the term ". . ." is a constant in an accepted framework. If the latter condition is not fulfilled, the expression is not a statement.) Since (*a*) follows from (*c*) and (*b*), (*a*) is likewise analytic.

Thus it is clear that if someone accepts the framework of numbers, then he must acknowledge (*c*) and (*b*) and hence (*a*) as true statements. Generally speaking, if someone accepts a framework of entities, then he is bound to admit its entities as possible designata. Thus the question of the admissibility of entities of a certain type or of abstract entities in general as designata is reduced to the question of the acceptability of those entities. Both the nominalistic critics, who refuse the status of designators or names to expressions like "red", "five", etc., because they deny the existence of abstract entities, and the skeptics, who express doubts concerning the existence and demand evidence for it, treat the question of existence as a theoretical question. They do, of course, not mean the internal question; the affirmative answer to this question is analytic and trivial and too obvious for doubt or denial, as we have seen. Their doubts refer rather to the framework itself; hence they mean the external question. They believe that only after making sure that there really are entities of the kinds in question are we justified in accepting the framework by incorporating the linguistic forms into our language. However, we have seen that the external question is not a theoretical question but rather the practical question whether or not to accept those linguistic forms. This acceptance is not in need of a theoretical justification (except with respect to expediency and fruitfulness), because it does not imply a belief or assertion. Ryle says that the "Fido"-Fido principle is "a grotesque theory". Grotesque or not, Ryle is wrong in calling it a theory. It is rather the practical decision to accept certain frameworks. Maybe Ryle is historically right, with respect to those whom he mentions as previous representatives of the principle, viz. John Stuart Mill, Frege, and Russell. If these philosophers regarded the acceptance of a framework of entities as a theory, an assertion, they were victims of the same old, metaphysical confusion. But it is certainly wrong to regard my semantical method as involving a belief in the reality of abstract entities, since I reject a thesis of this kind as a metaphysical pseudo-statement.

The critics of the use of abstract entities in semantics overlook the fundamental difference between the acceptance of a framework of entities and an internal assertion, e.g., an assertion that there are elephants or electrons or prime numbers greater than a million. Whoever makes an internal assertion is certainly obliged to justify it by providing evidence, empirical evidence in the case of electrons, logical proof in the case of the prime numbers. The demand for a theoretical justification, correct in the case of internal assertions, is sometimes wrongly applied to the acceptance of a framework of entities. Thus, for example, Ernest Nagel[9] asks for "evidence relevant for affirming with warrant that there are such entities as infinitesimals or propositions". He characterizes the evidence required in these cases—in distinction, to the empirical evidence in the case of electrons—as "in the broad sense logical and dialectical". Beyond this no hint is given as to what might be regarded as relevant evidence. Some nominalists regard the acceptance of abstract entities as a kind of superstition or myth, populating the world with fictitious or at least dubious entities, analogous to the belief in centaurs or demons. This shows again the confusion mentioned, because a superstition or myth is a false (or dubious) internal statement.

Let us take as example the natural numbers as cardinal numbers, i.e., in contexts like "Here are three books". The linguistic forms of the framework of numbers, including variables and the general term "number" are generally used in our common language of communication; and it is easy to formulate explicit rules for their use. Thus the logical characteristics of this framework are sufficiently clear (while many internal questions, i.e., arithmetical questions, are, of course, still open). In spite of this, the controversy concerning the external question of the ontological reality of numbers continues. Suppose that one philosopher says: "I believe that there are numbers as real entities. This gives me the right to use the linguistic forms of the numerical framework and to make semantical statements about numbers as designata of numerals". His nominalistic opponent replies: "You are wrong; there are no numbers. The numerals may still be used as meaningful expressions. But they are not names, there are no entities designated by them. Therefore the word 'number' and numerical variables must not be used (unless a way were found to introduce them as merely abbreviating devices, a way of translating them into the nominalistic thing language)." I cannot think of any possible evidence that would be regarded as relevant by both philosophers, and therefore, if actually found, would decide the controversy or at least make one of the opposite theses more probable than the other. (To construe the numbers as classes or properties of the second level, according to the Frege-Russell method does, of course, not solve the controversy, because the first philosopher would affirm and the second deny the existence of classes or properties of the second level.) Therefore I feel compelled to regard the external question as a pseudo-question, until both parties to the controversy offer a common interpretation of the question as a cognitive question; this would involve an indication of possible evidence regarded as relevant by both sides.

There is a particular kind of misinterpretation of the acceptance of abstract entities in various fields of science and in semantics, that needs to be cleared up. Certain early British empiricists (e.g., Berkeley and Hume) denied the existence of abstract entities on the ground that immediate experience presents us only with particulars, not with universals, e.g., with this red patch, but not with Redness or Color-in-General; with this scalene triangle, but not with Scalene Triangularity or Triangularity-in-General. Only entities belonging to a type of which examples were to be found within immediate experience could be accepted as ultimate constituents of reality. Thus, according to this way of thinking, the existence of abstract entities could be asserted only if one could show either that some abstract entities fall within the given, or that abstract entities can be defined in terms of the types of entity which are given. Since these empiricists found no abstract entities within the realm of sense-data, they either denied their existence, or else made a futile attempt to define universals in terms of particulars. Some contemporary philosophers, especially English philosophers following Bertrand Russell, think in basically similar terms. They emphasize a distinction between the data (that which is immediately given in consciousness, e.g. sense-data, immediately past experiences, etc.) and the constructs based on the data. Existence or reality is ascribed only to the data; the constructs are not real entities; the corresponding linguistic expressions are merely ways of speech not actually designating anything (reminiscent of the nominalists' *flatus vocis*). We shall not criticize here this general conception. (As far as it is a principle of accepting certain entities and not accepting others, leaving aside any ontological, phenomenalistic and nominalistic pseudo-statements, there cannot be any theoretical objection to it.) But if this conception leads to the view that other philosophers or scientists who accept abstract entities thereby assert or imply their occurrence as immediate data, then such a view must be rejected as a misinterpretation. References to space-time points, the electromagnetic field, or electrons in physics, to real or complex numbers and their functions in mathematics, to the excitatory potential or unconscious complexes in psychology, to an inflationary trend in economics, and the like, do not imply the assertion that entities of these kinds occur as immediate data. And the same holds for references to abstract entities as designata in semantics. Some of the criticisms by English philosophers against such references give the impression that, probably due to the misinterpretation just indicated, they accuse the semanticist not so much of bad metaphysics (as some nominalists would do) but of bad psychology. The fact that they regard a semantical method involving abstract entities not merely as doubtful and perhaps wrong, but as manifestly absurd, preposterous and grotesque, and that they show a deep horror and indignation against this method, is perhaps to be explained by a misinterpretation of the kind described. In fact, of course, the semanticist does not in the least assert or imply that the abstract entities to which he refers can be experienced as immediately given either by sensation or by a kind of rational intuition. An assertion of this kind would indeed be very dubious psychology. The psychological question as to which kinds of entities do and which do not occur as immediate data is entirely irrelevant for semantics, just as it is for physics, mathematics, economics, etc., with respect to the examples mentioned above.[10]

5. Conclusion

For those who want to develop or use semantical methods, the decisive question is not the alleged ontological question of the existence of abstract entities but rather the question whether the use of abstract linguistic forms or, in technical terms, the use of variables beyond those for things (or phenomenal data), is expedient and fruitful for the purposes for which semantical analyses are made, viz. the analysis, interpretation, clarification, or construction of languages of communication, especially languages of science. This question is here neither decided nor even discussed. It is not a question simply of yes or no, but a matter of degree. Among those philosophers who have carried out semantical analyses and thought about suitable tools for this work, beginning with Plato and Aristotle and, in a more technical way on the basis of modern logic, with C. S. Peirce and Frege, a great majority accepted abstract entities. This does, of course, not prove the case. After all, semantics in the technical sense is still in the initial phases of its development, and we must he prepared for possible fundamental changes in methods. Let us therefore admit that the nominalistic critics may possibly be right. But if so, they will have to offer better arguments than they did so far. Appeal to ontological insight will not carry much weight. The critics will have to show that it is possible to construct a semantical method which avoids all references to abstract entities and achieves by simpler means essentially the same results as the other methods.

The acceptance or rejection of abstract linguistic forms, just as the acceptance or rejection of any other linguistic forms in any branch of science, will finally be decided by their efficiency as instruments, the ratio of the results achieved to the amount and complexity of the efforts required. To decree dogmatic prohibitions of certain linguistic forms instead of testing them by their success or failure in practical use, is worse than futile; it is positively harmful because it may obstruct scientific progress. The history of science shows examples of such prohibitions based on prejudices deriving from religious, mythological, metaphysical, or other irrational sources, which slowed up the developments for shorter or longer periods of time. Let us learn from the lessons of history. Let us grant to those who work in any special field of investigation the freedom to use any form of expression which seems useful to them; the work in the field will sooner or later lead to the elimination of those forms which have no useful function. *Let us be cautious in making assertions and critical in examining them, but tolerant in permitting linguistic forms.*

Notes

1. The terms "sentence" and "statement" are here used synonymously for declarative (indicative, propositional) sentences.

2. In my book *Meaning and Necessity* (Chicago, 1947) I have developed a semantical method which takes propositions as entities designated by sentences (more specifically, as intensions of sentences). In order to facilitate the understanding of the systematic development, I added some informal, extra-systematic explanations concerning the nature of propositions. I said that the term "proposition" "is used neither for a linguistic expression nor for a subjective, mental occurence, but rather for something objective that may or may not be exemplified in nature. . . . We apply the term 'proposition' to any entities of a certain logical type, namely, those that may be expressed by (declarative) sentences in a language" (p. 27). After some more detailed discussions concerning the relation between propositions and facts, and the nature of false propositions, I added: "It has been the purpose of the preceding remarks to facilitate the understanding of our conception of propositions. If, however, a reader should find these explanations more puzzling than clarifying, or even unacceptable, he may disregard them" (p. 31) (that is, disregard these extra-systematic explanations, not the whole theory of the propositions as intensions of sentences, as one reviewer understood). In spite of this warning, it seems that some of those readers who were puzzled by the explanations, did not disregard them but thought that by raising objections against them they could refute the theory. This is analogous to the procedure of some laymen who by (correctly) criticizing the ether picture or other visualizations of physical theories, thought they had refuted those theories. Perhaps the discussions in the present paper will help in clarifying the role of the system of linguistic rules for the introduction of a framework of entities on the one hand, and that of extra-systematic explanations concerning the nature of the entities on the other.

3. W. V. Quine was the first to recognize the importance of the introduction of variables as indicating the acceptance of entities. "Theontology to which one's use of language commits him comprises simply the objects that he treats as falling . . . within the range of values of his variables" ("Notes on Existence and Necessity", *Journal of Philos.*, 40 (1943), pp. 113–127, see p. 118; compare also his "Designation and Existence", *ibid.*, 36 (1939), pp. 701–9, and "On Universals", *Journal of Symbolic Logic*, 12 (1947), pp. 74–84).

4. For a closely related point of view on these questions see the detailed discussions in Herbert Feigl, *Existential Hypotheses*, forthcoming in *Philosophy of Science*, 1950.

5. Paul Bernays, *Sur le platonisme dans les mathématiques* (*L'En-seignement math.*, 34 [1935], pp. 52–69). W. V. Quine, see footnote p. 65, and a recent paper *On What There Is* (*Review of Metaphysics, 2* [1948], pp. 21–38). Quine does not acknowledge the distinction which I emphasize above, because according to his general conception there are no sharp boundary lines between logical and factual truth, between questions of meaning and questions of fact, between the acceptance of a language structure ant the acceptance of an assertion formulated in the language. This conception, which seems to deviate considerably from customary ways of thinking, will be explained in his forthcoming book, *Foundations of Logic*. When Quine in the article mentioned above classifies my logicistic conception of mathematics (derived from Frege and Russell) as "platonic realism" (p. 33), this is meant (according to a personal communication from him) not as ascribing to me agreement with Plato's metaphysical doctrine of universals, but merely as referring to the fact that I accept a language of mathematics containing variables of higher levels. With respect to the basic attitude to take in choosing a language form (an "ontology" in Quine's terminology, which seems to me misleading), there appears now to be agreement between us: "the obvious counsel is tolerance and an experimental spirit" (op. cit., p. 38).

6. See Carnap, *Scheinprobleme in der Philosophie; das Fremdpsy-chische und der Realismusstreit*, Berlin, 1928. Morilz Schlick, *Positivismus und Realismus*, reprinted in *Gesammelie Aufsätze*, Wien 1938.

7. See *Introduction to Semantics*, Cambridge Mass.; 1942; *Meaning and Necessity*, Chicago, 1947. The distinction I have drawn in the latter book between the method of the name-relation and the method of intension and extension is not essential for our present discussion. The term "designation" is here used in a neutral way; it may be understood as referring to the name-relation or to the intension-relation or to the extension-relation or to any similar relations used in other semantical methods.

8. G. Ryle, *Meaning and Necessity* (*Philosophy*, 24 (1949), pp. 69–76).

9. E. Nagel, Review of Carnap, *Meaning and Necessity* (*Journal of Philos.*, 45 (1948), pp. 467–72).

10. Wilfrid Sellars (*Acquaintance and Description Again*, in *Journal of Philos.* 46 (1949), pp. 496–504, see pp. 502 f.) analyzes clearly the roots of the mistake "of taking the designation relation of semantic theory to be a reconstruction of being present to an experience".

Originally published in 1969, this essay is the cornerstone of Sellars's account of "verbal behaviorism," which is an empirical model for thought based entirely on rules for language use.

WILFRID SELLARS

Language as Thought and as Communication

My aim in this paper is to throw light from several directions on the intimate connections which exist between conceptual thinking and the linguistic behavior which is said to 'express' it. The position which I shall ultimately delineate and defend, though behavioristic in its methodological orientation is not, initial appearances to the contrary, behavioristic in its substantive contentions. It can, nevertheless, be characterized as an attempt to give a naturalistic interpretation of the intentionality of conceptual acts.

The early sections (I–IV) stress the essentially rule-governed character of linguistic behavior. I argue that a proper understanding of the nature and status of linguistic rules is a *sine qua non* of a correct interpretation of the sense in which linguistic behavior can be said to *be* (and not merely to *express*) conceptual activity. The second, and larger part of the paper (Sections Vff.) is devoted to exploring the sense (or senses) in which language can be said to 'express' thought. A distinction is drawn between three different contexts in which the verb occurs. It is argued that they involve radically different meanings which, if confused, blur the distinction between language as conceptual act and language as means of communication, and preclude the possibility of an adequate philosophy of language.

I

There are many interesting questions about the exact meaning or meanings of the term 'rule' in non-philosophical contexts. What, for example, is the difference between a 'rule' and a 'principle'? Are principles simple 'first' rules in that they are not special applications of more general rules? Or is the primary difference that rules can be arbitrary? Or are principles rules for choosing rules? Is the principle of induction, for example, a higher order rule for choosing law-like statements, themselves construed as extra-logical rules of inference? Though these questions are intrinsically interesting and relevant to the general topic of this paper, I shall not discuss them. For however the domain of norms and standards is to be stratified and botanized, the term 'rule' has acquired over the years a technical and generic sense in which it applies to general statements concerning that which ought or ought not to be done or to be the case, or to be permissible or not permissible—distinctions which can be put in many different ways.

For our purposes, then, a rule is roughly a general 'ought' statement. Such statements have been traditionally divided into hypothetical and categorical 'oughts,' or, as it has often misleadingly been put, 'imperatives.' The distinction between hypothetical and categorical oughts is an important one, though I believe that they are far more intimately related than is ordinarily taken to be the case.[1]

Hypothetical oughts have the form "if one wants X, one ought to do Y." They transpose a relation of implication between a state of affairs X and a doing of Y into an implication appropriate to practical reasoning. In spite of their crucial importance to a theory of normative discourse, I shall have nothing to say about them, save by implication.

As far as anything I have so far said is concerned, a categorical ought is simply one that is not, in the familiar Kantian sense, a hypothetical ought. I shall continue my division informally by calling attention to the most familiar variety of general categorical oughts, those, namely, of the form

If one is in C, one ought to do A.

Notice that although this proposition is conditional in form, it is not, in the Kantian sense, a hypothetical ought; and it is *as* contrasted with the latter that, even though it is conditional, it is called categorical. By application and the use of modus ponens one can derive conclusions of the form

S ought to do A

which not only are *not* hypothetical oughts, but are categorical (non-iffy) statements. Notice, by contrast, that from "If one wants X, one ought to do A," together with "S wants X" it is *not* correct to infer "S ought to do A."

The important feature, for our purposes, of general categorical oughts of the above form is that for actual existence to conform to these oughts is a matter of the agents to which they apply *doing A* when they are actually in the specified circumstance C; and this, in turn, a matter of their setting about doing A when they *believe* that the circumstances are C.

It follows that the 'subjects' to which these rules apply must have the concepts of *doing A* and *being in C*. They must have, to use a current turn of phrase, the appropriate 'recognitional capacities.' Furthermore, for the rule itself to play a role in bringing about the conformity of 'is' to 'ought,' the agents in question must conceive of actions A *as* what ought to be done in circumstances C. This requires that they have the concept of what it is for an action to be called for by a certain kind of circumstance.

II

Importantly different from rules of the above form—which may be called, in a straightforward sense, *rules of action*—are rules that specify not what someone ought to do, but how something *ought to be*. Of these an important sub class has the form:

Xs ought to be in state φ, whenever such and such is the case.

The purpose of such a rule is achieved to the extent that it comes to be the case that Xs are in state φ when such and such is indeed the case. This time, however, the conformity of actual existence to the ought does not, in general, require that the Xs which are, in a sense, the *subjects* of the rule, i.e. that to which it applies, have the concept of what it is to be in state φ or of what it is for such and such to be the case. This is obvious when the Xs in question are inanimate objects, as in the example:

Clock chimes ought to strike on the quarter hour.

Now ought-to-be's (or *rules of criticism* as I shall also call them), though categorical in form, point beyond themselves in two ways. In the first place they imply (in some sense of this protean term) a *reason*, a *because* clause. The exploration of this theme would seem to take us back to the excluded topic of hypothetical imperatives. In the second place, though ought-to-be's are carefully to be distinguished from ought-to-do's they have an essential connection with them. The connection is, roughly, that ought-to-be's imply ought-to-do's. Thus the ought-to-be about clock chimes implies, roughly,

(Other things being equal and where possible) one ought to bring it about that clock chimes strike on the quarter hour.

This rule belongs in our previous category, and is a rule of action. As such it requires that the item to which *it* applies (persons rather than chimes) have the appropriate concepts or recognitional capacities.

The distinction between ought-to-do's (rules of action) and ought-to-be's (rules of criticism) stands out clearly when the examples are suitably chosen. A possibility of confusion arises, however, when the ought-to-be's concern persons rather than inanimate objects. Consider, for example,

One ought to feel sympathy for bereaved people.

This example is interesting for two reasons: (1) It is a rule conformity to which requires that the subjects to which it applies have the concept of what it is to be bereaved. In this respect it is like a rule of action. (2) In the absence of a clear theory of action one might think of *feeling sympathy* as an action. Thus a casual and uninformed look might lead to the subsumption of the example under the form

One ought to do A, if C.

It is clear on reflection, however, that feeling sympathy is an action only in that broad sense in which anything expressed by a verb in the active voice is an action.

Nor should it be assumed that all ought-to-be's which apply to persons and concern their being in a certain state whenever a certain circumstance obtains are such that the conformity to them of actual fact requires that the persons in question have the concept of this circumstance. The point is of decisive importance for our problem. To set the stage, consider ought-to-be's pertaining to the training of animals.

These rats ought-to-be in state φ, whenever C.

The conformity of the rats in question to this rule does not require that they have a concept of C, though it does require that they be able to respond differentially to cues emanating from C. Since the term 'recognitional capacity' is one of those accordion words which can be used now in one sense now in another, it is a menace to sound philosophy.

On the other hand, the subjects of the ought-to-do's corresponding to these ought-to-be's, i.e. the trainers, must have the concept both of the desirable state φ and of the circumstances in which the animals are to be in it.

If we now return to the sympathy example, we notice another interesting feature. If we compare the ought-to-be with the corresponding ought-to-do,

(Other things being equal and where possible) one ought to bring it about that people feel sympathy for the bereaved,

we see that the 'subjects' of the ought-to-be (i.e., those who ought to feel sympathy) coincide with the 'subjects' of the corresponding ought-to-do (i.e., those who ought to bring it about that people feel sympathy for the bereaved). It is the same items (people) who are the *agent*-subjects of the ought-to-do and the *subject-matter* subjects of the ought-to-be.

III

It is obvious, from the above considerations, that if *all* rules of language were ought-to-do's we would be precluded from explaining what it is to have concepts in terms of rules of language. Now many rules of language *are* ought-to-do's thus,

(Other things being equal) one ought to say such and such, if in C

and as such they can be efficacious in linguistic activity only to the extent that people have the relevant concepts. It is therefore of the utmost importance to note that many of the rules of language which are of special interest to the epistemologist are ought-to-be's rather than ought-to-do's. For only by taking this fact into account is it possible to carry out a program according to which (a) linguistic activity is, in a primary sense, conceptual activity; (b) linguistic activity is through and through rule-governed.

Much attention has been devoted of late to linguistic *actions*[2] where the term 'action' is taken in the strict sense of what an agent does, a piece of conduct, a performance—the *practical* sense of action, as contrasted with the general metaphysical sense in which action is contrasted with passion. The topic of linguistic actions, whether performatory, locutionary, illocutionary, perlocutionary,[3] or perhaps, elocutionary is an important one. Indeed, it is important not only for a theory of communication, but for epistemology, for there are, indeed, linguistic *actions* which are of essential interest to the epistemologist: thus asking questions and seeking to answer them. On the other hand it can scarcely be over-emphasized that to approach language in terms of the paradigm of *action* is to make a commitment which, if the concept of action is taken seriously, and the concept of rule is taken seriously, leads, to (a) the Cartesian idea of linguistic episodes as *essentially* the sort of thing brought about by an agent whose conceptualizing is not linguistic; (b) an inability to understand the rule-governed character of this conceptualizing itself, as contrasted with its overt expression. For if thought is analogous to linguistic activity to the extent implied by Plato's metaphor 'dialogue in the soul,' the idea that overt speech is *action* and its rules *rules of action* will generate the idea that all inner speech is *action* and *its* rules *rules of action*, which leads to paradox and absurdity without end.

I propose, instead that the epistemologist, while recognizing that language is an instrument of communication, should focus attention on language as the bearer of conceptual activity. This is not to say that the two aspects can be separated as with a knife. Indeed, by pointing out that ought-to-be's imply ought-to-do's we have already recognized that language users exist at the level of agents. Roughly, to be a being capable of conceptual activity, is to be a being which acts, which recognizes norms and standards, and which engages in practical reasoning. It is, as Kant pointed out, one and the same reason which is in some of its activities 'theoretical,' and in some of its activities 'practical.' Of course, if one gives to 'practical' the specific meaning *ethical* then a fairly sharp separation of these activities can be maintained. But if one means by 'practical' *pertaining to norms*, then so-called theoretical reason is as larded with the practical as is practical reasoning itself.

IV

Even if it be granted than many of the linguistic oughts which are of special interest to an epistemologist are ought-to-be's, the fact that ought-to-be's and ought-to-do's are conceptually inseparable might be thought to preclude a linguistic approach to conceptual abilities. Clearly *primary* epistemic ought-to-do's (and by calling them 'primary' I mean simply that they are not the unfolding of ought-to-be's, whether as primary they are categorical or hypothetical), pertaining to the systematic use of linguistic abilities and propensities to arrive at correct linguistic representations of the way things are, presuppose the possession of concepts by the agents to which they apply. And since all ought to-be's unfold into ought-to-do's which, in their turn, presuppose concepts, the outlook for linguistic theory of concepts would seem to be dark indeed. Yet the fundamental clues for a resolution of the problem have already been given.

To fix our ideas, let us consider an example which, though simplified to its bare bones contains the essence of the matter:

(Ceteris paribus) one ought to respond to red objects in sunlight by uttering or being disposed to utter 'this is red.'

This *ought-to-be* rule must not be confused with (fictitious) *ought-to-do* rule,

(Ceteris paribus) one ought to say 'this is red' in the presence of red objects in sunlight.

The latter presupposes that those to whom it applies have the concepts of 'red' objects,' 'sunlight,' and, even more important, of what it is to *say* 'this is red.' In other words, they must already have the conceptual framework of what it is to do something in a circumstance.

The distinction between *saying* and *uttering*, or being disposed to utter, is diagnostic of the difference between the 'ought-to-do' and the 'ought-to-be.' It might be objected that to use language meaningfully is to *say* rather than merely utter. But to merely utter is to parrot, and we need a concept which mediates between merely uttering and saying.

Notice that the ought-to-do which corresponds to the above ought-to-be, namely

One ought to bring it about *(ceteris paribus)* that people respond to red objects in sunlight by uttering or being disposed to utter 'this is red'

presupposes that *its* agent subjects have a conceptual framework which includes the concepts of a red object, or sunlight, of uttering 'this is red,' of what it is to do or bring about something, and of what it is for an action to be called for by a circumstance.

On the other hand, this ought-to-do does *not* presuppose that the subjects in which the disposition to utter 'this is red' in the presence of red objects in sunlight *is to be brought about* have any of these concepts.

But what of the objection that the *subject-matter* subjects of the ought-to-be coincide with the agent subjects of the ought-to-do and hence that they too must have the concepts in question? The answer should be obvious; the members of a linguistic community are *first* language *learners* and only potentially 'people,' but *subsequently* language *teachers*, possessed of the rich conceptual framework this implies. They start out by being the *subject-matter* subjects of the ought-to-be's and graduate to the status of agent subjects of the ought-to-do's. Linguistic ought-to-be's are translated into *uniformities* by training. As Wittgenstein has stressed, it is the linguistic community as a self-perpetuating whole which is the minimum unit in terms of which conceptual activity can be understood.

Furthermore there are radically different kinds of linguistic ought-to-be's: not only word-object ought-to-be's (or, as I have called them elsewhere, language entry transitions),[4] but also the ought-to-be's formulated by formation and transformation rules.

The oughts governing utterances as perceptual responses to the environment are not ought-to-do's—though, as the pragmatists have emphasized, perception as an element in enquiry occurs in a context of actions, epistemic and otherwise. Similarly the oughts governing inference are not ought-to-do's. Inferring is not a *doing* in the conduct sense—which, however, by no means implies that it is not a *process*. Again, as the pragmatists have stressed, inference as an element in enquiry occurs in the context of action, epistemic and otherwise.

A language is a many-leveled structure. There are not only the ought-to-be's which connect linguistic responses to extra-linguistic objects, but also the equally essential ought-to-be's which connect linguistic responses to *linguistic* objects. There could be no training of language users, unless this were the case. Finally, there would be no language training unless there were the uniformities pertaining to the use of practical language, the language of action, intention, of 'shall' and 'ought,' which, as embodying epistemic norms and standards, is but one small (but essential) part of the conceptual structure of human agency.

One isn't a full-fledged member of the linguistic community until one not only *conforms* to linguistic ought-to-be's (and may-be's) by exhibiting the required uniformities, but grasps these ought-to-be's and may-be's themselves (i.e., knows the rules of the language.) One must, therefore, have the concept of oneself as an agent, as not only the *subject-matter* subject of ought-to-be's but the *agent*-subject of ought-to-do's. Thus, even though conceptual activity rests on a foundation of *conforming* to ought-to-be's of *uniformities* in linguistic behavior, these uniformities exist in an ambience of action, epistemic or otherwise. To be a language user is to conceive of oneself as an agent subject to rules. My point has been that one can grant this without holding that all meaningful linguistic episodes are *actions* in the conduct sense, and all linguistic rules, rules for doing.

A living language is a system of elements which play many different types of roles, and no one of these types of role make sense apart from the others. Thus, while the mere concept of a kind of vocalizing being a response by a human organism in specified circumstances to a certain kind of object does make sense in isolation, this concept is not as such the concept of the vocalizing as a *linguistic response*. For to classify an item as linguistic involves relating it to just such a system as I have been sketching. 'Word' goes not only with 'object' but with 'person,' 'ought-to-be's,' 'ought-to-do's' and much, much more.

V

Within the framework sketched above, I propose to explore the idea that insofar as it has conceptual meaning, language is essentially a means whereby one thinker can express his thoughts to others. Now the term 'thought' has a wide range of application, including such items as assumptions, the solving of problems, wishes, intentions, and perceptions. It is also ambiguous, sometimes referring to *what* is thought, sometimes to the *thinking* of it. To limit the range of my paper, I shall concentrate on thought as belief, and since the latter term shares the ambiguity indicated above, I note that for the time being at least, I shall be concerned with believings rather than things believed.

The following characterization of the state of believing something will serve to get the discussion under way

Jones believes that-p = Jones has a settled disposition to think that-p.

It would be foolhardy—indeed downright mistaken—to claim that this formula captures 'the' meaning of believes, and even more so to put it by saying that 'a belief is a settled disposition to think that something is the case.' For, as with most, if not all, of the words in which philosophers are interested, we are confronted with a cluster of senses which resemble each other in the family way.

To say that the senses of cognate expressions bear a family resemblance to one another must not be taken to imply that they present themselves as a family, nor even that they constitute a family. Aristotle seems to have thought that philosophically interesting concepts present themselves to us as families in which, with a little effort, we can discern the fathers, mothers, aunts, uncles, and cousins of various degrees. In some cases something like this may be true. But the matter is rarely so simple, and there is more than a little truth to the idea that the families are 'created' by reconstruction (hopefully rational) or regimentation rather than found.[5]

If the above account of belief gets us started, it does so by confronting us with the equally problematic concepts of *disposition* and *thinking that-p*. Before stepping into these quicksands, let us ostensibly make matters worse by turning our attention from *believing* itself to the more complicated concept of the *expression* of belief. For sound philosophical strategy calls for the examination of concepts as they function in larger contexts, rather than subjecting them to scrutiny in splendid isolation. By taking elusive concepts together, one may limit the degrees of freedom which enable them separately to elude our grasp. If beliefs are to be construed as dispositions, this strategy would have us seek to relate the sense in which beliefs are 'expressed' to the sense in which the dispositions of things and persons are manifested by what they do. This suggests the schema

x expresses Jones' belief that-p = x is a manifestation of Jones' settled disposition to think that-p.

If the right hand side of this attempted explication were clearcut and unambiguous, substantial progress would have been made. But it isn't; and our only hope is that a spark of clarity may result from rubbing unclarities together.

A first unclarity concerns what it is for a disposition to be 'manifested' by a doing, and how the class of doings by which a given disposition is manifested is to be delimited. If the 'disposition' is of the familiar kind to which we refer by such expressions as 'an angry disposition' or, perhaps, by such a term as 'humility' then it would seem that, depending on circumstances, any of a wide range of episodes could be its manifestation. Indeed, there is a sense in which, depending on circumstances, any of a wide range of episodes could count as a 'manifestation' of Jones' belief that-p. But, to characterize belief that-p as a settled disposition to *think that-p*, is, if sound, to narrow things down in an interesting way. For to do so, is to introduce a conceptual tie between the designation of the disposition and the kind of episodes which can be said, at least in a primary sense, to 'manifest' it.

For if we ask what episodes manifest a disposition to V, when 'V' represents a verb which stands for a doing (e.g. 'laugh') the answer must be, in the first instance, episodes of V-ing (e.g. laughing). We have consequently committed ourselves to the idea that it is episodes of *thinking that-p* which are, in a primary sense at least, manifestations of Jones' disposition, *to think that-p;* and consequently that it is episodes of thinking that-p which are, in a primary sense, manifestations of Jones' belief that-p. This gives us the schema

x is a primary manifestation of Jones' belief that-p → x is a thinking that-p.

But now our troubles really begin. For there is a *prima facie* tension between 'being a thinking that-p' and being a 'manifestation' of anything. The latter term carries with it the implication of 'making something manifest,' i.e., apparent, (roughly) perceptible, observable. But, we are tempted to expostulate, what need be less 'manifest' than an episode of thinking that-p.

It might be thought that all we need do is replace 'manifestation' by a term which lacks this implication. And there are, indeed, such terms at hand—thus 'realization,' 'actualization.' The statements

episodes of thinking that-p are *realizations* of the settled disposition to think that-p

episodes of thinking that-p are *actualizations* of the settled disposition to think that-p

trip easily off the metaphysically trained tongue. But they are ruled out by our strategy. For the concept with which we are concerned is that of the *expression* of a belief, and 'expression,' clearly has the same implication of 'overtness' or 'perceptibility' as does the 'manifestation' to which our initial intuitions have led us.

The boulder may have slipped, but perhaps it has not rolled to the bottom. Our task may ultimately prove to be like that of Sisyphus, but perhaps we are not yet forced to make a new beginning. To continue is to look for a way of making coherent the idea that episodes of thinking that-p are the primary *expressions* (with all that this implies) of the belief that-p.

To do so within the allotted space however, I must abandon the leisurely dialectic which consults intuition at each stage of the argument, and instead must draw upon the familiarity of standard philosophical moves. In terms of this new strategy, the obvious move is to espouse a form of logical behaviorism according to which, in first approximation, 'thinking that-p' is, in its most episodic sense, to be equated with 'candidly and spontaneously uttering "p"'[6] where the person, call him Jones, who utters 'p' is doing so *as one who knows the language to which 'p' belongs.* I need not remind you of all the troubles which beset this move. Some of them will be taken into account as the argument moves along. But since, in any case, my strategy remains in a broad sense dialectical, the fact that the above equation suffers from serious inadequacies need not prevent it from playing an essential role in the argument.

The phrase 'candidly and spontaneously' is intended to sum up an open-ended set of conditions without which the suggestion can't get off the ground. Jones' thinking that-p obviously cannot be a quoting of 'p' or uttering it on the stage in the course of acting. The qualifying phrase also clearly rules out the case where Jones is lying, i.e., using words to deceive. Somewhat less obviously it is intended to imply that Jones is not choosing his words to express his convictions. He is neither lying nor speaking truthfully. In a sense, as we shall see, he is not *using* the words at all.

According to the behavioristic position we are now considering, thinking that-p is, in its *primary episodic* sense, thinking-out-loud that-p. As thinking-out-loud, an utterance of 'p' is not directed to an audience. It is not, as such, a social act. Explicit performatives (e.g. 'I promise') are clearly out of place in utterances which are, in the desired sense, to be thinkings-out-loud. Nor is it appropriate to characterize thinkings-out-loud in terms of the categories of illocutionary performance—at least those which require an audience (e.g. 'statement,' 'avowal,' 'argument')[7]—even though exactly similar utterances would, *in a context of 'communication,'* be appropriately so characterized.

VI

It is important to realize that the ways in which we classify linguistic expressions are not only bound up with the jobs they do, but with the purposes for which the classification is made. Since these purposes tend, for obvious reasons, to concern the role of language as a means of communication, i.e., as that by which we give information, warn, make statements, predict, describe, etc., we should not be surprised, our behaviorist will tell us, if expressions which, as candidly uttered in *non-communicative* contexts, are thinking-out-loud, are classified in a way which is conceptually tied to communication, and, hence, to functions of quite a different order of complexity. One needs only think of the difference between the purely logical characterization of 'it is not raining' as the 'negation' of 'it is raining,' and characterizing it as the 'denial' of the latter, or note the social implications of classifying a word as a *referring* expression.

Thus the ways in which common sense, and not only common sense, classifies linguistic expressions, and the verbs which it uses to describe what people do with them, are heavily weighted in the direction of linguistic *performances* in a context of *communication*. That it is legitimate to view language in this way is not to be doubted. Indeed, it is philosophically important to be clear about the categories in terms of which the variety of ways in which language functions in inter-personal exchange are to be understood. But there is a danger that exclusive concern with this perspective will obscure those connections between thought and language where the latter is *not* functioning as a means of communication.

The point is not that there are failures of communication, e.g. the supposed hearer may be an inanimate object mistaken for a man or a foreigner. It is not even that there are soliloquies, if by this is meant cases of 'talking to oneself.' It is the more radical point that thinking-out-loud is a form of meaningful speech which doesn't consist in talking *to* anyone at all, even oneself, and hence is not, in any ordinary sense, *talking*.

VII

But before I develop this point let me return to the formula we were considering before this digression on the orientation toward contexts of communication of the categories in terms of which common sense, linguistics, and many philosophies of language approach linguistic behavior. The formula was

x is a primary expression of Jones' belief that-p
= x is a primary manifestation of his settled disposition to think that-p
(i.e., is a thinking that-p).

The implications of the term 'manifestation' (and, for that matter, of 'expression') led us in the direction of a logical behaviorism according to which the relevant sense of 'thinking that-p' is 'thinking-out-loud that-p.' Thus reinterpreted, the formula becomes

x is a primary expression of Jones' belief that-p
= x is a primary manifestation of Jones' settled disposition to think-out-loud that-p (i.e., is a thinking-out-loud that-p).

It will be remembered that the point of this behavioristic move was to assimilate the sense in which an episode is a primary *expression* (implying overtness) of a belief to the sense in which an episode of, for example, a piece of litmus paper turning red is a *manifestation* (implying overtness) of its disposition to turn red.

It should be noted in passing that in the case of the litmus paper we seem required to expand the characterization of the disposition into

disposition to turn red, *if put in acid.*

This generates the suspicion that if we are to continue with our strategy, we must similarly expand our analysis of 'Jones believes that-p' into

Jones has a settled disposition to think-out-loud that-p, if . . .

If what? There many pitfalls here, though we can, perhaps, cover them up temporarily with something like 'if the question whether-p arises.' To do so, however, would immediately confront us with a more serious difficulty. For it simply isn't the case that if a person believes that-p, he utters 'p' let alone thinks-out-loud that-p, whenever the question whether-p arises.

Confronted by this fact, we are strongly tempted to abandon our strategy and say that if a person believes that-p, then (other things being equal) whenever the question whether-p arises, he tends to *think* (*not* think-out-loud) that-p; to which we might add that if the circumstances are appropriate he may *express* his thought by uttering (saying?) 'p.'

VIII

On the other hand, if, however, we are to continue with our original strategy, we must resolutely put aside the temptation to draw the kind of distinction between *thought* and its *expression* which this formulation implies, and continue with the intriguing idea that an uttering of 'p' which is a primary expression of a belief that-p is not merely an *expression* of a thinking that-p, but is itself a *thinking*, i.e., a thinking-out-loud that-p.

Yet the preceding remarks do remind us that we must take into account the fact that there is a sense of 'express' in which we can be said to express our thoughts by *using* language for this purpose. Thus, we express our thought that-p by *saying* 'p.' Can we sophisticate our logical behaviorism to do justice to this fact?

Let us take a closer look at the words 'thought' and 'express,' First the latter: it will be noticed that the reference to observability implied by the term 'manifestation' in the context 'manifestation of the disposition to think that-p' was absorbed by the behaviorist into the phrase which describes the disposition. Thus, '*manifestation* of the disposition to *think* that-p,' became, in effect '*actualization* of the disposition to think-*out-loud* that-p.'

Thus the behaviorist's formula becomes, in effect,

x is a primary expression of Jones' belief that-p
= x is a manifestation of Jones' settled disposition to think that-p

= x is an actualization of Jones' settled disposition to think-out-loud that-p
(i.e., x is a thinking-out-loud that-p).

It is only too clear that by pushing this analysis of the context 'expression of belief' in this direction the behaviorist has lost contact with the idea that people *express* their beliefs by *using* language. The point can be put simply—indeed bluntly—by saying that the concept of the *actualization of a disposition* is not, as such, the concept of an *action*, whereas *expressing their beliefs* is something people *do*.

The statement

Jones, by saying 'p', expressed his belief that-p

requires an interpretation of *saying p* as an action which is undertaken by Jones *in order to express (to someone)* his belief *that-p*. If we suspect that Jones is lying, we could equally describe him as saying "p", but we would then go on to say something like

Jones, by saying 'p', *pretended* to believe that-p.

In neither case could Jones' saying 'p' be construed as a case of *thinking* (even 'out loud') that-p. Thus were Jones speaking truthfully, the thinking immediately involved, if any, would be of the sort described by such formulas as

Jones thought that saying '. . .' would express his belief that-p
Jones intended to express his belief that-p by saying '. . .'

or, in the case of lying

Jones intended to pretend to believe that-p by saying '. . . .'

Thus, granted the validity of the concept of thinking-out-loud, the thinking-out-loud which, were it to occur, would be immediately involved in the situation formulated by

Jones, by uttering '. . .,' expressed his belief that-p

would be *not*

Jones thought-out-loud that-p

but rather

Jones thought-out-loud that saying '. . .' would express his belief that-p

or, where Jones is lying,

Jones thought-out-loud that he would pretend to believe that-p by saying '. . .'

Needless to say, the latter thinking-out-loud would be self-frustrating in the presence of the audience he intends to deceive.

IX

If we leave behaviorism aside for a moment, we can add a new dimension to the discussion by noting that the term 'express' in contexts pertaining to thought has two radically different senses. The difference can be brought out by relating these senses to two different contexts, namely,

(1) *Jones* expressed his thought (belief) that-p by saying . . .
(2) *Jones' utterance* of 'p' expressed his thought that-p

I shall call the former the 'action' sense of express, and the latter, for want of a better term, the 'causal' sense. Both, as we shall see, are to be distinguished from a third sense illustrated by the context

Jones' utterance of 'p' expressed *the* thought that-p

where the phrase '*the* thought that-p' stands for an abstract entity, a thought in Frege's sense (i.e., in one sense of this term, a 'proposition'). I shall call this the logical (or semantical) sense of 'express.'

Although my ultimate aim is to show how a logical behaviorist might draw these distinctions, my initial move will be to discuss them in more traditional terms. I shall, therefore, construct a regimented (I dare not say idealized) model according to which, in the course of learning to speak a language, a child acquires the capacity to be in mental states which are *counterparts*, in a sense to be analyzed, of the utterances which come to belong to his repertory of linguistic behavior. The idea can be blocked out in two steps:

(a) A mental episode which is a thinking that-p is correlated, in a certain linguistic community, with a piece of linguistic behavior which stands for (expresses in the logical or semantical sense) the thought (proposition) that-p
(b) In the initial stages of the child's mastery of the language, whenever it has a thought that-p, this thought is manifested in a purely involuntary way by the corresponding verbal behavior.

As our model for understanding the sense in which the uttering of 'p' is the involuntary manifestation of a thinking that-p, let us take the instinctive connection between a pain and a piece of unlearned pain behavior. The fact that a connection between states A and B of a child is, in some sense, *learned* rather than *instinctive*, *acquired* rather than *part of its initial equipment*, by no means entails that either A or B is under the child's voluntary control. Not all learning to *do* something in a broad sense of 'do' consists in the addition of new behaviors to the stock of things that are under one's voluntary control.

The key feature of our model is that the acquired connection between the mental act and the verbal behavior is not to be construed on the action model of 'using the behavior to express one's thought.' Thus, verbal behavior is not in our child's voluntary control in that, although, *once the language is learned*, a necessary and sufficient condition of the child saying 'p' is that it thinks that-p, the saying is the involuntary manifestation of the thinking.

Notice that the model allows the child a rich vocabulary, including the language of intention and resolve as well as the language in which matters-of-fact are stated. It also allows that the child learns to verbalize about verbal behavior and even about the mental acts of which its verbal behavior is the involuntary manifestation.

X

We are now in a position to weaken our model and still make our point. We need not suppose that the child remains a chatterbox. We can suppose it to acquire the ability to keep its thoughts to itself in the sense that it can effectively tell itself to keep quiet, without ceasing to think. We can grant that to this limited extent its verbal behavior becomes under its voluntary control. When it is thinking without speaking, we shall say that it is in a keeping-its-thoughts-to-itself frame of mind. When not in this frame of mind, it thinks out loud.[8] Thus, 'Thinking out loud' remains the primary form in which thinking occurs. The child's keeping its thoughts to itself can be compared to the opening of a general switch which breaks (or, to mix metaphors) short circuits the initial acquired connection between thoughts and verbal behavior.

At this stage, the child has no conception of locutionary acts (e.g. predicting, telling) as verbal behavior which can be engaged in whether or not one is thinking the corresponding thoughts. It has no concept of *saying "p" without thinking that-p.*

On the other hand, it is perfectly capable of having concepts of *actions* involving thinking out loud. Thus, wondering out loud about the weather; "I shall wonder out loud about the likelihood of rain." It is important to see that this by no means entails that there is such a thing as an action of *thinking out loud that-p*. Even in our more sophisticated framework there is no such thing as an *action* of thinking that-p, though there is the action of *deliberating* (i.e., deliberating out loud) what to do. By granting, as we must, that it can conceive of actions consisting of thinkings out loud, we admit a further sense in which its verbal behavior (*as* thinkings out loud) would be under its voluntary control.

The child's verbal behavior would express its thoughts, but, to put it paradoxically, the child could not express them.

Notice, also, that although its linguistic behavior would be meaningful, and we could say of each of its utterances what, specifically it meant, e.g.

Jones' utterance meant 'it is raining,'

It would, on our assumptions, be incorrect to say, for example

Jones, by uttering '. . .' meant (to convey) . . .

For the latter supposes that Jones has the concept of an action of uttering '. . . .' as a piece of linguistic behavior which could exist independently of its being the "spontaneous verbal expression" of the corresponding mental act. There being no such action as bringing about a specific mental act, there could be no such thing as bringing about a thinking out loud for the purpose of conveying a thought.

In other words, just as our regimenting fiction enables us to draw a distinction between a sense in which a mode of verbal behavior can *express* thoughts without being *used to express* them, so it enables us to distinguish between the context

utterance of E (in L) means____

and the sense of 'means,' closely related to 'intends,' which involves the context

Jones, by uttering E, means (to convey) . . .

The familiar saw that words have meaning only because people mean things by them is harmless if it tells us that words have no meaning in abstraction from their involvement in the verbal behavior of language users. It is downright mistaken if it tells us that for an expression to have a certain sense or reference is for it to be *used* by people *to convey* the corresponding thought. Rather, we should say, it is because the expression has a certain meaning that it can be effectively used to convey the corresponding thought.

XI

Let us now return to the initial accounts we gave of belief and its expression. The first thing to note is that if we were to reformulate them in terms of our model we would get something like the following schema:

Jones believes that-p = Jones has a settled disposition to think that-p, if the question occurs to him whether-p, and, indeed, to think out loud that-p, unless he is in a keeping-his-thoughts-to-himself frame of mind.[9]

We also get the following formulae with respect to 'expression of belief':

x is a primary actualization of Jones' belief that-p → x is a thinking that-p (and, indeed, a thinking out loud that-p unless he is in a keeping-his-thoughts-to himself frame of mind).

x is a primary expression of Jones' belief that-p → x is a thinking out loud that-p.

Thus, where Jones is in a thinking out loud frame of mind, the verbal behavior is both an *actualization of* and, in the 'causal' sense, an *expression of* his belief, both a *thinking* and an *expression of thought.*

XII

But what will our logical behaviorist say to all this? Clearly he will be unhappy about our uncritical acceptance of mental acts as covert inner episodes. What moves might he make? He may well accept our initial formula

Jones believes that-p = Jones has a settled disposition to think that-p.

But he will emphasize the 'settled,' which we have not yet done, and will call attention to the fact that it presumably contrasts with something. It is not obvious what the contrasting adjective should be, but it, too, should apply to dispositions. Let us, he suggests, try 'proximate,' drawing on the contrast between 'settled' and 'near the surface.' Another appropriate contrast would be provided by 'short term.'

Objects, as is well known, can have causal properties which are not so to speak, immediately available. Thus iron attracts filings, *if* it has been treated in a certain way. A *proximate* disposition can roughly be characterized as one which is immediately available.

Our logical behaviorist, consequently, suggests that

Jones believes that-p = Jones has the *settled* disposition to have *short term, proximate* dispositions to think-out-loud that-p, if the question whether-p arises, and he is in a thinking-out-loud frame of mind.

In other words, our logical behaviorist construes the contrast between fleeting thought episodes and settled beliefs as falling *within* the broad category of dispositions, and hence construes the 'covertness' of thoughts as simply a special case of the covertness of dispositions. Flammability, he reminds us, is not a covert flame.

Many features of our previous discussion can be fitted into this framework, once its distinctive character is understood. Thus, the behaviorist substitutes for the previous account of the child's candid and spontaneous verbal behavior as the expression (in the 'causal' sense) of classically conceived *episodes* of thought, an account according to which a

thinking-out-loud that-p

is simply an 'actualization' of a

short term proximate, disposition to think-out-loud that-p.

In the non-behavioristic model we stipulated that the child be unable to verbalize without thinking the appropriate thought, in other words, that only if it has the mental act of thinking that-p does it utter 'p.' In the behavioristic reconstruction framework, the corresponding stipulation would be that all utterances of 'p' be thinking-out-loud that-p.

Both stipulations could be formulated in the same words, thus 'the child utters "p" only in the course of thinking out loud that-p.' But the two concepts of thinking out loud are radically different. In the non-behavioristic model, the phrase 'thinking-out-loud' referred to thoughts together with their verbal expression. In the behavioristic reconstruction it is to be taken as an unanalyzed expression which means roughly the same as 'candid spontaneous verbal behavior,' but serves, by its hyphenated mode of composition, to emphasize that the basic meaningfulness of candid, spontaneous verbal behavior is *not* to be construed in terms of its being the reverberation at the tip of the tongue of covert episodes which are thoughts properly speaking, in accordance with the schema

x is candid, spontaneous verbal behavior = is an expression[10] of thought

XIII

It is important not to confuse logical behaviorism with what might be called logical physicalism. I mean by the latter the view which denies that, to quote Chisholm, "when we analyze the kind of meaning that is involved in natural language we need some concepts we do not need in physics or behavioristics."[11] Chisholm thinks that to deny the need for such an irreducible concept is tantamount to trying to "analyze the semantics . . . of natural language in a physicalistic vocabulary of a behavioristic psychology with no undefined semantical term and no reference to thoughts."[12]

In the essay which led to the correspondence from which I am quoting, I had argued that the concept of meaning which belongs in the context

E(in L) means____

is not to be analyzed in terms of a reference to 'thoughts.' Thus I rejected any analysis along *either* of the following lines

E(in L) means____ = *candid and spontaneous utterances* of F causally express thoughts pertaining to____

E(in L) means____ = *speakers of L* use E to express their thoughts pertaining to____

where 'thought' is to be taken as referring to classically conceived inner episodes or mental acts.

On the other hand, though I denied that 'means' in the sense appropriate to the context 'E(in L) means____' is to be analyzed (defined) in terms of a reference to thoughts, I also argued that it cannot be analyzed in physicalistic terms. From Chisholm's point of view this was a blatant attempt to have my cake and eat it. As he saw it, to *admit* that "to analyze the kind of meaning that is involved in natural language" we need a distinctively semantical term ('means') which *cannot* be analyzed in physicalistic terms, but *deny* that the explication of this distinctively semantical term requires a reference to *thoughts* has all the appearance of paradox.

The correspondence went on at some length, and although some progress was made, the issue was never really joined. As I now diagnose the situation some ten years later, the cause of this failure was my inability to clarify adequately two points:

(a) The exact nature of statements of the form 'E(in L) means____'
(b) The exact relation of the concept of *meaning* to that of *thought*.

The space which remains is too short to do anything more than indicate the moves I should have made.

My basic move should have been to clarify along the lines of the present paper the distinction between the contexts

person expresses

and

utterance expresses.

My second move should have been to give a more adequate clarification of the concept of meaning as it occurs in the context 'expression (in L) means____' (as contrasted with the context 'person, by uttering E, means____'). At the time of the correspondence I was unable to do much more than offer the rather cryptic suggestion that statements of this form are (a) *sui generis*, (b) *convey* (rather than *describe*) how the subject expression is used, by exhibiting an expression in the hearer's active vocabulary which has the same job—the idea being that by rehearsing his use of the latter, he will be able to grasp the use of the former. As I have since argued,[13] to say what an expression means is to *classify* it by the use of a sortal predicate the application of which implies that the expression in question does the job in its language which is done in the speaker's language by an expression from which the predicate is formed. Thus, roughly

'und' (in German) means *and*

has the form

'und's (in German) are ·and·s

where '·and·' is a sortal predicate of the kind in question.

But above all I should have made it clear that in my view the fundamental concept pertaining to thinking is thinking-out-loud as conceived by our logical behaviorists.[14] This is not to say that I agree with him in rejecting the classical conception of thoughts as inner episodes in a non-dispositional sense. Rather I accept mental acts in something like the classical sense, but argue that the concept of such acts is, in a sense I have attempted to clarify, a derivative concept.

Finally, I should have emphasized my total commitment to the thesis that the concept of thought essentially involves that of intentionality in the following sense. To say of a piece of verbal behavior that it is a thinking-out-loud, is to commit oneself to say of it that it *means something*, while to say of it specifically that it is a thinking-out-loud that-p, is to commit oneself to say of it that it is a piece of verbal behavior which means *p*.

Thus, at the primary level, instead of analyzing the intentionality or aboutness of verbal behavior in terms of its expressing or being used to express classically conceived thoughts or beliefs, we should recognize that this verbal behavior is *already thinking in its own right*, and its intentionality or aboutness is simply the appropriateness of classifying it in terms which relate to the linguistic behavior of the group to which one belongs.

Notes

1. For an exploration of this and related issues, see my *Science and Metaphysics* (London, Routledge and Kegan Paul, 1968), Chapter VI (especially sections XIV–XVII).

2. I have in mind particularly John Austin and his students. The best statement of this approach is to be found in Austin's *How to do Things with Words* (London, Oxford University Press, 1963).

3. For an explanation and defense of these distinctions see Austin's *How to do Things with Words*.

4."Some Reflections on Language Games," *Philosophy of Science*, Vol. 21, No. 3, 1954 (Reprinted as Chapter 11 in *Science, Perception and Reality*), It is important to note that a full discussion would refer to may-be's (or permitteds) as well as ought-to-be's—otherwise the concept of 'free' as opposed to 'tied' (stimulus bound) linguistic activity, essential to any account of the functioning of a conceptual system, would be left out of the picture.

5. Equally dangerous are such mephorical contrasts as those between 'paradigm' and 'borderline,' 'shadow' and 'penumbra.' All suggest a sequential strategy according to which, once we find the thread, we know how to begin and what kinds of difficulty to expect.

6. Similarly, 'wondering whether-p' would be equated with 'uttering "p?"', 'wishing that-p' with 'uttering "would (that) p"' and 'deciding to do A' with uttering 'I shall do A.'

7. We can grant that a thinking-out-loud that-p might be a constituent of a reasoning-out-loud or a deliberating-out-loud on a certain topic.

8. The concept of 'thinking out loud' appropriate to this model should not be equated with thinking-out-loud as construed by the behavioristic position we have been considering. The latter does not recognize 'mental episodes' in the sense required by the present model.

9. The 'if the question occurs to him whether-p' condition can be taken to cover all cases in which, where the alternatives 'p' and 'not p' are relevant to his course of thought, he thinks that-p, even if the question whether-p is not actually raised.

10.'Expression' in the causal sense, i.e., a manifestation at the 'surface' of a covert process which is its cause.

11. *Minnesota Studies in the Philosophy of Science*, Vol. II, p. 523.

12. *Ibid.*

13. Most recently in *Science and Metaphysics*, Chapter III.

14. The priority in question, to use Aristotle's distinction, is in the order of knowing as contrasted with the order of being. As an analogy, notice that concepts pertaining to things as perceived by the senses are prior in the order of knowing to concepts of micro-physical particles, whereas (for the Scientific Realist) micro-physical particles are prior in the order of being to objects as perceived by the senses.

In this essay, Davidson presents an argument that it is futile to hold that meaning and truth are relative to a language or set of concepts, since the criterion for an expression being meaningful in a language is its translatability.

DONALD DAVIDSON

On the Very Idea of a Conceptual Scheme

Philosophers of many persuasions are prone to talk of conceptual schemes. Conceptual schemes, we are told, are ways of organizing experience; they are systems of categories that give form to the data of sensation; they are points of view from which individuals, cultures, or periods survey the passing scene. There may be no translating from one scheme to another, in which case the beliefs, desires, hopes and bits of knowledge that characterize one person have no true counterparts for the subscriber to another scheme. Reality itself is relative to a scheme: what counts as real in one system may not in another.

Even those thinkers who are certain there is only one conceptual scheme are in the sway of the scheme concept; even monotheists have religion. And when someone sets out to describe "our conceptual scheme," his homey task assumes, if we take him literally, that there might be rival systems.

Conceptual relativism is a heady and exotic doctrine, or would be if we could make good sense of it. The trouble is, as so often in philosophy, it is hard to improve intelligibility while retaining the excitement. At any rate that is what I shall argue.

We are encouraged to imagine we understand massive conceptual change or profound contrasts by legitimate examples of a familiar sort. Sometimes an idea, like that of simultaneity as defined in relativity theory, is so important that with its addition a whole department of science takes on a new look. Sometimes revisions in the list of sentences held true in a discipline are so central that we may feel that the terms involved have changed their meanings. Languages that have evolved in distant times or places may differ extensively in their resources for dealing with one or another range of phenomena. What comes easily in one language may come hard in another, and this difference may echo significant dissimilarities in style and value.

But examples like these, impressive as they occasionally are, are not so extreme but that the changes and the contrasts can be explained and described using the equipment of a single language. Whorf, wanting to demonstrate that Hopi incorporates a metaphysics so alien to ours that Hopi and English cannot, as he puts it, "be calibrated," uses English to convey the contents of sample Hopi sentences.[1] Kuhn is brilliant at saying what things were like before the revolution using—what else?—our post-revolutionary idiom.[2] Quine gives us a feel for the "pre-individuative phase in the evolution of our conceptual scheme,"[3] while Bergson tells us where we can go to get a view of a mountain undistorted by one or another provincial perspective.

The dominant metaphor of conceptual relativism, that of differing points of view, seems to betray an underlying paradox. Different points of view make sense, but only if there is a common coordinate system on which to plot them; yet the existence of a common system belies the claim of dramatic incomparability. What we need, it seems to me, is some idea of the considerations that set the limits to conceptual contrast. There are extreme suppositions that founder on paradox or contradiction; there are modest examples we have no trouble understanding. What determines where we cross from the merely strange or novel to the absurd?

We may accept the doctrine that associates having a language with having a conceptual scheme. The relation may be supposed to be this: if conceptual schemes differ, so do languages. But speakers of different languages may share a conceptual scheme provided there is a way of translating one language into the other. Studying the criteria of translation is therefore a way of focusing on criteria of identity for conceptual schemes. If conceptual schemes aren't associated with languages in this way, the original problem is needlessly doubled, for then we would have to imagine the mind, with its ordinary categories, operating with a language with *its* organizing structure. Under the circumstances we would certainly want to ask who is to be master.

Alternatively, there is the idea that *any* language distorts reality, which implies that it is only wordlessly if at all that the mind comes to grips with things as they really are. This is to conceive language as an inert (though necessarily distorting) medium independent of the human agencies that employ it; a view of language that surely cannot be maintained. Yet if the mind can grapple without distortion with the real, the mind itself must be without categories and concepts. This featureless self is familiar from theories in quite different parts of the philosophical landscape. There are, for example, theories that make freedom consist in decisions taken apart from all desires, habits and dispositions of the agent; and theories of knowledge that suggest that the mind can observe the totality of its own perceptions and ideas. In each case, the mind is divorced from the traits that constitute it; a familiar enough conclusion to certain lines of reasoning, as I said, but one that should always persuade us to reject the premisses.

We may identify conceptual schemes with languages, then, or better, allowing for the possibility that more than one language may express the same scheme, sets of intertranslatable languages. Languages we will not think of as separable from souls; speaking a language is not a trait a man can lose while retaining the power of thought. So there is no chance that someone can take up a vantage point for comparing conceptual schemes by temporarily shedding his own. Can we then say that two people have different conceptual schemes if they speak languages that fail of intertranslatability?

In what follows I consider two kinds of case that might be expected to arise: complete, and partial, failures of translatability. There would be complete failure if no significant range of sentences in one language could be translated into the other; there would be partial failure if some range could be translated and some range could not (I shall neglect possible asymmetries.) My strategy will be to argue that we cannot make sense of total failure, and then to examine more briefly cases of partial failure.

First, then, the purported cases of complete failure. It is tempting to take a very short line indeed: nothing, it may be said, could count as evidence that some form of activity could not be interpreted in our language that was not at the same time evidence that that form of activity was not speech behavior. If this were right, we probably ought to hold that a form of activity that cannot be interpreted as language in our language is not speech behavior. Putting matters this way is unsatisfactory, however, for it comes to little more than making translatability into a familiar tongue a criterion of languagehood. As fiat, the thesis lacks the appeal of self-evidence; if it is a truth, as I think it is, it should emerge as the conclusion of an argument.

The credibility of the position is improved by reflection on the close relations between language and the attribution of attitudes such as belief, desire and intention. On the one hand, it is clear that speech requires a multitude of finely discriminated intentions and beliefs. A person who asserts that perseverance keeps honor bright must, for example, represent himself as believing that perseverance keeps honor bright, and he must intend to represent himself as believing it. On the other hand, it seems unlikely that we can intelligibly attribute attitudes as complex as these to a speaker unless we can translate his words into ours. There can be no doubt that the relation between being able to translate someone's language and being able to describe his attitudes is very close. Still, until we can say more about *what* this relation is, the case against untranslatable languages remains obscure.

It is sometimes thought that translatability into a familiar language, say English, cannot be a criterion of languagehood on the grounds that the relation of translatability is not transitive. The idea is that some language, say Saturnian, may be translatable into English, and some further language, like Plutonian, may be translatable into Saturnian, while Plutonian is not translatable into English. Enough translatable differences may add up to an untranslatable one. By imagining a sequence of languages, each close enough to the one before to be acceptably translated into it, we can imagine a language so different from English as to resist totally translation into it. Corresponding to this distant language would be a system of concepts altogether alien to us.

This exercise does not, I think, introduce any new element into the discussion. For we should have to ask how we recognized that what the Saturnian was doing was *translating* Plutonian (or anything else). The Saturnian speaker might tell us that that was what he was doing or rather, we might for a moment assume that that was what he was telling us. But then it would occur to us to wonder whether our translations of Saturnian were correct.

According to Kuhn, scientists operating in different scientific traditions (within different "paradigms") "live in different worlds."[4] Strawson's *The Bounds of Sense* begins with the remark that "It is possible to imagine kinds of worlds very different from the world as we know it."[5] Since there is at most one world, these pluralities are metaphorical or merely imagined. The metaphors are, however, not at all the same. Strawson invites us to imagine possible non-actual worlds, worlds that might be described, using our present language, by redistributing truth values over sentences in various systematic ways. The clarity of the contrasts between worlds in this case depends on supposing our scheme of concepts, our descriptive resources, to remain fixed. Kuhn, on the other hand, wants us to think of different observers of the same world who come to it with incommensurable systems of concepts. Strawson's many imagined worlds are seen (or heard)—anyway described—from the same point of view. Kuhn's one world is seen from different points of view. It is the second metaphor we want to work on.

The first metaphor requires a distinction within language of concept and content: using a fixed system of concepts (words with fixed meanings) we describe alternative universes. Some sentences will be true simply because of the concepts or meanings involved, others because of the way of the world. In describing possible worlds, we play with sentences of the second kind only.

The second metaphor suggests instead a dualism of quite a different sort, a dualism of total scheme (or language) and uninterpreted content. Adherence to the second dualism, while not inconsistent with adherence to the first, may be encouraged by attacks on the first. Here is how it may work.

To give up the analytic-synthetic distinction as basic to the understanding of language is to give up the idea that we can clearly distinguish between theory and language. Meaning, as we might loosely use the word, is contaminated by theory, by what is held to be true. Feyerabend puts it this way:

> Our argument against meaning invariance is simple and clear. It proceeds from the fact that usually some of the principles involved in the determinations of the meanings of older theories or points of view are inconsistent with the new . . . theories. It points out that it is natural to resolve this contradiction by eliminating the troublesome . . . older principles, and to replace them by principles, or theorems, of a new . . . theory. And it concludes by showing that such a procedure will also lead to the elimination of the old meanings.[6]

We may now seem to have a formula for generating distinct conceptual schemes. We get a new out of an old scheme when the speakers of a language come to accept as true an important range of sentences they previously took to be false (and, of course, vice versa). We must not describe this change simply as a matter of their coming to view old falsehoods as truths, for a truth is a proposition, and what they come to accept, in accepting a sentence as true, is not the same thing that they rejected when formerly they held the sentence to be false. A change has come over the meaning of the sentence because it now belongs to a new language.

This picture of how new (perhaps better) schemes result from new and better science is very much the picture philosophers of science, like Putnam and Feyerabend, and historians of science, like Kuhn, have painted for us. A related idea emerges in the suggestion of some other philosophers, that we could improve our conceptual lot if we were to tune our language to an improved science. Thus both Quine and Smart, in somewhat different ways, regretfully admit that our present ways of talking make a serious science of behavior impossible. (Wittgenstein and Ryle have said similar things without regret.) The cure, Quine and Smart think, is to change how we talk. Smart advocates (and predicts) the change in order to put us on the scientifically straight path of materialism; Quine is more concerned to clear the way for a purely extensional language. (Perhaps I should add that I think our *present* scheme and language are best understood as extensional and materialist.)

If we were to follow this advice, I do not myself think science or understanding would be advanced, though possibly morals would. But the present question is only whether, if such changes were to take place, we should be justified in calling them alterations in the basic conceptual apparatus. The difficulty in so calling them is easy to appreciate. Suppose that in my office of Minister of Scientific Language I want the new man to stop using words that refer, say, to emotions, feelings, thoughts and intentions, and to talk instead of the physiological states and happenings that are assumed to be more or less identical with the mental riff and raff. How do I tell whether my advice has been heeded if the new man speaks a new language? For all I know, the shiny new phrases, though stolen from the old language in which they refer to physiological stirrings, may in his mouth play the role of the messy old mental concepts.

The key phrase is: for all I know. What is clear is that retention of some or all of the old vocabulary in itself provides no basis for judging the new scheme to be the same as, or different from, the old. So what sounded at first like a thrilling discovery—that truth is relative to a conceptual scheme—has not so far been shown to be anything more than the pedestrian and familiar fact that the truth of a sentence is relative to (among other things) the language to which it belongs. Instead of living in different worlds, Kuhn's scientists may, like those who need Webster's dictionary, be only words apart.

Giving up the analytic-synthetic distinction has not proven a help in making sense of conceptual relativism. The analytic-synthetic distinction is however explained in terms of something that may serve to buttress conceptual relativism, namely the idea of empirical content. The dualism of the synthetic and the analytic is a dualism of sentences some of which are true (or false) both because of what they mean and because of their empirical content, while others are true (or false) by virtue of meaning alone, having no empirical content. If we give up the dualism, we abandon the conception of meaning that goes with it, but we do not have to abandon the idea of empirical content: we can hold, if we want, that *all* sentences have empirical content. Empirical content is in turn explained by reference to the facts, the world, experience, sensation, the totality of sensory stimuli, or something similar. Meanings gave us a way to talk about categories, the organizing structure of language, and so on; but it is possible, as we have seen, to give up meanings and analyticity while retaining the idea of language as embodying a conceptual scheme. Thus in place of the dualism of the analytic-synthetic we get the dualism of conceptual scheme and empirical content. The new dualism is the foundation of an empiricism shorn of the untenable dogmas of the analytic-synthetic distinction and reductionism—shorn, that is, of the unworkable idea that we can uniquely allocate empirical content sentence by sentence.

I want to urge that this second dualism of scheme and content, of organizing system and something waiting to be organized, cannot be made intelligible and defensible. It is itself a dogma of empiricism, the third dogma. The third, and perhaps the last, for if we give it up it is not clear that there is anything distinctive left to call empiricism.

The scheme-content dualism has been formulated in many ways. Here are some examples. The first comes from Whorf, elaborating on a theme of Sapir's. Whorf says that:

> . . . language produces an organization of experience. We are inclined to think of language simply as a technique of expression, and not to realize that language first of all is a classification and arrangement of the stream of sensory experience which results in a certain world-order . . . In other words, language does in a cruder but also in a broader and more versatile way the same thing that science does . . . We are thus introduced to a new principle of relativity, which holds that all observers are not led by the same physical evidence to the same picture of the universe, unless their linguistic backgrounds are similar, or can in some way be calibrated.[7]

Here we have all the required elements: language as the organizing force, not to be distinguished clearly from science; what is organized, referred to variously as "experience," "the stream of sensory experience," and "physical evidence"; and finally, the failure of intertranslatability ("calibration"). The failure of intertranslatability is a necessary condition for difference of conceptual schemes; the common relation to experience or the evidence is what is supposed to help us make sense of the claim that it is languages or schemes that are under consideration when translation fails. It is essential to this idea that there be something neutral and common that lies outside all schemes. This common something cannot, of course, be the *subject matter* of contrasting languages, or translation would be possible. Thus Kuhn has recently written:

> Philosophers have now abandoned hope of finding a pure sense-datum language . . . but many of them continue to assume that theories can be compared by recourse to a basic vocabulary consisting entirely of words which are attached to nature in ways that are unproblematic and, to the extent necessary independent of theory . . . Feyerabend and I have argued at length that no such vocabulary is available. In the transition from one theory to the next words change their meanings or conditions of applicability in subtle ways. Though most of the same signs are used before and after a revolution e.g. force, mass, element, compound, cell—the ways in which some of them attach to nature has somehow changed. Successive theories are thus, we say, incommensurable.[8]

"Incommensurable" is, of course, Kuhn and Feyerabend's word for "not intertranslatable." The neutral content waiting to be organized is supplied by nature.

Feyerabend himself suggests that we may compare contrasting schemes by "choosing a point of view outside the system or the language." He hopes we can do this because "there is still human experience as an actually existing process"[9] independent of all schemes.

The same, or similar, thoughts are expressed by Quine in many passages: "The totality of our so-called knowledge or beliefs . . . is a man-made fabric which impinges on experience only along the edges . . .";[10] ". . . total science is like a field of force whose boundary conditions are experience";[11] "As an empiricist I . . . think of the conceptual scheme of science as a tool . . . for predicting future experience in the light of past experience."[12] And again:

> We persist in breaking reality down somehow into a multiplicity of identifiable and discriminable objects. . . . We talk so inveterately of objects that to say we do so seems almost to say nothing at all; for how else is there to talk? It is hard to say how else there is to talk, not because our objectifying pattern is an invariable trait of human nature, but because we are bound to adapt any alien pattern to our own in the very process of understanding or translating the alien sentences.[13]

The test of difference remains failure or difficulty of translation: ". . . to speak of that remote medium as radically different from ours is to say no more than that the translations do not come smoothly."[14] Yet the roughness may be so great that the alien has an "as yet unimagined pattern beyond individuation."[15]

The idea is then that something is a language, and associated with a conceptual scheme, whether we can translate it or not, if it stands in a certain relation (predicting, organizing, facing or fitting) to experience (nature, reality, sensory promptings). The problem is to say what the relation is, and to be clearer about the entities related.

The images and metaphors fall into two main groups: conceptual schemes (languages) either *organize* something, or they *fit* it (as in "he warps his scientific heritage to fit his . . . sensory promptings").[16] The first group contains also *systematize, divide up* (the stream of experience); further examples of the second group art *predict, account for, face* (the tribunal of experience). As for the entities that get organized, or which the scheme must fit, I think again we may detect two main ideas: either it is reality (the universe, the world, nature), or it is experience (the passing show, surface irritations, sensory promptings, sense data, the given).

We cannot attach a clear meaning to the notion of organizing a single object (the world, nature, etc.) unless that object is understood to contain or consist in other objects. Someone who sets out to organize a closet arranges the things in it. If you are told not to organize the shoes and shirts, but the closet itself, you would be bewildered. How would you organize the Pacific Ocean? Straighten out its shores, perhaps, or relocate its islands, or destroy its fish.

A language may contain simple predicates whose extensions are matched by no simple predicates, or even by any predicates at all, in some other language. What enables us to make this point in particular cases is an ontology common to the two languages, with concepts that individuate the same objects. We can be clear about breakdowns in translation when they are local enough, for a background of generally successful translation provides what is needed to make the failures intelligible. But we were after larger game: we wanted to make sense of there being a language we could not translate at all. Or, to put the point differently, we were looking for a criterion of languagehood that did not depend on, or entail, translatability into a familiar idiom. I suggest that the image of organizing the closet of nature will not supply such a criterion.

How about the other kind of object, experience? Can we think of a language organizing *it*? Much the same difficulties recur. The notion of organization applies only to pluralities. But whatever plurality we take experience to consist in—events like losing a button or stubbing a toe, having a sensation of warmth or hearing an oboe—we will have to individuate according to familiar principles. A language that organizes *such* entities must be a language very like our own.

Experience (and its classmates like surface irritations, sensations and sense data) also makes another and more obvious trouble for the organizing idea. For how could something count as a language that organized *only* experiences, sensations, surface irritations or sense data? Surely knives and forks, railroads and mountains, cabbages and kingdoms also need organizing.

This last remark will no doubt sound inappropriate as a response to the claim that a conceptual scheme is a way of coping with sensory experience; and I agree that it is. But what was under consideration was the idea of *organizing* experience, not the idea of *coping with* (or fitting or facing) experience. The reply was apropos of the former, not the latter, concept. So now let's see whether we can do better with the second idea.

When we turn from talk of organization to talk of fitting we turn our attention from the referential apparatus of language—predicates, quantifiers, variables and singular terms—to whole sentences. It is sentences that predict (or are used to predict), sentences that cope or deal with things, that fit our sensory promptings, that can be compared or confronted with the evidence. It is sentences also that face the tribunal of experience, though of course they must face it together.

The proposal is not that experiences, sense data, surface irritations or sensory promptings are the sole subject matter of language. There is, it is true, the theory that talk about brick houses on Elm Street is ultimately to be construed as being about sense data or perceptions, but such reductionistic views are only extreme, and implausible, versions of the general position we are considering. The general position is that sensory experience provides all the *evidence* for the acceptance of sentences (where sentences may include whole theories). A sentence or theory fits our sensory promptings, successfully faces the tribunal of experience, predicts future experience, or copes with the pattern of our surface irritations, provided it is borne out by the evidence.

In the common course of affairs, a theory may be borne out by the available evidence and yet be false. But what is in view here is not just actually available evidence;

it is the totality of possible sensory evidence past, present and future. We do not need to pause to contemplate what this might mean. The point is that for a theory to fit or face up to the totality of possible sensory evidence is for that theory to be true. If a theory quantifies over physical objects, numbers or sets, what it says about these entities is true provided the theory as a whole fits the sensory evidence. One can see how, from this point of view, such entities might be called posits. It is reasonable to call something a posit if it can be contrasted with something that is not. Here the something that is not is sensory experience—at least that is the idea.

The trouble is that the notion of fitting the totality of experience, like the notions of fitting the facts, or being true to the facts, adds nothing intelligible to the simple concept of being true. To speak of sensory experience rather than the evidence, or just the facts, expresses a view about the source or nature of evidence, but it does not add a new entity to the universe against which to test conceptual schemes. The totality of sensory evidence is what we want provided it is all the evidence there is; and all the evidence there is is just what it takes to make our sentences or theories true. Nothing, however, no *thing*, makes sentences and theories true: not experience, not surface irritations, not the world, can make a sentence true. *That* experience takes a certain course, that our skin is warmed or punctured, that the universe is finite, these facts, if we like to talk that way, make sentences and theories true. But this point is put better without mention of facts. The sentence "My skin is warm" is true if and only if my skin is warm. Here there is no reference to a fact, a world, an experience, or a piece of evidence.[17]

Our attempt to characterize languages or conceptual schemes in terms of the notion of fitting some entity has come down, then, to the simple thought that something is an acceptable conceptual scheme or theory if it is true. Perhaps we better say *largely* true in order to allow sharers of a scheme to differ on details. And the criterion of a conceptual scheme different from our own now becomes: largely true but not translatable. The question whether this is a useful criterion is just the question how well we understand the notion of truth, as applied to language, independent of the notion of translation. The answer is, I think, that we do not understand it independently at all.

We recognize sentences like "'Snow is white' is true if and only if snow is white" to be trivially true. Yet the totality of such English sentences uniquely determines the extension of the concept of truth for English. Tarski generalized this observation and made it a test of theories of truth: according to Tarski's Convention T, a satisfactory theory of truth for a language L must entail, for every sentence *s* of L, a theorem of the form "*s* is true if and only if *p*" where "*s*" is replaced by a description of *s* and "*p*" by *s* itself if L is English, and by a translation of *s* into English if L is not English.[18] This isn't, of course, a definition of truth, and it doesn't hint that there is a single definition or theory that applies to languages generally. Nevertheless, Convention T suggests, though it cannot state, an important feature common to all the specialized concepts of truth. It succeeds in doing this by making essential use of the notion of translation into a language we know. Since Convention T embodies our best intuition as to how the concept of truth is used, there does not seem to be much hope for a test that a conceptual scheme is radically different from ours if that test depends on the assumption that we can divorce the notion of truth from that of translation.

Neither a fixed stock of meanings, nor a theory-neutral reality, can provide, then, a ground for comparison of conceptual schemes. It would be a mistake to look further for such a ground if by that we mean something conceived as common to incommensurable schemes. In abandoning this search, we abandon the attempt to make sense of the metaphor of a single space within which each scheme has a position and provides a point of view.

I turn now to the more modest approach: the idea of partial rather than total failure of translation. This introduces the possibility of making changes and contrasts in conceptual schemes intelligible by reference to the common part. What we need is a theory of translation or interpretation that makes no assumptions about shared meanings, concepts or beliefs.

The interdependence of belief and meaning springs from the interdependence of two aspects of the interpretation of speech behavior: the attribution of beliefs and the interpretation of sentences. We remarked before that we can afford to associate conceptual schemes with languages because of these dependencies. Now we can put the point in a somewhat sharper way. Allow that a man's speech cannot be interpreted without knowing a good deal about what he believes (and intends and wants), and that fine distinctions between beliefs are impossible without understood speech; how then are we to interpret speech or intelligibly to attribute beliefs and other attitudes? Clearly we must have a theory that simultaneously accounts for attitudes and interprets speech—a theory that rests on evidence which assumes neither.

I suggest, following Quine, that we may without circularity or unwarranted assumptions accept certain very general attitudes towards sentences as the basic evidence for a theory of radical interpretation. For the sake of the present discussion at least we may depend on the attitude of accepting as true, directed at sentences, as the crucial notion. (A more full-blooded theory would look to other attitudes towards sentences as well, such as wishing true, wondering whether true, intending to make true, and so on.) Attitudes are indeed involved here, but the fact that the main issue is not begged can be seen from this: if we merely know that someone holds a certain sentence to be true, we know neither what he means by the sentence nor what belief his holding it true represents. His holding the sentence true is thus the vector of two forces: the problem of interpretation is to abstract from the evidence a workable theory of meaning and an acceptable theory of belief.

The way this problem is solved is best appreciated from undramatic examples. If you see a ketch sailing by and your companion says, "Look at that handsome yawl," you may be faced with a problem of interpretation. One natural possibility is that your friend has mistaken a ketch for a yawl, and has formed a false belief. But if his vision is good and his line of sight favorable it is even more plausible that he does not use the word "yawl" quite as you do, and has made no mistake at all about the position of the jigger on the passing yacht. We do this sort of off the cuff interpretation all the time, deciding in favor of reinterpretation of words in order to preserve a reasonable theory of belief. As philosophers we are peculiarly tolerant of systematic malapropism, and practised at interpreting the result. The process is that of constructing a viable theory of belief and meaning from sentences held true.

Such examples emphasize the interpretation of anomalous details against a background of common beliefs and a going method of translation. But the principles involved must be the same in less trivial cases. What matters is this: if all we know is what sentences a speaker holds true, and we cannot assume that his language is our own, then we cannot take even a first step towards interpretation without knowing or assuming a great deal about the speaker's beliefs. Since knowledge of beliefs comes only with the ability to interpret words, the only possibility at the start is to assume general agreement on beliefs. We get a first approximation to a finished theory by assigning to sentences of a speaker conditions of truth that actually obtain (in our own opinion) just when the speaker holds those sentences true. The guiding policy is to do this as far as possible, subject to considerations of simplicity, hunches about the effects of social conditioning, and of course our common sense, or scientific, knowledge of explicable error.

The method is not designed to eliminate disagreement, nor can it; its purpose is to make meaningful disagreement possible, and this depends entirely on a foundation—*some* foundation—in agreement. The agreement may take the form of widespread sharing of sentences held true by speakers of "the same language," or agreement in the large mediated by a theory of truth contrived by an interpreter for speakers of another language.

Since charity is not an option, but a condition of having a workable theory, it is meaningless to suggest that we might fall into massive error by endorsing it. Until we have successfully established a systematic correlation of sentences held true with sentences held true, there are no mistakes to make. Charity is forced on us;—whether we like it or not, if we want to understand others, we must count them right in most matters. If we can produce a theory that reconciles charity and the formal conditions for a theory, we have done all that could be done to ensure communication. Nothing more is possible, and nothing more is needed.

We make maximum sense of the words and thoughts of others when we interpret in a way that optimizes agreement (this includes room, as we said, for explicable error, i.e. differences of opinion). Where does this leave the case for conceptual relativism? The answer is, I think, that we must say much the same thing about differences in conceptual scheme as we say about differences in belief: we improve the clarity and bite of declarations, of difference, whether of scheme or opinion, by enlarging the basis of shared (translatable) language or of shared opinion. Indeed, no clear line between the cases can be made out. If we choose to translate some alien sentence rejected by its speakers by a sentence to which we are strongly attached on a community basis, we may be tempted to call this a difference in schemes; if we decide to accommodate the evidence in other ways, it may be more natural to speak of a difference of opinion. But when others think differently from us, no general principle, or appeal to evidence, can force us to decide that the difference lies in our beliefs rather than in our concepts.

We must conclude, I think, that the attempt to give a solid meaning to the idea of conceptual relativism, and hence to the idea of a conceptual scheme, fares no better when based on partial failure of translation than when based on total failure. Given the underlying methodology of interpretation, we could not be in a position to judge that others had concepts or beliefs radically different from our own.

It would be wrong to summarize by saying we have shown how communication is possible between people who have different schemes, a way that works without need of what there cannot be, namely a neutral ground, or a common coordinate system. For we have found no intelligible basis on which it can be said that schemes are different. It would be equally wrong to announce the glorious news that all mankind—all speakers of language, at least—share a common scheme and ontology. For if we cannot intelligibly say that schemes are different, neither can we intelligibly say that they are one.

In giving up dependence on the concept of an uninterpreted reality, something outside all schemes and science, we do not relinquish the notion of objective truth—quite the contrary. Given the dogma of a dualism of scheme and reality, we get conceptual relativity, and truth relative to a scheme. Without the dogma, this kind of relativity goes by the board. Of course truth of sentences remains relative to language, but that is as objective as can be. In giving up the dualism of scheme and world, we do not give up the world, but reestablish unmediated touch with the familiar objects whose antics make our sentences and opinions true or false.

Notes

Presidential Address delivered before the Seventieth Annual Eastern Meeting of the American Philosophical Association in Atlanta, December 28, 1973.

1. B. L. Whorf, "The Punctual and Segmentative Aspects of Verbs in Hopi."
2. T. S. Kuhn, *The Structure of Scientific Revolutions.*
3. W. V. Quine, "Speaking of Objects," p. 24.
4. T. S. Kuhn, *The Structure of Scientific Revolutions*, p. 134.
5. Peter Strawson, *The Bounds of Sense*, London, 1966, p. 15.
6. Paul Feyerabend, "Explanation, Reduction, and Empiricism," in *Scientific Explanation, Space, and Time: Minnesota Studies in the Philosophy of Science*, Vol. III, Minneapolis. 1962, p. 82.
7. Benjamin Lee Whorf, *Language, Thought and Reality: Selected Writings of Benjamin Lee Whorf*, ed. J. B. Carroll, New York, 1956, p. 55.
8. Thomas Kuhn, "Reflection on my Critics" in *Criticism and the Growth of Knowledge*, eds. I. Lakatos and A. Musgrave, Cambridge, 1970, pp. 266, 267.

9. Paul Feyerabend, "Problems of Empiricism," in *Beyond the Edge of Certainty*, ed. R. G. Colodny, Englewood Cliffs, New Jersey, 1965, p. 214.

10. W.V.O. Quine, "Two Dogmas of Empiricism," reprinted in *From a Logical Point of View*, 2nd edition. Cambridge, Mass., 1961, p. 42.

11. *Ibid.*

12. *Ibid.*, p. 44.

13. W.V.O. Quine, "Speaking of Objects," reprinted in *Ontological Relativity and Other Essays*, New York. 1969, p. 1.

14. *Ibid.*, p. 25.

15. *Ibid.*, p. 24.

16. "Two Dogmas of Empiricism," p. 46.

17. These remarks arc defended in my "True to the Facts," *The Journal of Philosophy*, Vol. 66 (1969), pp. 748–764.

18. Alfred Tarski, "The Concept of Truth in Formalized Languages," in *Logic, Semantics, Metamathematics,* Oxford, 1956.

Putnam offers the now famous Twin Earth thought experiment in order to defend the thesis that the meaning of a term is at least in part settled by what exists in the world.

HILARY PUTNAM

Meaning and Reference

Unclear as it is, the traditional doctrine that the notion "meaning" possesses the extension/intension ambiguity has certain typical consequences. The doctrine that the meaning of a term is a concept carried the implication that meanings are mental entities. Frege, however, rebelled against this "psychologism." Feeling that meanings are *public* property—that the *same* meaning can be "grasped" by more than one person and by persons at different times—he identified concepts (and hence "intensions" or meanings) with abstract entities rather than mental entities. However, "grasping" these abstract entities was still an individual psychological act. None of these philosophers doubted that understanding a word (knowing its intension) was just a matter of being in a certain psychological state (somewhat in the way in which knowing how to factor numbers in one's head is just a matter of being in a certain very complex psychological state).

Secondly, the timeworn example of the two terms 'creature with a kidney' and 'creature with a heart' does show that two terms can have the same extension and yet differ in intension. But it was taken to be obvious that the reverse is impossible: two terms cannot differ in extension and have the same intension. Interestingly, no argument for this impossibility was ever offered. Probably it reflects the tradition of the ancient and medieval philosophers, who assumed that the concept corresponding to a term was just a conjunction of predicates, and hence that the concept corresponding to a term must a*lways* provide a necessary and sufficient condition for falling into the extension of the term. For philosophers like Carnap, who accepted the verifiability theory of meaning, the concept corresponding to a term provided (in the ideal case, where the term had "complete meaning") a *criterion* for belonging to the extension (not just in the sense of "necessary and sufficient condition," but in the strong sense of *way of recognizing* whether a given thing falls into the extension or not). So theory of meaning came to rest on two unchallenged assumptions:

(1) That knowing the meaning of a term is just a matter of being in a certain psychological state (in the sense of "psychological state," in which states of memory and belief are "psychological states"; no one thought that knowing the meaning of a word was a continuous state of consciousness, of course).

(2) That the meaning of a term determines its extension (in the sense that sameness of intension entails sameness of extension).

I shall argue that these two assumptions are not jointly satisfied by *any* notion, let alone any notion of meaning. The traditional concept of meaning is a concept which rests on a false theory.

Are Meanings in the Head?

For the purpose of the following science-fiction examples, we shall suppose that somewhere there is a planet we shall call Twin Earth. Twin Earth is very much like Earth: in fact, people on Twin Earth even speak *English*. In fact, apart from the differences we shall specify in our science-fiction examples, the reader may suppose that Twin Earth is *exactly* like Earth. He may even suppose that he has a *Doppelganger*—an identical copy—on Twin Earth, if he wishes, although my stories will not depend on this.

Although some of the people on Twin Earth (say, those who call themselves "Americans" and those who call themselves "Canadians" and those who call themselves "Englishmen," etc.) speak English, there are, not surprisingly, a few tiny differences between the dialects of English spoken on Twin Earth and standard English.

One of the peculiarities of Twin Earth is that the liquid called "water" is not H_2O but a different liquid whose chemical formula is very long and complicated. I shall abbreviate this chemical formula simply as XYZ. I shall suppose that XYZ is indistinguishable from water at normal temperatures and pressures. Also, I shall suppose that the oceans and lakes and seas of Twin Earth contain XYZ and not water, that it rains XYZ on Twin Earth and not water, etc.

If a space ship from Earth ever visits Twin Earth, then the supposition at first will be that 'water' has the same meaning on Earth and on Twin Earth. This supposition will be corrected when it is discovered that "water" on Twin Earth is XYZ, and the Earthian space ship will report somewhat as follows.

"On Twin Earth the word 'water' means XYZ."

Symmetrically, if a space ship from Twin Earth ever visits Earth, then the supposition at first will be that the word 'water' has the same meaning on Twin Earth and on Earth. This supposition will be corrected when it is discovered that "water" on Earth is H_2O, and the Twin Earthian space ship will report:

"On Earth the word 'water' means H_2O."

Note that there is no problem about the extension of the term 'water': the word simply has two different meanings (as we say); in the sense in which it is used on Twin Earth, the sense of water_{TE}, what *we* call "water" simply isn't water, while in the sense in which it is used on Earth, the sense of $water_E$, what the Twin Earthians call "water" simple isn't water. The extension of 'water' in the sense of $water_E$ is the set of all wholes consisting of H_2O molecules, or something like that; the extension of water in the sense of $water_{TE}$ is the set of all wholes consisting of XYZ molecules, or something like that.

Now let us roll the time back to about 1750. The typical Earthian speaker of English did not know that water consisted of hydrogen and oxygen, and the typical Twin-Earthian speaker of English did not know that "water" consisted of XYZ. Let $Oscar_1$ be such a typical Earthian English speaker, and let $Oscar_2$ be his counterpart on Twin Earth. You may suppose that there is no belief that $Oscar_1$ had about water that $Oscar_2$ did not have about "water." If you like, you may even suppose that $Oscar_1$ and $Oscar_2$ were exact duplicates in appearance, feelings, thoughts, interior monologue, etc. Yet the extension of the term 'water' was just as much H2O on Earth in 1750 as in 1950; and the extension of the term 'water' was just as much XYZ on Twin Earth in 1750 as in 1950. $Oscar_1$ and $Oscar_2$ understood the term 'water' differently in 1750 *although they were in the same psychological state*, and although, given the state of science at the time, it would have taken their scientific communities about fifty years to discover that they understood the term 'water' differently. Thus the extension of the term 'water' (and, in fact, its "meaning" in the intuitive preanalytical usage of that term) is *not* a function of the psychological state of the speaker by itself.[1]

But, it might be objected, why should we accept it that the term 'water' had the same extension in 1750 and in 1950 (on both Earths)? Suppose I point to a glass of water and say "this liquid is called water." My "ostensive definition" of water has the following empirical presupposition: that the body of liquid I am pointing to bears a certain sameness relation (say, *x is the same liquid as y*, or *x is the* $same_L$ *as y*) to most of the stuff I and other speakers in my linguistic community have on other occasions called "water." If this presupposition is false because, say, I am—unknown to me—pointing to a glass of gin and not a glass of water, then I do not intend my ostensive definition to be accepted. Thus the ostensive definition conveys what might be called a "defeasible" necessary and sufficient condition: the necessary and sufficient condition for being water is bearing the relation $same_L$ to the stuff in the glass; but this is the necessary and sufficient condition only if the empirical presupposition is satisfied. If it is not satisfied, then one of a series of, so to speak, "fallback" conditions becomes activated.

The key point is that the relation $same_L$ is a *theoretical* relation: whether something is or is not the same liquid as *this* may take an indeterminate amount of scientific investigation to determine. Thus, the fact that an English speaker in 1750 might have called XYZ "water," whereas he or his successors would not have called XYZ water in 1800 or 1850 does not mean that the "meaning" of 'water' changed for the average speaker in the interval. In 1750 or in 1850 or in 1950 one might have pointed to, say, the liquid in Lake Michigan as an example of "water." What changed was that in 1750 we would have mistakenly thought that XYZ bore the relation $same_L$ to the liquid in Lake Michigan, whereas in 1800 or 1850 we would have known that it did not.

Let us now modify our science-fiction story. I shall suppose that molybdenum pots and pans *can't* be distinguished from aluminum pots and pans save by an expert. (This could be true for all I know, and, *a fortiori*, it could be true for all I know by virtue of "knowing the meaning" of the words *aluminum* and *molybdenum.*) We will now suppose that molybdenum is as common on Twin Earth as aluminum is on Earth, and that aluminum is as rare on Twin Earth as molybdenum is on Earth. In particular, we shall assume that "aluminum" pots and pans are made of molybdenum on Twin Earth. Finally, we shall assume that the words 'aluminum' and 'molybdenum' are *switched* on Twin Earth: 'aluminum' is the name of *molybdenum*, and 'molybdenum' is the name of *aluminum.* If a space ship from Earth visited Twin Earth, the visitors from Earth probably would not suspect that the "aluminum" pots and pans on Twin Earth were not made of aluminum, especially when the Twin Earthians *said* they were. But there is one important difference between the two cases. An Earthian metallurgist could tell very easily that "aluminum" was molybdenum, and a Twin Earthian metallurgist could tell equally easily that aluminum was "molybdenum." (The shudder quotes in the preceding sentence indicate Twin Earthian usages.) Whereas in 1750 no one on either Earth or Twin Earth could have distinguished water from "water," the confusion of aluminum with "aluminum" involves only a part of the linguistic communities involved.

This example makes the same point as the preceding example. If Oscar$_1$ and Oscar$_2$ are standard speakers of Earthian English and Twin Earthian English, respectively, and neither is chemically or metallurgically sophisticated, then there may be no difference at all in their psychological states when they use the word 'aluminum'; nevertheless, we have to say that 'aluminum' has the extension *aluminum* in the idiolect of Oscar$_1$ and the extension *molybdenum* in the idiolect of Oscar$_2$. (Also we have to say that Oscar$_1$ and Oscar$_2$ mean different things by 'aluminum'; that 'aluminum' has a different meaning on Earth than it does on Twin Earth, etc.) Again we see that the psychological state of the speaker does *not* determine the extension (or the "meaning," speaking preanalytically) of the word.

Before discussing this example further, let me introduce a *non*-science-fiction example. Suppose you are like me and cannot tell an elm from a beech tree. We still say that the extension of 'elm' in my idiolect is the same as the extension of 'elm' in anyone else's, viz., the set of all elm trees, and that the set of all beech trees is the extension of 'beech' in *both* of our idiolects. Thus 'elm' in my idiolect has a different extension from 'beech' in your idiolect (as it should). Is it really credible that this difference in extension is brought about by some difference in our *concepts?* My *concept* of an elm tree is exactly the same as my concept of a beech tree (I blush to confess). If someone heroically attempts to maintain that the difference between the extension of 'elm' and the extension of 'beech' in *my* idiolect is explained by a difference in my psychological state, then we can always refute him by constructing a "Twin Earth" example—just let the words 'elm' and 'beech' be switched on Twin Earth (the way 'aluminum' and "molybdenum' were in the previous example). Moreover, suppose I have a *Doppelganger* on Twin Earth who is molecule for molecule "identical" with me. If you are a dualist, then also suppose my Doppelganger thinks the same verbalized thoughts I do, has the same sense data, the same dispositions, etc. It is absurd to think *his* psychological state is one bit different from mine: yet he "means" *beech* when he says "elm," and *I* "mean" *elm* when I say "elm." Cut the pie any way you like, "meanings" just ain't in the *head!*

A Sociolinguistic Hypothesis

The last two examples depend upon a fact about language that seems, surprisingly, never to have been pointed out: that there is *division of linguistic labor.* We could hardly use such words as 'elm' and 'aluminum' if no one possessed a way of recognizing elm trees and aluminum metal; but not everyone to whom the distinction is important has to be able to make the distinction. Let us shift the example; consider *gold.* Gold is important for many reasons: it is a precious metal; it is a monetary metal; it has symbolic value (it is important to most people that the "gold" wedding ring they wear really consist of gold and not just *look* gold); etc. Consider our community as a "factory": in this "factory" some people have the "job" of *wearing gold wedding rings*; other people have the "job" of selling gold wedding rings; still other people have the job of *telling whether or not something is really gold.* It is not at all necessary or efficient that every one who wears a gold ring (or a gold cufflink, etc.), or discusses the "gold standard," etc., engage in buying and selling gold. Nor is it necessary or efficient that every one who buys and sells gold be able to tell whether or not something is really gold in a society where this form of dishonesty is uncommon (selling fake gold) and in which one can easily consult an expert in case of doubt. And it is *certainly* not necessary or efficient that every one who has occasion to buy or wear gold be able to tell with any reliability whether or not something is really gold.

The foregoing facts are just examples of mundane division of labor (in a wide sense). But they engender a division of linguistic labor: every one to whom gold is important for any reason has to *acquire* the word 'gold'; but he does not have to acquire the *method of recognizing* whether something is or is not gold. He can rely on a special subclass of speakers. The features that are generally thought to be present in connection with a general name—necessary and sufficient conditions for membership in the extension, ways of recognizing whether something is in the extension, etc.—are all present in the linguistic community *considered as a collective body;* but that collective body divides the "labor" of knowing and employing these various parts of the "meaning" of 'gold.'

This division of linguistic labor rests upon and presupposes the division of *non*linguistic labor, of course. If only the people who know how to tell whether some metal is really gold or not have any reason to have the word 'gold' in their vocabulary, then the word 'gold' will be as the word 'water' was in 1750 with respect to that subclass of speakers, and the other speakers just won't acquire it at all. And some words do not exhibit any division of linguistic labor: 'chair', for example. But with the increase of division of labor in the society and the rise of science, more and more words begin to exhibit this kind of division of labor. 'Water', for example, did not exhibit it at all before the rise of chemistry. Today it is obviously necessary for every speaker to be able to recognize water (reliably under normal conditions), and probably most adult speakers even know the necessary and sufficient condition "water is H_2O," but only a few adult speakers could distinguish water from liquids that superficially resembled water. In case of doubt, other speakers would rely on the judgment of these "expert" speakers. Thus the way of recognizing possessed by these "expert" speakers is also, through them, possessed by the collective linguistic body, even though it is not possessed by each individual member of the body, and in this way the most *recherché* fact about water may become part of the *social* meaning of the word although unknown to almost all speakers who acquire the word.

It seems to me that this phenomenon of division of linguistic labor is one that it will be very important for sociolinguistics to investigate. In connection with it, I should like to propose the following hypothesis:

> hypothesis of the universality of the division of linguistic labor:
> Every linguistic community exemplifies the sort of division of linguistic labor just described; that is, it possesses at least some terms whose associated "criteria" are known only to a subset of the speakers who acquire the terms, and whose use by the other speakers depends upon a structured cooperation between them and the speakers in the relevant subsets.

It is easy to see how this phenomenon accounts for some of the examples given above of the failure of the assumptions (1 and 2). When a term is subject to the division of linguistic labor, the "average" speaker who acquires it does not acquire anything that fixes its extension. In particular, his individual psychological state *certainly* does not fix its extension; it is only the sociolinguistic state of the collective linguistic body to which the speaker belongs that fixes the extension.

We may summarize this discussion by pointing out that there are two sorts of tools in the world: there are tools like a hammer or a screwdriver which can be used by one person; and there are tools like a steamship which require the cooperative activity of a number of persons to use. Words have been thought of too much on the model of the first sort of tool.

Indexicality and Rigidity

The first of our science-fiction examples—'water' on Earth and on Twin Earth in 1750—does not involve division of linguistic labor, or at least does not involve it in the same way the examples of 'aluminum' and 'elm' do. There were not (in our story, anyway) any "experts" on water on Earth in 1750, nor any experts on "water" on Twin Earth. The example *does* involve things which are of fundamental importance to the theory of reference and also to the theory of necessary truth, which we shall now discuss.

Let W_1 and W_2 be two possible worlds in which I exist and in which this glass exists and in which I am giving a meaning explanation by pointing to this glass and saying "This is water." Let us suppose that in W_1 the glass is full of H_2O and in W_2 the glass is full of XYZ. We shall also suppose that W_1 is the *actual* world, and that XYZ is the stuff typically called "water" in the world W_2 (so that the relation between English speakers in W_1 and English speakers in W_2 is exactly the same as the relation between English speakers on Earth and English speakers on Twin Earth). Then there are two theories one might have concerning the meaning of 'water':

> (1) One might hold that 'water' was *world-relative* but *constant* in meaning (i.e., the word has a constant relative meaning). On this theory, 'water' means the same in W_1 and W_2; it's just that water is H_2O in $W_{1,}$ and water is XYZ in W_2.
>
> (2) One might hold that water is H_2O in all worlds (the stuff called "water" in W_2 isn't water), but 'water' doesn't have the same meaning in W_1 and W_2.

If what was said before about the Twin Earth case was correct, then (2) is clearly the correct theory. When I say "*this* (liquid) is water," the "this" is, so to speak, a *de re* "this"—i.e., the force of my explanation is that "water" is whatever bears a certain equivalence relation (the relation we called "*same*$_L$" above) to the piece of liquid referred to as "this" *in the actual world.*

We might symbolize the difference between the two theories as a "scope" difference in the following way. On theory (1), the following is true:

> (1') (For every world *W*) (For every *x* in *W*) (*x* is water ≡ *x* bears *same*$_L$ to the entity referred to as "this" in *W*)

while on theory (2):

> (2') (For every world *W*) (For every *x* in *W*) (*x* is water ≡ *x* bears *same*$_L$, to the entity referred to as "this" in the actual world W_1).

I call this a "scope" difference because in (1′) 'the entity referred to as "this"' is within the scope of 'For every world *W*'—as the qualifying phrase 'in *W*' makes explicit—whereas in (2′) 'the entity referred to as "this"' means "the entity referred to as 'this' *in the actual world*,' and has thus a reference *independent* of the bound variable 'W'.

Kripke calls a designator "rigid" (in a given sentence) if (in that sentence) it refers to the same individual in every possible world in which the designator designates. If we extend this notion of rigidity to substance names, then we may express Kripke's theory and mine by saying that the term 'water' is *rigid*.

The rigidity of the term 'water' follows from the fact that when I give the "ostensive definition": "*this* (liquid) is water," I intend (2′) and not (1′).

We may also say, following Kripke, that when I give the "ostensive definition "*this* (liquid) is water," the demonstrative 'this' is *rigid.*

What Kripke was the first to observe is that this theory of the meaning (or "use," or whatever) of the word 'water' (and other natural-kind terms as well) has startling consequences for the theory of necessary truth.

To explain this, let me introduce the notion of a *cross-world relation.* A two-term relation *R* will be called *cross-world* when it is understood in such a way that its extension is a set of ordered pairs of individuals *not all in the same possible world.* For example, it is easy to understand the relation *same height as* as a cross-world relation: just understand it so that, e.g., if x is an individual in a world W_1 who is 5 feet tall (in W_1) and y is an individual in W_2 who is 5 feet tall (in W_2), then the ordered pair x, y belongs to the extension of *same height as.* (Since an individual may have different heights in different possible worlds in which that same individual exists, strictly speaking, it is not the ordered pair x, y that constitutes an element of the extension of *same height as*, but rather the ordered pair *x-in-world-* W_1, *y-in-world-* W_2.)

Similarly, we can understand the relation $same_L$ (same liquid as) as a cross-world relation by understanding it so that a liquid in world W_1 which has the same important physical properties (in W_1) that a liquid in W_2 possesses (in W_2) bears $same_L$ to the latter liquid.

Then the theory we have been presenting may be summarized by saying that an entity x, in an arbitrary possible world, is *water* if and only if it bears the relation $same_L$ (construed as a cross-world relation) to the stuff *we* call "water" in the actual world.

Suppose, now, that I have not yet discovered what the important physical properties of water are (in the actual world)—i.e., I don't yet know that water is H_2O. I may have ways of *recognizing* water that are successful (of course, I may make a small number of mistakes that I won't be able to detect until a later stage in our scientific development), but not know the microstructure of water. If I agree that a liquid with the superficial properties of "water" but a different microstructure *isn't really water,* then my ways of recognizing water cannot be regarded as an analytical specification of what *it is to be* water. Rather, the operational definition, like the ostensive one, is simply a way of pointing out a standard—pointing out the stuff *in the actual world* such that, for x to be water, in *any* world, is for x to bear the relation $same_L$ to the *normal* members of the class of *local* entities that satisfy the operational definition. "Water" on Twin Earth is not water, even if it satisfies the operational definition, because it doesn't bear $same_L$ to the *local* stuff that satisfies the operational definition, and local stuff that satisfies the operational definition but has a microstructure different from the rest of the local stuff that satisfies the operational definition isn't water either, because it doesn't bear $same_L$ to the *normal* examples of the local "water."

Suppose, now, that I discover the microstructure of water—that water is H_2O. At this point I will be able to say that the stuff on Twin Earth that I earlier *mistook* for water isn't really water. In the same way, if you describe, not another planet in the actual universe, but another possible universe in which there is stuff with the chemical formula XYZ which passes the "operational test" for *water*, we shall have to say that that stuff isn't water but merely XYZ. You will not have described a possible world in which "water is XYZ," but merely a possible world in which there are lakes of XYZ, people drink XYZ (and not water), or whatever. In fact, once we have discovered the nature of water, nothing counts as a possible world in which water doesn't have that nature. Once we have discovered that water (in the actual world) is H_2O, *nothing counts as a possible world in which water isn't H_2O.*

On the other hand, we can perfectly well imagine having experiences that would convince us (and that would make it rational to believe that) water *isn't* H2O. In that sense, it is conceivable that water isn't H_2O. It is conceivable but it isn't possible! Conceivability is no proof of possibility.

Kripke refers to statements that are rationally unrevisable (assuming there are such) as *epistemically necessary*. Statements that are true in all possible worlds he refers to simply as necessary (or sometimes as "metaphysically necessary"). In this terminology, the point just made can be restated as: a statement can be (metaphysically) necessary and epistemically contingent. Human intuition has no privileged access to metaphysical necessity.

In this paper, our interest is in theory of meaning, however, and not in theory of necessary truth. Words like 'now', 'this', 'here' have long been recognized to be *indexical*, or *token-reflexive*—i.e., to have an extension which varies from context to context or token to token. For these words, no one has ever suggested the traditional theory that "intension determines extension." To take our Twin Earth example: if I have a *Doppelganger* on Twin Earth, then when I think "I have a headache," *he* thinks "I have a headache." But the extension of the particular token of 'I' in his verbalized thought is himself (or his unit class, to be precise), while the extension of the token of 'I' in *my* verbalized thought is *me* (or my unit class, to be precise). So the same word, 'I', has two different extensions in two different idiolects; but it does not follow that the concept I have of myself is in any way different from the concept my *Doppelganger* has of himself.

Now then, we have maintained that indexicality extends beyond the *obviously* indexical words and morphemes (e.g., the tenses of verbs). Our theory can be summarized as saying that words like 'water' have an unnoticed indexical component: "water" is stuff that bears a certain similarity relation to the water *around here*. Water at another time or in another place or even in another possible world has to bear the relation $same_L$ to *our* "water" *in order to be water*. Thus the theory that (1) words have "intensions," which are something like concepts associated with the words by speakers; and (2) intension determines extension—cannot be true of natural-kind words like 'water' for the same reason it cannot be true of obviously indexical words like 'I'.

The theory that natural-kind words like 'water' are indexical leaves it open, however, whether to say that 'water' in the Twin Earth dialect of English has the same *meaning* as 'water' in the Earth dialect and a different extension—which is what we normally say about 'I' in different idiolects—thereby giving up the doctrine that "meaning (intension) determines extension," or to say, as we have chosen to do, that difference in extension is *ipso facto* a difference in meaning for natural-kind words, thereby giving up the doctrine that meanings are concepts, or, indeed, mental entities of *any* kind.[2]

It should be clear, however, that Kripke's doctrine that natural-kind words are rigid designators and our doctrine that they are indexical are but two ways of making the same point.

We have now seen that the extension of a term is not fixed by a concept that the individual speaker has in his head, and this is true both because extension is, in general, determined *socially*—there is division of linguistic labor as much as of "real" labor—and because extension is, in part, determined *indexically*. The extension of our terms depends upon the actual nature of the particular things that serve as paradigms, and this actual nature is not, in general, fully known to the speaker. Traditional semantic theory leaves out two contributions to the determination of reference—the contribution of society and the contribution of the real world; a better semantic theory must encompass both.

Notes

1. See fn 2, p. 710 below, and the corresponding text.

2. Our reasons for rejecting the first option—to say that 'water' has the same meaning on Earth and on Twin Earth, while giving up the doctrine that meaning determines reference—are presented in "The Meaning of 'Meaning.'" They may be illustrated thus: Suppose 'water' has the same meaning on Earth and on Twin Earth. Now, let the word 'water' become phonemically different on Twin Earth—say, it becomes 'quaxel.' Presumably, this is not a change in meaning per se, on any view. So 'water' and 'quaxel' have the same meaning (although they refer to different liquids). But this is highly counterintuitive. Why not say, then, that 'elm' in my idiolect has the same meaning as 'beech' in your idiolect, although they refer to different trees?

In this essay, Putnam makes the case for a reconstruction of realism.

HILARY PUTNAM

Realism with a Human Face

Part One: Realism

In this essay I hope it will become clear that my indebtedness to Kant is very large, even if it must be "this side idolatry." For me, at least, almost all the problems of philosophy attain the form in which they are of real interest only with the work of Kant. Now, however, I want to do something which a *true* Kant lover might regard as virtually blasphemous: I want to begin this essay by meditating on a remark of Nietzsche's. I trust that the remark is one that Kant would not have been offended by.

In *The Birth of Tragedy* Nietzsche writes that "as the circle of science grows larger it touches paradox at more places." Part One of this essay will be a meditation on this wonderful aphorism. My interest is not in Nietzsche (although he is immensely interesting), nor in Nietzsche's text, but in the remark itself; which is to say that the remark, as I wish to understand it here, is entangled with the thought and experience of our own time, not Nietzsche's. The remark is about "the circle of science," however, and so I want to look at science, and at how the world can become more paradoxical as the circle of scientific knowledge enlarges. Nietzsche's remark could be illustrated with materials from just about any scientific field, but I want to consider just two examples here.

My first example is from an area which is familiar to a few, but highly esoteric stuff to most educated people: the field of quantum mechanics. It is not my purpose here to talk technicalities, so I will not try to describe the theory at all. What I will rather attempt to describe is a discussion which started almost as soon as quantum mechanics itself started and which is still going on—the discussion of "how to interpret" quantum mechanics.

Such discussions are not unprecedented in the history of science, but the *reasons* for the dispute are highly unusual. Let me try to state those reasons in a highly schematized form. The theory, as it was formulated by Bohr and also (somewhat differently) by von Neumann applies to a dynamical system—say, a system of elementary particles, or a system of fields and particles. As in classical physics, the system can be quite small—one or two or three particles—or it can "in principle" be quite large. But—here is the curious feature which was *not* present in classical physics—any application of the theory requires that, *in addition* to the "system" being talked about, there be "apparatus" or an "observer" which is *not* included in the system. In principle, then, there is no "quantum mechanical theory of the whole universe."[1]

The wise men of the founding generation of quantum mechanics—men like Eugene Wigner—talked of a "cut between the system and the observer." The apparatus, which eventually makes the measurement which test the predictions of the theory, is said to be on the "observer's" side of the "cut." In Bohr's own version of the so-called Copenhagen Interpretation (which is actually a family of interpretations due to Bohr, von Neumann, Heisenberg, Wigner, and others, all different to a larger or a smaller extent), *every property of the system is considered to have meaning and existence only in relation to a particular measuring apparatus in a particular experimental situation.* In addition, the measuring apparatus is supposed to be satisfactorily describable (as far as its function in the experiment goes) using only the language and the mathematical formulas of classical physics (including special relativity). Thus, on Bohr's view, quantum mechanics does not make classical physics simply *obsolete*; rather, it presupposes classical physics in a way in which, for example, it would be absurd to claim that Newtonian physics presupposes medieval physics. The use of quantum mechanics to describe the "system" presupposes the use of a theory most people would consider incompatible with quantum mechanics—classical physics—to describe the apparatus!

This is paradoxical enough, but the dependence of quantum physics on classical physics (in Bohr's version of the Copenhagen Interpretation) is not the paradox I am trying to direct attention to.

Let me go back to a remark I made a moment ago: the remark that, in principle, there is no "quantum mechanical theory of the whole universe." It is part of the appeal of Newton's vision—and I speak of Newton's *vision* because Newton's physics had a peculiar *visualizability* that had an enormous amount to do with its impact on theology, philosophy, psychology, the whole culture—that it presents us with (what the seventeenth century took to be) a "God's-Eye View" of the whole universe. The universe is a giant machine, and if you are a materialist, then we ourselves are just subsystems in the giant machine. If you are a Cartesian dualist, then our bodies are just subsystems in the giant machine. Our measurements, our observations, insofar as they can be described physically, are just interactions *within* the whole shebang. The dream of a picture of the universe which is so complete that it actually includes the theorist-observer in the act of picturing the universe is the dream, of a physics which is also a metaphysics (or of a physics which once and for all makes metaphysics unnecessary). Even dualists like Descartes dreamed the dream; they just felt we have to have an additional fundamental science, a fundamental science of Psychology to describe "the soul or the mind or the intellect," to carry out the dream completely. That dream has haunted Western culture since the seventeenth century. You could describe it as the dream of a circle of science which has expanded until there is nothing outside of itself—and hence, no paradoxes left for it to touch! Anyone who has ever done work, experimental or mathematical, with a *real* scientific theory must have felt this dream.

But Bohr's Copenhagen Interpretation gives up precisely this dream! Like Kant, Bohr felt that the world "in itself" was beyond the powers of the human mind to picture; the new twist—one Kant would never have accepted—is that even the "empirical world," the world of our experience, cannot be completely described with just *one* picture, according to Bohr. Instead, we have to make a "complementary" use of different classical pictures—wave pictures in some experimental situations, particle pictures in others—and give up the idea of a single picturable account to cover all situations.

Bohr's ideas were highly controversial, and remain so today. The first of the ideas that I mentioned—that quantum mechanics essentially presupposes the use of classical physics (to describe the measuring apparatus)—does not, I think, stand up. Von Neumann's classical work showed us how to analyze measurement in purely quantum mechanical terms.[2] But the "cut between the observer and the system" has proved more robust, and it is this cut and the idea of the relativity of physical concepts to the experimental situation that are the heart of the Bohr interpretation. Very few physicists today would understand "complementarity" as referring primarily to the complementary use of *classical* concepts, as Bohr did. In what follows, that aspect of Bohr's thought will not occupy us further.

To see how far opponents of the Copenhagen Interpretation are willing to go, let me describe a problem that was immediately raised in connection with the Copenhagen view(s), as well as an anti-Copenhagen response to the same problem, one that was, however, proposed many years later.

Suppose I have a system that is described as completely as quantum mechanics knows how to describe one. Descriptions, in quantum mechanics, are called "states,"[3] and a description that is as complete as the formalism allows is called a "maximal state" (also called a "wave function" or a "psi function"). For the sake of definiteness, imagine that the system is a radium atom about to undergo radioactive decay. Simplifying matters somewhat, let us say that at the future time *t* the atom may either be in the original state, call it A, or in a "decayed" state, B. (In other words, the atom may either have emitted or may have failed to emit one or more quanta of radiation.) The "indeterministic" character of the theory is *not* reflected in the mathematical formalism at all! Mathematically, the formalism—the famous Schroedinger equation—tells one that the atom will undergo a transition from its original state, call it A, into a new state $A^{\#}$. The fact that the atom may either have decayed (into state B) or not decayed (stayed in state A) is reflected *not* by the presence of a statistical element in the Schroedinger equation itself, as one would expect in the case of a normal stochastic theory, but rather by the fact that the new state $A^{\#}$ is, in a certain sense, a "superposition" of the two alternative possibilities A and B.

This feature of the theory was seized upon by opponents of the Copenhagen Interpretation from the beginning—and the opponents included Einstein as well as Schroedinger himself. "Aha!" they cried, "You see, the so-called 'superposition' of A and B is not really a complete description at all. When you say 'the system will be in state $A^{\#}$' what that means is that the system will *either* be in state A or in state B.

Quantum mechanics is just not a complete description of physical reality. Its so-called 'maximal states,' such as A#, are only partial descriptions."

Defenders of the Copenhagen Interpretation[4] replied that the prediction that the atom will go into state A# refers to what the atom will do when it is isolated—*a fortiori*, when *no* measurement is made. If a measurement is made at time *t*, then the measurement "throws" the system into either the state A or the state B. The deterministic transition

A——>A#

governs the evolution of the isolated radium atom. (This transition is so "nonclassical" that any attempt to actually *picture* it is inappropriate, the defenders of the Copenhagen Interpretation say.) The stochastic transition

A# ——> *either* A *or* B

governs the measurement interaction. (This stochastic transition is the famous "collapse of the wave packet.")

I must ask non-scientists to excuse what must sound like a lapse into technicality; what I am setting the stage for is not the exposition of the scientific theory, but rather the presentation of a surprising event in the recent history of science—one whose significance I shall leave it to the reader to judge.

The event I refer to is the appearance on the scene some years ago of the so-called Many-Worlds Interpretation of quantum mechanics. This interpretation, which was proposed by Everett and De Witt,[5] and for a time supported by John Wheeler, still has some enthusiastic proponents among quantum cosmologists. But it sounds more like something from the latest science fiction best seller than like a theory expounded by serious scientists.

What the theory says can be explained (informally, of course) with the aid of my little example of the atom which does or does not undergo radioactive decay. According to the Many-Worlds Interpretation, the *entire cosmological universe* is a "system" in the sense of quantum mechanics. Thus the "cut between the observer and the system" is simply rejected. This interpretation aims at restoring the feature of the Newtonian *Weltanschauung* that I referred to as its "God's-Eye View" of the world—restoring that feature at virtually any price. Moreover, according to this interpretation, the Schroedinger equation[6] is the only equation governing physical processes—the universe evolves *deterministically* according to this view; the indeterminism thought to be characteristic of quantum mechanics is also rejected. There is no "reduction of the wave packet." What happens in an experimental situation like the one described, according to the Many-Worlds Interpretation, is not that the universe makes an indeterministic "jump" into either the state A or the state B when the measurement is made,[7] but that the universe "splits" into two parallel worlds (mathematically, one of these is represented by the "relative state" A and the other by the "relative state" B). In one of these "parallel worlds" or "branches" the atom decays; in the other it does not.

But what about the observer, say *me*? Well, if I am the observer, then—according to Everett and De Witt and their supporters—I will have *two* "future selves" at the time *t*. Each of my future selves will, of course, think that it is the only "Hilary Putnam" and that its "branch" is the "whole world." But each of my future selves will be wrong. There will be two Hilary Putnams, one experiencing a "world in which the atom did not decay" and one experiencing a "world in which the atom decayed"!

As a philosopher, I am fascinated by the appearance of the Many-Worlds Interpretation as a cultural phenomenon. This is so similar to what we have seen over and over again in the history of metaphysics! A well-known poet (Derek Walcott) once riddled, "What is the difference between a philosopher and a ruler?" The answer was a pun: "A ruler will only stretch to one foot, but a philosopher will go to any length." But the pun contains a deep observation; it *is* part of our philosophical tradition that at least one kind of philosopher will go to any length to preserve what he regards as a central metaphysical principle, a principle that is "necessary" in the peculiar philosophical sense of "necessary." What is startling is to observe a metaphysical system as daring as any being born in the unexpected locus of a discussion among physicists about how to understand the deepest and the most accurate physical theory we possess.

Obviously, no one proposed anything as extreme as the Many-Worlds Interpretation until many other suggestions which are not as extreme had been tried out and rejected. And I cannot emphasize too strongly that only a small minority—an extremely small minority—of physicists feels any discomfort with the Copenhagen Interpretation to the present day. But there is and always has been a small minority—which included Einstein and Schroedinger, as I remarked—which does feel discomfort, and which tried and still tries to find a "God's-Eye View" to replace the "cut between the system and the observer."

At the beginning, opponents of the quantum mechanical orthodoxy looked for what were called "hidden variables." The idea was that quantum mechanics is an *incomplete* description of the physical world, and that if we found out how to complete it, by adding the missing parameters (the "hidden" ones), we would simultaneously get rid of the "objectionable" features—indeterminism, the clash with "realist" intuitions—*and* perceive that quantum mechanics is not giving us the ultimate physical processes, but only a kind of statistically average description of processes. The most famous attempt of this kind was made by David Bohm, whose interpretation has recently been revived and modified by J. S. Bell. The problems with this approach were summarized by Hans Reichenbach in his book on the foundations of quantum mechanics,[8] in the form of what he called a Principle of Anomaly. The principle says that there are, indeed, various ways of supplementing quantum mechanics with "hidden variables," but all of them require the postulation of instantaneous action at a distance, "clairvoyance" on the part of the "system" (that is, it acts, in certain situations, as if it "knew" which measurement was going to be made in the future), or other "causal anomalies." Although Reichenbach's attempt at a mathematical demonstration of this

Principle of Anomaly cannot be accepted, an argument more recently offered by Bell shows that he is right. Since I am looking at the history of physics from a cultural, as well as from a logical, point of view, let me remark that the truth of the Principle of Anomaly accounts for the fact that, although there are, indeed, a number of hidden variable interpretations around, none of them convinces anyone but the inventor and (if he is lucky) up to six friends.

It is only in the light of the failure—or what the scientific community has perceived as the failure—of these many attempts to restore the God's-Eye View conception of physics while continuing to accept the framework of quantum mechanics that one can understand why anyone would even be tempted to try anything as metaphysically dramatic as the Many-Worlds Interpretation. In the Many-Worlds Interpretation there are no "hidden variables"—*every* fact is *completely* described by the "maximal state" of the whole Universe, with all its "branches." Of course, many facts are "hidden" from this particular "self." But no fact is hidden from God, or from any omniscient mind, since the omniscient observer knows the "state function of the whole Universe," and that state function codes *all* the information about *all* the "branches"—all the "parallel worlds." And it codes it in good old everyday quantum mechanical language, the language of "states"—there is no supplementation with "hidden variables" that are not describable in the existing formalism.

Of course, this is a queer sense of "no hidden variables," at least from a layman's point of view. *Whole parallel worlds and other selves that I can't observe*—aren't *these* "hidden variables" with a vengeance? Not from the point of view of the Omniscient Quantum Physicist—and it is the Omniscient Quantum Physicist's point of view that this interpretation tries to capture.

Again, in this interpretation, there are no "nonlocal interactions"—the splitting of the world into parallel worlds vitiates the proof of Bell's Theorem—and, in particular, there is no "reduction of the wave packet." The space-time structure is that of relativistic physics (which is why it is cosmologists that are especially attracted to it). And the logic is classical logic. Only one problem remains:[9] all this talk of "other worlds" is, after all, only a *picture*, and the picture, if we accept it, does nothing for us but give us metaphysical comfort. At no point does this wild ontological extravaganza really change the practice of physics in any way. It only reassures us that a God's-Eye View is still possible.

Actually, it doesn't really do that. For, alas, we don't find that this picture is one we can *believe*. What good is a metaphysical picture one can't believe?

I began this essay with a quotation from Nietzsche. I hope that the discussion I just reviewed illustrates the truth of the aphorism that I took as the subject for my musings here: "As the circle of science grows larger, it touches paradox at more places." *Indeed!* Quantum mechanics is a beautiful example of the way in which increased understanding can make the world a more paradoxical place.

I shall shortly place by the side of this example a very different illustration of the same fact. But before I leave quantum mechanics, let us consider for a moment the nature of the paradox involved. The problem is often posed as a clash between our desire to interpret quantum mechanics realistically and our desire to preserve the principle that one cannot send causal signals faster than light. But this way of explaining what is paradoxical about the present state of our understanding of quantum mechanics is too formalistic. Rather than viewing the paradox as a "clash between realism and locality," I myself prefer to go back to the discussion as it was when Bohr first put forward his Copenhagen Interpretation.

Although von Neumann did not accept the claim that classical physics must be used on the "observer" side of the "cut between the system and the observer," he certainly agreed that there was such a cut, as did all the proponents of the Copenhagen Interpretation in that period. And I suggest that—as was, indeed, felt at the time—it was the need for and presence of such a cut that is the most paradoxical feature of the theory. "Locality" enters the discussion when we consider whether we can change or reinterpret the theory so as to avoid the need for the cut; but so do many other issues (can we change classical logic? can we change classical probability theory?[10] are "parallel worlds" intelligible?). Although the discussion in the last ten years has fixated on Locality and on Bell's Theorem, these issues are best considered as forming the technical background to the problem. What is paradoxical is the upshot, the need to recognize a cut between the observer and the system in any quantum mechanical description of physical reality. And we feel this to be a paradox precisely because what it means to have a cut between the observer and the system is, as I said at the outset, that a great dream is given up—the dream of a description of physical reality as it is apart from observers, a description which is objective in the sense of being "from no particular point of view." In short, I contend that it is the clash with "realism" in this sense that we consider paradoxical; our unwillingness to give up our belief in locality of course figures as well, in that physicists refuse to restore "realism" by just adopting some ad hoc nonlocal theory for the sake of satisfying our discomfort, but it should go without saying that ad hoc ways out of a paradoxical situation are not acceptable.

Logic and the God's-Eye View

My next example comes from logic—more precisely, from the response of modern logic to the most ancient of logical paradoxes, the puzzle of the Liar. Rather than consider the statement "All Cretans are liars" (uttered by a Cretan),[11] modern treatments begin with some such example as the following sentence:

(I) The sentence (I) is false.

I suppose someone might think that it is illegitimate to use "(I)" to name an expression which contains "(I)" itself as a proper part, but many forms of "self-reference" are quite harmless. (Consider: "Write down the sentence I am uttering in your notebook.") In any case, the suggestion that we throw self-reference out of the language turns out to be excessively costly; in fact, Gödel showed that as long as our language contains number theory, there will always be ways of constructing sentences that refer to themselves. So we shall stipulate that (I) cannot be denied the status of a proper sentence *merely* on the ground that it mentions itself. But then, it seems, we have a paradox.

We normally develop the paradox by observing that if the sentence (I) is true, then it must be false. But how do we do this? We have to accept the principle that *to say of a sentence that it is true is equivalent to asserting the sentence.* Tarski, the founder of the modern logical theory of these matters,[12] used "Snow is white" as his example of a typical sentence, and the requirement that any satisfactory treatment of truth must enable us to show that

"Snow is white" is true if and only if snow is white

has become a famous example in the philosophical as well as in the logical literature. Now, if we accept sentence (I) as having a truth-value at all (if it doesn't, then it is not in the scope of Tarski's theory), it follows by the principle just mentioned that

(i) "(I) is false" is true if and only if (I) is false,

and hence

(ii) "(I) is false" is true if and only if "(I) is false" is false

—which is a contradiction!

So far no inconsistency has actually resulted. We assumed that "(I) is false" has a truth-value, and that assertion has now been refuted. We cannot consistently assert either that (I) is true or that (I) is false. But why should we *want* to assert either? Is it not natural to say that (I) is neither true nor false?

Indeed it is. But now another paradox arises to haunt us—the paradox Charles Parsons has called the Strong Liar. One form is:

(II) The sentence (II) is either false or lacks a truth-value.

The sentence (II) is paradoxical because, if we try to avoid the previous argument by denying that (II) has a truth-value, that is by asserting

(II) lacks a truth-value,

then it obviously follows that

(II) is either false or lacks a truth-value

—and the sentence (II) is one that we discover ourselves to have just asserted! So we must agree that (II) is true; which means that we have contradicted ourselves.

To Tarski it seemed—and this is the orthodox view among logicians to the present day—that in a properly regimented language we could avoid such paradoxes by giving up the idea that there is a universal and unitary notion of truth—that is, by giving up the idea that "is true" is the same predicate no matter what language we are speaking of. In addition, he maintained that if I say of a sentence in a language L that it is true or false, my assertion belongs to a different language—a "meta-language," call it meta-L. No language is allowed to contain its own truth-predicate. ("Semantically closed languages are inconsistent.")

Self-reference as such is not ruled out. There can be such a sentence as:

(III) The sentence (III) is not true-in-L,

but this sentence will not belong to L itself, but only to meta-L. Since it is not well-formed in L, it is, of course, true that it is not true-in-L. And since this is exactly what it *says* in meta-L, it *is* true in meta-L. By recognizing how truth is relative to language, we can see how (III) is nonsense (and not true) in the "object language" L and true in the meta-language meta-L, and this dissolves the paradox.

It remains to determine if Tarski has succeeded, or if he has only pushed the antinomy out of the formal language and into the informal language which he himself employs when he explains the significance of his formal work. In seeing this, the thing to keep in mind, I repeat, is that Tarski did *not*—as has sometimes been inaccurately claimed—ban self-reference as such. (As I remarked, the cost of banning all possible forms of self-reference from language is much too high.) Rather, he abandoned the idea that we have a unitary notion of truth. If each language has its own truth-predicate, and the notion "true-in-L," where L is a language, is itself expressible in a different language (a meta-language) but not in L itself, the "semantical paradoxes" can all be avoided. But in what language is Tarski himself supposed to be saying all this?

Tarski's theory introduces a "hierarchy of languages." There is the object language (this can be any language which is itself free of such "semantical" notions as reference and truth); there is the meta-language, the meta-meta-language, and so on. For every finite number *n*, there is a meta-language of level *n*. These languages form a hierarchy. Using the so-called transfinite numbers, one can even extend the hierarchy into the transfinite—there are meta-languages of higher and higher *infinite* orders. The paradoxical aspect of Tarski's theory, indeed of any hierarchical theory, is that one has to stand outside the whole hierarchy even to formulate the statement that the hierarchy exists. But what is this "outside place"—"informal language"—supposed to be? It cannot be "ordinary language," because ordinary language, according to Tarski, is semantically closed and hence inconsistent. But neither can it be a regimented language, for no regimented language can make semantic generalizations about itself or about languages on a higher level than itself.

This brings us to a philosophically important possibility: the possibility of denying that our informal discourse constitutes a "language." This position was taken by Bertrand Russell and recently revived by Charles Parsons in one of the most profound papers on the Liar paradoxes of recent decades.[13] According to this position, the informal discourse in which we say "Every language has a meta-language, and the truth predicate for the language belongs to that meta-language, not to the language itself" is not itself a part of any language, but a "speech act" which is *sui generis*.

The problem is that the inferences we draw from such "systematically ambiguous" statements (am I allowed to call them "statements"?) as

(V) Every language L has a meta-language ML

exactly resemble the inferences we draw from an ordinary universal statement such as "All men are mortal." Given the additional premise that L_1 L_2, L_3, . . . are languages, anyone who accepts (V) is immediately able to conclude that

L_1 has a meta-language ML_1
L_2 has a meta-language ML_2

in just the way that anyone who accepts "All men are mortal" is immediately able to conclude (given the additional premise that Tom, Dick, and Harry are men) that Tom is mortal, Dick is mortal, and Harry is mortal. Yet, according to Parsons's suggestion, systematically ambiguous discourse is a primitive and irreducible kind of discourse, not to be understood on the model of other kinds of language use.

In spite of my great respect for Parsons, not to say for Bertrand Russell, I confess that I cannot understand this position at all. One could, after all, formally escape the paradox by insisting that all "languages" properly so-called are to be written with ink other than red, and reserving red ink for discourse which generalizes about all "languages properly so-called." Since generalizations about "all languages" which are printed in red ink would not include the Red Ink Language in which they are written (the Red Ink Language is *sui generis*), we cannot derive the Strong Liar or other semantic paradoxes. But this looks like a formalistic trick rather than an appealing, let alone a compelling, philosophical resolution of a conceptual difficulty. In what language do we express the fact that "Generalizations about the Non–Red Ink Languages do not include the Red Ink Languages in their scope"? Think it or say it but never write it in *ink*? (It cannot be written in a Red Ink Language without violating Tarski's strictures against "semantically closed languages," because it refers to all Red Ink Languages.) Or should we write it in pencil but not in ink, to avoid semantic closure? As Douglas Edwards asked some years ago (in his senior thesis at Harvard), "Can the Semantics of Systematically Ambiguous Discourse be Stated even in Systematically Ambiguous Discourse?"

Perhaps the real thought is that some forms of discourse can be understood without presupposing the notion of truth at all. But then, why not claim that *all* discourse can be understood without presupposing the notion of truth at all? (As Richard Rorty seems to do.) Or perhaps the suggestion is that these things cannot be "said" but can only be "shown." But the problem is that the things which we are "shown" when Systematic Ambiguity is explained to us are shown by being *said*. The idea that there are discursive thoughts which cannot be "said" is just the formalistic trick that I said I don't understand.

I do not wish to claim any particular originality for these reflections, apart from my particular formulation here. In a famous philosophical paper, Kurt Gödel, made it quite clear that he did not think the semantic paradoxes had been solved (as opposed to the set theoretic paradoxes, which he did think had been solved). I have heard other logicians say that what we have done is push the semantic paradoxes out of the formalized languages we construct so that we don't have to worry about them. But it is time to reflect on what this situation means.

First, let us reflect on the history of these puzzles. At least in a crude form (for instance, the joke about the Cretan), they are very old. And logic was quite a sophisticated business in Stoic times, in medieval times, in Leibniz's time, as well as in the nineteenth century. Yet no one seems to have regarded them as terribly serious business before Russell. So the first problem we face, as we move away from the technicalities, is: why have these puzzles recently become a subject for such strenuous examination?

I am not a historian of science, so I will not attempt to answer this question. It may be, however, that it required the formalization of logic (which came to the center of world logical attention with the appearance of Boole's logical investigations in the late 1840s), the development of a logic of relations and of multiple generality, which was the contribution of Peirce and Frege in the 1870s and 1880s, *and* the idea of a single symbolic language adequate for the formalization of all of science, which was the contribution of Frege in 1878 followed by Russell and Whitehead in the first decades of the present century, to bring this problem to the forefront of logical attention. (There still remains the problem of why it was Russell and not Frege who did so, but I will not venture a conjecture about this.) If this is right—and this is the way Russell views the matter—it is not until we try to construct a totalistic symbolic language like that of *Principia Mathematica* that the semantic paradoxes cease to look like mere curiosities, or idle "brain teasers." What could have been regarded in this way before suddenly threatens a whole logical system, the fruit of decades of work by some of the greatest logicians of all time (I am thinking of Frege, Russell, and Whitehead as engaged in a single collective enterprise here), with inconsistency. If the system is a formalization of our whole extant mathematical and deductive-logical knowledge, that it should be inconsistent from the very start is intolerable. Some way has to be found to avoid this—even a device as desperate as Russell's "Systematic Ambiguity" or Tarski's "Levels of Language."

In short, what we have here is not a paradox which *first arises* as the circle of science grows larger, as was the case with the cut between the observer and the system in quantum mechanics, but rather a paradox which was already noticed (or almost noticed) but which looked totally unimportant until the circle of science got big enough. In a sense, it was the importance of the semantic paradoxes that was the scientific discovery, not their existence.

The paradoxes themselves, however, are hardly less paradoxical than the solutions to which the logical community has been driven. For in giving up the idea that we can generalize about "all languages," in giving up the idea that we have a single unitary notion of truth applicable to any language whatsoever, we have arrived at a strange position—a position, I want to suggest, somehow reminiscent of the position we find ourselves in quantum mechanics.

To bring out the analogy I have in mind, let us go back to the problem with the idea of Systematic Ambiguity. The problem may be put this way: if *you* construct a hierarchy of languages, then no paradox arises if I generalize over *your* whole hierarchy, provided I do not regard *my* "informal meta-language" as lying anywhere in *your* hierarchy of languages. In short, I can generalize over as large a totality of languages as I want (excluding totalities which include my own language or languages which themselves contain my own language), but the language in which I do the generalizing must always lie outside the totality over which I generalize. Substitute "the observer" for "I" in this formulation, and you get: There is always a cut between the observer's language and the totality of languages he generalizes over. The "God's-Eye View"—the view from which absolutely all languages are equally part of the totality being scrutinized—is forever inaccessible.

If we formulate the principle of the "cut between the observer and the system" in quantum mechanics by saying that the observer can take as large a totality as he wishes as the system (excluding totalities which include himself in the act of performing the measurement), but that he himself (or at least a part of himself) must always lie outside the system, then the analogy is complete. And it is more than a formal analogy; it is an *epistemic* analogy. The same notion of a "God's-Eye View," the same epistemic ideal of achieving a view from an "Archimedean point"—a point from which we can survey observers as if they were not *ourselves*, survey them as if we were, so to speak, *outside our own skins*—is involved in both cases. The same notion that ideal knowledge is *impersonal* is involved. That we should not be able to attain this ideal in practice is not paradoxical—we never expected really to attain it in practice. But that there should be *principled difficulties with the ideal itself*—that it should turn out that we can no longer visualize what it would *mean* to attain the ideal—this is a fact which constitutes for us, constituted as we are, the most profound of paradoxes.

In the second part of this essay I shall discuss the significance all this has for philosophy. I shall try to connect the failure of the ideal of a God's-Eye View with the central problems of Western philosophy from the time of Kant. I shall argue that the fashionable panacea of relativism—even if it is given a new name, such as "deconstruction" or even "pragmatism" (by Richard Rorty)—is not the only, or the right, reaction to that failure. Since this is a Kant Lecture, let me say that these issues were, of course, close to Kant's own interests, however much the outcome I have sketched here would have distressed him. Kant was deeply torn between the idea that all knowledge is partly our own construction and the idea that knowledge must yield what I have called a "God's-Eye View." Yet the idea that there are *limits to knowledge*, and that we find ourselves in "antinomies"—another word for paradoxes—when we try to go beyond those limits is also a Kantian idea. To Kant it looked as if what was beyond the limits was "transcendent metaphysics"; today it begins to seem as if part of what was once considered *within* the limits, within Kant's "world of experience," cannot be fully brought under the Kantian "regulative idea of Nature." ("Nature" for Kant included the notion of a totally unified system of natural laws; a "cut between the observer and the system" would have been as distasteful to Kant as it was to be, more than a century later, to Einstein.)

There is also a reason to mention Einstein at this point. Einstein failed to carry through his project of overthrowing the Copenhagen Interpretation and restoring the Kantian regulative idea of Nature. But it would be wrong to view him as just a nostalgic reactionary (as some quantum physicists came close to doing). There is a part of all of us which sides with Einstein—which wants to see the God's-Eye View restored in all its splendor. The struggle within ourselves, the struggle to give up or to retain the old notions of metaphysical reality, objectivity, and impersonality, is far from over.

Part Two: Relativism

The death of metaphysics is a theme that entered philosophy with Kant. In our own century, a towering figure (some would say, *the* towering figure in philosophy), Ludwig Wittgenstein, sounded that note both powerfully and in a uniquely personal way; and he did not hesitate to lump epistemology together with metaphysics. (According to some of Wittgenstein's interpreters, what is today called "analytic philosophy" was, for Wittgenstein, the most confused form of metaphysics!) At the same time, even the man on the street could see that metaphysical discussion did not abate. A simple induction from the history of thought suggests that metaphysical discussion is not going to disappear as long as reflective people remain in the world. As Gilson said at the end of a famous book, "Philosophy always buries its undertakers."

The purpose of this essay is not to engage in a further debate about the question: "Is (or: "In what sense is") metaphysics dead?" I take it as a fact of life that there is a sense in which the task of philosophy is to overcome metaphysics and a sense in which its task is to continue metaphysical discussion. In every philosopher there is a part that cries, "This enterprise is vain, frivolous, crazy—we must say 'Stop!'" and a part that cries, "This enterprise is simply reflection at the most general and most abstract level; to put a stop to it would be a crime against reason." *Of course* philosophical problems are unsolvable; but as Stanley Cavell once remarked, "there are better and worse ways of thinking about them."

What I just said could have been said at virtually any time since the beginning of modernity. I also take it—and this too is something I am not going to argue, but take as another fact of life, although I know that there are many who would disagree—that the enterprises of providing a *foundation* for Being and Knowledge—a successful description of the Furniture of the World or a successful description of the Canons of Justification—are enterprises that have disastrously failed, and we could not have seen this until these enterprises had been given time to prove their futility (although Kant did say something like this long ago). There *is* a sense in which the futility of something that was called metaphysics and the futility of something that was called epistemology is a sharper, more painful problem for our period—a period that hankers to be called "postmodern" rather than modern.

What I want to do is lay out some principles that we should *not* abandon in our despair at the failure of something that was called metaphysics and something that was called epistemology. It will soon be evident that I have been inspired to do this, in large part, by a very fruitful ongoing exchange with Richard Rorty, and this essay may be viewed as yet another contribution to that exchange. For Rorty, as for the French thinkers whom he admires, two ideas seem gripping. (1) The failure of our philosophical "foundations" is a failure of the whole culture, and accepting that we were wrong in wanting or thinking we could have a foundation requires us to be *philosophical revisionists*. By this I mean that, for Rorty or Foucault or Derrida, the failure of foundationalism makes a difference to how we are allowed to talk in ordinary life—a difference as to whether and when we are allowed to use words like "know," "objective," "fact," and "reason." The picture is that philosophy was not a reflection *on* the culture, a reflection some of whose ambitious projects failed, but a *basis*, a sort of pedestal, on which the culture rested, and which has been abruptly yanked out. Under the pretense that philosophy is no longer "serious" there lies hidden a gigantic seriousness. If I am right, Rorty hopes to be a doctor to the modern soul. (2) At the same time, Rorty's analytic past shows up in this: when he rejects a philosophical controversy, as, for example, he rejects the "realism/antirealism" controversy, or the "emotive/cognitive" controversy, his rejection is expressed in a Carnapian tone of voice—he *scorns* the controversy.

I am often asked just where I disagree with Rorty. Apart from technical issues—of course, any two philosophers have a host of technical disagreements—I think our disagreement concerns, at bottom, these two broad attitudes. I hope that philosophical reflection may be of some real cultural value; but I do not think it has been the pedestal on which the culture rested, and I do not think our reaction to the failure of a philosophical project—even a project as central as "metaphysics"—should be to abandon ways of talking and thinking which have practical and spiritual weight. I am not, in that sense, a philosophical revisionist. And I think that what is important in philosophy is not just to say, "I reject the realist/antirealist controversy," but to show that (and how) both sides *misrepresent* the lives we live with our concepts. That a controversy is "futile" does not mean that the rival pictures are unimportant. Indeed, to reject a controversy without examining the pictures involved is almost always just a way of *defending* one of those pictures (usually the one that claims to be "antimetaphysical"). In short, I think philosophy is both more important and less important than Rorty does. It is not a pedestal on which we rest (or have rested until Rorty). Yet the illusions that philosophy spins are illusions that belong to the nature of human life itself, and that need to be illuminated. Just saying "That's a pseudo-issue" is not of itself therapeutic; it is an aggressive form of the metaphysical disease itself.

These remarks are, of course, much too general to serve as answers to the grand question "After Metaphysics What?" But no one philosopher can answer that question. "After metaphysics" there can only be *philosophers*—that is, there can only be the search for those "better and worse ways of thinking" that Cavell called for. In the rest of this essay I want to begin such a search by laying out some principles. I hope that this may eventually provoke Rorty to indicate which of the principles I list he can accept, and which ones his philosophical revisionism would lead him to scorn.

Warrant and Communal Agreement

I shall begin by laying out some principles concerning warranted belief and assertion. Since "justification" is a notion that applies to only certain sorts of statements,[14] I shall use John Dewey's technical term "warranted assertibility" (or just "warrant," for short) instead of the term "justification."

The first is the one with which Rorty is certain to disagree, and it sets the stage for all the others:

> (1) In ordinary circumstances, there is usually a fact of the matter as to whether the statements people make are warranted or not.

Some of the principles that follow are likely to puzzle or disquiet various philosophers (including Rorty); but let me list the whole group before I deal with the "disquiets." Here are the others:[15]

> (2) Whether a statement is warranted or not is independent of whether the majority of one's cultural peers would *say* it is warranted or unwarranted.
>
> (3) Our norms and standards of warranted assertibility are historical products; they evolve in time.
>
> (4) Our norms and standards always reflect our interests and values. Our picture of intellectual flourishing is part of, and only makes sense as part of, our picture of human flourishing in general.
>
> (5) Our norms and standards of *anything*—including warranted assertibility—are capable of reform. There are better and worse norms and standards.

Although there is a tension—some will say, an unbearable tension—between these principles, I do not think I am the first to believe that they can and should be held jointly. From Peirce's earliest writing, they have, I believe, been held by pragmatists, even if this particular formulation is new. However, my defense of them will not depend on the arguments of particular pragmatist predecessors.

Let me begin my discussion with the first two principles: the existence of such a thing as "warrant" and its independence from the opinion of one's cultural peers.

There is *one* way of defending these principles which is sure to provoke objections from antirealists and/or nonrealists: that is to posit the existence of trans-historical "canons" of warranted belief which *define* warrant, independently of whether any given person or culture is able to state those canons. But that is not the way in which one should defend the independence of warrant from majority opinion. Rather than viewing the fact that warrant is independent of majority opinion as a fact about a transcendent reality, one should recognize that it is nothing but a property of the concept of warrant itself; or, since talk of "properties of concepts" has led some philosophers to overwork the analytic/synthetic distinction, let me say simply that it is a central part of our picture of warrant. To say that whether or not it is warranted in a given problematical situation to accept a given judgment is independent of whether a majority of one's peers would *agree* that it is warranted in that situation is just to show that one has the concept of warrant.

Indeed, that this is so is shown by the *praxis* of the Relativists themselves. They know very well that the majority of their cultural peers are not convinced by Relativist arguments, but they keep on arguing because they think they are *justified* (warranted) in doing so, and they share the picture of warrant as independent of majority opinion. But, it may be objected, surely the Relativist can reformulate his view so as to avoid this argument? Instead of claiming that he is describing our ordinary notion of warrant, the careful Relativist ought to say he is proposing a *better* concept. "Yes, this is a feature of our ordinary concept of warrant," the Relativist ought to admit, "but it is a *bad* feature."

But what can "bad" possibly mean here but "based on a wrong metaphysical picture"? And how can a Relativist speak of *right* and *wrong* metaphysical pictures? I am, of course, assuming the Relativist is a Relativist about *both* truth and warrant; a Realist about truth who happens to be a Relativist about warrant (there actually are such philosophers, I believe) can consistently hold that "I can't justify this belief, but I nonetheless believe that it is *true* that a statement S is warranted if and only if the majority of one's cultural peers would agree that it is warranted." Such a philosopher can hold without self-refutation that his own belief is true but not warranted; but there is a kind of pragmatic inconsistency about his position. The point I have just made is one that I have often made in the past: Relativism, just as much as Realism, assumes that one can stand within one's language and outside it at the same time. In the case of Realism this is not an immediate contradiction, since the whole content of Realism lies in the claim that it makes sense to think of a God's-Eye View (or, better, of a "View from Nowhere"); but in the case of Relativism it constitutes a self-refutation.

Let me now discuss the last of my five principles, and in particular the claim, which is the heart of that principle, that "there are better and worse norms and standards." And this time I *shall* discuss Rorty's position.

Superficially, it might seem that Rorty and I agree on this. He often speaks of finding better ways of talking and acting, ways that enable us to "cope better." Why shouldn't changing our norms and standards sometimes enable us to "cope better"?

But in one crucial place[16] he says of reforms that they are not "better by reference to a previously known standard, but just better *in the sense that they come to seem clearly better than their predecessors.*" It is at precisely this point that I get the feeling that we do not agree at all.

The gloss Rorty puts on his own notion of "new and better ways of talking and acting"—*in the sense that they come to seem clearly better than their predecessors*—amounts to a rejection, rather than a clarification, of the notion of "reforming" the ways we are doing and thinking invoked in my fifth principle. Indeed, for many statements *p* it may well be the case that if those among us who want us to adopt standards according to which *p* is warranted win out, we will cope better in the sense that it will come to seem to us that we are coping better, and if those among us who want us to adopt standards according to which not-*p* is warranted win out, we will also cope better *in the sense that it will come to seem to us that we are coping better.* For example, since the community Rorty speaks of is normally all of Western culture, it could happen that a neofascist tendency wins out, and people cope better in the sense that *it comes to seem to them that they are coping better by dealing savagely with those terrible Jews, foreigners, and communists*, while if the forces of good win out it will also be the case that people cope better *in the sense that it comes to seem to them that they are.* Of course, Rorty himself would not feel "solidarity" with the culture if it went the first way. But the point is that *this* concept of "coping better" is not the concept of there being *better* and *worse* norms and standards at all. Just as it is internal to our picture of warrant that warrant is logically independent of the opinion of the majority of our cultural peers, so it is internal to our picture of "reform" that whether the outcome of a change is good (a reform) or bad (the opposite) is logically independent of whether it *seems* good or bad. (That is why it makes sense to argue that something most people take to be a reform in fact isn't one.) I believe, therefore, that Rorty *rejects* my fifth principle.

Is Rorty trapped in the same bind as the Relativist, then? Well, his views are certainly much more nuanced than are typical Relativist views. He has also changed them, often in ways I approve of. So I am not sure just what he is prepared to defend. But I shall take the risk of putting forward an amalgam of Rorty's published views as the view I *think* he holds now.

In *Philosophy and the Mirror of Nature* Rorty distinguished between "normal" and "hermeneutic" discourse. Discourse is normal when the culture is in agreement on the relevant standards and norms. Talk about tables and chairs is normal discourse in our culture; we all have pretty much the same ways of answering such questions as "Are there enough chairs for the dinner party tonight?" When there is unresolvable disagreement, discourse which attempts to bridge the paradigm-gap is forced to be "hermeneutic."

What happens when someone *criticizes* the accepted cultural norms and standards? Here, I think Rorty's answer is that I *can* say of the critic's views (I assume, for the sake of the example, that I agree with the critic in question) that they are "true," "more rational," or whatever seems appropriate, but these semantic and epistemic adjectives are really used *emotively*. I am "complimenting" the critic's proposals, not saying that they have particular attributes. In particular, when Rorty argues that his own views are more helpful philosophically, have more content, than the views he criticizes, he is engaged in hermeneutic discourse (which is to say, in rhetoric). But what is the purpose of his rhetoric?

It may be that we will behave better if we become Rortians—we may be more tolerant, less prone to fall for various varieties of religious intolerance and political totalitarianism. If that is what is at stake, the issue is momentous indeed. But a fascist could well agree with Rorty at a very abstract level—Mussolini, let us recall, supported pragmatism, claiming that it sanctions unthinking activism.[17] If our aim is tolerance and the open society, would it not be better to argue for these directly, rather than to hope that these will come as the byproduct of a change in our metaphysical picture?

It seems more likely to me that, most of the time anyway, Rorty really thinks that metaphysical realism is *wrong*. We will be better off if we listen to him in the sense of having fewer false beliefs; but this, of course, is something he cannot admit he really thinks. I think, in short, that the attempt to say that *from a God's-Eye View there is no God's-Eye View* is still there, under all that wrapping.

To round out this part of the discussion, let me say a word about principle 3: the principle that says that norms and standards of warrant evolve in time. (Principle 4 is saved for discussion in a later section of this essay.) In one sense, the "historicity" of norms and standards is just a fact of life, but it is nonetheless necessary to have some picture of *how* norms and standards change. Although historians can do a far better job than I could hope to of painting such a picture, let me refer schematically to two important ways. (1) As Nelson Goodman has long emphasized, norms, standards, and judgments about particular cases often *conflict*. When this happens, we are often pushed to a special kind of philosophical reflection which we might call *reconstructive reflection*. Goodman's great contribution, I think, has been to urge that reconstructive reflection does not lose its value just because the dream of a *total* and *unique* reconstruction of our system of belief is hopelessly Utopian; we can learn a great deal from partial and even fragmentary reconstructions, and we can learn a great deal from reconstructing our beliefs in alternative ways. "Delicate mutual adjustment" of beliefs, norms, and standards to one another is a fertile source of change in all three. (2) There is a kind of *feedback loop*: relying on our existing norms and standards of warrant, we discover facts which themselves sometimes lead to a change in the pictures that inform those norms and standards (and thus, indirectly, to a change in the norms and standards themselves). The discovery of the anomalous phenomena which led to the successor theories to Newtonian physics—relativity and quantum mechanics—and of the post-Newtonian methodologies which went with those theories is an example in point.

The principle just discussed (the third in my list) was that our norms and standards are *historical objects*—they evolve and change in time; and the fifth, and last, was that our norms and standards can be *reformed*. The third and fifth principles must, of course, be understood as conditioning each other: the fact is not just that we *do* change our norms and standards, but that doing so is often an improvement. An improvement judged from where? From within *our* picture of the world, of course. But from within that picture itself, *we* say that "better" isn't the same as "*we* think it's better." And if my "cultural peers" don't agree with me, sometimes I *still* say "better" (or "worse"). There are times when, as Stanley Cavell puts it, I "rest on myself as my foundation."[18]

Realism with a Small "r" and with an "R"

The attempt to say that warrant (and truth) is just a matter of communal agreement[19] is, then, simultaneously a misdescription of the notions we actually have and a self-refuting attempt to both have and deny an "absolute perspective." Are we then forced to become "metaphysical realists"—at the end of the day, if not at the beginning? Is there no middle way?

If saying what we say and doing what we do is being a "realist," then we had better be realists—realists with a small "r." But metaphysical versions of "realism" go beyond realism with a small "r" into certain characteristic kinds of philosophical fantasy. Here I agree with Rorty.

Here is one feature of our intellectual practice that these versions have enormous difficulty in accommodating. On the one hand, trees and chairs—the "thises and thats we can point to"—are paradigms of what we call "real," as Wittgenstein remarked.[20] But consider now a question about which Quine, Lewis, and Kripke all disagree: what is the relation between the tree or the chair and the space-time region it occupies? According to Quine, the chair and the electromagnetic and other fields that make it up and the space-time region that contains these fields are one and the same: so the chair *is* a space-time region. According to Kripke, Quine is just wrong: the chair and the space-time region are two numerically distinct objects. (They have the same mass, however!) The proof is that the chair *could have occupied a different space-time region*. According to Quine, modal predicates are hopelessly vague, so this "proof" is worthless. According to Lewis, Quine is right about the chair but wrong about the modal predicates: the correct answer to Kripke is that if the chair could have been in a different place, as we say, what that means is that a *counterpart* of this chair could have been in that place; not that *this very chair* (in the sense of the logical notion of identity [=]) could have been in that place.

Well, who is right? Are chairs really *identical* with their matter, or does a chair somehow coexist in the same space-time region with its matter while remaining numerically distinct from it? And is their matter really identical with the fields? And are the fields really identical with the space-time regions? To me it seems clear that at least the first, and probably all three, of these questions are nonsensical. We can formalize our language in the way Kripke would and we can formalize our language in the way Lewis would, and (thank God!) we can leave it unformalized and not pretend that the ordinary language "is" obeys the same rules as the sign " = " in systems of formal logic. Not even God could tell us if the chair is "identical" with its matter (or with the space-time region); and not because there is something He doesn't know.

So it looks as if even something as paradigmatically "real" as a chair has aspects that are conventional. *That the chair is blue is paradigmatically a "reality" and yet that the chair [is/is not/we don't have to decide] a space-time region is a matter of convention.*

And what of the space-time region itself? Some philosophers think of points as location *predicates*, not objects. So a space-time region is just a set of properties (if these philosophers are right) and not an object (in the sense of concrete object) at all, if this view is right. Again, it doesn't so much seem that there is a "view" here at all, as yet *another* way we could reconstruct our language. But how can the existence of a concrete object (the space-time region) be a matter of *convention*? And how can the identity of A (the chair) and B (the space-time region) be a matter of *convention*? The realist with a small "r" needn't have an answer to these questions. It is just a fact of life, he may feel, that certain alternatives are equally good while others are visibly forced. But metaphysical realism is not just the view that there are, after all, chairs, and some of them are, after all, blue, and we didn't just *make all that up*. Metaphysical realism presents itself as a powerful transcendental picture: a picture in which there is a fixed set of "language-independent" objects (some of which are abstract and others are concrete) and a fixed "relation" between terms and their extensions. What I am saying is that the picture only partly agrees with the commonsense view it purports to interpret; it has consequences which, from a commonsense view, are quite absurd. There is nothing wrong at all with holding on to our realism with a small "r" and jettisoning the Big "R" Realism of the philosophers.

Although he was far from being a Big "R" realist, Hans Reichenbach had a conception of the task of philosophy[21] which, if it had succeeded, might well have saved Realism from the objection just raised: the task of philosophy, he wrote, is to *distinguish what is fact and what is convention ("definition") in our system of knowledge*. The trouble, as Quine pointed out, is that the philosophical distinction between "fact" and "definition" on which Reichenbach depended has collapsed. As another example, not dissimilar to the one I just used, consider the conventional character of any possible answer to the question, "Is a point identical with a series of spheres that converge to it?" We know that we can take extended regions as the primitive objects and "identify" points with sets of concentric spheres, and all geometric facts are perfectly well represented. We know that we can also take points as primitives and take spheres to be sets of points. But the very statement "we can do either" assumes a diffuse background of empirical facts. Fundamental changes in the way we do physics could change the whole picture. So "convention" does not mean *absolute convention*—truth by stipulation, free of every element of "fact." And, on the other hand, even when we see such a "reality" as a tree, the possibility of that perception is dependent on a whole conceptual scheme, on a language in place. What is factual and what is conventional is a matter of degree; we cannot say, "These and these elements of the world are the raw facts; the rest is convention, or a mixture of these raw facts with convention."

What I am saying, then, is that elements of what we call "language" or "mind" *penetrate so deeply into what we call "reality" that the very project of representing ourselves as being "mappers" of something "languages-independent" is fatally compromised from the very start.* Like Relativism, but in a different way, Realism is an impossible attempt to view the world from Nowhere. In this situation it is a temptation to say, "So we make the world," or "our language makes up the world," or "our culture makes up the world"; but this is just another form of the same mistake. If we succumb, once again we view the world—the only world we know—as a *product.* One kind of philosopher views it as a product from a raw material: Unconceptualized Reality. The other views it as a creation *ex nihilo. But the world isn't a product. It's just the world.*

Where are we then? On the one hand—this is where I hope Rorty will sympathize with what I am saying—our image of the world cannot be "justified" by anything but its success as judged by the interests and values which evolve and get modified at the same time and in interaction with our evolving image of the world itself. Just as the absolute "convention/fact" dichotomy had to be abandoned, so (as Morton White long ago urged)[22] the absolute "fact/value" dichotomy has to be abandoned, and for similar reasons. On the other hand, it is part of that image itself that the world is not the product of our will—or our dispositions to talk in certain ways, either.

Notes

Part One and Part Two of this essay were delivered individually as Kant Lectures at Stanford University in the fall of 1987.

"Realism with a Human Face," reprinted by permission of the publisher from *Realism with a Human Face* by Hilary Putnam, edited and introduced by James Conant, pp. 3–29, Cambridge, Mass.: Harvard University Press, Copyright © 1990 by the President and Fellow of Harvard College.

1. This is denied, however, by the so-called Many-Worlds Interpretation of quantum mechanics, which is discussed later in this chapter.

2. J. von Neumann, *Mathematical Foundations of Quantum Mechanics* (Princeton, N.J.; Princeton University Press, 1955). I interpret von Neumann's interpretation in my "Quantum Mechanics and the Observer," chapter 14 of *Realism and Reason* (Cambridge; Cambridge University Press, 1975), which is volume 3 of my *Philosophical Papers.*

3. In what follows, I am deliberately identifying states with their descriptions to simplify the exposition.

4. The defense to the objection described in the texts is von Neumann's. Bohr himself would have said that the transition A——>A# is a purely formal one, which has no meaning apart from a particular experimental situation. If the experimental situation is that a measurement is made at time *t* to find out if the atom decayed or not, then the appropriate classical picture is that the atom was already in state A or in state B (that is, it had already emitted radiation or it

had not) and the measurement finds out which; but this is *only* a "classical picture," albeit the one appropriate to *that* experimental situation. The question "But what state is the atom in at time *t* if *no* measurement is made?" is scientifically meaningless, in Bohr's view.

5. Hugh Everett, '"Relative State' Formulation of Quantum Mechanics," in B. S. De Witt and N. Graham, *The Many-Worlds Interpretation of Quantum Mechanics* (Princeton, N.J.: Princeton University Press, 1973).

6. More precisely, the Dirac equation, or whatever successor that equation may have when quantum mechanics and relativity theory are finally reconciled.

7. Strictly speaking, the states A and B would have to be replaced by appropriate states of the entire cosmological universe in this argument, on the Many- Worlds Interpretation.

8. Hans Reichenbach, *Philosophical Foundations of Quantum Mechanics* (Berkeley: University of California Press, 1948).

9. Actually, another problem remains with the Many-Worlds Interpretation: namely, the difficulty of interpreting the notion of probability if all possible worlds are equally "real."

10. This has been proposed by Itamar Pitowski. See his communication in *Physical Review Letters,* 48 (1982): 1299.

11. Strictly speaking, this sentence is paradoxical only on the supposition that (1) every Cretan other than the speaker tells at least one lie—otherwise the sentence is straightforwardly false; and (2) the speaker himself always utters the truth, with the possible exception of this one occasion—otherwise, if the first supposition holds, the sentence is straightforwardly true. It is to avoid these empirical suppositions that the paradox needs to be reformulated as it is above.

12. A. Tarski, "The Concept of Truth in Formalized Languages" (1933), reprinted in his *Logic, Semantics, Metamathematics* (Oxford: Oxford University Press, 1956), pp. 152-278.

13. Charles Parsons, "The Liar Paradox," in *Philosophy in Mathematics* (Ithaca, N.Y.: Cornell University Press, 1987).

14. For example, if I am sincerely convinced that I had eggs for breakfast, it makes sense to ask if I am right, but no sense to ask if I have a "justification."

15. Readers of *Reasont Truth, and History* (Cambridge: Cambridge University Press, 1981) will recognize that each of these principles played a role in the argument of that book.

16. Richard Rorty, *Consequences of Pragmatism* (Minneapolis; University of Minnesota Press, 1982), p. xxxvii.

17. See Ralph Barton Perry, *The Thought and Character of William James* (Boston: Little, Brown, 1935), vol. 2, p. 575. For a criticism of Perry's partial concession to Mussolini's view see Peter Skagestad's "Pragmatism and the Closed Society: A Juxtaposition of Charles Peirce and George Orwell," in *Philosophy and Social Criticism,* 2 (1986): 307-329.

18. *The Claim of Reason* (Oxford: Oxford University Press, 1979), p. 125.

19. Something like this view is ascribed to Wittgenstein in Kripke's *Wittgenstein on Rules and Private Language* (Cambridge, Mass.: Harvard University Press, 1982). In conversation, Stanley Cavell has suggested to me that this makes it sound as if Wittgenstein thought that truth and warrant are a matter of etiquette—wanting to find a justified (or a true) hypothesis is like wanting to use the same fork my "cultural peers" use, on such a story. But Wittgenstein would not have thought *this* is a description of *our* form of life at all.

20. I.udwig Wittgenstein, *Wittgenstein's Lectures on Mathematics,* ed. Cora Diamond (Oxford: Blackwell, 1971), Lecture 25. The remark "thises and thats we can point to" is from this lecture.

21. Hans Reichenbach, *Philosophy of Space and lime* (New York: Dover, 1958).

22. Morton White, *Towards Reunion in Philosophy* (Cambridge, Mass.: Harvard University Press, 1956).

In this essay, Putnam revisits and defends Dewey's thought that democracy is in part the epistemic project of making our social lives more "intelligent."

HILARY PUTNAM

A Reconsideration of Deweyan Democracy

I. Introduction

I want to discuss a philosopher whose work at its best illustrates the way in which American pragmatism (at *its* best) avoided both the illusions of metaphysics and the pitfalls of skepticism: John Dewey. While Dewey's output was vast, one concern informed all of it; even what seem to be his purely epistemological writings cannot be understood apart from that concern. That concern is with the meaning and future of democracy. I shall discuss a philosophical justification of democracy that I believe one can find in Dewey's work. I shall call it *the epistemological justification of democracy* and although I shall state it in my own words, I shall deliberately select words which come from Dewey's own philosophical vocabulary.

The claim, then, is this: Democracy is not just a form of social life among other workable forms of social life; it is the precondition for the full application of intelligence to the solution of social problems. The notions from Dewey's vocabulary that I have employed are, of course, *intelligence* (which Dewey contrasts with the traditional philosophical notion of *reason*) and *problem solving*. First, let me say a word about the sense in which such a claim, if supported, can be called a *justification* of a form of social life.

In *Ethics and the Limits of Philosophy*,[1] Bernard Williams draws a very useful distinction between two senses in which one might attempt to justify ethical claims. One is an Utopian sense: One might try to find a justification for ethical claims that would actually convince skeptics or amoralists and persuade them to change their ways. (This is like finding a "proof" that Hitler was a bad man that Hitler himself would have had to accept.) Williams rightly concludes that this is an unrealistic objective.

> When the philosopher raised the question of what we shall have to say to the skeptic or amoralist, he should rather have asked what we shall have to say about him. The justification he is looking for is in fact designed for the people who are largely within the ethical world, and the aim of the discourse is not to deal with someone who probably will not listen to it, but to reassure, strengthen, and give insight to those who will. . . . If, by contrast, the justification is addressed to a community that is already an ethical one, then the politics of ethical discourse, including moral philosophy, are significantly

> different. The aim is not to control the enemies of the community or its shirkers but, by giving reason to people already disposed to hear it, to help in continually creating a community held together by that same disposition.[2]

Here Williams's conception of moral philosophy seems to be exactly Dewey's conception. Yet Williams ignores not only the historical figure John Dewey, but the very possibility of Dewey's particular justification. Instead, Williams considers just two ways in which ethical claims could "objectively" be justified, and associates these two lands of justification with Aristotle and Kant, respectively.[3] Even though Williams considers Kantian and Aristotelian strategies of justification to be the only possible ones, he might still have left room for a discussion of Dewey. Some commentators have seen a sense in which Dewey might be an Aristotelian, even though he was much more of an empiricist than Aristotle.[4] But when Williams discusses Aristotelian strategies—strategies of justification based on conceptions of human flourishing—something very strange happens. "Human flourishing" is defined in an entirely individualistic sense. Thus, after repeating the remark that "the answer to Socrates' question [How should one live?] cannot be used by those who (from the perspective of the rest) most need it,"[5] Williams goes on to say:

> Still, this does not cast us to the opposite extreme, that the answer is simply meant to keep up the spirits of those within the system, give them more insight, and help them to bring up their children. The answer does that, but not only that. On Aristotle's account a virtuous life would indeed conduce to the well-being of the man who has had a bad upbringing, even if he cannot see it. The fact that he is incurable, and cannot properly understand the diagnosis, does not mean that he is not ill.[6]

An *Aristotelian* justification, in the only sense that Williams considers, is one that can be given to each nondefective human being (each human being who is not "ill"). In short, the only hope for an objective foundation for ethics[7] that Williams considers is what might be called a "medical" justification—an "objective" justification for ethics that would show, in some sense of "ill" that does not beg the question, that the amoral or immoral man is ill. Moreover, the only place that such a justification could originate, according to Williams, is in "some branch of psychology."[8] Williams is skeptical about that possibility, although he says that "[i]t would be silly to try to determine a priori and in a few pages whether there could be such a theory."[9] The aim mentioned earlier, "not to control the enemies of the community or its shirkers but, by giving reason to people already disposed to hear it, to help in continually creating a community held together by that same disposition"[10]—has been radically reinterpreted.

However, when Williams explains why it is unlikely that there will ever be a "branch of psychology" that will provide us with "objective" foundations for ethics, he makes a very interesting remark:

> Any adequate psychology of character will presumably include the truth, in some scientifically presentable form, that many people are horrible because they are unhappy, and

> conversely: where their unhappiness is not something specially defined in ethical terms, but is simply basic unhappiness—misery, rage, loneliness, despair. That is a well-known and powerful fact; but it is only one in a range of equally everyday facts. Some who are not horrible, and who try hard to be generous and to accommodate others' interests, are miserable, and from their ethical state. They may be victims of a suppressed self-assertion that might once have been acknowledged but now cannot be, still less overcome or redirected. There is also the figure, rarer perhaps than Callicles supposed, but real, who is horrible enough and not miserable at all but, by any ethological standard of the bright eye and the gleaming coat, dangerously flourishing. For people who want to ground the ethical life in psychological health, it is something of a problem that there can be such people at all.[11]

Williams does go on to question whether the latter sort of people really exist, or whether it is simply an illusion that they do. What I want to call your attention to here is not the worry about whether such people really exist, but the reference to "any ethological standard of the bright eye and the gleaming coat."[12] Apparently, an "objective" standard of human flourishing would regard us as if we were tigers (or perhaps squirrels)! Williams describes a standard of human flourishing that ignores everything that Aristotle himself would have regarded as typically human. Dewey, on the other hand, thought of us primarily in terms of our capacity to intelligently initiate action, to talk, and to experiment.

Not only is Dewey's justification a social justification—that is, one addressed to the community as a whole rather than to each member of the community—it is also an *epistemological* justification, and this too is a possibility that Williams ignores. As I stated earlier, the possibility that Williams considers is a "medical" justification; a proof that if you are amoral then you are in some way "ill." If we tried to recast Dewey's justification in such terms, then we would have to say that society which is not democratic is in a certain way ill; but the medical metaphor is, I think, best dropped altogether.

II. The Noble Savage and the Golden Age

Although John Dewey's arguments are largely ignored in contemporary moral and political philosophy, his enterprise—the enterprise of justifying democracy—is alive and well. John Rawls's monumental *A Theory of Justice*,[13] for example, attempts both to produce a rationale for democratic institutions and a standpoint from which to criticize the failures of those institutions. This could also serve as a description of Dewey's project. But there are scholars in disciplines other than philosophy, and to some extent even scholars of philosophy, who consider the very enterprise of justifying democracy a wrong-headed one. One objection comes from anthropologists and other social scientists,[14] although it is by no means limited to them.[15] These relativist social scientists are sometimes also radicals when it comes to their own cultures, but they strongly oppose any attempt by members of liberal democratic cultures to prescribe change for traditional societies. In the most extreme case (the case I have in mind is an essay by a radical economist, Stephen Marglin),[16] they reject the idea that we can criticize traditional societies even for such sexist practices as female circumcision. Marglin defends his point of view in part by defending an extreme relativism,[17] but I think there is something else at work—something which one finds in the arguments of many social scientists who are not nearly as sophisticated as Marglin: Not to be too nice about it, what I think we are seeing is the revival of the myth of the Noble Savage.

Basically, traditional societies are viewed by these thinkers as so superior to our own societies that we have no right to disturb them in any way. To see what is wrong with this view, let us for the moment focus on the case of male chauvinism in traditional societies.

One argument that is often used to justify a relativistic standpoint is virtually identical to an argument that is used by reactionaries in our own culture, and it is surprising that these social scientists fail to see this. At bottom, the idea is that people in traditional societies are "content"—they are not asking for changes and we have no right to say that they should be asking for changes, because in so doing we are simply imposing a morality that comes from a different social world. It is important, in discussing this to separate two questions: the question of paternalistic intervention on one hand, and the question of moral judgment, moral argument, and persuasion on the other. It is not part of Dewey's view, for example, that benevolent despots should step in and correct social ills wherever they may exist. It is time to let Dewey speak for himself:

> The conception of community of good may be clarified by reference to attempts of those in fixed positions of superiority to confer good upon others. History shows that there have been benevolent despots who wished to bestow blessings on others. They have not succeeded except when their actions have taken the indirect form of changing the conditions under which those lived who were disadvantageously placed. The same principle holds of reformers and philanthropists when they try to do good to others in ways which leave passive those to be benefited. There is a moral tragedy inherent in efforts to further the common good which prevent the result from being either good or common—not good, because it is at the expense of the active growth of those to be helped, and not common because these have no share in bringing the result about. The social welfare can be advanced only by means which enlist the positive interest and active energy of those to be benefited or "improved." The traditional notion of the great man, of the hero, works harm. It encourages the idea that some "leader" is to show the way; others are to follow in imitation. It takes time to arouse minds from apathy and lethargy, to get them to thinking for themselves, to share in making plans, to take part in their execution. But without active cooperation both in forming aims and in carrying them out there is no possibility of a common good.[18]

The true paternalists are those who object to *informing* the victims of male chauvinism, or of other forms of oppression, of the injustice of their situation and of the existence of alternatives. Their argument is a thinly disguised utilitarian one. Their conception of the good is basically "satisfaction" in one of the classic utilitarian senses; in effect they are saying that the women (or whoever the oppressed may be) are satisfied, and that the "agitator" who "stirs them up" is the one who is guilty of creating *dissatisfaction*. But Dewey is no utilitarian. (He was a consequentialist, but he was no utilitarian.) The fact that someone feels satisfied with a situation means little if the person has no information or false information concerning either her own capacities or the existence of available alternatives to her present way of life. The real test is not what women who have never heard of feminism say about their situation; indeed, it is hard to see how the situation of a chauvinist woman in India is different from the situation of a chauvinist woman in this country thirty years ago who had never been exposed to feminist ideas. Such women might well have answered a questionnaire by saying that they were satisfied with their lives; but after realizing the falsity of the beliefs on which the acceptance of their lives had been based, the same women not only felt dissatisfied with those lives, but they sometimes felt ashamed of themselves for having allowed such a belief system to be imposed upon them. One of Dewey's fundamental assumptions is that people value growth more than pleasure. To keep the oppressed from learning so that they remain "satisfied" is, in a phrase originated by Peirce, to "block the path of inquiry."

What the radical social scientists are in fact proposing is an "immunizing strategy," a strategy by which the rationales of oppression in other cultures can be protected from criticism. If this is based on the idea that the aspirations to equality and dignity are confined to citizens of Western industrial democracies, then the events of Tien-an-men Square in the spring of 1989 speak a more powerful refutation of that view than any words I could write here.

At the other extreme, at least politically, from the "Noble Savage" argument against attempting to justify democratic institutions is an argument found in the recent writings of Alasdair MacIntyre.[19] MacIntyre gives a sweeping philosophical resumé of the history of Western thought which endorses the idea that one system of ethical beliefs can "rationally defeat" another system and insists that there can be progress in the development of world views. MacIntyre's argument, however, is haunted by the suggestion that such progress fundamentally stopped somewhere between the twelfth and fourteenth centuries, and that we have been retrogressing ever since.

MacIntyre's conception of rationality is based largely on the work of Thomas Kuhn[20] but with certain interesting omissions. Like Kuhn, MacIntyre believes that world views such as Confucianism, or Aristotelianism, or utilitarianism cum empiricism are often incommensurable. At the same time, MacIntyre believes that the adherents of a world view can incorporate elements from another world view, or even in exceptional cases, scrap their world view and go over to another by a kind of wholesale conversion. What makes such a wholesale conversion rational is that the new paradigm dissolves difficulties that the old paradigm is unable to escape either by straightforwardly answering the questions, or by showing why and how they are not genuine questions at all. Moreover, the new paradigm solves problems in a way that an honest adherent of the old paradigm must acknowledge as superior to anything his or her paradigm can supply.[21] Of course, the new paradigm must not at the same time lose the ability to answer what its adherents must admit are genuine questions that the old paradigm could answer.

MacIntyre makes one application[22] of this idea that startled me. According to MacIntyre, the great Scholastic synthesis of Aquinas and his successors was rationally superior, in this sense, to Aristotelian philosophy.[23] What is startling about this is that, according to MacIntyre, a key ingredient which enabled Scholastic philosophy to handle problems and internal difficulties that the Aristotelian system could not solve was the notion of original sin![24]

What makes this startling is that if the new system *could* solve or dissolve problems that the old system could not, it also purchased difficulties that the old system did not face. Christianity took over from Judaism the notion of a Fall, but it interpreted that notion in a way in which traditional Judaism, for the most part, refused to do. The specifically Christian notion of original sin is unintelligible apart from the Christian notion of a Redeemer. That is, no religion would or could hold that we are compelled to sin or that our nature is so fundamentally corrupt that we cannot help sinning, unless it was prepared to provide a Redeemer to help us (or at least *some* of us) out of this predicament. I don't mean that this was the only option open to Christianity as a matter of logic, but it was the only option open to Christianity as a matter of its own history and traditions.

MacIntyre speaks[25] of the great medieval synthesis of Revelation and Greek philosophy which requires both the notions of original sin and of a triune God. If Christianity is to be viewed as the resolution of a set of problems and difficulties that a scientific or metaphysical system may be called upon to explain, dissolve, or reformulate, then surely the question of the *intelligibility* and the *logical coherence* of its fundamental notions must arise. Of course, if we view Christianity in a different way, for example, as Kierkegaard viewed it,[26] as not something that we accept on the basis of reason at all, then the problem does not arise in the same way (or the notion of "intelligibility" becomes a very different one).

The fact is that the methodological conceptions that MacIntyre defends are deeply flawed. I said that MacIntyre leaves certain things out of Kuhn's account of paradigm change in science. What he leaves out, in fact, is simply *experiment*. But the pragmatists recognized the value of experimentation. Dewey, of course, comes from the pragmatist tradition, and while the founder of pragmatism, Charles Sanders Peirce, eventually repudiated both the label "pragmatism" and much that William James and Dewey associated with that word, the two famous articles that Peirce published in *Popular Science Monthly* in 1877 and 1878, "The Fixation of Belief" and "How to Make Our Ideas Clear,"[27] remain the founding documents of the movement to the present day. In the first of those articles, Peirce discusses a methodology closely related to the one that MacIntyre proposes. He calls that the methodology of "What is Agreeable to Reason."[28] Peirce tells us, I think rightly, that what we have learned—learned by trying that method, and trying again and again throughout the long history of our culture— is that it simply does not work. The method of "What is Agreeable to Reason" by itself, without fallibilism, without experimentation, has never been able to lead to the successful discovery of laws of nature, nor has it been able to lead to resolutions of metaphysical disputes that would command the consensus of intelligent men and women. In place of the method of "What is Agreeable to Reason" (and the other failed methods that Peirce calls the methods of "tenacity" and "authority"),[29] Peirce proposes the "scientific method." By employing the scientific method Peirce does not mean following some rule book, say John Stuart Mill's, or Francis Bacon's, or Rudolf Carnap's. What he means is testing one's ideas in practice, and maintaining an attitude of fallibilism toward them. To judge ideas simply on the basis of their ability to resolve difficulties without putting them under strain, without testing them, without trying to falsify them is to proceed prescientifically. Peirce would agree with MacIntyre that rational decision between paradigms requires reflection and discussion. More than any scientific philosopher of his time, Peirce stressed that scientific method is not *just* a matter of experimentation, but experimentation and testing remain crucial in the formation of rational beliefs about matters of fact.

I know that MacIntyre will say that this criticism passes him by. Far from claiming that rationality is just "out there," available to all properly trained human minds, as traditional rationalists did, MacIntyre insists that rationality (but not truth) is relative to one's paradigm.[30] No historical or universalistic account of rationality can be given at all, he insists. And, he argues, rejecting claims to unrevisable possession of truth makes one a fallibilist. The charm of MacIntyre's writing lies precisely in displaying how such a "postmodern" mind can come to such traditional conclusions! But I cannot accept this defense for two reasons. First, although rationality is relative and historical (perhaps *too* relative and historical!), in MacIntyre's view, there is a fixed principle governing rational discussion *between* paradigms, which allows one paradigm to sometimes "rationally defeat" another. It is in the application of *this* principle that MacIntyre is forced back upon what amounts to "What is Agreeable to [MacIntyre's] Reason." The claim that he is only conceding what any "honest" adherent of the defeated paradigm would have to concede is a bit of persiflage that, in a different context, MacIntyre would be the first to see through. Second, fallibilism in the sense of giving up the a priori is not all there is to Peirce's sense of fallibilism. Peirce's fallibilism requires that one see experimentation, in the widest sense of that term, as the decisive element in rational paradigm change. MacIntyre might reply that reliance on experimentation is only rational "relative to" the contemporary scientific paradigm. But if that were his reply, then this is just where MacIntyre and pragmatism decisively part company.

If I am disturbed by the suggestion haunting MacIntyre's writing that we have been retrogressing ever since the late Middle Ages (a suggestion that has been put forward much more blatantly in Allan Bloom's best seller, *The Closing of the American Mind*),[31] it is because the politics which such views can justify are nothing less than appalling. As many historians have reminded us, the Roman Catholic Church practiced torture through much of its long history. There was a total contempt for what are today regarded as human rights (of course, MacIntyre knows this), and there was terrible persecution of religious minorities. As a Jew, I am particularly worried by the possibility that the sufferings that the Church inflicted upon Jews could someday be "justified" as exercises of a paradigm which had "rationally defeated" the Jewish world view.

What the defenders of the Noble Savage and the defenders of the Golden Age have in common is that their doctrines tend to immunize institutionalized oppression from criticism. The immunizing strategies are different, but they have this in common: they give up the idea that it would be good for the victims of oppression to know of alternative ways of life, alternative conceptions of their situation, and to be free to see for themselves which conception is better. Both Noble Savagers and Golden Agers block the path of inquiry.

III. Dewey's Metaphysics (Or Lack Thereof)

From what "premises" does Dewey derive the claim that I imputed to him, that is, that democracy is a precondition for the full application of intelligence to solving social problems? As we shall shortly see, the underlying premises are some very "ordinary" assumptions. Dewey believes (as we all do, when we are not playing the skeptic) that there are better and worse resolutions to human predicaments—to what he calls "problematical situations."[32] He believes that of all the methods for finding better resolutions, the "scientific method" has proved itself superior to Peirce's methods of "tenacity," "authority," and "What is Agreeable to Reason." For Dewey, the scientific method is simply the method of experimental inquiry combined with free and full discussion—which means, in the case of social problems, the maximum use of the capacities of citizens for proposing courses of action, for testing them, and for evaluating the results. And, in my view, that is all that Dewey really needs to assume.

Of course, a conventional analytic metaphysician would not hold this view. In analytic philosophy today, one cannot simply assume that intelligent people are able to distinguish better resolutions to problematical situations from worse resolutions even after experimentation, reflection and discussion; one first must show that better and worse resolutions to problematical situations exist. This is, for example, what bothers Bernard Williams. For Bernard Williams there could only be facts about what forms of social life are better and worse if such facts issued from "some branch of psychology."[33] Lacking such a "branch of psychology" (and Williams thinks it very unlikely there will ever be one), we have no basis for believing that one form of social life can be better than another except in a relativist sense, that is, unless the judgment of better or worse is explicitly made relative to the principles and practices of "some social world or other."[34] For Williams the distinction between facts which are relative in this way and facts which are "absolute" is omnipresent; there can not be "absolute" facts of the kind Dewey thinks intelligent people are able to discover.[35] Dewey, as I read him, would reply that the whole notion of an "absolute" fact is nonsensical.

However, it is a fact that, while at one time analytic philosophy was an antimetaphysical movement (during the period of Logical Positivism), it has recently become the most pro-metaphysical movement. And from a metaphysician's point of view, one can never begin with an epistemological premise that people are able to tell whether A is better or worse than B; one must first show that, in "the absolute conception of the world," there are such possible facts as "better" and "worse." A metaphysical-reductive account of what "good" is must precede any discussion of what is better than what. In my view, Dewey's great contribution was to insist that we neither have nor require a "theory of everything," and to stress that what we need instead is insight into how human beings resolve problematical situations. But again, it is time to let Dewey speak for himself:

> [Philosophy's] primary concern is to clarify, liberate and extend the goods which inhere in the naturally generated functions of experience. It has no call to create a world of "reality" *de novo*, nor to delve into secrets of Being hidden from common sense and science. It has no stock of information or body of knowledge peculiarly its own; if it does not always become ridiculous when it sets up as a rival of science, it is only because a particular philosopher happens to be also, as a human being, a prophetic man of science. Its business is to accept and to utilize for a purpose the best available knowledge of its own time and place. And this purpose is criticism of beliefs, institutions, customs, policies with respect to their bearing upon good. This does not mean their bearing upon *the* good, as something itself attained and formulated in philosophy. For as philosophy has no private score of knowledge or of methods for attaining truth, so it has no private access to good. As it accepts knowledge of facts and principles from those competent in inquiry and discovery, so it accepts the goods that are diffused in human experience. It has no Mosaic or Pauline authority of revelation entrusted to it. But it has the authority of intelligence, of criticism of these common and natural goods.[36]

Here Dewey uses the notion of "intelligence." This notion, however, is not meant to be a metaphysical notion. Dewey contrasts this notion of intelligence with the traditional philosophical notion of reason. Intelligence, for Dewey, is not a transcendental faculty; it is simply the ability to plan conduct, to learn relevant facts, to make experiments, and to profit from the planning, the facts, and the experiments. The notion is admittedly vague, but we do have the ability to determine whether persons are more or less intelligent with respect to the conduct of their activities in particular areas. In a number of places Dewey connects intelligence with the ability for developing new capacities for acting effectively in an environment with what he calls "growth."

IV. Habermas's and Apel's Epistemological Justifications for Democracy

If Deweyan insights and argumentative strategies have been largely ignored by analytic philosophers in recent years, they have in a sense been rediscovered, although with a difference, in recent continental philosophy. Both Jürgen Habermas[37] and Karl-Otto Apel[38] give epistemological justifications for democracy that have a definite relation to Dewey's arguments. I think we can better understand Dewey's view by comparing it with their epistemological justifications for democracy.

Both Habermas and Apel present arguments that are at least in part "transcendental arguments," but the term must be taken with caution. Neither Apel nor Habermas believes in the possibility of a transcendental deduction of a system of categories which will give the a priori structure of the world of experience, in the style of Kant. For Apel and Habermas, "transcendental argument" is simply inquiry into the presuppositions of things that we do—for example, the presuppositions of the activity of arguing about whether something should or should not be done. Their work cannot be simply assimilated to the philosophical work of pragmatists like Dewey (which may be a good reason to compare and contrast it with that work), for it rests on the notion of internal relations between concepts (i.e., the notion of analytic truth). Dewey was extremely leery of such a notion, and he certainly would not have given it a prominent place in any exposition of his views. Moreover, Apel, in particular, seems to view philosophy as consisting entirely of transcendental argument (although Habermas allows both "transcendental" and empirical considerations to play a role), and Dewey would certainly have rejected such a conception.

In Apel's presentation of the argument,[39] the act of stating something has certain formal presuppositions: the speaker implicitly or explicitly claims that what he is saying is true (if the statement is descriptive) or normatively right (if the statement is normative), or possesses still other kinds of validity (in the case of other kinds of statements).[40] The speaker implicitly or explicitly claims to be sincere: "I say that p, but I am not sincere in saying this" is self-defeating, if intended as a "constative" speech act (an act of asserting that p). The speaker implicitly or explicitly claims to be able to give reasons: in most circumstances, "I claim that p, but I can give no reason" will fail in a rational discussion. And there are still other conditions of this kind that need not concern us in this sketch of the position.[41]

Apel and Habermas further explain that the idea of a fully justified statement is that the statement can withstand tests and criticism. This is implicit in the practice of discussing whether or not a given statement really is fully justified. At the same time, they draw on the work of Peirce and the later work of Wittgenstein to argue that the idea of a statement whose complete and final warrant is wholly available to the speaker him or herself—who neither needs nor can profit from the data of others—is an empty and fallacious idea. The idea of a statement which is true (or normatively right) or one which can withstand tests and criticism, is empty unless we allow any statement claimed to be true to be tested by an ongoing community of testers, or at any rate, critics. The upshot is that if I am a participant in a rational discussion (or wish to be, and therefore refrain from pragmatically contradicting my declared intention to participate in such a discussion), then I am committed to the idea of a possible community of inquirers.

So far this may not seem to have anything to do with democracy, although it does concern pragmatist models of inquiry, Wittgenstein's private language argument,[42] and other philosophical models. But what sort of community must the ideal community of inquirers be? A community which is competent to determine what is true and false (or any other sort of validity that can be rationally discussed) must be such that anyone in that community can criticize what is put forward knowing that his or her criticism will be heard and discussed. If some criticisms are simply ignored, then the possibility of an "immunizing strategy" rears its ugly head; we are back at the method of "What is Agreeable to Reason," or worse, the methods of "tenacity" or (still worse) "authority."[43] In short, the community must be one which respects the principles of intellectual freedom and equality.

Although the argument just summarized has clear points of agreement and overlap with Dewey's view, there are strong differences. Habermas and Apel claim to show that the moral obligations fundamental to democratic politics can be derived from the obligation not to perform "pragmatically contradictory" speech-acts. That is, they would claim, each member of the community of inquirers has the obligation to make only statements which are (as far as one knows) true, sincere, and supported by reasons. But such a derivation, even if correct, surely is backward. We are not concerned with the ethical or democratic life only or even primarily because we have to live that way in order to discover and tell the truth, be sincere, and have reasons; rather, being sincere and telling the truth are among the obligations that we sometimes undertake in connection with the ethical life. Moreover, the obligation to discover and to tell the truth is a defeasible obligation. For example, we should not try to discover any more truths about better ways to make bacteriological weapons or nerve gasses. Indeed, if the whole human race could agree not to try to discover any more truths about better ways to make atom bombs, that would be a good thing. I don't mean that it would be a good thing if we stopped doing physics altogether, and I recognize that pursuing pure physics will undoubtedly lead to discoveries that can be used to make weapons. But the fact remains that there is a difference between trying to discover fundamental laws of nature and trying to discover specific engineering applications. Refusing to discover specific engineering applications is, after all, refusing to even try to discover some truths that human beings are capable of discovering and that have bearing on rational arguments. Yet the decision that, for weighty moral reasons, we are better off not knowing certain things is at times perfectly justified. Indeed, someone who thought that we had an obligation to discover the most effective ways to torture people and a further obligation to publicize that knowledge would be a monster.

But this observation seems to undercut much of the force of Habermas's and Apel's arguments. After all, the anti-democratic despot need not be insincere when saying what he or she believes to be the truth. He or she may honestly believe that an authoritarian society is the best society. He or she may refuse to allow that belief to be put to the test because the despot believes that the moral cost of such a test would be much too high. If, for example, the despot is convinced that trying democratic modes of social organization would lead to enormous amounts of suffering, he or she may feel that while not allowing them to be tried, or even discussed, is unfortunate epistemologically, and prevents his or her beliefs from having as much warrant as they might otherwise have, not trying them is not only morally justified, but morally required. The problem with the arguments of Habermas and Apel is that what is required for the optimal pursuit of truth may not be what is required for human flourishing or even for human survival.

Apel's reply to this objection is that when the anti-democratic despot puts forward this argument, then, by the very act of offering an argument, he or she undertakes to listen to reasons on the other side. If this is right, the despot's behavior is pragmatically self-contradictory. But I do not see the force of this reply at all. Avoiding "pragmatic self-contradiction" in this highly sophisticated sense can hardly be the supreme maxim governing human life!

It seems to me that Dewey does have an answer to this kind of objection, but it is not a "transcendental" answer. Dewey believes, and he recognizes that this is an empirical hypothesis, that it is simply not true that democratic societies (and Dewey was a democratic socialist) cannot survive without producing massive unhappiness, or that ordinary people are not capable of making the decisions and taking the responsibilities that they must make and take if democracy is to function effectively. As a matter of empirical fact, the arguments offered by the despot and by all who defend special privilege are rationalizations, that is, they are offered in what is, at bottom, bad faith. I quote:

> All special privilege narrows the outlook of those who possess it, as well as limits the development of those not having it. A very considerable portion of what is regarded as the inherent selfishness of mankind is the product of an inequitable distribution of power—inequitable because it shuts out some from the conditions which direct and evoke their capacities, while it produces a one-sided growth in those who have privilege. Much of the alleged unchangeableness of human nature signifies only that as long as social conditions are static and distribute opportunity unevenly, it is absurd to expect change in men's desires and aspirations. Special privilege always induces a stand pat and reactionary attitude on the part of those who have it; in the end it usually provokes a blind rage of destruction on the part of those who suffer from it. The intellectual blindness caused by privileged and monopolistic possession is made evident in "rationalization" of the

> misery and cultural degradation of others which attend its existence. These are asserted to be the fault of those who suffer, to be the consequence of their own improvidence, lack of industry, willful ignorance, etc. There is no favored class in history which has not suffered from distorted ideas and ideals, just as the deprived classes suffered from inertia and underdevelopment.[44]

The critical thrust of this discussion is unmistakable. Democracy may, as Winston Churchill said, be "better than all the other systems which have actually been tried," but it by no means provides full opportunity for the use of "social intelligence" in Dewey's sense. For the use of "social intelligence," as Dewey makes clear, is incompatible, on the one hand, with denying the underprivileged the opportunity to develop and use their capacities, and, on the other hand, with the rationalization of entrenched privilege. Dewey's justification is a critical justification of democracy, one that calls as much for the reform of democracy as for its defense. But what I wish to call attention to here, by contrasting Dewey's argument with Habermas's and Apel's arguments, is its thoroughgoing dependence on empirical hypotheses. For Dewey, the justification of democracy rests at every point on arguments which are not at all transcendental, but which represent the fruit of our collective experience. Deweyan philosophy exemplifies the very methodology for which it argues.

V. Dewey and James

While Dewey's social philosophy seems, as far as it goes, entirely correct, his moral philosophy is less satisfactory when we try to apply it to individual existential choices. To see why, consider the famous example of an existential choice that Sartre employed in *Existentialism and Humanism*.[45] It is World War II, and Pierre has to make an agonizing choice. He has to choose between joining the Resistance, which means leaving his aging mother alone on the farm, or staying and taking care of his mother, but not helping to fight the enemy. Dewey's recommendation to use intelligently guided experimentation in solving ethical problems does not really help in Pierre's case. Pierre is not out to "maximize" the "good," however conceived; he is out to do what is right. Like all consequentialists, Dewey has trouble doing justice to considerations of what is right. This is not to say that Dewey's philosophy never applies to individual existential choices. Some choices are just dumb. But Pierre is not dumb. Neither of the alternatives he is considering is in any way stupid. Yet he cannot just flip a coin.

There are, of course, problems of individual choice which can be handled just as one should handle social problems. If, for example, I cannot decide which school my child should attend, I may decide to experiment. I may send the child to a school with the idea that if it doesn't work out, I can take her out and put her in a different school. But that is not the sort of problem that Pierre faces. Pierre is not free to experiment.

What some philosophers say about such a situation is that the agent should look for a policy such that, if everyone in a similar situation were to act on that policy, the consequences would be for the best. He or she should then act on that policy. Sometimes that is reasonable, but in Pierre's situation it isn't. One of the things that is at stake in Pierre's situation is Pierre's need to decide who Pierre is. Individuality is at stake; and individuality in this sense is not just a "bourgeois value" or an Enlightenment idea. In the Jewish tradition one often quotes the saying of Rabbi Susiah, who said that in the hereafter the Lord would not ask him, "Have you been Abraham?," or "Have you been Moses?," or "Have you been Hillel?," but "Have you been Susiah?" Pierre wants to be Pierre; or as Kierkegaard would say, he wants to become who he already is.[46] And this is not the same thing as wanting to follow the "optimal policy"; or perhaps it is—perhaps the optimal policy in such a case is, in fact, to "become who you are." But doing that is not something that the advice to use "the scientific method" can help you very much with, even if your conception of the scientific method is as generous as Dewey's.

There are various possible future continuations of Pierre's story, no matter what decision he makes. Years afterward, if he survives, Pierre may tell the story of his life (rightly or wrongly) depicting his decision (to join the Resistance or to stay with his mother) as clearly the right decision, with no regrets or doubts, whatever the costs may have turned out to be. Or he may tell his story depicting his decision as the wrong decision, or depicting it as a "moral dilemma" to which there was no correct answer.[47] But part of the problem Pierre faces at the time he makes the decision is that he doesn't even know that he faces a "moral dilemma."

William James somewhere quotes an aphorism of Kierkegaard's (whom he could not have read, since Kierkegaard had not been translated into any language James read) to the effect that "We live forward but we understand backward."[48] That is exactly Pierre's situation. Dewey's advice to consider "consummatory experiences" is of no use in this case, even if we restrict ourselves to consummatory experiences which are intelligently brought about and "appraised." For if Pierre considers only his own consummatory experiences, then he is horrendously selfish, but if he tries to consider all relevant consummatory experiences, then he is involved with a hopelessly vague question. This is often the case when we try to think like consequentialists in real life.

It was precisely this sort of situation that William James was addressing when he wrote the famous essay "The Will to Believe"[49] (which James later said should have been titled "The *Right* to Believe"). Although this essay has received a great deal of hostile criticism, I believe that its logic is, in fact, precise and impeccable, but I will not try to defend that claim here. For James it is crucial for understanding situations like Pierre's that we recognize at least three of their features: that the choice Pierre faces is "forced," that is, these are the only options realistically available to him; that the choice is "vital"—it matters deeply to him; and that it is not possible for Pierre to decide what to do on intellectual grounds. In such a situation—and only in such a situation—James believes that Pierre has the right to believe and to act "running ahead of scientific evidence."[50] The storm of controversy around "The Will to Believe" was largely occasioned by the fact that James took the decision to believe or not to believe in God to be a decision of this kind. Because religious (and even more anti-religious) passions are involved, most of the critics do not even notice that the argument of "The Will to Believe" is applied by James and is meant to apply to all existential decisions.[51] Most critics also have not noticed that it is meant to apply to the individual's choice of a philosophy, including pragmatism itself.[52]

James believed, as Wittgenstein did,[53] that religious belief is neither rational nor irrational but arational. It may, of course, not be a viable option for those who are committed atheists or committed believers. But those for whom it is a viable option may be in a situation completely analogous to the one Sartre imagines (or so James believed). For James, however, the need to "believe ahead of the evidence" is not confined to religious and existential decisions. It plays an essential role in science itself. Although this is hardly controversial nowadays, it was what caused the most controversy when the lecture, "The Will to Believe" was repeated for the graduate students at Harvard University.[54] James's point—which anticipated an idea that historians of science have documented very well in recent years—was that the great innovators in science (as well as their partisans) very often believe their theories despite having very little evidence, and defend them with enormous passion.

The scientific community's acceptance of Einstein's theory of relativity provides a very nice example of James's point. By way of background, let me explain that Max Planck was an early convert to Einstein's theory of special relativity. He played a crucial role in bringing that theory to the attention of elite physicists.[55] At that time, however, Einstein's theory appeared to lead to exactly the same predictions as Poincaré's theory, which also incorporated Lorentz transformations. (In Poincaré's theory there is still an absolute rest that cannot be detected experimentally because of the Lorentz contractions.) According to Gerald Holton, who recently related the story to me, the physicists in Berlin met with Planck on one occasion and drove him to the wall by demanding that he provide an experimental reason for preferring Einstein's theory over Poincaré's. Planck could not do this. Instead he said, "*Es ist mir eigentlich mehr sympatisch*" (it's simply more sympatico). Einstein himself had an equally passionate belief in his own general theory of relativity. When asked what he would have said if the eclipse experiment had turned out the wrong way, Einstein responded, "I would have felt sorry for the Lord God."

James made a point not just about the history of science, although he was quite right about that. His claim—a claim which the logical positivists paradoxically helped to make part of the conventional philosophy of science with their sharp distinction between context of discovery and context of justification—was that science would not progress if scientists never believe or defend theories except on sufficient evidence. When it comes to the institutional decision, the decision made by academically organized science, to accept a theory or not, then it is important to apply the scientific method; in "the context of justification" (although James did not use that jargon) James was all on the side of scrupulous attention to evidence. Even before logical positivism appeared, however, James recognized that there is another moment in scientific procedure—the discovery moment—during which the same constraints cannot be applied.

Perhaps even the positivists might not have gone as far as James. Even the positivists might have said that in the context of discovery it is all right to think of a theory, and propose it for testing without sufficient evidence, but even the individual scientist should not become a believer in his or her theory before it has been fully tested. To this, James would say, in company with many historians and sociologists of science nowadays, that if scientists took that advice, too many good theories would never get tested at all. Enormous numbers of theories are proposed every day, and only a very small number really are eventually tested. The willingness of individuals to "believe ahead of the evidence" thus plays a crucial role in empirical science itself.

The situation with respect to religion is, of course, quite different. Even though the physicist or the molecular biologist who invents a theory, or the advocates who find the theory "*sympatisch*," may believe the theory ahead of the evidence, the eventual acceptance by the scientific community depends on public confirmation. In the case of religious belief however—*pace* Alasdair MacIntyre—there is never public confirmation. Perhaps the only One who can "verify" that God exists is God Himself.[56] The Pierre case, moreover, is still a third kind of case.[57] In that case, as I already remarked (following an observation by Ruth Anna Putnam),[58] Pierre may come to feel afterward that he made the right choice (although he will hardly be able to "verify" that he did), but there is no guarantee that he will "know" later whether he did. James would say that in each of these cases it is valuable, both from the point of view of the individual and of the public, that there should be individuals who make such choices.

James thought that every single human being must make decisions of the kind that Pierre had to make, even if they are not as dramatic (of course, this was Sartre's point as well). Our best energies, James argued, cannot be set free unless we are willing to make the sort of existential commitment that this example illustrates. Someone who only acts when the "estimated utilities" are favorable does not live a meaningful human life. For instance, even if I choose to devote my life to a calling whose ethical and social value is certain, say, to comforting the dying, helping the mentally ill, curing the sick, or relieving poverty, I still have to decide, not whether it is good that someone should do that thing, but whether it is good that I, Hilary Putnam, do that thing. The answer to that question cannot be a matter of well-established scientific fact, no matter how generously "scientific" is defined.

This existentialist note is unmistakable in the quotation from Fitzjames Stephen[59] with which James ends *The Will to Believe*:

> "What do you think of yourself? What do you think of the world?. . . . These are questions with which all must deal as it seems good to them. They are riddles of the Sphinx, and in some way or other we must deal with them. . . . In all important transactions of

> Life we have to take a leap in the dark. . . . If we decide to leave the riddles unanswered, that is a choice. If we waver in our answer, that too is a choice; but whatever choice we make, we make it at our peril. If a man chooses to turn his back altogether on God and the future, no one can prevent him. No one can show beyond reasonable doubt that he is mistaken. If a man thinks otherwise, and acts as he thinks, I do not see how any one can prove that he is mistaken. If a man thinks otherwise, and acts as he thinks, I do not see how any one can prove that he is mistaken. Each must act as he thinks best, and if he is wrong so much the worse for him. We stand on a mountain pass in the midst of whirling snow and blinding mist, through which we get glimpses now and then of paths which may be deceptive. If we stand still, we shall be frozen to death. If we take the wrong road, we shall be dashed to pieces. We do not certainly know whether there is any right one. What must we do? 'Be strong and of a good courage.' Act for the best, hope for the best, and take what comes. . . . If death ends all, we cannot meet death better."[60]

The life of Rudolf Carnap is a beautiful example of James's point. No doubt Carnap thought that his entire adult life was based on rational principles, and that at each point he could cogently and rationally justify what he did. This includes his commitment to socialism, as well as his commitment to logical positivism (which he called "the scientific conception of the world" in a famous manifesto).[61] He believed in logical positivism not only for what he considered its intrinsic correctness, but also as a means to "social transformation." Yet those of us who look back on Carnap's life can see that he was making exactly the "leaps in the dark" that Fitzjames Stephen described.

James's existentialism is all the more remarkable because he had not read a single existentialist writer (except Nietzsche, whom he pitied[62] and read without any sensitivity). At the same time, James never failed to see the need for a check on existential commitment. For James, my right to my own existential commitments stops where it infringes upon the similar right of my neighbor. Indeed, James described the principle of tolerance ("our ancient national doctrine of live and let live") as having "a far deeper meaning than our people now seem to imagine it to possess."[63] If reason (or "intelligence") cannot decide what my ultimate commitment should be, it can certainly decide from long and bitter experience that fanaticism is a terrible and destructive force. James always tempered a sympathetic understanding of the need for commitment with a healthy awareness of the horrors of fanaticism.

If Dewey is less sensitive than James to the limits of intelligence as a guide to life, it is perhaps because of Dewey's dualistic conception of human goods. For Dewey there are fundamentally two, and only two, dominant dimensions to human life: the aesthetic dimension and the social dimension, which for Dewey meant the struggle for a better world, a better society, and for the release of human potential. Dewey was criticized for seeing all of life as social action; he could and did always reply that on the contrary, in the last analysis he saw all "consummatory experience" as aesthetic. The trouble with this answer is that a bifurcation of goods into social goods, which are attained through the use of instrumental rationality, and consummatory experiences, which are ultimately aesthetic, too closely resembles a similar positivist or empiricist division of life into the prediction and control of experiences and the enjoyment of experiences. James, I think, succumbs less than Dewey to the temptation to offer a metaphysics of terminal goods.

VI. Conclusion

If, in spite of these criticisms, I still take John Dewey as one of my philosophical heroes, it is because his reflection on democracy never degenerates into mere propaganda for the democratic status quo. It is true that Dewey's optimism about human potential is not something which has been proven right beyond all doubt, nor does Dewey claim that it has. As Dewey emphatically reminds us, however, neither has pessimism about human potential been proven to be right. On the contrary, to the extent that previously oppressed groups have been given the opportunity to develop their capacities, those capacities have always been surprising.

I would like to close by saying a little more about this critical dimension of Dewey's thought. When Dewey speaks of using the scientific method to solve social problems, he does not mean relying on experts who, Dewey emphasizes, could not solve social problems. For one thing, experts belong to privileged classes and are affected by the rationalizations of which Dewey spoke. As an elite, they are accustomed to telling others how to solve their social problems. For Dewey, social problems are not resolved by telling other people what to do. Rather, they are resolved by releasing human energies so that people will be able to act for themselves.[64] Dewey's social philosophy is not simply a restatement of classical liberalism; for, as Dewey says,

> The real fallacy [of classical liberalism] lies in the notion that individuals have such a native or original endowment of rights, powers and wants that all that is required on the side of institutions and laws is to eliminate the obstructions they offer to the "free" play of the natural equipment of individuals. The removal of obstructions did not have a liberating effect upon such individuals as were antecedently possessed of the means, intellectual and economic, to take advantage of the changed social conditions. But it left all others at the mercy of the new social conditions brought about by the freed powers of those advantageously situated. The notion that men are equally free to act if only the same legal arrangements apply equally to all—irrespective of differences in education, in command of capital, and that control of the social environment which is furnished by the institution of property—is a pure absurdity, as facts have demonstrated. Since actual, that is, effective, rights and demands are products of interactions, and are not found in the original and isolated constitution of human nature, whether moral or psychological, mere elimination of obstructions is not enough. The latter merely liberates force and ability as that happens to be distributed by past accidents of history. This "free"

> action operates disastrously as far as the many are concerned. The only possible conclusion, both intellectually and practically, is that the attainment of freedom conceived as power to act in accord with choice depends upon positive and constructive changes in social arrangements.[65]

We too often forget that Dewey was a radical. But he was a radical democrat, not a radical scoffer at "bourgeois democracy." For Dewey, our democracy is not something to be spurned, nor is it something with which we should be satisfied. Our democracy is an emblem of what could be. What could be is a society that develops the capacities of all its men and women to think for themselves, to participate in the design and testing of social policies, and to judge the results. Perhaps for Dewey education plays the role that revolution plays in the philosophy of Karl Marx. Not that education is enough. Education is a means by which people can acquire capacities, but they have to be empowered to use those capacities. In the above passage, Dewey lists a number of things that stand in the way of that empowerment. Nevertheless, education is a precondition for democracy if democracy is a precondition for the use of intelligence to solve social problems. The kind of education that Dewey advocated did not consist in a Rousseauistic belief in the native goodness of every child, or in an opposition to discipline in public schools, or in a belief that content need not be taught. As Dewey's writings on education show, he was far more hard-headed and realistic than the "progressive educators" in all of these respects. Dewey did insist, however, that education must not be designed to teach people their place, or to defer to experts, or to accept uncritically a set of opinions. Education must be designed to produce men and women who are capable of learning on their own and of thinking critically. The extent to which we take the commitment to democracy seriously is measured by the extent to which we take the commitment to education seriously. In these days, saying these words fills me with shame for the state of democracy at the end of the twentieth century.

Notes

1. Bernard Williams, *Ethics and the Limits of Philosophy* (London: Fontana, 1985).
2. *Ibid.* 26–27.
3. *Ibid.* 29.
4. See, e.g., James Gouinlock, introduction to *The Moral Writings of John Dewey*, ed. James Gouinlock (New York: Hafner, 1976), xxiii.
5. Williams, 40.
6. *Ibid.*
7. Although Williams also considers the Kantian strategy, he concludes that it is unworkable, and that if any objective justification could be given—which he doubts—it would have to be along Aristotelian lines.
8. Williams, 45.
9. *Ibid.*

10. *Ibid.* 27.
11. *Ibid.* 45–46.
12. *Ibid.* 46.
13. John Rawls, *A Theory of Justice* (Cambridge, MA: Harvard University Press, 1971).
14. See, *e.g.*, Frédérique A. Marglin & Stephen A. Marglin eds., *Dominating Knowledge* (Oxford: Oxford University Press, 1990).
15. See, *e.g.*, Michael Walzer, *Interpretation and Social Criticism* (Cambridge, MA: Harvard University Press, 1987). In his recent work, Walzer seems to be searching for a middle path between relativistic social scientists and moral philosophers like John Rawls.
16. Stephen Marglin, "Towards the Decolonization of the Mind," in *Dominating Knowledge*, 1–29.
17. *Ibid.*
18. John Dewey and J. H. Tufts, *Ethics*, rev. ed. (New York: Holt, 1936).
19. These arguments are set forth in Alasdair MacIntyre, *After Virtue*, 2nd ed. (Notre Dame, IN: University of Notre Dame Press, 1984), and its successor, Alasdair MacIntyre, *Whose Justice? Which Rationality?* (Notre Dame, IN: University of Notre Dame Press, 1988).
20. Thomas Kuhn, *The Structure of Scientific Revolutions* (Chicago: University of Chicago Press, 1962).
21. Here MacIntyre's thinking resonates more with Stephen Toulmin's than with Kuhn's.
22. MacIntyre, *Whose Justice? Which Rationality?* chapters 9–11.
23. MacIntyre, *After Virtue*, 205.
24. *Ibid.* 181.
25. See *ibid.* 182.
26. See Søren Kierkegaard, *Concluding Unscientific Postscript*, trans. David F. Swenson (Princeton: Princeton University Press, 1941).
27. Charles Sanders Peirce, "The Fixation of Belief" and "How to Make Our Ideas Clear," reprinted in *Writings of Charles S. Peirce*, ed. Christian J. Kloesl (Bloomington: Indiana University Press, 1986), 3.242–276.
28. Peirce, "Fixation," 256.
29. *Ibid.* 230, 251.
30. MacIntyre, *After Virtue*, 9–10.
31. Allan Bloom, *The Closing of the American Mind* (New York: Simon and Schuster, 1987).
32. John Dewey, *Logic* (New York: Holt, 1938), 280.
33. Williams, 45.
34. *Ibid.* 150.
35. For a discussion of Williams's metaphysical views, see Hilary Putnam, "Objectivity and the Science/Ethics Distinction," in *The Quality of Life*, ed. Martha Nussbaum and Amartya Sen (Oxford: Clarendon Press, 1993).
36. Dewey, *Experience and Nature*, 407–08.
37. See Jürgen Habermas, *The Theory of Communicative Action*, trans. Thomas McCarthy (Boston: Beacon Press, 1984); Habermas, "Wahrheitstheorien," in *Wirklichkeit und Reflexion: Festschrift fiir W. Schutz*, ed. H. Fahrenbach (Pfüllingen, 1973), 211–65.
38. See Karl-Otto Apel, *Diskurs und Verantwortung: Das Problem des Ubergangs zur Postkonventionellen Moral*, 1985.
39. *Ibid.* Habermas refers to this argument repeatedly in *The Theory of Communicative Action*, but it is not given explicitly at any one place in that book. One can, nevertheless, get a pretty clear view of how Habermas understands the argument from the first chapter of volume I of that work, and Habermas's own statement of the argument that appears in Habermas, "Wahrheitstheorien."

40. It may be noticed that even though Habermas and Apel are, like Dewey, "cognitivists" in ethics, they accept a dichotomy between normative and descriptive statements that Dewey would have regarded as an untenable dualism.

41. While I would of course agree with these other conditions, I would not attach weight to the claim that they express "internal relations," that is, that they are analytic. But neither would I attach much weight to the fact that they are not (in my view) analytic. The important thing is that they are "necessarily relative to our present body of knowledge." Hilary Putnam, *Philosophical Papers, Volume I: Mathematics, Matter, and Method* (Cambridge: Cambridge University Press, 1976), 237–249. Although American analytic philosophers, who have been disabused of the notion of analyticity by Quine, will be quick to point out that a "paradigm shift" might someday lead us to abandon the very notions of truth and statement making in favor of we-know-not-what "successor notions." Furthermore, they will argue, the fact that we do not as of this time know what it would be like to have such "successor concepts" makes such talk empty, even if the claim that there are not "analytic" truths in this area is correct.

42. Ludwig Wittgenstein, *Philosophical Investigations*, trans. G.E.M. Anscombe (New York: Macmillan, 1953), paragraphs 243–326.

43. See Peirce, "The Fixation of Belief," 29.

44. Dewey and Tufts, *Ethics*, 385–86.

45. Jean-Paul Sartre, *Existentialism and Humanism*, trans. P. Mairet (London: Methuen, 1948).

46. Kierkegaard, 116.

47. See also Ruth Anna Putnam, "Weaving Seamless Webs," *Philosophy* 62 (April, 1987), 207–220. Ruth Anna Putnam uses as an example of a "moral dilemma" the predicament of a pacifist who must decide whether and to what extent he or she is willing to participate in the war effort, for example, by serving in a non-combat capacity. As she says, "sometimes only within the frame of a whole life, and sometimes only within the frame of the life of a whole community, can these decisions be evaluated." *Ibid.* 216.

48. William James, *Pragmatism* (Cambridge, MA: Harvard University Press, 1975), 107.

49. William James, "The Will to Believe" (first published in 1897), in *The Will to Believe and Other Essays in Popular Philosophy* (Cambridge, MA: Harvard University Press, 1979).

50. *Ibid.* 29.

51. This conclusion is clear not only from the essay itself, but from many other essays in which James offers similar arguments.

52. See James, *Pragmatism*, 281 ("[W]hether the pragmatic theory of truth is true really, they [the pragmatists] cannot warrant—they can only believe it. To their hearers they can only propose it, as I propose it to my readers, as something to be verified ambulando, or by the way in which its consequences may confirm it."); "William James, *The Meaning of Truth* (Cambridge, MA: Harvard University Press, 1975).

53. Wittgenstein's views can be found in twenty printed pages of notes taken by some of his students on his lectures on religious belief. Reprinted in Ludwig Wittgenstein, *Lectures and Conversations on Aesthetics. Psychology and Religious Belief*, ed. Cyril Barrett (Oxford: Blackwell, 1966).

54. See Edgar Arthur Singer, Jr., *Modern Thinkers and Present Problems: An Approach to Modern Philosophy Through Its History* (New York: Henry Holt, 1923), 218–20.

55. Planck was also responsible for publishing Einstein's paper in the journal Planck edited.

56. This is not to say that religious belief is unwarranted. I believe that it is "warranted," although not by evidence. This stance is intimately connected with a sense of existential decision.

57. See Sartre.

58. See Ruth Anna Putnam.

59. J. Stephen, *Liberty, Equality, Fraternity* (1874).

60. Quotation from James Fitzjames Stephen in William James, "The Will to Believe," 33.

61. Rudolf Carnap, Hans Hahn, and Otto Neurath, "The Scientific Conception of the World: The Vienna Circle," in *Empiricism and Sociology*, ed. Marie Neurath and Robert S. Cohen (Boston: Reidel, 1973), 300–19.

62. See William James, *Varieties of Religious Experience*, first published in 1902 (Cambridge, MA: Harvard University Press, 1985), 296–7 (referring to "poor Nietzsche").

63. William James, *Talks to Teachers on Psychology and to Students on Some of Life's Ideals*, first published in 1899 (Cambridge, MA: Harvard University Press, 1983), 5. The entire concluding paragraph of the preface, from which this quotation is taken, is a paean to tolerance and an attack on "the pretension of our nation to inflict its inner ideals and institutions *vi et armis* upon Orientals." (James was referring to the Philippines.)

64. An example that comes to mind is the energies that were released when Polish workers formed Solidarity.

65. John Dewey, "Philosophies of Freedom," in *Freedom in the Modern World*, ed. Horace Meyer Kallen (New York: Coward-McCann, 1928), 236–71; quoted passage on 249–50.

Rorty presents here his case for a reconstruction of the notion of "the world" either as a platitude regarding knowledge's object or as whatever is not currently up for debate.

RICHARD RORTY

The World Well Lost

The notion of alternative conceptual frameworks has been a commonplace of our culture since Hegel. Hegel's historicism gave us a sense of how there might be genuine novelty in the development of thought and of society. Such a historicist conception of thought and morals was, we may see by hindsight, rendered possible by Kant, himself the least historicist of philosophers. For Kant perfected and codified the two distinctions that are necessary to develop the notion of an "alternative conceptual framework"—the distinction between spontaneity and receptivity and the distinction between necessary and contingent truth. Since Kant, we find it almost impossible not to think of the mind as divided into active and passive faculties, the former using concepts to "interpret" what "the world" imposes on the latter. We also find it difficult not to distinguish between those concepts which the mind could hardly get along without and those which it can take or leave alone—and we think of truths about the former concepts as "necessary" in the most proper and paradigmatic sense of the term. But as soon as we have this picture of the mind in focus, it occurs to us, as it did to Hegel, that those all-important a priori concepts, those which determine what our experience or our morals will be, might have been different. We cannot, of course, imagine what an experience or a practice *that* different would be like, but we can abstractly suggest that the men of the Golden Age, or the inhabitants of the Fortunate Isles, or the mad, might shape the intuitions that are our common property in different molds, and might thus be conscious of a different "world."

Various attacks on the contrast between the observed and the theoretical (in, e.g., Kuhn, Feyerabend, and Sellars) have led recently to a new appreciation of Kant's point that to change one's concepts would be to change what one experiences, to change one's "phenomenal world." But this appreciation leads us to question the familiar distinction between spontaneity and receptivity. The possibility of different conceptual schemes highlights the fact that a Kantian unsynthesized intuition can exert no influence on how it is to be synthesized—or, at best, can exert only an influence we shall have to describe in a way as relative to a chosen conceptual scheme as our description of everything else. Insofar as a Kantian intuition is effable, it is just a perceptual judgment, and thus not *merely* "intuitive." Insofar as it is ineffable, it is incapable of having an explanatory function. This dilemma—a parallel to that which Hegelians raised concerning the thing-in-itself—casts doubt on the notion of a faculty of "receptivity." There seems no need to postulate an intermediary between the physical thrust of the stimulus upon the organ and the full-fledged conscious judgment that the properly programmed organism forms in consequence. Thus there is no need to split the organism up into a receptive wax tablet on the one hand and an "active" interpreter of what nature has there imprinted on the other. So the Kantian point that different a priori concepts would, if there could be such things, give a different phenomenal world gives place either to the straightforward but paradoxical claim that different concepts give us different worlds, or to dropping the notion of "conceptual framework" altogether. 'Phenomenal' can no longer be given a sense, once Kantian "intuitions" drop out. For the suggestion that our concepts shape neutral material no longer makes sense once there is nothing to serve as this material. The physical stimuli themselves are not a useful substitute, for the contrast between the "posits" which the inventive mind constructs to predict and control stimuli, and the stimuli themselves, can be no more than a contrast between the effable world and its ineffable cause.[1]

The notion of *alternative* conceptual frameworks thus contains the seeds of doubt about the root notion of "conceptual framework," and so of its own destruction. For once the faculty of receptivity and, more generally, the notion of neutral material becomes dubious, doubt spreads easily to the notion of conceptual thought as "shaping" and thus to the notion of the World-Spirit moving from one set of a priori concepts to the next.

But the doubts about the Hegelian picture produced by an attack on the given/interpretation distinction are vague and diffuse by comparison with those which result from attacking the necessary/contingent distinction. Quine's suggestion that the difference between a priori and empirical truth is merely that between the relatively difficult to give up and the relatively easy brings in its train the notion that there is no clear distinction to be drawn between questions of meaning and questions of fact. This, in turn, leaves us (as Quine has pointed out in criticizing Carnap) with no distinction between questions about alternative "theories" and questions about alternative "frameworks."[2] The philosophical notion of "meaning," against which Quine is protesting is, as he says, the latest version of the "idea idea"—a philosophical tradition one of whose incarnations was the Kantian notion of "concept." The notion of a choice among "meaning postulates" is the latest version of the notion of a choice among alternative conceptual schemes. Once the necessary is identified with the analytic and the analytic is explicated in terms of meaning, an attack on the notion of what Harman has called the "philosophical" sense of 'meaning' becomes an attack on the notion of "conceptual framework" in any sense that assumes a distinction of kind between this notion and that of "empirical theory."[3]

So far we have seen how criticisms of givenness and of analyticity both serve to dismantle the Kantian notion of "conceptual framework"—the notion of "concepts necessary for the constitution of experience, as opposed to concepts whose application is necessary to control or predict experience." I have been arguing that without the notions of "the given" and of "the a priori" there can be no notion of "the constitution of experience." Thus there can be no notion of alternative experiences, or alternative worlds, to be constituted by the adoption of new a priori concepts. But there is a simpler and more direct objection to the notion of "alternative conceptual framework," to which I now wish to turn. This objection has recently been put forward, in connection with Quine's thesis of indeterminacy, by Davidson and Stroud.[4] The argument is verificationist, and turns on the unrecognizability of persons using a conceptual framework different from our own (or, to put it another way, the unrecognizability as a *language* of anything that is not translatable into English). The connection between Quine's attack on "conventionalist" notions of meaning and this verificationist argument is supposed to be as follows: if one thinks of "meaning" in terms of the discovery of the speech dispositions of foreigners rather than in terms of mental essences (ideas, concepts, chunks of the crystalline structure of thought), then one will not be able to draw a clear distinction between the foreigner's using words different in meaning from any words in our language and the foreigner's having many false beliefs. We can and must play off awkward translations against ascriptions of quaint beliefs, and vice versa, but we will never reach the limiting case of a foreigner all or most of whose beliefs must be viewed as false according to a translating scheme that pairs off all or most of his terms as identical in meaning with some terms of English. We will not reach this case (so the Davidsonian argument goes) because any such translation scheme would merely show that we had not succeeded in finding a translation at all.

But (to extend Davidson's argument a bit) if we can never find a translation, why should we think that we are faced with language users at all? It is, of course, possible to imagine humanoid organisms making sounds of great variety at one another in very various circumstances with what appear to be various effects upon the interlocutors' behavior. But suppose that repeated attempts systematically to correlate these sounds with the organisms' environment and behavior fail. What should we say? One suggestion might be that the analytic hypotheses we are using in our tentative translation schemes use concepts that we do not share with the natives—because the natives "carve up the world" differently, or have different "quality spaces" or something of the sort. But could there be a way of deciding between this suggestion and the possibility that the organisms' sounds are *just* sounds? Once we imagine different ways of carving up the world, nothing could stop us from attributing "untranslatable languages" to *anything* that emits a variety of signals. But, so this verificationist argument concludes, this degree of open-endedness shows us that the purported notion of an untranslatable language is as fanciful as that of an invisible color.

It is important to note that Quinean arguments against analyticity and for the indeterminacy of translation are not necessary for this argument. The argument stands on its own feet—Quine's only contribution to it being to disparage the possibility that 'meaning' can mean something more than what is contextually defined in the process of predicting the foreigner's behavior. To adopt this view of meaning is all that is required to suggest that the notion of "people who speak our language but believe nothing that we believe" is incoherent.[5] To *show* that it is incoherent, however—to complete the argument—one would have to show in detail that no amount of nonlinguistic behavior by the foreigner could be sufficient to underwrite a translation that made all or most of his beliefs false.[6] For it might be the case, for example, that the way in which the foreigner dealt with trees while making certain sounds made it clear that we had to translate some of his utterances as "These are not trees," and so on for everything else with which he had dealings. Some of his utterances might be translated as: "I am not a person," "These are not words," "One should never use *modus ponens* if one wishes valid arguments," "Even if I were thinking, which I am not, that would not show that I exist." We might ratify these translations by showing that his nonlinguistic ways of handling himself and others showed that he actually did hold such paradoxical beliefs. The only way to show that this suggestion cannot work, would be actually to tell the whole story about this hypothetical foreigner. It might be that a story could be told to show the coherence of these false beliefs with each other and with his actions, or it might not. To show that Davidson and Stroud were right would be to show that, indeed, no such story was tellable.

There is, I think, no briefer way to decide on the soundness of this a priori argument against the possibility of alternative conceptual frameworks than to run over such possible stories. But this inconclusiveness is a feature this argument has in common with all interesting verificationist anti-skeptical arguments. It conforms to the following pattern: (1) the skeptic suggests that our own beliefs (about, e.g., other minds, tables and chairs, or how to translate French) have viable alternatives which unfortunately can never be known to hold but which justify the suspension of judgment; (2) the anti-skeptic replies that the very meaning of the terms used shows that the alternatives suggested are not merely dubious but in principle unverifiable, and thus not reasonable alternatives at all; (3) the skeptic rejoins that verificationism confuses the *ordo essendi* with the *ordo cognoscendi* and that it may well be that some alternative is true even though we shall never know that it is; (4) the anti-skeptic replies that the matter is not worth debating until the skeptic spells out the suggested alternative in full detail, and insinuates that this cannot be done; (5) the controversy degenerates into a dispute about assuming the burden of proof, with the skeptic claiming that it is not up to him to build up a coherent story around his suggested alternative but rather up to the anti-skeptic to show a priori that this cannot be done.

In the case at hand, the skeptic is the fan of "alternative conceptual frameworks," practicing his skepticism on a global scale by insinuating that our entire belief structure might dissolve, leaving not a wrack behind, to be replaced by a complete but utterly dissimilar alternative: The Davidsonian anti-skeptic is in the position of asking how one could come to call any pattern of behavior evidence for such an alternative. The skeptic replies that perhaps we could *never* come to do so, but this merely shows how complete our egocentric predicament is. And so it goes.[7]

In this case, however (unlike the case of limited skepticism about whether, e.g., 'pain' or 'red' means to me what it does to you), the skeptic's global approach gives him a significant dialectical advantage. For he can here sketch what might bring about the actualization of his suggested alternative without being caught up in disagreement about how to interpret concrete experimental results. He can simply refer us to ordinary scientific and cultural progress extrapolated just beyond the range of science fiction. Consider, he will say, the following view of man's history and prospects. Our views about matter and motion, the good life for man, and much else have changed in subtle and complicated ways since the days of the Greeks. Many of the planks in Neurath's boat have been torn up and relaid differently. But since (1) we can describe why it was "rational" for each such change to have occurred, and (2) *many* more of our beliefs are the same as Greek beliefs than are different (e.g., our belief that barley is better than nettles and freedom than slavery, that red is a color, and that lightning often precedes thunder), we should not yet wish to talk about "an alternative conceptual framework." And yet we must admit that even the relatively slight refurbishings of the boat which have occupied the past two thousand years are enough to give us considerable difficulty in knowing just *how* to translate some Greek sentences, and just *how* to explain the "rationality" of the changes that have intervened. Again, the various shifts that have taken place in our understanding of the subject matter of the beliefs we purportedly "share" with the Greeks (resulting from, e.g., the development of new strains of nettles, new forms of slavery, new ways of producing color perceptions, and new explanations of the sound of the thunder and the look of the lightning) make us a little dubious about the claim to shared belief. They create the feeling that here too we may be imposing on history rather than describing it. Let us now extrapolate from ourselves to the Galactic civilization of the future, which we may assume to have moved and reshaped 10^{50} planks in the boat we are in, whereas since Aristotle we have managed to shift only about 10^{20}. Here the suggestion that we interpret these changes as a sequence of rational changes in views about a common matter seems a bit forced, and the fear that even the most empathic Galactic historians of science "won't really understand us properly" quite appropriate. So, our skeptic concludes, the Davidson-Stroud point that to describe in detail the Galactic civilization's beliefs is automatically to make them merely alternative theories within a common framework is not enough. Granting this point, we can still see that it is rational to expect that the incommunicably and unintelligibly novel will occur, even though, *ex hypothesi*, we can neither write nor read a science-fiction story that describes Galactic civilization. Here, then, we have a case in which there really is a difference between the *ordo cognoscendi* and the *ordo essendi*, and no verificationist argument can apply.

To intensify the antinomy we confront here, let us agree for the sake of argument that it is a necessary condition for an entity to be a person that it have or once have had the potentiality for articulating beliefs and desires comparable in quantity and complexity to our own. The qualifications are required if we are to include infants and the insane while excluding dogs and the simpler sort of robots. But the same qualifications will, of course, give trouble when we come to cases where it is not clear whether we are educating a person by developing his latent potentialities (as by teaching a child a language) or transforming a thing into a person (as by clamping some additional memory units onto the robot). Bating this difficulty for the moment, however, let us simply note that this formulation has the consequence that ascribing personhood, ascribing a language, and ascribing beliefs and desires go hand in hand. So, if Davidson is right, ascribing personhood and ascribing mostly the *right* beliefs and mostly the *appropriate* desires go hand in hand. This means that we shall never be able to have evidence that there exist persons who speak languages in principle untranslatable into English or hold beliefs all or most of which are incompatible with our own.

Despite this, however, we can extrapolate to a story about how just such persons might come into existence. So it seems that the world may come to be full of persons whom we could never conceivably recognize as such. A Galactic time-traveler come among us, we now realize, would eventually be forced to abandon his original presumption that we were persons when he failed to correlate our utterances with our environment in any way that enabled him to construct an English-Galactic lexicon. Our initial assumption that the Galactic emissary was a person would be frustrated by the same sort of discovery. How sad that two cultures who have so much to offer each other should fail to recognize each other's existence! What pathos in the thought that we, time-traveling among our Neanderthal ancestors, might stand to them as the Galactic stands to us! But the situation is even worse than that, for reasons I hinted at earlier. We can now see that, for all we know, our *contemporary* world is filled with unrecognizable persons. Why should we ignore the possibility that the trees and the bats and the butterflies and the stars all have their various untranslatable languages in which they are busily expressing their beliefs and desires to one another? Since their organs suit them to receive such different stimuli and to respond in such different ways, it is hardly surprising that the syntax and the primitive predicates of their languages bear no relation to our own.

The inclusion of this last possibility may suggest that something has gone wrong. Perhaps we should not have been so ready to admit the possibility of extrapolation. Perhaps we were too hasty in thinking that attributions of personhood and of articulate belief went hand in hand—for surely we know in advance that butterflies are not persons and therefore know in advance that they will have no beliefs to express. For myself, however, I see nothing wrong with the proposed extrapolation, and I do not see what 'known in advance not to be a person' could mean when applied to the butterfly save that the butterfly doesn't seem human. But there is no particular reason to think that our remote ancestors or descendants would seem human right off the bat either. Let the notion of a person be as complex and multiply criterioned as you please, still I do not think that it will come unstuck from that of a complex interlocked set of beliefs and desires, nor that the latter notion can be separated from that of the potentiality for translatable speech. So I think that to rule the butterflies out is to rule out the Galactics and the Neanderthals, and that to allow extrapolation to the latter is to allow for the possibility that the very same beliefs and desires which our Galactic descendants will hold are being held even now by the butterflies. We can dig in our heels and say that terms like 'person', 'belief, 'desire', and 'language' are ultimately as token—reflexive as 'here' and 'now' or 'morally right', so that in each case essential reference is made to where we are. But that will be the *only* way of ruling out the Galactic, and thus the *only* way of ruling out the butterfly.

If this seems puzzling, I think it will seem less so if we consider some parallels. Suppose we say that there is no poetry among the Patagonians, no astronomy among the aborigines, and no morality among the inhabitants of the planet Mongo. And suppose a native of each locale, protesting against our parochial view, explains that what they have is a *different* sort of poetry, astronomy, or morals, as the case may be. For the Patagonian, neither Homer nor Shelley nor Mallarmé nor Dryden look in the least like poets. He admits, however, that Milton and Swinburne are both faintly reminiscent, in the same only vaguely describable respect, of the paradigms of Patagonian poesy. Those paradigms strike him as clearly fulfilling some of the roles in his culture which our poets fulfill in ours, though not all. The aborigine knows nothing of the equinoxes and the solstices, but he does distinguish planets from stars. However, he uses the same term to refer to planets, meteors, comets, and the sun. The stories he tells about the movements of these latter bodies are bound up with a complicated set of stories about divine providence and cure of diseases, whereas the stories told about the stars have to do exclusively with sex. The inhabitants of the planet Mongo appear shocked when people tell the truth to social equals, and surprised and amused when people refrain from torturing helpless wanderers. They seem to have no taboos at all about sex, but a great many about food. Their social organizations seem held together half by a sort of lottery, and half by brute force. The inhabitants of Mongo, however, profess to be revolted by the Earthlings' failure to grasp the moral point of view, and by our apparent confusion of morality with etiquette and with expedients for ensuring social order.

In the three cases just cited the question, Is it a different *sort* of poetry (or astronomy, or morality), or do they simply have *none?* is obviously not the sort of question it is very important to answer. I suggest that the question, Are the Galactics, or the butterflies, different sorts of persons than ourselves or not persons at all? is also not very important. In the three cases mentioned, one can extend the argument indefinitely by pressing for further details. In the global case, where *ex hypothesi* no translation scheme will work, we cannot. But in the global case (having beliefs *tout court*), as in the particular cases of having beliefs about astronomy or about right and wrong, what is in question is just the best way of predicting, controlling, and generally coping with the entities in question. In the course of figuring this out, we encounter some of the same hard questions I referred to above—the questions that arise when coping with such borderline cases as fetuses, prelinguistic infants, computers, and the insane—Do they have civil rights? Must we try to justify ourselves to them? Are they thinking or acting on instinct? Are they holding beliefs or merely responding to stimuli? Is that a word to which they assign a sense, or are they just sounding off on cue? I doubt that many philosophers believe any longer that procedures for answering such questions are built into "our language" waiting to be discovered by "conceptual analysis." But if we do not believe this, perhaps we can be content to say, in the global case, that the question, Might there be alternative conceptual frameworks to our own, held by persons whom we could never recognize as persons? is the same case. I doubt that we can ever adumbrate general ways of answering questions like, Is it a conceptual framework very different from our own, or is it a mistake to think of it as a language at all? Is it a person with utterly different organs, responses, and beliefs, with whom communication is thus forever impossible, or rather just a complexly behaving thing?

This "don't-care" conclusion is all I have to offer concerning the antinomy created by the Davidson-Stroud argument on the one hand and the skeptic's extrapolation on the other. But this should not be thought of as denigrating the importance of what Davidson and Stroud are saying. On the contrary, I think that, having seen through this antinomy and having noticed the relevance of the original argument to our application of the notion of "person," we are now in a better position to see the importance that it has. This importance can be brought out by (a) looking at the standard objection to the coherence theory of truth ("it cuts truth off from the world") and (b) recurring to our previous discussion of the Kantian roots of the notion of "conceptual framework."

Consider first the traditional objection to coherence theories of truth which says that, although our only *test* of truth must be the coherence of our beliefs with one another, still the *nature* of truth must be "correspondence to reality." It is thought a sufficient argument for this view that Truth is One, whereas alternative equally coherent sets of beliefs are Many.[8] In reply to this argument, defenders of coherence and pragmatic theories of truth have argued that our so-called "intuition" that Truth is One is simply the expectation that, if all perceptual reports were in, there would be one optimal way of selecting among them and all other possible statements so as to have one ideally proportioned system of true beliefs. To this reply, the standard rebuttal is that there would clearly be many such possible systems, among which we could choose only on aesthetic grounds. A further, and more deeply felt, rebuttal is that it is the *world* that determines the truth. The accident of which glimpses of the world our sense organs have vouchsafed us, and the further accidents of the predicates we have entrenched or the theories whose proportions please us, may determine what we have a right to believe. But how could they determine the *truth*?[9]

Now the Davidson-Stroud argument supplies a simple, if temporizing, answer to this standard objection to the coherence theory. Since most of our beliefs (though not any particular one) simply *must* be true—for what could count as evidence that the vast majority of them were not?—the specter of alternative conceptual frameworks shrinks to the possibility that there might be a number of equally good ways to modify slightly our present set of beliefs in the interest of greater predictive power, charm, or what have you. The Davidson-Stroud point makes us remember, among other things, what a very small proportion of our beliefs are changed when our paradigms of physics, or poetry, or morals, change—and makes us realize how few of them *could* change. It makes us realize that the number of beliefs that changed among the educated classes of Europe between the thirteenth and the nineteenth centuries is ridiculously small compared to the number that survived intact. So this argument permits us to say: it is just not the case that there are "alternative" coherent global sets of beliefs. It is perfectly true that there will always be areas of inquiry in which alternative incompatible sets of beliefs are "tied." But the fact that we shall *always* be holding mostly true beliefs and, thus, presumably be "in touch with the world" the vast majority of the time makes this point seem philosophically innocuous. In particular, the claim that, since Truth is One and, therefore, is "correspondence," we must resurrect a foundationalist epistemology to explain "how knowledge is possible" becomes otiose.[10] We shall automatically be "in touch with the world" (most of the time) whether or not we have any incorrigible, or basic, or otherwise privileged or foundational statements to make.

But this way of dealing with the claim that "it is the *world* that determines what is true" may easily seem a fraud. For, as I have been using it, the Davidson-Stroud view seems to perform the conjuring trick of substituting the notion of "the unquestioned vast majority of our beliefs" for the notion of "the world." It reminds us of such coherence theorists as Royce, who claim that our notion of "the world" is just the notion of the ideally coherent contents of an ideally large mind, or of the pragmatists' notion of "funded experience"—those beliefs which are not at the moment being challenged, because they present no problems and no one has bothered to think of alternatives to them. In all these cases—Davidson and Stroud, Royce, Dewey—it may well seem that the issue about truth is just being ducked. For our notion of the world—it will be said—is not a notion of unquestioned beliefs, or unquestionable beliefs, or ideally coherent beliefs, but rather of a hard, unyielding, rigid *être-en-soi* which stands aloof, sublimely indifferent to the attentions we lavish upon it. The true realistic believer will view idealisms and pragmatisms with the same suspicion with which the true believer in the God of our Fathers will view, for example, Tillich's talk of an "object of ultimate concern."[11]

Now, to put my cards on the table, I think that the realistic true believer's notion of the world is an obsession rather than an intuition. I also think that Dewey was right in thinking that the only intuition we have of the world as determining truth is just the intuition that we must make our new beliefs conform to a vast body of platitudes, unquestioned perceptual reports, and the like. So I am happy to interpret the upshot of the Davidson-Stroud argument in a Deweyan way.

But I have no arguments against the true believer's description of our so-called "intuitions." All that can be done with the claim that "only the *world* determines truth" is to point out the equivocation in the realists' own use of 'world'. In the sense in which "the world" is just whatever that vast majority of our beliefs not currently in question are currently thought to be about, there is of course no argument.[12] If one accepts the Davidson-Stroud position, then "the world" will just be the stars, the people, the tables, and the grass—all those things which nobody except the occasional "scientific realist" philosopher thinks might not exist. The fact that the vast majority of our beliefs must be true will, on this view, guarantee the existence of the vast majority of the things we now think we are talking about. So in one sense of 'world'—the sense in which (except for a few fringe cases like gods, neutrinos, and natural rights) we now know perfectly well what the world is like and could not possibly be wrong about it—there is no argument about the point that it is the world that determines truth. All that "determination" comes to is that our belief that snow is white is true because snow is white, that our beliefs about the stars are true because of the way the stars are laid out, and so on.

But this trivial sense in which "truth" is "correspondence to reality" and "depends upon a reality independent of our knowledge" is, of course, not enough for the realist.[13] What he wants is precisely what the Davidson-Stroud argument prevents him from having—the notion of a world *so* "independent of our knowledge" that it might, for all we know, prove to contain none of the things we have always thought we were talking about. He wants to go from, say, "we might be wrong about what the stars are" to "none of the things we talk about might be anything like what we think they are." Given this projection from, as Kant would say, the "conditioned" to the "unconditioned," it is no wonder that antinomies are easily generated.

The notion of "the world" as used in a phrase like 'different conceptual schemes carve up the world differently' must be the notion of something *completely* unspecified and unspecifiable—the thing-in-itself, in fact. As soon as we start thinking of "the world" as atoms and the void, or sense data and awareness of them, or "stimuli" of a certain sort brought to bear upon organs of a certain sort, we have changed the name of the game. For we are now well within some particular theory about how the world is. But for purposes of developing a controversial and nontrivial doctrine of truth as correspondence, only an utterly vague characterization in some such terms as 'cause of the impacts upon our receptivity and goal of our faculty of spontaneity' will do. "Truth" in the sense of "truth taken apart from any theory" and "world" taken as "what determines such truth" are notions that were (like the terms 'subject' and 'object', 'given' and 'consciousness') made for each other. Neither can survive apart from the other.

To sum up this point, I want to claim that "the world" is either the purely vacuous notion of the ineffable cause of sense and goal of intellect, or else a name for the objects that inquiry at the moment is leaving alone: those planks in the boat which are at the moment not being moved about. It seems to me that epistemology since Kant has shuttled back and forth between these two meanings of the term 'world', just as moral philosophy since Plato has shuttled back and forth between 'the Good' as a name for an ineffable touchstone of inquiry which might lead to the rejection of *all* our present moral views, and as a name for the ideally coherent synthesis of as many of those views as possible. This equivocation seems to me essential to the position of those philosophers who see "realism" or "the correspondence theory of truth" as controversial or exciting theses.

To remove altogether the "realistic" temptation to use the word 'world' in the former vacuous sense, we should need to eschew once and for all a whole galaxy of philosophical notions that have encouraged this use—in particular, the Kantian distinctions I discussed at the outset. For suppose we have a simple theory of the eye of the mind either getting, or failing to get, a clear view of the natures of kinds of things—the sort of theory we get, say, in parts of Aristotle's *Posterior Analytics*. Then the notion of alternative sets of concepts will make no clear sense. *Noûs* cannot err. It is only when we have some form of the notion that the mind is split between "simple ideas" or "passively received intuitions" on the one hand and a range of complex ideas (some signifying real, and some only nominal, essences) on the other, that *either* the coherence theory of truth *or* the standard objections to it can begin to look plausible. Only then is the notion plausible that inquiry consists in getting our "representations" into shape, rather than simply describing the world. If we no longer have a view about knowledge as the result of manipulating *Vorstellungen*, then I think we can return to the simple Aristotelian notion of truth as correspondence with reality with a clear conscience—for it will now appear as the uncontroversial triviality that it is.

To develop this claim about the way in which Kantian epistemology is linked with the notion of a nontrivial correspondence theory of truth and thus with the "realist's" notion of "the world" would require another paper, and I shall not try to press it further. Instead I should like to conclude by recalling some of the historical allusions I have made along the way, in order (as Sellars says) to place my conclusions in philosophical space. I said at the outset that the notion of "conceptual framework" and, thus, that of "alternative conceptual framework" depend upon presupposing some standard Kantian distinctions. These distinctions have been the common target of Wittgenstein, Quine, Dewey, and Sellars. I can now express the same point by saying that the notion of "the world" that is correlative with the notion of "conceptual framework" is simply the Kantian notion of a thing-in-itself, and that Dewey's dissolution of the Kantian distinctions between receptivity and spontaneity and between necessity and contingency thus leads naturally to the dissolution of the true realistic believer's notion of "the world." If you start out with Kant's epistemology, in short, you will wind up with Kant's transcendental metaphysics. Hegel, as I suggested earlier, kept the epistemology, but tried to drop the thing-in-itself, thus making himself, and idealism generally, a patsy for realistic reaction. But Hegel's historical sense—the sense that nothing, including an a priori concept, is immune from cultural development—provided the key to Dewey's attack on the epistemology that Hegel shared with Kant. This attack was blunted by Dewey's use of the term 'experience' as an incantatory device for blurring every possible distinction, and so it was not until more sharply focused criticisms were formulated by Wittgenstein, Quine, and Sellars that the force of Dewey's point about "funded experience" as the "cash-value" of the notion of "the world" could be seen. But now that these criticisms have taken hold, the time may have come to try to recapture Dewey's "naturalized" version of Hegelian historicism. In this historicist vision, the arts, the sciences, the sense of right and wrong, and the institutions of society are not attempts to embody or formulate truth or goodness or beauty. They are attempts to solve problems—to modify our beliefs and desires and activities in ways that will bring us greater happiness than we have now. I want to suggest that this shift in perspective is the natural consequence of dropping the receptivity/spontaneity and intuition/concept distinctions, and more generally of dropping the notion of "representation" and the view of man that Dewey has called "the spectator theory" and Heidegger, the "identification of *physis* and *idea*." Because the idealists kept this general picture and occupied themselves with redefining the "object of knowledge," they gave the idealism and the "coherence theory" a bad name—and realism and the "correspondence theory" a good one. But if we can come to see both the coherence and correspondence theories as noncompeting trivialities, then we may finally move beyond realism and idealism. We may reach a point at which, in Wittgenstein's words, we are capable of stopping doing philosophy when we want to.

Notes

1. T. S. Kuhn, "Reflections on My Critics," in I. Lakatos and A. Musgrave, eds., *Criticism and the Growth of Knowledge* (New York: Cambridge, 1970), p. 276, says that "the stimuli to which the participants in a communication breakdown respond are, under pain of solipsism, the same" and then continues by saying that their "programming" must be so also, since men "share a history . . . a language, an every day world, and most of a scientific one." On the view I should like to support, the *whole* anti-solipsist burden is borne by the "programming," and the "stimuli" (like the noumenal unsynthesized intuitions) drop out. If a stimulus is thought of as somehow "neutral" in respect to different conceptual schemes, it can be so only, I would argue, by becoming "a wheel that can be turned though nothing else moves with it." (Cf. Ludwig Wittgenstein, *Philosophical Investigations* [New York: Macmillan, 1958], I, 271.)

2. See W. V. Quine, "On Carnap's View on Ontology," in *The Ways of Paradox* (New York: Random House, 1966), pp. 126–134.

3. See Gilbert Harman, "Quine on Meaning and Existence, I," *Review of Metaphysics*, XXI, 1 (September 1967): 124–151, p. 142.

4. I first became aware of this argument, and of the importance of the issues I am here discussing, on reading the sixth of the Locke Lectures which Davidson gave at Oxford in 1970. These lectures are at present still unpublished, and I am most grateful to Davidson for permission to see the manuscript, and also the manuscript of his 1971 University of London Lectures on "Conceptual Relativism"—the more especially as I want to turn Davidson's argument to purposes for which he would have slim sympathy. After reading Davidson's unpublished material, I read Barry Stroud's presentation of a partially similar argument in "Conventionalism and the Indeterminacy of Translation," in *Words and Objections: Essays on the Work of W. V. Quine*, ed. Davidson and J. Hintikka (Dordrecht: Reidel, 1969), esp. pp. 89–96. Stroud and Davidson concur in rejecting the notion of "alternative conceptual frameworks," but Davidson goes on to draw explicitly the radical conclusion that "most of our beliefs must be true." It is this latter conclusion on which I shall be focusing in this paper. (Addendum, 1981: Although Davidson has not yet published his Locke Lectures in full, the material most relevant to this paper has appeared in his "On the Very Idea of a Conceptual Scheme," *Proceedings of the American Philosophical Association*, 17 [1973–74], pp. 5–20.)

5. I have argued elsewhere ("Indeterminacy of Translation and of Truth," *Synthese*, 23 [1972]: 443–462) that Quine's doctrine that there is no "matter of fact" for translations to be right or wrong about, is philosophical overkill, and that the "idea idea" is adequately discredited by attacks on the Kantian distinctions discussed above.

6. The importance of this point was shown me by Michael Friedman. I am grateful also to Michael Williams for criticisms of my general line of argument.

7. I have tried to develop this view of the course of the argument between verificationists and skeptics in "Verificationism and Transcendental Arguments, *Noûs*, V, 1 (February 1971): 3–14, and in "Criteria and Necessity," *Noûs*, VIII, 4 (November 1973): 313–329.

8. For a recent formulation of this objection, see John L. Pollock, "Perceptual Knowledge," *Philosophical Review*, LXXX, 3 (July 1971): 290–292.

9. This sort of question is at the root of the attempt to distinguish between a "theory of truth" and a "theory of evidence" in reply to such truth-as-assertibility theorists as Sellars—see Harman's criticism of Sellars on this point in "Sellars' Semantics," *Philosophical Review*, LXXIX, 3 (July 1970): 404–419, pp. 409ff., 417ff.

10. See Pollock, *op. cit.*, for a defense of the claim that, once we reject a coherence theory of justification, such an explanation in foundationalist terms becomes necessary.

11. For examples of the programmatic passion that realism can inspire, see the "Platform of the Association for Realistic Philosophy," in *The Return to Reason*, ed. John Wild (Chicago: Henry Regnery, 1953); and the "Program and First Platform of Six Realists," in Edwin B. Holt *et al., The New Realism* (New York: Macmillan, 1912), pp. 471ff.

12. I say "are currently thought to be about" rather than "are about" in order to skirt an issue that might be raised by proponents of a "causal theory of reference." Such a theory might suggest that we are in fact now talking about (referring to) what the Galactics will be referring to, but that the Galactics might know what this was and we might not. (The relevance of such theories of reference was pointed out to me by Michael Friedman and by Fred Dretske.) My own view, which I cannot develop here, is that an attempt to clarify epistemological questions by reference to "reference" will always be explaining the obscure by the more obscure—explicating notions ("knowledge," "truth") which have some basis in common speech in terms of a contrived and perpetually controversial philosophical notion. See Essay 7, below. [Rorty, "Is There a Problem about Fictional Discourse?" in his *Consequences of Pragmatism* (Minneapolis: University of Minnesota Press, 1982), pp. 110–138.]

13. I do not wish to be taken as suggesting the triviality of Tarski's semantic theory, which seems to me not a theory relevant to epistemology (except perhaps, as Davidson has suggested,

to the epistemology of language learning). I should regard Tarski as founding a new subject, not as solving an old problem. I think that Davidson is right in saying that, in the sense in which Tarski's theory is a correspondence theory, "it may be the case that no battle is won, or even joined between correspondence theories and others" ("True to the Facts," *Journal of Philosophy*, LXVI, 21 [Nov. 6, 1969] : 748–764, p. 761). The philosophically controversial "correspondence theory of truth" to which coherence and pragmatic theories were supposed alternatives is not the theory Strawson (quoted by Davidson, *op. cit.*, p. 763) identifies as "to say that a statement is true is to say that a certain speech-episode is related in a certain conventional way to something in the world exclusive of itself." For this latter view would, as far as it goes, be perfectly acceptable to, e.g., Blanshard or Dewey.

In this essay, Rorty argues that since there are no noncircular arguments for one's intellectual and cultural practices, ethnocentrism is not only unavoidable but legitimate.

RICHARD RORTY

Solidarity or Objectivity?

There are two principal ways in which reflective human beings try, by placing their lives in a larger context, to give sense to those lives. The first is by telling the story of their contribution to a community. This community may be the actual historical one in which they live, or another actual one, distant in time or place, or a quite imaginary one, consisting perhaps of a dozen heroes and heroines selected from history or fiction or both. The second way is to describe themselves as standing in immediate relation to a nonhuman reality. This relation is immediate in the sense that it does not derive from a relation between such a reality and their tribe, or their nation, or their imagined band of comrades. I shall say that stories of the former kind exemplify the desire for solidarity, and that stories of the latter kind exemplify the desire for objectivity. Insofar as a person is seeking solidarity, she does not ask about the relation between the practices of the chosen community and something outside that community. Insofar as she seeks objectivity, she distances herself from the actual persons around her not by thinking of herself as a member of some other real or imaginary group, but rather by attaching herself to something which can be described without reference to any particular human beings.

The tradition in Western culture which centers around the notion of the search for Truth, a tradition which runs from the Greek philosophers through the Enlightenment, is the clearest example of the attempt to find a sense in one's existence by turning away from solidarity to objectivity. The idea of Truth as something to be pursued for its own sake, not because it will be good for oneself, or for one's real or imaginary community, is the central theme of this tradition. It was perhaps the growing awareness by the Greeks of the sheer diversity of human communities which stimulated the emergence of this ideal. A fear of parochialism, of being confined within the horizons of the group into which one happens to be born, a need to see it with the eyes of a stranger, helps produce the skeptical and ironic tone characteristic of Euripides and Socrates. Herodotus' willingness to take the barbarians seriously enough to describe their customs in detail may have been a necessary prelude to Plato's claim that the way to transcend skepticism is to envisage a common goal of humanity—a goal set by human nature rather than by Greek culture. The combination of Socratic alienation and Platonic hope gives rise to the idea of the intellectual as someone who is in touch with the nature of things, not by way of the opinions of his community, but in a more immediate way.

Plato developed the idea of such an intellectual by means of distinctions between knowledge and opinion, and between appearance and reality. Such distinctions conspire to produce the idea that rational inquiry should make visible a realm to which nonintellectuals have little access, and of whose very existence they may be doubtful. In the Enlightenment, this notion became concrete in the adoption of the Newtonian physical scientist as a model of the intellectual. To most thinkers of the eighteenth century, it seemed clear that the access to Nature which physical science had provided should now be followed by the establishment of social, political, and economic institutions which were in accordance with Nature. Ever since, liberal social thought has centered around social reform as made possible by objective knowledge of what human beings are like—not knowledge of what Greeks or Frenchmen or Chinese are like, but of humanity as such. We are the heirs of this objectivist tradition, which centers around the assumption that we must step outside our community long enough to examine it in the light of something which transcends it, namely, that which it has in common with every other actual and possible human community. This tradition dreams of an ultimate community which will have transcended the distinction between the natural and the social, which will exhibit a solidarity which is not parochial because it is the expression of an ahistorical human nature. Much of the rhetoric of contemporary intellectual life takes for granted that the goal of scientific inquiry into man is to understand "underlying structures," or "culturally invariant factors," or "biologically determined patterns."

Those who wish to ground solidarity in objectivity—call them "realists"—have to construe truth as correspondence to reality. So they must construct a metaphysics which has room for a special relation between beliefs and objects which will differentiate true from false beliefs. They also must argue that there are procedures of justification of belief which are natural and not merely local. So they must construct an epistemology which has room for a kind of justification which is not merely social but natural, springing from human nature itself, and made possible by a link between that part of nature and the rest of nature. On their view, the various procedures which are thought of as providing rational justification by one or another culture may or may not really *be* rational. For to be truly rational, procedures of justification *must* lead to the truth, to correspondence to reality, to the intrinsic nature of things.

By contrast, those who wish to reduce objectivity to solidarity—call them "pragmatists"—do not require either a metaphysics or an epistemology. They view truth as, in William James' phrase, what is good for *us* to believe. So they do not need an account of a relation between beliefs and objects called 'correspondence,' nor an account of human cognitive abilities which ensures that our species is capable of entering into that relation. They see the gap between truth and justification not as something to be bridged by isolating a natural and transcultural sort of rationality which can be used to criticize certain cultures and praise others, but simply as the gap between the actual good and the possible better. From a pragmatist point of view, to say that what is rational for us now to believe may not be *true*, is simply to say that somebody may come up with a better idea. It is to say that there is always room for improved belief, since new evidence, or new hypotheses, or a whole new vocabulary, may come along.[1] For pragmatists, the desire for objectivity is not the desire to escape the limitations of one's community, but simply the desire for as much intersubjective agreement as possible, the desire to extend the reference of "us" as far as we can. Insofar as pragmatists make a distinction between knowledge and opinion, it is simply the distinction between topics on which such agreement is relatively easy to get and topics on which agreement is relatively hard to get.

"Relativism" is the traditional epithet applied to pragmatism by realists. Three different views are commonly referred to by this name. The first is the view that every belief is as good as every other. The second is the view that "true" is an equivocal term, having as many meanings as there are procedures of justification. The third is the view that there is nothing to be said about either truth or rationality apart from descriptions of the familiar procedures of justification which a given society—*ours*—uses in one or another area of inquiry. The pragmatist holds the ethnocentric third view. But he does not hold the self-refuting first view, nor the eccentric second view. He thinks that his views are better than the realists', but he does not think that his views correspond to the nature of things. He thinks that the very flexibility of the word "true"—the fact that it is merely an expression of commendation—insures its univocity. The term "true," on his account, means the same in all cultures, just as equally flexible terms like "here," "there," "good," "bad," "you," and "me" mean the same in all cultures. But the identity of meaning is, of course, compatible with diversity of reference, and with diversity of procedures for assigning the terms. So he feels free to use the term "true" as a general term of commendation in the same way as his realist opponent does—and in particular to use it to commend his own view.

However, it is not clear why "relativist" should be thought an appropriate term for the ethnocentric third view, the one which the pragmatist *does* hold. For the pragmatist is not holding a positive theory which says that something is relative to something else. He is, instead, making the purely *negative* point that we should drop the traditional distinction between knowledge and opinion, construed as the distinction between truth as correspondence to reality and truth as a commendatory term for well-justified beliefs. The reason that the realist calls this negative claim "relativistic" is that he cannot believe that anybody would seriously deny that truth has an intrinsic nature. So when the pragmatist says that there is nothing to be said about truth save that each of us will commend as true those beliefs which he or she finds good to believe, the realist is inclined to interpret this as one more positive theory about the nature of truth: a theory according to which truth is simply the contemporary opinion of a chosen individual or group. Such a theory would, of course, be self-refuting.

But the pragmatist does not have a theory of truth, much less a relativistic one. As a partisan of solidarity, his account of the value of cooperative human inquiry has only an ethical base, not an epistemological or metaphysical one. Not having *any* epistemology, *a fortiori* he does not have a relativistic one.

The question of whether truth or rationality has an intrinsic nature, of whether we ought to have a positive theory about either topic, is just the question of whether our self-description ought to be constructed around a relation to human nature or around a relation to a particular collection of human beings, whether we should desire objectivity or solidarity. It is hard to see how one could choose between these alternatives by looking more deeply into the nature of knowledge, or of man, or of nature. Indeed, the proposal that this issue might be so settled begs the question in favor of the realist, for it presupposes that knowledge, man, and nature *have* real essences which are relevant to the problem at hand. For the pragmatist, by contrast, "knowledge" is, like "truth," simply a compliment paid to the beliefs which we think so well justified that, for the moment, further justification is not needed. An inquiry into the nature of knowledge can, on his view, only be a sociohistorical account of how various people have tried to reach agreement on what to believe.

The view which I am calling "pragmatism" is almost, but not quite, the same as what Hilary Putnam, in his recent *Reason, Truth, and History*, calls "the internalist conception of philosophy."[2] Putnam defines such a conception as one which gives up the attempt at a God's eye view of things, the attempt at contact with the nonhuman which I have been calling "the desire for objectivity." Unfortunately, he accompanies his defense of the antirealist views I am recommending with a polemic against a lot of the other people who hold these views—e.g., Kuhn, Feyerabend, Foucault, and myself. We are criticized as "relativists." Putnam presents "internalism" as a happy *via media* between realism and relativism. He speaks of "the plethora of relativistic doctrines being marketed today"[3] and in particular of "the French philosophers" as holding "some fancy mixture of cultural relativism and 'structuralism.'"[4] But when it comes to criticizing these doctrines all that Putnam finds to attack is the so-called "incommensurability thesis": vis., "terms used in another culture cannot be equated in meaning or reference with any terms or expressions *we* possess."[5] He sensibly agrees with Donald Davidson in remarking that this thesis is self-refuting. Criticism of this thesis, however, is destructive of, at most, some incautious passages in some early writings by Feyerabend. Once this thesis is brushed aside, it is hard to see how Putnam himself differs from most of those he criticizes.

Putnam accepts the Davidsonian point that, as he puts it, "the whole justification of an interpretative scheme . . . is that it renders the behavior of others at least minimally reasonable by *our* lights."[6] It would seem natural to go on from this to say that we cannot get outside the range of those lights, that we cannot stand on neutral ground illuminated only by the natural light of reason. But Putnam draws back from this conclusion. He does so because he construes the claim that we cannot do so as the claim that the range of our thought is restricted by what he calls "institutionalized norms," publicly available criteria for settling all arguments, including philosophical arguments. He rightly says that there are no such criteria, arguing that the suggestion that there are is as self-refuting as the "incommensurability thesis." He is, I think, entirely right in saying that the notion that philosophy is or should become such an application of explicit criteria contradicts the very idea of philosophy.[7] One can gloss Putnam's point by saying that "philosophy" is precisely what a culture becomes capable of when it ceases to define itself in terms of explicit rules, and becomes sufficiently leisured and civilized to rely on inarticulate know-how, to substitute *phronesis* for codification, and conversation with foreigners for conquest of them.

But to say that we cannot refer every question to explicit criteria institutionalized by our society does not speak to the point which the people whom Putnam calls "relativists" are making. One reason these people are pragmatists is precisely that they share Putnam's distrust of the positivistic idea that rationality is a matter of applying criteria.

Such a distrust is common, for example, to Kuhn, Mary Hesse, Wittgenstein, Michael Polanyi, and Michael Oakeshott. Only someone who did think of rationality in this way would dream of suggesting that "true" means something different in different societies. For only such a person could imagine that there was anything to pick out to which one might make "true" relative. Only if one shares the logical positivists' idea that we all carry around things called "rules of language" which regulate what we say when, will one suggest that there is no way to break out of one's culture.

In the most original and powerful section of his book, Putnam argues that the notion that "rationality . . . is defined by the local cultural norms" is merely the demonic counterpart of positivism. It is, as he says, "a scientistic theory inspired by anthropology as positivism was a scientistic theory inspired by the exact sciences." By "scientism" Putnam means the notion that rationality consists in the application of criteria.[8] Suppose we drop this notion, and accept Putnam's own Quinean picture of inquiry as the continual reweaving of a web of beliefs rather than as the application of criteria to cases. Then the notion of "local cultural norms" will lose its offensively parochial overtones. For now to say that we must work by our own lights, that we must be ethnocentric, is merely to say that beliefs suggested by another culture must be tested by trying to weave them together with beliefs we already have. It is a consequence of this holistic view of knowledge, a view *shared* by Putnam and those he criticizes as "relativists," that alternative cultures are not to be thought of on the model of alternative geometries. Alternative geometries are irreconcilable because they have axiomatic structures, and contradictory axioms. They are *designed* to be irreconcilable. Cultures are not so designed, and do not have axiomatic structures. To say that they have "institutionalized norms" is only to say, with Foucault, that knowledge is never separable from power—that one is likely to suffer if one does not hold certain beliefs at certain times and places. But such institutional backups for beliefs take the form of bureaucrats and policemen, not of "rules of language" and "criteria of rationality." To think otherwise is the Cartesian fallacy of seeing axioms where there are only shared habits, of viewing statements which summarize such practices as if they reported constraints enforcing such practices. Part of the force of Quine's and Davidson's attack on the distinction between the conceptual and the empirical is that the distinction between different cultures does not differ in kind from the distinction between different theories held by members of a single culture. The Tasmanian aborigines and the British colonists had trouble communicating, but this trouble was different only in extent from the difficulties in communication experienced by Gladstone and Disraeli. The trouble in all such cases is just the difficulty of explaining why other people disagree with us, of reweaving our beliefs so as to fit the fact of disagreement together with the other beliefs we hold. The same Quinean arguments which dispose of the positivists' distinction between analytic and synthetic truth dispose of the anthropologists' distinction between the intercultural and the intracultural.

On this holistic account of cultural norms, however, we do not need the notion of a universal transcultural rationality which Putnam invokes against those whom he calls "relativists." Just before the end of his book, Putnam says that once we drop the notion of a God's-eye point of view we realize that:

> we can only hope to produce a more rational *conception* of rationality or a better *conception* of morality if we operate from *within* our tradition (with its echoes of the Greek agora, of Newton, and so on, in the case of rationality, and with its echoes of scripture, of the philosophers, of the democratic revolutions, and so on . . . in the case of morality.) We are invited to engage in a truly human dialogue.[9]

With this I entirely agree, and so, I take it, would Kuhn, Hesse, and most of the other so-called "relativists"—perhaps even Foucault. But Putnam then goes on to pose a further question:

> Does this dialogue have an ideal terminus? Is there a *true* conception of rationality, an ideal morality, even if all we ever have are our conceptions of these?

I do not see the point of this question. Putnam suggests that a negative answer—the view that "there is only the dialogue"—is just another form of self-refuting relativism. But, once again, I do not see how a claim that something does not exist can be construed as a claim that something is relative to something else. In the final sentence of his book, Putnam says that "The very fact that we speak of our different conceptions as different conceptions of *rationality* posits a *Grenzbegriff*, a limit-concept of ideal truth." But what is such a posit supposed to do, except to say that from God's point of view the human race is heading in the right direction? Surely Putnam's "internalism" should forbid him to say anything like that. To say that *we* think we're heading in the right direction is just to say, with Kuhn, that we can, by hindsight, tell the story of the past as a story of progress. To say that we still have a long way to go, that our present views should not be cast in bronze, is too platitudinous to require support by positing limit-concepts. So it is hard to see what difference is made by the difference between saying "there is only the dialogue" and saying "there is also that: to which the dialogue converges."

I would suggest that Putnam here, at the end of the day, slides back into the scientism he rightly condemns in others. For the root of scientism, defined as the view that rationality is a matter of applying criteria, is the desire for objectivity, the hope that what Putnam calls "human flourishing" has a transhistorical nature. I think that Feyerabend is right in suggesting that until we discard the metaphor of inquiry, and human activity generally, as converging rather than proliferating, as becoming more unified rather than more diverse, we shall never be free of the motives which once led us to posit gods. Positing *Grenzbegriffe* seems merely a way of telling ourselves that a nonexistent God would, if he did exist, be pleased with us. If we could ever be moved solely by the desire for solidarity, setting aside the desire for objectivity altogether, then we should think of human progress as making it possible for human beings to do more interesting things and be more interesting people, not as heading towards a place which has somehow been prepared for humanity in advance. Our self-image would employ images of making rather than finding, the images used by the Romantics to praise poets rather than the images used by the Greeks to praise mathematicians. Feyerabend seems to me right in trying to develop such a self-image for us, but his project seems misdescribed, by himself as well as by his critics, as "relativism."[10]

Those who follow Feyerabend in this direction are often thought of as necessarily enemies of the Enlightenment, as joining in the chorus which claims that the traditional self-descriptions of the Western democracies are bankrupt, that they somehow have been shown to be "inadequate" or "self-deceptive." Part of the instinctive resistance to attempts by Marxists, Sartreans, Oakeshottians, Gadamerians and Foucauldians to reduce objectivity to solidarity is the fear that our traditional liberal habits and hopes will not survive the reduction. Such feelings are evident, for example, in Habermas' criticism of Gadamer's position as relativistic and potentially repressive, in the suspicion that Heidegger's attacks on realism are somehow linked to his Nazism, in the hunch that Marxist attempts to interpret values as class interests are usually just apologies for Leninist takeovers, and in the suggestion that Oakeshott's skepticism about rationalism in politics is merely an apology for the status quo.

I think that putting the issue in such moral and political terms, rather than in epistemological or metaphilosophical terms, makes clearer what is at stake. For now the question is not about how to define words like "truth" or "rationality" or "knowledge" or "philosophy," but about what self-image our society should have of itself. The ritual invocation of the "need to avoid relativism" is most comprehensible as an expression of the need to preserve certain habits of contemporary European life. These are the habits nurtured by the Enlightenment, and justified by it in terms of an appeal of Reason, conceived as a transcultural human ability to correspond to reality, a faculty whose possession and use is demonstrated by obedience to explicit criteria. So the real question about relativism is whether these same habits of intellectual, social, and political life can be justified by a conception of rationality as criterionless muddling through, and by a pragmatist conception of truth.

I think that the answer to this question is that the pragmatist cannot justify these habits without circularity, but then neither can the realist. The pragmatists' justification of toleration, free inquiry, and the quest for undistorted communication can only take the form of a comparison between societies which exemplify these habits and those which do not, leading up to the suggestion that nobody who has experienced both would prefer the latter. It is exemplified by Winston Churchill's defense of democracy as the worst form of government imaginable, except for all the others which have been tried so far. Such justification is not by reference to a criterion, but by reference to various detailed practical advantages. It is circular only in that the terms of praise used to describe liberal societies will be drawn from the vocabulary of the liberal societies themselves. Such praise has to be in *some* vocabulary, after all, and the terms of praise current in primitive or theocratic or totalitarian societies will not produce the desired result. So the pragmatist admits that he has no ahistorical standpoint from which to endorse the habits of modern democracies he wishes to praise. These consequences are just what partisans of solidarity expect. But among partisans of objectivity they give rise, once again, to fears of the dilemma formed by ethnocentrism on the one hand and relativism on the other. Either we attach a special privilege to our own community, or we pretend an impossible tolerance for every other group.

I have been arguing that we pragmatists should grasp the ethnocentric horn of this dilemma. We should say that we must, in practice, privilege our own group, even though there can be no noncircular justification for doing so. We must insist that the fact that nothing is immune from criticism does not mean that we have a duty to justify everything. We Western liberal intellectuals should accept the fact that we have to start from where we are, and that this means that there are lots of views which we simply cannot take seriously. To use Neurath's familiar analogy, we can *understand* the revolutionary's suggestion that a sailable boat can't be made out of the planks which make up ours, and that we must simply abandon ship. But we cannot take his suggestion seriously. We cannot take it as a rule for action, so it is not a live option. For some people, to be sure, the option *is* live. These are the people who have always hoped to become a New Being, who have hoped to be converted rather than persuaded. But we—the liberal Rawlsian searchers for consensus, the heirs of Socrates, the people who wish to link their days dialectically each to each—cannot do so. Our community—the community of the liberal intellectuals of the secular modern West—wants to be able to give a *post factum* account of any change of view. We want to be able, so to speak, to justify ourselves to our earlier selves. This preference is not built into us by human nature. It is just the way *we* live now.[11]

This lonely provincialism, this admission that we are just the historical moment that we are, not the representatives of something ahistorical, is what makes traditional

Kantian liberals like Rawls draw back from pragmatism.[12] "Relativism," by contrast, is merely a red herring. The realist is, once again, projecting his own habits of thought upon the pragmatist when he charges him with relativism. For the realist thinks that the whole point of philosophical thought is to detach oneself from any particular community and look down at it from a more universal standpoint. When he hears the pragmatist repudiating the desire for such a standpoint he cannot quite believe it. He thinks that everyone, deep down inside, *must* want such detachment. So he attributes to the pragmatist a perverse form of his own attempted detachment, and sees him as an ironic, sneering aesthete who refuses to take the choice between communities seriously, a mere "relativist." But the pragmatist, dominated by the desire for solidarity, can only be criticized for taking his own community *too* seriously. He can only be criticized for ethnocentrism, not for relativism. To be ethnocentric is to divide the human race into the people to whom one must justify one's beliefs and the others. The first group—one's *ethnos*—comprises those who share enough of one's beliefs to make fruitful conversation possible. In this sense, everybody is ethnocentric when engaged in actual debate, no matter how much realist rhetoric about objectivity he produces in his study.[13]

What is disturbing about the pragmatist's picture is not that it is relativistic but that it takes away two sorts of metaphysical comfort to which our intellectual tradition has become accustomed. One is the thought that membership in our biological species carries with it certain "rights," a notion which does not seem to make sense unless the biological similarities entail the possession of something nonbiological, something which links our species to a nonhuman reality and thus gives the species moral dignity. This picture of rights as biologically transmitted is so basic to the political discourse of the Western democracies that we are troubled by any suggestion that "human nature" is not a useful moral concept. The second comfort is provided by the thought that our community cannot wholly die. The picture of a common human nature oriented towards correspondence to reality as it is in itself comforts us with the thought that: even if our civilization is destroyed, even if all memory of our political or intellectual or artistic community is erased, the race is fated to recapture the virtues and the insights and the achievements which were the glory of that community. The notion of human nature as an inner structure which leads all members of the species to converge to the same point, to recognize the same theories, virtues, and works of art as worthy of honor, assures us that even if the Persians had won, the arts and sciences of the Greeks would sooner or later have appeared elsewhere. It assures us that even if the Orwellian bureaucrats of terror rule for a thousand years the achievements of the Western democracies will someday be duplicated by our remote descendants. It assures us that "man will prevail," that something reasonably like *our* world-view, *our* virtues, *our* art, will bob up again whenever human beings are left alone to cultivate their inner natures. The comfort of the realist picture is the comfort of saying not simply that there is a place prepared for our race in our advance, but also that we now know quite a bit about what that place looks like. The inevitable ethnocentrism to which we are all condemned is thus as much a part of the realist's comfortable view as of the pragmatist's uncomfortable one.

The pragmatist gives up the first sort of comfort because he thinks that to say that certain people have certain rights is merely to say that we should treat them in certain ways. It is not to give a *reason* for treating them, in those ways. As to the second sort of comfort, he suspects that the hope that something resembling *us* will inherit the earth is impossible to eradicate, as impossible as eradicating the hope of surviving our individual deaths through some satisfying transfiguration. But he does not want to turn this hope into a theory of the nature of man. He wants solidarity to be our *only* comfort, and to be seen not to require metaphysical support.

My suggestion that the desire for objectivity is in part a disguised form of the fear of the death of our community echoes Nietzsche's charge that the philosophical tradition which stems from Plato is an attempt to avoid facing up to contingency, to escape from time and chance. Nietzsche thought that realism was to be condemned not only by arguments from its theoretical incoherence, the sort of argument we find in Putnam and Davidson, but also on practical, pragmatic, grounds. Nietzsche thought that the test of human character was the ability to live with the thought that there was no convergence. He wanted us to be able to think of truth as:

> a mobile army of metaphors, metonyms, and anthromorphisms—in short a sum of human relations, which have been enhanced, transposed, and embellished poetically and rhetorically and which after long use seem firm, canonical, and obligatory to a people.[14]

Nietzsche hoped that eventually there might be human beings who could and did think of truth in this way, but who still liked themselves, who saw themselves as *good* people for whom solidarity was *enough*.[15]

I think that pragmatism's attack on the various structure-content distinctions which buttress the realist's notion of objectivity can best be seen as an attempt to let us think of truth in this Nietzschean way, as entirely a matter of solidarity. That is why I think we need to say, despite Putnam, that "there is only the dialogue," only *us*, and to throw out the last residues of the notion of "trans-cultural rationality." But this should not lead us to repudiate, as Nietzsche sometimes did, the elements in our movable host which embody the ideas of Socratic conversation, Christian fellowship, and Enlightenment science. Nietzsche ran together his diagnosis of philosophical realism as an expression of fear and resentment with his own resentful idiosyncratic idealizations of silence, solitude, and violence. Post-Nietzschean thinkers like Adorno and Heidegger and Foucault have run together Nietzsche's criticisms of the metaphysical tradition on the one hand with his criticisms of bourgeois civility, of Christian love, and of the nineteenth century's hope that science would make the world a better place to live, on the other. I do not think that there is any interesting connection between these two sets of criticisms. Pragmatism seems to me, as I have said, a philosophy of solidarity rather than of despair. From this point of view, Socrates' turn away from the gods, Christianity's turn from an Omnipotent Creator to the man who suffered on the Cross, and the Baconian turn from science as contemplation of eternal truth to science as instrument of social progress, can be seen as so many preparations for the act of social faith which is suggested by a Nietzschean view of truth.[16]

The best argument we partisans of solidarity have against the realistic partisans of objectivity is Nietzsche's argument that the traditional Western metaphysico-epistemological way of firming up our habits simply isn't working anymore. It isn't doing its job. It has become as transparent a device as the postulation of deities who turn out, by a happy coincidence, to have chosen *us* as their people. So the pragmatist suggestion that we substitute a "merely" ethical foundation for our sense of community—or, better, that we think of our sense of community as having no foundation except shared hope and the trust created by such sharing—is put forward on practical grounds. It is *not* put forward as a corollary of a metaphysical claim that the objects in the world contain no intrinsically action-guiding properties, nor of an epistemological claim that we lack a faculty of moral sense, nor of a semantical claim that truth is reducible to justification. It is a suggestion about how we might think of ourselves in order to avoid the kind of resentful belatedness—characteristic of the bad side of Nietzsche—which now characterizes much of high culture. This resentment arises from the realization, which I referred to at the beginning of this chapter, that the Enlightenment's search for objectivity has often gone sour.

The rhetoric of scientific objectivity, pressed too hard and taken too seriously, has led us to people like B. F. Skinner on the one hand and people like Althusser on the other—two equally pointless fantasies, both produced by the attempt to be "scientific" about our moral and political lives. Reaction against scientism led to attacks on natural science as a sort of false god. But there is nothing wrong with science, there is only something wrong with the attempt to divinize it, the attempt characteristic of realistic philosophy. This reaction has also led to attacks on liberal social thought of the type common to Mill and Dewey and Rawls as a mere ideological superstructure, one which obscures the realities of our situation and represses attempts to change that situation. But there is nothing wrong with liberal democracy, nor with the philosophers who have tried to enlarge its scope. There is only something wrong with the attempt to see their efforts as failures to achieve something which they were not trying to achieve—a demonstration of the "objective" superiority of our way of life over all other alternatives. There is, in short, nothing wrong with the hopes of the Enlightenment, the hopes which created the Western democracies. The value of the ideals of the Enlightenment is, for us pragmatists, just the value of some of the institutions and practices which they have created. In this essay I have sought to distinguish these institutions and practices from the philosophical justifications for them provided by partisans of objectivity, and to suggest an alternative justification.

Notes

1. This attitude toward truth, in which the consensus of a community rather than a relation to a nonhuman reality is taken as central, is associated not only with the American pragmatic tradition but with the work of Popper and Habermas. Habermas' criticisms of lingering positivist elements in Popper parallel those made by Deweyan holists of the early logical empiricists. It is important to see, however, that the pragmatist notion of truth common to James and Dewey is not dependent upon either Peirce's notion of an "ideal end of inquiry" nor on Habermas' notion of an "ideally free community." For criticism of these notions, which in my view are insufficiently ethnocentric, see my "Pragmatism, Davidson and Truth," in Rorty's *Objectivity, Relativism, and Truth, Philosophical Papers, Volume 1* (Cambridge: Cambridge University Press, 1991), pp.126–161, and "Habermas and Lyotard on Postmodernity" in Rorty's *Essays on Heidegger and Others, Philosophical Papers, Volume 2* (Cambridge: Cambridge University Press, 1991), pp. 164–176.

2. Hilary Putnam, *Reason, Truth, and History* (Cambridge: Cambridge University Press, 1981), pp. 49–50.

3. Ibid., p. 119.

4. Ibid., p. x.

5. Ibid., p. 114.

6. Ibid., p. 119. See Davidson's "On the very idea of a conceptual scheme," in his *Inquiries into Truth and Interpretation* (Oxford: Oxford University Press, 1984) for a more complete and systematic presentation of this point.

7. Putnam, p. 113.

8. Ibid., p. 126.

9. Ibid., p. 216.

10. See, e.g., Paul Feyerabend, *Science in a Free Society* (London: New Left Books, 1978), p. 9, where Feyerabend identifies his own view with "relativism (in the old and simple sense of Protagoras)." This identification is accompanied by the claim that " 'Objectively' there is not much to choose between anti-semitism and humanitarianism." I think Feyerabend would have served himself better by saying that the scare-quoted word "objectively" should simply be dropped from use, together with the traditional philosophical distinctions which buttress the subjective-objective distinction, than by saying that we may keep the word and use it to say the sort of thing Protagoras said. What Feyerabend is really against is the correspondence theory of truth, not the idea that some views cohere better than others.

11. This quest for consensus is opposed to the sort of quest for authenticity which wishes to free itself from the opinion of our community. See, for example, Vincent Descombes' account of Deleuze in *Modern French Philosophy* (Cambridge: Cambridge University Press, 1980), p. 153: "Even if philosophy is essentially demystificatory, philosophers often fail to produce authentic critiques; they defend order, authority, institutions, 'decency,' everything in which the ordinary person believes." On the pragmatist or ethnocentric view I am suggesting, all that critique can or should do is play off elements in "what the ordinary person believes" against other elements. To attempt to do more than this is to fantasize rather than to converse. Fantasy may, to be sure, be an incentive to more fruitful conversation, but when it no longer fulfills this function it does not deserve the name of "critique."

12. In *A Theory of Justice* Rawls seemed to be trying to retain the authority of Kantian "practical reason" by imagining a social contract devised by choosers "behind a veil of ignorance"—using the "rational self-interest" of such choosers as a touchstone for the ahistorical validity of certain social institutions. Much of the criticism to which that book was subjected, e.g., by

Michael Sandel in his *Liberalism and the Limits of Justice* (Cambridge: Cambridge University Press, 1982), has centered on the claim that one cannot escape history in this way. In the meantime, however, Rawls has put forward a meta-ethical view which drops the claim to ahistorical validity. Concurrently, T. M. Scanlon has urged that the essence of a "contractualist" account of moral motivation is better understood as the desire to justify one's action to others than in terms of "rational self-interest." See Scanlon, "Contractualism and Utilitarianism," in A. Sen and B. Williams, eds., *Utilitarianism and Beyond* (Cambridge: Cambridge University Press, 1982). Scanlon's emendation of Rawls leads in the same direction as Rawls' later work, since Scanlon's use of the notion of "justification to others on grounds they could not reasonably reject" chimes with the "constructivist" view that what counts for social philosophy is what can be justified to a particular historical community, not to "humanity in general." On my view, the frequent remark that Rawls' rational choosers look remarkably like twentieth-century American liberals is perfectly just, but not a criticism of Rawls. It is merely a frank recognition of the ethnocentrism which is essential to serious, nonfantastical, thought. I defend this view in "The Priority of Democracy to Philosophy" and "Postmodernist Bourgeois Liberalism" in Part III of Rorty's *Objectivity, Relativism, and Truth, Philosophical Papers, Volume.*

13. In an important paper called "The Truth in Relativism," included in his *Moral Luck* (Cambridge: Cambridge University Press, 1981), Bernard Williams makes a similar point in terms of a distinction between "genuine confrontation" and "notional confrontation." The latter is the sort of confrontation which occurs, asymmetrically, between us and primitive tribespeople. The belief-systems of such people do not present, as Williams puts it, "real options" for us, for we cannot imagine going over to their view without "self-deception or paranoia." These are the people whose beliefs on certain topics overlap so little with ours that their inability to agree with us raises no doubt in our minds about the correctness of our own beliefs. Williams' use of "real option" and "notional confrontation" seems to me very enlightening, but I think he turns these notions to purposes they will not serve. Williams wants to defend ethical relativism, defined as the claim that when ethical confrontations are merely notional "questions of appraisal do not genuinely arise." He thinks they *do* arise in connection with notional confrontations between, e.g., Einsteinian and Amazonian cosmologies. (See Williams, p. 142.) This distinction between ethics and physics seems to me an awkward result to which Williams is driven by his unfortunate attempt to find *something* true in relativism, an attempt which is a corollary of his attempt to be "realistic" about physics. On my (Davidsonian) view, there is no point in distinguishing between true sentences which are "made true by reality" and true sentences which are "made by us," because the whole idea of "truth-makers" needs to be dropped. So I would hold that there is *no* truth in relativism, but this much truth in ethnocentrism: we cannot justify our beliefs (in physics, ethics, or any other area) to everybody, but only to those whose beliefs overlap ours to some appropriate extent. (This is not a theoretical problem about "untranslatability," but simply a practical problem about the limitations of argument; it is not that we live in different worlds than the Nazis or the Amazonians, but that conversion from or to their point of view, though possible, will not be a matter of inference from previously shared premises.)

14. Nietzsche, "On Truth and Lie in an Extra-Moral Sense," in *The Viking Portable Nietzsche*, Walter Kaufmann, ed. and trans., pp. 46–47.

15. See Sabina Lovibond, *Realism and Imagination in Ethics* (Minneapolis: University of Minnesota Press, 1983), p. 158: "An adherent of Wittgenstein's view of language should equate that goal with the establishment of a language-game in which we could participate ingenuously, while retaining our awareness of it as a specific historical formation. A community in which such a language-game was played would be one . . . whose members understood their own form of life and yet were not embarrassed by it."

16. See Hans Blumenberg, *The Legitimation of Modernity* (Cambridge, Mass.: MIT Press, 1982), for a story about the history of European thought which, unlike the stories told by Nietzsche and Heidegger, sees the Enlightenment as a definitive step forward. For Blumenberg, the attitude of "self-assertion," the kind of attitude which stems from a Baconian view of the nature and purpose of science, needs to be distinguished from "self-foundation," the Cartesian project of grounding such inquiry upon ahistorical criteria of rationality. Blumenberg remarks, pregnantly, that the "historicist" criticism of the optimism of the Enlightenment, criticism which began with the Romantics' turn back to the Middle Ages, undermines self-foundation but not self-assertion.

Written in the wake of Rawls's turn to a "political not metaphysical" liberal theory, Rorty argues that we should begin with our democratic commitments and fashion a philosophy to suit.

RICHARD RORTY

The Priority of Democracy to Philosophy

Thomas Jefferson set the tone for American liberal politics when he said "it does me no injury for my neighbor to say that there are twenty Gods or no God."[1] His example helped make respectable the idea that politics can be separated from beliefs about matters of ultimate importance—that shared beliefs among citizens on such matters are not essential to a democratic society. Like many other figures of the Enlightenment, Jefferson assumed that a moral faculty common to the typical theist and the typical atheist suffices for civic virtue.

Many Enlightenment intellectuals were willing to go further and say that since religious beliefs turn out to be inessential for political cohesion, they should simply be discarded as mumbo jumbo—perhaps to be replaced (as in twentieth-century totalitarian Marxist states) with some sort of explicitly secular political faith that will form the moral consciousness of the citizen. Jefferson again set the tone when he refused to go that far. He thought it enough to privatize religion, to view it as irrelevant to social order but relevant to, and possibly essential for, individual perfection. Citizens of a Jeffersonian democracy can be as religious or irreligious as they please as long as they are not "fanatical." That is, they must abandon or modify opinions on matters of ultimate importance, the opinions that may hitherto have given sense and point to their lives, if these opinions entail public actions that cannot be justified to most of their fellow citizens.

This Jeffersonian compromise concerning the relation of spiritual perfection to public policy has two sides. Its absolutist side says that every human being, without the benefit of special revelation, has all the beliefs necessary for civic virtue. These beliefs spring from a universal human faculty, conscience—possession of which constitutes the specifically human essence of each human being. This is the faculty that gives the individual human dignity and rights. But there is also a pragmatic side. This side says that when the individual finds in her conscience beliefs that are relevant to public policy but incapable of defense on the basis of beliefs common to her fellow citizens, she must sacrifice her conscience on the altar of public expediency.

The tension between these two sides can be eliminated by a philosophical theory that identifies justifiability to humanity at large with truth. The Enlightenment idea of "reason" embodies such a theory: the theory that there is a relation between the ahistorical essence of the human soul and moral truth, a relation which ensures that free and open discussion will produce "one right answer" to moral as well as to scientific questions.[2] Such a theory guarantees that a moral belief that cannot be justified to the mass of mankind is "irrational," and thus is not really a product of our moral faculty at all. Rather, it is a "prejudice," a belief that comes from some other part of the soul than "reason." It does not share in the sanctity of conscience, for it is the product of a sort of pseudoconscience—something whose loss is no sacrifice, but a purgation.

In our century, this rationalist justification of the Enlightenment compromise has been discredited. Contemporary intellectuals have given up the Enlightenment assumption that religion, myth, and tradition can be opposed to something ahistorical, something common to all human beings qua human. Anthropologists and historians of science have blurred the distinction between innate rationality and the products of acculturation. Philosophers such as Heidegger and Gadamer have given us ways of seeing human beings as historical all the way through. Other philosophers, such as Quine and Davidson, have blurred the distinction between permanent truths of reason and temporary truths of fact. Psychoanalysis has blurred the distinction between conscience and the emotions of love, hate, and fear, and thus the distinction between morality and prudence. The result is to erase the picture of the self common to Greek metaphysics, Christian theology, and Enlightenment rationalism: the picture of an ahistorical natural center, the locus of human dignity, surrounded by an adventitious and inessential periphery.

The effect of erasing this picture is to break the link between truth and justifiability. This, in turn, breaks down the bridge between the two sides of the Enlightenment compromise. The effect is to polarize liberal social theory. If we stay on the absolutist side, we shall talk about inalienable "human rights" and about "one right answer" to moral and political dilemmas without trying to back up such talk with a theory of human nature. We shall abandon metaphysical accounts of what a right is while nevertheless insisting that everywhere, in all times and cultures, members of our species have had the same rights. But if we swing to the pragmatist side, and consider talk of "rights" an attempt to enjoy the benefits of metaphysics without assuming the appropriate responsibilities, we shall still need something to distinguish the sort of individual conscience we respect from the sort we condemn as "fanatical." This can only be something relatively local and ethnocentric—the tradition of a particular community, the consensus of a particular culture. According to this view, what counts as rational or as fanatical is relative to the group to which we think it necessary to justify ourselves—to the body of shared belief that determines the reference of the word "we." The Kantian identification with a central transcultural and ahistorical self is thus replaced by a quasi-Hegelian identification with our own community, thought of as a historical product. For pragmatist social theory, the question of whether justifiability to the community with which we identify entails truth is simply irrelevant.

Ronald Dworkin and others who take the notion of ahistorical human "rights" seriously serve as examples of the first, absolutist, pole. John Dewey and, as I shall shortly be arguing, John Rawls serve as examples of the second pole. But there is a third type of social theory—often dubbed "communitarianism"—which is less easy to place. Roughly speaking, the writers tagged with this label are those who reject both the individualistic rationalism of the Enlightenment and the idea of "rights," but, unlike the pragmatists, see this rejection as throwing doubt on the institutions and culture of the surviving democratic states. Such theorists include Robert Bellah, Alasdair MacIntyre, Michael Sandel, Charles Taylor, early Roberto Unger, and many others. These writers share some measure of agreement with a view found in an extreme form both in Heidegger and in Horkheimer and Adorno's *Dialectic of Enlightenment*. This is the view that liberal institutions and culture either should not or cannot survive the collapse of the philosophical justification that the Enlightenment provided for them.

There are three strands in communitarianism that need to be disentangled. First, there is the empirical prediction that no society that sets aside the idea of ahistorical moral truth in the insouciant way that Dewey recommended can survive. Horkheimer and Adorno, for example, suspect that you cannot have a moral community in a disenchanted world because toleration leads to pragmatism, and it is not clear how we can prevent, "blindly pragmatized thought" from losing "its transcending quality and its relation to truth."[3] They think that pragmatism was the inevitable outcome of Enlightenment rationalism and that pragmatism is not a strong enough philosophy to make moral community possible.[4] Second, there is the moral judgment that the sort of human being who is produced by liberal institutions and culture is undesirable. MacIntyre, for example, thinks that our culture—a culture he says is dominated by "the Rich Aesthete, the Manager, and the Therapist"—is a *reductio ad absurdum* both of the philosophical views that helped create it and of those now invoked in its defense. Third, there is the claim that political institutions "presuppose" a doctrine about the nature of human beings and that such a doctrine must, unlike Enlightenment rationalism, make clear the essentially historical character of the self. So we find writers like Taylor and Sandel saying that we need a theory of the self that incorporates Hegel's and Heidegger's sense of the self's historicity.

The first claim is a straightforward empirical, sociological-historical one about the sort of glue that is required to hold a community together. The second is a straightforward moral judgment that the advantages of contemporary liberal democracy are outweighed by the disadvantages, by the ignoble and sordid character of the culture and the individual human beings that it produces. The third claim, however, is the most puzzling and complex. I shall concentrate on this third, most puzzling, claim, although toward the end I shall return briefly to the first two.

To evaluate this third claim, we need to ask two questions. The first is whether there is any sense in which liberal democracy "needs" philosophical justification at all.

Those who share Dewey's pragmatism will say that although it may need philosophical articulation, it does not need philosophical backup. On this view, the philosopher of liberal democracy may wish to develop a theory of the human self that comports with the institutions he or she admires. But such a philosopher is not thereby justifying these institutions by reference to more fundamental premises, but the reverse: He or she is putting politics first and tailoring a philosophy to suit. Communitarians, by contrast, often speak as though political institutions were no better than their philosophical foundations.

The second question is one that we can ask even if we put the opposition between justification and articulation to one side. It is the question of whether a conception of the self that, as Taylor says, makes "the community constitutive of the individual"[5] does in fact comport better with liberal democracy than does the Enlightenment conception of the self. Taylor summarizes the latter as "an ideal of disengagement" that defines a "typically modern notion" of human dignity: "the ability to act on one's own, without outside interference or subordination to outside authority." On Taylor's view, as on Heidegger's, these Enlightenment notions are closely linked with characteristically modern ideas of "efficacy, power, unperturbability."[6] They are also closely linked with the contemporary form of the doctrine of the sacredness of the individual conscience—Dworkin's claim that appeals to rights "trump" all other appeals. Taylor, like Heidegger, would like to substitute a less individualistic conception of what it is to be properly human—one that makes less of autonomy and more of interdependence.

I can preview what is to come by saying that I shall answer "no" to the first question about the communitarians' third claim and "yes" to the second. I shall be arguing that Rawls, following up on Dewey, shows us how liberal democracy can get along without philosophical presuppositions. He has thus shown us how we can disregard the third communitarian claim. But I shall also argue that communitarians like Taylor are right in saying that a conception of the self that makes the community constitutive of the self does comport well with liberal democracy. That is, if we *want* to flesh out our self-image as citizens of such a democracy with a philosophical view of the self, Taylor gives us pretty much the right view. But this sort of philosophical fleshing-out does not have the importance that writers like Horkheimer and Adorno, or Heidegger, have attributed to it.

Without further preface, I turn now to Rawls. I shall begin by pointing out that both in *A Theory of Justice* and subsequently, he has linked his own position to the Jeffersonian ideal of religious toleration. In an article called "Justice as Fairness: Political not Metaphysical," he says that he is "going to apply the principle of toleration to philosophy itself," and goes on to say:

> The essential point is this: as a practical political matter no general moral conception can provide the basis for a public conception of justice in a modern democratic society. The social and historical conditions of such a society have their origins in the Wars of

> Religion following the Reformation and the development of the principle of toleration, and in the growth of constitutional government and the institutions of large market economies. These conditions profoundly affect the requirements of a workable conception of political justice: such a conception must allow for a diversity of doctrines and the plurality of conflicting, and indeed incommensurable conceptions of the good affirmed by the members of existing democratic societies.[7]

We can think of Rawls as saying that just as the principle of religious toleration and the social thought of the Enlightenment proposed to bracket many standard theological topics when deliberating about public policy and constructing political institutions, so we need to bracket many standard topics of philosophical inquiry. For purposes of social theory, we can put aside such topics as an ahistorical human nature, the nature of selfhood, the motive of moral behavior, and the meaning of human life. We treat these as irrelevant to politics as Jefferson thought questions about the Trinity and about transubstantiation.

Insofar as he adopts this stance, Rawls disarms many of the criticisms that, in the wake of Horkheimer and Adorno, have been directed at American liberalism. Rawls can agree that Jefferson and his circle shared a lot of dubious philosophical views, views that we might now wish to reject. He can even agree with Horkheimer and Adorno, as Dewey would have, that these views contained the seeds of their own destruction. But he thinks that the remedy may be not to formulate better philosophical views on the same topics, but (for purposes of political theory) benignly to neglect these topics. As he says:

> since justice as fairness is intended as a political conception of justice for a democratic society, it tries to draw solely upon basic intuitive ideas that are embedded in the political institutions of a democratic society and the public traditions of their interpretation. Justice as fairness is a political conception in part because it starts from within a certain political tradition. We hope that this political conception of justice may be at least supported by what we may call "overlapping consensus," that is, by a consensus that includes all the opposing philosophical and religious doctrines likely to persist and gain adherents in a more or less just constitutional democratic society.[8]

Rawls thinks that "philosophy as the search for truth about an independent metaphysical and moral order cannot . . . provide a workable and shared basis for a political conception of justice in a democratic society."[9] So he suggests that we confine ourselves to collecting, "such settled convictions as the belief in religious toleration and the rejection of slavery" and then "try to organize the basic intuitive ideas and principles implicit in these convictions into a coherent conception of justice."[10]

This attitude is thoroughly historicist and antiuniversalist.[11] Rawls can wholeheartedly agree with Hegel and Dewey against Kant and can say that the Enlightenment attempt to free oneself from tradition and history, to appeal to "Nature" or "Reason," was self-deceptive.[12] He can see such an appeal as a misguided attempt to make philosophy do what theology failed to do. Rawls's effort to, in his words, "stay on the surface, philosophically speaking" can be seen as taking Jefferson's avoidance of theology one step further.

On the Deweyan view I am attributing to Rawls, no such discipline as "philosophical anthropology" is required as a preface to politics, but only history and sociology. Further, it is misleading to think of his view as Dworkin does: as "rights-based" as opposed to "goal-based." For the notion of "basis" is not in point. It is not that we know, on antecedent philosophical grounds, that it is of the essence of human beings to have rights, and then proceed to ask how a society might preserve and protect these rights. On the question of priority, as on the question of the relativity of justice to historical situations, Rawls is closer to Walzer than to Dworkin.[13] Since Rawls does not believe that for purposes of political theory, we need think of ourselves as having an essence that precedes and antedates history, he would not agree with Sandel that for these purposes, we need have an account of "the nature of the moral subject," which is "in some sense necessary, non-contingent and prior to any particular experience."[14] Some of our ancestors may have required such an account, just as others of our ancestors required such an account of their relation to their putative Creator. But *we*—we heirs of the Enlightenment for whom justice has become the first virtue—need neither. As citizens and as social theorists, we can be as indifferent to philosophical disagreements about the nature of the self as Jefferson was to theological differences about the nature of God.

This last point suggests a way of sharpening up my claim that Rawls's advocacy of philosophical toleration is a plausible extension of Jefferson's advocacy of religious toleration. Both "religion" and "philosophy" are vague umbrella terms, and both are subject to persuasive redefinition. When these terms are broadly enough defined, everybody, even atheists, will be said to have a religious faith (in the Tillichian sense of a "symbol of ultimate concern"). Everybody, even those who shun metaphysics and epistemology, will be said to have "philosophical presuppositions."[15] But for purposes of interpreting Jefferson and Rawls, we must use narrower definitions. Let "religion" mean, for Jefferson's purposes, disputes about the nature and the true name of God—and even about his existence.[16] Let "philosophy" mean, for Rawls's purposes, disputes about the nature of human beings and even about whether there is such a thing as "human nature."[17] Using these definitions, we can say that Rawls wants views about man's nature and purpose to be detached from politics. As he says, he wants his conception of justice to "avoid . . . claims about the essential nature and identity of persons."[18] So presumably, he wants questions about the point of human existence, or the meaning of human life, to be reserved for private life. A liberal democracy will not only exempt opinions on such matters from legal coercion, but also aim at disengaging discussions of such questions from discussions of social policy. Yet it will use force against the individual conscience, just insofar as conscience leads individuals to act so as to threaten democratic institutions. Unlike Jefferson's, Rawls's argument against fanaticism is not that it threatens truth about the characteristics of an antecedent metaphysical and moral order by threatening free discussion, but *simply* that it threatens freedom, and thus threatens justice. Truth about the existence or nature of that order drops out.

The definition of "philosophy" I have just suggested is not as artificial and ad hoc as it may appear. Intellectual historians commonly treat "the nature of the human subject" as the topic that gradually replaced "God" as European culture secularized itself. This has been the central topic of metaphysics and epistemology from the seventeenth century to the present, and, for better or worse, metaphysics and epistemology have been taken to be the "core" of philosophy.[19] Insofar as one thinks that political conclusions require extrapolitical grounding—that is, insofar as one thinks Rawls's method of reflective equilibrium[20] is not good enough—one will want an account of the "authority" of those general principles.

If one feels a need for such legitimation, one will want either a religious or a philosophical preface to politics.[21] One will be likely to share Horkheimer and Adorno's fear that pragmatism is not strong enough to hold a free society together. But Rawls echoes Dewey in suggesting that insofar as justice becomes the first virtue of a society, the need for such legitimation may gradually cease to be felt. Such a society will become accustomed to the thought that social policy needs no more authority than successful accommodation among individuals, individuals who find themselves heir to the same historical traditions and faced with the same problems. It will be a society that encourages the "end of ideology," that takes reflective equilibrium as the only method needed in discussing social policy. When such a society deliberates, when it collects the principles and intuitions to be brought into equilibrium, it will tend to discard those drawn from philosophical accounts of the self or of rationality. For such a society will view such accounts not as the foundations of political institutions, but as, at worst, philosophical mumbo jumbo, or, at best, relevant to private searches for perfection, but not to social policy.[22]

In order to spell out the contrast between Rawls's attempt to "stay on the surface, philosophically speaking" and the traditional attempt to dig down to "philosophical foundations of democracy," I shall turn briefly to Sandel's *Liberalism and the Limits of Justice*. This clear and forceful book provides very elegant and cogent arguments against the attempt to use a certain conception of the self, a certain metaphysical view of what human beings are like, to legitimize liberal politics. Sandel attributes this attempt to Rawls. Many people, including myself, initially took Rawls's *A Theory of Justice* to be such an attempt. We read it as a continuation of the Enlightenment attempt to ground our moral intuitions on a conception of human nature (and, more specifically, as a neo-Kantian attempt to ground them on the notion of "rationality"). However, Rawls's writings subsequent to *A Theory of Justice* have helped us realize that we were misinterpreting his book, that we had overemphasized the Kantian and underemphasized the Hegelian and Deweyan elements. These writings make more explicit than did his book Rawls's metaphilosophical doctrine that "what justifies a conception of justice is not its being true to an order antecedent to and given to us, but its congruence with our deeper understanding of ourselves and our aspirations, and our realization that, *given our history and the traditions embedded in our public life*, it is the most reasonable doctrine *for us*."[23]

When reread in the light of such passages, *A Theory of Justice* no longer seems committed to a philosophical account of the human self, but only to a historico-sociological description of the way we live now.

Sandel sees Rawls as offering us "deontology with a Humean face"—that is, a Kantian universalistic approach to social thought without the handicap of Kant's idealistic metaphysics. He thinks that this will not work, that a social theory of the sort that Rawls wants requires us to postulate the sort of self that Descartes and Kant invented to replace God—one that can be distinguished from the Kantian "empirical self" as choosing various "contingent desires, wants and ends," rather than being a mere concatenation of beliefs and desires. Since such a concatenation—what Sandel calls a "radically situated subject"[24]—is all that Hume offers us, Sandel thinks that Rawls's project is doomed.[25] On Sandel's account, Rawls's doctrine that "justice is the first virtue of social institutions" requires backup from the metaphysical claim that "teleology to the contrary, what is most essential to our personhood is not the ends we choose but our capacity to choose them. And this capacity is located in a self which must be prior to the ends it chooses."[26]

But reading *A Theory of Justice* as political rather than metaphysical, one can see that when Rawls says that "the self is prior to the ends which are affirmed by it,"[27] he need not mean that there is an entity called "the self" that is something distinct from the web of beliefs and desires that that self "has." When he says that "we should not attempt to give form to our life by first looking to the good independently defined,"[28] he is not basing this "should" on a claim about the nature of the self. "Should" is not to be glossed by "because of the intrinsic nature of morality"[29] or "because a capacity for choice is the essence of personhood," but by something like "because *we*—we modern inheritors of the traditions of religious tolerance and constitutional government—put liberty ahead of perfection."

This willingness to invoke what *we* do raises, as I have said, the specters of ethnocentrism and of relativism. Because Sandel is convinced that Rawls shares Kant's fear of these specters, he is convinced that Rawls is looking for an "'Archimedean point' from which to assess the basic structure of society"—a "standpoint neither compromised by its implication in the world nor dissociated and so disqualified by detachment."[30] It is just this idea that a standpoint can be "compromised by its implication in the world" that Rawls rejects in his recent writings. Philosophically inclined communitarians like Sandel are unable to envisage a middle ground between relativism and a "theory of the moral subject"—a theory that is not about, for example, religious tolerance and large market economies, but about human beings as such, viewed ahistorically. Rawls is trying to stake out just such a middle ground.[31] When he speaks of an "Archimedian point," he does not mean a point outside history, but simply the kind of settled social habits that allow much latitude for further choices. He says, for example,

> The upshot of these considerations is that justice as fairness is not at the mercy, so to speak, of existing wants and interests. It sets up an Archimedean point for assessing the social system without invoking a priori considerations. The long range aim of society is settled in its main lines irrespective of the particular desires and needs of its present members. . . . There is no place for the question whether men's desires to play the role of superior or inferior might not be so great that autocratic institutions should be accepted, or whether men's perception of the religious practices of others might not be so upsetting that liberty of conscience should not be allowed.[32]

To say that there is no place for the questions that Nietzsche or Loyola would raise is not to say that the views of either are unintelligible (in the sense of "logically incoherent" or "conceptually confused"). Nor is it to say that they are based on an incorrect theory of the self. Nor is it *just* to say that our preferences conflict with theirs.[33] It is to say that the conflict between these men and us is so great that "preferences" is the wrong word. It is appropriate to speak of gustatory or sexual preferences, for these do not matter to anybody but yourself and your immediate circle. But it is misleading to speak of a "preference" for liberal democracy.

Rather, we heirs of the Enlightenment think of enemies of liberal democracy like Nietzsche or Loyola as, to use Rawls's word, "mad." We do so because there is no way to see them as fellow citizens of our constitutional democracy, people whose life plans might, given ingenuity and good will, be fitted in with those of other citizens. They are not crazy because they have mistaken the ahistorical nature of human beings. They are crazy because the limits of sanity are set by what we can take seriously. This, in turn, is determined by our upbringing, our historical situation.[34]

If this short way of dealing with Nietzsche and Loyola seems shockingly ethnocentric, it is because the philosophical tradition has accustomed us to the idea that anybody who is willing to listen to reason—to hear out all the arguments—can be brought around to the truth. This view, which Kierkegaard called "Socratism" and contrasted with the claim that our point of departure may be simply a historical event, is intertwined with the idea that the human self has a center (a divine spark, or a truth-tracking faculty called "reason") and that argumentation will, given time and patience, penetrate to this center. For Rawls's purposes, we do not need this picture. We are free to see the self as centerless, as a historical contingency all the way through. Rawls neither needs nor wants to defend the priority of the right to the good as Kant defended it, by invoking a theory of the self that makes it more than an "empirical self," more than a "radically situated subject." He presumably thinks of Kant as, although largely right about the nature of justice, largely wrong about the nature and function of philosophy.

More specifically, he can reject Sandel's Kantian claim that there is a "distance between subject and situation which is necessary to any measure of detachment, is essential to the ineliminably *possessive* aspect of any coherent conception of the self."[35] Sandel defines this aspect by saying, "I can never fully be constituted by my attributes . . . there must always be some attributes I *have* rather than am." On the interpretation of Rawls I am offering, we do not need a categorical distinction between the self and its situation. We can dismiss the distinction between an attribute of the self and a constituent of the self, between the self's accidents and its essence, as "merely" metaphysical.[36] If we are inclined to philosophize, we shall want the vocabulary offered by Dewey, Heidegger, Davidson, and Derrida, with its built-in cautions against metaphysics, rather than that offered by Descartes, Hume, and Kant.[37] For if we use the former vocabulary, we shall be able to see moral progress as a history of making rather than finding, of poetic achievement by "radically situated" individuals and communities, rather than as the gradual unveiling, through the use of "reason," of "principles" or "rights" or "values."

Sandel's claim that "the concept of a subject given prior to and independent of its objects offers a foundation for the moral law that . . . powerfully completes the deontological vision" is true enough. But to suggest such a powerful completion to Rawls is to offer him a poisoned gift. It is like offering Jefferson an argument for religious tolerance based on exegesis of the Christian Scriptures.[38] Rejecting the assumption that the moral law needs a "foundation" is just what distinguishes Rawls from Jefferson. It is just this that permits him to be a Deweyan naturalist who needs neither the distinction between will and intellect nor the distinction between the self's constituents and its attributes. He does not *want* a "complete deontological vision," one that would explain *why* we should give justice priority over our conception of the good. He is filling out the consequences of the claim that it is prior, not its presuppositions.[39] Rawls is not interested in conditions for the identity of the self, but only in conditions for citizenship in a liberal society.

Suppose one grants that Rawls is not attempting a transcendental deduction of American liberalism or supplying philosophical foundations for democratic institutions, but simply trying to systematize the principles and intuitions typical of American liberals. Still, it may seem that the important questions raised by the critics of liberalism have been begged. Consider the claim that we liberals can simply dismiss Nietzsche and Loyola as crazy. One imagines these two rejoining that they are quite aware that their views unfit them for citizenship in a constitutional democracy and that the typical inhabitant of such a democracy would regard them as crazy. But they take these facts as further counts against constitutional democracy. They think that the kind of person created by such a democracy is not what a human being should be.

In finding a dialectical stance to adopt toward Nietzsche or Loyola, we liberal democrats are faced with a dilemma. To refuse to argue about what human beings should be like seems to show a contempt for the spirit of accommodation and tolerance, which is essential to democracy. But it is not clear how to argue for the claim that human beings ought to be liberals rather than fanatics without being driven back on a theory of human nature, on philosophy. I think that we must grasp the first horn. We have to insist that not every argument need to be met in the terms in which it is presented. Accommodation and tolerance must stop short of a willingness to work within any vocabulary that one's interlocutor wishes to use, to take seriously any topic that he puts forward for discussion. To take this view is of a piece with dropping the idea that a single moral vocabulary and a single set of moral beliefs are appropriate for every human community everywhere, and to grant that historical developments may lead us to simply *drop* questions and the vocabulary in which those questions are posed.

Just as Jefferson refused to let the Christian Scriptures set the terms in which to discuss alternative political institutions, so we either must refuse to answer the question "What sort of human being are you hoping to produce?" or, at least, must not let our answer to this question dictate our answer to the question "Is justice primary?"[40] It is no more evident that democratic institutions are to be measured by the sort of person they create than that they are to be measured against divine commands. It is not evident that they are to be measured by anything more specific than the moral intuitions of the particular historical community that has created those institutions. The idea that moral and political controversies should always be "brought back to first principles" is reasonable if it means merely that we should seek common ground in the hope of attaining agreement. But it is misleading if it is taken as the claim that there is a natural order of premises from which moral and political conclusions are to be inferred—not to mention the claim that some particular interlocutor (for example, Nietzsche or Loyola) has already discerned that order. The liberal response to the communitarians' second claim must be, therefore, that even if the typical character types of liberal democracies *are* bland, calculating, petty, and unheroic, the prevalence of such people may be a reasonable price to pay for political freedom.

The spirit of accommodation and tolerance certainly suggests that we should seek common ground with Nietzsche and Loyola, but there is no predicting where, or whether, such common ground will be found. The philosophical tradition has assumed that there are certain topics (for example, "What is God's will?," "What is man?," "What rights are intrinsic to the species?") on which everyone has, or should have, views and that these topics are prior in the order of justification to those at issue in political deliberation. This assumption goes along with the assumption that human beings have a natural center that philosophical inquiry can locate and illuminate. By contrast, the view that human beings are centerless networks of beliefs and desires and that their vocabularies and opinions are determined by historical circumstance allows for the possibility that there may not be enough overlap between two such networks to make possible agreement about political topics, or even profitable discussion of such topics.[41] We do not conclude that Nietzsche and Loyola are crazy because they hold unusual views on certain "fundamental" topics; rather, we conclude this only after extensive attempts at an exchange of political views have made us realize that we are not going to get anywhere.[42]

One can sum up this way of grasping the first horn of the dilemma I sketched earlier by saying that Rawls puts democratic politics first, and philosophy second. He retains the Socratic commitment to free exchange of views without the Platonic commitment to the possibility of universal agreement—a possibility underwritten by epistemological doctrines like Plato's Theory of Recollection[43] or Kant's theory of the relation between pure and empirical concepts. He disengages the question of whether we ought to be tolerant and Socratic from the question of whether this strategy will lead to truth. He is content that it should lead to whatever intersubjective reflective equilibrium may be obtainable, given the contingent make-up of the subjects in question. Truth, viewed in the Platonic way, as the grasp of what Rawls calls "an order antecedent to and given to us," is simply not relevant to democratic politics. So philosophy, as the explanation of the relation between such an order and human nature, is not relevant either. When the two come into conflict, democracy takes precedence over philosophy.

This conclusion may seem liable to an obvious objection. It may seem that I have been rejecting a concern with philosophical theories about the nature of men and women on the basis of just such a theory. But notice that although I have frequently said that Rawls *can be content* with a notion of the human self as a centerless web of historically conditioned beliefs and desires, I have not suggested that he *needs* such a theory. Such a theory does not offer liberal social theory a *basis*. If one *wants* a model of the human self, then this picture of a centerless web will fill the need. But for purposes of liberal social theory, one can do without such a model. One can get along with common sense and social science, areas of discourse in which the term "the self" rarely occurs.

If, however, one has a taste for philosophy—if one's vocation, one's private pursuit of perfection, entails constructing models of such entities as "the self," "knowledge," "language," "nature," "God," or "history," and then tinkering with them until they mesh with one another—one *will* want a picture of the self. Since my own vocation is of this sort, and the moral identity around which I wish to build such models is that of a citizen of a liberal democratic state, I commend the picture of the self as a centerless and contingent web to those with similar tastes and similar identities. But I would not commend it to those with a similar vocation but dissimilar moral identities—identities built, for example, around the love of God, Nietzschean self-overcoming, the accurate representation of reality as it is in itself, the quest for "one right answer" to moral questions, or the natural superiority of a given character type. Such persons need a more complex and interesting, less simple-minded model of the self—one that meshes in complex ways with complex models of such things as "nature" or "history." Nevertheless, such persons may, for pragmatic rather than moral reasons, be loyal citizens of a liberal democratic society. They may despise most of their fellow citizens, but be prepared to grant that the prevalence of such despicable character types is a lesser evil than the loss of political freedom. They may be ruefully grateful that their private senses of moral identity and the models of the human self that they develop to articulate this sense—the ways in which they deal with their aloneness—are not the concern of such a state. Rawls and Dewey have shown how the liberal state can ignore the difference between the moral identities of Glaucon and of Thrasymachus, just as it ignores the difference between the religious identities of a Catholic archbishop and a Mormon prophet.

There is, however, a flavor of paradox in this attitude toward theories of the self. One might be inclined to say that I have evaded one sort of self-referential paradox only by falling into another sort. For I am presupposing that one is at liberty to rig up a model of the self to suit oneself, to tailor it to one's politics, one's religion, or one's private sense of the meaning of one's life. This, in turn, presupposes that there is no "objective truth" about what the human self is *really* like. That, in turn, seems a claim that could be justified only on the basis of a metaphysico-epistemological view of the traditional sort. For surely if anything is the province of such a view, it is the question of what there is and is not a "fact of the matter" about. So my argument must ultimately come back to philosophical first principles.

Here I can only say that if there were a discoverable fact of the matter about what there is a fact of the matter about, then it would doubtless be metaphysics and epistemology that would discover that meta-fact. But I think that the very idea of a "fact of the matter" is one we would be better off without. Philosophers like Davidson and Derrida have, I think, given us good reason to think that the *physis–nomos, in se–ad nos,* and objective–subjective distinctions were steps on a ladder that we can now safely throw away. The question of whether the reasons such philosophers have given for this claim are themselves metaphysico-epistemological reasons, and if not, what sort of reasons they are, strikes me as pointless and sterile. Once again, I fall back on the holist's strategy of insisting that reflective equilibrium is all we need try for—that there is no natural order of justification of beliefs, no predestined outline for argument to trace. Getting rid of the idea of such an outline seems to me one of the many benefits of a conception of the self as a centerless web. Another benefit is that questions about whom we need justify ourselves to—questions about who counts as a fanatic and who deserves an answer—can be treated as just further matters to be sorted out in the course of attaining reflective equilibrium.

I can, however, make one point to offset the air of light-minded aestheticism I am adopting toward traditional philosophical questions. This is that there is a moral purpose behind this light-mindedness. The encouragement of light-mindedness about traditional philosophical topics serves the same purposes as does the encouragement of light-mindedness about traditional theological topics. Like the rise of large market economies, the increase in literacy, the proliferation of artistic genres, and the insouciant pluralism of contemporary culture, such philosophical superficiality and light-mindedness helps along the disenchantment of the world. It helps make the world's inhabitants more pragmatic, more tolerant, more liberal, more receptive to the appeal of instrumental rationality.

If one's moral identity consists in being a citizen of a liberal polity, then to encourage light-mindedness may serve one's moral purposes. Moral commitment, after all, does not require taking seriously all the matters that are, for moral reasons, taken seriously by one's fellow citizens. It may require just the opposite. It may require trying to josh them out of the habit of taking those topics so seriously. There may be serious reasons for so joshing them. More generally, we should not assume that the aesthetic is always the enemy of the moral. I should argue that in the recent history of liberal societies, the willingness to view matters aesthetically—to be content to indulge in what Schiller called "play" and to discard what Nietzsche called "the spirit of seriousness"—has been an important vehicle of moral progress.

I have now said everything I have to say about the third of the communitarian claims that I distinguished at the outset: the claim that the social theory of the liberal state rests on false philosophical presuppositions. I hope I have given reasons for thinking that insofar as the communitarian is a critic of liberalism, he should drop this claim and should instead develop either of the first two claims: the empirical claim that democratic institutions cannot be combined with the sense of common purpose predemocratic societies enjoyed, or the moral judgment that the products of the liberal state are too high a price to pay for the elimination of the evils that preceded it. If communitarian critics of liberalism stuck to these two claims, they would avoid the sort of terminal wistfulness with which their books typically end. Heidegger, for example, tells us that "we are too late for the gods, and too early for Being." Unger ends *Knowledge and Politics* with an appeal to a *Deus absconditus*. MacIntyre ends *After Virtue* by saying that we "are waiting not for a Godot, but for another—doubtless very different—St. Benedict."[44] Sandel ends his book by saying that liberalism "forgets the possibility that when politics goes well, we can know a good in common that we cannot know alone," but he does not suggest a candidate for this common good.

Instead of thus suggesting that philosophical reflection, or a return to religion, might enable us to re-enchant the world, I think that communitarians should stick to the question of whether disenchantment has, on balance, done us more harm than good, or created more dangers than it has evaded. For Dewey, communal and public disenchantment is the price we pay for individual and private spiritual liberation, the kind of liberation that Emerson thought characteristically American. Dewey was as well aware as Weber that there is a price to be paid, but he thought it well worth paying. He assumed that no good achieved by earlier societies would be worth recapturing if the price were a diminution in our ability to leave people alone, to let them try out their private visions of perfection in peace. He admired the American habit of giving democracy priority over philosophy by asking, about any vision of the meaning of life, "Would not acting out this vision interfere with the ability of others to work out their own salvation?" Giving priority to that question is no more "natural" than giving priority to, say, MacIntyre's question "What sorts of human beings emerge in the culture of liberalism?" or Sandel's question "Can a community of those who put justice first ever be more than a community of strangers?" The question of which of these questions is prior to which others is, necessarily, begged by *everybody*. Nobody is being any more arbitrary than anybody else. But that is to say that nobody is being arbitrary at all. Everybody is just insisting that the beliefs and desires they hold most dear should come first in the order of discussion. That is not arbitrariness, but sincerity.

The danger of re-enchanting the world, from a Deweyan point of view, is that it might interfere with the development of what Rawls calls "a social union of social unions,"[45] some of which may be (and in Emerson's view, should be) very small indeed. For it is hard to be both enchanted with one version of the world and tolerant of all the others. I have not tried to argue the question of whether Dewey was right in this judgment of relative danger and promise. I have merely argued that such a judgment neither presupposes nor supports a theory of the self. Nor have I tried to deal with Horkheimer and Adorno's prediction that the "dissolvent rationality" of the Enlightenment will eventually cause the liberal democracies to come unstuck.

The only thing I have to say about this prediction is that the collapse of the liberal democracies would not, in itself, provide much evidence for the claim that human societies cannot survive without widely shared opinions on matters of ultimate importance—shared conceptions of our place in the universe and our mission on earth. Perhaps they cannot survive under such conditions, but the eventual collapse of the democracies would not, in itself, show that this was the case—any more than it would show that human societies require kings or an established religion, or that political community cannot exist outside of small city-states.

Both Jefferson and Dewey described America as an "experiment." If the experiment fails, our descendants may learn something important. But they will not learn a philosophical truth, any more than they will learn a religious one. They will simply get some hints about what to watch out for when setting up their next experiment. Even if nothing else survives from the age of the democratic revolutions, perhaps our descendants will remember that social institutions *can* be viewed as experiments in cooperation rather than as attempts to embody a universal and ahistorical order. It is hard to believe that this memory would not be worth having.

Notes

1. Thomas Jefferson, *Notes on the State of Virginia*, Query XVII, in *The Writings of Thomas Jefferson*, ed. A. A. Lipscomb and A. E. Bergh (Washington, D.C., 1905), 2: 217.

2. Jefferson included a statement of this familiar Scriptural claim (roughly in the form in which it had been restated by Milton in *Areopagitica*) in the preamble to the Virginia Statute

for Religious Freedom: "truth is great and will prevail if left to herself, . . . she is the proper and sufficient antagonist to error, and has nothing to fear from the conflict, unless by human interposition disarmed of her natural weapons, free argument and debate, errors ceasing to be dangerous when it is permitted freely to contradict them" (ibid., 2: 302).

3. Max Horkheimer and Theodor W. Adorno, *Dialectic of Enlightenment* (New York: Seabury Press, 1972), p. xiii.

4."For the Enlightenment, whatever does not conform to the rule of computation and utility is suspect. So long as it can develop undisturbed by any outward repression, there is no holding it. In the process, it treats its own ideas of human rights exactly as it does the older universals . . . Enlightenment is totalitarian" (ibid., p. 6). This line of thought recurs repeatedly in communitarian accounts of the present state of the liberal democracies; see, for example, Robert Bellah, Richard Madsen, William Sullivan, Ann Swidler, and Steven Tipton, *Habits of the Heart: Individualism and Commitment in American Life* (Berkeley: University of California Press, 1985): "There is a widespread feeling that the promise of the modern era is slipping away from us. A movement of enlightenment and liberation that was to have freed us from superstition and tyranny has led in the twentieth century to a world in which ideological fanaticism and political oppression have reached extremes unknown in previous history" (p. 277).

5. Charles Taylor, *Philosophy and the Human Sciences*, vol. 2 of *Philosophical Papers* (Cambridge: Cambridge University Press, 1985), p. 8.

6. Ibid., p. 5.

7. John Rawls, "Justice as Fairness: Political not Metaphysical," *Philosophy and Public Affairs* 14 (1985): 225. Religious toleration is a constantly recurring theme in Rawls's writing. Early in *A Theory of Justice* (Cambridge, Mass.: Harvard University Press, 1971), when giving examples of the sort of common opinions that a theory of justice must take into account and systematize, he cites our conviction that religious intolerance is unjust (p. 19). His example of the fact that "a well-ordered society tends to eliminate or at least to control men's inclinations to injustice" is that "warring and intolerant sects are much less likely to exist" (p. 247). Another relevant passage (which I shall discuss below) is his diagnosis of Ignatius Loyola's attempt to make the love of God the "dominant good": "Although to subordinate all our aims to one end does not strictly speaking violate the principles of rational choice . . . it still strikes us as irrational, or more likely as mad" (pp. 553–4).

8. Rawls, "Justice as Fairness," pp. 225–6. The suggestion that there are many philosophical views that will *not* survive in such conditions is analogous to the Enlightenment suggestion that the adoption of democratic institutions will cause "superstitious" forms of religious belief gradually to die off.

9. Ibid., p. 230.

10. Ibid.

11. For Rawls's historicism see, for example, *Theory of Justice*, p. 547. There, Rawls says that the people in the original position are assumed to know "the general facts about society," including the fact that "institutions are not fixed but change over time, altered by natural circumstances and the activities and conflicts of social groups." He uses this point to rule out, as original choosers of principles of justice, those "in a feudal or a caste system," and those who are unaware of events such as the French Revolution. This is one of many passages that make clear (at least read in the light of Rawls's later work) that a great deal of knowledge that came late to the mind of Europe is present to the minds of those behind the veil of ignorance. Or, to put it another way, such passages make clear that those original choosers behind the veil exemplify a certain modern type of human being, not an ahistorical human nature. See also p. 548, where Rawls says, "Of course in working out what the requisite principles [of justice] are, we must rely upon current knowledge as recognized by common sense and the existing scientific consensus.

We have to concede that as established beliefs change, it is possible that the principles of justice which it seems rational to choose may likewise change."

12. See Bellah et al., *Habits of the Heart*, p. 141, for a recent restatement of this "counter-Enlightenment" line of thought. For the authors' view of the problems created by persistence in Enlightenment rhetoric and by the prevalence of the conception of human dignity that Taylor identifies as "distinctively modern," see p. 21: "For most of us, it is easier to think about to get what we want than to know exactly what we should want. Thus Brian, Joe, Margaret and Wayne [some of the Americans interviewed by the authors] are each in his or her own way confused about how to define for themselves such things as the nature of success, the meaning of freedom, and the requirements of justice. Those difficulties are in an important way created by the limitations in the common tradition of moral discourse they—and we—share." Compare p. 290: "the language of individualism, the primary American language of self-understanding, limits the way in which people think."

To my mind, the authors of *Habits of the Heart* undermine their own conclusions in the passages where they point to actual moral progress being made in recent American history, notably in their discussion of the civil-rights movement. There, they say that Martin Luther King, Jr., made the struggle for freedom "a practice of commitment within a vision of America as a community of memory" and that the response King elicited "came from the reawakened recognition by many Americans that their own sense of self was rooted in companionship with others who, though not necessarily like themselves, nevertheless shared with them a common history and whose appeals to justice and solidarity made powerful claims on our loyalty" (p. 252). These descriptions of King's achievement seem exactly right, but they can be read as evidence that the rhetoric of the Enlightenment offers at least as many opportunities as it does obstacles for the renewal of a sense of community. The civil-rights movement combined, without much strain, the language of Christian fellowship and the "language of individualism," about which Bellah and his colleagues are dubious.

13. See Michael Walzer, *Spheres of Justice* (New York: Basic, 1983), pp. 312 ff.

14. Michael Sandel, *Liberalism and the Limits of Justice* (Cambridge: Cambridge University Press, 1982), p. 49.

15. In a recent, as yet unpublished, paper, Sandel has urged that Rawls's claim that "philosophy in the classical sense as the search for truth about a prior and independent moral order cannot provide the shared basis for a political conception of justice" presupposes the controversial metaphysical claim that there is no such order. This seems to me like saying that Jefferson was presupposing the controversial theological claim that God is not interested in the name by which he is called by human beings. Both charges are accurate, but not really to the point. Both Jefferson and Rawls would have to reply, "I have no arguments for my dubious theological-metaphysical claim, because I do not know how to discuss such issues, and do not want to. My interest is in helping to preserve and create political institutions that will foster public indifference to such issues, while putting no restrictions on private discussion of them." This reply, of course, begs the "deeper" question that Sandel wants to raise, for the question of whether we *should* determine what issues to discuss on political or on "theoretical" (for example, theological or philosophical) grounds remains unanswered.

16. Jefferson agreed with Luther that philosophers had muddied the clear waters of the gospels. See Jefferson's polemic against Plato's "foggy mind" and his claim that "the doctrines which flowed from the lips of Jesus himself are within the comprehension of a child; but thousands of volumes have not yet explained the Platonisms engrafted on them; and for this obvious reason, that nonsense can never be explained" (*Writings of Thomas Jefferson*, 14: 149).

17. I am here using the term "human nature" in the traditional philosophical sense in which Sartre denied that there was such a thing, rather than in the rather unusual one that Rawls gives

it. Rawls distinguishes between a "conception of the person" and a "theory of human nature," where the former is a "moral ideal" and the latter is provided by, roughly, common sense plus the social sciences. To have a theory of human nature is to have "general facts that we take to be true, or true enough, given the state of public knowledge in our society," facts that "limit the feasibility of the ideals of person and society embedded in that framework" ("Kantian Constructivism in Moral Theory," *Journal of Philosophy* 88 [1980]: 534).

18. Rawls, "Justice as Fairness," p. 223.

19. In fact, it has been for the worse. A view that made politics more central to philosophy and subjectivity less would both permit more effective defenses of democracy than those that purport to supply it with "foundations" and permit liberals to meet Marxists on their own, political, ground. Dewey's explicit attempt to make the central philosophical question "What serves democracy?" rather than "What permits us to argue for democracy?" has been, unfortunately, neglected. I try to make this point in "Philosophy as Science, as Metaphor, and as Politics" (in *Essays on Heidegger and Others*).

20. That is, give-and-take between intuitions about the desirability of particular consequences of particular actions and intuitions about general principles, with neither having the determining voice.

21. One will also, as I did on first reading Rawls, take him to be attempting to supply such legitimation by an appeal to the rationality of the choosers in the original position. Rawls warned his readers that the original position (the position of those who, behind a veil of ignorance that hides them from their life chances and their conceptions of the good, select from among alternative principles of justice) served simply "to make vivid . . . the restrictions that it seems reasonable to impose on arguments for principles of justice and therefore on those principles themselves" (*Theory of Justice*, p. 18).

But this warning went unheeded by myself and others, in part because of an ambiguity between "reasonable" as defined by ahistorical criteria and as meaning something like "in accord with the moral sentiments characteristic of the heirs of the Enlightenment." Rawls's later work has, as I have said, helped us come down on the historicist side of this ambiguity; see, for example, "Kantian Constructivism": "the original position is not an axiomatic (or deductive) basis from which principles are derived but a procedure for singling out principles most fitting to the conception of the person most likely to be held, at least implicitly, in a democratic society" (p. 572). It is tempting to suggest that one could eliminate all reference to the original position from *A Theory of Justice* without loss, but this is as daring a suggestion as that one might rewrite (as many have wished to do) Kant's *Critique of Pure Reason* without reference to the thing-in-itself. T. M. Scanlon has suggested that we can, at least, safely eliminate reference, in the description of the choosers in the original position, to an appeal to self-interest. ("Contractualism and Utilitarianism," in *Utilitarianism and Beyond*, ed. Bernard Williams and Amartya Sen [Cambridge: Cambridge University Press, 1982]). Since justifiability is, more evidently than self-interest, relative to historical circumstance, Scanlon's proposal seems to be more faithful to Rawls's overall philosophical program than Rawls's own formulation.

22. In particular, there will be no principles or intuitions concerning the universal features of human psychology relevant to motivation. Sandel thinks that since assumptions about motivation are part of the description of the original position, "what issues at one end in a theory of justice must issue at the other in a theory of the person, or more precisely, a theory of the moral subject" (*Liberalism and the Limits of Justice*, p. 47). I would argue that if we follow Scanlon's lead (note 21) in dropping reference to self-interest in our description of the original choosers and replacing this with reference to their desire to justify their choices to their fellows, then the only "theory of the person" we get is a sociological description of the inhabitants of contemporary liberal democracies.

23. Rawls, "Kantian Constructivism," p. 519. Italics added.

24. Sandel, *Liberalism and the Limits of Justice*, p. 21. I have argued for the advantages of thinking of the self as just such a concatenation in chapter 2 of *Contingency, Irony, and Solidarity* (Cambridge: Cambridge University Press, 1989). When Sandel cites Robert Nozick and Daniel Bell as suggesting that Rawls "ends by dissolving the self in order to preserve it" (*Liberalism and the Limits of Justice*, p. 95), I should rejoin that it may be helpful to dissolve the metaphysical self in order to preserve the political one. Less obliquely stated: It may be helpful, for purposes of systematizing our intuitions about the priority of liberty, to treat the self as having no center, no essence, but *merely* as a concatenation of beliefs and desires.

25. "Deontology with a Humean face either fails as deontology or recreates in the original position the disembodied subject it resolves to avoid" (ibid., p. 14).

26. Ibid., p. 19.

27. Rawls, *Theory of Justice*, p. 560.

28. Ibid.

29. It is important to note that Rawls explicitly distances himself from the idea that he is analyzing the very idea of morality and from conceptual analysis as the method of social theory (ibid., p. 130). Some of his critics have suggested that Rawls is practicing "reductive logical analysis" of the sort characteristic of "analytic philosophy"; see, for example, William M. Sullivan, *Reconstructing Public Philosophy* (Berkeley: University of California Press, 1982), pp. 94ff. Sullivan says that "this ideal of reductive logical analysis lends legitimacy to the notion that moral philosophy is summed up in the task of discovering, through the analysis of moral rules, both primitive elements and governing principles that must apply to any rational moral system, *rational* here meaning 'logically coherent'" (p. 96). He goes on to grant that "Nozick and Rawls are more sensitive to the importance of history and social experience in human life than were the classic liberal thinkers" (p. 97). But this concession is too slight and is misleading. Rawls's willingness to adopt "reflective equilibrium" rather than "conceptual analysis" as a methodological watchword sets him apart from the epistemologically oriented moral philosophy that was dominant prior to the appearance of *A Theory of Justice*. Rawls represents a reaction against the Kantian idea of "morality" as having an ahistorical essence, the same sort of reaction found in Hegel and in Dewey.

30. Sandel, *Liberalism and the Limits of Justice*, p. 17.

31. ". . . liberty of conscience and freedom of thought should not be founded on philosophical or ethical skepticism, nor on indifference to religious and moral interests. The principles of justice define an appropriate path between dogmatism and intolerance on the one side, and a reductionism which regards religion and morality as mere preferences on the other" (Rawls, *Theory of Justice*, p. 243). I take it that Rawls is identifying "philosophical or ethical skepticism" with the idea that everything is just a matter of "preference," even religion, philosophy, and morals. So we should distinguish his suggestion that we "extend the principle of toleration to philosophy itself" from the suggestion that we dismiss philosophy as epiphenomenal. That is the sort of suggestion that is backed up by reductionist accounts of philosophical doctrines as "preferences" or "wish fulfillments" or "expressions of emotion" (see Rawls's criticism of Freudian reductionism in ibid., pp. 539ff.). Neither psychology nor logic nor any other theoretical discipline can supply non-question-begging reasons why philosophy should be set aside, any more than philosophy can supply such reasons why theology should be set aside. But this is compatible with saying that the general course of historical experience may lead us to neglect theological topics and bring us to the point at which, like Jefferson, we find a theological vocabulary "meaningless" (or, more precisely, useless). I am suggesting that the course of historical experience since Jefferson's time has led us to a point at which we find much of the vocabulary of modern philosophy no longer useful.

32. Ibid., pp. 261–2.

33. The contrast between "mere preference" and something less "arbitrary," something more closely related to the very nature of man or of reason, is invoked by many writers who think of "human rights" as requiring a philosophical foundation of the traditional sort. Thus my colleague David Little, commenting on my "Solidarity or Objectivity?" (above), says "Rorty appears to permit criticism and pressure against those societies [the ones we do not like] *if we happen to want to* criticize and pressure them in pursuit of some interest or belief we may (at the time) have, and for whatever ethnocentric reasons we may happen to hold those interests or beliefs" ("Natural Rights and Human Rights: The International Imperative," in *National Rights and Natural Law: The Legacy of George Mason*, ed. Robert P. Davidow [Fairfax, Va.: George Mason University Press, 1986], pp. 67–122; italics in original). I would rejoin that Little's use of "happen to want to" presupposes a dubious distinction between necessary, built-in, universal convictions (convictions that it would be "irrational" to reject) and accidental, culturally determined convictions. It also presupposes the existence of such faculties as reason, will, and emotion, all of which the pragmatist tradition in American philosophy and the so-called existentialist tradition in European philosophy try to undercut. Dewey's *Human Nature and Conduct* and Heidegger's *Being and Time* both offer a moral psychology that avoids oppositions between "preference" and "reason."

34. "Aristotle remarks that it is a peculiarity of men that they possess a sense of the just and the unjust and that their sharing a common understanding of justice makes a polis. Analogously one might say, in view of our discussion, that a common understanding of justice as fairness makes a constitutional democracy" (Rawls, *Theory of Justice*, p. 243). In the interpretation of Rawls I am offering, it is unrealistic to expect Aristotle to have developed a conception of justice as fairness, since he simply lacked the kind of historical experience that we have accumulated since his day. More generally, it is pointless to assume (with, for example, Leo Strauss) that the Greeks had already canvassed the alternatives available for social life and institutions. When we discuss justice, we cannot agree to bracket our knowledge of recent history.

35. Sandel, *Liberalism and the Limits of Justice*, p. 20.

36. We can dismiss other distinctions that Sandel draws in the same way. Examples are the distinction between a voluntarist and a cognitive account of the original position (ibid., p. 121), that between "the identity of the subject" as the "product" rather than the "premise" of its agency (ibid., p. 152), and that between the question "Who am I?" and its rival as "the paradigmatic moral question," "What shall I choose?" (ibid., p. 153). These distinctions are all to be analyzed away as products of the "Kantian dualisms" that Rawls praises Hegel and Dewey for having overcome.

37. For some similarities between Dewey and Heidegger with respect to anti-Cartesianism, see my "Overcoming the Tradition," in Richard Rorty, *Consequences of Pragmatism* (Minneapolis: University of Minnesota Press, 1982).

38. David Levin has pointed out to me that Jefferson was not above borrowing such arguments. I take this to show that Jefferson, like Kant, found himself in an untenable halfway position between theology and Deweyan social experimentalism.

39. Sandel takes "the primacy of the subject" to be not only a way of filling out the deontological picture, but also a necessary condition of its correctness: "If the claim for the primacy of justice is to succeed, if the right is to be prior to the good in the interlocking moral and foundational sense we have distinguished, then some version of the claim for the primacy of the subject must succeed as well" (*Liberalism and the Limits of Justice*, p. 7). Sandel quotes Rawls as saying that "the essential unity of the self is already provided by the conception of the right" and takes this passage as evidence that Rawls holds a doctrine of the "priority of the self" (ibid., p. 21). But consider the context of this sentence. Rawls says: "The principles of justice and their

realization in social forms define the bounds within which our deliberations take place. The essential unity of the self is already provided by the conception of right. Moreover, in a well-ordered society this unity is the same for all; everyone's conception of the good as given by his rational plan is a sub-plan of the larger comprehensive plan that regulates the community as a social union of social unions" (*Theory of Justice*, p. 563). The "essential unity of the self," which is in question here, is simply the system of moral sentiments, habits, and internalized traditions that is typical of the politically aware citizen of a constitutional democracy. This self is, once again, a historical product. It has nothing to do with the nonempirical self, which Kant had to postulate in the interests of Enlightenment universalism.

40. This is the kernel of truth in Dworkin's claim that Rawls rejects "goal-based" social theory, but this point should not lead us to think that he is thereby driven back on a "rights-based" theory.

41. But one should not press this point so far as to raise the specter of "untranslatable languages." As Donald Davidson has remarked, we would not recognize other organisms as actual or potential language users—or, therefore, as persons—unless there were enough overlap in belief and desire to make translation possible. The point is merely that efficient and frequent communication is only a necessary, not a sufficient, condition of agreement.

42. Further, such a conclusion is *restricted* to politics. It does not cast doubt on the ability of these men to follow the rules of logic or their ability to do many other things skillfully and well. It is thus not equivalent to the traditional philosophical charge of "irrationality." That charge presupposes that inability to "see" certain truths is evidence of the lack of an organ that is essential for human functioning generally.

43. In Kierkegaard's *Philosophical Fragments*, to which I have referred earlier, we find the Platonic Theory of Recollection treated as the archetypal justification of "Socratism" and thus as the symbol of all forms (especially Hegel's) of what Bernard Williams has recently called "the rationalist theory of rationality"—the idea that one is rational only if one can appeal to universally accepted criteria, criteria whose truth and applicability all human beings can find "in their heart." This is the philosophical core of the Scriptural idea that "truth is great, and will prevail," when the idea is dissociated from the idea of "a New Being" (in the way that Kierkegaard refused to dissociate it).

44. See Jeffrey Stout's discussion of the manifold ambiguities of this conclusion in "Virtue Among the Ruins: An Essay on MacIntrye," *Newe Zeitschrift für Systematische Theologie und Religionsphilosophie* 26 (1984): 256–73, especially 269.

45. This is Rawls's description of "a well-ordered society (corresponding to justice as fairness)" (*Theory of Justice*, p. 527). Sandel finds these passages metaphorical and complains that "intersubjective and individualistic images appear in uneasy, sometimes unfelicitous combination, as if to betray the incompatible commitments contending within" (*Liberalism and the Limits of Justice*, pp. 150ff.). He concludes that "the moral vocabulary of community in the strong sense cannot in all cases be captured by a conception that [as Rawls has said his is] 'in its theoretical bases is individualistic.'" I am claiming that these commitments will look incompatible only if one attempts to define their philosophical presuppositions (which Rawls himself may occasionally have done too much of), and that this is a good reason for not making such attempts. Compare the Enlightenment view that attempts to sharpen up the theological presuppositions of social commitments had done more harm than good and that if theology cannot simply be discarded, it should at least be left as fuzzy (or, one might say, "liberal") as possible. Oakeshott has a point when he insists on the value of theoretical muddle for the health of the state.

Elsewhere Rawls has claimed that "there is no reason why a well-ordered society should encourage primarily individualistic values if this means ways of life that lead individuals to pursue their own way and to have no concern for the interest of others" ("Fairness to Goodness," *Philosophical Review* 84 [1975]: 550). Sandel's discussion of this passage says that it "suggests a deeper sense in which Rawls' conception is individualistic," but his argument that this suggestion is correct is, once again, the claim that "the Rawlsian self is not only a subject of possession, but an antecedently individuated subject" (*Liberalism and the Limits of Justice*, pp. 61ff.). This is just the claim I have been arguing against by arguing that there is no such thing as "the Rawlsian self" and that Rawls does not want or need a "theory of the person." Sandel says (p. 62) that Rawls "takes for granted that every individual consists of one and only one system of desires," but it is hard to find evidence for this claim in the texts. At worst, Rawls simplifies his presentation by imagining each of his citizens as having only one such set, but this simplifying assumption does not seem central to his view.

In this essay, Cornel West makes the case for a reconstruction of religious belief in terms of the historical contexts that give rise to them.

CORNEL WEST

Dispensing with Metaphysics in Religious Thought

A historicist turn has occurred in contemporary philosophy which has not yet awakened some theologians from their dogmatic slumber. Ironically, this turn—enacted by Thomas Kuhn, Richard Rorty, and others—is less radical and thorough than that initiated in theology by Ernst Troeltsch at the turn of the century. But who among our most influential religious thinkers invokes Troeltsch these days?

In this brief chapter I shall argue that historicism is indispensable for contemporary religious thought. I understand historicism as the view that structured social practices constitute the sources for standards which adjudicate between conflicting theories and interpretations. I then will suggest that this acceptance of historicism (an acceptance of our finitude and fallibilism) entails a rejection of old-style metaphysics.

Historicism in itself is a philosophically uninteresting perspective. It functions primarily in a critical and negative manner. It becomes philosophically controversial only when one tries to make it into a philosophical viewpoint. I hold that historicism should be understood as merely claiming that background prejudices, presuppositions, and prejudgments are requisite for any metaphysical or ontological reflections on the way the world is. This means that those metaphysical or ontological projects which hide and conceal their background conditions are deceptive and deficient. There is no doubt that metaphysical and ontological reflections should continue. In fact, these reflections are inescapable for finite human animals suspended in webs of significance we ourselves spin (to invoke Max Weber's famous phrase popularized by Clifford Geertz). Yet since these metaphysical or ontological reflections are never free of a particular set of presuppositions, prejudices, and prejudgments, metaphysics and ontology in the grand mode or in the old sense are anachronistic, antiquated, and, most important, unwarranted. Instead, metaphysics and ontologies are always relative to specific traditions, theories, and particular sets of social practices. In short, the Age of Metaphysics is over, yet inescapable metaphysical reflections will and must go on.

My conception of historicism requires that we try to approach the metaphysical schemes of contemporary philosophers as anthropologists approach the cosmological schemes of Hopi Indians. The aim here is not to remove ourselves from our own background assumptions and presuppositions, but rather to demystify the highbrow philosophical debates, to demythologize the aura of profundity and solemnity of the debates themselves.

Seen in this way, crucial philosophical debates are less about the way the world is or the legitimate grounds of knowledge and more about how self-critical interlocutors (as bearers of particular traditions) in specific modes of inquiry project and preserve regulative self-images and guiding vocabularies that promote various aims and purposes. For example, the basic aim of philosophical realists in our time is to defend what some authoritative institutional practices, such as those of the scientific community or of some religious community, say that the world really is. Secular realists hold that what the secular priesthood, that is, the scientific community, says about the world is the way the world really is. For secular realists, the self-correcting character of scientific practices ensures that their grasp of Reality is the most reliable we have.

Religious realists hold that what an ecclesiastical priesthood says about the world is the way the world is. For them, the nonrational character of religious discourse signifies just how right they must be regarding an entity or power that transcends human reason. For both types of realists (secular or religious), it is Reality which ultimately serves as the arbiter of which theories or interpretations are accepted and warranted.

For historicists, secular realism is an intellectual strategy adopted by those who promote the authority of the secular priesthood. The aim of this strategy is to convince themselves and others that their acceptance of this authority is rational *independent of the aims and purposes of the secular priesthood.* I reject secular realism because its notion of rationality is deceptive and deficient. The predominant concepts of rationality accepted in the scientific community are inseparable from the aims and purposes of this community, that is, to predict and control phenomena. Yet even if one accepts, as good historicists do, that the scientific community fulfills this aim better than any other competitors, for example, communities of magicians or numerologists, one need not be seduced by an ideology of secular realism. The issue of whether scientific explanations provide the best predictions of phenomena because they are true or whether they are true because they yield the best predictions becomes a perennially circular one—precisely because the notion of truth in the scientific community is value-laden, that is, integral to its aims of prediction and control. To put it crudely, the idea of a true theory that predicts poorly is unintelligible and unacceptable in the scientific community.

Similarly, religious realism is an intellectual strategy adopted by those who accept the authority of particular ecclesiastical (or personal) interpretations. The purpose here is to convince one's self and others that these interpretations are true *regardless of their role and junction in one's life.* I reject religious realism because it rests upon a faulty notion of religious "truth." The truth-claims of religious communities are inseparable from the aims and purposes of those communities, that is, to provide meaning and value in human lives. Yet if one holds, as some Christian historicists do, that certain Christian communities do this better than other communities, one need not accept religious realism in order to be religious. The issue of whether certain religious communities provide the best meaning and value in human lives because they are true or whether they are true because they yield the best meaning and value in human lives becomes inescapably circular—precisely because the notion of truth in religious communities is value-laden, that is, integral to its aims of providing meaning and value. The notion of a true religion that does not sustain people through the crises and traumas of life is unintelligible and unacceptable for religious communities. In fact, as Pascal and Kierkegaard noted, the ideology of religious realism may sap some of the authenticity of religious faith by robbing it of existential risk and anxiety. In this way, old-style metaphysics may even harm one's religious faith.

Historicists have often been accused of being closet idealists or vulgar relativists. Since they reject using Reality as the ultimate standard to adjudicate between conflicting viewpoints, they are portrayed as either disbelieving in sense-independent objects or claiming that there are no rational standards to distinguish better and worse interpretations. My sort of historicism indeed rejects Reality as the ultimate standard since reality-claims are theory-laden, that is, our truth-claims are mediated by our theories. But sense-independent objects indeed do exist according to our best theories. So to reject Reality as the standard by which we accept theories of reality is not the same as rejecting the existence of Reality per se. Rather, it is to reject value-neutral and theory-free notions of Reality as standards for philosophical arbitration.

Nor is my historicism reducible to vulgar relativism. There are rational standards to adjudicate between better and worse theories or interpretations, yet these standards are relative to our common aims and purposes. Intersubjective agreement is requisite for feasible and effective standards. This does not mean that Reality is simply what people can agree on. Rather, it means that common aims and purposes are required if there are to be rational standards which help determine acceptable and unacceptable theories and interpretations.

In conclusion, I suggest that acceptable forms of metaphysical reflections are those of synoptic narratives and overarching vocabularies that provide enhancing self-images and enabling coping techniques for living. The greatness (and weakness) of the grand metaphysicians of old is not the logical consistency and theoretical coherence of their systems but rather the qualities of mind and forms of life that are imaged and enacted in their discourses. My sort of historicism does not see the threat to legitimate metaphysical reflection coming from philosophers but rather from the deep crisis in synecdochic narrative practices in our postmodern culture.

Since the high modernism of Proust, Joyce, and Kafka, our narrative strategies have shunned self-confident notions of social belonging and innocent ideas of "capturing the whole" of things. And as Jean-François Lyotard has argued in *The Postmodern Condition*, we are witnessing an increasing incredulity toward master- or meta-narratives, be they Christian, Marxist, or liberal. We live in a time of cultural disarray and social decay, an age filled with ruins and fragments. Hence, our intellectual landscapes are littered with allegorical tales of deterioration rather than dramative narratives of reconciliation. The only truly totalizing story that can credibly encompass all of us is a nuclear holocaust narrative.

In stark contrast to Huston Smith, my historicism compels me to conclude that dispensing with old-style metaphysics is a crucial step toward more legitimate (and much less ambitious) modes of metaphysical reflection. Yet even these more legitimate narrative modes may have highly limited potency and pertinence in a world in which any sense of the whole has been lost. Without such a sense, there can be only truncated (especially nostalgic) forms of metaphysical reflections. And without vital narratives, narrativity itself becomes more and more an object of metaphysical reflection. In fact, the great metaphysical project of our time—Paul Ricoeur's metaphysics of narrativity in *Time and Narrative*—may be symptomatic of the end of old-style and legitimate forms of metaphysics. If this be so, both Huston Smith's metaphysical realism and my narrativistic historicism are "vestigial clingings to long lost ways, the planting of feet on a world that is gone."

Susan Haack reviews the traditional dialectic between the epistemological foundationalist and coherentist, and she proposes a unique synthesis with "foundherentism."

SUSAN HAACK

Double-Aspect Foundherentism

A New Theory of Empirical Justification

I make no apology for my allegiance to the Neologistic Typographical school of philosophy. I could, I admit, wish my new terminology more euphonious; but I hope its ugliness may be excused for the sake of the way it wears its sense on its sleeve.

Foundationalism and coherentism are not exhaustive of possible styles of theory of epistemic justification. This is just as well, for neither will do. Coherentism cannot allow the relevance of experience to empirical justification; foundationalism can allow it only by way of the thesis that there are some beliefs which are justified exclusively by experience and not at all by the support of other beliefs, and which constitute the ultimate grounds of all other justified beliefs. Foundherentism is an intermediate theory which (unlike coherentism) allows the relevance of experience but (unlike experientialist foundationalism) requires neither privileged beliefs justified exclusively by experience nor an essentially one-directional notion of evidential support.[1]

Like foundationalist theories of an experientialist stripe, foundherentism faces the objection that, since there can be only causal and not logical relations between a subject's experiences and his beliefs, experience cannot be relevant to justification. The objection rests on the false assumption that justification is a purely logical concept.[2] The foundherentist theory developed will be a double-aspect theory, combining causal and evaluative elements.

I make no apology for doing epistemology, nor for doing it by way of an investigation of the concept of justification. It is held in some quarters that the issues of the epistemological tradition are misconceived, and should be abandoned or replaced,[3] This fashionable cynicism has been encouraged by a conviction that the traditional problems have not been resolved either by foundationalism or by coherentism. I share that conviction. The pessimistic conclusion, however, is obviously too hasty if the traditionally rival theories do not exhaust the options.

My goal is explication: to remain close to the contours of our pre-analytic conception of justification (good evidence, convincing reasons, acceptably-grounded belief), but allowing an element of stipulation where those contours are fuzzier than theory demands. The project is undertaken not from the perspective of a detached spectator of our epistemic practices, nor from the perspective of an uncritical participant, but from the perspective of a critical participant. It is not presupposed that there is any guarantee that our commonsense ideas of good evidence, strong reasons, etc., will turn out to be fully coherent, nor that the presuppositions about human cognitive capacities and limitations built into them will turn out to be fully defensible; but in fact the commonsense conceptions seem to withstand critical scrutiny rather robustly.

The *explicandum* is: A is more/less justified, at t, in believing that p, depending on, . . . This choice already indicates some substantial presuppositions: that it is the personal locution, not an impersonal locution like "the belief that p is justified," which is the more primitive; that justification comes in degrees; that whether or to what degree a person is justified in believing something may change over time.

The procedure will be gradually to refine an initial, intuitively plausible but vague formula. The first approximation is: A is more/less justified, at t, in believing that p, depending on how good his evidence is. I am inclined to regard this initial formula as close to trivial (indeed, to think of "justified" as in effect epistemologists' portmanteau word for what in ordinary parlance would most often be expressed in the less technical vocabulary of strong or flimsy reasons, a weak or overwhelming case, good or unconvincing evidence, etc). In the context of current epistemological debate, however, it should be conceded that even this innocuous-seeming formula is not quite innocent of presuppositions; it indicates a preference for an evidentialist over an extrinsic approach.

Successive elaborations of the initial formula will depend on articulating the relations between the causal and the evaluative elements of the concept of justification, fundamental to which will be the distinction between the state and content senses of "belief," henceforth marked as "S-belief" *versus* "C-belief." The first stage, couched in terms of causal relations between A's S-beliefs and other, including perceptual, states of A, will characterize what is called, in an obvious extension of the state/content distinction, "A's S-evidence with respect to p." The second stage will be a manoeuvre by which to arrive, from the characterization of A's S-evidence with respect to p (which consists of certain states of A), at a characterization of A's C-evidence with respect to p (which consists of certain sentences or propositions). The third, evaluative stage will complete the explication by characterizing "how good" in "how good A's C-evidence with respect to p is."

What is on offer will be at best a sketch of a theory, and more than somewhat uneven in its level of detail. The reason is, mainly, that this is, at least for the present, the best I can do.

How justified a person is in believing something depends, not just on *what* he believes, but on *why* he believes it; "why he believes it" being a matter of what it is, in his S-beliefs and experiences, on which his having the S-belief in question depends.[4] (This is one reason for thinking the personal locution primitive.)

The initiating causes of A's S-belief that p—whatever was involved in his coming to believe that p originally—should be distinguished from the causes operative at the time at which his degree of justification is at issue. These may be the same, but they may be different; and when they are different, it is on the causes operative at the time in question that justification depends.[5] (This is why the *explicandum* includes the condition, "at t")

What causes someone to believe something, at a time, is often a matter of a balance of forces; some factors, that is, incline him towards believing that p, others incline him against it, with the former outweighing the latter. Both sustaining and inhibiting causes are relevant to an assessment of degree of justification.[6]

Some sustaining or inhibiting factors are states of the person concerned; others are not. Only causes of A's S-belief which are states of A will figure in the characterization of his evidence.[7]

"The causal nexus, at t, of A's S-belief that p" will refer to those states of A which are operative at t, whether sustaining or inhibiting, in the vector of forces resulting in A's believing that p. The phrase is meant to suggest a mesh of S-beliefs interconnected with each other, with the subject's perceptual experiences, his desires and fears, etc. The causal nexus of an S-belief is to include the states which directly sustain or inhibit the S-belief, the states which sustain or inhibit those states, and so on. The idea is that our criteria of justification are neither simply atomistic nor unqualifiedly holistic: they focus on those elements of the whole constellation of A's states at t which bear a causal relation, sustaining or inhibiting, to the particular S-belief in question.

Before even an initial explication of "A's evidence with respect to p" is possible it is necessary to distinguish evidential from non-evidential components of the causal nexus of an S-belief. Belief states, perceptual states, introspective states, and memory traces will count as evidential; other states, such as the subject's desires or fears, his being under the influence of alcohol or panic, will not. That such states contribute to sustaining/inhibiting an S-belief may have a bearing on the likelihood that the C-belief is true; nevertheless, they are ordinarily regarded as the kind of thing which affects a person's reaction to or judgement of his evidence, not as themselves part of his evidence. That such non-evidential states belong to the causal nexus of an S-belief may be a necessary part of an explanation of how it is that the subject believes something despite the flimsiness of his evidence;[8] but it is not relevant to the calculation of the degree to which he is justified.

We now have the necessary apparatus for a preliminary explication of "A's S-evidence with respect to p."[9] "A's S-reasons for believing that p" will refer to those S-beliefs which sustain A's S-belief that p; "A's current sensory S-evidence for believing that p" to the perceptual states which sustain A's S-belief that p; "A's past sensory S-evidence for believing that p" to the perceptual traces which sustain A's S-belief that p; "A's sensory S-evidence for believing that p" to A's current and past sensory S-evidence for believing that p; "A's current introspective S-evidence for believing that p" to the introspective states which sustain A's S-belief that p; "A's past introspective S-evidence for believing that p" to the introspective traces which sustain A's S-belief that p; "A's introspective S-evidence for believing that p" to A's current and past introspective S-evidence for believing that p; "A's experiential S-evidence for believing that p" to A's sensory and introspective S-evidence for believing that p; and "A's S-evidence for believing that p" to A's S-reasons and experiential S-evidence for believing that p. "A's S-evidence against believing that p" will be characterized like "A's S-evidence for believing that p," but with "inhibit" for "sustain"; and "A's S-evidence with respect to p" will refer to A's S-evidence for believing that p and A's S-evidence against believing that p. "A's direct S-evidence with respect to p" will refer to those evidential states which directly sustain/inhibit his S-belief that p, "A's indirect_1 S-evidence with respect to p" will refer to those which directly sustain/inhibit his direct S-evidence with respect to p, . . . , and so on.

A's S-reasons with respect to p are themselves S-beliefs of A's, with respect to which A may have further S-evidence, but A's experiential S-evidence with respect to p consists of non-belief states of A, not the kind of thing with respect to which A has, or needs, evidence. Experiential S-evidence sustains/inhibits S-beliefs, not *vice versa*; this is the sense in which A's experiential S-evidence is his *ultimate* S-evidence. (This is the important truth that experientialist foundationalism tries to accommodate—but in a forced and unnatural way.)

The pre-analytic notion of "the evidence of the senses" is not innocent of theory. Human beings, according to the commonsense picture, perceive things and events in the world; we interact, by means of our senses, with those things and events; these interactions are what "sensory experience" refers to. By and large our senses are good, reliable ways of detecting what goes on around us; but in unfavorable circumstances one may be unable to see or hear, etc., clearly, and may misperceive, and in extremely unfavorable circumstances where one's senses are grossly disordered one may even "perceive" what is not there at all.

The intention is to represent both the positive and the negative aspects of this picture. In what follows "perceptual state" will be given a somewhat lax interpretation, to allow it to include states phenomenologically indistinguishable from perceptual states in the strict sense; but in due course the commonsense assumption that perceptual states are ordinarily the result of one's sensory interactions with things and events in the world will be built in.

Introspective S-evidence is included as a kind of experiential S-evidence in the belief that it is also part of the commonsense picture that a human being has some means of scanning (some of) his own mental states and processes. But nothing will be said about introspection here beyond the observation that perceptual S-evidence and introspective S-evidence are treated as distinct categories in order to avoid any elision of perception into introspective awareness of one's own mental states. Such an elision would betray the commonsense presumption that what we perceive is the things around us—a presumption I wish to preserve.

As the role played by perceptual states locates the relevance of current sensory experience to justification, the role played by perceptual (and introspective) traces locates the role of memory, in the sense represented by: "A remembers seeing/hearing/. . . ."[10] Here again the terminology will be used with deliberate laxness. "Perceptual (introspective) traces" will be allowed possibly to include states which are indistinguishable by the subject from those which are the present traces of past perceptual (introspective) states. This distinction of perceptual state/perceptual trace, of current/past sensory S-evidence, is very crude. Perception isn't really instantaneous, but an ongoing process. But degree of justification can change in the course of the process, as, e.g., one gets a better look at a thing. So, to mitigate the crudeness somewhat, perceptual states should be construed not as instantaneous but as having some (unspecified, and gerrymanderable) duration.

A person's S-beliefs are frequently maintained, in whole or part, by his hearing, seeing, or remembering hearing or seeing, what someone else says or writes. Such testimonial S-evidence enters the picture by way of A's sensory S-evidence; as when A's S-belief that p is sustained by his remembering hearing B say that p, and his S-beliefs that B is well-informed, has no strong motive for deceit, etc. (It is assumed that, if A doesn't understand B's language, if he has the S-belief that p, his hearing B say "p*" will not form part of its causal nexus.)[11]

A's S-evidence with respect to p consists of (a gerrymandered collection of) states of A. But in the evaluative stage "evidence" will have to mean "C-evidence," for it is sentences or propositions, not states of a person, which can support or undermine each other, be consistent or inconsistent with each other, cohere or fail to cohere as an explanatory story, etc. So a bridge is needed from S- to C-evidence. "A's C-reasons for believing that p" will refer to the C-beliefs A's believing which constitute A's S-reasons for believing that p; "A's experiential C-evidence for believing that p" to sentences or propositions to the effect that A is in (a) certain state(s)—the state(s) which constitute A's experiential S-evidence for believing that p; "A's C-evidence for believing that p" will refer to A's C-reasons for believing that p and A's experiential C-evidence for believing that p; "A's C-evidence against believing that p" will be characterized like "A's C-evidence for believing that p," but with "against" for "for"; and "A's C-evidence with respect to p" will refer to A's C-evidence for believing that p and A's C-evidence against believing that p. A's direct, indirect$_1$, etc., C-evidence with respect to p are distinguished in parallel to the corresponding distinctions for A's S-evidence.

This was couched with deliberate vagueness in terms of "sentences or propositions." The main advantage of this deliberate vagueness is that, because of the lack of clear criteria of identity for propositions, it temporarily puts off the hard question, what sorts of characterizations of perceptual (etc.) states might be appropriate here. Our ordinary ways of describing "the evidence of the senses" offer some clues. What justifies me in thinking there's a woodpecker in the oak tree?—"my seeing it, the fact that I can see it," is a natural answer; an answer, however, often enough qualified or hedged, as: "but I only got a glimpse," or "but it's against the light," and possibly revised more radically, as: "well, it looked just as *if* there was a bird there." It seems desirable to tie "A's sensory evidence" at least loosely to "how it looks (etc.) to A"; but at the same time to respect the commonsense distinction of more and less favorable circumstances—a good look is better evidence than a glimpse, seeing a thing in good light and full view better evidence than seeing it partly hidden and at dusk,. . . , and so on. For these (and other) reasons I am inclined to favor characterizations along the lines of "A is in the sort of perceptual state a normal subject would be in when looking at a rabbit three feet away in good light," "in the sort of state a normal subject would be in when getting a brief glimpse of a fast-moving rabbit at dusk," . . . , etc. This is how, though "perceptual state" has been allowed to include states phenomenologically indistinguishable from those resulting from one's sensory interactions with the world, the presupposition that normally perception *is* the result of such interactions is retained.

There is another significant asymmetry built in at the level of C-evidence between A's reasons and his experiential evidence. A's C-reasons with respect to p will consist of propositions which may be true or may be false. His experiential C-evidence, however, will consist of propositions *all of which are true*. This is no reinstatement of any sort of infallibilism with respect to perceptual or introspective beliefs; it is just that the propositions concerned are to the effect that A is in such-and-such a perceptual (etc.) state, and they are all true because *ex hypothesi* A *is* in that state. This feature guarantees what may be called the "experiential anchoring" of justified empirical beliefs.

How justified someone is in believing something, then, according to the second approximation, depends on how good his C-evidence is. The remaining problem is to explicate "how good."

The explication to be offered aspires to represent the gradational character of justification; not, however, to give anything like a numerical scale of degrees of justification, or even anything as ambitious as criteria for a linear ordering, but only to say what factors raise, and what lower, the degree to which someone is justified in a belief.

The model is not, as a foundationalist's might be, how one determines the soundness or otherwise of a mathematical proof, but how one determines the reasonableness or otherwise of entries in a crossword puzzle. This model is more hospitable to a gradational account. But the main motivation is that it permits pervasive mutual support, rather than encouraging an essentially one-directional conception. The clues are the analogues of the subject's experiential evidence, already filled-in entries the analogue of his reasons. The clues don't depend on the entries, but the entries are, in varying degree, interdependent; these are the analogues of asymmetries already noted between experiential evidence and reasons.

How reasonable one's confidence is that a certain entry in a crossword puzzle is correct depends on how much support is given to this entry by its clue and any already filled-in intersecting entries; how reasonable, independently of the entry in question, one's confidence is that those intersecting entries are correct; and how many of them have been completed. Analogously, how good A's C-evidence with respect to p is would depend on:

(1) how *favorable* A's direct C-evidence with respect to p is;
(2) how *secure* A's direct C-reasons with respect to p are, *independently of the C-belief that p;*
(3) how *comprehensive* A's C-evidence with respect to p is.

It should be noted that, although clause (2) mentions explicitly only A's direct C-evidence with respect to p, its application takes one progressively outward, to the appraisal of A's indirect_1, indirect_2, . . . , etc., C-evidence with respect to p. For in considering how independently secure A's direct C-reasons are, it will be necessary to consider how well his indirect_1 C-evidence supports them, and how independently secure his indirect_1 C-reasons are, . . . , and so on.

C-evidence may be favorable or unfavorable with respect to a C-belief, with its being conclusive representing one extreme, and its precluding the truth of the proposition in question representing the other. C-evidence may be favorable but not conclusive, supportive to a greater or lesser degree; or unfavorable but not fatal, undermining to a greater or lesser degree. One might say that at the upper limit E makes it certain that p, at the lower limit E makes it certain that not p; and that E is more supportive the more likely it makes it that p, more undermining the more unlikely it makes it that p. But this, though true enough, is not very helpful, since "E makes it certain that p," "E makes it likely that p," and so forth are little more than verbal variants on the locutions in need of explication. One might say, a little more helpfully, that if E is conclusive it leaves no room for alternatives to p, and if it is favorable but not conclusive it is the more supportive the less room it leaves for alternatives to p. I can't resist calling this "the Petrocelli Principle."

With respect to the limit cases, I suggest the following rather straightforward characterization. E is conclusive with respect to p just in case its p-extrapolation (the result of adding p to it) is consistent, and its not-p-extrapolation inconsistent; E is fatal with respect to p just in case its not-p-extrapolation is consistent, and its p-extrapolation inconsistent.

The characterization of degrees of supportiveness less than collusiveness presents more difficulty. The Petrocelli Principle offers some clues, but not enough, I think, to determine a unique solution. It directs us, at any rate, to look at the success of p relative to its competitors. So here is a tentative first move: A proposition C[p] is a competitor of p iff (i) given E, it precludes p, and (ii) the C[p]-extrapolation of E is better explanatorily integrated than E is. A strong characterization of supportiveness might run somewhat as follows: E is supportive to some degree with respect to p just in case the addition of p to it improves its explanatory integration more than the addition of any of its competitors does; E is the more supportive with respect to p the more the addition of p to it improves its explanatory integration more than the addition of the nearest of its competitors does. A weaker characterization would go, rather, along these lines: E is supportive to some degree with respect to p just in case the addition of p to E improves its explanatory integration; E is the more supportive with respect to p the more the addition of p to it improves its explanatory integration more than the more of its competitors do. The crossword analogy pulls one somewhat in the direction of the weaker characterization, which I am therefore inclined to favor—though not by a very large margin.

I had formerly favored the conjecture that E is supportive with respect to p just in case its p-extrapolation is better explanatorily integrated than its not-p-extrapolation, and the more supportive the more its p-extrapolation is better explanatorily integrated than its not-p-extrapolation. But I no longer think this can be correct: the problem is that if p is potentially explanatory of E or some component of E, it is not to be expected that not-p will be a rival potential *explanans*. (For this reason, the proposal was also not well motivated by the crossword analogy.) This now-rejected characterization of supportiveness was prompted in part by its isomorphism with the characterization of conclusiveness. With either of the characterizations now on the table, I note, at least an analogy of structure can be sustained: conclusiveness is a matter of the superiority of p over its *negation* with respect to *consistency* with E; supportiveness is a matter of the superiority of p over its *competitors* with respect to the *explanatory integration* of E.

The proposed characterization is not equivalent to more familiar accounts appealing to deductive implication and inductive support of p by E; and where it differs it has certain advantages.

Although, if E is conclusive with respect to p, it deductively implies p, the converse is not true without exception. If E is itself inconsistent, E deductively implies p, but it does not qualify as conclusive with respect to p. If E is inconsistent, not only its not-p-extrapolation but also its p-extrapolation is inconsistent too. This upshot, that inconsistent evidence with respect to p is, as I shall say, indifferent, is surely more plausible than the foundationalist line that it is conclusive; and it is achieved without succumbing to the excessively strenuous coherentist thesis that if there is any inconsistency in A's belief-set, he is not justified in any of his beliefs.

The intuition is much stronger that there is such a thing as favorable-but-not-conclusive evidence than it is that there is such a thing as "inductive implication" or "inductive logic"—certainly if "logic" is taken to indicate relations susceptible of a purely syntactic characterization.[12] My approach to "E is supportive (favorable but not conclusive) with respect to p" has, from this point of view, at least the negative advantage of requiring no appeal to an "inductive logic" which is prone to paradox at best, maybe mythical at worst. Perhaps it also has a positive advantage. At least, by appealing to the notion of explanatory integration in the explication of supportiveness foundherentism borrows some of the intuitive appeal of the notions of (on the foundationalist side) inference to the best explanation and (on the coherentist side) explanatory coherence. Like these more familiar notions, it should be construed as undemanding with respect to truth; i.e., as requiring the truth neither of *explicantia* nor *explicanda*. The notion of inference to the best explanation is, so to speak, both *one-directional* and *optimizing* in character; the notion of explanatory coherence has neither characteristic. The explication tentatively proposed here looks rather closer to the latter, coherentist notion, since, first, explanatory integration is taken to be a property possessed in varying degrees by sets of propositions; and, second, because of my weak preference for the weaker characterization the p-extrapolation of E does not have to be better explanatorily integrated than all C[p]-extrapolations for E to count as supportive with respect to p.

How favorable E is with respect to p is not sufficient by itself to determine degree of justification. If A's direct C-evidence with respect to p includes other beliefs of his, the degree to which he is justified in believing that p will also depend on the degree to which he is justified in believing those C-reasons. The possibility of mutual dependence is not precluded; it could be that A's C-reasons with respect to p include some C-belief, say the C-belief that z, one of A's C-reasons with respect to which is the C-belief that p. The point of the qualification "independently of the C-belief that p" in clause (2) is to avoid the danger of circularity this would otherwise present.

The idea of independent security is easiest to grasp in the context of the crossword analogy.

How reasonable one's confidence is that 4 across (in figure 1) is correct depends, *inter alia*, on how reasonable one's confidence is that 2 down is correct. True, how reasonable one's confidence is that 2 down is correct in turn depends, *inter alia*, on how reasonable one's confidence is that 4 across is correct. But in judging how reasonable one's confidence is that 4 across is correct one need not, for fear of getting into a vicious circle, ignore the support given it by 2 down; it is enough that one judge how reasonable one's confidence is that 2 down is correct *leaving aside the support given it by 4 across*. And this is also how the account of the independent security of A's C-reasons with respect to p avoids circularity.

The crossword analogy also shows the way around another potential objection. The degree of independent security of A's C-reasons with respect to p has been explained in terms of the degree to which A is justified, independently of the C-belief that p, in believing his direct C-reasons with respect to p. So, since "justified" occurs on the right-hand side, won't the explication be ineliminable? No—but the explanation is a bit tricky, and easier to see in the case of the crossword puzzle. In figuring out how reasonable one's confidence in some entry is, one will eventually reach a point where the issue is not how well some entry is supported by others, but how well it is supported by its clue. Analogously, in appraising how justified A is, independently of the C-belief that p, in believing his C-reasons with respect to that belief, one will

1 H	2 I	3 P			
	4 R	U	B	5 Y	
6 R	A	T		7 A	N
8 E	T		9 O	R	
	10 E	R	O	D	E

ACROSS
1. A cheerful start (3)
4. She's a jewel (4)
6. No, it's Polonius (3)
7. An article (2)
8. A visitor from outside fills this space (2)
9. What's the alternative? (2)
10. Dick Tropin did this to York: it wore 'im out (5)

DOWN
2. Angry Irish rebels? (5)
3. Have a shot at an Olympic event (3)
5. A measure of one's back garden (4)
6. What's this all about? (2)
9. The printer hasn't got my number (2)

Consider 4 across: RUBY

How reasonable it is to think this is correct depends on:
- (1) the clue
- (2) how likely it is that IRATE is correct
- (3) how likely it is that PUT is correct
- (4) how likely it is that YARD is correct

How reasonable it is to think IRATE is correct depends on:
- (i) the clue
- (ii) how likely it is that HIP is correct (which also depends on IRATE and PUT)
- (iii) how likely it is that RAT is correct (which also depends on IRATE and RE)
- (iv) how likely it is that ET is correct (which also depends on IRATE)
- (v) how likely it is that ERODE is correct (which also depends on IRATE, OO, and YARD)
- (vi) how likely it is that RUBY is correct

How reasonable it is to think PUT is correct depends on:
- (a) the clue
- (b) how likely it is that HIP is correct (which also depends on IRATE and PUT)
- (c) how likely it is that RAT is correct (which also depends on IRATE and RE)
- (d) how likely it is that RUBY is correct

How reasonable it is to think YARD is correct depends on:
- (A) the clue
- (B) how likely it is that AN is correct (which also depends on YARD)
- (C) how likely it is that OR is correct (which also depends on YARD and OO)
- (D) how likely it is that ERODE is correct (which also depends on YARD, IRATE, and OO)
- (E) how likely it is that RUBY is correct

Figure 1

eventually reach a point where the issue is not how well some belief is supported by other C-beliefs, but how well it is supported by experiential C-evidence. And here the question of justification doesn't arise. But doesn't this mean that the account is lapsing into a kind of foundationalism? No. What it means is that "justified" eventually drops out of the *explicans* as one reaches the question, how well some belief(s) is (are) supported by experiential C-evidence; this does not require that any beliefs be justified exclusively by experiential C-evidence, nor, *a fortiori*, that all other justified beliefs be justified by the support of such beliefs.

There is an asymmetry to be noted between the role of A's C-reasons for believing that p and his C-reasons against believing that p. A is more [less] justified in believing that p the more [less] justified he is, independently of the C-belief that p, in believing his C-reasons for believing that p; but the less [more] justified in believing that p the more [less] justified he is, independently of the C-belief that p, in believing his C-reasons against believing that p.

Degree of supportiveness and degree of independent security together are still insufficient to determine degree of justification; there is also the dimension of comprehensiveness. The comprehensiveness condition is the nearest analogue, in my account, of the more familiar total evidence requirement on inductions. Unlike this requirement and like the comprehensiveness condition imposed by some coherentists, however, it is not a factor determining degree of supportiveness but a separate criterion entering into the determination of degree of justification.

Comprehensiveness promises to be tougher to spell out even than supportiveness and independent security; the crossword analogy isn't much help here, and the characterization of "A's evidence" cannot be extrapolated in any easy way to "evidence," *simpliciter*. Perhaps fortunately, the role of comprehensiveness is most prominent negatively, when one judges someone unjustified in some belief or justified only to a modest degree because of their failure to take some relevant evidence into account. It is worth noting that "failure to take relevant evidence into account" includes failure, for instance, to take a closer look; so the comprehensiveness condition should be construed to include experiential evidence.

Even in advance of further analysis it is clear that the dimension of comprehensiveness is not likely to yield a linear ordering. And there is a further complication because relevance of evidence is itself a matter of degree: an indeterminacy about how to weigh failure to take a lot of marginally relevant evidence into account relative to failure to take just a bit of more centrally relevant evidence into account.[13] Relevance of evidence is being taken to be an objective matter. What evidence appears to A to be relevant depends on various background beliefs of A's, which may be true or may be false.[14] What evidence *is* relevant, however, coincides with what evidence appears to A to be relevant only if A's background beliefs are true. (This partly explains why, though justification is not, *judgements* of justification are always perspectival; I judge how much of the relevant evidence you have taken into account by reference to what I take to be relevant.)

It can now be seen that inconsistency in one's belief-set does carry a price, though a lesser price than the coherentist exacts. Inconsistency in one's C-evidence with respect to some belief has the consequence that one is not justified in that belief. To avoid this a subject whose belief-set is inconsistent will have to keep the incompatible parts of his belief-set apart from each other; and this can be achieved only at the price of failure sometimes to take relevant evidence into account—which itself lowers the degree of justification of the beliefs it affects.

"A is more justified in believing that p the more favorable his direct C-evidence with respect to p is, the more [less] independently secure his C-reasons for [against] believing that p are, and the more comprehensive his C-evidence with respect to p is." This is a bit more specific than the first and second attempts, but it still leaves the question, what the minimal conditions are for A's being justified to *any* degree in believing that p.

One necessary condition is that there *be* such a thing as A's C-evidence with respect to p; if his S-belief were the result simply of a blow to the head, or of one of those pills philosophers are fond of imagining, he would not be justified at all. Furthermore, since it is the justification of empirical beliefs which is at issue, it is necessary that A's C-evidence include some experiential C-evidence. Another necessary condition has already been suggested: A's C-evidence must be favorable with respect to p. Presumably also some minimal standard of comprehensiveness is necessary; it is tempting to suggest that A's C-evidence must at least include all the relevant evidence A possesses—but this is unfortunately too demanding.[15] With respect, finally, to the question of the minimal standards of independent security, the obvious suggestion is that A must be justified to some degree in believing his direct C-reasons for believing that p; but the asymmetry between reasons for and reasons against means that no such obvious suggestion offers itself on the negative side.

What about the upper end of the scale? Our ordinary talk of someone's being "completely justified" in believing something is highly context-dependent; it means something like: "in the circumstances—including such matters as how important it is to be right about whether p, whether it is A's particular business to know whether p, etc.—A has taken sufficient care in seeking out and assessing relevant evidence that he doesn't count as having been epistemically negligent or as epistemically blameworthy in believing that p." This may be represented by "A is *completely* justified in believing that p," which would refer to a context-dependent area somewhere vaguely in the upper range of the scale of justification. Its vagueness and context-dependence is what makes this ordinary conception useful for practical purposes (and for the statement of Gettier-type paradoxes), but severely limits its theoretical usefulness. What one might call the philosophical conception, however—"COMPLETE justification," which would require one's C-evidence to be conclusive and maximally comprehensive, and one's C-reasons to be maximally independently secure—is of *only* theoretical interest, since it is doubtful that it is ever actually achieved.

Complex as this has been, it is far from complete, either in depth or in breadth. I have helped myself to a whole slew of concepts, some of which have been left completely unexplicated, and of none of which a fully satisfactory account has been given. This cannot be excused by appeal to the fact that the pre-analytic concept of justification is itself vague, for one purpose of explication is to improve precision; nor by the fact that any explication must end somewhere, for the concepts on which I have relied are hardly so transparent as to be prime candidates for this status. In partial mitigation, however, it may be observed that close relatives of some of the concepts needed (explanatory integration, comprehensiveness) are already current in the literature, and that the foundherentist is free to borrow the best efforts of rival theorists to spell them out.

But let me conclude by dwelling rather on the prospects than on the problems for the proposed approach. Were there time, it would be desirable to say something about how the impersonal locution, "the belief that p is more/less justified . . .," may be given sense; about how to accommodate the idea that belief as well as justification comes in degrees; about how the gradational character of supportiveness may draw the teeth of the lottery paradox and its up-and-back structure the teeth of the "infinite regress argument"[16] for foundationalism; . . . ; about what light the crossword analogy might throw on the matter of procedures of inquiry; . . . , and so on.

Since I dare allow myself only one more paragraph, however, let me devote it to some observations about the affinity of double-aspect foundherentism with (a very modest, reformist style of) meta-epistemological naturalism.[17] Our criteria for appraising degree of justification, I have suggested, have built into them certain assumptions about human cognitive capacities and limitations—assumptions about our perceptual capacities and limitations being prominent here. These assumptions, though of a high degree of generality and abstraction, seem manifestly synthetic; so when it comes to the question of the appropriateness or otherwise of our criteria of justification to the goal of inquiry (roughly, their truth-indicativeness), it is not to be expected that meta-epistemological arguments of a purely *a priori* character will suffice. There is no reason to anticipate that meta-epistemological issues could simply be handed over to psychology to adjudicate ("the senses are a means of detecting information about things and events around us" is not readily classifiable either as belonging to psychology rather than philosophy, or as belonging to philosophy rather than psychology, but is most plausibly located in the border territory between them). But there is reason to anticipate that work in the psychology of perception may have a contributory relevance. At any rate, from the foundherentist perspective, with its acknowledgement of the legitimacy of justification *via* relations of mutual support among beliefs, the idea is very congenial that, if the assumptions about perception presupposed by an epistemological theory prove to be embedded, also, in plausible psychological theorizing, then—to a degree depending on the plausibility of the theory and the intimacy of the embedding—this would be favourable to those assumptions, and to the epistemological theory.[18] These remarks do not, of course, in themselves constitute a ratification of the foundherentist criteria; but perhaps they will serve to make foundherentism attractive to some naturalists, as a very modest, reformist naturalism is to foundherentists.

Notes

An ancestor of this paper was read at Brown University, the University of Rochester, the Moral Sciences Club, Cambridge, and the London School of Economics in 1987–88; I am grateful for helpful comments made on those occasions, and to Andrew Swann for helpful correspondence about the concept of independent security. The present version, prepared with the help of a Max Orowitz research grant from the University of Miami for the summer of 1991, was delivered as an invited paper at the American Philosophical Association meetings in December 1991, Peter Hare replying.

1. See also Haack, S., "Theories of Knowledge: an Analytic Framework," *Proceedings of the Aristotelian Society,* LXXXIII, 1982–83, 143–57.

2. See also Haack, S., "What is 'the Problem of the Empirical Basis', and does Johnny Wideawake Solve it?", *British Journal for the Philosophy of Science* 42, 1991, 269–89.

3. See also Haack, S., "Recent Obituaries of Epistemology," *American Philosophical Quarterly*, 27.3, 1990, 199–220.

4. Suppose that A (a patient) and B (his doctor) both believe the same thing: that A's symptoms are not indicative of serious heart disease; but that A's belief rests only on his having read somewhere that in 10% of cases these symptoms are not serious, whereas B's rests on the results of the numerous reliable tests to which A has been submitted. B, surely, is more justified than A in believing that A's symptoms are not serious.

5. Suppose that initially A's belief that his symptoms are not serious is largely a matter of wishful thinking; but that subsequently he is informed of the results of the tests, and it is this which then maintains his belief. He is, surely, more justified at the later than at the earlier time in believing that his symptoms are not serious.

6. For example, B's belief that A's symptoms are not serious is maintained, it may be supposed, by his knowledge of the test results and his beliefs about the reliability of the tests, which outweigh his belief that in 90% of cases such symptoms are indicative of serious heart disease.

7. The perceptual state of A which one might describe as his seeing the dog in the room, for instance, will count as part of his evidence, but there being a dog in the room will not.

8. Implicit in this is an embryo theory about the nature of wishful thinking: that a person's desire that p be the case contributes to his believing that it *is* the case by leading him to exaggerate the significance of weak or marginal evidence. This was taken to be the explanation of A's optimism in footnotes 4 and 5. There is a similar phenomenon which might be called "fearful thinking."

9. Two—or at least one-and-a-half—caveats are needed here. The first is that S-beliefs which belong to the causal nexus of A's S-belief that p not in virtue of their sustaining or inhibiting some S-belief which sustains or inhibits the S-belief that p, etc., but in virtue of their causal relations to some non-belief state in the causal nexus of A's S-belief that p, should be excluded from A's S-evidence. The second is that it may be necessary to exclude evidential states which are causally related to A's S-belief, but in the wrong way. ("Deviant causal chains" are a logical

possibility dear to philosophers' hearts, but casually enough disregarded in our pre-analytic conceptual scheme.)

10. Memory also crops up in a second form: to say "A remembers that p" is to say that he earlier came to believe that p, and now still believes it, he has not forgotten it. (It also, of course, in ordinary usage, implies that p is true.) How justified A is in what may be called a "persisting belief" will depend, as with all beliefs, on how good his evidence is—his evidence at the time at which the question of justification is at issue, that is. This needn't mean that it has to be said that I am not justified, for instance, in my present belief that my high school English teacher was called "Miss Wright"; this persisting belief is now sustained by past experiential S—evidence—of seeing and hearing the name used by myself and others.

11. Here is one place where the logical possibility of deviant causal chains mentioned in footnote 9 looks potentially awkward. What if A's hearing B say "p*"—which means in B's language, which however A doesn't understand, what "p" means in A's language—somehow causes A to believe that p?

12. This is why, rather than saying that the concept of justification is partly causal and partly logical ("causical," as I called it in "Rebuilding the Ship While Sailing on the Water," in *Perspectives on Quine*, eds Barrett, R. and Gibson, R., Blackwell's, Oxford, 1990, 111–27) I now prefer to say more neutrally that it is partly causal and partly evaluative. Whether the notion of supportive evidence qualifies as "logical" depends, I am now inclined to think, on whether the notion of explanatory integration could be explicated in a purely syntactical manner. I rather doubt this; but cannot offer a well thought-out argument here.

13. This loose talk of "a lot" and "just a bit" of evidence will rightly raise suspicions that a problem of relativity to language may impede further explication here.

14. Suppose you and I are both on an appointments committee. You think a certain candidate should be ruled out of consideration because his handwriting indicates that he is not trustworthy. I think graphology is bunk and scoff at your "evidence." You think how the candidate writes his "p's," say, is relevant evidence with respect to his honesty; I think it is utterly irrelevant.

15. In part because, given A's other beliefs, some of the relevant evidence he possesses may not appear relevant to A; but mainly because it would lead back to the undesirable consequence that if there is any inconsistency in A's belief-set, he is not justified in any of his beliefs.

16. So-called. Actually, "the no tolerable alternatives argument" would be both more accurate and more to the present point; which is that the account of independent security offered here contains the necessary elements of a reply to the foundationalist allegation, no less crucial than the claim that an infinite regress of reasons cannot be justifying, that mutual support is inevitably viciously circular.

17. See also "Rebuilding the Ship," section II, and "The Two Faces of Quine's Naturalism," forthcoming in *Synthese*. "Very modest" is intended, first, to indicate that I sympathize, not with a revolutionary style of naturalism which would rule the traditional projects misconceived and propose that they be superseded by new, natural-scientific projects, but with a reformist style which would undertake the traditional projects in a naturalistic way. It is intended, second, to indicate that I sympathize, not with a scientistic style of reformist naturalism which would hand the traditional projects over to the natural sciences for adjudication, but with a much less ambitious style which would deny that the these projects can be undertaken wholly *a priori*, and acknowledge the contributory relevance of considerations from, for example, the psychology of perception, to those projects.

18. The picture of perception built into my account of justification is in many, though not all, respects much like the picture defended and elaborated by J. J. Gibson in *The Senses Considered*

as Perceptual Systems (Houghton Mifflin, Boston, Massachusetts, 1966); "New Reasons for Realism" (*Synthese*, 17, 1967); and *The Ecological Approach to Visual Perception* (Houghton Mifflin, Boston, Massachusetts, 1979, and Lawrence Erlbaum Associates, Hillsdale, New Jersey, and London, 1986.) It may be worth noting that Gibson opens the first of the books mentioned with a quotation from Thomas Reid, philosopher of commonsense *par excellence*. But, of course, not all psychologists agree with Gibson's approach. I was introduced to Gibson's work by Kelley, D., *The Evidence of the Senses*, Louisiana State University Press, Baton Rouge and London, 1986, though the use I make of it is rather different from Kelley's.

In this paper, Posner offers a summary of his "anti-theory" and pragmatic conception of law and legal judgment.

RICHARD A. POSNER

Pragmatic Adjudication

Pragmatism is at one level a philosophical position, just as scientific realism, transcendental idealism, existentialism, utilitarianism, and logical positivism are. It is the level well-illustrated by a recently published book in which Richard Rorty and his critics go at each other hammer and tongs over such questions as whether language reflects reality, whether free will is compatible with a scientific outlook, and whether such questions are even meaningful.[1] My concern is at a different level, with an issue in "applied" pragmatism, although after listening to Professor Grey's paper at the conference about the independence of legal from philosophical pragmatism I realize that this term maybe inapt.[2] I shall take up that issue at the end of this essay. The "applied" issue that is my subject till then is whether adjudication, particularly appellate adjudication, can or should be pragmatic.

The issue is at once spongy and, for me at least, urgent. It is spongy because "pragmatism" is such a vague term. Among the Supreme Court Justices who have been called "pragmatists" are Oliver Wendell Holmes, Louis Brandeis, Felix Frankfurter, Robert Jackson, William O. Douglas, William Brennan, Lewis Powell, John Paul Stevens, Edward White, and now Stephen Breyer; others could easily be added to the list.[3] Among theorists of adjudication, the label has been applied not only to those who call themselves pragmatists, of whom there are now quite a number, but also to Ronald Dworkin, who calls pragmatism, at least Rorty's conception of pragmatism, an intellectual meal fit only for a dog (and I take it he does not much like dogs).[4] Some might think the inclusion of Frankfurter in my list even more peculiar than the inclusion of Dworkin. But it is justified by Frankfurter's rejection of First Amendment absolutism, notably in the flag-salute cases, and to his espousal of a "shocks the conscience" test for substantive due process. This is a refined version of Holmes' "puke" test—a statute or other act of government violates the Constitution if and only if it makes you want to throw up.[5] Can it be an accident that Frankfurter announced his test in a case about pumping the stomach of a suspect for evidence?[6]

The "puke" test is shorthand for Holmes' more considered formulation, in his dissent in *Lochner*: a statute does not work a deprivation of "liberty" without due process of law within the meaning of the due process clauses of the Fifth and Fourteenth Amendments "unless it can be said that a rational and fair man necessarily would admit that the statute proposed [opposed?] would infringe fundamental principles as they have been understood by the traditions of our people and our law."[7] By "fundamental principles" Holmes meant principles of morality so deeply rooted in the judge's being that the judge would find their rejection incomprehensible. The qualification "the traditions of our people and our law" is significant, however, as I shall explain later.

What makes the issue of whether adjudication is or should be pragmatic an urgent one for me is that my critics do not consider my theory of adjudication pragmatic at all. They think it is in the spirit of logical positivism, from which pragmatists try to distance themselves. The logical positivists believed that moral assertions, because they are neither tautological nor verifiable empirically, have no truth value at all—are matters purely of taste or of unreasoned emotion.[8] Jeffrey Rosen, for example, argues that my book *Overcoming Law* endorses a visceral, personalized, ruleless, free-wheeling, unstructured conception of judging.[9] And well before I thought of myself as a pragmatist, I was criticized for being "a captive of a thin and unsatisfactory epistemology," which is just the sort of criticism that a purely emotive theory of judging would invite.[10] Am I, then, backsliding? I had better try to make clear what I think pragmatic adjudication is.

I

An initial difficulty is that pragmatic adjudication cannot be derived from pragmatism as a philosophical stance. For it would be entirely consistent with pragmatism the philosophy *not* to want judges to be pragmatists, just as it would be entirely consistent with utilitarianism not to want judges to conceive their role as being to maximize utility. One might believe for example that overall utility would be maximized if judges confined themselves to the application of rules, because discretionary justice, with all the uncertainty it would create, might be thought on balance to reduce rather than to increase utility. Similarly, a pragmatist committed to judging a legal system by the results the system produced might think that the best results would be produced if the judges did not make pragmatic judgments but simply applied rules. He might, by analogy to rule utilitarians, be a "rule pragmatist."

So pragmatic adjudication will have to be defended—pragmatically—on its own terms rather than as a corollary of philosophical pragmatism. (This would be necessary anyway, because of the vagueness of the philosophical concept.) But what exactly is to be defended? I do not accept Dworkin's definition: "the pragmatist thinks judges should always do the best they can for the future, in the circumstances, unchecked by any need to respect or secure consistency in principle with what other officials have done or will do."[11] That is Dworkin the polemicist speaking. But if his definition is rewritten as follows—"a pragmatist judge always tries to do the best he can do for the present and the future, unchecked by any felt *duty* to secure consistency in principle with what other officials have done in the past"—then I can accept it as a working definition of the concept of pragmatic adjudication. On this construal the difference between, say, a judge who is a legal positivist in the strong sense of believing that the law is a system of rules laid down by legislatures and merely applied by judges, and a pragmatic judge, is that the former is centrally concerned with securing consistency with past enactments, and the latter is concerned with securing consistency with the past only to the extent that decisions in accordance with precedent may happen to conduce to producing the best results for the future.

II

What does the pragmatic approach to judging entail? What are the pros and cons (pragmatically evaluated, of course)? And is it, on balance, the right approach for judges to take?

Consider to begin with the differences in the way the judicial positivist and the judicial pragmatist might weigh or order the materials bearing on the decision of a case. By "judicial positivist" I mean a judge who believes not only that the positivist account of law is descriptively accurate—that the meaning of law is exhausted in positive law—but also that the positivist account should guide judicial decision-making in the strong sense that no right should be recognized or duty imposed that does not have its source in positive law. (A weaker sense will be considered later.) The judicial positivist would begin and usually end with a consideration of cases, statutes, administrative regulations, and constitutional provisions—all these and only these being "authorities" to which the judge must defer in accordance with the principle that a judge who is not a pragmatist has a duty to secure consistency in principle with what other officials have done in the past. If the authorities all line up in one direction, the decision of the present case is likely to be foreordained, because to go against the authorities would, unless there are compelling reasons to do so, violate the duty to the past. The most compelling reason would be that some other line of cases had adopted a principle inconsistent with the authorities directly relevant to the present case. It would be the judges' duty, by comparing the two lines and bringing to bear other principles manifest or latent in case law, statute, and constitutional provision, to find the result in the present case that would promote or cohere with the best interpretation of the legal background as a whole.

The pragmatist judge has different priorities. That judge wants to come up with the best decision having in mind present and future needs, and so does not regard the maintenance of consistency with past decisions as an end in itself, but only as a means for bringing about the best results in the present case. He is not uninterested in past decisions, in statutes, and so forth. Far from it. For one thing, these are repositories of knowledge, even, sometimes, of wisdom, and so it would be folly to ignore them even if they had no authoritative significance. For another, a decision that destabilized the law by departing too abruptly from precedent might, on balance, have bad results.

There is often a tradeoff between rendering substantive justice in the case under consideration and maintaining the law's certainty and predictability. This tradeoff, which is perhaps clearest in cases in which a defense of statute of limitations is raised, will sometimes justify sacrificing substantive justice in the individual case to consistency with previous cases or with statutes or, in short, with well-founded expectations necessary to the orderly management of society's business. Another reason not to ignore the past is that often it is difficult to determine the purpose and scope of a rule without tracing the rule to its origins.

The pragmatist judge thus regards precedent, statutes, and constitutions both as sources of potentially valuable information about the likely best result in the present case and as signposts that he must be careful not to obliterate or obscure gratuitously, because people may be relying upon them. But because the pragmatist judge sees these "authorities" merely as sources of information and as limited constraints on his freedom of decision, he does not depend upon them to supply the rule of decision for the truly novel case. For that he looks also or instead to sources that bear directly on the wisdom of the rule that he is being asked to adopt or modify.

Some years ago the Supreme Court held that if there are two possible grounds for dismissing a suit filed in federal court, one being that it is not within the court's jurisdiction and the other being that the suit has no merit, and if the jurisdictional ground is unclear but the lack of merit is clear, the court can dismiss the suit on the merits without deciding whether there is jurisdiction.[12] This approach is "illogical." Jurisdiction is the power to decide the merits of a claim; so a decision on the merits presupposes jurisdiction. The pragmatic justification for occasionally putting the merits cart before the jurisdictional horse begins by asking why federal courts have a limited jurisdiction and have made rather a fetish of keeping within its bounds. The answer I think is that these are extraordinarily powerful courts and the concept of limited jurisdiction enables them both to limit the occasions for the exercise of power and to demonstrate self-restraint.[13] But if the lack of merits of a case is clear, a decision so holding will not enlarge federal judicial power but will merely exercise it well within its outer bounds. If, therefore, the question of jurisdiction is unclear in a case whose lack of merit is clear, the prudent and economical course may be to skip over the jurisdictional question and dismiss the case on the merits.

Here is another example of the difference between positivistic and pragmatic adjudication. When oil and gas first became commercially valuable, the question arose whether they should be treated like other "mobile" resources, such as wild animals, where the rule of the common law was (and is) that you have no property right until you take possession of the animal, or, instead, like land and other "stable" property, title to which can be obtained by recording a deed in a public registry or by some other paper record without the owner's having to take physical possession of the good.[14] A judicial positivist who was asked whether only possessory rights should be recognized in oil and gas would be likely to start with the cases on property rights in wild animals and consider whether oil and gas are enough "like" them to justify subsuming these minerals under the legal concept *ferae naturae*, which would mean enforcing only property rights obtained by possession. (So no one could own oil until it was pumped to the surface.) The pragmatic judge would be more inclined to start with the teachings of natural-resources economists and oil and gas engineers, to use the advice of these experts to decide which regime of property rights (possessory or title) would produce the better results when applied to oil and gas, and only then to examine the wild-animal cases and other authorities to see whether they might block the decision that would be best for the exploitation of oil and gas.

I am aware that the pragmatic judge may fall on his face. He may not be able to understand what the petroleum engineers and the economists are trying to tell him or to translate it into a workable legal rule. The plodding positivist, his steps wholly predictable, will at least promote stability in law, a genuine public good, and the legislature can always step in and prescribe an economically sound scheme of property rights. That is pretty much the history of property rights in oil and gas. Perhaps nothing better could realistically be expected. But American legislatures, in contrast to European parliaments, are so sluggish when it comes to correcting judicial mistakes that a heavy burden of legal creativity falls inescapably on the shoulders of the judges. I do not think that the judges can bear the burden unless they are pragmatists. But I admit that they will not be able to bear it comfortably until changes in legal education and practice make law a more richly theoretical and empirical, and less formal and casuistic, field.

My third example is a current focus of controversy, the issue of the enforceability of contracts of surrogate motherhood. In holding that they are unenforceable the Supreme Court of New Jersey in the *Baby M* case engaged in a labored and rather windy tour of legal sources and concepts, overlooking the two issues, both factual in the broad sense, that would matter most to a pragmatist.[15] The first is whether women who agree to be surrogate mothers typically or at least frequently experience intense regret when the moment comes to surrender the newborn baby to the father and his wife. The second is whether contracts of surrogate motherhood are typically or frequently exploitive in the sense that the surrogate mother is a poor woman who enters into the contract out of desperation. If the answers to both questions are "no," then, given the benefits of the contracts to the signatories, the pragmatist judge would probably enforce such contracts.[16]

These examples should help us see that although both the positivist and the pragmatist are interested in the authorities *and* the facts (broadly construed—I am not talking only or even mainly about the facts developed at a trial through testimony, exhibits, and cross-examination), the positivist starts with and gives more weight to the authorities, while the pragmatist starts with and gives more weight to the facts. This is the most succinct description of pragmatic adjudication that I can come up with. It helps, incidentally, to explain two features of Holmes' judicial philosophy that seem at first glance antipathetic to pragmatic adjudication: his lack of interest, of which Brandeis complained, in economic and other data, and his reluctance to overrule previous decisions. A pragmatic judge believes that the future should not be the slave of the past, but he need not have faith in any particular bodies of data as guides to making the decision that will best serve the future. If like Holmes you lacked confidence that you or anyone else had any very clear idea of what the best decision on some particular issue would be, the pragmatic posture would be one of reluctance to overrule past decisions, since the effect of overruling would be to sacrifice certainty and stability for a merely conjectural gain.

I have said nothing about the pragmatic judge's exercising a "legislative" function, although the kind of facts that he would need in order to decide the oil and gas case in pragmatic fashion would be the kind that students of administrative law call "legislative" to distinguish them from the sort of facts ("adjudicative") that judge and jury, cabined by the rules of evidence, are called upon to find. Holmes said that judges were "interstitial" legislators whenever they were called upon to decide a case the outcome of which was not dictated by unquestioned authorities. This is a misleading usage because of the many differences in procedures, training, experience, outlook, knowledge, tools, timing, constraints, and incentives between judges and legislators. Scope is not the only difference, as Holmes' formulation suggests. What he should have said was that judges are rulemakers as well as rule appliers. A judge is a different kind of rulemaker from a legislator. An appellate judge has to decide in particular cases whether to apply an old rule unmodified, modify and apply the old rule, or create and apply a new rule. If he is a pragmatist he will be guided in this decision-making process by the goal of making the choice that will produce the best results. To make that choice he will have to do more than consult cases, statutes, regulations, constitutions, conventional legal treatises, and other orthodox legal materials.

III

I want to examine a little more systematically the objections to the pragmatic approach to judging. One objection to inviting the judge, as I just did, to stray beyond the boundaries of the orthodox legal materials of decision is that he is not trained to analyze and absorb the theories and data of social science. The example of Brandeis is not reassuring. Although Brandeis was a brilliant man of wide intellectual interests, his forays into social science whether as advocate or as judge were far from an unqualified success. Indeed, most social scientists today would probably agree that Brandeis' indefatigable industry in marshaling economic data and viewing them through the lens of economic theory was largely misguided. It led him to support (and to try to make a part of the law) such since-discredited policies as limiting women's employment rights, fostering small business at the expense of large, and encouraging public utility and common carrier regulation. Holmes, as I have said, had reservations about the reliability of social scientific theories, but his unshakable faith in the eugenics movement, an early twentieth-century product of social and biological theory, undergirds his most criticized opinion (incidentally one joined by Brandeis)—*Buck v. Bell.*[17] One of the deformities of the majority opinion in *Roe v. Wade* is that the opinion makes it seem that the issue of abortion rights is a medical one and that the reason for invalidating state laws forbidding abortion is simply that they interfere with the autonomy of the medical profession—a "practical" angle reflecting Justice Blackmun's long association with the Mayo Clinic.[18] The effects of abortion laws on women, children, and the family, which are the effects that are important to evaluating the laws, are not considered.

A second and related objection to the use of nonlegal materials to decide cases is that it is bound often to degenerate into "gut reaction" judging. I think that this appraisal is basically correct, provided the phrase "gut reaction" is taken figuratively rather than literally, but that the word "degenerate" is too strong. Cases do not wait upon the accumulation of some critical mass of social scientific knowledge that will enable the properly advised judge to arrive at the decision that will have the best results. The decisions of the Supreme Court in the area of sexual and reproductive autonomy, for example, came in advance of reliable, comprehensive, and accessible scholarship on sexuality, the family, and the status of women. The court had to decide whether capital punishment is cruel and unusual punishment at a time when the scientific study of the deterrent effects of capital punishment was just beginning. When the court decided to re-district the nation according to the "one man, one vote" principle it cannot have had a clear idea about the effects, which political scientists still do not agree upon more than thirty years later. The examples are not limited to the Supreme Court or to constitutional law. Common law judges had to resolve such issues as whether to extend the domain of strict liability, substitute comparative negligence for contributory negligence, simplify the rules of occupiers' liability, excuse breach of contract because of impossibility of performance, limit consequential damages, enforce waivers of liability, and so forth long before economists and economically minded lawyers got around to studying the economic consequences of these choices. When judges try to make the decision that will produce the "best results," without having any body of organized knowledge to turn to for help in making that decision, it seems that they must rely on their intuitions.

The fancy term for the body of bedrock beliefs that guide decision is natural law. Does this mean that the pragmatic approach to adjudication is just another version of the natural-law approach? I think not. The pragmatist does not look to God or other transcendental sources of moral principle to validate his departures from statute or precedent or other conventional "sources" of law. He has not the confidence of secure foundations and this should make him a little more tentative, cautious, and piecemeal in imposing his vision of the Good on society in the name of legal justice. If Holmes really thought he was applying a "puke" test to statutes challenged as unconstitutional rather than evaluating those statutes for conformity with transcendental criteria, this would help explain his restrained approach to constitutional adjudication. On the other hand, a pragmatic justice such as Robert Jackson, who unlike Holmes had a rich background of involvement in high-level political questions, was not bashful in drawing upon his extrajudicial experience for guidance to the content of constitutional doctrine.[19] The pragmatic judge is not always a modest judge.

The reason that using the "puke" test or one's "gut reactions" or even one's prejudicial high-governmental experiences to make judicial decisions sounds scandalous[20] is that the legal profession, and particularly its academic and judicial branches, want the added legitimacy that accrues to the decisions of people whose opinions are grounded in expert knowledge. The expert knowledge of another discipline is not what is wanted, although it is better than no expert knowledge at all. Both the law professor and the judge feel naked before society when the positions they take on novel cases, however carefully those positions are dressed up in legal jargon, are seen to reflect unstructured intuition based on personal and professional (but nonjudicial) experiences, and on character and temperament, rather than on disciplined, rigorous, and articulate inquiry.

Things are not quite so bad as that. It is not as if American judges were chosen at random and made political decisions in a vacuum. Judges of the higher American courts are generally picked from the upper tail of the population distribution in terms of age, education, intelligence, disinterest, and sobriety. They are not tops in all these departments but they are well above average, at least in the federal courts because of the elaborate preappointment screening of candidates for federal judgeships. Judges are schooled in a profession that sets a high value on listening to both sides of an issue before making up one's mind, on sifting truth from falsehood, and on exercising a detached judgment. Their decisions are anchored in the facts of concrete disputes between real people. Members of the legal profession have played a central role in the political history of the United States, and the profession's institutions and usages are reflectors of the fundamental political values that have emerged from that history. Appellate judges in nonroutine cases are expected to express as best they can the reasons for their decision in signed, public documents (the published decisions of these courts) and this practice creates accountability and fosters a certain reflectiveness and self-discipline. None of these things guarantees wisdom, especially since the reasons given for a decision are not always the real reasons behind it. But at their best American appellate courts are councils of wise elders and it is not completely insane to entrust them with responsibility for deciding cases in a way that will produce the best results in the circumstances rather than just deciding cases in accordance with rules created by other organs of government or in accordance with their own previous decisions, although that is what they will be doing most of the time.

Nor do I flinch from another implication of conceiving American appellate courts in the way that I have suggested. It is that these courts will tend to treat the Constitution and the common law, and to a lesser extent bodies of statute law, as a kind of putty that can be used to fill embarrassing holes in the legal framework. In the case of property rights in oil and gas, a court could take the position that it had no power to create new rules and must therefore subsume these newly valuable resources under the closest existing rule, the rule governing wild animals. It might even take the position that it had no power to enlarge the boundaries of existing rules, and in that event no property rights in oil and gas would be recognized until the legislature created a system of property rights for these resources. Under this approach, if Connecticut has a crazy law (as it did until *Griswold v. Connecticut* struck it down) forbidding married couples to use contraceptives, but no provision of the Constitution limits state regulation of the family, then the crazy law will stand until it is repealed or the Constitution amended to invalidate it.[21] Or if the Eighth Amendment's prohibition against cruel and unusual punishments has reference only to the *method* of punishment or to the propriety of punishing *at all* in particular circumstances (for example, for simply being poor, or an addict), then a state can with constitutional impunity sentence a sixteen-year-old to life imprisonment without possibility of parole for the sale of one marijuana cigarette, which in fact seems to be the Supreme Court's current view, one that I find very difficult to stomach.[22] I do not think a pragmatic Justice of the Supreme Court *would* stomach it, although he would give due weight to the implications for judicial caseloads of bringing the length of prison sentences under judicial scrutiny, and to the difficulty of working out defensible norms of proportionality. The pragmatic judge does not think that he should throw up his hands and say "sorry, no law to apply" when he is confronted with outrageous conduct that the framers of the Constitution neglected to foresee and make specific provision for.

Oddly, this basic principle of pragmatic judging has received at least limited recognition by even the most orthodox judges, with respect to statutes. It is accepted that if reading a statute the way it is written produces absurd results, the judges may rewrite it.[23] Most judges do not put it quite this way—they say that statutory interpretation is a search for meaning and Congress can't have meant the absurd result—but it comes to the same thing. And, at least in this country, common law judges reserve the right to "rewrite" the common law as they go along. I am merely suggesting that a similar approach, prudently employed, is the pragmatic approach to constitutional adjudication as well.

I do not belittle the dangers of the approach. People can feel very strongly about a subject and be quite wrong. Certitude is not the test of certainty. A wise person realizes that even his unshakable convictions may be wrong—but not all of us are wise. In a pluralistic society, moreover, which the United States seems to be more and more every year, a judge's unshakable convictions may not be shared by enough other people that he can base a decision on those convictions and be reasonably confident that it will be accepted. So the wise judge will try to check his convictions against those of some broader community of opinion, as suggested by Holmes in his dissent in *Lochner*. It was not irrelevant, from a pragmatic standpoint, to the outcome of *Brown v. Board of Education* that official racial segregation had been abolished outside the South and that it bore a disturbing resemblance to Nazi racial laws.[24] It was not irrelevant to the outcome of *Griswold v. Connecticut* that, as the court neglected to mention, only one other state (Massachusetts) had a similar law. If I were writing an opinion invalidating the life sentence in my hypothetical marijuana case I would look at the punishments for this conduct in other states and in the foreign countries, such as England and France, that we consider in some sense our peers. For if a law could be said to be contrary to world public opinion I would consider this a reason, not compelling but not negligible either, for regarding a state law as unconstitutional even if the Constitution's text had to be stretched a bit to cover it. The study of other laws, or of world public opinion as crystallized in foreign law and practices, is a more profitable inquiry than trying to find some bit of eighteenth-century evidence for thinking that maybe the framers of the Constitution wanted courts to make sure that punishments prescribed by statute were proportional to the gravity, or difficulty of apprehension, or profitability, or some other relevant characteristic of the crime. If I found such evidence I would think it a valuable bone to toss to a positivist or formalist colleague but I would not be embarrassed by its absence because I would not think myself duty-bound to maintain consistency with past decisions.

I would even think it pertinent to the pragmatic response to my hypothetical marijuana case to investigate or perhaps even just to speculate (if factual investigation proved fruitless) about the psychological and social meaning of imprisoning a young person for his entire life for the commission of a minor crime. What happens to a person in such a situation? Does he adjust? Deteriorate? What is the likely impact on his family, and on the larger society? How should one feel as a judge if one allows such a punishment to be imposed? And are these sentences for real, or are preposterously severe sentences soon commuted? Could it be that the deterrent effect of so harsh a sentence will be so great that the total number of years of imprisonment for violation of the drug laws will be reduced, making the sacrifice of this young person a utility-maximizing venture after all? Is utility the right criterion here? Is the sale of marijuana perhaps far more destructive than some ivory-tower judge or professor thinks? Do judges become callous if a large proportion of the criminal cases that they review involve very long sentences? If a defendant appealed who received "only" a five-year sentence, would the appellate judge's reaction be, "Why are you complaining about such a trivial punishment?"[25]

The response to the hypothetical case of the young man sentenced to life for selling marijuana is bound in the end to be an emotional rather than a closely reasoned one, because so many imponderables enter into that response, as my questions were intended to indicate. But emotion is not pure glandular secretion. It is influenced by experience, information, and imagination, and can thus be disciplined by fact.[26] Indignation or disgust founded on a responsible appreciation of a situation need not be thought a disreputable motive for action, even for a judge; it is indeed the absence of any emotion in such a situation that would be discreditable. It would be nice, though, if judges and law professors were more knowledgeable practitioners or at least consumers of social science (broadly defined to include history and philosophy), so that their "emotional" judgments were better informed.

My earlier reference to the ages of judges suggests another objection to pragmatic adjudication. Aristotle said, and I agree, that young people tend to be forward-looking. Their life lies ahead of them and they have only a limited stock of experience to draw upon in coping with the future, while old people tend to be backward-looking because they face an opposite balance between past and future.[27] If, therefore, a pragmatic judge is forward-looking, does that mean that we should invert the age profile of judges? Should Holmes have been made a judge at thirty and put out to pasture at fifty? Or, on the contrary, is it not the case that judges perform an important "balance wheel" function, one that requires them to be backward-looking, one that is peculiarly apt, therefore, for the aged? Have I not argued this myself, and also pointed out that, contrary to the conventional view, the great failing of the German judges in the Nazi period was not their positivism but their insistence on interpreting and applying the laws of the New Order to further the aims, the spirit, of those laws?[28]

These criticisms pivot on an ambiguity in the term "forward-looking." If it is meant to carry overtones of disdain for history, origins, and traditions, then the criticisms I have mentioned are entirely just. But I do not myself understand "forward-looking" in that sense. I understand it to mean that the past is valued not in itself but only in relation to the present and the future. That relation may be a very important one. It may be that the best the judge can do for the present and the future is to insist that breaks with the past be duly considered. That would be entirely consistent with pragmatism; it would be positivism-as-pragmatism. All that would be missing would be a sense of reverence for the past, a felt "duty" of continuity with the past. That reverence, that sense of duty, would be inconsistent with the forward-looking stance, and hence with pragmatism.

I think, likewise, that pragmatism is wholly neutral with regard to the question of whether the law should be dominated by rules or by standards. The pragmatist rejects the idea that law is not law unless it consists of rules, because that kind of conceptual analysis is not pragmatic. But he is open to any pragmatic argument in favor of rules, for example, that judges cannot be trusted to make intelligent decisions unless they are guided by rules or that decisions based on standards produce uncertainty disproportionate to any gain in flexibility. A pragmatic judge thus need not be recognizable by a distinctive style of judging. What would be distinctive would be that the style of thinking (which might be encapsulated as positivist or formalist rhetoric) owed nothing to ideas about the nature of law or the moral duty to abide by past decisions or some other nonpragmatic grounding of judicial attitudes. I likewise leave open just what are the criteria for the "best results" for which the pragmatic judge is striving. They are not what is best for the particular case without consideration of the implications for other cases. Pragmatism will not tell us what is best but, provided there is a fair degree of value consensus among the judges, as I think there is, it can help judges seek the best results unhampered by philosophical doubts.

The greatest danger of judicial pragmatism is intellectual laziness. It is a lot simpler to react to a case than to analyze it. The pragmatic judge must bear in mind at all times that he is a judge and that this means that he must consider all the legal materials and arguments that are or can be brought to bear upon the case. If legal reasoning is modestly defined as reasoning with reference to distinctive legal materials such as statutes and legal doctrines and to the law's traditional preoccupations, for example, with stability and the right to be heard and the other "rule of law" virtues, then it ought to be an ingredient of every legal decision, though not necessarily the be-all and end-all of the decision.[29] Just as some people think that an artist must prove that he is a competent draftsman before he should be taken seriously as an abstract artist, so I believe that a judge must prove—anew in every case—that he is a competent legal reasoner before he should be taken seriously as a pragmatic judge.

To put this point differently, the pragmatic judge must never forget that he is a judge and that the role of a judge is constraining as well as empowering. Several years ago the Chicago public schools were unable to open at the beginning of the school year because the state refused to approve the school district's budget. An injunction was sought to compel the schools to open, on the ground that their closure violated a judicial decree forbidding de facto racial segregation in the city's public schools. The basis on which the injunction was sought was not that the state's refusal to approve the budget had been motivated by any racial animus—there was no suggestion of that—but that the ultimate goal of the judicial decree, which was to improve the education and life prospects of black children in Chicago, would be thwarted if the schools were not open to educate them. The trial judge granted the request for an injunction, and did so on an avowedly pragmatic ground: the cost to Chicago's schoolchildren, of whatever race, of being denied an education. My court reversed.[30] We could not find any basis in federal law for the injunction.

The desegregation decree had not commanded the city to open the public schools on some particular date, or for that matter to open them at all, or even to *have* public schools, let alone to flout a state law requiring financial responsibility in the administration of the public school system. It seemed to us that what the judge had done was not so much pragmatic as lawless. Even if one rejects the view, as do I, that pragmatism requires judges to eschew pragmatic adjudication, they must not ignore the good of compliance with settled rules of law. If a federal judge is free to issue an injunction that has no basis in federal law, merely because he thinks the injunction will have good results, then we do not have pragmatic adjudication; we have judicial tyranny, which few Americans consider acceptable even if they are persuaded that the tyrant can be counted on to be generally benign.

The judge in the Chicago school case was guilty of what might be called myopic pragmatism, which may be Dworkin's conception of pragmatism. The only consequence that the judge took into consideration in deciding whether to issue the injunction was that children enrolled in the public schools would be deprived of schooling until the schools opened. The consequence that he ignored was the consequence for the political and governmental systems of granting federal judges an uncanalized discretion to intervene in political disputes. Had the power that the judge claimed been upheld, you can be sure that henceforth the financing of Chicago's public schools would be determined by a federal judge rather than by elected officials. The judge thought that unless he ordered the schools to open, the contending parties would never agree on a budget. The reverse was true. Only the fact that the schools were closed exerted pressure on the parties to settle their dispute. And indeed, as soon as we lifted the injunction, the parties came to terms and the schools opened. The consequence that the judge ignored was a consequence for the schoolchildren as well as for other members of society, so that it is possible that even the narrowest group affected by the decree would, in the long run, have been hurt had the decree been allowed to stand.

If intellectual laziness is a danger of pragmatic adjudication, and I think it is, it is also a danger of not being pragmatic. The conventional judge is apt not to question his premises. If he thinks that "hate speech" is deeply harmful, or that banning hate speech would endanger political liberty, he is not likely to take the next step, which is to recognize that he may be wrong and to seek through investigation to determine whether he is wrong.[31] The deeper the belief—the closer it lies to our core values—the less likely we are to be willing to question it. Our disposition will be not to question but to defend. As Peirce and Dewey emphasized, doubt rather than belief is the spur to inquiry; and doubt is a disposition that pragmatism encourages, precisely in order to spur inquiry. One reason that attitudes toward hate speech are held generally as dogmas rather than hypotheses—one reason that so little is known about the actual consequences of hate speech—is that a pragmatic approach has not been taken to the subject.

IV

I have been trying to explain my conception of pragmatic adjudication and to defend it against the critics of pragmatic: adjudication. But I would not like to leave the impression that I think pragmatic adjudication is *the* right way for all courts to go. Philosophical pragmatism, although one can find echoes or anticipations of it in German philosophy and elsewhere (Hume, Nietzsche, and Wittgenstein, for example), is basically an American philosophy, and it may not travel well to other countries. The same may be true for pragmatic adjudication. Concretely, the case for such adjudication is weaker in a parliamentary democracy than in a U.S.-style checks and balances federalist democracy. Many parliamentary systems (notably the English, which is the one I know best) are effectively unicameral and, what is more, the parliament is controlled by the executive. The legislative branch of so highly centralized a system can pass new laws pretty easily and rapidly and word them clearly. If the courts identify a gap in existing law, they can have reasonable confidence that it will be quickly filled by Parliament, so that only a temporary injustice will be done if the judges refrain from filling the gap themselves. English judges thus can afford to be stodgier, more rule-bound, less pragmatic than our judges; the cost in substantive injustice is lower.

Some parliamentary systems have a federal structure, some have constitutional review, and some have both. Some, the English for example, have neither. The ones that have neither have much clearer law, whereas to determine someone's legal obligation in the United States will often require consideration of state law (and perhaps the laws of several states), federal statutory law (and sometimes federal common law), and state and federal constitutional law. Our government is one of the most decentralized in the world. We have effectively a tricameral federal legislature, since the president through his veto power and his role in one of the major political parties is a full participant in the legislative process. This tricameral structure makes it extremely difficult to pass laws, let alone clearly worded laws (unclear wording in a contract or a statute facilitates agreement on the contract or statute as a whole by deferring resolution of the most contentious points). Moreover, the tricameral federal structure is layered on top of similarly three-headed state legislatures. American courts cannot, if they want "the best results," leave all rulemaking to legislatures, for that would result in legal gaps and perversities galore. The lateral-entry character of the American judiciary, the absence of uniform criteria for appointment, the moral, intellectual, and political diversity of the nation (and hence, given the previous two points, of the judges), the individualistic and antiauthoritarian character of the population, and the extraordinary complexity and dynamism of the society are further obstacles to American judges confining themselves to the application of rules laid down by legislatures, regulators, or the framers of the Constitution.

I am exaggerating the differences between the systems. But it is more natural for an English, Austrian, or Danish judge to think of himself or herself as mainly just a rule applier than it is for an American judge to do so, and since there are good pragmatic arguments in favor of judicial modesty, it is far from clear that English, Austrian, or Danish judges would be right on pragmatic grounds to become pragmatic adjudicators. I do not think that U.S. appellate judges have a choice.

V

I said I would come back to the question of whether it is accurate to describe this as a paper in "applied" pragmatism. I conjecture two relations between philosophical and legal pragmatism. First, the tendency of most philosophical speculation—and what makes it a proper staple of college education—is to shake up a person's presuppositions, so that if he happens to be a judge or lawyer reading philosophy he is likely to feel the presuppositions that define his professional culture shift beneath him. Philosophy, especially the philosophy of pragmatism, incites doubt, and doubt incites inquiry, making the judge less of a dogmatic, more of a pragmatic, adjudicator.

Second, philosophy, theology, and law have, to a significant extent, parallel conceptual structures. This is not surprising, because Christian theology was so heavily influenced by Greek and Roman philosophy, and Western law by Christianity. The orthodox versions of the three systems of thought have rather similar views on matters such as scientific and moral realism, free will, and mind-body dualism. A challenge to any of the systems, therefore, is a challenge to all three. Pragmatism in its role (which it shares with logical positivism, and here it should be pointed out that to the nonspecialist the similarities among the characteristic modern schools of philosophy are more conspicuous than the differences)[32] as skeptical challenger to orthodox philosophy encourages a skeptical view of the foundations of orthodox law with its many parallels to orthodox philosophy. That is why Rorty, who rarely discusses legal issues, is cited so frequently in law reviews.

Philosophical pragmatism does not dictate legal pragmatism or any other jurisprudential stance. But it may play a paternal and enabling role in relation to pragmatic theories of law, including the theory of pragmatic adjudication that I have tried to sketch in this paper.

Notes

This paper is the revised text of a talk given on November 3, 1995, at a conference on "The Revival of Pragmatism" sponsored by the Center for the Humanities of the City University of New York. I thank Scott Brewer, William Eskridge, Lawrence Lessig, Martha Nussbaum, Eric Posner, and Cass Sunstein, along with the commenters and other participants at the conference, for very helpful comments on an earlier draft.

1. Herman J. Saatkamp, ed., *Rorty & Pragmatism: The Philosopher Responds to His Critics* (Nashville: Vanderbilt University Press, 1995). Professor Hilary Putnam's talk at the conference was very much of this character.

2. See also Matthew H. Kramer, "The Philosopher-Judge: Some Friendly Criticisms of Richard Posner's Jurisprudence," *Modern Law Review* 59 (1996): 465, 475–78, where he states that "Metaphysical or philosophical pragmatism is a relativist position which denies that knowledge can be grounded on absolute foundations. Methodological or intellectual pragmatism is a position that attaches great importance to lively debate and open-mindedness and flexibility in the sciences, the humanities and the arts. Political pragmatism is a position that attaches great importance to civil liberties and to tolerance and to flexible experimentation in the discussions and institutions that shape the arrangements of human intercourse. . . . [T]hese three modes of pragmatism do not entail one another."

3. See, for example, Daniel A. Farber, "Reinventing Brandeis: Legal Pragmatism for the Twenty-First Century," *University of Illinois Law Review* (1995): 163.

4. For a list of pragmatists, see Richard A. Posner, *Overcoming Law* (Cambridge: Harvard University Press, 1995): 388–89. See also Richard Rorty, "The Banality of Pragmatism and the Poetry of Justice," in *Pragmatism in Law and Society*, edited by Michael Brint and William Weaver (1991). p. 89, and Ronald Dworkin, "Pragmatism, Right Answers, and True Banality," in *ibid.*, pp. 359, 360.

5. See Posner, *Overcoming Law*, p. 192.

6. *Rochin v. California*, 342 U.S. 165 (1952).

7. *Lochner v. New York*, 198 U.S. 45, 76 (1905) (Holmes' dissenting opinion).

8. Some are; for example, "murder is bad," since badness is built into the definition of "murder" (as distinct from "killing"), at least the popular as distinct from the legal definition. The distinction is important, because some forms of murder in the legal sense, such as a cuckold's killing the adulterer in flagrante delicto, are not considered morally wrong by a significant part of the community.

9. Rosen, "Overcoming Posner," *Yale Law Journal* 105 (1995): 581, 584–96.

10. Paul M. Bator, "The Judicial Universe of Judge Richard Posner," *University of Chicago Law Review* 52 (1985): 1146, 1161.

11. Ronald Dworkin, *Law's Empire* (Cambridge: Belknap Press, 1986), p. 161.

12. *Norton v. Mathews*, 427 U.S. 524, 532 (1976).

13. To quote Isabel in *Measure for Measure*, Act II, sc. 2, ll. 108–10: "Oh, it is excellent to have a giant's strength: but it is tyrannous to use it like a giant."

14. A chair, for example: it moves only when someone moves it, whereas gravity or air pressure will cause oil and gas to flow into an empty space even if no (other) force is applied. I think that when the animal rules were first applied to oil and gas, these resources were erroneously thought to have an internal principle of notion, to "move on their own," like animals. I set to one side property that is not physical at all, i.e., intellectual property.

15. Re *Baby M*, 537 A.2d 1227 (N.J. 1988).

16. See generally Richard A. Posner, *Sex and Reason* (Cambridge: Harvard University Press, 1992), pp. 420–28.

17. *Buck v. Bell*, 274 U.S. 200, 207 (1927) ("Three generations of imbeciles are enough").

18. *Roe v. Wade*, 410 U.S. 113 (1973).

19. Quite the contrary. As he said in his famous concurrence in the steel-seizure case, "That comprehensive and undefined presidential powers hold both practical advantages and grave dangers for the country will impress anyone who has served as legal adviser to a President in time of transition and public anxiety. While an interval of detached reflection may temper teachings of that experience, they probably are a more realistic influence on my views than the conventional materials of judicial decision which seem unduly to accentuate doctrine and legal fiction." *Youngstown Sheet & Tube Co. v. Sawyer*, 343 U.S. 579, 634 (1952) (Jackson, J., concurring).

20. Making the statement by Justice Jackson that I quoted in the preceding footnote remarkable for its candor; but am I mistaken in sensing a faintly apologetic tone?

21. See *Griswold v. Connecticut*, 381 U.S. 479 (1965).

22. See *Harmelin v. Michigan*, 501 U.S. 957 (1991).

23. See, for example, *Burns v. United States*, 501 U.S. 129,137, (1991); *Green v. Bock Laundry Machine Co.*, 490 U.S. 504, 527 (1989) (Scalia, J., concurring).

24. Which for these purposes however included the District of Columbia! See *Bolling v. Sharpe*, 347 U.S. 497 (1954).

25. I believe in fact that this is increasingly the reaction of federal appellate judges, as federal sentences become ever longer and the number of criminal appeals even greater.

26. I refer the reader once again to the striking quotation from Justice Jackson, in *Harmelin v. Michigan*. This is the theme of Martha C. Nussbaum's 1993 Gifford Lectures (to be published by Cambridge University Press), *Upheavals of Thought: A Theory of the Emotions*. One would not expect, for example, a person who had become genuinely, disinterestedly convinced that the Holocaust had never occurred to feel the same concern about anti-Semitism that people who believed it had occurred would tend to have.

27. I elaborate upon Aristotle's view in Chapter 5 of my book *Aging and Old Age* (1995).

28. As I argue in *ibid.*, Chapter 8. Posner, *Overcoming Law*, p. 155, discusses the issue of law in Nazi Germany. I would not be inclined to swing to the other extreme and blame Nazi jurisprudence on pragmatism. National Socialism was not a pragmatic faith.

29. As in Joseph Raz, "On the Autonomy of Legal Reasoning," in Raz, *Ethics in the Public Domain: Essays in the Morality of Law and Politics* 310 (1994).

30. *United States v. Board of Education*, 11 F.3d 668 (7th Cir. 1993).

31. My discussion of this subject was stimulated by a very interesting paper by Michel Rosenfeld, "Pragmatism, Pluralism and Legal Interpretation: Posner's and Rorty's Justice without Metaphysics Meets Hate Speech," in Dickstein, ed., *The Revival of Pragmatism* (Durham: Duke University Press, 1998), pp. 324–343.

32. Hilary Putnam's brand of pragmatism, for example, as is plain from his paper in Dickstein, *The Revival of Pragmatism*, pp. 37–53, is a position within, rather than against, analytic philosophy.

In this essay tour of his Making It Explicit, *Robert Brandom outlines his inferentialist program in semantics and maps its consequences in epistemology and practical reasoning..*

ROBERT BRANDOM

From Truth to Semantics

A Path through Making It Explicit

It was when I said,
"There is no such thing as the truth,"
That the grapes seemed fatter.
The fox ran out of his hole.

You. . . You said,
"There are many truths.
But they are not part of a truth."
Then the tree, at night, began to change.
—Wallace Stevens "On the Road Home"

1

The master concept of the theory of meaning presented in *Making It Explicit*[1] is *inference*, not *truth.* Of course there are a lot of questions about how such an inferential role semantics might be made to work; a good bit of the book is given over to addressing these challenges.

My aim there is to work out the substitutional and anaphoric fine structure of inferential roles in sufficient detail to shed light from a new direction on a host of familiar issues—not the least of which being the *representational* dimension of thought and talk, I try in the opening chapters of the book to motivate an approach to meaning that starts with the social practices of giving and asking for reasons—one that sees semantic contentfulness as a status conferred upon states and performances by the role they play in such a set of practices. The idea is that inferring, or taking one remark to furnish a *reason* for another, is a sort of *doing* that we can get an initial grip on independently of other semantic ideas—one that may then be parlayed into a deeper understanding of such more traditional semantic notions as truth and representation.

David Lewis is my paradigm of a philosopher who fully faces up to the obligation to show what it is about the *use* of expressions that establishes their association with semantically relevant whatnots—the obligation I take to distinguish *philosophical* semantics from formal semantics (which is entitled simply to stipulate the association, at least for atomic expressions). Lewis already had a well worked-out semantics, based on the association of sentence tokenings with sets of possible worlds. His question (in "Languages and Language") was accordingly how to conceive the use of sentences so as to establish such an association. His answer takes the form of his theory of convention. I start from the other end, with an account of implicitly normative social practices, in terms of attributing commitments and entitlements. The transition to semantics takes the form of a specification of the consequential structure such deontic scorekeeping must have in order to count as *inferentially* articulated—that is, as a game of giving and asking for *reasons*.

However successful that attempt to root semantics in pragmatics, and however interesting the results, the overall approach may still seem perverse. Why tie one hand behind one's back by taking on the task of explaining semantic content by eschewing initial appeal to a notion of truth and truth conditions? Why, apart from a low craving for novelty, should one not rely on truth for the basic concept of one's semantic theory? One may very well hope that stereoscopic vision will provide added depth of perception, and so seek to lay a novel conceptual perspective alongside a more familiar one. But is there any more specific reason to think that starting an account of meaning with the notion of truth conditions is a mistake—that it limits our vision or constricts our explanatory reach in some predictable way?

I claim that a proper understanding of the important *expressive* role played by truth locutions leads to the realization that that role precisely disqualifies them from playing a fundamental *explanatory* role in accounts of the nature of propositional contentfulness. That critical argument is quite independent of the inferential semantic idiom I go on to recommend in the constructive portion of the project (while nonetheless setting some relatively demanding criteria of adequacy for a successor theory). Someone who accepts this argument might want to respond to the diagnosis it offers with quite a different sort of theoretical therapy—though not one that treats truth conditions as prior in the order of semantic explanation to that of propositional contentfulness.

The most sophisticated and successful account I know of the expressive role of the concept of truth—of what one is *doing* in deploying truth talk—is an *anaphoric* theory. Such theories originate with Grover, Camp, and Belnap's *prosentential theory of truth*. The version I favor understands locutions such as ". . . is true" and its relatives as *proform-forming operators*. In the simplest case, "That is true", is a *prosentence*, which relates to, and inherits its content from, an anaphoric antecedent—for instance someone else's tokening of "Snow is white",—in the same way that a pro*noun* such as 'he' relates to and inherits its content from an anaphoric antecedent—for instance, someone else's tokening of 'Tarski'.

As the authors of the original theory introduce them by analogy to pronouns, prosentences are defined by four conditions:

- They occupy all grammatical positions that can be occupied by declarative sentences, whether free-standing or embedded.
- They are generic, in that *any* declarative sentence can be the antecedent of some prosentence.
- They can be used anaphorically either in the lazy way or in the quantificational way.
- In each use, a prosentence will have an anaphoric antecedent that determines a class of admissible sentential substituends for the prosentence (in the lazy case, a singleton). This class of substituends determines the significance of the prosentence associated with it.

Anaphora is a relation according to which the content of one tokening is determined by its relation to another tokening or class of tokenings: its anaphoric antecedent(s). The anaphoric dependent is *not* in general replaceable by its antecedent. Understanding an anaphoric dependent—such as, according to the sort of theory in question, a sentence formed using the word 'true' (or, indeed, 'refers')—is accordingly a two-stage process. First, one computes the class of antecedent tokenings. Then, one determines the content of the anaphoric dependent, as a function of the contents of its antecedents.

Such an approach to truth talk has many advantages. Unlike those—including traditional pragmatic theories, and performative theories—that Blackburn has called 'Boo/Hurrah' theories, anaphoric accounts smoothly handle embedded uses of 'true'. For instance, when 'true' is used in the antecedent of a conditional—as in "If it is true that the moon is made of green cheese, then there must have been very large or very numerous space mammals"—no commitment is being undertaken, no assertion endorsed, no pro-attitude expressed by the utterance of the sentence "It is true that the moon is made of green cheese". Yet it is clearly propositionally contentful, and makes an essential contribution to the content of the conditional claim. Embedded prosentences are as straightforwardly interpretable as embedded sentences. Unlike redundancy theories, such as Ramsey's, the anaphoric approach can handle sentence nominalizations, as in "Goldbach's conjecture is true",—the phrase 'Goldbach's conjecture' simply picks out the class of anaphoric antecedents of the whole prosentence by describing it.[2] And unlike simple disquotational theories, anaphoric approaches to truth talk are designed from the start to deal with quantificational cases.

For pro*nouns*, on which pro*sentences* are modeled, come in two flavors: what Geach calls 'lazy' pronouns, which can in the simplest cases be replaced without alteration in content by their antecedents, and quantificational pronouns, such as the 'it' in "Any positive integer is odd if *it* is not even". Just so with prosentences. "Everything McDowell says is true", is an example of a quantificational prosentence. Just as quantificationally bound anaphoric pro*nouns* let us say things we cannot say without them, so too do quantificationally bound anaphoric pro*sentences*. Tarski showed that languages with truth-locutions can be strictly expressively more powerful than languages without them. Quantificational prosentences are one of the prime reasons.[3]

The anaphoric approach smoothly handles cases in which the anaphoric antecedent contains indexicals, demonstratives, anaphoric dependents, and expressions in foreign languages—all of which cause trouble for straightforwardly disquotational theories. Thus if the antecedent of my utterance of "That is true", is your utterance of "I am hungry", the second stage of the computation of the content of my remark must adjust the indexical from your mouth to mine, and yield something equivalent in my mouth to "You are hungry", *not* the simply disquoted "I am hungry", which means something different in my mouth than in yours. Here the important thing is that anaphora is a relation between *tokenings* of expressions. Incautiously stated redundancy or disquotational theories, remaining at the level of expression *types*, get these cases wrong. In a similar way, at this stage in the evaluation of the content of an anaphoric dependent one must adjust for differences in availability of demonstratives and pronouns, and for changes in language. Again, the anaphoric approach deals appropriately with sentential modifiers. If the anaphoric dependent on a claim that-p is of the form "That *was* true", or "That is *not* true", or "That is *possibly* true", or "That is *probably* true", then at the second stage one cannot simply disquote the antecedent. One must apply the same sentential operator to it that is applied in the anaphoric dependent—yielding "It was the case that-p", "Not-p", "Possibly-p", "Probably-p", and so on.

So disquotational theories offer an oversimplified picture of the second stage of the evaluation of the content of anaphoric dependent expressions formed using 'true'. But they also oversimplify the first stage: the computation of the class of anaphoric antecedents. Disquotational theories take as their paradigm cases where the truth-claim contains a quote name of the anaphoric antecedent: "'Snow is white', is true". But other sorts of names can be used to specify the antecedent, as in "Goldbach's conjecture is true". Or the antecedent can be specified by description: "The first sentence on this page is true". Here disquotation simply offers a bad theory of the process of determining the anaphoric antecedent. For in fact, prosentences can use all the referential apparatus of the language to do that job. One can no more 'disquote' the demonstrative 'that' in "That is true", than one gets to a statement of Goldbach's conjecture by disquoting it. A proper account of the use of 'true' requires more articulated accounts of both stages of anaphoric evaluation.[4]

Further, though the original authors of the theory do not point this out, it has become clear that the theory that construes 'true' as a prosentence-forming operator generalizes smoothly and naturally to a treatment of 'refers' as a pro*noun*-forming operator. Its basic employment is in the construction of what may be called *anaphorically indirect definite descriptions*. These are expressions such as "the one Kissinger referred to [represented, described, talked about] as 'almost a third-rate intellect'", understood as a pronoun whose anaphoric antecedent is some utterance by Kissinger. A full-fledged pronominal or anaphoric theory of 'refers' talk can be generated by first showing how other uses of 'refers' and its cognates can be paraphrased so that 'refers' appears only inside indirect descriptions, and then explaining the use of these descriptions as pronouns formed by applying the 'refers' operator to some antecedent-specifying locution. Specifying the expressive role of 'refers' or 'denotes' in this way then permits the recursive generation of the Tarski biconditionals in a straightforward fashion. So treating 'true' as an operator that applies to a sentence nominalization and produces a prosentence anaphorically dependent upon the nominalized sentence token, and 'refers' as an operator that applies to an expression picking out a term tokening and produces a pronoun anaphorically dependent upon them accordingly permits a single theory form to explain the use of all legitimate semantic talk about truth *and* reference in purely anaphoric terms.

A feature dear to the hearts of the originators of the prosentential theory is its metaphysical parsimony. For what in the past were explained as attributions of a special and mysterious *property* (truth) are exhibited instead as uses of grammatical proforms anaphorically referring only to the sentence tokenings that are their antecedents. The approach is intended to be, as one might say, *ontologically deflating*—or at least unexciting. One important and often overlooked advantage of anaphoric accounts of the expressive role of 'true' (and 'refers') is that they are immune to a powerful and influential argument that Boghossian has deployed to urge that this sort of parsimony must undercut itself and lapse into incoherence.[5] The general worry is that the force of deflationist claims depends on the contrast between predicates (such as '. . . has a mass of more than ten grams') that do, and those (such as '. . . is true') that do not, correspond to properties. Such contrasts seem to presuppose a robust correspondence theory of the contents of some predicates—at least those the semantic deflationist finds unproblematic, paradigmatically those of natural science. But consistently following out the rejection of robust correspondence theories of content requires treating using an expression as a predicate as all there is to expressing a property, and using a declarative sentence to make a true claim to be all there is to stating a fact. So on a deflationary construal, one is forbidden to deny that the predicate '. . . is true' denotes a property. In this way, theories that deny that truth is a property can be seen to be conceptually unstable.

Notice, however, that this argument depends on treating ". . . is true" as a predicate. If it is, then since that expression is used to make claims and state facts, it must, on deflationary accounts, be taken to express a property. But the essence of the anaphoric approach to truth talk is precisely to take issue with this grammatical presupposition. According to those accounts, ". . . is true" expresses a prosentence-forming operator. Its syntax and grammar are quite distinct from those of predicates, to which it bears only the sort of surface similarity that quantificational expressions bear to genuine singular terms. The part of speech ". . . is true" is assimilated to by these theories does not have a directly denotational semantics. Rather, tokenings formed using ". . . is true", but inherit their significance anaphorically, by an entirely distinct mechanism. So when it is claimed here that ". . . is true" does not express a property, this means that it is not even of the right grammatical form to do so—any more than 'no-one' is of the right form to pick out an individual, although there are some features of its use that could mislead one on this point. Further, this claim is not made ad hoc to avoid the sort of theoretical circularity Boghossian points out, but is motivated by ground-level considerations having to do with the unifying a variety of uses of 'true' and 'refers' in a theoretically perspicuous way.

Now *if* the *expressive* roles of 'true' and 'refers' are to be understood along these lines—and arguing that they *can* be so understood of course falls far short of showing that they *must* be—then one is precluded from making certain sorts of fundamental *explanatory* appeals to the notion of truth, and hence of truth conditions. In particular, I think that one cannot explain the notion of *anaphora* that is relied upon by broadly prosentential theories without appealing to an antecedent notion of *propositional content*—what in the simplest cases is inherited by a prosentence from its anaphoric antecedent. That is, one cannot entitle oneself to employ a notion of anaphora in one's semantic theory unless one is already entitled to use a notion of propositional content. Thus if one's explanation of 'true', and hence of truth conditions, is dependent upon a notion of anaphora, one cannot without circularity explain the notion of propositional contents in terms of truth or truth conditions.[6]

Now one *can* say of anything that has a propositional content that it has truth conditions. According to the prosentential approach, that will be true of anything that can be expressed by declarative sentences or the corresponding 'that' clauses. One will further be able to *express* propositional contents by saying what their truth conditions are. And this expressive role means further that one can even *explain* the meaning of unfamiliar locutions by *expressing* their truth conditions in terms of more familiar ones—as one would do in saying 'Schnee ist weiss' is true if and only if snow is white. But it is, according to the anaphoric account of the expressive role 'true', wrong (though tempting) to think that one can therefore explain what propositional contentfulness is in general in terms of possession of truth conditions. So deflationists ought to acknowledge the possibility of *expressing* semantic content truth-conditionally, while denying the possibility of *explaining* semantic content in general truth-conditionally. This result will be unpalatable insofar as one cannot see how else one might begin to think about contentfulness than in terms of truth conditions.[7]

Indeed, I suspect that appreciation of this point is partly responsible for the relative lack of attention that semantic theorists have paid to prosentential theories of 'true'. While it might be acknowledged that such theories are expressively adequate, in the absence of a convincing and independently available account of propositional contentfulness, and of anaphora, they are not evidently of much explanatory use. Prom this point of view, one of the virtues of the account developed in *Making It Explicit* is that it makes available an independent account of propositional content in terms of inferential roles—one that can be used to define anaphoric prosentences, and hence to say what one is *doing* in talking about truth and truth conditions. Similarly, the discussion of substitution inferences offers an account of the conceptual role of singular terms that is independent of and antecedent to any account of term *reference*—one that can be used to define anaphoric pro*nouns* by their inheritance of substitution-inferential roles from their antecedents, and hence to say what one is doing in using 'refers' talk.

The view put forward in *Making It Explicit* accordingly differs from previous 'deflationary' approaches to truth talk in a number of ways:

- The anaphoric theory, which sees 'true' and 'refers' as anaphoric proform-forming operators has technical and theoretical advantages over more standard disquotational approaches.
- It is not deflationary about the *expressive* role of these traditional semantic locutions. On the contrary, it seeks to codify in a unified fashion the ways in which this vocabulary lets us say things we could not say without it. These include the generalizations formulated by the quantificational uses of proforms, local explanations of content by specifying truth conditions, and the interpersonal conveying of information. *Expressive* deflationism is just wrong: Tarski showed us long ago that the addition of a truth-locution to a language strictly increases its expressive power,
- It is, rather, deflationary about the *explanatory* role of these locutions, in particular, their suitability for explaining what propositional contentfulness consists in.
- Far from being content with this merely negative posture, however, it faces head-on the constructive obligation of such explanatory deflationism: the obligation to produce a detailed alternative to explaining propositional contentfulness in terms of possession of truth conditions.

2

Indeed, the book consists of an extended response to this challenge. The project is oriented by a methodological commitment to explain the *meanings* of linguistic expressions in terms of their *use*. The explanatory strategy is to begin with an account of social practices, identify the particular structure they must exhibit in order to qualify as specifically *linguistic* practices, and then consider what different sorts of semantic contents those practices can confer on states, performances, and expressions caught up in them in suitable ways. The result is a new kind of conceptual role semantics. It is at once firmly rooted in actual practices of producing and consuming speech acts, and sufficiently finely articulated to make clear how those practices are capable of conferring a rich variety of kinds of content—not just *narrow* contents, but also *broad* contents. The pragmatic significances of different sorts of speech acts are rendered theoretically in terms of how those performances affect the commitments (and entitlements to those commitments) acknowledge or otherwise acquired by those whose performances they are. That is, the account of linguistic practice is couched in a normative metalanguage of *scorekeeping* on commitments and entitlements.

The next step is to say what structure such a set of social practices must have in order to qualify as specifically discursive practice. This is a matter of moving from pragmatics to semantics. The defining characteristic of discursive practice is the production and consumption of specifically propositional contents. It is argued that propositional contentfulness should be understood in terms of specifically *inferential* articulation; propositions are what can serve as premises and conclusions of inferences, that is, can serve as and stand in need of reasons. The fundamental speech act—the one whose presence is necessary and sufficient for the practices involved to qualify as *linguistic* practices—is *assertion.* Assertion is the staking of claims that are inferentially articulated in the basic sense of both standing in need of reasons and being fit to serve as reasons.

The notion of *substitution* and substitutional inferences is used to show how expressions such as singular terms and predicates, which cannot directly play the inferential role of premise or conclusion in an argument, nonetheless can play an indirectly inferential role in virtue of their systematic contributions to the directly inferential roles of sentences in which they occur. Then, the notion of anaphora (whose paradigm is the relation between a pronoun and its antecedent) and anaphoric inheritance of substitutional commitment is used to show how even unrepeatable expressions such as demonstrative tokenings play substitution-inferential roles, and hence express conceptual contents.

The result is a kind of *conceptual role semantics* that is distinguished first by the nature of the functional system with respect to which such roles are individuated and attributed: what is appealed to is role in the implicitly normative linguistic social practices of a community, rather than the behavioral economy of a single individual. This is what makes it possible to characterize broad content, and not merely narrow content. It is also different from familiar ways of using the notion of conceptual role in conceiving of the conceptual in terms of specifically inferential articulation, and in its elaboration of the fundamental substitutional and anaphoric substructures of that inferential articulation.

The major explanatory challenge for those who approach semantics from the side of inference is to explain the representational dimension of semantic content—to construe referential relations in terms of inferential ones. In *Making It Explicit*, the representational properties of semantic contents are explained as consequences of the essentially *social*, perspectival character of inferential practice. Words such as the 'of' that expresses intentional directedness, and 'about' and 'represents' in their philosophically significant uses, have the expressive role they do—making representational relations explicit—in virtue of the way they figure in *de re* ascriptions of propositional attitudes. These are the tropes used to say explicitly what someone is thinking *about*, what a belief *represents*, what a claim is true *of*. The strategy is to offer a discursive scorekeeping account of the practices that constitute using locutions to express such *de re* ascriptions, and hence of how expressions must be used in order to mean 'of', 'about', or 'represents'. This account of what is expressed by the fundamental explicitly representational locutions then makes possible an explanation of the *objectivity* of concepts. It takes the form of a specification of the particular sort of inferential structure social scorekeeping practices must have in order to institute objective norms—norms according to which the correctness of an application of a concept answers to the facts about the object to which it is applied, in such a way that anyone (indeed everyone) in the linguistic community may be wrong about it.

The relation of expression between what is implicit in what practitioners do and what is explicit in what they say structures the story at two different levels. At the basic level, the question is how the capacity to entertain principles—and so to know that something is the case—arises out of the capacity to engage in practices—to know how to do something in the sense of being able to do it. What must practitioners be able to do in order to be able thereby to say that things are thus and so, that is, to express something explicitly? The first level of the account of expression accordingly consists in explaining—making theoretically explicit—the implicit structure of linguistic practices in virtue of which they count as making anything explicit at all.

The second level of the account of expression consists in working out a theory of the expressive role distinctive of *logical* vocabulary. The claim is that logical vocabulary is distinguished by its function of expressing explicitly within a language the features of the use of that language that confer conceptual contents on the states, attitudes, performances, and expressions whose significances are governed by those practices. Conditionals serve as a paradigm illustrating this expressive role. According to the inferential approach to semantics and the deontic scorekeeping approach to pragmatics, practitioners confer determinate propositional contents on states and expressions in part by their scorekeeping practice of treating the acknowledgment of one doxastic commitment (typically through assertional utterance of a sentence) as having the pragmatic significance of an undertaking of further commitments that are related to the original commitment as its inferential consequences. At the basic level, treating the claim expressed by one sentence as an inferential consequence of the claim expressed by another sentence is something practitioners can do, and it is because such practical attitudes can be implicit in the way they respond to each other's performances that their sentences come to mean what they do. With the introduction of conditional locutions linking sentences, however, comes the expressive power to say explicitly that one claim is a consequence of another. The expressive role distinctive of conditionals is making implicit inferential commitments explicit in the form of declarative sentences—sentences the assertion of which acknowledges a propositionally contentful doxastic commitment. In a similar way, at the basic level, scorekeepers can treat the claims expressed by two sentences as incompatible: namely by treating commitment to one as in practice precluding entitlement to the other. The introduction of a locution with the expressive power of negation makes it possible to express such implicit practical scorekeeping attitudes explicitly—by saying that two claims are incompatible (one entails the negation of the other). Identity and quantificational expressions are analyzed on this model as making explicit the substitutional relations characteristic of singular terms and predicates respectively, and further locutions are considered that play a corresponding expressive role in making anaphoric relations explicit.

So the book presents an *expressive theory of logic*. On this view, the philosophical significance of logic is not that it enables those who master the use of logical locutions to *prove* a special class of claims—that is, to entitle themselves to a class of commitments in a formally privileged fashion. The significance of logical vocabulary lies rather in what it lets those who master it *say*—the special class of claims it enables them to *express*. Logical vocabulary endows practitioners with the expressive power to make explicit as the contents of claims just those implicit features of linguistic practice that confer semantic contents on their utterances in the first place. Logic is the organ of semantic self-consciousness. It brings out into the light of day the practical attitudes that determine the conceptual contents members of a linguistic community are able to express—putting them in the form of explicit claims, which can be debated, for which reasons can be given and alternatives proposed and assessed. The formation of concepts—by means of which practitioners can come to be aware of anything at all—comes itself to be something of which those who can deploy logical vocabulary can be aware. Since plans can be addressed to, and intentional practical influenced exercised over, just those features of things of which agents can become explicitly aware by the application of concepts, the formation of concepts itself becomes in this way for the first time an object of conscious deliberation and control.

Explaining the features of the use of logical vocabulary that confer its characteristic sort of semantic content is accordingly explaining how the sort of expressive power the theorist requires to explain the features of the use of nonlogical vocabulary that confer semantic content on it can become available to those whose linguistic practice is being theorized about. It is this fact that sets the expressive scope of the project. The aim is twofold: to make explicit deontic score-keeping social practices that suffice to confer conceptual contents on nonlogical sentences, singular terms, and predicates in general, and to make explicit the deontic scorekeeping social practices in virtue of which vocabulary can be introduced as playing the expressive roles characteristic of a variety of particular logical locutions. How much logical vocabulary is worth reconstructing in this fashion? Neither more nor less than is required to make explicit within the language the deontic scorekeeping social practices that suffice to confer conceptual contents on nonlogical vocabulary in general. At that point it has been specified what practices a theorist must attribute to a community in order to be interpreting its members as engaging not just in specifically linguistic practices, but in linguistic practices that endow them with sufficient expressive power to say how their practices confer conceptual content on their states, attitudes, performances, and expressions. That is, they can express the pragmatic and semantic theory of the book. Along this expressive dimension, the project eats its own tail, or lifts itself up by its own bootstraps—presenting an explanation of what it is to say something that is powerful enough to explain what it itself is saying.

It is as part of this project that an account is offered of the crucial anaphoric expressive role played by traditional semantic vocabulary: paradigmatically, 'true' and 'refers' or 'denotes'. Doing so requires the whole pragmatically grounded semantic apparatus of *inferential* relations among the claimables expressed by sentences, inferentially significant *substitutional* relations among the conceptual structures expressed by subsentential expressions such as singular terms and predicates, and the substitutionally significant *anaphoric* relations among unrepeatable tokenings that make possible such fundamental features of empirical discourse as deixis and indexicality. According to this story, 'true' and 'refers' are bits of logical vocabulary that make explicit essential features of the complex process of coordinating our linguistic scorekeeping so as to be able to extract inferentially useful information from the remarks of those whose commitments differ from ours. What we say using traditional semantic vocabulary cannot be said without it. But one of the basic lessons of the whole story is that we understand that vocabulary best if it makes its appearance near the end of our semantic explanations, rather than near the beginning.

Notes

1. Harvard University Press, 1994.
2. The version of the anaphoric approach that is developed in Chapter Five of *Making It Explicit* differs from the original prosentential theory in seeing locutions like ". . . is true" as prosentence-forming operators, which can attach to a whole variety of singular terms that serve to specify the class of anaphoric antecedents. Some are quote names of the antecedents, others are descriptions, or indexicals picking them out, sentence nominalization, and so on.
3. Of course it is possible for broadly disquotational approaches to find a place for quantificational uses of 'true'. Nonetheless, these uses are incorporated in a more natural way in the prosentential approach, by means of the analogy between lazy and quantificational uses of pro*nouns*.
4. I provide the details in Chapter Five of *Making It Explicit*.
5. Paul Boghossian, "The Status of Content", *The Philosophical Review*, April, 1990. I have in mind the argument epitomized on p. 181 in the claim that: ". . . the denial that a given predicate refers to or expresses a property only makes sense on a robust construal of predicate reference. . . . But if this is correct, the denial, is that the truth predicate refers to a property, must itself be understood as framed in terms of a robust notion of reference. . . ."
6. This argument is reminiscent of one Dummett offers against the availability of truth—conditional semantic theories to those endorsing redundancy theories of truth. I think there is something to the analogy, but I think the particular role assigned to the notion of anaphora makes this is a good argument, while I am not convinced that Dummett's is.
7. Thus Boghossian, for instance, just *assumes* that content must be understood in terms of truth conditions [op. cit., p. 173]. It should not be surprising that those who start from such a presupposition then find theories that take a deflationary attitude toward the explanatory use of 'true' insupportable.

Price argues, against Rorty-style views, that the concept of truth is an indispensable component of cognitive and social life.

HUW PRICE

Truth as Convenient Friction

In a recent paper, Richard Rorty[1] begins by telling us why pragmatists such as himself are inclined to identify truth with justification:

> Pragmatists think that if something makes no difference to practice, it should make no difference to philosophy. This conviction makes them suspicious of the distinction between justification and truth, for that distinction makes no difference to my decisions about what to do. (*ibid.*, p. 19)

Rorty goes on to discuss the claim, defended by Crispin Wright, that truth is a normative constraint on assertion. He argues that this claim runs afoul of this principle of no difference without a practical difference:

> The need to justify our beliefs and desires to ourselves and to our fellow agents subjects us to norms, and obedience to these norms produces a behavioral pattern that we must detect in others before confidently attributing beliefs to them. But there seems no occasion to look for obedience to an *additional* norm—the commandment to seek the truth. For—to return to the pragmatist doubt with which I began—obedience to that commandment will produce no behavior not produced by the need to offer justification. (*ibid.*, p. 26)

Again, then, Rorty appeals to the claim that a commitment to a norm of truth rather than a norm of justification makes no behavioral difference.

This is an empirical claim, testable in principle by comparing the behavior of a community of realists (in Rorty's sense) to that of a community of pragmatists. In my view, the experiment would show that the claim is unjustified, indeed, false. I think that there is an important and widespread behavioral pattern that depends on the fact that speakers do take themselves to be subject to such an additional norm. Moreover, it is a behavioral pattern so central to what we presently regard as a worthwhile human life that no reasonable person would knowingly condone the experiment. Ironically, it is also a pattern that Rorty of all people cannot afford to dismiss as a pathological and dispensable by-product of bad philosophy. For it is conversation itself, or at any rate a central and indispensable part of conversation as we know it—roughly, interpersonal dialogue about "factual" matters.[2]

In other words, I want to maintain that in order to account for a core part of ordinary conversational practice, we must allow that speakers take themselves and their fellows to be governed by a norm stronger than that of justification. Not only is this a norm which speakers acknowledge they may fail to meet, even if their claims are well justified—this much is true of what Rorty calls the *cautionary* use of truth[3]—but also, more significantly, it is a norm which speakers immediately assume to be breached by someone with whom they disagree, *independently of any diagnosis of the source of the disagreement*. Indeed, this is the very essence of the norm of truth, in my view. It gives disagreement its immediate normative character, a character on which dialogue depends, and a character which no lesser norm could provide.

This fact about truth has been overlooked, I think, because the norm in question is *so* familiar, so much a given of ordinary linguistic practice, that it is very hard to see. Ordinarily we look through it, rather than at it. In order to make it visible, we need a sense of how things would be different without it. Hence, in part, my reason for beginning with Rorty. Although I disagree with Rorty about the behavioral consequences of a commitment to "a distinction between justification and truth," I think that the issue of the behavioral consequences of such a commitment embodies precisely the perspective we need, in order to bring into focus this fundamental aspect of the normative structure of dialogue.

In sharing Rorty's concern with the role of truth in linguistic practice, I share one key element of his pragmatism. But my kind of pragmatism about truth is not well marked on contemporary maps, and hence my second reason for beginning with Rorty. Rorty has explored the landscape of pragmatist approaches to truth more extensively than most pragmatist writers, past or present, and at different times has been inclined to settle in different parts of it. By locating my own kind of pragmatism with respect to views that Rorty has visited or canvassed, I hope to show that there is a promising position that he and others pragmatists have overlooked.

As noted, my view rests on the claim that a norm of truth plays an essential and little-recognized role in assertoric dialogue. In pursuit of this conclusion, it will turn out to be helpful to distinguish three norms, in order of increasing strength, roughly: sincerity, justification, and truth itself. Though somewhat crudely drawn, these distinctions will suffice to throw into relief the crucial role of the third norm in linguistic practice. My strategy will be to contrast assertion as we know it with some nonassertoric uses of language. In these latter cases, I will argue, the two weaker norms still apply. Moreover, it turns out that some of the basic functions of assertoric discourse could be fulfilled in an analogous way, by a practice which lacked the third norm. But it will be clear, I hope, that that practice would not support dialogue as we know it. What is missing—what the third norm provides—is the automatic and quite unconscious sense of engagement in common purpose that distinguishes assertoric dialogue from a mere roll call of individual opinion. Truth is the grit that makes our individual opinions engage with one another. Truth puts the cogs in cognition, at least in its public manifestations.[4]

To use a Rylean metaphor, my view is thus that truth supplies factual dialogue with its essential esprit de corps. As the metaphor is meant to suggest, what matters is that speakers think that there is such a norm—that they take themselves to be governed by it—not that their view be somehow confirmed by science or metaphysics. Science has already done its work, in pointing out the function of the thought in the lives of creatures like us. This may suggest that a commitment to truth is like a commitment to theism, an analogy which Rorty himself draws, against Wright, in the paper with which I began. In effect, Rorty's point is that it is one thing to establish that we do employ a realist notion of truth, a normative notion stronger than justification; quite another to establish that we ought to do so. As in the case of theism, we might do better to wean ourselves of bad realist habits.

There are several important differences between the two cases, however. First, the behavioral consequences of giving up theism are significant but hardly devastating.[5] But if I am right about the behavioral role of truth, the consequences of giving up truth would be very serious indeed, reducing the conversation of mankind to a chatter of disengaged monologues.[6]

Second, it is doubtful whether giving up truth is really an option open to us. I suspect that people who think it is an option have not realized how deeply embedded the idea of truth is in linguistic practice, and therefore underestimate the extent of the required change in two ways. They fail to see how radically different from current practice a linguistic practice without truth would have to be, and they overestimate our capacity to change our practices in general to move from here to there (underestimating the practical inflexibility of admittedly contingent practices).[7]

Third, and most interestingly of all, the issue of the status of truth is enmeshed with the terms of the problem, in a way which is quite uncharacteristic of the theism case. Metaphysical conclusions tend to be cast in semantic vocabulary. Theism is said to be in error in virtue of the fact that its claims are not *true*, that its terms fail to *refer*. For this reason, it is uniquely difficult to formulate a meaningful antirealism about the semantic terms themselves. In my view the right response to this is not to think (with Paul Boghossian)[8] that we thereby have a transcendental argument for semantic realism. Without an intelligible denial, realism is no more intelligible than antirealism. The right response—as Rorty himself in any case urges—is to be suspicious of the realist-antirealist debate itself.[9] Rorty, however, ties rejection of the realist-antirealist debate to rejection of a notion of truth distinct from justification, and of the idea of representation. I think this is the wrong path to the right conclusion. We should reject the metaphysical stance not by rejecting truth and representation, but by recognizing that in virtue of the most plausible story about the function and origins of these notions, they simply do not sustain that sort of metaphysical weight.

Concerning his own view of truth, Rorty describes himself as oscillating between Jamesian pragmatism, on the one hand, and deflationism, on the other: "swing[ing] back and forth between trying to reduce truth to justification and propounding some form of minimalism about truth."[10] My own view is neither of these alternatives, but has something in common with each. On the one hand, it is certainly some sort of minimalism about truth, but not the familiar sort that Rorty has in mind—not "Tarski's breezy disquotationalism," as he calls it (*ibid.*, p. 21). I agree with familiar disquotationalist minimalists such as W. V. Quine[11] and Paul Horwich[12] that truth is not a substantial property, about the nature of which there is an interesting philosophical issue. Like them, I think that the right approach to truth is to investigate its function in human discourse—to ask what difference it makes to us to have such a concept. Unlike such minimalists, however, I do not think the right answer to this question is that truth is merely a grammatical device for disquotation. I think that it has a far more important function, which requires that it be the expression of a norm. But like other minimalists, again, I think that there is no further question of interest to philosophy, once the question about function has been answered.

On the other hand, my view of truth is also pragmatist, for it explicates truth in terms of its role in practice. (This is also true of standard disquotational views, of course, although they ascribe the truth predicate a different role in practice.) In another sense, it conflicts with pragmatism, for it opposes the proposal that we identify truth with justification. This contrast reflects a deep tension within pragmatism. From Peirce and James on, pragmatists have often been unable to resist the urge to join their opponents in asking "What is truth?" (Indeed, the pragmatist position as a whole is often characterized in terms of its answer to this question.) Pragmatism thus turns its back on alternative paths to philosophical illumination about truth, even though these alternative paths—explanatory and genealogical approaches—are at least compatible with, if not mandated by, the pragmatist doctrine that we understand problematic notions in terms of their practical significance.

Rorty himself is well aware of this tension within pragmatism. In "Pragmatism, Davidson, and Truth," for example (*op. cit.*), he notes that James is less prone than Peirce to try to answer the "ontological" or reductive question about truth, and suggests that Davidson may be thought of as a pragmatist in the preferable nonreductive sense.[13] As he swings between pragmatism and deflationism, then, Rorty himself is at worst only intermittently subject to this craving for an *analysis* of truth. All the same, it seems to me that he is never properly aware of the range of possibilities for nonreductive pragmatism about truth. In particular, he is not properly aware of the possibility that such a pragmatism might find itself explaining the fact that the notion of truth in ordinary use is (and perhaps ought to be, in whatever sense we might make of this) one that conflicts with the identification of truth with justification: a normative goal of inquiry, stronger than any norm of justification, of the very kind that realists about truth—opponents both of pragmatism and of minimalism—mistakenly sought to analyze. In other words, Rorty seems to miss the possibility that the right thing for the explanatory pragmatist to say might be that truth is a goal of inquiry distinct from norms of justification, and that the realist's mistake is to try to *analyze* this normative notion, rather than simply to investigate its function and genealogy. It is this latter possibility that I want to defend.

I. Falsity and Lesser Evils

As I have said, I want to argue that truth plays a crucial role as a norm of assertoric discourse. It is not the only such norm, however, and a good way to highlight the distinctive role of truth is to distinguish certain weaker norms, and to imagine a linguistic practice which had those norms but not truth.[14] By seeing what such a practice lacks, we see what truth adds.

There are at least two weaker norms of assertion, in addition to any distinctive norm of truth.[15] The weakest relevant norm seems to be that embodied in the principle that it is prima facie appropriate to assert that *p* only when one believes that *p*—prima facie, because of course many other factors may come into play in determining the appropriateness of a particular assertion in a particular context. Let us call this the norm of *subjective assertibility*.[16] The norm is perhaps best characterized in negative form—that is, in terms of the conditions under which a speaker may be censured for failing to meet it:

> (Subjective assertibility) A speaker is incorrect to assert that *p* if she does not believe that *p*; to assert that *p* in these circumstances provides prima facie grounds for censure, or disapprobation.

The easiest way to see that this norm has very little to do with truth is to note that it is analogous to norms which operate with respect to utterances which we do not take to be truth apt. Prima facie, it is inappropriate to request a cup of coffee when one does not want a cup of coffee, but this does not show that requests or expressions of desires are subject to a norm of truth. In effect, this norm is simply that of sincerity, and some such norm seems to govern much conventional behavior. Conventions often depend on the fact that communities censure those who break them in this specific sense, by acting in bad faith.

The second norm is that of (personal) *warranted assertibility*. Roughly, '*p*' is warrantedly assertible by a speaker who not only believes that *p*, but is *justified* in doing so. The qualification 'personal' recognizes the fact that there are different kinds and degrees of warrant or justification, some of them more subjective than others. For example, is justification to be assessed with reference to a speaker's actual evidence as she (presently?) sees it, or by some less subjective lights? For the moment, for a degree of definiteness, let us think of it in terms of subjective coherence—a belief is justified if supported by a speaker's other current beliefs. This is what I shall mean by *personal* warranted assertibility.

Again, this second norm is usefully characterized in negative or censure form:

> (Personal warranted assertibility) A speaker is incorrect to assert that *p* if she does not have adequate (personal) grounds for believing that *p*; to assert that *p* in these circumstances provides prima facie grounds for censure.

A person who meets both the norms just identified may be said to have done as much as possible, *by her own current lights*, to ensure that her assertion that *p* is in order. Obviously, realists will say that her assertion may nevertheless be incorrect. Subjective assertibility and (personal) warranted assertibility do not guarantee truth. To an extent, moreover, most pragmatists are likely to agree. Few people who advocate reducing truth to (or replacing truth by) a notion of warranted assertibility have personal warranted assertibility in mind. Rather, they imagine some more objective, community-based variant, according to which a belief is justified if it coheres appropriately with the other beliefs of one's community. If we call this *communal* warranted assertibility, then the point is that we can make sense of a gap between the personal and communal notions. A belief may be justified in one sense but not the other.

Pragmatists and realists may thus agree that there is a normative dimension distinct from subjective assertibility and personal warranted assertibility—an assertion may be *wrong*, despite meeting these norms. This does not yet establish that the normative standard in question need be marked in ordinary discourse. In principle, it might be a privileged or theoretical notion, useful in expert second-order reflection on linguistic practice but unnecessary in folk talk about other matters. In practice, however, there seems a very good reason why it should not remain restricted in this way. Unless individual speakers recognize such a norm, the idea that they might *improve* their views by consultation with the wider community is simply incoherent to them. (It would be as if we gave a student full marks in an exam, and then told him that he would have done better if his answers had agreed with those of other students.)

It may seem that as yet, this argument does not favor realism over pragmatism. If the normative standard an individual speaker needs to acknowledge is that of the community as a whole, there is as yet no pressure to a notion of truth beyond community-wide warranted assertibility. But what constitutes the relevant community? At any given stage, is not the relation of a given community to its possible present and future extensions just like that of the individual to her community? If so, then the same argument applies at this level. At each stage, the actual community needs to recognize that it may be wrong by the standards of some broader community.[17]

The pragmatist might now seem obliged to follow Peirce, in identifying truth with warranted assertibility in the ideal limit of inquiry. The useful thing about this limit, in this context, is that it transcends any actual community. But in my view, as I will explain below (and as Rorty in some moods already case agrees), a better move for a pragmatist is to resist the pressure to *identify* truth with anything—in other words, simply to reject the assumption that an adequate philosophical account of truth needs to answer the question "What is truth?" Better questions for a pragmatist to ask are the explanatory ones: Why do we have such a notion? What job does it do in language? What features does it need to have to play this role? And how would things be different if we did not have it?

For the moment, we have the beginnings of an answer to the last question. If we did not have a normative notion in addition to the norms of subjective assertibility and personal warranted assertibility, the idea that we might improve our commitments by seeking to align them with those of our community would be simply incoherent. I will call this the *passive* account of the role of the third norm—passive, because it does not yet provide an active or causal role for a commitment to truth. Later, I will argue that the third norm not only creates the conceptual space for argument, in this passive sense, but actively encourages speakers to participate.[18]

II. The Third Norm in Focus

The best way to bring the third norm into focus is again to consider its negative or censure form:

(Truth) If not-*p*, then it is *incorrect* to assert that *p*; if not-*p*, there are prima facie grounds for censure of an assertion that *p*.

The important point is that this provides a norm of assertion which we take it that a speaker may fail to meet, even if she does meet the norms of subjective assertibility and (personal) warranted assertibility. We are prepared to make the judgment that a speaker is *incorrect*, or *mistaken*, in this sense, simply on the basis that we are prepared to make a contrary assertion; in advance, in other words, of any judgment that she fails to meet one or other of the two weaker norms.[19]

One of the reasons why this third norm is hard to distinguish from the two weaker norms of assertibility is that when we apply it in judging a fellow speaker right or wrong, the basis for our judgment lies in our own beliefs and evidence. It is not as though we are in a position to make the judgment from the stance of reality itself, as it were. I think this can make it seem as if application of this norm involves nothing more than reassertion of the original claim (in the case in which we judge it correct), or assertion of the negation of the original claim (in the case in which we judge it incorrect). Construed in these terms, our response contains nothing problematic for orthodox disquotational versions of the deflationary view, of course. Reassertion of this sort is precisely one of the linguistic activities which disquotational truth facilitates. Construed in these terms, then, there is no need for truth to be a distinct *norm*.

Our response is not merely reassertion, or assertion of the negation of the original claim, however. If it were, it would involve no commendation or criticism of the original utterance. This nonnormative alternative is hard to see, I think, because the norm in question is so familiar and so basic. As a result, it is difficult to see the immense difference the norm makes to the character of disagreements. But it comes into focus, I think, if we allow ourselves to imagine a linguistic practice which allowed reassertion and contrary assertion, but without this third normative dimension. What we need to imagine, in other words, is a linguistic community who use sentences to express their beliefs, and have a purely disquotational truth predicate, but for whom disagreements have no normative significance, except insofar as it is related to the weaker norms of assertibility.

This imaginative project is not straightforward, of course. Indeed, it is not clear that it is entirely coherent. If there is a third norm of the kind in question, is not it likely to be constitutive of the very notions of assertion and belief? If so, what sense is there in trying to imagine an assertoric practice which lacked this norm?

Well, let us see. What we need is the idea of a community who take an assertion—or rather the closest thing they have to what we call an assertion—to be *merely* an expression of the speaker's opinion. The relevant idea is familiar in the case of expressions of desires and preferences. It is easy to imagine a community—we are at least close to it ourselves—who have a language in which they give voice to psychological states of these kinds, not by *reporting* that they hold them (which would depend on assertion), but directly, in conventional linguistic forms tailored specifically for this purpose.

Think of a community who use language primarily for expressing preferences in restaurants, for example. (Perhaps the development of such a restricted language from scratch is incoherent, but surely we might approach it from the other direction. Imagine a community of dedicated lunchers, whose language atrophies to the bare essentials.) In this community we would expect a norm analogous to subjective assertibility: essentially, a normative requirement that speakers use these conventional expressions sincerely. Less obviously, such a practice might also involve a norm analogous to personal warranted assertibility. In other words, expressed preferences might be censured on the grounds that they were not well founded, by the speaker's own lights (for example, on the grounds they did not cohere with the speaker's other preferences and desires). In this practice there need be no place for a norm analogous to truth, however—no idea of an objective standard, over and above personal warranted assertibility, which preferences properly aim to meet.

At least to a first approximation, we can imagine a community who treat expressions of beliefs in the same way. They express their beliefs—that is, let us say, the kind of behavioral dispositions which we would characterize as beliefs—by means of a speech act we might call the *merely-opinionated assertion* (MOA, for short). These speakers—"Mo'ans," as I called them in another article[20]—criticize each other for insincerity and for lack of coherence, or personal warranted assertibility. But they go no further than this. In particular, they do not treat a disagreement between two speakers as an indication that, necessarily, one speaker or the other is mistaken—in violation of some norm. On the contrary, they allow that in such a case it may turn out that both speakers have spoken correctly, by the only two standards the community takes to be operable. Both may be sincere, and both, in their own terms, may have good grounds for their assertion.[21]

A speech community of this imagined kind could make use of a disquotational truth predicate, as a device to facilitate agreement with an expression of opinion made by another speaker. 'That's true' would function much like 'Same again', or 'Ditto', used in a bar or restaurant. Just as 'Same again' serves to indicate that one has the same preference as a previous speaker, 'That's true' would serve to indicate that one holds the same opinion as the previous speaker. The crucial point is that if the only norms in play are subjective assertibility and personal warranted assertibility, introducing disquotational truth leaves everything as it is. It does not import a third norm.

The difficulty we have in holding on to the idea of such a community stems from our almost irresistible urge to see the situation in terms of our own normative standards. There really is a third norm, we are inclined to think, even if these simple creatures do not know it. If two of them make incompatible assertions then one of them must be objectively incorrect, even if by their lights they both meet the only norms they themselves recognize. (I think even pragmatists will be inclined to say this, even though they want to equate the relevant kind of incorrectness not with falsity but with lack of some kind of justification more objective than that of personal warrant.) But the point of the story is precisely to bring this third norm into sharp relief, and hence I am quite happy to allow challenges to the story on these grounds, which rely on the very conclusion I want to draw. *For us*, there is a third norm. But why is that so? Where does the third norm come from? What job does it do—what difference does it make to our lives? And what features must it have in order to do this job?

III. What Difference Does the Third Norm Make?

Let us return to the Mo'ans, and their merely-opinionated assertions. Recall that Mo'ans use linguistic utterances to express their "beliefs," as well as other psychological states, such as preferences and desires. Where they differ from us is in the fact that they do not take a disagreement between two speakers in this belief-expressing linguistic dimension to indicate that one or another speaker must be at fault. They recognize the possibility of fault consisting in failure to observe one of the two norms of subjective assertibility or personal warranted assertibility, but lack the idea of the third norm, that of truth itself. This shows up in the fact that by default, disagreements are of a no-fault kind, in the way that expressions of different preferences often are for us.

What does it take to add the third norm to such a practice? Do the Mo'ans need to come to believe that there is a substantial property that the attitudes they use MOAs to express may have or lack—perhaps the property of corresponding to how things are in the world, perhaps that of being what their opinions are fated to converge on in the long run? Does adoption of the third norm depend on a piece of folk metaphysics of this kind? Not at all, in my view. The practice the Mo'ans need to adopt is simply that whenever they are prepared to assert (in the old MOA sense) that *p*, they also be prepared to ascribe fault to anyone who asserts not-*p*, independently of any grounds for thinking that that person fails one of the first two norms of assertibility. Perhaps they also need to be prepared to commend anyone who asserts that *p*, or perhaps failure-to-find-fault is motivation enough in this case. At any rate, what matters is that disagreement itself be treated as grounds for disapproval, as grounds for thinking that one's interlocutor has fallen short of some normative standard.

At this point it is worth noting what may seem a serious difficulty. If the Mo'ans do not *already* care about disagreements, why should they care about disagreements about normative matters? Suppose that we two are Mo'ans, that you assert that *p*, and that I assert that not-*p*. If this initial disagreement does not bother me, why should it bother me when—trying to implement the third norm—you go on to assert that I am "at fault," or "incorrect"? Again, I simply disagree; and if the former disagreement does not bite then nor will the latter. And if what was needed to motivate me to resolve our disagreement was *my* acceptance that I am "at fault," then motivation would always come too late. If I accept this at all, it is only after the fact—after the disagreement has been resolved in your favor.

To get the sequence right, then, I must be motivated by your disapproval itself. This is an important point. It shows that if there could be an assertoric practice which lacked the third norm, we could not add that norm simply by adding a normative predicate. Insofar—so very far, in my view—as terms such as 'true' and 'false' carry this normative force in natural languages, they must be giving voice to something more basic: a fundamental practice of expressions of attitudes of approval and disapproval, in response to perceptions of agreement and disagreement between expressed commitments. I will return to this point, for it is the basis of an important objection to certain other accounts of truth.

Imagine for the moment that the Mo'ans could add the third norm by adding a normative predicate, or pair of predicates ('correct' and 'incorrect', say). What would be the usage rule for these predicates? Simply that one be prepared to assert that p is correct if and only if one is prepared to assert that p; and to assert that p is incorrect if and only if one is prepared to assert that not-p. In other words, the usage rule is something very close to the disquotational schema ('p' is true if and only if p). As a result, the present proposal, that the truth predicate is an explicit expression of the third norm, already seems well on the way to an explanation of the disquotational functions of truth. We have already noted that the converse argument does not go through. A practice which lacked the third norm could still make use of a disquotational truth predicate.[22]

For the moment, we are interested in the function of the third norm. Why might the invention of such a norm be useful? What distinctive job does it do? We already have one answer to the latter question, and hence possibly to the former, in the passive account. Without a norm stronger than that of warranted assertibility *for me*, or *for us*, the idea of improving *my*, or *our*, current commitments would be incoherent. The third norm functions to create the conceptual space for the idea of further improvement. To do this job, we need a norm stronger than that of warranted assertibility for any *actual* community. (Of course, this does not yet show that we need something more than Peircean ideal assertibility, but one thing at a time.)

We can do better than the passive account, however. The third norm does not just hold open the conceptual space for the idea of improvement. It positively encourages such improvement, by motivating speakers who disagree to try to resolve their disagreement. Without the third norm, differences of opinion would simply slide past one another. Differences of opinion would seem as inconsequential as differences of preference. With the third norm, however, disagreement automatically becomes normatively loaded. The third norm makes what would otherwise be no-fault disagreements into unstable social situations, whose instability is only resolved by argument and consequent agreement—and it provides an immediate incentive for argument, in that it holds out to the successful arguer the reward consisting in her community's positive evaluation of her dialectical position. If reasoned argument is generally beneficial—beneficial in some long-run sense—then a community of Mo'ans who adopt this practice will tend to prosper, compared to a community who do not.

I will call this the *active* account of the role of the third norm. In effect, it contends that the fact that speakers take their belief-expressing utterances to be subject to the third norm plays a causal, carrot-and-stick role in encouraging them to settle their differences, in cases in which initially they disagree. The force of these carrots and sticks should not be overstated, however. In any given case, we are free not to give voice to our third-norm-grounded disapproval. If we do express it, the speakers with whom we disagree are free not to rise to the bait. Many factors may determine what happens in any particular case. My claim is simply that the third norm adds something new to the preferential mix. In particular, it gives rise to a new preferential pressure toward resolution of the disagreement in question—a pressure which would not exist in its absence, which does not exist for the Mo'ans, and which could not exist for us, if we did not care in general about the approval and disapproval of our fellows. The third norm depends on the fact that (to varying extents in varying circumstances) we do care about these things. It exploits this fact about us to make disagreements matter, in a way in which they would not otherwise matter. But the third norm does not come for free, with a general disposition to seek the approval of our fellows. What we have but the Mo'ans lack is an additional, special purpose, disposition: the disposition to disapprove of speakers with whom we disagree. This disposition is the mark of the third norm.

As in the case of the passive account of the role of the third norm, we need to be careful that this active account does not viciously presuppose the very notions for which it seeks to account. The notion of disagreement requires particular care. For one thing, recognition that one differs from a previous speaker must take some form more basic than the belief that he or she has said something "false," for otherwise there could not be a convention of applying this normative predicate when one perceives that one differs. For another, there is an important sense in which, on the proposed account, it is the practice of applying the third norm which creates the disagreement, where initially there was mere difference. Properly developed, the view seems likely to be something like this. There is a primitive incompatibility between certain behavioral commitments[23] of a single individual, which turns on the impossibility of both doing and not doing any given action A—both having and not having a cup of coffee, for example. All else—both the public perceived incompatibility of "conflicting" assertions by different speakers, and the private perceived incompatibility essential to reasoning—is by convention, and depends on the third norm.

Obviously, much more needs to be said about this. At another level, much also needs to be said about the possible advantages of such a mechanism for resolving differences—about its long-run advantages, for example, both compared to the case in which there is no such mechanism and compared to the case in which there is some different mechanism, such as deference to social rank. For immediate purposes, however, my claim does not depend on this latter work. For the present, my claim is simply that truth does play the role of this third norm, in providing the friction characteristic of factual dialogue as we know it. (I also claim, roughly, that this is perhaps the most interesting fact about truth, from a philosophical perspective.) In principle, this claim could be true, even though the practice in question was not advantageous. In principle, truth, and with it dialogue, could turn out to be a bad thing for the species, biologically considered.[24] No matter; it would still be true that we would not have understood truth until we understood its role in this debilitating practice.

Is talk of dialogue really essential here? Could not we say simply that the third norm is what distinguishes a genuinely assertoric linguistic practice from the "merely opinionated" assertoric practice of the Mo'ans? The distinguishing mark of genuine assertion is thus that by default, difference is taken as a sign of *fault*, of breach of a normative standard.

It would not strictly be incorrect to say this, in my view, but it ought to seem unsatisfying, by pragmatist lights. A pragmatist is interested in the practical significance of the notions of truth and falsity, in the issue of what difference possession of these notions makes to our lives. According to the view just suggested, the answer will be something like this. The difference that truth and falsity make is that they make our linguistic practice genuinely assertoric, rather than Mo'an. "I see that," the pragmatist will then say, "But what practical difference does *that* difference make, over and above the obvious difference—that is, over and above the fact that we approve and disapprove of some of our fellow speakers on occasions on which we would not otherwise do so?"

My own answer to the new question is that these habits of approval and disapproval tend to encourage dialogue, by providing speakers with an incentive to resolve disagreements. It is true that at this point the pragmatist's question—"What difference does *that* make?"—can be (indeed, should be) asked all over again. The importance I have here attached to dialogue rests in part on the gamble that this question will turn out to have an interesting answer, in terms of the long-run advantages of pooled cognitive resources, agreement on shared projects, and so on. But not entirely. Dialogue seems such a central part of our linguistic and social lives that the difference between a world without dialogue and our world is much greater than *merely* the difference between MOAs and genuine assertions. So even if it were to turn out that the development of dialogue had been an historical accident, of no great value to the species biologically considered, it would still be true that the most interesting behavioral consequence of the third norm would be dialogue, and not merely the more-than-merely-Mo'an assertion which makes dialogue possible.[25]

Recall that I began by challenging Rorty's claim that no behavioral consequences flow from a distinction between justification and truth. In one sense, my challenge does indeed amount to pointing out that the third norm—a notion of truth stronger than justification—brings with it the following behavioral difference: a disposition to criticize, or at least disapprove of, those with whom one disagrees. But if this were all the challenge amounted to, Rorty would be entitled to reply that of course there is this difference, but that this difference makes no interesting further difference. Hence the importance of dialogue, in my view, which turns a small difference in normative practice into a big difference in the way in which speakers engage with one another (and thereby ensures that Rorty's claim fails in an interesting rather than an insignificant way).

IV. Peirce Regained?

Now to the question deferred above. Does the third norm need to be other than a more-than-merely-personal notion of justification? In particular, could not it be a Peircean flavor of ideal warranted assertibility? I have several responses to this suggestion.

First, I think that the proposal is mistakenly motivated. As I said in the introduction, I think it stems from the tendency, still too strong in Peirce, to ask the wrong question about truth. If we think that the philosophical issue is "What is truth?" then naturally we will want to find an answer—something with which we may identify truth. Then, given standard objections to metaphysical answers, it is understandable that Peirce's alternative should seem attractive. But the attraction is that of methadone compared to heroin. Far better, surely, from a pragmatist's point of view, to rid ourselves of the craving for analysis altogether. To do this, we need to see that the basic philosophical needs that analysis seemed to serve can be met in another mode altogether: by explanation of the practices, rather than reduction of their objects. (Moreover, the explanatory project has the potential to allow us realist truth without the metaphysical disadvantages. The apparent disadvantages of realist truth emerge in the light of the reductive project, for it is from this perspective that it seems mysterious what truth could be. If we no longer feel obliged to ask the question, we will not be troubled by the fact that it is so hard to answer. We lose the motivation for seeking something else—something less "mysterious" than correspondence—with which to identify truth.)

"I accept all that," the pragmatist might say. "Nevertheless, perhaps it is true of the notion of truth (as we find it in practice), that it is identical (in some interesting sense) to ideal warranted assertibility. Should you not therefore allow, at least, the possibility that a Peircean account is the correct one?"

Two points in response to this: the first, an old objection, is that it is very unclear what the notion of the ideal limit might amount to, or even that it is coherent. For example, could not actual practice be improved or idealized in several dimensions, not necessarily consistent with one another? In this sense, then, the Peircean pragmatist seems a long way from offering us a concrete proposal.[26]

The second point—also an old point, for as Hilary Putnam observes, it is essentially the naturalistic fallacy[27]—concerns the nature of the proposed identification of truth with ideal warranted assertibility. Truth is essentially a normative notion. Its role in making disagreements matter depends on its immediate motivational character. Why should ideal warranted assertibility have this character? If someone tells me that my beliefs are not those of our infinitely refined future inquirers, why should that bother me? My manners are not those of the palace, but so what? In other words, it is hard to see how such an identification could generate the immediate normativity of truth.[28] (It seems more plausible that we begin with truth and define the notion of the ideal limit in terms of it: what makes the limit ideal is that it reaches truth. This does not tell us how and why we get into this particular normative circle in the first place.)

I have not yet mentioned what seems to me to be the most telling argument against the pragmatist identification of truth with warranted assertibility (in Peircean form or otherwise). It often seems to be suggested (by Rorty himself, among others—see the quotes with which I began), that instead of arguing about truth, we could argue about warranted assertibility. This seems to me to miss a crucial point. Without truth, the wheels of argument do not engage; disagreements slide past one another. This is true of disagreements about any matter whatsoever. In particular, it is true of disagreements about warranted assertibility. If we did not already have truth, in other words, we simply could not argue about warranted assertibility. For we could be aware that we have different opinions about what is warrantedly assertible, without that difference of opinion seeming to matter. What makes it matter is the fact that we subscribe to a practice according to which disagreement is an indication of culpable error, on one side or other; in another words, that we already take ourselves to be subject to the norms of truth and falsity.[29]

The crucial point is thus that assertoric dialogue requires an intolerance of disagreement. This needs to be present already in the background, a pragmatic presupposition of judgment itself. I am not a maker of assertions, a judger, at all, unless I am already playing the game to win, in the sense defined by the third norm. Since winning is already characterized in terms of truth, the idea of a conversational game with some alternative point is incoherent. It is like the idea of a game in which the primary aim is to compete—this idea is incoherent, because the notion of competition already presupposes a different goal.[30]

There is a connection here with an old objection to relativism, which tries to corner the relativist by asking her whether she takes her own relativistic doctrine to be true, and if so in what sense. The best option for the relativist is to say that she takes the doctrine to be true in the only sense she allows, namely, the relativistic one. When her opponent replies, "Well, in that case you should not be troubled by the fact that I disagree, because you recognize that what is true for me need not be true for you, and vice versa," the relativist has a reply. She can argue that truth is relative to communities, not to individual speakers, and hence that disagreements do not necessarily dissolve in this way.

My pragmatist opponents fare less well against an analogous argument, I think. The basic objection to their position is that in engaging with me in argument about the nature of truth (as about anything else), they reveal that they take themselves to be subject to the norm whose existence they are denying. If they did not take themselves to be subject to it, they would be in the same boat as the Mo'ans, with no reason to treat the disagreement between us as a cause for concern. They affirm *p*, I affirm not-*p*; but by their lights, this should be like the case in which they say "Yes" and I say "No," in answer to the question "Would you like coffee?" (This is what it should be like even if *p* is of the form '*q* is warrantedly assertible'.) The disagreement simply would not bite.

V. Truth as Convenient Fiction?

The third norm thus requires a notion of truth that differs from justification, even of a Peircean ideal variety. In this sense, then, the present account is realist rather than pragmatist about truth. In another sense, however, the view surely seems antirealist. After all, I have argued that what matters is that speakers take there to be a norm of truth, not that there actually be such a norm, in some speaker-independent sense. Is this not antirealism, or more precisely, in the current jargon, a form of *fictionalism* about truth?

If so, could, this be a satisfactory outcome? If truth does play the role I have claimed for it in dialogue, would not the realization that it is a fiction undermine that linguistic practice, by making it the case that we could no longer consistently feel bound by the relevant norms?

Let us call this objection the threat of *dialogical nihilism*. In my view, it is not a practical threat. I think that in practice we find it impossible to stop caring about truth. This is not an argument for realism, of course. The discovery that our biological appetites are not driven by perception of pre-existing properties—the properties of being tasty, sexually attractive, or whatever—does not lessen the force of those appetites, but no one thinks that this requires a realist view of the properties concerned. Even if nihilism were a practical threat, this would not be reason for thinking that the claim that truth is a fiction is *false*, by the lights of the game as currently played. It might be a pragmatic reason for keeping the conclusion quiet, but that is a different matter altogether (especially according to my realist opponents).

So even if the present view is correctly characterized as a form of fictionalism about truth, the nihilism objection is far from conclusive. But are the labels 'fictionalism' or 'antirealism' really appropriate? The need for caution stems from the fact that this approach to truth threatens to deprive both sides of the realism-antirealism debate of conceptual resources on which the debate seems to depend. As I noted earlier, the relevant metaphysical issues tend themselves to be framed in terms of truth, and related notions. A theory is said to be in error if its claims are not *true*, or if its terms fail to *refer*, for example. So the issue of the status of truth is here enmeshed with the terms of the problem, in a way which is quite uncharacteristic of metaphysical issues about other notions. As a result, it may be impossible to formulate a meaningful antirealism or fictionalism about the semantic terms themselves. This does not mean that we have to be realists about semantic notions, but only that if we are not realists we should be cautious about calling ourselves antirealists (or fictionalists), if these categories presuppose the very notions we want to avoid being realist about.

This may sound like an impossible trick, but in fact the kind of distinction we need is familiar elsewhere. It is the distinction between someone who "talks god talk" and espouses atheism, and someone who rejects the theological language game altogether (on Carnapian pragmatic grounds, say). These are two very different ways of rejecting theism. In the present case, the point is that we may consistently reject semantically-grounded realism about the semantic notions themselves, so long as we do so by avoiding theoretical use of semantic notions altogether, rather than by relying on those notions to characterize our departure from realism. (Why "theoretical use"? Because there is nothing to stop us continuing to use these semantic notions in a deflationary or disquotational sense.)

It might be suggested that we can sidestep this difficulty altogether by casting the relevant metaphysical issues in ontological rather than semantic terms. On this view, the relevant issue is whether truth exists, not whether (some) truth ascriptions are true. Against this suggestion, however, it is arguable that the relevant metaphysical issues arise initially from data concerning human linguistic usage, and only become metaphysical in the light of substantial semantic assumptions about the functions of the language concerned—for example, that it is truth conditional, or referential, in function. If so, then truth is once again enmeshed with the terms of the problem. And even if we concede the possibility of the ontological shift, the authority of Quine, Carnap and others may perhaps be invoked in support of a deflationary attitude to ontology, with the result that the realist-antirealist issue still dissolves.[31]

These issues are complex, and deserve a much more detailed examination than I can give them here. For present purposes, I simply flag the following as a possible outcome (of considerable plausibility, in my view). In common with other deflationary approaches to truth, the present account not only rejects the idea that there is a substantial metaphysical issue about truth (a substantial issue about the truthmakers of claims about truth, for example). Because it is about truth, it also positively prevents "reinflation." In other words, it seems to support a general deflationary attitude to issues of realism and antirealism. If so, then deflationism about truth is not only not to be equated with fictionalism, but tends to undermine the fictional-nonfictional distinction, as applied in the metaphysical realm.[32]

As I noted at the beginning, the present account of truth is hard to find on contemporary maps. In part, as should now be clear, this is because it combines elements not normally thought to be compatible. In one sense it is impeccably pragmatist, for example, for it appeals to nothing more than the role of truth in linguistic practice. Yet it rejects the pragmatist's *ur*-urge, to try to identify truth with justification. Again, it defends a kind of truth commonly seen as realist, but does so from a pragmatist starting point, without the metaphysics that typically accompanies such a realist view of truth. So in thinking about how to characterize this account of truth, we should be sensitive to the possibility that our existing categories—fictionalism, realism, and perhaps pragmatism itself—may need to be reconfigured. If so, then putting the position on the map is not like noticing a small country (Lichtenstein, perhaps) that previously we had overlooked. It is more like discovering a geographical analogue of the platypus, a region which our pre-existing cartographical conventions seemed a priori to disallow.

I began with Rorty's claim that the distinction between justification and truth makes no difference in practical life, no difference to our "decisions about what to do." Rorty regards a commitment to a notion of truth stronger than justification as a relic of a kind of religious deference to external authority. He recommends that just as we have begun to rid ourselves of theism, we should rid ourselves of the "representationalist" dogma that our beliefs are answerable to standards beyond ourselves. For Rorty, then, realist truth is a quasi-religious myth, which we would do better without.

Despite my reservations about the fictionalist label, I have agreed that truth is in some sense a myth, or at least a human creation.[33] But I have denied that in providing a norm stronger than justification, a commitment to truth makes no behavioral difference. On the contrary, I have argued, it plays an essential role in a linguistic practice of great importance to us, *as we currently are*. It is not clear whether we could coherently be otherwise, whether we could get by without the third norm. If so, however, then the result would be a very different language game. My main claim is that we have not understood truth until we understand its role in the game we currently play.

Notes

The first version of this paper was written for a conference in honor of Richard Rorty at the Australian National University in 1999. I am grateful to participants at that conference and to many subsequent audiences for much insightful discussion of these ideas.

1. "Is Truth a Goal of Inquiry? Donald Davidson versus Crispin Wright," in his *Truth and Progress: Philosophical Papers*, Volume 3 (New York: Cambridge, 1998), pp. 19–42.

2. Irony aside, nothing here turns on whether by 'conversation' I mean the same as Rorty. For me, what matters is the role of truth in the kind of interpersonal linguistic interaction I will call factual or assertoric dialogue, or simply dialogue. I do not claim that dialogue exhausts conversation, in Rorty's sense or any other. I used scare quotes on 'factual' above in anticipation of the suggestion that the notion of factuality in play might depend on that of truth, in a way which would create problems for my own account of the role of truth in dialogue. There is no

such difficulty, in my view. On the contrary, I take the perceived "factuality" or "truth-aptness" of the utterances in question to be part of the explanandum of the kind of account here proposed; cf. footnote 23.

3."Pragmatism, Davidson, and Truth," in *Objectivity, Relativism, and Truth: Philosophical Papers*, Volume 1 (New York: Cambridge, 1991), pp. 126–50, see p. 128.

4. If private cognition depends on the norms of public dialogue then truth plays the same role, at second hand, in the private sphere. This is a plausible extension of the present claim, in my view, but I will not try to defend it here.

5. At least compared to the alternative.

6."Global *Waiting for Godot,*" as a member of an audience in Dundee suggested I put it. Even more seriously, as noted above, giving up truth might silence our own "internal" rational dialogues.

7. Jonathan Rée makes a point of this kind against Rorty: "[C]ontingencies can last a very long time. Our preoccupations with love and death may not be absolute necessities, but they are not a passing fad either, and it is a safe bet that they will last as long as we do"—"Strenuous Unbelief," *London Review of Books*, XX, 20 (October 15, 1998): 7–11, here p. 11.

8."The Status of Content," *Philosophical Review*, XCIX, 2 (April 1990): 157–84.

9. A realist could object that a commitment to the third norm might be useful and yet in error, but Rorty cannot. It is fair for him to object against Wright that this commitment might be like theism, because Wright takes metaphysics seriously. By Wright's professed standards, then, the theism objection poses a real threat.

10. "Is Truth a Goal of Inquiry? Donald Davidson versus Crispin Wright," see p. 21.

11. *Philosophy of Logic* (Englewood Cliffs, NJ: Prentice-Hall, 1970).

12. *Truth* (Cambridge: Blackwell, 1990).

13. Robert Brandom makes a similar point in "Pragmatism, Phenomenalism, and Truth Talk," *Midwest Studies in Philosophy*, XXII (1988): 75–93.

14. For present purposes I can remain open-minded on the question as to whether such a practice is really possible. Perhaps a truth-like norm is essential to any practice which deserves to be called linguistic. At any rate, my use of the following linguistic thought experiment does not depend on denying this possibility.

15. In what sense "weaker"? In the sense, at least, that they apply to a wider range of linguistic behaviors. 'Less specialized' might be a better term.

16. This corresponds to a common use of the term 'assertibility condition', as for example when it is said that the subjective assertibility condition for the indicative conditional 'If p then q' is a high conditional credence in q given p.

17. Cf. Rorty's remark that, "[f]or any audience, one can imagine a better-informed audience"—"Is Truth a Goal of Inquiry? Donald Davidson versus Crispin Wright," see p. 22.

18. This account has prescriptive and nonprescriptive readings. The former uses the notion of improvement full-voice, saying that if speakers are to improve their commitments, they need the idea of the third norm. But as N. J. J. Smith pointed out to me, it could well be objected that the relevant notion of improvement simply presupposes the third norm, and therefore cannot provide any independent rationale for adopting it. No such circularity undermines the nonprescriptive reading, however, whose point is that because our existing conversational practice does take for granted such a notion of improvement, it thereby reveals its commitment to a third norm.

19. Note the contrast with Rorty's cautionary use of "true." In that use, we say of a claim that we take to be well justified that it might not be true. In the present use, we say of a claim that we might even allow to be well justified by its speaker's own lights that it is not true. It is the difference between mere caution and actual censure.

20. "Three Norms of Assertibility, or How the MOA Became Extinct," *Philosophical Perspectives*, XII (1988): 241–54. The present section and the next draw significantly on that paper.

21. As I noted earlier, my use of this example does not depend on the claim that such a linguistic practice be possible. It is doubtful whether notions such as belief, assertion, and opinion are really load bearing, in the imagined context. Much of the effect of the example could be achieved in another way, however, by imposing suitable restrictions on real linguistic practices—by imagining self-imposed restrictions on what we are allowed to say. One way to approach the Mo'an predicament from our own current practice would be to adopt the convention that whenever we would ordinarily assert '*p*' we express ourselves instead by saying 'My own opinion is that *p*'.

22. A defender of the disquotational view might argue that although there is a third norm, it is not the function of the truth predicate to express it. This will be a difficult position to defend, however. If any predicate—'correct', for example—expresses the third norm, then that predicate will function as a disquotational predicate, for the reason just mentioned. Hence it will have been pointless to maintain that true itself is not normative. So the disquotationalist needs to claim that the third norm is not expressed at all in this predicative form, and that seems implausible.

23. This is another place where circularity threatens. We need to be sure that the psychological states mentioned at this point are not thought of as already "factual" or "representational" in character, in a way which presupposes truth. Insofar as it is truth-involving, the "factual" character of the domain in question needs to be part of the explanandum—something that emerges from, rather than being presupposed by, the pragmatic account of the origins and consequences of "truth talk." In my view, one of the attractive features of this approach is that it offers the prospect that the uniformity of "factual," truth-involving talk might be compatible with considerable plurality in the nature and functions of the underlying psychological states. It thus offers an attractive new form for expressivist intuitions. Cf. my *Facts and the Function of Truth* (New York: Blackwell, 1988), chapter 8; "Metaphysical Pluralism," *Journal of Philosophy*, LXXXIX, 8 (August 1992): 387–409, §IV, and "Immodesty without Mirrors: Making Sense of Wittgenstein's Linguistic Pluralism," in Max Kölbel and Bernhard Weiss, eds., *Wittgenstein's Lasting Significance* (New York: Routledge, forthcoming).

24. Even if not dangerous on its own, the third norm might become so in combination with some particularly deadly source of intractable disagreements, such as religious commitment. More generally, the thought that argument is sometimes dangerous suggests a link between the concerns of this paper and the motivations of the Pyrrhonian skeptics. On the present view of truth, the question whether we could get by without truth seems closely related to that as to whether we could live as thoroughgoing Pyrrhonian skeptics.

25. This point would acquire new and even stronger force, if it were to be established that private cognition rests on the norms of public dialogue, in the way suggested in footnote 4.

26. As Rorty notes (in "Pragmatism, Davidson, and Truth," see p. 130), Michael Williams makes a point of this kind: "[W]e have no idea what it would be for a theory to be ideally complete and comprehensive . . . or of what it would be for inquiry to have an end"—"Coherence, Justification, and Truth," *Review of Metaphysics*, xxxiv (1980–81): 243–72, see p. 269.

27. *Meaning and the Moral Sciences* (New York: Routledge, 1978), p. 108.

28. It may seem that this argument begs the question against the pragmatist, by assuming that there is an epistemologically relevant gap between ideal warranted assertibility and truth. But the issue is not whether we need some norm in addition to ideal warranted assertibility, but whether ideal warranted assertibility itself could be immediately normative, in the way in which truth is. No one disputes that the manners of the palace are normative for those who live there—that is what it is to be manners—but it is an open question whether they are or should

be normative for the rest of us. Similarly for ideal assertibility, except that in this case no one lives at the limit, so that there is no one for whom the question is not open.

29. I noted above that the same point applies to the normative predicates themselves. If we were not already disposed to take disagreement to matter, we could not do so simply by adding normative predicates, for disagreement about the application of those predicates would be as frictionless as disagreement about anything else. My claim is thus that the notions of truth and falsity give voice to more primitive implicit norms, which themselves underpin the very possibility of "giving voice" at all. In effect, the above argument rests on the observation that this genealogy cannot be reversed: if we start with a predicate—warrantedly assertible or any other—then we have started too late. (I suspect that by "giving voice," I mean something close to "making explicit," in Brandom's sense.)

30. Here, incidentally, we see the essential flaw in the pious sentiments of Grantland Rice (1880–1954):

For when the One Great Scorer comes,
To write against your name,
He marks—not that you won or lost—
But how you played the game.

The One Great Scorer might assign marks on this basis, for divine purposes. *Pace* Rice, however, we could not play the game in question with such marks as our primary goal, for then it would be a different game altogether.

31. I defend the first of these two options in "Naturalism without Representationalism," in Mario de Caro and David Macarthur, eds., *Naturalism in Question* (Cambridge: Harvard, 2003) and the second in "Metaphysical Pluralism"; and "Naturalism and the Fate of the M-worlds," *Proceedings of the Aristotelian Society*, Supp. Vol. LXXI (1997): 247–67.

32. Rorty often says that he wants to walk away from realist-antirealist disputes. In other words, he does not think that there is an interesting philosophical question as to whether our commitments "mirror" reality. The above argument suggests that like other deflationists about truth, I have reason to follow Rorty in walking away from these issues. (In particular, my defense of truth over justification does not force me to stay.)

33. In the light of the argument above, this is a point more about the genealogy than about the reality of truth.

In this paper, Misak draws on a refined Peircean conception of truth to argue for an epistemic conception of deliberative democracy.

CHERYL MISAK

Making Disagreement Matter

Pragmatism and Deliberative Democracy

1. Introduction

There is a direct connection between deliberative democracy and the pragmatist theory of truth. The deliberative democrat thinks that correct political decisions can only be reached by free and open deliberation. And the pragmatist, at least the kind of pragmatist who follows the founder of the doctrine, C. S. Peirce, thinks that correctness or truth in any kind of discourse is that which would be the upshot of unlimited deliberation and inquiry.[1] Indeed, pragmatists have always wanted to bring moral and political judgments under our cognitive scope—under the scope of correctness, truth, falsity, knowledge, error, and reason. Peirce was the least explicit in conducting this task (but see Misak 2004), whereas James and Dewey were very explicit. The tradition has been continued by contemporary pragmatists such as Hilary Putnam and Jürgen Habermas. Moral and political judgments aim at getting things right and the best way of achieving or approximating that aim is to engage in reasoning, debate, and the consideration of different perspectives and evidence.

It is unsurprising that so many pragmatists are moral cognitivists, as Peirce's theory of truth, on which true beliefs are those that would be undefeated by deliberation and inquiry, seems tailor-made for cognitivism. It leaves the prospects for cognitivism intact, as it does not require a causal connection between our beliefs and physical objects. Moral and political judgments cannot be candidates for truth and falsity on a theory of truth that, for instance, has it that judgments are true if and only if they correspond to the mind-independent or physical world.

The Peircean account of truth is entirely general—that is, it is applicable in principle to any discourse or domain of inquiry.[2] A true belief, Peirce maintained, is one that is "unassailable by doubt" (*Collected Papers*, 5.416).[3] It is a belief that would forever stand up to deliberation or inquiry; not lead to disappointment; be "indefeasible" or not defeated, were deliberation to be pursued as far as it could fruitfully go (*CP* 5.569, 6.485). Truth is a stable property—a belief is either true (indefeasible) or not. And truth is not a matter for some particular community—if a belief is indefeasible, it would stand up to whatever could be thrown at it, by any community of inquirers.

In *Truth, Politics, Morality*, I presented a sustained defense of this pragmatist cognitivism. The starting point of that argument was that we take ourselves in morals and politics to aim at the right answer—i.e., at the truth, rather than at what my own standards point to (what is justified by my lights) or at what community standards point to (what is justified by our lights). We try to get things right, we distinguish between thinking that we are right and being right, we criticize the beliefs and actions of others, we think that we can improve our judgments, and we take ourselves to be able to learn by listening to others, by putting ourselves in another's shoes, by examining the arguments of the other side, by broadening our horizons, and so forth. We think that "rational" persuasion, not brow-beating or force, is the appropriate way to get people to agree with us. Indeed, we want others to *agree* with us, not to merely mouth what we say or fall in line with it.

That is, our practices—what we find when we examine morals and politics—point to cognitivism. The pragmatist is of course committed to keeping philosophical theories true to practice. As Peirce writes: "We must not begin by talking of pure ideas,—vagabond thoughts that tramp the public roads without any human habitation,—but must begin with men and their conversation" (*CP* 8.112). This commitment to respecting practice is not itself without arguments in its support: for instance, a theory of *x* must take seriously what *x* is like, or it runs the risk of not being a theory of *x*, but a theory of something else instead.

Nonetheless, two related difficulties press upon cognitivism and its thought that the practice of moral and political deliberation suggests that moral and political beliefs fall under the scone of truth and reason. One is that there is much disagreement in moral and political deliberation. We often find issues to be contestable, thorny, and underdetermined. The cognitivist must tell us how we can understand our aim to be getting the right answer when in morals and politics there is such widespread disagreement about what is the right answer. The cognitivist must convince us that our practices *really do* point in the direction of cognitivism rather than, say, skepticism.

The other difficulty is that the starting point of the argument for cognitivism turns on the purported fact that *we take ourselves* to be committed to open deliberation and to getting the right answer. What if some groups do not take themselves to be so committed—what if some take their moral and political decisions to aim merely at doing what is best for themselves, their ethnic group, their nation, or their class? What if some groups argue that we ought *not* to pursue inclusive deliberative methods of political decision-making? What if they argue for totalitarian methods or straight voting, for example? We can't simply rest on the appealing thought that deliberation, conversation, and taking seriously the views of others is the right way to proceed. And when we give the required justification for open deliberation, we must not beg the question in favor of the liberal democratic values we may hold dear.

A significant part of *Truth, Politics, Morality* was engaged in showing that the pragmatist/cognitivist can address these problems. I will not here rehearse the arguments regarding the first problem—that about disagreement—but in Section 3 I will add an important thought. What primarily concerns me here is the second issue—the argument in favor of deliberation.

Unfortunately, there has been very little satisfying work done in this domain. The first chapter of *Truth, Politics, Morality* is a catalog of failed attempts. I offered my own argument for deliberation later in that book and will speak to that argument in Section 2. I will then improve matters by discussing a new argument by Huw Price. We shall see that one of the virtues of Price's contribution to these debates is that he can be seen as bringing together the two problems set out above: he shows that open deliberation aimed at truth is justified, because only it can explain why disagreements matter to us.

2. Deliberation and its Connection to Belief and Assertion

David Estlund (1997) and Henry Richardson (1994) are two deliberative democrats who see the need for providing a justification for the deliberative method. Their argument has affinities with my own and a summary of it will give the reader a sense of what is required. Estlund and Richardson ask us to assume that we aim at impartiality in our political decision-making. Once we assume that, it becomes clear that we have a preference for deliberative over random ways of achieving this aim. We do not think, for instance, that flipping a coin is a good way of making our decisions, even though coin-flipping does exemplify a kind of impartiality. The fact that we have this preference betrays the fact that we think that it is important to respect certain standards. A legitimate procedure must be answerable to reasons—it must pay attention to the reasons that matter. If, for instance, a vote (which also exemplifies a kind of impartiality) resulted in a policy that scuttled our fundamental values, we would reject the result of the vote. (No doubt this is part of the reason why referenda are not the most appropriate basis for political decision-making.) Since reasons come to light primarily in debate and deliberation, a legitimate procedure must proceed by debate and deliberation. Coin-flipping and straight voting cannot guarantee that reasons will be respected and so we reject them as methods of political decision-making. Deliberation is the only method that is justified for those who hold that random methods of impartiality are not preferable over methods which pay attention to reasons. Note the cognitivism here: political decision-making must be responsive to *reasons*.

The Estlund and Richardson argument is an argument about moral and political decision-making. It starts with the assumption that we aim at impartiality, which, if it is indeed our aim, is our aim only in moral and political discourse.[4] My argument, on the other hand, is entirely general: it is applicable to any kind of discourse.

And my argument will not ask us to assume anything so contentious as the thought that everyone aims at impartiality. Some of Estlund's and Richardson's opponents will very clearly not aim at impartiality: on the contrary, they will aim at a partial decision. They will want to eliminate the "other" in their midst and have their political decision-making serve only a homogenous group.[5] This is another way of saying that the Estlund and Richardson argument is not successful against those who contend that their aim is not to get an answer that is correct for everyone, but rather an answer for their group only. Or it is another way of saying that those who assume that impartiality is our aim already sign up to the liberal democratic values in question—the values of inclusiveness, of letting everyone have their say, etc. But at least Estlund and Richardson offer us a good argument in favor of deliberation in those cases in which our opponents agree that they aim at impartiality.

We shall see in Section 3 that Price's argument is as general as my own: indeed, he doesn't even mention moral and political discourse. And we shall see that it is similarly uncontentious, for both Price and I base our arguments on something everyone does: assert, believe, and engage with others.

The argument I presented in *Truth, Politics, Morality* (73ff.) is as follows. Reflect on the difference between the phrases "I suspect that *p*" or "it seems to me that *p*," on the one hand, and "I believe that *p*" or "I assert that *p*," on the other. What I do when I use the first two phrases is distance myself from the obligations that come with belief and assertion. (From here on I will simply discuss belief, although everything I say applies equally to assertion.)

Those obligations can be summarized by saying that if I believe that *p*, I commit myself to defending *p*—to arguing that I am, and others are, warranted in believing *p*. Working out what it is to have warrant for a belief will no doubt be a difficult and controversial business. But that does not interfere with the thought that to believe commits one to engage in the business of justification, whether or not one can live up to the commitment. Failing to incur the commitment, failing to see that one is required to offer reasons for one's belief, results in the degradation of belief to mere opinion or to dogmatism.

A more precise way of making this point is to say that when I believe *p*, I commit myself to saying what could speak for or against *p* and to giving up *p* in the face of sustained evidence and argument against it. A belief, in order to be a belief, is such that it is responsive to or answerable to reasons and evidence. That is a very part of what is to have a belief—it is a *constitutive norm* of belief. Part of what it is to hold a belief, as opposed to being in some other mental state, such as entertaining an interesting but idle thought, lying about what one believes, or holding a dogmatic opinion, is that there must be something that can speak for or against a belief and that belief must be responsive to what can speak for or against it. Some cognitive states—those not appropriately connected to reasons—are not deserving of the label "belief."

Of course, the reasons standing behind a belief need not be explicitly acknowledged—I might believe and act habitually, but for reasons nonetheless. When I stop at the red light, I need not articulate to myself the reasons for stopping, but the reasons are nonetheless there. I would articulate them if asked.

The idea that belief must turn on reasons certainly fits with a large part of the psychological reality of belief. A believer thinks that her belief fits best with the evidence and argument. I cannot get myself to believe that *p* by deciding that if the coin I am about to flip lands heads, I will believe it, and if it lands tails, I will not. In order to believe *p* I have to be convinced that I have good reason to believe it. Here we have something like the Estlund and Richardson point. But it is not that aiming at impartiality requires us to pay attention to the reasons that matter. It is that *believing* requires us to pay attention to the reasons that matter.

A corollary of this point about the constitutive nature of belief is that, as Bernard Williams has argued, we cannot decide to believe—we cannot get ourselves, by an act of will alone, to believe that something is the case. We can only believe on reasons. Raz (1999, 10–11) has rightly pointed out that much of the discussion about whether we can choose to believe would have been better conducted if attention had been paid to the fact that beliefs normally belong to the active side of our lives, not the passive. Beliefs do not just come upon us—we reach for them. We respond to reasons. We can decide to believe something only in the sense that we can decide to deliberate. We might then conclude that we have good reason to believe *p*, but we cannot pick a belief and decide to believe it, not caring where the reasons may fall.

There are countless nuances that need to be articulated here—involving the states of denial, irrational belief (belief based on faulty reasons, but reasons nonetheless), *akrasia*, etc. These nuances are beyond the scope of this paper, but we would do well to articulate just one of them. Notice that if I were convinced that my coin had some special power to deliver true beliefs, then I might well get myself to believe *p* by its flip. In this case I have made a prior (and most likely mistaken) judgment that my coin delivers beliefs that fit the evidence and argument. I still aim at getting beliefs that would fit with and respond to the reasons, I simply go about the business in a wrongheaded or irrational way. But if I decide to believe *p* because an expert believes it, I need not be making such a mistake. I might have very good reason to think that the expert is the best deliverer of beliefs that are properly keyed to the evidence and argument. So if I take my physician's diagnoses as being probably correct, whether or not I learn about the underlying causes and biology myself, what I acquire are genuine beliefs.

In moral and political inquiry, however, we must be careful with the notion of an expert. Everyone who is engaged with others is engaged in moral and political deliberation. And anyone, whatever their formal training, might be very good at it. So if I am interested in what kindness requires in a particular difficult situation, I might consult an especially kind person, but I need not take advice from anyone with a particular sort of training.[6] It is part and parcel of deliberative democracy that each individual is an equal participant in deliberation. The pragmatist position outlined here is very much in step with that.

The central point is that any method for arriving at genuine beliefs must be a method that is driven by reasons and experience. The argument embraces more than the Estlund and Richardson argument because everyone has beliefs, whereas not everyone aims at impartiality. Everyone ought to expose herself to reasons by engaging in debate and deliberation, for inquiry and deliberation are implicated in believing and asserting.

Once that point is accepted, we can see further relationships between Peirce's account of truth and deliberative democracy. For another constitutive norm of belief is that belief aims at the truth. A belief is such that it is responsive to the reasons that matter and it aims at getting things right. The best way to achieve this aim is to engage in inquiry. For if you want to have your decisions governed by reasons, then you will have to expose yourself to reasons—you will have to engage in debate and deliberation. And were we to get beliefs that, after sustained inquiry, were not defeated by reasons, then there would be nothing more we could ask of them: they would be true.

Let me present Peirce's view another way. He illuminates the concept of truth by giving an account of the role of truth in inquiry and deliberation. As Wiggins (2002) puts it, we can get leverage on the concept of truth, or get a fix on it, by exploring its connection with our practices of belief and inquiry. The role played by truth in these practices is that it is our aim in belief and inquiry. But, of course, we have other, more proximate or more local aims when we believe and inquire. We aim to get beliefs that are fruitful, that fit with the evidence, that have explanatory and predictive power, that are consistent with other well-grounded beliefs, and so forth, if a belief were such that it would survive all the challenges we could put to it, if it would meet all of the local aims of inquiry, then there is nothing more we could ask of it—it would be true. "Truth," if you like, is a catch-all for the local aims of inquiry. If the local aims were to be forever satisfied, then the aim of truth would be satisfied as well.

Clearly, if we want true beliefs, we should expose them to these challenges—to experience and argument that might overturn them. Better to find out now that a belief is defeated, rather than down the line. A physicist who refused to take into account any of the experimental results of, say American physicists, would be adopting a very bad method for getting beliefs that would stand up to reasons. Similarly, those engaged in moral or political deliberation who denigrate or ignore the experiences of those with a certain skin color, gender, or religion are also adopting a method unlikely to reach the truth.

Deliberation is justified because it is the best way of exposing and communicating the reasons that matter and democratic deliberation is justified because we need to expose *all* of the reasons that matter, not just a subset of them.

I have suggested that what it is to assert, to make a claim, to believe, to judge, is to be engaged in a process of justification. It is to commit oneself to giving reasons—to be prepared, in the appropriate circumstances, to justify the claim to others and to oneself. And it is to commit oneself to being open and responsive to evidence and argument. If (to use a well-known Peircean contrast) we are to retain the distinction between mere tenacity (holding on to our opinions come what may) and belief, then our beliefs, including our beliefs about what is right or wrong and just or unjust, must in principle be responsive to evidence and argument. To put it bluntly, deliberative democracy in political philosophy is the right view, because deliberative democracy in epistemology is the right view.

3. Price on Truth and Disagreement

Now let us turn to Huw Price's argument. He starts with the pragmatist thought that the best way to get leverage on a concept is to examine its role in practice. We must get away from the habit of searching for reductive analyses and adopt, rather, the pragmatist alternative to philosophical illumination.[7] We can understand something important about a concept (in this instance, the concept of truth) by understanding its practical significance—by investigating its function in human discourse.

Price examines our practice and finds that it requires a robust notion of truth. The pragmatist of Rorty's stripe fails to see that when you examine practice, you find that truth is not just solidarity or what this or that community happens to find best to believe. When you examine practice, you in fact find that the goal of inquiry is truth as we have always thought of it—something stable and independent of what this or that person or community might think. Speakers take themselves to be subject to the norm of truth—not just the norms of sincerity, justification, warrant, or keeping in step with the beliefs of the community, for example. Price thinks that "in practice we find it impossible to stop caring about truth" (2003, 187).

His argument for this contention is that the behavior pattern that betrays the commitment to truth is so central to what we presently regard as a worthwhile human life that no reasonable person would experiment with trying to do without the norm of truth (168). No reasonable person would try to rest with the aim of getting beliefs that are warranted or justified by current community standards. For the norm of truth plays an essential, indeed a constitutive, role in assertion and dialogue as we know them. To do without truth is to silence our conversations—both our conversations with others and our own internal conversations.

"The very essence of the norm of truth," argues Price, is to give disagreement "its immediate normative character" (168). It is to make disagreement matter: "Without truth, the wheels of argument do not engage; disagreements slide past one another" (185). In order to really *engage* others in conversation or dialogue, we have to see their disagreement as implying a mistake on someone's part. Otherwise, we are merely talking past each other.

The flip side of this point is that without truth, we could not find the conceptual space to formulate the idea of improving upon our beliefs. Indeed, the norm of truth encourages improvement by motivating speakers who disagree to try to resolve the disagreement. For disagreement, again, implies a mistake on someone's part.[8]

Price brings the norm of truth into focus (and shows that it plays the above distinct and critical roles in linguistic practice) by asking us to imagine a community that uses language primarily for expressing preferences in restaurants—a community of speakers that obeys only the weaker norms of subjective assertibility (sincerity) and personal warranted assertibility (justification). The norm of sincerity says that to assert that *p* without believing that *p* provides grounds for censure or disapprobation. The norm of justification says that to assert that *p* without having adequate personal grounds for believing that *p* provides reasons for censure or disapprobation. A person who meets both of these norms may be said to have done as much as possible, by her own current lights, to ensure that her assertion that *p* is in good order. These speakers can criticize each other for being insincere or for making personally unjustified statements, but not for failing to tell the truth. They have merely-opinionated assertions (MOAs)—hence Price's name "Mo'ans" for the members of this fictional community (177).

Mo'ans are like dedicated lunchers whose language atrophies to the bare essentials (177). They might criticize expressed preferences on the ground that they were not sincere or on the ground that they were not well-founded by the speaker's own lights. ("You always say that you want the goat, but when it arrives, you don't eat it!") The Mo'ans, that is, use linguistic utterances to express their "beliefs," preferences, and desires. They differ from us in that they do not take disagreement to indicate that one or the other speaker is at fault or mistaken. They do not say "goat tastes disgusting and if you disagree, you are mistaken." Disagreements are of a no-fault kind.

A Mo'an, in other words, cannot be criticized for getting things wrong, even when she is not talking about what she would like to eat, but about whether there is *E. coli* in the petri dish or whether there is milk in the refrigerator. For Mo'ans do not treat a disagreement between two speakers as an indication that one speaker has made a mistake.

We can now see how our linguistic practice differs from that of Mo'ans. In our practice, we can distinguish between telling the truth and being sincere. I can be sincere (say what I really believe) without telling the truth. The converse is also possible: I can tell the truth and be insincere. I can say what someone orders me to say and if I don't believe it and it happens to be true, I will have insincerely uttered a truth. We can also distinguish between being justified and telling the truth. I can have the best possible (personal) justification for *p* and yet *p* can be false. The converse is again possible: *p* can be true and I can lack justification for it. Mo'ans are unable to make these distinctions.

By noting such differences, we can see what the third norm—the norm of truth—adds to our practice. The main difference, Price tells us, is that in the Mo'ans' linguistic practice we cannot find dialogue and argumentation as we know them. We cannot, that is, find the *engagement* of individual opinions, as opposed to the mere roll call of individual opinions (169). The third norm adds something new to a practice governed merely by the first two norms: it adds "the grit that makes our individual opinions engage with one another" (169). Price thinks that the difficulty we have in holding on to the idea of such a community as the Mo'ans stems from our almost irresistible urge to see the situation in terms of our own normative standards. There really is a third norm, we are inclined to think, even if these simple creatures don't know it. If two of them make incompatible assertions, then one of them must be objectively incorrect, even if by their lights they both meet the only norms they themselves recognize (178).

To add the norm of truth, Price argues, Mo'ans need not believe that there is a substantial *property* that mere expressions of opinion lack, "the property of corresponding to how things are in the world [or] of being what their opinions are fated to converge on in the long run" (179). The adoption of the third norm does not depend on such a "piece of folk metaphysics."[9] All that Mo'ans need to adopt is the following practice: if they assert that *p*, then they must be prepared to ascribe fault to anyone who asserts ~*p*. All that they need to do is treat disagreement to be itself grounds for disapproval. "True" and "false" give voice to this fundamental practice—the practice of dialogue with bite. We have "a norm which speakers immediately assume to be breached by someone with whom they disagree, *independently of any diagnosis of the source of the disagreement*" (168).[10] We need the notion of truth because it underpins the practice of engaging with others.

4. Deliberation and Disagreement

Deliberative democrats would do well to draw the following moral from Price's argument: if we really deliberate; if we really engage with others when we deal with moral and political issues, if disagreement matters, then we have no choice but to see ourselves as abiding by the norm of truth and taking ourselves to aim at truth. In the following statement, the affinities between Price's argument and the argument I presented in Section 2 should be clear:

> The crucial point is thus that assertoric dialogue requires an intolerance of disagreement. This needs to be present already in the background, a pragmatic presupposition of judgement itself. I am not a maker of assertions, a judger, at all, unless I am already playing the game to win, in the sense defined by the third norm. (186)

Assertion, judgment, and belief presuppose or require that one aims at getting things right, where "getting things right" means getting to the answer not merely justified by me, or by my community, but justified *tout court*.

Many substantial and interesting questions concerning the amount of disagreement that is tolerable in morals and politics will arise here. Surely in those matters more akin to preferences, we ought to agree to disagree—matters such as whether one ought to give money to Oxfam or to one's struggling family. And some questions involving diverse cultural and religious norms will also seem to have underdetermined answers. Here I must refer the reader to my *Truth, Politics, Morality* for a sustained discussion of how the pragmatist view outlined here can accommodate, and even applaud, diversity and disagreement while maintaining that we aim at the truth.

If we can step back from these questions, we see that we in fact have a nice result. Recall that one of the obstacles in the way of cognitivism was that it seemed to rest on the *claim* that we *take ourselves* in moral and political decision-making to aim at the truth. The objection then was that perhaps not everyone takes themselves to aim at truth or perhaps we *ought not* to take ourselves to aim at truth. If aiming at the truth is optional, perhaps we ought to wean ourselves of this habit, just as we might think that we ought to wean ourselves of the habit of thinking that God exists. The fact that many employ a notion of God does not show that God exists. Similarly, the fact that some take themselves to aim at the truth does not show that there is a truth at which we aim. Price's response to this kind of objection is as follows:

> First, the behavioural consequences of giving up theism are significant but hardly devastating. But if I am right about the behavioural role of truth, the consequences of giving up truth would be very serious indeed, reducing the conversation of mankind to a chaotic chatter of disengaged monologues. Second, it is doubtful whether giving up truth is really an option open to us. I suspect that people who think it is an option have not realised how deeply embedded the idea of truth is in linguistic practice and therefore underestimate the extent of the required change. (170)

Trying to give up the concept of truth is not something we can do, for it would require too radical a change in our practices of communication and engagement with others. We do assert, we do believe, we do engage with others, we do take disagreement to matter. These practices are central to who we are—to suggest that we give them up is a spurious recommendation. Even if we could give them up, we wouldn't want to. It is not just that we *take ourselves* to aim at something more than personal justification and community-wide justification. We *do* aim at something more and could not even make the attempt to stop. The deliberative democrat can thus adopt cognitivism with an easy conscience: the very fact that we believe, assert, and argue shows that it is the only reasonable position to adopt.

It is worth pausing here to notice that the strength of this kind of argument varies from proponent to proponent. In its strongest, and least plausible, form, it is a transcendental argument such as that put forward by Habermas (1990) and Apel (1990). They argue that democratic norms are necessarily presupposed by the very act of communication and thus the norms are necessary truths. In a more modest form, Joseph Heath (1998) argues that in certain kinds of inquiry, we have needs for convergence or for taking disagreement to be unacceptable. When debating about physical or natural events, when debating in a court of law about what happened in a traffic accident, or when debating about what is right and wrong, we are under pressure, to varying degrees, to agree. It is not acceptable for someone to say that contradictory descriptions of who jumped the curb are both in fact correct. Disagreement, that is, matters in this kind of inquiry.

The arguments that Price and I make are somewhere in between these two poles. We argue that human beings are the kind of being that makes assertions, has beliefs, and takes disagreement to matter in those areas of inquiry that are, for want of a better word, "objective." To say that disagreement doesn't matter, to say that we don't aim at the truth, is to make a serious mistake about the kind of beings we are and to suggest a revision in practice that we can't and won't make.

Of course, as I have suggested, deciding where disagreement matters in moral and political inquiry will be especially interesting. As Peirce thought, morality falls somewhere between the highly subjective domain of taste and the much more objective domain of physical science. But morality nonetheless frequently aims at the truth and is such that disagreement matters. This is the terrain on which the debate about morals ought to be conducted.

Nonetheless, the deliberative democrat need not be thwarted by the fact that there is disagreement in morals and politics. For the fact that such disagreement often matters to us suggests that we frequently aim at getting the right answers to our questions about what we ought to do and about how we ought to treat others. The only alternative is to take disagreement not to point to a mistake and, in the ensuing void, fight to the last for your own opinion.[11] If there is no explanation of the fact that you and I disagree—no appeal to the idea of a mistake—then we are left with the looming possibility that there is nothing we could get right or wrong. And if there is nothing to get right or wrong, then there seems no reason against pursuing our own preferences. The challenge here, which I think can be met by the pragmatist, is to provide a view according to which we aim at the truth, despite sometimes being drawn to the idea that a particular judgment that something is wrong amounts to the claim that I and like-minded sorts were brought up to dislike it.

Where disagreement does not matter—if you and I disagree about whether it is best to give money to Oxfam, where it will alleviate suffering abroad, or to the United Way, where it will relieve suffering locally—we will want to say that there is no truth of the matter here. The answer is underdetermined—either answer is acceptable. We will, to use that familiar expression, agree to disagree; I will not condemn you for making a mistake and you will not condemn me for making a mistake. But where disagreement does matter—if you and I disagree about whether Canada ought to join in the war against Iraq—we will want to say that there is a truth of the matter here, despite the fact of our intractable disagreement and lack of clarity about how to resolve it. This kind of disagreement will issue in censure or disapprobation. And this type of disagreement is such that, if we want to resolve it, we will have to deliberate, listen to the views of others, and consider the reasons. We will have to be deliberative democrats.

Notes

"Making Disagreement Matter: Pragmatism and Deliverative Democracy" by Cheryl Misak. *Journal of Speculative Philosophy*, 18.1, pp. 9–22. Copyright © 2004 The Pennsylvania State University. Reproduced by permission of Penn State Press.

I thank David Dyzenhaus for helpful comments on a draft of this paper.

1. It is important to see that this is not an analytic definition of truth, but a distinctively pragmatic elucidation of truth. It is an illumination of the concept of truth, brought about by paying attention to the relationship between truth and inquiry. See Misak (1990, chap. 1) and Wiggins (2004).

2. See Misak (1990; 2000; 2004) for details about how it is at home in science and in mathematics.

3. Hereafter given as *CP*; numerals refer to volume and paragraph number.

4. Note that all such discourses, like judicial discourse, are likely to be a mix of moral and factual inquiry.

5. See Misak (2000) for a sustained discussion of this kind of opponent, exemplified by Carl Schmitt, who at one point was held in high regard by the Nazis.

6. See Misak (2000, 96–97) for a discussion of expertise.

7. Price fails to see that this thought is Peirce's thought. He makes the common, but by now unacceptable, mistake of taking Peirce to be offering a reductive analysis of truth, rather than trying to set out truth's role in practice. See Misak (1990, chap. 1), Wiggins (2002; 2003), and Hookway (2000) for the argument that Peirce's theory of truth must be seen as the distinctively pragmatic theory he intended it to be.

8. Others have also argued, as have I, that the notions of improvement and mistake require a robust concept of truth (see Misak 2000, 77, 90–91). Price notes that Rorty can identify improvements and mistakes by contrasting a belief with the beliefs of the community. But given that we also want to be able to say that a community's beliefs can be mistaken and can be improved, we are directed to something more like Peirce's account of truth, according to which the community's belief can be contrasted with the belief that would stand up to inquiry, were inquiry to proceed as far as it fruitfully could go.

9. See Misak (2000; forthcoming) for the argument that Peirce's account of truth meets the antimetaphysical standards of the disquotationalist. That is, Price is wrong to take Peirce's position as metaphysical, let alone as folk metaphysical.

10. Crispin Wright (1992) argues that a mark of those discourses that go beyond the minimal truth-predicate—a mark of, for want of a better word, an objective discourse—is that disagreement is taken to arise from some fault or mistake. Wright thinks that moral discourse fails to meet this standard. See Misak (forthcoming) for discussion.

11. This again is the suggestion of Carl Schmitt. See Misak (2000) for a sustained discussion of how even Schmitt will make assertions and have beliefs, thus betraying his commitment to the truth.

Works Cited

Apel, Karl-Otto. 1990. "Is the Ethics of the Ideal Communication Community a Utopia?" In *The Communicative Ethics Controversy*, ed. S. Benhabib and F. Dallmayr. Cambridge: MIT Press.

Estlund, David. 1997. "Beyond Fairness and Deliberation: The Epistemic Dimension of Democratic Authority." In *Deliberative Democracy*, ed. J. Bohman and W. Rehg. Cambridge: MIT Press.

Habermas, Jürgen. 1990. "Discourse Ethics: Notes on a Program of Philosophical Justification." In *Moral Consciousness and Communicative Action*, trans. Lenhardt and Weber Nicholsen. Boston: MIT Press.

Heath, Joseph. 1998. "A Pragmalist Theory of Convergence." In *Pragmatism*, ed. C. Misak. *Canadian Journal of Philosophy*, supp. vol.

Hookway, Christopher. 2000. *Truth, Rationality, and Pragmatism: Themes From Peirce*. Oxford: Oxford University Press.

Misak, Cheryl. 1990. *Truth and the End of Inquiry: A Peircean Account of Truth*. Oxford: Clarendon Press.

———. 2000. *Truth, Politics, Morality*. London: Routledge.
———. 2004. "C. S. Peirce on Vital Matters." In *The Cambridge Companion to Peirce*, ed. C. Misak. Cambridge: Cambridge University Press.
———. Forthcoming. "Deflationism and Pragmatism."
Peirce, C. S. 1931. *Collected Papers of Charles Sanders Peirce*, vols. 1–6. Ed. C. Hartshorne and P. Weiss. Cambridge, MA: Harvard University Press.
———. 1958. *Collected Papers of Charles Sanders Peirce*, vols. 7–8. Ed. A. Burks. Cambridge, MA: Harvard University Press.
Price, Huw. 2003. "Truth As Convenient Friction." The *Journal of Philosophy*, vol. C, no. 4.
Raz, Joseph. 1999. *Engaging Reason: On the Theory of Value and Action*. Oxford: Oxford University Press.
Richardson, Henry. 1994. *Practical Reasoning About Final Ends*. Cambridge: Cambridge University Press.
Wiggins, David. 1991. "Truth, and Truth as Predicated of Moral Judgements." In *Needs, Values, Truth*, 2d ed. Oxford: Basil Blackwell.
———. 1998. "C. S. Peirce: Belief, Truth, and Going from the Known to the Unknown." In *Pragmatism*, ed. C. Misak. *Canadian Journal of Philosophy*, supp. vol.
———. 2002. "An Indefinabilist cum Normative View of Truth and the Marks of Truth." In *What is Truth?*, ed. R. Shantz. Berlin: Walter De Gruyter.
———. 2004. "Reflections on Inquiry and Truth Arising from Peirce's Method for the Fixation of Belief." In The *Cambridge Companion to Peirce*, ed. C. Misak. Cambridge: Cambridge University Press.
Williams, Bernard. 1973. "Deciding to Believe." In *Problems of the Self*. Cambridge: Cambridge University Press.
Wright, Crispin. 1992. *Truth and Objectivity*. Cambridge, MA: Harvard University Press.

CREDITS

Brandom, Robert. "From Truth to Semantics." *Philosophical Issue*, Issue 8: Truth (1997): 141–54.

Carnap, Rudolf. "Empiricism, Semantics, and Ontology," 205–21 in *Meaning and Necessity*. Chicago: University of Chicago Press, 1956. Reprinted with permission.

Davidson, Donald. "On the Very Idea of a Conceptual Scheme." Reprinted with permission of the American Philosophical Association.

Dewey, John. "Creative Democracy: The Task Before Us," 224–30 in *The Later Works Volume 14: 1939–1941* © 1988, 2008 by the Board of Trustees, Southern Illinois University, reproduced by permission of the publisher.

Goodman, Nelson. *Ways of Worldmaking* (Hackett, 1978). Reprinted by permission of Hackett Publishing Company, Inc. All rights reserved.

———. "The New Riddle of Induction," 59–83 in *Fact, Fiction, and Forecast*. Cambridge, Mass.: Harvard University Press. Copyright © 1979, 1983 by Nelson Goodman.

Haack, Susan. "Double-Aspect Foundherentism: A New Theory of Empirical Justification." *Philosophy and Phenomenological Research* 53, no. 1 (March 1993): 113–28.

Hook, Sidney. "The Democratic Way of Life," in *Reason, Social Myths, and Democracy*. New York: Humanities Press, 1940. Reproduced by permission of Ernest B. Hook.

Misak, Cheryl. "Making Disagreement Matter: Pragmatism and Deliverative Democracy." *Journal of Speculative Philosophy* 18.1 (2004): 9–22. Copyright © 2004 The Pennsylvania State University. Reproduced by permission of Penn State Press.

Posner, Richard. "Pragmatic Adjudication." *Cardozo Law Review* 18:1 (1996): 1–20. Reprinted with permission.

Putnam, Hilary. "Meaning and Reference." *Journal of Philosophy* LXX, 19 (November 1973): 699–711. Reprinted by permission.

———"Realism with a Human Face." Chapter 1 in *Realism with a Human Face*. Cambridge, Mass.: Harvard University Press.

———"A Reconsideration Deweyan Democracy." *Southern California Law Review* 63 (1990): 1671–97. Reprinted by permission.

Price, Hew. "Truth as Convenient Fiction." *Journal of Philosophy* C, 4 (April 2003): 167–90.

Quine, W. V. "Natural Kinds," 114–38 in *Ontological Relativity*. New York: Columbia University Press, 1969. Reprinted with permission of the publisher.

———"Two Dogmas of Empiricism." *The Philosophical Review* 69 (1951): 20–43. © 1951, Sage School of Philosophy at Cornell. Used by permission of the present publisher, Duke University Press.

———"On What There Is" *The Review of Metaphysics* 2 (1948): 21–38. Copyright © 1948 by *The Review of Metaphysics*. Reprinted with permission.

Rorty, Richard. "The Priority of Democracy to Philosophy," from *Objectivity, Relativism, and Truth: Philosophical Papers*. Cambridge: Cambridge University Press, 1991. Copyright © 1991 Cambridge University Press. Reprinted with permission.

Sellars, Wilfred. "Language as Thought and Communication." *Philosophy and Phenomenological Research* 29, no. 4 (1969). Reproduced with permission of Blackwell Publishing Ltd.

West, Cornel. "Dispensing with Metaphysics in Religious Thought." *Religion and Intellectual Life* 3.3 (Spring 1986). Reprinted with permission of *CrossCurrents*.

INDEX